Workplace Law Handbook 2009

Edited by Alex Davies

Workplace Law Group
Second Floor, Daedalus House
Station Road, Cambridge CB1 2RE

Tel. 0871 777 8881
Fax 0871 777 8882
info@workplacelaw.net
www.workplacelaw.net

ISBN 978-1-905766-63-5

Published by
Workplace Law Network
Second Floor
Daedalus House
Station Road
Cambridge CB1 2RE
Tel. 0871 777 8881
Fax. 0871 777 8882
Email info@workplacelaw.net
www.workplacelaw.net

Design and layout by Workplace Law Group and Amnet Systems Ltd.
Printed and bound by Oriental Press, Dubai.

Cover design by Gary Jobson
Cover images: istockphoto.com

Contents

Contents

Workplace Law Network
www.workplacelaw.net

Contents

Contents

Contents

Contents

Comment...

Editor's introduction

Alex Davies is the Project Editor at Workplace Law Group. She has a wide range of experience in publishing, having completed a BA (Hons) Publishing degree in 2001, and worked on several business titles in a freelance capacity.

Welcome to the 2009 edition of the *Workplace Law Handbook*.

It has been an interesting year in employment law, with an emphasis on looking to the future, and reflecting on the wider issues surrounding the workplace. Workers' rights have been placed high on the agenda, with plans for a new Equality Bill, extensions to flexible working arrangements, a review of agency workers' rights, and changes to the process for hiring migrant workers. Maternity leave provisions have also changed, and sex discrimination laws have been extended to further protect the worker.

However, as John Hutton, Secretary of State for Business, Enterprise and Regulatory Reform, put it earlier this year, "having a multiplicity of employment rights won't amount to a great deal if you can't get a job in the first place". With global markets predicting a recession and the phrase 'credit crunch' looming large on every newspaper, there has never been a better time to ensure your workplace, and workforce, is as productive, competitive and efficient as possible.

The *Workplace Law Handbook* is here to help you do just that. In a handy, simple-to-use, A-Z format, its content is written in concise, easy-to-understand, jargon-free language, on the subjects you need to know about. This year's edition contains ten brand new chapters, and all of the content has been extensively updated to keep it fresh, current and informative.

Workplace Law Group has also had an eventful year. On 7 May we were awarded the prestigious Business Website of the Year award from the Periodical Publishers Association, in recognition of our newly-relaunched website – www.workplacelaw.net – and the *Workplace Law Magazine*, which is now in its fourth year. We're very proud of our achievement, and feel that our network – which now has over 50,000 members – is one of the liveliest, most contemporary and informative sources of reference for employers in the UK.

This year has also seen us stacking the shelves of the brand-new Workplace Law Bookshop, to offer a wider choice of products to enable employers to search for the information they need, when they need it. Check it out at www.workplacelaw.net/Bookshop – where you will see the new *Handbook* takes pride of place.

This is the sixth edition of the *Handbook*, and its continued success as our flagship title is in no small way down to the feedback and criticism that we receive each year from our readers. The *Handbook* is designed to be *the* reference guide for employers and managers on all aspects of employment law, health and safety and premises management, and so, as with all aspects of the Workplace Law Network, it is designed with the reader in mind. Need to know the number of toilets you are legally obliged to provide to employees? It's in here (p.683). How to work out your staff's annual holiday entitlement? You'll find it within these pages (p.403). What about your requirements under the WEEE Regulations? That's all included too (p.744). In fact, these 808 pages contain a whopping 184 chapters and comment pieces – and we've managed to shrink it into a smaller, lighter, more user-friendly format than last year – to avoid the risk of WRULDs (see p.776) and eye strain (p.305). We'd love to know what you think of the new design, and indeed the content. Please email me at alex.davies@workplacelaw.net with your thoughts.

As ever, this *Handbook* has been compiled by the generosity and expertise of our ever-growing family of lawyers, specialists, consultants and practitioners, and I would like to thank all 106 of them for their contributions.

A. Davies.

About Workplace Law Group

Established in 1995, Workplace Law has grown to become one of the UK's leading providers of legal information and advice. We specialise in delivering plain-English advice and information to suit your needs.

The Workplace Law Network is a membership organisation keeping over 50,000 professionals, including facilities managers, health and safety officers, and personnel managers, up to date with the legal issues affecting the workplace.

Premium members have access to an extensive range of in-depth guidance and case reports, updated daily, on all areas of health and safety, building management and employment law. Premium members also have exclusive access to a panel of top solicitors and experts who can answer specific queries about legal issues in the workplace.

Workplace Law is also now one of the UK's leading health and safety and HR training and consultancy firms, providing public and in-house training in accredited qualifications such as IOSH Managing Safely, IOSH Directing Safely and the NEBOSH National General Certificate, as well as the CIPD Certificate in Personnel and Practice and Certificate in Employment Relations Law and Practice. We also undertake general risk assessments, fire risk assessments, health and safety audits and project work, and on the employment side, provide employers with practical HR and legal support.

Workplace Law is dedicated to helping businesses get to grips with the requirements of the law. Please let us know how we can help you and your organisation.

www.workplacelaw.net

T. +44 (0)871 777 8881
F. +44 (0)871 777 8882

Workplace Law Group
Second Floor, Daedalus House
Station Road
Cambridge
CB1 2RE

The contributors

*berwin leighton paisner

Berwin Leighton Paisner is a leading law firm based in the City of London. We pride ourselves on our superb client base including many leading companies and financial institutions. We strive to lead the market in the excellence of our service delivery.

We are well known for our extraordinary success in developing market leadership positions within the real estate, corporate and finance areas. We distinguish ourselves by working with our clients in creative and innovative ways to achieve commercial solutions.

www.blplaw.com

Ian De Freitas, Partner
ian.defreitas@blplaw.com

Ian is a Partner at Berwin Leighton Paisner. He deals with all forms of intellectual property disputes as well as handling defamation, privacy and harassment cases. He has a particular focus on the technology and publishing sectors.

Jagdeep Tiwana, Senior Associate
jagdeep.tiwana@blplaw.com

Jagdeep Tiwana is a Senior Associate with leading City law firm, Berwin Leighton Paisner LLP. Jagdeep specialises in health and safety law, regulatory litigation and compliance. She has extensive experience in the health and safety arena, having prosecuted for both the HSE and local authorities. Jagdeep also defends cases involving health and safety and other regulatory offences and undertakes her own advocacy in courts throughout the UK.

Fiona Clark, Associate
fiona.clark@blplaw.com

Fiona Clark is an Associate at Berwin Leighton Paisner specialising in employment law. She advises on both contentious matters, including unfair dismissal, discrimination and restrictive covenants, and non-contentious matters such as drafting contracts of employment and staff handbooks.

Mark Kaye, Senior Assistant
mark.kaye@blplaw.com

Mark advises on a broad range of employment matters with a particular emphasis on non-contentious corporate finance and PFI transactions, including frequently advising in relation to the application or otherwise of TUPE.

Jackie Thomas, Assistant Solicitor
jackie.thomas@blplaw.com

Jackie specialises in all aspects of employment law, and advises on both contentious and non-contentious employment law issues, including executive service contracts, discrimination and issues arising from the termination of employment.

Nicole Hallegua, Assistant Solicitor
nicole.hallegua@blplaw.com

Nicole Hallegua has acted on numerous contentious and non-contentious employment matters including wrongful dismissal, unfair dismissal, and race and sex discrimination cases. In particular, she has been involved in a large high-profile constructive dismissal and sex discrimination claim for a financial institution involving more than 20 witnesses and a four-week trial.

Lizzie Mead, Junior Associate
lizzie.mead@blplaw.com

Lizzie Mead is a Junior Associate in the Employment Pensions and Incentives Group of Berwin Leighton Paisner. She advises on both contentious and non-contentious employment law issues.

BIRD & BIRD

Bird & Bird is an international commercial law firm which combines leading-edge legal expertise with an indepth understanding of chosen industry sectors including aviation and aerospace, banking and financial services, communications, electronics, information technology, life sciences, media and sports. In each of these sectors we provide a full range of legal services and have full service capability from all our offices.

We work with some of the world's most innovative and technologically advanced companies and have a long established reputation for providing cutting-edge legal advice to clients operating at the forefront of their sectors. With offices all over the world we are strategically placed to offer local expertise within a global context helping our clients to realise their business goals both domestically and internationally.

www.twobirds.com

Elizabeth Upton, Senior Solicitor
elizabeth.upton@twobirds.com

Elizabeth Upton is a Senior Solicitor working in the Commercial Department at Bird & Bird. She advises clients on a wide range of IT matters including the licensing of software, agreements for the provision of internet services, online terms and conditions and other legal implications of ecommerce. In addition, as a member of Bird & Bird's Information Law Group, Elizabeth regularly advises on data protection and privacy issues for all types of business and has recently been involved in a data protection audit for a large group of UK companies. Elizabeth has particular experience of advising on the use of personal data in the online environment.

Rhian Hill, Associate
rhian.hill@twobirds.com

Rhian joined Bird & Bird's Commercial Group in September 2006, having joined the firm as a Trainee Solicitor in 2004. She provides general commercial and technology advice in the public and private sectors. Rhian provides general data protection compliance advice including drafting and reviewing data protection policies and employee monitoring policies, and advises on a variety of Freedom of Information and Data Protection compliance issues.

Solicitors

Law firm BPE is based in Cheltenham, and clients range from private investors, to dynamic entrepreneurs, high street chains, public institutions, blue chip multi-nationals, and a foreign Government. Legal services supplied range from corporate, company commercial, commercial property, commercial litigation, insolvency, employment, tax / trusts and wills, PI for Insurers and volume residential property.

www.bpe.co.uk

John Turnbull, Solicitor
john.turnbull@bpe.co.uk

John specialises in all aspects of employment law, dealing particularly with defending claims for unfair dismissal, disability and sex discrimination, and drafting bespoke contracts and handbooks.

John Murphy, Associate
john.murphy@bpe.co.uk

John uses his experience as a former in-house lawyer to benefit employers in their dealings with employees. His knowledge of employment law is extensive and is particularly detailed when it comes to dismissals, redundancies, outsourcing and business transfers.

His common-sense approach and excellent communication skills guarantee that clients' issues are always fully understood and that the most sensible and appropriate advice is given.

Andrea Bateman, Associate
andrea.bateman@bpe.co.uk

The vast majority of Andrea's time is spent working on behalf of employers looking for pragmatic and decisive advice on employment issues. Andrea carries out both contentious and non-contentious work and in addition to her broad knowledge of employment law, she has particular expertise in discrimination, flexible working, post-employment restrictions, redundancy and business transfers (TUPE).

Bureau Veritas UK & Ireland provide a broad range of consulting and laboratory services to companies operating within the built and natural environments.

Our services are deployed to a wide range of clients and sectors, including major blue chip companies, offshore operators, consumer products, and local authorities.

The built environment division closely monitors and evaluates risks relating to people working within the workplace and any other type of building. The built environment has a major influence on health, welfare, morale and productivity of employees, contractors and visitors alike. Managing these risk factors is a key issue for all organisations and new legal precedents are being set to ensure statutory requirements are met.

Bureau Veritas UK & Ireland has the expert knowledge, resource and expertise to support organisations in providing a safe and healthy workplace, providing a comprehensive management solution.

www.uk.bureauveritas.co.uk

Mick Dawson, Commercial Director
mick.dawson@uk.bureauveritas.com

Mick is Commercial Director within the Occupational Safety and Health division of Bureau Veritas and has been advising on asbestos issues for over 17 years. He is a Chartered Environmentalist and holds the BOHS Certificate of Competence in Asbestos. As well as being a tutor and examiner for the BOHS proficiency modules and S301 oral exam he is an approved assessor for the NIACS practical assessment.

Mick is a founding member of ATAC and currently sits on the Management Committee and chairs the Training sub-committee.

Sally Goodman, Technical Director
sally.goodman@uk.bureauveritas.com

Sally is Technical Director - Corporate Responsibility Services at Bureau Veritas HS&E Limited, where she is involved in sustainable development strategy and systems, corporate social responsibility, international environmental management systems and environmental supply chain management.

Mark Webster, Principal Consultant
mark.webster@uk.bureauveritas.com

Mark Webster is a Principal Consultant – Industrial Performance and Permitting Group within Bureau Veritas HS&E Limited. He is an Associate member of the Institute of Environmental Management and Assessment (IEMA), a registered (IEMA) environmental auditor and an Associate member of the Chartered Institute of Wastes Management.

Mark has 17 years' experience in the environmental field, principally related to waste management involving many varied projects such as preparation of Application Site Reports,

PPC Permit applications and SPMPs, landfill engineering and monitoring, pre-acquisition and due diligence environmental auditing. More recently Mark has primarily been involved with PPC permit variations and applications for industrial processes.

Colin Malcolm, Principal Consultant
colin.malcolm@uk.bureauveritas.com

Colin Malcolm has an MA in Environmental Management, is a Full Member of the Institute of Environmental Management and Assessment (IEMA) and sits on the IEMA Full Membership assessment panel. Colin has particular experience in working within industry on environmental legislation compliance and in particular IPPC; Environmental Management System implementation; training development and delivery; and waste, energy and resource efficiency auditing. Colin is a registered environmental panel advisor for the Government Envirowise programme, an approved Low Carbon Energy Assessor for the Chartered Institution of Building Services Engineers (CIBSE) and is a licensed Building Research Establishment Environmental Assessment Method Offices assessor (BREEAM).

Stephen Day, Head of Fire Science
stephen.day@uk.bureauveritas.com

Stephen heads Fire Science at the London laboratories of Bureau Veritas UK & Ireland Consulting, having over 20 years' experience in front line fire, safety, and radiological activities. His role has given him experience in a wide range of incidents and emergencies and includes commissioning and running a UKAS accredited laboratory and health and safety auditing. He has investigated many sites contaminated with radioactivity throughout the UK as well as in Russia, advised on remediation options, and acted as technical advisor to LARRMACC.

Fabien Joly-de-Bresillon, Head of Energy Services
fabien.joly-de-bresillon@uk.bureauveritas.com

Fabien Joly de Bresillon leads the Energy Services business in Bureau Veritas, which has extensive experience of working on energy issues with Building and Property owners, managers and occupiers.

Ben Shuster, Consultant
ben.shuster@uk.bureauveritas.com

Ben has worked in Bureau Veritas' Corporate Responsibility Services division as a Consultant since 2004. Since joining, he has been primarily involved in environmental / energy / CSR audit and assurance work, developing and maintaining environmental management systems (EMS) and the preparation of environmental awareness training material.

In addition to EMS work, Ben is a qualified BREEAM assessor; a methodology for assessing the environmental performance of buildings. The BREEAM system assesses buildings, at both the operational and design phase, in areas such as energy and water use, transport infrastructure, pollution, land use and ecology and building management.

In addition to his work at Bureau Veritas, Ben has worked for the Energy Conservation and Solar Centre; conducting energy audits and implementing building energy reduction action plans. He has conducted similar reviews for Bureau Veritas, and is also involved with energy-related aspects of environmental management system implementation, such as the collection and analysis of energy consumption data and the formulation and coordination of energy conservation plans.

Ben is a graduate member of the Institute of Energy, an Associate Member of the Institute of Environmental Management & Assessment and specialised in Energy Policy and Environmental Technology at Imperial College, London.

Mahendra Mistry
mahendra.mistry@uk.bureauveritas.com

Mahendra is a graduate Electrical Engineer with 31 years' experience. He started his career with the National Coal Board and specialised in high voltage distribution and motor control in explosive atmospheres. He then moved on as a design engineer for a leading industrial controls manufacturer. He became plant engineer for Electrolux, which is the largest domestic appliance manufacturer, looking after all site facilities and manufacturing plant.

He has spent the last 15 years with Bureau Veritas, a leading engineering inspection, testing and certification company. Mahendra progressed to become technical head of the electrical section, setting standards for safe electrical inspection and testing. He represents the company on national and international standards committees for electrical installations. He also works closely with the HSE on electrical accidents to produce safer systems of work and machine electrical safety.

Kevin McFahn, Engineering Specialist
kevin.mcfahn@uk.bureauveritas.com

Kevin is one of two Engineering Specialists within Bureau Veritas Inspection Limited with national responsibility for the maintenance of technical standards within the discipline.

Other duties involve selection and training of new engineers, auditing to ensure accreditation of the business under UKAS and representing the business within SAFed and on BSI technical committees.

Kevin also works as a consultant for Machinery Directive issues on a worldwide basis. He also acts for Bureau Veritas in the capacity of a Notified Body for Annex IV machines under the Machinery Directive. He holds a B.Sc (Hons) and is a Mechanical Engineer with over 30 years' experience in the industry.

Simon Ient, Business Unit Director of Acoustics and Vibration
simon.ient@uk.bureauveritas.com

Simon is Practice Leader for the Acoustics and Vibration Division within the HSE Consulting Group. He runs a team of 37 professionals specialising in environmental, occupational and structural noise and vibration issues.

On a technical level Simon is currently managing work associated with environmental management of the HRL Centrica Energy Barrow Gas terminal and associated sites as well as providing health and safety support services.

The Butler & Young Group of companies provides professional, practical advice and support on a wide range of construction projects. Its development has seen it grow to a company with over 200 professional staff in all disciplines and over 20 offices nationwide. Building on its success the Butler & Young Group now has a family of companies providing a multi-disciplined construction consultancy, comprising building control, fire engineering, health and safety, DDA auditing, environmental engineering and asbestos surveys through to structural design and party wall surveying. The Butler & Young Group provides an effective and efficient service with experts in all fields of the building industry. This enables it to provide completed schemes, which are on budget, on time, and satisfy all statutory obligations.

www.byl.co.uk

Dave Allen, Head of Quality and Standards
dave.allen@byl.co.uk

Dave Allen is the Head of Quality and Standards at Butler and Young Group and is responsible for setting technical policy in the group and ensuring a quality service is maintained through technical and procedural auditing. He has 23 years' experience in Building Control dealing with projects as diverse as towers in Canary Wharf and listed barns in Herefordshire. He is actively involved in building control working groups and has recently been involved in the implementation of a new IT system in Butler & Young.

Steve Cooper, Standards and Warranty Manager
steven.cooper@byl.co.uk

Steve Cooper is the Standards and Warranty Manager for Butler and Young Group and is a member of the Association of Building Engineers. He has over 20 years' experience in the construction industry having spent most of that time in Building Control. During this time he has been employed in both the private and public sector and has experience in dealing with the full spectrum of building work from the refurbishment of historic buildings to modern methods of construction. Recently the Government has placed a great deal of emphasis on reducing carbon emissions in Building Regulations and they are likely to be used as the driver for the move to the Code For Sustainable Homes. Steve has been providing training on this subject.

C/M/S/ Cameron McKenna

CMS Cameron McKenna is a full service international law firm advising businesses, financial institutions, governments and other public sector bodies. With 130 partners and over 700 other lawyers, CMS Cameron McKenna has a strong network of offices throughout the UK, CEE and Western Europe. Our lawyers have strong expertise in many legal areas including facilities management, construction, health and safety, projects and project finance, real estate, environment, financial services, corporate, energy and natural resources, insurance and reinsurance, technology, lifesciences, intellectual property, human resources, pensions, competition, European law, arbitration and litigation. The Facilities Management and Construction practice offers a full range of legal services to clients from all sectors of the industry and is highly regarded as a leader in its field.

www.law-now.com

Rupert Choat, Partner and Solicitor Advocate
rupert.choat@cms-cmck.com

Rupert Choat is a Partner and Solicitor Advocate at CMS Cameron McKenna LLP, specialising in facilities management and construction for over ten years. Rupert has made numerous programmes for the Einstein Network and often speaks at seminars and other events. He is widely published in journals from the UK to Australia and regularly contributes to Building magazine as well as CMS' market leading Law-Now alert service.

Jan Burgess, Solicitor Advocate
jan.burgess@cms-cmck.com

Jan Burgess is a Solicitor Advocate practising health and safety law in England, Wales and Scotland. Her client base consists of a large number of multinational companies, many of them engaged in the highly regulated oil and gas industry in the North Sea. Her recent experience includes a number of high profile matters - including fatalities both onshore and offshore. In addition to representing companies in health and safety prosecutions and fatal accident inquiries / coroners' inquests she provides regular advice on current and forthcoming legislation in this area.

Amy Thickett, Solicitor
amy.thickett@cms-cmck.com

Amy Thickett is a Solicitor in CMS Cameron McKenna's employment team. Her experience includes drafting employment contracts, directors' service agreements and staff handbooks, drafting and advising on severance agreements, advising on individual dismissal issues, redundancy issues and employee aspects of corporate mergers and acquisitions.

Her litigation experience includes handling Employment Tribunal claims for unfair dismissal, constructive unfair dismissal, disability discrimination, race discrimination and whistleblowing.

Sarah Ozanne, Solicitor
sarah.ozanne@cms-cmck.com

Sarah has specialised in employment since qualifying with the firm in 2001. She advises on all areas of employment law, both contentious and non-contentious. Her experience includes advising on employment aspects of mergers, disposals and acquisitions, real estate transactions, outsourcings and PPP and PFI transactions. She also advises on stand-alone employment issues, including the drafting of relevant employment documentation.

GREENWOODS
SOLICITORS LLP

Greenwoods Solicitors LLP is a commercial law firm, considered by the current edition of *The Legal 500* to be a "regional heavyweight" in the East Anglia region. We provide quality legal advice and pragmatic solutions to our local, national and international clients.

Whilst not one of the largest regional firms, we have been successful in identifying the market in which we are best placed to operate. By knowing who we want to work for and having the right lawyers we have been able to focus and develop our strengths to give those clients the very best service.

We know the importance of building strong working relationships with our clients. We seek to understand their objectives, the commercial environment within which they operate and their need for practical legal advice. We are proactive, we look for solutions (rather than just problems) and adopt a 'can-do' attitude. We are committed to drafting legal documents in plain English and to communicating with our clients in a straightforward way.

www.greenwoods.co.uk

Kathryn Gilbertson, Director
kgilbertson@greenwoods.co.uk

Kathryn Gilbertson is a Director and heads up the Business Defence Team at Greenwoods Solicitors LLP.

She led the successful defence of Gillian Beckingham, architect, who was charged with seven counts of manslaughter following the UK's largest outbreak of Legionnaire's disease.

Kathryn advises on all aspects of regulatory law, including corporate manslaughter; health and safety issues; food safety and trading law matters.

A recognised leader in her field, she has a reputation for an innovative approach to regulatory compliance issues and for her astute commercial awareness. Kathryn's team offer a 24/7 one stop regulatory and crisis management service.

Robert Dillarstone, Director
rdillarstone@greenwoods.co.uk

A Director, Robert heads the employment and employee benefits work.

Having acted in cases both before the Court of Appeal and the House of Lords, Robert's strength lies in his commercial, practical and personable approach to delivering solutions to clients.

Robert is acknowledged by the legal directories as a leader in his field. The 2006 edition of *The Legal 500* states that Robert "heads a two-partner team that has an excellent reputation as far afield as the City" whilst Chambers and Partners *A Client's Guide to the Legal Profession 2007* states that "the Peterborough-based team is headed by the 'talented and effective' director, Robert Dillarstone, who 'never ducks an issue'." He has been advising on high-level contentious and pre-dismissal issues as well as the current hot potato that is TUPE. Highlights have included advice to a large media plc on the employment, TUPE and restructuring aspects of its acquisition of a group of radio companies.

The contributors

Lisa Jinks, Senior Solicitor
ljinks@greenwoods.co.uk

Lisa is a Senior Solicitor who has substantial experience in all aspects of employment law, having qualified in 1992. Her all-round expertise includes corporate immigration advice, an area that Lisa built up since joining Greenwoods Solicitors LLP.

One of Lisa's key responsibilities is employmentlaw@work, the department's up-to-the minute email update service which has been a great success since its launch in 2002. As such, Lisa has become the firm's 'guru' on the latest happenings in employment law, at both UK and European level. Lisa also takes a lead role in producing the department's client training programme, particularly informing clients on crucial latest developments.

John Macaulay, Director
jmacaulay@greenwoods.co.uk

A Director, John joined Greenwoods Solicitors LLP in 1989 and has specialised in employment and discrimination law since qualifying in 1991. John has a wealth of experience in advising on all aspects of employment law and has spent significant time 'at the sharp end', arguing clients' cases at Tribunal.

The 2006 edition of *The Legal 500* states that John is "highly regarded by clients". Chambers and Partners' *A Client's Guide to the Legal Profession 2007* also recognises John's expertise, remarking on his "impressive understanding of the employer's point of view," and noting that he is "highly capable of appreciating the challenges facing business and industry".

John leads the Department's training programme, delivering seminars and workshops, both regionally and nationally, on a wide range of topics such as discrimination, data protection, workplace consultation, stress at work and cyber liability to diverse audiences including HR professionals, owners / managers, in-house lawyers, doctors and occupational health professionals.

Natalie Turner, Solicitor
ncturner@greenwoods.co.uk

Natalie joined the firm from Prettys in Ipswich where she trained and subsequently qualified as a Solicitor in September 2004. She is particularly experienced in a range of employment law issues including handling Employment Tribunal claims, advising clients on dismissals, grievances and disciplinary procedures, preparation of contracts and policies and advising clients on the employment aspects of business acquisitions and disposals.

Natalie's role in the team includes all aspects of employment law. With her previous legal experience, Natalie is well placed to advise on these areas.

Workplace Law Network
www.workplacelaw.net

Kennedys
Legal advice in black and white

Kennedys is known primarily as an insurance-driven commercial litigation practice, although the firm is also recognised for skills in the non-contentious commercial field, particularly within the insurance, construction and transport industries. Kennedys has a fast-growing reputation for its work in employment law and the healthcare and insolvency sectors.

Kennedys' approach in all matters is recognising that the 'product' required by clients is the economic resolution of the claim, not merely the legal services necessary along the way. The firm looks at the commercial issues relevant to each case. All Kennedys' fee earners work with this philosophy in mind. Having acted for individuals and organisations involved in many of the major cases in this area, including the trial resulting from the Hatfield rail crash, Kennedys' Health and Safety team is widely recognised as a leader in its field.

www.kennedys-law.com

Daniel McShee, Partner
d.mcshee@kennedys-law.com

Daniel McShee specialises in disaster litigation, public inquiries, criminal law in industry and health and safety prosecutions and enforcement actions. He has a particular interest in the law of corporate manslaughter having been involved in a number of such actions and writes and presents regularly on this and other related topics.

Susan Cha, Solicitor
s.cha@kennedys-law.com

Susan Cha advises and defends companies and individuals in police and HSE investigations and prosecutions arising out of work-related accidents and incidents. She also has extensive experience of public inquiry work.

David Wright, Solicitor
d.wright@kennedys-law.com

David Wright specialises in advising organisations and individuals who are under investigation or being prosecuted by the authorities in relation to work-related accidents. He also advises, presents and writes regularly on health and safety and other regulatory issues. His clients include railway companies, NHS trusts, manufacturers, construction companies and property developers.

A substantial commercial law firm with offices in Birmingham and London offering a full range of legal services – both nationally and internationally. The number of people in the firm ensures that it has strength in depth with a dedicated team of people who pride themselves on their ability to give advice to clients which is prompt, technically correct and commercial. One of Martineau Solicitors' strengths is an ability to think creatively and constructively with a view to solving problems and enabling transactions to be completed to its clients' maximum advantage. The close working relationship between departments enables the firm to provide an efficient and effective specialist service. With accreditations in ISO9001 and Investors in People, its commitment to both quality and people is clearly demonstrated, whilst it constantly looks for ways to improve its service delivery and reduce costs by means of technology.

www.martineau-uk.com

Nicola Cardenas-Blanco, Solicitor
nicola.cardenas-blanco@martineau-uk.com

Nicola Cardenas-Blanco is a Solicitor in the Commercial Disputes Management team, specialising in regulatory issues and representing both corporate and educational clients. Nicola has been involved in matters concerning workplace fatalities, asbestos exposure and related issues, product liability and a variety of other workplace health and safety concerns. Nicola deals with claims involving negligence, contract and breach of statutory duty, and additionally in relation to educational clients, human rights and judicial review.

Jo Bradbury, Solicitor
joanne.bradbury@martineau-uk.com

Jo is a Solicitor in the Employment and Pensions Group at Martineau Solicitors. She joined the group in September 2005 having completed her training contract with the firm. Jo undertakes a broad range of contentious and non-contentious employment work, acting for both claimants and respondents. Jo also has experience in defending discrimination claims in respect of access to membership of public sector pension schemes.

Gemma Cawthray, Solicitor
gemma.cawthray@martineau-uk.com

Gemma Cawthray is a Solicitor specialising in employment law at Martineau Solicitors. She qualified into the Employment and Pensions Group in September 2007 after completing her training contract with the firm and spent eight months of her training within the employment team. Gemma advises on a variety of contentious and non-contentious employment law issues and acts for a broad range of private companies, public sector bodies and educational establishments.

Michelle Billingsley, Solicitor
michelle.billingsley@martineau-uk.com

Michelle Billingsley is a Solicitor in the Employment and Pensions Group at Martineau. She joined the Group as a Solicitor on qualification in September 2008, having completed her training contract with the firm. Michelle spent eight months in the Group prior to qualification and during that time she gained experience in a variety of contentious and non-contentious employment matters. Her non-contentious experience includes the drafting of contracts of employment, policies and procedures, compromise agreements and articles. Her contentious work largely includes preparing claims on behalf of Respondents.

David Browne, Solicitor
david.browne@martineau-uk.com

David Browne is a Solicitor in the Employment and Pensions Group at Martineau Solicitors. He joined the group in September 2007 having completed his training contract with the firm. David undertakes a broad range of contentious and non-contentious employment work, acting for both claimants and respondents. David is also a member of the Employment Lawyers Association.

Mills & Reeve is amongst the UK's largest full service law firms with offices in Birmingham, Cambridge, London and Norwich. The firm provides a full range of commercial legal services and focuses on providing quality, pragmatic, commercial advice to businesses, institutions and individuals in the UK and internationally. The firm has a national reputation for its advice to clients across a range of sectors including: property, private client, higher and further education, healthcare, insurance and technology. Mills & Reeve was recognised as one of the top three firms in the UK in *The Lawyer*'s annual awards. The firm has more recently been listed in *The Sunday Times* Top 100 Best Companies to work for and has also been recognised as one of the country's top employers by the Corporate Research Foundation.

www.mills-reeve.com

Kathryn Haigh, Solicitor
kathryn.haigh@mills-reeve.com

Kathryn is a Solicitor specialising in employment law at Mills & Reeve based in the Cambridge office. Kathryn has extensive experience in dealing with Employment Tribunal claims, including discrimination cases, and regularly advises on managing difficult employment situations such as long term sickness absence, performance management and termination. Kathryn's recent work includes advising on the employment aspects of a business share sale, advising on the variation of employees' contracts of employment and reviewing employment policies in light of the new Age Discrimination Regulations.

Anna Youngs, Solicitor
anna.youngs@mills-reeve.com

Anna is a Solicitor at Mills & Reeve, specialising in Employment Law in the Birmingham office. She works for a range of private companies and public sector bodies. Her recent work includes advising on collective redundancy procedures, including collective redundancy litigation, advising on the implications of a recent merger and the subsequent restructuring process, acting on complex disability claims and advising on the TUPE implications of transfers from the public sector to the private sector. Anna carries out advocacy at the Employment Tribunal and prepares a wide range of training materials for clients.

Pinsent Masons

Pinsent Masons LLP is one of the most highly regarded property law firms. The firm's strategy is to be recognised as the pre-eminent legal advisor serving the needs of the energy and utilities, financial services and insurance, government, infrastructure and construction, manufacturing and engineering, real estate, technology and facilities management industries. The team was a finalist in the category of Real Estate Team of the Year at The Lawyer Awards 2008. The firm ranks in the UK top 15 law firms and is one of Europe's leaders. Clients benefit from the depth of industry knowledge of the firm's teams of specialist lawyers who provide a comprehensive service in health and safety, employment, PPP/PFI projects, dispute resolution (property and commercial), commercial property, planning, environment and sustainability, corporate and commercial, data protection, pensions, insolvency and taxation.

www.pinsentmasons.com

Stuart Wortley, Partner
stuart.wortley@pinsentmasons.com

Stuart leads the firm's national Property Litigation team comprising lawyers in Birmingham, Leeds and London. He worked from the Leeds office for nine years but is now based in London. He advises on all aspects of property law (in particular cases involving landlord and tenant issues) but concentrates on resolving disputes and finding solutions to property-related problems. He acts for government departments, banks, property developers, property investment companies and corporate clients.

Jonathan Riley, Partner
jonathan.riley@pinsentmasons.com

Jonathan is a Partner in the firm's Planning and Environmental Unit. He trained at a leading city firm and has extensive experience as a specialist planning solicitor acting for both the private and public sectors. He formerly combined private practice with being a lecturer in law at Keble College, Oxford.

Michael Ryley, Partner
michael.ryley@pinsentmasons.com

Michael Ryley joined Pinsent Masons as a Partner in January 1998. He heads the firm's Employment Group and is based in the London office. Save for a period spent working in Tokyo, Michael has spent his entire career to date in the City of London, advising a wide range of clients on all aspects of employment law and human resources strategy. Although his practice includes advice in contentious matters, Michael spends the bulk of his time advising on the employment law aspects of mergers and acquisitions, outsourcings, PFI schemes and facilities management contracts. As such he is recognised as an expert on TUPE and is well known as a writer on the employment law issues which arise in such projects. His extensive bibliography includes *Employment Law Aspects of Mergers and Acquisitions – A Practical Guide*, *Employment Law for the Construction Industry* and many articles for professional journals. He is a Contributing Editor of the CIPD / Jordans Employment Law Service, for which he writes the TUPE section. He is on the Editorial Board of *Facilities Management Legal Update* and is a member of the CBI's Employee Relations Panel.

Kevin Boa, Partner
kevin.boa@pinsentmasons.com

Kevin Boa is a partner in the Property Group and qualified in England and Scotland. He specialises in advice on commercial property transactions and projects. He has experience in advising developers, banks, landlords and tenants in PFI, development, retail, office, industrial, leisure and healthcare work.

Siobhan Cross, Partner
siobhan.cross@pinsentmasons.com

Siobhan Cross is a Partner in the Property team. She advises on asset management and landlord and tenant matters. She has acted for a wide range of clients and her expertise is recognised in the leading directories. She has acted and continues to act for a number of landowners in relation to issues concerning the location of communications apparatus on their land and arising under the Communications Code, including a major national transport provider and a large central London Estate.

Martin Damms, Senior Associate
martin.damms@pinsentmasons.com

Martin is a Senior Associate in the Planning and Environment Unit in the Property Group. Martin represents both private and public sector clients in a wide range of contentious and non-contentious planning and related matters, including planning applications, appeals, section 106 obligations and judicial review relating to housing, retail, leisure and minerals developments and particularly town centre regeneration schemes. He also covers highways issues and has acted for and against local authorities in compulsory purchase proceedings and compensation proceedings.

Louise Townsend, Senior Associate
louise.townsend@pinsentmasons.com

Louise Townsend is a Senior Associate in the Outsourcing, Technology and Commercial Group at Pinsent Masons. She specialises in data protection and freedom of information compliance and speaks regularly at seminars and workshops on data protection and freedom of information. She is co-author of a book on data protection and pensions, holds the ISEB qualifications in data protection and freedom of information and is an accredited ISEB trainer.

Michael Smith, Senior Associate
michael.smith@pinsentmasons.com

Michael is a Senior Associate in the firm's specialist Property Litigation team, forming part of the Property Group. He advises on all aspects of property law with an emphasis on opposed and unopposed lease renewals, telecommunications related property matters, forfeiture and possession actions, as well as advising on contentious issues arising in all types of commercial transactions. He currently acts for a wide variety of clients, including government departments, listed companies, property developers, property investments companies and banks.

Joseph Murphy, Associate
joe.murphy@pinsentmasons.com

Joseph Murphy is an Associate in the Property Litigation Group working on all aspects of contentious property work including all aspects of landlord and tenant. Joseph has a particular specialism in complex rights to light cases, and in trespass. He acts for a variety of clients including government departments, universities, developers and investment companies, including a number of listed companies.

As a leading provider of multi-disciplinary consultancy services worldwide Scott Wilson offers comprehensive advice and support on all building-related topics. By providing asset management advice such as strategic planning, feasibility studies, space planning, project management and health and safety advice, Scott Wilson enables the client to manage their assets in the most economical and beneficial way for their business. Scott Wilson has extensive experience of providing services under the CDM Regulations and general health and safety advice to clients, such as audits, policies, procedures, asbestos management plans and workplace inspections. Scott Wilson's wide range of services also includes considerable experience in project management where the company has been involved in projects ranging from minor works to significant new buildings such as Portsmouth's Spinnaker Tower.

www.scottwilson.com

Andrew Richardson, Associate, Health and Safety Services
andrew.richardson@scottwilson.com

Andrew Richardson is an Associate in Health and Safety Services for Scott Wilson. He is a chartered civil engineer with over 30 years' experience of designing and project managing an extensive range of projects including commercial, industrial, military and historic buildings. On moving into health and safety ten years ago, he carried out the role of Planning Supervisor under the CDM Regulations. He holds a NEBOSH General Certificate in Occupational Safety and Health. At Scott Wilson, as well as providing services under the CDM Regulations, he is part of the team responsible for the health and safety of over 600 people at 20 offices throughout England. He has also developed and presented a number of safety-related courses, including CDM and Working at Height. He provides health and safety consultancy advice to many respected companies and organisations.

TaylorWessing

Taylor Wessing is a powerful source of legal support for organisations doing business in or with Europe and is based primarily in the UK, France and Germany, with further offices in Brussels, Alicante, Dubai and Shanghai. A market leader in advising IP and technology-rich industries, Taylor Wessing boasts a strong reputation in the corporate, finance and real estate sectors alongside indepth experience across the full range of legal services including tax, commercial disputes and employment.

www.taylorwessing.com

Dana Shunmoogum, Senior Associate
d.shunmoogum@taylorwessing.com

Dana Shunmoogum is a Senior Associate in the Pensions Group. Dana qualified in September 2001. She joined Taylor Wessing's Pensions Group in London in July 2006 having previously practiced in the Mayer Brown International pensions group. Dana advises both sponsoring employers and trustees of pensions schemes in all areas of pensions law and practice. Her experience ranges from general scheme advisory and documentation work arising from the administration of occupational pensions schemes, and the winding up of such schemes, to litigation. Dana also advises on the pensions aspects of corporate transactions. Dana's recent work includes:

- advice in connection with the closure of a number of defined benefit schemes to new joiners and to future accruals (involving the breakage of the link to final salary);
- advice on the possible demerger of a scheme into two separate schemes;
- advising a professional trustee company in relation to obtaining compensation from the Financial Assistance Scheme;
- advising a major institutional lender on the moral hazard risks of a proposed re-financing;
- issuing proceedings to seek directions on the beneficiaries eligible to share in a scheme's assets on winding-up.

Dana is a member of the Association of Pension Lawyers (APL) and is a regular speaker on the APL Introductory Course. She has also had a number of articles published.

Hugh Merritt, Associate
h.merritt@taylorwessing.com

Hugh is an Associate in the Corporate Department who specialises in providing advice on financial services law and regulation to City of London financial institutions, investment funds and other regulated businesses.

His areas of expertise include Financial Services law and regulation and insurance regulation.

Emma Tracey, Associate
e.tracey@taylorwessing.com

Emma Tracey is an Associate in the Pensions Group. She joined the group on qualification in September 2006, having trained with the firm. She has recently become an associate member of the Association of Pension Lawyers. Both during her training contract and since qualification Emma has gained experience on a variety of pensions law matters. These include Pensions Ombudsman complaints, corporate transactions and advising trustees on matters relating to winding up. Emma has also helped advise trustee boards on scheme documentation and the administration of occupational pension schemes.

Naomi Branston, Employment Lawyer
n.branston@taylorwessing.com

Naomi is a Specialist Employment Lawyer working in the firm's employment and pensions department. She has experience in all aspects of employment law. Her non-contentious experience includes the drafting of contracts of employment, consultancy agreements, employee handbooks and compromise agreements. She has also assisted in corporate transactions and company restructuring exercises requiring advice on transfers of undertaking and redundancy procedure. Her contentious experience includes the conduct of Employment Tribunal proceedings, principally on behalf of Respondents. Naomi also speaks fluent German and provides English employment law advice to a number of German clients with interests in the UK.

Mark McCanney, Associate
m.mccanney@taylorwessing.com

Mark McCanney is an Associate in the Employment and Pensions Group. Mark has advised corporate clients and individuals on a number of day-to-day employment issues such as unfair dismissal, maternity and parental leave, disciplinary and grievance procedures, redundancy and employment policies. He provides ad hoc employment advice to a number of European and US clients who require accurate, commercial advice often within short timeframes. Recent work has included advising a large corporate client in defending a race discrimination claim, preparing for an Employment Tribunal for a large US client and reviewing the handbook and employment contracts of several US start-up companies. Mark is also part of the cross-firm Immigration Group and has advised on work permits and other immigration status issues. Mark has assisted the Group in preparing for the implementation of the new 'Points Based System' in the UK and the effect this will have on clients who rely on employing non-EU workers. Mark trained with the firm and qualified into the Employment and Pensions Group in September 2007.

Kathryn Clapp, Professional Support Lawyer
k.clapp@taylorwessing.com

Kathryn joined Taylor Wessing LLP's Employment Group in London in 2002 having previously practiced as an employment solicitor at Field Fisher Waterhouse and Garretts - Andersen Legal. She has experience of advising employers and senior executives on a broad range of contentious and non-contentious employment issues. She has advised on business transfers, outsourcings, collective redundancies as well as providing general advisory work to employers. Kathryn is the Employment Group's Professional Support Lawyer and in her current role she focuses on analysing the latest legal developments and their impact for clients. She provides internal legal training for fee earners within the Group and maintains and updates the Group's legal know-how resources. Kathryn writes for and edits the Firm's monthly Employment law client newsletter 'Law at Work', as well as writing articles for other Firm publications and legal journals. Kathryn is a member of the Employment Lawyers' Association.

Andrew Telling, Professional Support Lawyer
a.telling@taylorwessing.com

Andrew Telling is a Professional Support Lawyer. He focuses on analysing the latest legal and market practice developments in corporate law and their impact for our clients and the transactions we advise on. He also organises and updates our corporate legal know-how resources, prepares bulletins for clients and provides internal legal training for our lawyers. He worked for many years in the corporate departments of Linklaters and Allen & Overy, and draws on extensive transactional and advisory experience in public takeovers, private M&A, reverse takeovers, joint ventures, leveraged transactions, full list and AIM IPOs and secondary listings, demergers, members' and creditors' schemes of arrangement, capital reductions, rights issues, B share schemes, statutory transfer schemes, company rescue restructurings, group reorganisations and corporate governance.

Other contributors

Anderson Strathern: Alan Masson, Jill Bell and Debbie Fellows
www.andersonstrathern.co.uk

Anderson Strathern LLP is a dynamic and progressive full service law firm. The firm is focused on its client needs and achieving excellence in terms of the quality of advice and its overall service. Anderson Strathern's impressive client base includes commercial, heritage and public sector clients. The firm has recognised strengths in all aspects of property, corporate services, dispute resolution, employment, discrimination and private client management. Its parliamentary and public law team provides a unique service and is relevant to many areas of business. Anderson Strathern LLP is the only new appointment to The Scottish Executive Legal Framework Agreement Panel. While the majority of its client work has a Scottish focus, an increasing number of the firm's solicitors are dual qualified in England as well as Scotland and they act on behalf of clients on cross border transactions.

Alan Masson is a Partner in the Employment Unit and is accredited by the Law Society of Scotland as a specialist in employment law.

He has developed extensive employment law experience over many years in dealing with a wide range of issues, from the restructuring of the workforces in high profile insolvencies to the negotiation and variation of individual contracts of employment. He has handled workforce issues in acquisitions and mergers; contracting out in the public and private sectors; PFI and PPP projects; the restructuring and reorganisation of workforces including collective consultation issues; resolving industrial relations disputes; handling disciplinary and grievance issues at all levels; and problems involving all forms of statutory discrimination, bullying and harassment.

He is a regular speaker at employment law events organised by a variety of organisations and frequently undertakes training for employers and umbrella organisations in employment law matters.

He has written many articles for general readership consumption, published in *The Scotsman* and *Herald* newspapers, in magazines such as *CA Magazine* and online on www.workplacelaw.net.

Having joined Anderson Strathern to set up its Employment Unit, Jill Bell was appointed as Director of the Anderson Strathern Discrimination Law Service in 2002. Having worked in the area of employment law for nearly 20 years and been involved in many Employment Tribunal cases in both Scotland and England she now advises on all aspects of discrimination law as well as advising employers, service providers and educational establishments on 'best practice'. She has acted in a large number of discrimination claims including claims under the goods, facilities and services provisions of the discrimination legislation and advises Further and Higher Educational establishments on their obligations to students.

She has designed and delivered in-house training programmes for clients on equality and diversity including Equality Impact Assessment training and dealing with bullying and harassment.

Jill is a member of the Scottish Discrimination Lawyers Association, the Discrimination Law Association and Equality Exchange. She sits on the Law Society of Scotland's Diversity Committee and on the panel awarding specialist accreditation in discrimination law.

Debbie Fellows is an Associate in our Employment Unit. She has experience advising both employers and employees across a wide range of employment issues including unfair dismissal, redundancy, TUPE, contracts of employment, service contracts and discrimination as well as representing clients at Employment Tribunal.

Debbie regularly provides interactive training to clients on employment and discrimination issues and through this is committed to working with clients to ensure their compliance and understanding of Employment law.

She has a Masters degree in employment law and has a particular interest in Equal Pay, that being the subject of her Masters dissertation.

Ashurst: Marc Hanson
www.ashurst.com

Ashurst's specialist construction and facilities management team is a widely recognised market leader. It has been involved in many facilities management and construction projects ranging from procuring standalone maintenance contracts to major PFI / PPP infrastructure contracts.

The team is responsible for the drafting of the two standard form contracts produced for the facilities management industry, the Chartered Institute of Building Standard Form of Facilities Management Contract and, for the Property Advisers to the Civil Estate, the PACE Government Contract / Works / 10 Standard Form of Facilities Management Contract along with relevant volumes of Guidance Notes for the contracts.

Marc Hanson is head of the Facilities Management Team specialising in all aspects of facilities management law, from contract drafting to dispute resolution. He has extensive experience of advising property owners, contractors, institutions and public authorities in connection with major domestic and international projects. Significant clients include Prudential Assurance, BAA Lynton, Lattice Properties, Chelsfield and Greycoat.

Marc is well known in the industry and is author of the Chartered Institute of Building Standard Form FM contract, the government PACE GC / Works / 10 standard form of FM contract and *Guide to Facilities Management Contracts* (2nd Edition) published by Workplace Law Network. Marc is described as 'leading' lawyer in the *Chambers Guide to the Legal Profession*, and is a member of the British Institute of Facilities Management.

Biffa Waste Services: Phil Conran
www.biffa.co.uk

Biffa Waste Services is one of the UK's largest waste management companies, providing a wide portfolio of services including compliance services under Producer Responsibility. Biffa collects over four million tonnes of waste from one million households and 90,000 industrial and commercial customers each year, and handles a further four million tonnes for disposal. More than one million tonnes is now disposed of through treatment and recycling. Biffa also operates a number of local authority Civic Amenity sites and provides a national WEEE collection service from businesses.

Phil Conran is General Manager of Recycling Development at Biffa Waste Services which he joined in 1991. Initially responsible for the planning and implementation of recycling programmes for local authorities, he has spent the last 10 years heavily involved in the application of Producer Responsibility within the UK, starting with the development of one of the first Packaging Waste Regulations Compliance Schemes – Biffpack – and leading to his current position as Deputy Chairman of the Government's Advisory Committee on Packaging. He has been at the forefront of the debate over the development of the WEEE Regulations, being part of various government working groups and bodies such as the WEEE Advisory Group and set up the Transform Producer Compliance Scheme within Biffa which now has a 7% market share and includes members such as BT and DSG International.

The contributors

Blake Lapthorn Tarlo Lyons: Michael Brandman
www.bllaw.co.uk

Blake Lapthorn Tarlo Lyons provides the full range of legal services needed by companies and organisations, with an industry-focused approach through specialist industry sector groups. Combining specialist expertise with a strong commercial approach, the firm delivers results for clients, whether they are multinational companies, owner-managed businesses, government agencies or not-for-profit organisations.

The firm's size and locations gives it the breadth of experience and the depth of resources to provide the highest levels of service and the capacity to handle large and complex projects at very competitive rates. As well as the full range of corporate and commercial services, the industry sector group draws together leading advisors from different legal disciplines, to provide targeted advice built on an understanding of the issues faced by a particular sector.

Michael Brandman joined Blake Lapthorn Tarlo Lyons as a Partner in 1990.

He specialises in property litigation:

- advice and implementation of landlord's remedies for tenant default, including distress for rent, forfeiture and relief against forfeiture, statutory notices and fixed charge demands under the Landlord & tenant (Covenant) Act, section 146 Law of Property 1925, statutory demands under the Insolvency Act, applications for restraining orders;

- advice on tenant insolvency, dealing with liquidators and receivers.

Plus:

- Preparation of draft legal agreements for property transactions, including leasehold & freehold transfers, licences , property development and partnership agreements;

- advice on legal implications of property issues associated with estates;

- commercial property development; and

- commercial property investment.

Bond Pearce: Dale Collins
www.bondpearce.com

Bond Pearce is one of the UK's leading commercial law firms providing corporate, property and dispute resolution services to major businesses and the public sector throughout the UK and overseas. It competes nationally in key industry sectors of energy, real estate, insurance and retail.

The firm's significant growth in the last decade has been based on forging strong client relationships, delivering high quality advice with effective business solutions and recruiting excellent lawyers and support staff. In a recent survey of advisors to the FTSE 100, Bond Pearce was listed as 24th nationwide and first equal of all law firms in the south of England. With offices in Bristol, Exeter, London, Southampton and Plymouth, the firm dominates the south of England. Serviced offices in Cardiff, Edinburgh and Leeds have been set up to meet specific client needs in other parts of the UK.

Dale Collins is a Solicitor-Advocate and is recognised in the legal directories for his experience and expertise in the field of health and safety law. He has been a criminal advocate for over 18 years and has extensive advocacy experience in the criminal courts and before other tribunals both from a prosecution and defence perspective, having dealt with everything from pollution of watercourses to corporate manslaughter. Dale also has an MA in Environmental Law and is an experienced lecturer.

British Parking Association: Kelvin Reynolds
www.britishparking.co.uk

The British Parking Association (BPA) is the largest Professional Association in Europe representing organisations in the Parking and Traffic Management Industry. As the recognised authority within the parking industry, the BPA represents, promotes and influences the best interests of the parking and traffic management sectors throughout the UK and Europe. It provides its members with a range of benefits all aimed at helping the professional in their day-to-day work.

Kelvin Reynolds was appointed as Director of Technical Services for the British Parking Association in March 2004. He is responsible for the development and delivery of Technical Services to Association members, promoting industry best practice and Government liaison. He also produces industry Codes of Practice as well as being the UK Head of Safer Parking Scheme (Park Mark)(R).

Kelvin has significant experience in the management of parking in the private and public sector and was formerly Parking Services Manager at the City of London in the 1980s and 90s, and subsequently Transport and Infrastructure Manager at Bluewater, Europe's largest retail and leisure destination.

He was an elected member of the BPA Executive Council from 1989 to 1995 and has been a major contributor to the successful development of the BPA's Parkex International exhibition and conference event.

Kelvin is a UK Incorporated Engineer, a Fellow of the Highways Incorporated Engineers and has a Diploma in Highway and Traffic Engineering. He is also a Member of the IoD.

Charles Russell: Carolyn Haddon and Susan Thomas
www.cr-law.co.uk

Charles Russell's 242 years of diligent client service has given it a unique position as a firm which successfully combines traditional values with the progressive practices of a modern commercial firm. The result is a firm which enjoys a refreshing diversity of work. Through the quality, intelligence and commitment of our staff, we have achieved a balance which offers real benefits to our clients whether they are seeking legal advice for themselves, their family, or on behalf of their business.

We increasingly find that clients require a full range of legal services and so we are committed to providing legal services to both commercial and private clients. After all, where there is commerce there are people.

Carolyn Haddon joined Charles Russell as a Trainee Solicitor in September 2001 and qualified into the Employment and Pensions Service Group in September 2003. She specialises in all aspects of employment law, both contentious and non-contentious and is part of the immigration team which advises on corporate immigration issues.

Susan Thomas qualified in September 2005 and primarily advises corporate clients and not-for-profit organisations on all aspects of employment law, both contentious and non-contentious, including business reorganisation and transfers, discrimination, employment policies and procedures, parental rights and grievance and disciplinary issues.

Chivers Commercial: Catherine Edwards
www.chiverscommercial.co.uk

Chivers Commercial is an independent firm of chartered surveyors with indepth knowledge and experience of the commercial property market. The firm was established in 1946 and currently has four directors and two consultants, all of whom are chartered surveyors.

Catherine Edwards is a fellow of the Royal Institution of Chartered Surveyors and is currently Chairman of Chivers Commercial, having joined the firm as a Partner in December 1997. She carries out commercial agency, valuations for loan security and tax purposes, general professional work from landlord and tenant matters including dilapidations and Compulsory Purchase to boundary disputes and access audits for the Disability Discrimination Act 1995. She is a member of the Valuation, Commercial, Residential and Dispute Resolution faculties of the RICS. Chivers Commercial is an independent firm of chartered surveyors with in-depth knowledge and experience of the commercial property market. The firm was established in 1946 and currently has a team of 12, including four fellows of the RICS.

Cripps Harries Hall LLP: Roger Byard
www.crippslaw.com

Cripps Harries Hall LLP is a leading law firm based in the South East providing a wide range of legal services. We advise many high-profile clients including plcs, financial institutions, private companies, local and national government, charities and individuals. Our simple and effective strategy of concentrating resources in a single regional centre of excellence has enabled us to provide the maximum benefit to clients including being highly competitive on cost. Our core values of being Distinctive, Open and Committed underpin all that we do to provide the highest quality of service to our clients.

Roger Byard is a recognised leader in his field and has substantial experience in handling a wide range of employment issues, acting for both employers and employees. He advises on the appointment of senior executives, the management of grievance, disciplinary and dismissal proceedings, the reorganisation of businesses (including redundancy programmes), and discrimination. He has considerable experience of the Transfer of Undertakings (Protection of Employment) Regulations particularly in connection with changes in service provision.

Dundas & Wilson LLP: Mandy Laurie
www.dundas-wilson.com

Dundas & Wilson is a leading UK corporate law firm with over 80 partners and 300 other lawyers across our offices in London, Edinburgh and Glasgow. The core of the firm's strategy is its commitment to clients – and the firm has an enviable UK client base. D&W offer clients an integrated UK capability in the key areas of its practice and is continually expanding its London capabilities to further support this. D&W recruit and retain top quality personnel – not just lawyers, but at all levels throughout the firm – and this has played a large part in strengthening our client proposition and our position in the marketplace.

Mandy Laurie is a Partner in D&W's employment team and has considerable experience in representing clients in Employment Tribunals throughout the UK. Mandy regularly gives advice on potentially contentious issues and problems with an international focus. She has particular interest in discrimination and equality and has presented a number of seminars in this area.

Emaar Properties: Mick Dalton
www.emaar.com

Mick Dalton is the Senior Director, Asset Management, for Emaar Properties PJSC in Dubai, and the Immediate past chairman of the British Institute of Facilities Management, Group Operations Director Global Switch, Operations Director White & Case and Director of FM for Ernst & Young. Mick has over 20 years' experience in FM and is a regular speaker, author on technology in FM, Energy Performance and customer service.

Freeth Cartwright LLP: Vanessa di Cuffa, Raymond Joyce
www.freethcartwright.co.uk

Freeth Cartwright LLP is one of the UK's leading regional law firms. Our solicitors operate from offices in Nottingham, Birmingham, Derby, Leicester, and Manchester, and our client base reflects not only our regional strength but also our nationwide service delivery. We are committed to continuous improvement and our increasing success as a business is built on achieving success for our clients. We work in close partnership with clients, providing positive, practical solutions and clear, comprehensive advice.

Vanessa di Cuffa is a Senior Associate heading up the employment law practice at the Birmingham office of Freeth Cartwright LLP. She has extensive experience in dealing with Employment Tribunal claims, including unfair dimissal claims, breach of contract claims, redundancy and all aspects of discrimination claims. She works for a wide range of private companies and public sector clients and she has advised in all aspects of employment law, contentious and non-contentious. Some of her recent advice includes advising on a collective redundancy situation for a local authority and TUPE issues. She has defended complex disability and sex discrimination claims and many Age discrimination claims. She has also defended on some very complex constructive dismissal claims. She has a particular expertise in the equal pay claims in the public sector and she regularly appears in Tribunal doing advocacy. Vanessa regularly reviews policies and contracts and advises on the technical implications of TUPE transfers and re-structuring of companies. Vanessa delivers seminars and bespoke training and regularly produces articles for publication.

Raymond Joyce is a Solicitor, Chartered Civil Engineer, accredited adjudicator and mediator specialising in commercial law and dispute resolution with particular emphasis in the construction and engineering sectors. His expertise includes contract drafting, health and safety, professional negligence, litigation, arbitration and ADR.

Raymond is also the author of *The CDM Regulations 2007 Explained* and the previous titles on the former Construction (Design and Management) Regulations 1994 published by Thomas Telford and *A Commentary on Construction Contracts, Part II of the Housing Grants Construction and Regeneration Act 1996.*

Furniture Industry Research Association (FIRA): Phil Reynolds
www.fira.co.uk

For over half a century, the Furniture Industry Research Association (FIRA) has driven the need for higher standards through testing, research and innovation for the furniture and allied industries. New and better materials, improved processes and appropriate standards have been developed to enhance the quality of furniture and assist manufacturers and retailers to become more competitive. Information on our members' products can be found on the FIRA website.

A non-government-funded organisation, FIRA is supported by all sections of the furniture industry, ensuring ongoing research programmes that bring benefits to all and at the same time providing the Association with the influence and capability to help shape legislation and regulations.

Phil Reynolds is the Head of Commercial Services at FIRA. Phil is the Convenor of CEN TC207 WG 5 Contract & Educational Furniture, the European committee developing standards for furniture, and Chairman of BSI FW0/2, the equivalent British Standards Committee. Phil is a member of numerous other British, European and International Standards Committees.

Glass and Glazing Federation: Catherine Hogan
www.ggf.org.uk

The Glass and Glazing Federation (GGF) is the recognised leading authority and voice for employers and companies within the flat glass, glazing, window, home improvement, plastics

and applied window film industries in the UK. We have members in over 1,000 business locations – there is a GGF member in almost every UK town.

All our members have been vetted to ensure quality of service: this vetting process includes making a site visit to the company's premises, checking three years of their accounts and taking up references.

All our members work to a Code of Good Practice and to the technical standards laid out in the Federation's Glazing Manual.

Hempsons Solicitors: David Sinclair
www.hempsons.co.uk

Hempsons is one of the UK's leading law firms in the health sector, acting for both the NHS and private sector businesses providing healthcare services or products to the UK health sector. The firm also has a reputation as a leading charities practice, acting for many health, medical or research-related not-for-profit organisations.

David Sinclair is a dual-qualified Solicitor and safety practitioner, who was amongst the first practitioners in the UK to achieve Chartered Health and Safety Practitioner status. Trained originally as a mining engineer, David has a BSc Honours degree in Occupational Health and Safety and a Durham University postgraduate diploma in Environmental Management.

Howard Kennedy: Howard Lewis-Nunn
www.howardkennedy.com

Howard Kennedy is a leading law firm located in the heart of London´s West End, committed to providing clients with practical, commercial advice. Its aim is to assist its clients in achieving their objectives by providing proactive and well-managed legal services.

Howard Lewis-Nunn specialises in all aspects of employment law with particular experience in advocacy in Employment Tribunals. He regularly advises on employment policies and staff handbooks, and also advises on data protection issues in employment.

He has worked extensively on commercial and PFI projects, advising on employment issues arising from these transactions and the application of TUPE. He is a speaker on a wide range of issues, including managing reorganisations and handling disability claims.

Heating and Ventilating Contractors' Association: Bob Towse
www.hvca.org.uk

The HVCA is the UK's leading trade association for the hvacr industry, and was established in 1904. Bob Towse is Head of Technical and Safety for the Heating and Ventilating Contractors' Association (HVCA). He took on this role in 2001 and is responsible for technical and health and safety policy for the Association. Prior to joining the HVCA, Bob was technical manager and field operations manager for CORGI, the Council for Registered Gas Installers. Bob is a member of the Council of the Institution of Gas Engineers and Managers (IGEM).

Igrox: David Cross
www.igrox.co.uk

Igrox Ltd is an ISO 9001:2000 accredited company formed in 1976 to provide Methyl Bromide fumigation services to agriculture and container fumigation in ports around the UK. In 1983 these services were expanded to provide rodent and insect control treatments to industry and agriculture. In 2001 Igrox Ltd acquired the Dyno-Kil pest control business doubling the turnover of Igrox and more than doubling the number of staff. It is the aim of Igrox Ltd to provide safe and effective pest control services with no unwanted pesticide residues, no re-infestation and no adverse environmental conditions.

David Cross graduated from the Institute of Biology in 1984 and took up the position of leading research worker with the Forestry commission working on the control of woodland insect pests for three years. In 1988 he became a Pest Control Service Technician and was promoted to Field Biologist in 1991. He joined Igrox Ltd in 1996 where he has worked as Technical Services Consultant, Technical Manager and was promoted to Technical Director in 2004. Chief responsibilities include running the technical department, coordinating the ISO quality management procedures, trouble shooting, and developing bespoke services tailored for individual companies' pest control requirements.

IOSH: Nattasha Freeman
www.iosh.co.uk

IOSH is Europe's leading body for health and safety professionals. We have nearly 30,000 members worldwide, including more than 8,000 Chartered Safety and Health Practitioners. The Institution was founded in 1945 and is an independent, not-for-profit organisation that sets professional standards, supports and develops members and provides authoritative advice and guidance on health and safety issues. IOSH is formally recognised by the ILO as an international non-governmental organisation. Nattasha Freeman is IOSH's current president.

MacRoberts: David Flint
www.macroberts.com

As one of Scotland's leading commercial law firms, MacRoberts prides itself on being highly-attuned to clients' needs. Over many years, a huge range of leading British and international businesses, banks and other financial institutions have continued to trust MacRoberts' lawyers to lend a clear insight to the commercial and legal issues which face them. MacRoberts has the experience, the range of contacts and the specialist disciplines to help clients, large or small, individual or corporate, cut through extraneous matter and make the right decisions. In an increasingly frantic world there is no substitute for a commercial partner on whom you can rely. With offices in Glasgow and Edinburgh, staffed by partners who feature consistently in Scotland's legal *Who's Who*, MacRoberts is a firm which meets that essential client requirement.

David Flint is a Partner in the firm's Intellectual Property and Technology Law Group and specialises in all aspects of non-contentious intellectual property, with particular emphasis on computer-related contracts and issues. David is acknowledged as a leading expert in Intellectual Property Law, Computer / IT law, and European Law.

David has played a key role in a number of major commercial contract projects and on IP issues relating to the privatisation of British Energy plc. He advises a major Scottish University on IP and Technology matters and is engaged in advising a major Scottish company on IP issues arising out of the use of the Internet as a world-wide marketing medium.

David is a recognised authority on restrictive practices and Competition Law and, with qualifications from both Glasgow and Amsterdam Universities, also advises extensively on all aspects of EU Law including agency and distribution. He is a member of the CBI Competition Panel and the Joint Working Party on Competition Law of the UK Law Societies and Bars. David writes and lectures extensively in the UK and internationally in relation to his specialities.

Peters & Peters: Claire Lipworth and Dr Anna Odby
www.petersandpeters.co.uk

Peters & Peters is one of the leading firms in the areas of fraud, financial regulation, money laundering compliance and extradition. Its clients include corporates, governments, financial institutions, professionals and individuals.

Claire Lipworth is a Partner in Peters & Peters' Fraud and Regulatory Department. She specialises in contentious fraud and regulatory matters, in particular investigations brought by the Serious Fraud Office. Claire has significant expertise in HM Revenue & Customs money laundering and cash seizure cases and of all aspects of anti-money laundering compliance. She is also experienced in FSA investigations. Claire is increasingly involved in advising individuals in relation to cartel infringements under the Enterprise and Competition Acts. She also represents clients facing company directors' disqualification proceedings and disciplinary proceedings brought by their professional bodies. Claire trained at Peters & Peters, qualifying in 1992. She became a partner in 1999.

Dr Anna Odby is an Associate in Peters & Peters' Fraud and Regulatory Department. She specialises in business crime and regulatory advice, with particular expertise in money laundering regulation and compliance. A former university lecturer in Public Law and Human Rights Law, Anna holds a Doctorate in anti-money laundering law. She joined Peters & Peters in 2005 where she trained in civil and criminal fraud before qualifying.

PHS Washrooms: Andrew Johnston
www.phs.co.uk/washrooms

With over 40 years' experience, PHS Washrooms offers unrivalled standards of service based on a total commitment to customer satisfaction. With nationwide coverage, PHS Washrooms offer the strength and security of a national organisation with the reassurance of a fast, friendly, local service. Naturally, all PHS services are managed with respect for the environment and strictly according to the law.

Andrew Johnston is the Marketing Manager for PHS Washrooms. At PHS Washrooms the aim is simple – to provide the very best in quality Washroom Services to satisfy the wide ranging needs of customers.

Reynolds Porter Chamberlain: Fiona Montgomerie
www.rpc.co.uk

Reynolds Porter Chamberlain provides legal expertise to commercial and insurance clients across a wide range of practice areas. RPC has more than 260 lawyers and some of the sharpest minds in the UK legal market operating within its two divisions – commercial, which offers a full business law service across a wide range of industry sectors, and insurance, which stands alone in fulfilling the specialist needs of the insurance industry. Together, they provide a trusted, one-stop service to UK and international clients, working on projects spanning many jurisdictions.

RPC's commercial division acts for the full spectrum of corporate clients – from blue chip multinationals and listed PLCs to smaller entrepreneurial businesses. Among a range of practice areas are employment law and commercial dispute resolution. RPC's employment team comprises ten lawyers who deal with all aspects of employment law in this increasingly regulated field.

Fiona Montgomerie is a Senior Solicitor within the Dispute Resolution / Employment Group at Reynolds Porter Chamberlain LLP, a top 50 City law firm. She specialises in employers' liability and health and safety issues and has wide experience of workplace safety issues (from machinery safety to industrial disease). She has become closely involved in issues arising from stress at work, its prevention and litigation relating to it. She has an MA in health and safety law and is particularly interested in preventative work relating to health and safety in all business sectors. She advises in relation to non-contentious aspects of health and safety, as well as in relation to prosecutions and other litigation.

Rollits: Chris Platts
www.rollits.com

Rollits recognises that commercial problems require flexible and practical advice and draw on the skills of lawyers throughout the firm to provide a full spectrum of commercial legal services. Establishing close working relationships with clients enables us to understand their business and identify with their needs. We believe that quality legal services are vital to the operation of today's modern business and the Lexcel accreditation underlines our commitment to provide clients with the highest quality of service.

We do not believe in being 'all things to all men' and have developed specialist lawyers throughout the firm, dedicated to giving expert advice and guidance. Whilst we ensure that all work is carried out at an appropriate level, our high quality service includes partner involvement to a greater degree than normally provided by many law firms. We embrace the latest in information and communication technology to ensure immediate communication.

Chris Platts has been involved in health and safety law for 23 years. During that time he has represented a whole host of clients ranging from individuals to major enterprises. His present clients number among them a multinational company, major plcs, small and medium sized businesses together with individuals. He regularly advises clients on the health and safety implications of accidents, particularly fatal accidents, and has dealt with many inquests and prosecutions.

Chris advises clients on strategies following accidents, particularly with regard to investigation and appropriate responses to enforcing authorities in efforts to avoid possible prosecutions.

Security Industry Authority: Robert Buxton
www.the-sia.org.uk

The Security Industry Authority is responsible for regulating the private security industry in England, Wales and Scotland; we license individuals undertaking specific licensable activities within the private security industry and manage the Approved Contractor Scheme, which measures private security suppliers against independently assessed standards.

Robert Buxton spent many years with HM Customs and Excise in various roles including front-line anti-smuggling and drugs policy. It was as a law enforcement officer that Robert's career moved towards media relations when he became a Customs Law Enforcement spokesman, advising journalists on all aspects of Customs work and enforcement operations. Robert joined the Security Industry Authority in 2002 as the Media Relations Manager. It was early days for the SIA and Robert set up the media office to publicise the new Authority. He has since worked closely with the Home Office, the security industry and other stakeholders to promote the SIA, its aims and the licensing scheme. In June 2008, Robert was appointed Assistant Director of Marketing.

Society of Light and Lighting: Liz Peck
www.cibse.org

The Society of Light and Lighting acts as the professional body for lighting. It has over 2,000 members in the UK and worldwide, and carries out a full range of activities. The Society is a company limited by guarantee which is controlled by CIBSE.

Liz Peck studied Business and Finance at Sheffield Hallam University. She joined Concord Lighting in their customer service department in early 1999. When Concord merged with Marlin Lighting to form Concord:Marlin, she joined their Lighting Design department. Liz completed the LIF (Lighting Industry Federation) Certificate and then went on to complete an MSc in Light and Lighting at the Bartlett School of Architecture in London, as part of her continuing lighting education. She spent a further two years with Concord:Marlin before joining Philips Lighting as Senior Lighting Designer. Liz worked for Philips for just under five years, providing lighting design expertise on a huge variety of projects and applications, spanning the whole industry. She then had a brief spell with independent consultant, Urban Projects, before establishing her own lighting design consultancy, LPA Lighting, in December 2007. Liz has been an active Member of the Society for a number of years, sitting on the Newsletter and Communications Committee and both CIBSE and SLL Council. She took up the role as Secretary of the Society in February 2008.

The contributors

Suzy Lamplugh Trust: Jo Walker
www.suzylamplugh.org

The Suzy Lamplugh Trust is the only UK charity entirely devoted to providing everyone in society with the practical support and personal safety guidance they need to reduce their fear of crime and develop skills and strategies for keeping themselves safe. It was established in 1986. Their mission is to raise awareness of the importance of personal safety and to provide solutions that effect change in order to help people to avoid violence and aggression and live safer, more confident lives. It offers a range of training solutions including a series of popular personal safety training seminars.

Jo Walker is Campaigns and Communications Officer for Suzy Lamplugh Trust. She has worked there for six years and during this time she has written a number of articles on the subject of loneworking.

TripleAconsult: Elspeth Grant
www.tripleaconsult.co.uk

TripleAconsult looks at your overall business operations, identifies the risks and hazards and converts them into lasting benefits.

Elspeth Grant is a Professional Project Manager with many years' experience, having honed her skills whilst delivering multi-million pound IT and change management programmes for clients in retail and finance, local government and transportation sectors who is now using these skills in the complex world of workplace legislation. Elspeth uses the commercial disciplines (e.g. risk management, planning, financial control etc.) to deliver clear effective solutions. She has concentrated particularly on disability discrimination issues and is highly experienced in providing end to end solutions for clients with multiple property portfolios. By working closely with clients Elspeth builds long term relationships, helping clients to identify and resolve issues in a cost effective manner, by turning business risk into business benefit and addressing issues such as strategic plans, process and procedures, access assessments and by providing advice on auxiliary aids. Elspeth sits on the Guildford Borough Access Committee, writes regularly in the FM press on disability issues and presents to forums such as the BIFM.

Tyndallwoods Solicitors: Sue Conlan and Aliya Khan
www.tyndallwoods.co.uk

Tyndallwoods is a Birmingham Legal Practice undertaking a wide range of contentious and non contentious work. Our Immigration Team, while undertaking a very wide range of advice and advocacy has in the past mainly focused on human rights. We have now launched a tailored business unit within the Immigration Team, Migration for Business - MfB. Our highly experienced and specialist team has provided immigration services for more than 25 years and we are regularly cited as one of the leading firms in this area. Whilst Immigration Law changes constantly, 2008/9 will bring changes of particular importance when a new type of relationship between employer and employee is to be rolled out by Government in tandem with a points-based objective qualification system. The new system assess applicants against a wide range of criteria and brings significant additional responsibilities for those involved in migration which, if not complied with in full, can have serious consequences.

Initially with the Joint Council for the Welfare of Immigrants, then since February 1993 in private practice, Sue Conlan undertakes research, consultancy and training, for example with the OISC and with COMPAS at Oxford University.

Aliya Khan is a Legal Executive and a caseworker in the Migration for Business unit. She has been working with Tyndallwoods since 2003. She undertakes various applications and reviews such as Highly Skilled Migrants (HSMP), Work Permits for Tier 1 and Work Permits for Romanian and Bulgarian nationals, International Graduate Scheme applications, student applications and EEA nationals. Her main focus of work is with those who wish to seek employment in the UK or who are already working in the UK.

Underwoods: Kerry Underwood, Robert Males and Amanda Dorling
www.underwoods-solicitors.co.uk

Underwoods is a highly influential flagship firm and a model for other law firms. It provides a superlative service and with its unparalleled standards of client care Underwoods' glowing reputation is fully deserved. It has pioneered offshoring of legal work, contingency and conditional fees, menu pricing and fixed fees. It has an innovative and commercial approach and provides clients with secure websites for 24-7 access to their files.

Kerry Underwood is Senior Partner of Underwoods Solicitors and was a part-time Employment Tribunal chairman for eight years. He is a member of the Equal Opportunities' Commission panel of solicitors and the Disability Rights Commission panel. He is widely recognised as one of the country's top employment lawyers.

Robert Males has a wealth of experience in employment law and acts for companies ranging from sole practices up to the very largest organisations with international dimensions.

Robert is a leading expert in stress at work claims having recently represented the claimant in a leading case in the Court of Appeal.

Robert is well known for his swift and practical advice on a wide range of business issues. He has lectured to the legal profession both home and abroad on many areas with a particular interest in the Money Laundering Regulations.

Amanda Dorling is an Employment Solicitor with Underwoods Solicitors and specialises in discrimination law.

Amanda is regarded as a rising star in this most demanding and competitive of law firms.

Visor Consultants: Peter Power
www.visorconsultants.com

Since 1995, Visor Consultants have helped many organisations to much better anticipate and prepare for whatever risks and threats they might face. Clients range from multinational companies in several countries, to key UK Government Departments in the UK and many SMEs. Their core work focuses on the delivery of pioneering and bespoke Crisis and Business Continuity services. All consultants engaged with Visor have many years of real-time experience and between them have so far won four prestigious Business Continuity awards. Key services include corporate exercises, audits, workshops, presentations, media skills training, trauma / stress awareness and operational risk management.

In 2007 Visor launched a new service in Central London called 'Visor Virtual Office'. This provides a series of ready to use crisis management rooms in the West End and City as well as training for crisis teams ready to use them. Details are on the Visor website.

Peter Power is Managing Director of Visor Consultants (UK) Limited. His team regularly helps organisations plan and deliver highly successful scenario-based exercises as well as crisis management and business continuity workshops, corporate resilience courses and motivation sessions. He often appears on BBC, CNN and Sky TV News and has considerable real time experience gained at the front line of events such as terrorist sieges, bomb scenes, disasters, reputational crises, product recalls and other corporate dramas.

His knowledge of crisis decision-making is quoted in the UK Government (Cabinet Office) Guide on Integrated Emergency Management and he is the author of many other advice guidebooks including the original UK Government (DTI) booklet 'Preventing Chaos in a Crisis'. He is also listed in the UK Register of Expert Witnesses and is the primary author of the ubiquitous Gold, Silver and Bronze command structure, a Fellow of numerous industry associations and member of the Guild of Freemen of the City of London. Peter is also a member of the BSI Crisis Management Steering Group and the UK Security Review Committee (Resilience sub-group).

Water Regulations Advisory Scheme: Steve Tuckwell
www.wras.co.uk

The Water Regulations Advisory Scheme (WRAS) promotes knowledge of the Water Fittings Regulations and Water By-laws throughout the UK and encourages their consistent interpretation and enforcement for the prevention of waste, undue consumption, misuse, erroneous measurement or contamination of water supplies. Supported by the UK Water Suppliers, WRAS offers a free-to-use technical enquiry service for questions of general interpretation regarding the Water Fittings Regulations, which apply to all premises which have a connection to the public water supply.

WRAS publishes the Water Fittings and Materials Directory, available on the WRAS website, which lists water fittings and appliances of many types which have been assessed as complying with the requirements of the Regulations, ensuring their acceptability to the water suppliers who enforce these Regulations.

Alan Cox, Fire Safety Consultant
Alan started his fire and safety career with Warwick County Fire Service in 1963 and served as both an Operational and Fire Safety Inspecting Officer. In 1976 he transferred to the West Midlands Fire Service until 1978 when he moved to the NHS as the District Fire Safety Officer for West Birmingham Health Authority where he was also the West Midlands Regional Health Authority Fire Advisor and advisor to the DHSS. During his NHS career he worked and studied for six months in the USA looking at different approaches to fire safety. He was also responsible for developing a computerized Hospital Fire Evacuation Program that was used in many major hospitals.

In 1994 Alan moved to HSBC as their Senior Fire and Safety Officer responsible for the 80 countries in which the bank had a presence and in 2005 he set up his own Fire and Safety Consultancy. During his career with HSBC he established a global approach to fire safety, organized many international fire and safety conferences and developed a standardized method of protecting Computer Areas from fire.

During his career he has published a number of books on fire safety and made many specialist technical videos on subjects such as Hospital Evacuation, Fire Protection of Electronic Data Protection Areas, Fire Doors, Mail Room Safety and Working Safely with Asbestos.

Chris Streatfeild, Risk Management Consultant
Chris is a Risk Management Consultant with more than 20 years' experience in health and safety law and practice. He has trained the boards of some of Britain's best-known companies. Chris has held senior health and safety roles in a number of organisations including law firm Nabarro Nathanson, the Engineering Employers Federation (EEF) and British Steel. A Chartered Member of IOSH and IEMA, Chris has a NEBOSH Diploma, an MBA and a Masters in Health and Safety Law and Environmental Law.

Greta Thornbory, Occupational Health Consultant
Greta Thornbory is an Occupational Health and Educational Consultant with 30 years' experience in OH practice and teaching. During that time she has worked with government departments, professional bodies, pharmaceutical, educational and other companies, including several multi-nationals, on a variety of occupational health and safety projects. She also worked for the Royal College of Nursing for 12 years as a senior lecturer and programme director of both occupational health and continuing professional development, during which time she was responsible for many of the 95 Nursing Update programmes for the learning zone on BBC TV and was the RCN representative on the UN Environment and Development Round Table on Health and Environment.

She is now Consulting and CPD Editor of Occupational Health and is responsible for commissioning and editing the monthly multidisciplinary CPD articles and resources for professional updating purposes. She is the co-author with Joan Lewis of *Employment Law and Occupational health: a practical handbook* published in 2006 and is in the process of writing with specialist co-authors a text book on Public Health Nursing. Greta also authored Workplace Law Group's Special Report: *Occupational Health – Making the Business Case.*

Jayn Bond, HR Specialist

Jayn is a Chartered Fellow of the CIPD with over 18 years' experience in HR. She is commercially aware and has a pragmatic approach to her work which is underpinned with an in-depth knowledge of employment legislation and best practice. Jayn is Head of HR at Workplace Law Group and Course Director for our accredited CIPD certificate level courses. Jayn has been advising Chief Executives, Managing Directors and Senior Managers of SMEs, local authorities and not-for-profit organisations at both strategic and operational level for a number of years. Jayn has served a Lay Member on Stratford Employment Tribunal Panel for the last three years.

Paul Clarke, Fire Safety Enforcement Officer

Paul Clarke has worked for Cambridgeshire Fire and Rescue Service for 17 years and has five years' experience in fire safety. As the Fire Safety Enforcement Team Leader, Paul has responsibility for supporting six districts, ensuring the update and implementation of enforcement and legislative policies. He is also responsible for coordinating and delivering fire safety training to both existing fire safety advisors and also operational firefighters. Paul also devised and implemented the Service's Unwanted Fire Signals policy. This was a large piece of work which has succeeded in significantly reducing the number of automatic fire alarms that crews attend.

Bill Scholes, Chartered Health and Safety Practitioner

With an electrical engineering background, Bill Scholes has over 33 years' experience of the workplace. His career has spanned a variety of industries including steel, water, food production through to white goods, distribution, offices and call centres. He has been professionally involved with health and safety for nearly a decade, in that time holding senior management positions. His work experience has been invaluable in his role as a health and safety trainer and consultant (which he has been doing since 2003). In addition to being a NEBOSH examiner, he has for the past two years been the lead tutor for Workplace Law Group's NEBOSH General Certificate Programme.

Absence management

Anna Youngs, Mills & Reeve

Key points
- Keep accurate absence / attendance records.
- Monitor absence data.
- Consider whether the Disability Discrimination Act applies.

Legislation
- Access to Medical Reports Act 1988.
- Disability Discrimination Act 1995 (as amended).
- Employment Act 2002.

Absence problems
Although employers expect a certain amount of absence, high levels of absence can be disruptive, and expensive. Absence-related dismissals or disciplinary sanctions can lead to expensive tribunal claims and therefore it is important that employers handle absence carefully. The treatment of absences will depend on a number of factors including whether the absence is:

- persistent, frequent, short-term absence;
- long-term absence;
- sickness related; and/or
- unauthorised absences (including lateness).

Employers are liable to pay employees' statutory sick pay for certain periods. There may be an underlying cause for the absence, which could be sickness related, related to the employee's personal or domestic circumstances or could be due to a problem in the workplace. Establishing the cause may enable employers to work out a solution and manage absence more effectively.

This chapter gives a brief overview of some of the issues that arise in this complicated area of employee management.

Monitoring absence levels
Monitoring absence will assist in assessing how much working time is lost, and whether there are particular employees who have more time off than others. Monitoring also assists the employer to get to the cause of absences, and highlight any problems in any particular department or relating to any type of work.

Monitor absence by keeping detailed attendance records, showing when, and why, any individual employee has been absent and the duration of the absence (this will include a record of whether the absence was authorised).

Reducing absence levels
Employers should implement an absence management policy, which sets out how they will monitor absence, and what will happen as a result of employee absenteeism.

Most employers have trigger points for different stages of the absence management procedure. Some employers calculate 'working time lost'; others use the 'Bradford Factor', which is a long-standing HR tool.

The triggers and the procedure should be applied consistently, and at each stage the employee should be given an opportunity to explain their absences.

One tool that many employers have found to be effective in reducing absence levels is a return to work interview where some gentle quizzing of the employee about the reason for the absence, how they are feeling, what support they may need etc. is undertaken. It is not clear why this is so effective but some speculate that the reduction in absenteeism may be because some employees fear having to face a manager on their return to explain about their absence.

Other steps that can be taken to reduce absences include:

- induction and training for employees;
- training managers and supervisors to manage absence effectively;
- ensuring that the absence policy covers the provision of medical or self certificates to cover sickness absence;
- involving occupational health as appropriate, especially if there is no medical certificate to support self-certified absences;
- undertaking risk assessments in respect of any recurring causes of absence (including stress risk assessments if applicable); and
- keeping in contact with absent employees and throughout any process consult with the employee.

In all cases of sickness absence the employer should have an up-to-date report on the employee's medical condition. This may be a GP report, specialist advice, an Occupation Health report etc. The employer should not just ask for a 'report' but ask specific questions on diagnosis and prognosis in the employee's/employer's circumstances.

ACAS recommends that in all cases the employee should be told what improvement is expected and be warned of the likely consequences if no improvement occurs. If there is no improvement, ACAS recommends that employers take into account the following factors before deciding upon appropriate action:

- Performance;
- Likelihood of change in attendance levels;
- Any improvement already made;
- The availability of suitable alternative work (if appropriate); and
- The effect of past and future absences on the business.

Historically, an employee's length of service has been taken into account with their employment history when looking at appropriate sanctions for absenteeism, but this should not be a major factor given that the Employment Equality (Age) Regulations 2006 may render this discriminatory on the grounds of age.

Disability Discrimination Act 1995 (DDA)

Where the reason for absence is ill heath, employers must consider whether the DDA is applicable. This is not just the case for long-term absences, as a disability within the meaning of the DDA could result in an employer taking frequent short periods of absence.

Employers must consider whether there are any reasonable adjustments that can be made for a disabled employee. This may include adjusting the way in which a sickness absence policy is applied to a disabled employee.

In addition, dismissal or any other form of disciplinary sanction due to disability-related absence may be less favourable treatment for a reason related to a disability. This depends on the facts of the case, but given the complexities of the law under the DDA employers should be able to 'justify' their decisions as set out in the DDA. Generally, disability-related discrimination will not be justified unless adjustments have already been considered and, where reasonable, made.

The DDA says that an example of a reasonable adjustment is allowing disabled people time off work for rehabilitation, assessment or treatment.

This is one of the most complex areas of law. Many employers shy away from dismissing an employee who has a disability, fearing a claim of disability-related discrimination. Whilst dismissals in this context are hard to get right, that does not mean that it cannot be done.
If monitoring absence reveals an underlying medical condition, employers should:

■ get an up-to-date medical opinion to determine the extent of the condition, its likely duration and whether the levels of absence are likely to decrease to an acceptable level;
■ consider, in light of any medical report(s) and other information whether the illness may amount to a disability under the DDA; and
■ if the employee may be disabled, look at what reasonable adjustments can be made.

Dismissal or disciplinary action in respect of maternity-related absence is highly likely to amount to sex discrimination.

Additional points to note when dealing with unauthorised absence or lateness
Where absence is unauthorised and is not sickness-related, absence should be treated as a conduct issue. The Tribunals will look at the very least for the following steps to have been taken (as well as compliance with the Statutory Dismissal Procedures, which are being replaced in April 2009 with a new ACAS Code, and employer's own policy) before dismissal:

■ a fair review of the attendance record and reasons for absence;
■ an opportunity for the employee to have made representations; and
■ targets for improvement and warnings of dismissal if attendance does not improve.

If an employer believes that an employee has extended their annual leave through sickness absence, rather than actually being sick, a reasonable investigation must be carried out before taking disciplinary action.

Additional points to note when dealing with short-term certified sickness or uncertified absence
Short-term sickness absence can be dealt with as a capability issue. Special care must be taken if the employee could have a disability (as set out above).

If considering dismissal, check and consider the following:

■ Employee's prognosis and whether absence levels are likely to decrease and if so in what time-frame;
■ Whether the employee's attendance record has improved; and
■ The effect of the absences on the business, and whether temporary cover can address this.

Additional points to note when dealing with long-term sickness absence
If an employee has been off on long-term sickness absence, the risk that they

are covered by the DDA is increased. Particular points are:

- the employee's prognosis and whether absence levels are likely to decrease and if so in what time-frame;
- employee consent will be needed to get a medical opinion from a doctor appointed by the employer or the employee's own GP. If the employee refuses permission, employers must take action based on the information available to them;
- consider reasonable adjustments to the job or working arrangements, which may include finding an alternative role, or a phased return for the employee;
- whether the absence is caused in whole or in part because of a failure to make reasonable adjustments. If the employer has failed to meet the duty to make reasonable adjustments, dismissal is likely to be unfair and discriminatory. Employers may need to seek advice as to what adjustments would be reasonable and what can be taken into account when determining whether an adjustment is reasonable;

- consider whether the job can be covered by other employees or temporary replacements and how long the job can reasonably be kept open;
- be clear about sick pay arrangements and keep the employee informed; and
- a thorough investigation will be required before dismissal.

Ill health retirement may be an option, but this would not prevent an employee from making an Tribunal claim so consultation is again key.

The ACAS Advisory Booklet, *Managing Attendance and Employee Turnover* gives further detailed advice about how to manage different types of sickness absence.

See also: Disciplinary and grievance procedures, p.216; Leave, p.457; Medical records, p.491; Occupational health, p.537; Sickness leave, p.654

Sources of further information

HSE – Managing sickness absence and return to work: www.hse.gov.uk/sicknessabsence/index.htm

ACAS Code of Practice on Disciplinary and Grievance Procedures: www.acas.org.uk/media/pdf/9/5/CP01_1.pdf

ACAS: *Managing attendance and employee turnover*: www.acas.org.uk/index. aspx?articleid=1183

EHRC: www.equalityhumanrights.com/en/publicationsandresources/Disability/ Pages/Employment.aspx)

HSE: www.hse.gov.uk/sicknessabsence/index.htm)

Accessible environments

Elspeth Grant, TripleAconsult

Key points

- Accessible environments are essential with the Paralympics being held here in the UK in four years' time.
- An estimated one in five of the population are disabled with the majority of these having disabilities not related to wheelchairs.
- A truly accessible environment will only be achieved through a mix of management processes, training and physical changes.
- Strategic planning is an essential tool before accessible environments can be achieved.

Legislation

- Disability Discrimination Act 1995 and 2005 – introduced in three phases over nine years.
- Building Regulations – Part B (fire safety) and Part M (access to facilities and employment).
- British Standards – BS 5588 (fire safety) and BS 8300 (supporting Part M).
- Regulatory Reform (Fire Safety) Order 2005 – fire safety legislation based on risk assessment.

Introduction

This chapter examines accessible environments in the wider sense and how best these may be implemented in a manner that provides true benefits for organisations / companies, disabled and non-disabled people alike. This is particularly important in an economic climate where budgets are tight and every cost unit is likely to be questioned. The drivers for an accessible environment are a mix of legal, social, economic and personal. It should be remembered that no one knows what the future holds; any one of us might suddenly require an accessible environment. If implemented in a practical manner, accessible environments benefit businesses, organisations, disabled and non-disabled people.

In just four years' time, not only the Olympics but also the Paralympics will be held in the UK. This will present not only a sizeable revenue opportunity but also a challenge for those whose responsibility it is to ensure our environments are accessible for the thousands of disabled athletes and visitors who will accessing our environment during this time. Those organisations that ensure that their environments are fully accessible will be those that benefit the most.

An accessible environment can only be realised if the foundations are put in place by way of strategic planning. The strategy should provide a vision for the future and how it can be implemented. It should cover as a minimum internal and external communications, health and safety aspects, and the physical environment in addition to the delivery of products and services.

Last year, Trevor Phillips of the Equality and Human Rights Commission stated:

"Disabled people have two sources of discrimination: one is other people but the other is the world constructed by mankind … Disabled people should be able to get on with their lives and no one should question that."

Cost-effective accessible environments are achievable and real business benefits can be gained by all if the right approach is taken. A figure often quoted is the estimate by the CBI that disabled people account for a potential £50bn of spend in the country; however, some 13 years after the Disability Discrimination Act (1995) was originally passed, many still cannot access the employment opportunities, services or leisure facilities that they require. It is important to remember that an accessible environment is an asset which assists all users, not just disabled people.

Background information
Before implementing an accessible environment, it is important to understand some of the statistics relating to disabled people and the interrelationship between the legislation that supports accessibility. There is no longer a register of disabled people so these statistics are gathered from a number of sources and can vary considerably. The following statistics identify the approximate numbers of disabled people in the United Kingdom (believed to be over one in five of the population) and will help the focus of attention to be across the wide spectrum of disabilities:

- Wheelchair users – 600,000 (of which 50% can leave their wheelchairs for short periods);
- Reading difficulties including dyslexia – 2.5–6 million;
- Visual impairments – 2.5–3 million;
- Deaf or hard of hearing – 8.5 million; and
- Arthritis – over nine million.

These figures highlight that the vast majority of disabled people are not wheelchair users. In order to ensure that an environment is accessible the issues are far wider than the provision of an accessible WC and a ramp.

The legal requirement
In brief, Building Regulations Part B and M address the built environment whilst the DDA is focused on the people who use the building, which also includes the built environment. The result is that there is such a thing as a Part M-compliant workplace; however there is no such thing as a DDA-compliant workplace (so although a person can have a Part M-compliant workplace they could still be discriminatory under the DDA, as the latter is concerned with the activities and services provided within that area).

As the following paragraph, contained in Approved Document M, indicates, rather than the religious following of Building Regulations, the emphasis should be on solutions which really improve the environment for all disabled people:

"There is no obligation to adopt any particular solution contained in the Approved Document if you prefer to meet the requirement of the regulation in some other way."

Within the framework, designers have the option to:

- remove the feature;
- alter the feature so that it no longer has that effect;
- provide a reasonable means of avoiding the feature; and/or
- provide the service by a reasonably alternative means.

The Regulatory Reform Order (RRO) states that the 'Responsible Person' must ensure the safe evacuation of everyone from the building and that includes disabled people.

Building managers, Responsible People and fire competent people should take particular notice of the note in BS 5588 Part 8:

"Refuges are relatively safe waiting areas for short periods. They are not areas where disabled people should be left indefinitely until rescued by the fire brigade, or until the fire is extinguished. It is not acceptable to leave disabled people in refuges and if this was the process and people were to die then any criminal proceedings would be taken out against the Responsible Person."

Guidance from the Department of Communities and Local Government (CLG) on Means of Escape for Disabled People re-enforces this by stating very clearly that:

"... Under current fire safety legislation it is the responsibility of the person(s) having responsibility for the building to provide a fire safety risk assessment that includes an emergency evacuation plan that includes an emergency evacuation plan for all people likely to be in the premises, including disabled people, and how that plan will be implemented. Such an evacuation plan should not rely upon the intervention of the Fire and Rescue Service to make it work ..."

This is further backed up by the CLG Guidance on *Fire Safety Risk Assessment – Sleeping Accommodation*, section 3.4.3:

"Once a fire has started, been detected and a warning given, everyone in your premises should be able to escape to a place of total safety unaided and without the help of the fire and rescue service."

Responsible People should note that this guidance essentially means that 'stay put' fire evacuation plans for disabled people, which involve waiting for assistance for the fire and rescue services, are no longer appropriate or acceptable.

Strategic planning and implementation
A truly accessible environment will only be achieved through a mix of management processes, training and physical changes. Legally an employer or service provider must only take 'reasonable' steps to provide access; however, in order to obtain best business benefit and provide the 'best possible' environment for clients and employees, the key is to identify and resolve any barriers that may prevent a disabled person from fully participating on the same basis as a non-disabled person. It is good practice to consult with any appropriate groups of disabled people during the implementation of an accessible environment. As with any market and research activity, this both adds value and ensures that the environment meets the needs of the users.

Fundamental to successful access planning is to understand whether there is a requirement to be proactive as in an environment which is open to the public (a bingo hall, supermarket, rail station, school, university) or whether the environment is controlled (an office, staff area). For example, if the target environment is open to the public and a green field site, then Part M and Part B supported by management processes should be implemented throughout. However, if the environment is an existing office building and not open to the public then it may be more appropriate to identify potential physical barriers and, if no disabled person is currently employed, to implement access impact assessments for all employees to identify whether any alterations to the workplace should be made. Many organisations undertake expensive access assessments of their environment as a first step to the provision of an accessible environment without having first identified a strategic approach or a clear vision of how changes will be implemented.

As a general rule, it is recommended that an access strategy is documented to cover approaches to:

Internal communications
- Documentation of an access policy.
- Implementation of a staff communications policy.
- Provision of staff training in assisting disabled people.
- Implementation of non-discriminatory procedures including recruitment.

Health and safety
- Identification of all health and safety issues.
- Creation of overall strategy for means of escape for disabled people.
- Identification of those who may need assistance to evacuate.
- Integration of escape plans with any third party entities.
- Creation of Personal Emergency Evacuation Plans (PEEPs).

External communications
- Identification of the information needs of disabled people.
- Review of existing methods of communication and identifying any gaps in information needs; particularly via written media, the internet, websites, call centres, advertisements etc.
- Documentation of a communication strategy and implementation of service policies for disabled people.
- Provision of accessible booking facilities if appropriate, which must include the same discounts for those unable to book online.

- Provision of information on transportation for both private and public facilities.

Physical environment
- Access assessments of the environment and subsequent tracking of actions by priority and responsibility.
- Resolution of barriers identified during access assessments with a focus on high priority or high risk areas as recommended.
- Maintenance schedules taking into consideration access assessment recommendations.
- Refurbishments and/or new properties.

Products and services
- Development and implementation of products and service policies.
- Documentation of procedures for the provision of service to disabled customers.
- Devising a communication strategy for the public.

Monitoring and evaluation
- Establishment of a baseline for assessing critical success factors.
- Annual reviews and comprehensive reviews of progress.

Once issued, the access strategy will become a blueprint for the implementation of the accessible environment. Although the strategy will only refer to activities at a high level, the strategy must include timelines, responsibilities, monitoring procedures and critical success criteria. It is only at this point that further steps can be taken to reduce barriers for disabled people and to make physical changes.

Conclusion
Stephen Hawkins has had a scientific career which has spanned more than 40 years and his books and public appearances have made him an academic

celebrity and world-renowned theoretical physicist. Stephen is famous for his contributions to the fields of cosmology and quantum gravity, especially in the context of black holes, and his popular works in which he discusses his own theories and cosmology in general. He is also severely disabled. The question is – can society afford to ignore one in five of the population by preventing them from accessing our environments when any one of them could have the intellect and drive to provide answers to the challenges of our world?

It is essential for the economy that both disabled and non-disabled people are able to access employment, goods and services. If approached in a logical manner, it is possible to achieve an accessible environment without necessarily increasing cost. Identifying the issues and producing a cohesive plan is the key to achieving an accessible environment which meets the needs of both disabled and non-disabled people. What disabled people are asking for today, we may well be asking for tomorrow.

See also: Building Regulations, p.81; Disability access and egress, p.204; Disability legislation, p.209; Discrimination, p.222; Display screen equipment, p.238; Fire, means of escape, p.322; Lighting, p.469; Toilets, p.683

Sources of further information

Planning for inclusion and accessibility is a key aspect of building design and management, and considering the needs of disabled and less mobile people will only increase in importance as our working population gets older and in need of accessible environments. Workplace Law Group's *Making Buildings Accessible 2009: Special Report* contains essential guidance and key research on how to make buildings inclusive and accessible to all. Covering key legislation, practical examples, case studies and case law, this informative Special Report has all the information that building managers and FMs need to ensure their building is inclusive and accessible to all. For more information visit www.workplacelaw.net/Bookshop/SpecialReports.

Accident investigations

Daniel McShee, Kennedys

Key points
The investigation and analysis of work-related accidents and incidents forms an essential part of managing health and safety.

Legislation
- Health and Safety at Work etc. Act 1974.
- Management of Health and Safety at Work Regulations 1999.

Overview
HSE guidance on investigating accidents and incidents, which currently takes the form of combined workbook and guidance notes, emphasises that investigation and analysis of work-related accidents and incidents forms an essential part of managing health and safety. Further, it stresses that the learning of lessons from what is uncovered by accident and incident investigation lies at the heart of preventing further events.

There are legal reasons for investigating. Sections 2 and 3 of the Health and Safety at Work etc. Act 1974 (HSWA) impose general duties on employers to ensure that their employees and those affected by the conduct of their business are, so far as is reasonably practicable, not exposed to risks to their health and safety. Following an accident, in determining whether employers have met this duty, the HSE will often look to see if there have been previous incidents and whether these have been properly investigated as part of the employer's safety management system. A failure to investigate previous incidents or learn lessons from them will be deemed by the HSE to be an aggravating feature in any further incident.

Regulation 5 of the Management of Health and Safety at Work Regulations 1999 also requires employers to plan, organise, control, monitor and review their health and safety arrangements. Health and safety investigations form an essential part of this process.

In addition to legal reasons for investigating, there are also benefits from doing so – namely the prevention of further similar adverse events, which would include the prevention of business losses due to disruption, stoppage, lost orders, and the impact of criminal and civil legal actions.

Practical issues
It is the potential consequences and the likelihood of the adverse incident recurring that should determine the level of investigation, not simply the injury or ill health suffered on a particular occasion. Thus for example, when investigating an incident, the HSE would look to see whether there have been any near misses in the past.

It is essential that management and the workforce are fully involved in any investigation. Depending on the level of investigation, it may be that employees, management and directors of all levels will be involved.

It is essential that an investigation is reported directly to someone with the authority to make decisions and act on recommendations.

The urgency of an investigation will depend on the magnitude and immediacy of the risk involved. The general rule is that accidents and incidents should be investigated as soon as possible in order to ensure that evidence is not lost or that memories do not fade.

An investigation will involve analysis of all of the information available (i.e. the incident scene, witness evidence, documentary evidence, etc.) to identify what went wrong and determine what steps must be taken to prevent it happening again.

The HSE guidance sets out a step-by-step guide to health and safety investigations.

Step 1. Gathering information
This includes finding out what happened to establish whether there were any management failings. It is important to capture information as soon as possible. If necessary, work must stop to allow this to take place. If there is any doubt about the safety of a particular type of work, piece of machinery, etc., then this should be stopped for the duration of the investigation. In the event that this action is not taken, the HSE itself might serve a prohibition notice requiring the work activity to stop immediately where the inspector believes there to be a risk of serious personal injury.

Step 2. Analysing the information
Analysis involves examining all the facts to determine how the accident happened; both the direct and indirect causes. All information gathered should be assembled and examined to identify what information is relevant and what information is missing.

The analysis must be carried out in a systematic way so that all possible causes and the consequences and potential consequences of the adverse event are fully reviewed.

Step 3. Identifying suitable risk control measures
Where a proper investigation is undertaken, it should in most cases be possible to identify failings both direct and indirect – frontline and management – which led to the incident or accident taking place. This might include factors such as work pressures on performance, long hours, safety culture, etc. Once the failings have been clearly identified, this should assist in determining the remedial measures that should be implemented. All possible remedial measures should be risk assessed to ensure that making a change to a work activity, type of machinery, etc., does not in itself import greater risk than was present previously. If several risk control measures are identified, they should be carefully prioritised as a risk control action plan.

Step 4. The action plan and its implementation
At this stage, those people within the organisation who have the authority to make decisions and act on recommendations should be involved. It is good practice for those people to 'accept' the recommendations and to ensure that there is a proper action plan for implementation of the remedial measures identified. This would include a monitoring system to ensure that recommendations are indeed undertaken.

Analysis of major accidents shows that, even where previous incidents have been properly investigated in terms of identifying the failings and the appropriate remedial measures, it is the implementation of the recommendations that has failed to achieve any change and recommendations have become lost in the passage of time. Again, the HSE when investigating any incident will look to see whether any previous incidents could and should have been learned from, including the implementation of recommendations from any previous investigation.

The HSE recommends that the action plan should be based upon SMART objectives (Specific, Measurable, Agreed, Realistic and with Timescales).

A word of warning
Internal accident investigation reports are disclosable to the HSE. Although this fact should not impact on an employer's approach to its investigation or its findings, it is often the way in which those findings are expressed that can cause unnecessary difficulties for the employer and individual employees. In the circumstances, care should be taken when drafting investigation reports and those responsible for them should bear in mind that the reports will often have a wider audience than originally anticipated.

> *See also*: Health and safety at work, p.364; Health and safety inspections, p.381; Reporting of Injuries, Diseases and Dangerous Occurrences, p.628; Slips, trips and falls, p.657

Sources of further information

Investigating accidents and incidents – A workbook for employers, unions, safety representatives and safety professionals (HSE Books) ISBN: 0 7176 2827 2.

Agency and temporary workers

Fiona Clark, Berwin Leighton Paisner and Amanda Dorling, Underwoods

Key points

Usually, agency workers are supplied by an agency to a client business for temporary assignments. The agency and the client will enter into a contract for the supply of the named worker, and the worker will enter into a contract with the agency.

Usually, the agency will pay and have the right to discipline the worker, but the client will give the worker day-to-day instructions.

The main legal issues concerning an agency worker are whether he is self-employed and, if not, whether he is the employee of the agency or the client. These issues will determine the worker's entitlement to statutory employment rights and status for taxation purposes.

Temporary employees (i.e. those people directly employed with organisations on short-term contracts) will not be entitled to claim unfair dismissal, redundancy pay or certain maternity rights if they do not have sufficient continuous service.

Legislation

- Employment Agencies Act 1973.
- The Conduct of Employment Agencies and Employment Businesses Regulations 2003 (the Regulations).

Overview

Many employers use agency workers on short-term projects or to meet surges in demand. The most common agency arrangement is for the agency to supply temporary staff to clients, for which the agency charges a weekly fee. The worker submits his weekly timesheets to the agency, which pays the worker at an hourly rate.

In the case of more permanent positions, an employment agency may offer the client a different service, whereby the agency introduces potential candidates to the client, following which the successful candidate contracts directly with the client. Because the agency drops out of the picture, this is a standard employment relationship between the client and the worker.

Employed or self-employed?

It should be emphasised that there are, at present, no hard and fast rules as to whether the worker is employed or self-employed. Tribunals have reached different conclusions in cases with similar facts.

In general, workers find it difficult to establish that they are employees of the agency because the agency lacks sufficient day-to-day control over them. However, if the agency does exercise considerable control, a Tribunal may determine that the worker is its employee for either the whole relationship (known as an 'umbrella contract') or in relation to a particular assignment.

Agency workers also find it difficult to show that they are employees of the client, because there is no contractual relationship between the parties. Recently, several cases suggested that it may be possible to imply a contract of employment between the client and the worker (particularly in the case of long-serving workers). However, several EAT decisions in 2006 and 2007 moved away from this approach and now an employment contract will only be found to exist between the client and the worker where it is necessary to give effect to the reality of the relationship. As a result, it is now much less likely that an agency worker will be an employee of a client, particularly if there is a contract between the worker and the agency and there has been no change in circumstances since the initial supply of the worker by the agency.

Why an agency worker's employment status is important

In employment law terms, the main advantage of engaging an individual on a self-employed basis is that many employment rights do not apply. Unfair dismissal, redundancy payments and maternity rights, for example, may be claimed only by employees.

Additionally, if an individual is self-employed, he will pay income tax on trading income (formerly Schedule D) and pay National Insurance contributions at the self-employed rate. Business expenses may be set off against the individual's tax liability.

Importantly, whether or not an agency worker is deemed to be an employee of

the client, they are likely to be a 'worker' (thereby acquiring rights under other legislation such as the Working Time Regulations and anti-discrimination legislation) and the client is likely to be vicariously liable for any tortious actions committed by the worker while at work, mainly because it will exercise day-to-day control over the worker. It may also be liable to the worker for any claim by him for personal injury.

Standards for employment agencies

The Employment Agencies Act 1973 and subsequent Regulations impose certain standards on employment agencies. These include the requirement to obtain and provide certain information to workers and clients and to agree certain terms with them before providing any services.

Temporary workers

Employers of employees on temporary contracts should be aware of the Fixed-term Employees (Prevention of Less Favourable Treatment) Regulations 2002. They should also be aware that temporary employees will not be able to claim certain statutory rights if they lack sufficient continuity of service. Unfair dismissal requires one year's continuous service (in most cases); the right to receive a redundancy payment requires two years' continuous service; and statutory maternity pay is only payable where the woman, on the 15th week before her expected week of childbirth, has worked continuously for 26 weeks. However, a worker need not have acquired any length of service to make a discrimination claim.

Recent cases

Consistent Group Ltd v. Kalwak (2008) **IRLR 505 CA**

The claimants were Polish nationals. The defendant recruitment agency was involved in the provision of staff to work principally in the hotel industry, but also in food processing factories. The claimants had arranged for the agency to place them in work before they entered the UK. Upon their arrival in the UK, the agency accommodated them in a house where other Poles were already living. Money was deducted for accommodation and cleaning charges.

The contract that the claimants entered into with the agency was entitled 'Self employed sub-contractor's Contract for Services'. Under an 'Obligations' term of that contract it provided that:

- the claimants should provide services on an ad-hoc and casual basis;
- the claimants were not employed by the agency;
- there was no obligation upon the agency to provide work; and
- there was no obligation upon the claimant to accept work offered by the agency.

However, under a 'Substitution' term the agreement provided that where the claimants were assigned to a job they were to perform those services personally unless they could not, and that if a claimant was unable so to perform suitable substitute cover was to be provided by the claimant. The Employment Tribunal found that the claimants were employed by the agency. That decision was upheld by the Employment Appeal Tribunal but The Court of Appeal allowed an appeal by the agency and found that there was in fact no contract as any implied terms would be inconsistent with the express 'obligations' term.

James v. London Borough of Greenwich (2008) IRLR 302 CAMs
James worked for the council through an employment agency from 2001. In 2003 she left that agency and joined another agency which paid a better hourly wage.

She had a contract with the agency, and the agency had a contract with the council, but there was no express contract directly between Ms James and the council. After a period of sickness in August and September 2004 she was told that she was no longer required and that the agency had sent a replacement.

The Employment Tribunal found that the applicant was not an employee of the defendant under a contract of service and rejected her claim for unfair dismissal. That decision was upheld on appeal by the Employment Appeal Tribunal. The applicant appealed, contending that the Employment Tribunal should have considered whether there was an implied employment contract between her and the defendant, particularly in the light of the fact that she had been employed with the defendant for a number of years.

The Court of Appeal dismissed the appeal as whilst the defendant had provided work to the applicant for several years, the mere passage of time did not generate a legal obligation on the part of the defendant to provide her with work any more than it generated a legal obligation on her to do the work.

Recent developments

CBI and TUC Agreement
In May 2008 the CBI and TUC reached agreement on how fairer treatment for agency workers in the UK should be promoted, while not removing the important flexibility that agency work can offer both employers and workers. Agreement was reached that after 12 weeks in a given job there will be an entitlement to equal treatment with permanent employees. It was also agreed that equal treatment will be defined to mean at least the basic working and

employment conditions that would apply to the workers concerned if they had been recruited directly by that undertaking to occupy the same job.

EU Temporary (Agency) Workers Directive

On 9 June 2008 the draft Agency Workers Directive was discussed at the European Employment Council. At the Council political agreement was reached on the Agency Workers Directive. This is an important stage in the European process and breaks six years of deadlock on this issue. At the time of writing, the next stage is for the European Parliament to consider what has been agreed, in its second reading, before the Directive returns to the Council for final agreement. The revised wording of the Agency Workers Directive allows the UK to implement the May 2008 agreement between CBI and TUC. The main points of agreement in the Temporary Agency Workers Directive are:

- Equal treatment as of day one for temporary agency workers as well as regular workers in terms of pay and maternity leave.

- Possibility to derogate from this through collective agreements and through agreements between social partners at national level.
- Temporary agency workers to be informed about permanent employment opportunities in the user enterprise.
- Equal access to collective facilities such as a canteen, childcare facilities and transport service.
- EU Member States have to improve temporary agency workers access to training and childcare facilities in periods between their assignments so as to increase their employability.
- Member States have to ensure penalties for non-compliance by temporary agencies and enterprises.

See also: Employment status, p.282; Fixed-term workers, p.335; Self-employment, p.648

Sources of further information

Agency workers FAQs:
www.berr.gov.uk/employment/employment-agencies/faq/page23965.html

Workplace Law Group's *Working with Contractors 2008: Special Report* defines the difference between an employee and a contractor, and is essential reading for those involved in the appointment of contractors for work activities. It is designed to provide workplace managers with everything they need to know to ensure they, and the contractors they employ, meet their duties under health and safety and employment law. For more information visit www.workplacelaw.net/Bookshop/SpecialReports.

Alcohol and drugs in the workplace

Mandy Laurie, Dundas & Wilson

Key points

- There are legal obligations on employers to ensure a safe and healthy workplace for their employees.
- Employees have a right to work in a safe and healthy workplace and they have responsibilities for their own wellbeing and that of their colleagues.
- Ensuring health and safety in the workplace necessitates the regulation of the use of alcohol and drugs.
- Having clear guidelines regarding the use of alcohol and drugs in the workplace will assist employers in achieving regulation in this area.

Legislation

- Misuse of Drugs Act 1971.
- Health and Safety at Work etc. Act 1974.
- Road Traffic Act 1988.
- Transport and Works Act 1992.
- Management of Health and Safety at Work Regulations 1999.

Legal obligations on employers and employees

The Health and Safety at Work etc. Act 1974 and the Management of Health and Safety at Work Regulations 1999 place a general duty on employers to ensure, so far as is reasonably practicable, the health, safety and welfare of employees.

If an employer knowingly allows an employee under the influence of alcohol or drugs to continue working and this places the employee and/or others at risk, the employer could be prosecuted.

The Road Traffic Act 1988 and the Transport and Works Act 1992 require that drivers of road vehicles must not be under the influence of alcohol or drugs while driving, attempting to drive or when they are in charge of a vehicle.

The Transport and Works Act 1992 makes it a criminal offence for certain workers to be unfit through drink and/or drugs while working on railways, tramways and other guarded transport systems. The operators of the transport systems would also be guilty of an offence unless they had shown all due diligence in trying to prevent such an offence being committed.

The Misuse of Drugs Act 1971 makes it illegal for any person knowingly to permit drug use on their premises except in specified circumstances (e.g. when they have been prescribed by a doctor).

Regulation of alcohol and drugs in the workplace

It is important that employers regulate the use of alcohol and drugs in the workplace because failure to do so can lead to:

- poor performance and reduced productivity;
- lateness and absenteeism;

- accidents and therefore health and safety concerns;
- low morale and poor employee relations; and
- damage to the company reputation and customer relations.

The detrimental effects of drug and alcohol misuse in the workplace can be seen in the following statistics:

- A survey conducted by Alcohol Concern and DrugScope in 2001 reported that 60% of employers reported problems due to alcohol misuse and 27% reported problems due to drug misuse;
- A 2003 survey reported by Alcohol Concern suggested a strong link between absenteeism and alcohol use, and estimated that alcohol was a contributory factor in around 20-25% of all workplace accidents;
- In early 2004 the Health and Safety Executive (HSE) published a report into the scale and impact of illegal drug use by workers which found that overall, 13% of working respondents reported drug use in the previous year; and
- According to the HSE, alcohol is estimated to be responsible for between 3% and 5% of all absences from work in the UK, which equates to between eight and 14 million lost working days.

Alcohol and drug misuse by employees are two problems that increasing numbers of employers face. It is therefore essential that employers have policies and procedures to deal with such problems.

Employment policies and procedures
Policies on alcohol and drugs in the workplace should:

- set out the legal obligations behind the policy and summarise the aims of the policy;

- be clear as to whom the policy applies;
- make clear what will be considered to be alcohol and drug misuse and any specific rules / exceptions e.g. in relation to prescription medicines;
- set out the disciplinary action that will be taken following a breach of the policy;
- provide advice as to where help can be obtained and details of any support that the employer will provide; and
- assure staff that any alcohol or drug problem will be treated in strict confidence.

ACAS has recently issued a new set of guidelines entitled *Health, Work and Well Being* which provides information on producing alcohol and drug policies.

In addition to ensuring that there is a drug and alcohol policy in place, employers should:

- ensure that there are procedures in place to find out if an employee has an alcohol- or drug-related problem e.g. alcohol / drugs screening or medical examinations;
- seek to support the employee in the event that medical advice determines that they have an alcohol- or drug-related problem;
- ensure managers receive appropriate training to implement the policy and to ensure that it is applied consistently;
- consider placing the employee on alternative duties until they have combated their alcohol- or drug-related problem;
- consider the application of the Disability Discrimination Act 1995. Alcohol and drug addiction are not classified as disabilities (other than where addiction is a result of a substance being medically prescribed); therefore there is no requirement on an employer to make reasonable adjustments.

The symptoms of alcohol and drug addiction may, however, be classified as disabilities as the cause of the impairment is irrelevant, even when the cause falls within the exclusion list. Therefore depression or liver disease caused by alcohol dependency would count as an impairment;

- consider disciplinary action where an employee under the influence of alcohol or drugs places either himself or others at risk in the workplace;
- consider dismissal on grounds of capability or for some other substantial reason. Capability dismissals can include where an employee's performance falls below an acceptable standard, or where an employee is absent though ill health because of an alcohol- or drug-related problem; and
- consider reporting any criminal activity to the police. However, there is no obligation for an employer to do so.

In all cases of dismissal, employers should ensure that the statutory dismissal procedure is followed.

See also: Data protection, p.186; Driving at work, p.244; Monitoring employees, p.521; Smoking, p.660

Sources of further information

As an employer you are committed to providing a safe working environment for your employees. You are also committed to promoting the health and wellbeing of your employees. Alcohol and substance misuse can be detrimental to the health and performance of employees and may pose a potential risk to safety in the workplace and the welfare of other employees. Workplace Law Group's *Drug and Alcohol Policy and Management Guide, v.1.0* policy is designed to help protect employees from the dangers of alcohol, drug and other substance misuse and to encourage those with a drug or alcohol problem to seek help. For more information visit www.workplacelaw.net/Bookshop/PoliciesAndProcedures.

Asbestos

Mick Dawson, Bureau Veritas

Key points

Exposure to asbestos is hazardous to health. The three main conditions – asbestosis, lung cancer and mesothelioma – can all be fatal. Current HSE estimates put the death rate in the UK from asbestos-induced diseases at almost 4,000 a year and likely to increase until 2015 or later. Workers in the maintenance and construction trades comprise the largest group of people contracting the diseases, rather than those who worked in the old asbestos manufacturing and installation industry.

The use of asbestos in buildings and construction materials is now completely prohibited. Building owners and those in control of non-domestic premises have a duty to manage the asbestos-containing materials (ACM) within their buildings by formulating an asbestos management plan.

This will involve identifying whether buildings have ACM, assessing the risk from each occurrence and having a process to manage the ACM. In addition, any work on ACM or work that is likely to disturb ACM is regulated by the need for additional risk assessments prior to work taking place, control measures to prevent the spread of asbestos and evidence of training and competency. Depending on risk, work on some ACM may be restricted to HSE-licensed companies who must follow a notification procedure and carry out the work inside segregated work areas using specially trained operatives who undergo medical surveillance.

Legislation

The Control of Asbestos Regulations (CAR) 2006 is the single statutory instrument dealing with asbestos in the UK by implementing the 2003/18/EC amendment to the Asbestos Worker Protection Directive 83/477/EEC. The main parts are as follows:

- Risk Assessments to be undertaken and plans of work to be prepared for all work on asbestos.
- Work becomes licensable, notifiable and workers subject to medical surveillance if the Control Limit will be exceeded.

- Control Limit for all types of asbestos of 0.1 fibres per cubic centimetre (f/cm^3) of air measured over four hours.
- No requirement for licensing, notification or medical surveillance if worker exposure is judged to be "sporadic and of low intensity". This is defined as being below the Control Limit and:
  - short, non-continuous maintenance activities;
  - removal of non-degraded materials firmly linked in a matrix;
  - encapsulation or sealing of ACM in good condition; and
  - air and bulk sampling.

- Awareness training for those whose work may disturb the fabric of the building.
- Selection of Respiratory Protective Equipment (RPE) is based on reducing exposure as low as reasonably practical, not just below the Control Limit.

The Regulations

The provisions fall under the umbrella of the Health and Safety at Work etc. Act 1974. CAR 2006 is supported by two Approved Codes of Practice (ACoPs) and a number of guidance documents.

The primary purpose of the Regulation is to prevent and reduce asbestos exposure to building occupants, visitors and maintenance and construction workers.

The ACoPs give advice on the preferred method of compliance with the Regulation. This advice has special legal status which means that if you are prosecuted for a breach of health and safety law and it is proved that you did not follow the relevant provisions of an ACoP you will need to show that you have complied with the law in some other way or the court will find you at fault.

Approved Code of Practice, L127: The management of asbestos in non-domestic premises

Regulation 4 of the CAR 2006 imposes a more practical duty on those in control of buildings. The duty holder will have to:

- take reasonable steps to find ACM and check their condition;
- presume materials contain asbestos unless there is strong evidence they do not;
- make a written record of the location and condition and keep it up to date;
- assess the risk of exposure; and
- prepare a plan to manage that risk.

Regulation 4 is also known as the Duty to Manage and introduces the concept of an Asbestos Management Plan (or Plan). It applies to managing ACM in non-domestic premises, although the common parts of domestic premises are part of the Regulation. However, landlords have a duty to fulfil the same obligations under the Defective Premises Act 1974 (and also the Management of Health and Safety at Work Regulations 1999), and by taking actions in line with this ACoP they would be demonstrating a satisfactory level of compliance.

The duty holder is defined as being anyone with a contractual, or tenancy, obligation in relation to the maintenance and repair of buildings, or, where there is no contract, anyone in control of the buildings.

The duty holder will need to have in place a Plan explaining how the issues of asbestos within their buildings will be addressed. The Plan should consist of:

- details of each ACM and an explanation of the risk assessment (the algorithm);
- table of priorities and timescales;
- personnel and responsibilities;
- training for employees and contractors;
- procedures for preventing uncontrolled maintenance and building work;
- procedures for ensuring information on ACMs are made available to those that need it;
- arrangements for monitoring ACM; and
- arrangements for updating and reviewing the management plan.

A guidance booklet supports the ACoP: *HSG227 A comprehensive guide to managing asbestos in premises*. A summary of this guidance is reproduced in the free leaflet *INDG223 (rev. 3) A short guide to managing asbestos in premises.*

Management options

There are a number of options available to building managers to fulfil their duties under ACoP L127.

Option A

A comprehensive survey and removal programme would ensure full and thorough compliance. This, however, would be disruptive and extremely costly and the HSE does not advise this as the preferred approach.

Option B

Do nothing in the short term, assume that all unidentified materials contain asbestos and carry out a survey before any building or maintenance work is carried out. This would protect those coming into contact with asbestos but may lead to greater cost in the long run. In larger premises or multi-building portfolios, it would also be difficult to manage, and hence, prove the ACoP is being complied with.

Option C

Introduce a planned survey programme based on a management system that reviews the property stock and identifies where asbestos is more likely to be present, e.g. in buildings constructed between 1945 and 1985. Surveys would then be carried out in those buildings or areas where ACM are most likely to be present and the risk would be assessed on a case-by-case basis.

If the material is in good condition and unlikely to be disturbed, it can be left in place. An asbestos management system should be maintained and updated when action is taken, as well as ensuring that all information is made available to those who could come into contact with asbestos.

Asbestos surveys

The document *MDHS 100 Surveying, sampling and assessment of asbestos-containing materials* was originally published by the HSE in July 2001. It contains the recommended procedures for assessing asbestos risks and describes Type 1, 2 and 3 asbestos surveys. At the time of writing, the HSE has consulted stakeholders regarding updating MDHS 100 (to be renamed *Asbestos: The Surveyors' Guide*) and the new version is expected around Spring 2009. The main changes will be:

- Management Surveys – formally known as Type 1 (presumptive) and Type 2 (sampling) surveys.
- Demolition / Refurbishment Surveys – formally Type 3 surveys requiring a more rigorous inspection for ACM used within the building fabric.
- Greater clarity of the role of the survey in managing asbestos and the management plan.
- Greater clarity on the respective roles of the client and surveyor in the survey and what to expect from each other.
- Strengthening of the sections on competence and caveats.
- Detailed guidance on Demolition / Refurbishment surveys.

Approved Code of Practice and Guidance, L143: Control of Asbestos Regulations 2006

In general terms, those ACM posing the highest risk are those containing fibres that are less firmly bound and so have a greater potential for fibre release – spray coating, insulation and asbestos insulating board (AIB). Because it is likely that the Control Limit of 0.1 f/ml would be exceeded during removal, this work would usually need to be carried out by a licensed contractor who notifies the enforcing authority 14 days in advance by submitting a bespoke plan of work. From

1 September 2008 the Plan of Work no longer needs to be submitted with the notification form, but does need to be prepared prior to notification.

The ACoP expands on the concept of "sporadic and low intensity worker exposure" (see above) a phrase which appears in the EU Directive itself. As well as a comparison with the 0.1 f/cm^3 Control Limit, the Regulation also stipulates that if a peak level of 0.6f/cm^3 measured over ten minutes is not exceeded then the work is judged to be within this definition.

Other examples of work that fit the definition and would therefore not need a licensed contractor, notification to the enforcing authority, or medical surveillance of operatives include:

- materials firmly linked in a matrix will include asbestos cement, textured decorative coatings, bitumen, plastic resin or rubber, and cardboard, felt, gaskets and washers.
- Short non-continuous maintenance activities will include any one person carrying out work for less than one hour in a seven-day period, or all workers carrying out work for less than two hours in total.

However, all work with ACM, including those listed above, must be undertaken by trained workers following a risk assessment and with appropriate controls to prevent exposure.

The ACoP also outlines more defined and explicit training requirements in three areas:

1. Work on licensable ACM.
2. Work on non-licensable ACM.
3. Awareness training for maintenance, installation and construction workers.

Asbestos awareness training
Regulation 10 of CAR 2006 states that awareness training should be given to anyone whose work will disturb the fabric of the building where ACM could be hidden. This would include maintenance staff, electricians, plumbers, painters, HVAC engineers, IT installers and other contracting trades. The only buildings that are exempt would be those that are free from ACM. This does not mean that a building owner or occupier has to train the people themselves, but they will have to ask their suppliers how they intend to comply with the Regulation. This could be achieved by making it a condition of approved supplier status.

Guidance: *The Licensed Contractors' Guide, HSG247*
The ACoP is supported by a detailed guidance document published in 2006. *HSG247* consolidates five previous documents into one single reference point for licensed asbestos removal work.

The Guide embraces subjects such as licences, plans of work, training, PPE, enclosures, controlled removal techniques, waste disposal and decontamination.

Guidance: *The Non-Licensed Guide*
At the time of writing, the HSE plans to introduce a new document which will provide guidance on larger scale work with low risk asbestos materials. The Non-Licensed Guide will focus particularly on asbestos cement (replacing HSG 189/2 Working With Asbestos Cement) and textured coatings where, in the case of the latter, it will expand on the information already provided in L143. Work on textured coatings is subject to a specific exemption and does not require a licence or notification. Nor is it necessary for textured coatings to be removed prior

to a building being demolished. A newly designed good practice work method describes how this material should be removed safely by trained workers using specialist equipment inside a segregated work area.

The guide will cover the more complex and technically challenging work such as the construction of enclosures and airlocks, and reoccupation arrangements. It will also replace HSG213 Introduction to Asbestos Essentials by providing simpler guidance on work planning, use of task sheets, decontamination and waste handling.

Guidance: Minor Works (Asbestos Essentials)

There is additional guidance aimed at works of a minor nature or short duration that the building maintenance and allied trades may carry out. The previous HSG210 Asbestos Essentials Task Manual has been replaced by internet-based task sheets that describe a safe system of work to complete various repair or maintenance tasks which involve work on ACM. There are around 40 different task sheets available for download free of charge from the HSE Asbestos Homepage describing tasks such as how to carry out minor work on textured coatings or AIB, removing asbestos-containing electrical items and dealing with fly-tipped asbestos waste.

Prohibition and related provisions

The importation, supply and use of ACM containing brown and blue (amosite and crocidolite respectively) asbestos (generally comprising asbestos spray coatings, insulation products and AIB) have been formally prohibited since 1985. The importation, supply and use of chrysotile or white asbestos (such as asbestos cement products) was prohibited in 1999.

Using the prohibition dates can provide an indication of what products could be found in buildings if the date of construction is known.

Hazardous Waste Regulations 2005

The Hazardous Waste Regulations came into force in England and Wales in July 2005 and superseded the Special Waste Regulations 1996. Asbestos has now been reclassified as a 'hazardous' waste in line with the EU waste classification system.

The changes from the previous Regulations largely affect the registered waste carriers and licensed asbestos removal companies (defined as being 'consignors') who transport the waste to landfill after it has been removed from buildings.

However, building owners or occupiers are defined as being 'producers' of the waste. This means that their buildings need to be notified to the Environment Agency on an annual basis if more than 200kg of asbestos waste will be removed from their premises. This notification process can either be carried out by the producer or the consignor.

All asbestos products and waste have to be disposed of in accordance with the Regulations by means of a registered carrier (which can be the licensed asbestos removal contractor) under a consignment note procedure.

The Scottish Environmental Protection Agency (SEPA) still recognises the Special Waste Regulations 1996.

Checklist of key action points
- Assess the likelihood of ACM in your premises.
- Decide whether a survey is needed.
- Incorporate the survey information into an Asbestos Management Plan.
- Make this information available to anyone on site who may need it, e.g. contractors.
- Keep the information up to date.

- Assess whether removal or repair work will require a licensed or non-licensed contractor.
- Seek specialist advice if unsure of any of the above requirements.

See also: Hazardous waste, p.720

Sources of further information

HSE – Asbestos: www.hse.gov.uk/asbestos

Asbestos Removal Contractors Association: www.arca.org.uk/

Biological hazards

Chris Streatfeild, Risk Management Consultant

Key points

- Biological hazards include fungi, moulds, bacteria and viruses. The effects of biological contamination in humans can lead to mild conditions such as nausea through to potentially lethal conditions such as hepatitis.
- Biological agents are covered by the Control of Substances Hazardous to Health Regulations 2002 (COSHH), which impose a responsibility on employers to carry out a risk assessment for all hazardous substances.
- Thorough testing and good hygiene practice can help to control the risks of contamination. Under COSHH a biological agent includes any micro-organism, cell culture, or human endoparasite, whether or not genetically modified, which may cause infection, allergy, toxicity or otherwise create a hazard to human health.

Legislation

- Notification of Cooling Towers and Evaporative Condensers Regulations 1992.
- Management of Health and Safety at Work Regulations 1999.
- Genetically Modified Organisms (Contained Use) Regulations 2000 (as amended).
- Control of Substances Hazardous to Health Regulations 2002 (as amended).
- The Carriage of Dangerous Goods and Use of Transportable Pressure Equipment Regulations 2004.

Types of hazard

Many workplaces will find themselves exposed to biological risks, which must be properly controlled in order to avoid contamination. There are four principal types of biological agent:

1. *Fungi.* These produce spores which can cause allergic reactions when inhaled.
2. *Moulds.* These are a group of small fungi that thrive in damp conditions. They can bring on allergic reactions including athlete's foot and asthma.

3. *Bacteria.* These are very small single-celled organisms, which are gradually becoming immune to treatment. The effects of contamination in humans range from mild nausea to potentially lethal conditions such as legionnaires' disease and tuberculosis.
4. *Viruses.* These are minute non-cellular organisms, smaller than bacteria. As with the common cold, there is no way of controlling viruses other than the body's own natural defences. Extremely dangerous forms of virus include AIDS and hepatitis.

The HSE has provided guidance on a range of biohazards including influenza, SARS, legionella and zoonoses. This includes practical advice covering:

- What is the disease / condition?
- How do people get it?
- What are the symptoms?
- Where does it come from?
- What measures are there to control the disease / condition?
- What do you do if you or an employee contracts the disease / condition?

Workplace Law Network
www.workplacelaw.net

These are all essential areas that should be covered as part of a COSHH assessment.

The Approved List of Biological Agents provides a list of specific organisms covered. The criteria for classifying a biological agent in one of four groups are:

- *Group 1* – unlikely to cause human disease.
- *Group 2* – can cause human disease and may be a hazard to employees; it is unlikely to spread to the community and there is usually effective prophylaxis or treatment available.
- *Group 3* – can cause severe human disease and may be a serious hazard to employees; it may spread to the community, but there is usually effective prophylaxis or treatment available.
- *Group 4* – causes severe human disease and is a serious hazard to employees; it is likely to spread to the community and there is usually no effective prophylaxis or treatment available.

Practical scenarios
The risks from biological hazards are increased where a thorough cleaning and maintenance regime is not put in place. The presence of the legionella bacteria in water systems and air conditioning units can result in an outbreak of legionnaires' disease; the UK's most high-profile case occurred in Barrow-in-Furness in 2002, where seven people died.

Similarly, poor hygiene in the use and handling of food can increase the spread of biological hazards. Employers should put in place a policy for managing food in fridges in order to separate meats, cooked food, raw food and liquids so that the effect of minor spillages is minimised. Many employers also enforce a policy preventing workers from eating at their desks or on the shop floor, and ensure that food waste goes into special bins. The advantage here is that food waste can be dealt with specially (both inside and outside the building) to avoid attracting rodents – a further cause of the spread of disease.

The so-called hospital 'superbug' MRSA is perhaps one of the best-known biological hazards. In 2005, an NHS patient successfully sued a hospital, arguing that MRSA could be classified as a biological agent under the Control of Substances Hazardous to Health Regulations, and that the hospital had breached these Regulations by not ensuring its infection control policy was properly implemented. This approach, using health and safety legislation rather than pursuing more expensive, time-consuming and difficult to prove negligence claims, is likely to be used by an increasing number of claimants.

Risk assessments
A COSHH risk assessment should be undertaken to consider the risks arising from biological hazards. As with other risk assessments, the process should first identify the presence of biological agents in the workplace, and the people who might be affected by them. The assessment should take into account the features of a particular hazard (such as the legionella bacteria) and should evaluate the risk. Additional requirements will apply when handling and using genetically modified organisms (see www. hse.gov.uk/biosafety/gmo/law.htm). The most important principle underpinning the risk assessment is understanding the chain of infection. This recognises the notion that the breaking of any link in the chain will enable the infection to be prevented or controlled. In other words, preventing or controlling the source of the infection and its means of transmission or protecting

the potential hosts could each provide an effective level of control. However, as with any hierarchical model, the preferred and most effective method will always be to control as close to the source as possible. Reliance on protecting the host, using perhaps PPE, should always be regarded as a last resort.

In order to conduct a robust risk assessment it is important to carry out accurate monitoring in the form of environmental testing (such as air and water quality monitoring). The risks from biological hazards will be reduced through regular maintenance and cleaning, and through the exercise of good hygiene practice, reinforced through information, instruction, training and supervision.

Hopsital infections

Healthcare-associated infection (HAI) is an important cause of morbidity and mortality amongst hospital patients. The most well known are MRSA (Methicillin-resistant staphylococcus aureus) and Cdiff (Clostridium difficile.) Although these are potentially subject to health and safety regulation, the HSE does not generally deal with clinical matters. Extensive guidance and advice is provided by the Department of Health. However, employers should still ensure that HAIs are addressed as part of the risk assessment protocols performed.

The importance in managing HAIs is demonstrated in a recent report by the HSE on the investigation into outbreaks of Clostridium difficile at Stoke Mandeville Hospital, Buckinghamshire Hospitals NHS Trust. See also the Healthcare Commission report on the investigation into outbreaks of Clostridium difficile at Maidstone and Tunbridge Wells NHS Trust.

See also: COSHH, p.176; Legionella, p.461; Water quality, p.738

Sources of further information

HSE – guidance on influenza, SARS, legionella and zoonoses: www.hse.gov.uk/biosafety/diseases.htm

The Approved List of Biological Agents: www.hse.gov.uk/pubns/misc208.pdf

Department of Health: www.dh.gov.uk/en/Policyandguidance/ Healthandsocialcaretopics/Healthcareacquiredinfection/index.htm

HSE – *Stoke Mandeville Hospital report*: www.hse.gov.uk/healthservices/hospital-infect/stokemandeville.pdf

Healthcare Commission Report – *Maidstone and Tunbridge Wells NHS Trust*: www.healthcarecommission.org.uk/_db/_documents/Maidstone_and_Tunbridge_ Wells_investigation_report_Oct_2007.pdf

Bomb alerts

Andrew Richardson, Scott Wilson

Key points
The legislation that requires an employer to deal with bomb alerts is Regulation 8 of the Management of Health and Safety at Work Regulations 1999. Regulation 8 requires employers to put into place procedures for serious and imminent danger and for danger areas.

Legislation
- Health and Safety at Work etc. Act 1974.
- Management of Health and Safety at Work Regulations 1999.

Required procedures
The Regulations require employers to:

- establish and where necessary action appropriate procedures to be followed in the event of serious and imminent danger to persons at work;
- nominate sufficient numbers of competent persons to implement those procedures in so far as they relate to evacuation from the premises;
- inform any person at work of the nature of the hazard and of the steps taken or the steps to be taken to protect them from it;
- enable the persons concerned to stop work and proceed to a place of safety in the event of their being exposed to serious, imminent and unavoidable danger; and
- except in exceptional circumstances, require the persons concerned to be prevented from resuming work in any situation where there is still serious and imminent danger.

All emergency procedures have to be written down and effectively communicated to all personnel on the premises, including all visitors, contractors, etc. Details of the possible different types of bomb and the different steps required for each will need communicating to all employees. The procedures must identify the nature of the risk and should take into account the seriousness and danger that the risk poses. Responsibilities for specific employees – e.g. receptionists who may take the bomb threat call, maintenance staff who may need to shut down ventilation systems and wardens who may have a duty to ensure the work areas are rapidly evacuated and clear – should all be clearly identified. The person who has been designated as the competent person responsible for these procedures should be clearly identified and his role, responsibilities and authority detailed. Any other emergency procedures required under any other health and safety legislation in respect of dangerous substances, explosives, etc., should be included in the procedural document.

The procedural document must detail how and when the procedures should be implemented to allow people sufficient time to get to a place of safety and should allow for other emergencies that may occur at the same time. Work should not resume while a serious danger remains. Expert advice from authorities such as the police and fire brigade should be obtained if in doubt.

See also: Business Continuity Management, p.100; Emergency procedures and crisis management, p.256

Sources of further information

The website of the Centre for the Protection of National Infrastructure, a Government authority, has good basic information and useful links. Specific advice on bomb threat procedures can be found at www.cpni.gov.uk/ SecurityPlanning/bombThreats.aspx

Preparing for Emergencies – what you need to know: www.preparingforemergencies.gov.uk/

Expecting the unexpected – business continuity in an uncertain world (2003) is also available as a download at www.ukresilience.gov.uk/~/media/assets/ www.ukresilience.info/london_first%20pdf.ashx. Although aimed at the business community in London, it contains much relevant information.

Boundaries and party walls

Stuart Wortley, Pinsent Masons

Key points

■ The position of a boundary on a plan is normally only indicative, and its exact position normally has to be plotted on the ground.

■ Where possible, boundary disputes should be resolved between neighbours as soon as possible without recourse to litigation.

■ Works to a party wall need to conform to the procedures in the Party Wall etc. Act 1996.

■ The erection of a wall or fence may require planning permission if it exceeds certain heights.

Legislation

■ Town and Country Planning (General Permitted Development) Order 1995.
■ Party Wall etc. Act 1996.
■ Land Registration Act 2002.
■ Land Registration Rules 2003.
■ Antisocial Behaviour Act 2003.

Boundary lines

A boundary line is an invisible line between adjoining properties. Its position is ascertained from title deeds and documents, from plans and measurements referred to in these, and from inspection of the site. Frequently, precise positioning is not possible: plans, measurements and descriptions are not necessarily accurate when compared to what appears to be obviously long established on the ground.

There may be a structure along a boundary. This could be a wall or fence on one side of the boundary or a party wall with the boundary along its centre line. The external or (in the case of a multi-let building or terraced house) internal wall of a building may also be a boundary wall or a party wall.

Position of boundary lines

In relation to registered land, the general boundaries rule is that boundary lines on the Land Register are only to be taken as general indications as to their precise position (Land Registration Act 2002, section 60). This is the starting point for ascertaining the position of a boundary line but is no guarantee on a sale of premises. The commonly used standard conditions of sale reflect this by stating that a seller does not guarantee his property boundaries. An application, by the registered proprietor, may be made to the Chief Land Registrar to determine the exact line of the boundary (Land Registration Rules 2003, Part 10).

If an established boundary structure is reasonably close to this line, it is likely that structure will be immediately adjacent to, or, in the case of a party wall, on the true boundary line. In the case of ancient field boundaries, which can exist in developed areas, where there is or was a hedge and a ditch, the presumption is that the boundary is on the far side of the ditch from the hedge.

Ownership of a boundary

A boundary, as such, does not belong to anyone – it is simply the point at which two properties meet. However, the wall which marks the edge of a building will generally belong to that building and be the responsibility of the owner of the property on that side of the boundary line.

Covenants in title deeds to maintain walls or fences, and 'T' marks on the inside of a boundary line on a deeds plan in the title, are all indicators as to which owner is responsible for or owns the boundary structure. But this may not be conclusive. Where a wall divides two buildings, it will normally be a party wall.

Party walls

A party wall is a wall owned or used by two adjoining owners. Commonly, the boundary runs down the centre line and each owner is deemed to own the wall up to the centre line and to have rights over the other half. Special rules apply under the Party Wall etc. Act 1996. The provisions of this Act are very detailed and before taking any steps under it an owner should consult a surveyor or solicitor with specialist knowledge. The Act also details the different types of party wall. In buildings on several floors in multi-occupation, a floor / ceiling may also be a party structure within the Act.

New walls or fences along the boundary

There are limits on the height of man-made boundary structures which can be erected without obtaining planning legislation (Town and Country Planning (General Permitted Development) Order 1995). There is a maximum height of one metre above ground next to a highway and of two metres on all other boundaries. Anything higher will require planning permission.

The owner of land can put up a wall or fence on his land up to the boundary. It may also be possible to construct a wall or fence across a boundary.

Under the Party Wall etc. Act 1996, an owner may put up a new party wall, after appropriate statutory notices, if his neighbour agrees. If the neighbour does not agree, the new wall must be on the building owner's side, but footings may be placed on the adjoining owner's land. A new wall must not interfere with established rights such as rights of light to windows or rights of way.

Boundary structures next to highways may be subject to restrictions or controls, particularly next to access points and on corners where there are vision splays. While security fencing will be permitted in general, anything that is likely to cause harm to children and deterrents designed to injure trespassers, such as broken glass on top of walls, should be avoided as it is likely to result in civil or criminal liability if someone is in fact injured.

Maintaining the boundary structure

If you own the boundary structure, you will be responsible for maintaining it in a safe condition unless the deeds require the adjoining owner to do so. If it causes damage to the neighbouring property by collapse or by parts of it falling onto that property, you may be liable. You can and should insure against this risk.

Check your policy to see that this risk is covered. The cost of rebuilding in case of damage can also be included in your policy.

Existing structures on boundaries may have rights of support. Any activity on the adjoining property that lessens or removes that support will not generally be permissible. However, if the scheme of work is carried out to a party wall under the Party Wall etc. Act 1996, both building owners should have the comfort of having a scheme approved by independent surveyors.

Entry onto neighbouring land to carry out work

If you need access to the neighbouring property to repair or rebuild the boundary structure (which may actually be the wall of your building), your deeds may give you rights.

You also have limited rights for this under the Access to Neighbouring Land Act 1992 (but this does not allow new development). You need to give notice of your intentions to the owner and occupier of the adjoining property. If he is not willing to give you access, you can apply to the court for an order that he must give necessary access. You will be responsible for any damage caused to his property in the course of exercising the right.

The Party Wall etc. Act 1996 contains alternative arrangements for allowing entry onto adjoining land for carrying out work to party walls (and other party structures) and for excavations below the foundations of the neighbouring property. The Act has a strict regime of notices and counter-notices with detailed timescales and provisions for resolution by independent surveyors if the owners are unable to agree. The Act assumes the involvement of specialist surveyors, whose advice should be sought from the outset.

Hedges and trees

The Antisocial Behaviour Act 2003 contains provisions that enable a local authority, on receiving a complaint, to force remedial action in respect of evergreen hedges which are more than two metres high and which adversely affect the reasonable enjoyment of another person's

land. In such a case the owner can be required to ensure that the hedge is kept to a height of no more than two metres.

If there are trees or hedges belonging to a neighbouring property that actually overhang your boundary, you can trim the offending overhanging branches. However, you must return the trimmings to the owner of the tree or hedge. Before exercising this right, it is advisable to warn the neighbouring owner that you intend to do so.

Hedges in rural areas are increasingly subject to conservation controls, particularly where they are next to open or agricultural land. For example, hedges more than 20 metres long with open or agricultural land on at least one side may not be removed without the consent of the Countryside Agency.

Boundary disputes

The costs of taking legal action are usually out of all proportion to the value of the property concerned and only lead to soured relations between adjoining owners. Therefore try to resolve disputes by agreement.

If you agree terms, record them in writing and place a copy with each owner's deeds.

Where it is not possible to reach agreement, it is possible to apply to the court:

- for a declaration as to the correct position of the boundary;
- for an order for possession of any land on your side of the boundary which is occupied by another party, and damages for any loss you may have suffered. Damages may also be awarded based on the benefit which the party in occupation has enjoyed.

If the dispute is urgent (for example if your neighbour is carrying out works to a party wall without complying with the proper procedures) you may be able to apply for an order that the works be stopped whilst the dispute is considered by the court. However, if you ultimately lose the argument, damages and costs may be awarded against you.

If the Land Registry makes an error on the title plan as to the location of a boundary line, you may be able to claim to have the title plan corrected or a claim for compensation.

Under the Civil Procedure Rules, there is a duty on both parties to act reasonably in exchanging information and to try to avoid the need for court proceedings.

> *See also*: Buying and selling property, p.110; Landlord and tenant: possession issues, p.444; Property disputes, p.595

Sources of further information

Workplace Law Network provides premium members with unrestricted access to a comprehensive range of online information – factsheets, case reports and daily news items – on employment, health and safety and premises management. Members also benefit from an online advice service and a free subscription to the *Workplace Law Magazine*. For more information email membership@ workplacelaw.net or call our membership services team on 0871 777 8881.

Building Regulations

Dave Allen, Butler & Young Group

Key points

The Building Regulations are made under powers in the Building Act 1984. They apply in England and Wales, and the majority of building projects have to comply with them. They exist to ensure the health and safety of people in and around all types of building (i.e. domestic, commercial and industrial). They also provide for energy conservation and for access into and around buildings.

The Building Regulations contain various sections dealing with definitions, procedures, and what is expected in terms of the technical performance of building work. For example, they:

- define what types of building, plumbing and heating projects amount to 'building work' and make these subject to control under the Building Regulations;
- specify what types of building are exempt from control under the Building Regulations;
- set out the notification procedures to follow when starting, carrying out and completing building work; and
- set out the 'requirements' with which the individual aspects of building design and construction must comply in the interests of the health and safety of building users, energy conservation, and access into and around buildings.

What is 'building work'?

'Building work' is defined in Regulation 3 of the Building Regulations. The definition means that the following types of project amount to 'building work':

- the erection or extension of a building;
- the installation or extension of certain building services or fittings;
- an alteration project involving work that will temporarily or permanently affect the ongoing compliance of the building, service or fitting with the requirements relating to structure, fire or access to and use of buildings;
- the insertion of insulation into a cavity wall;
- the underpinning of the foundations of a building; and

certain works on a building's thermal elements, works carried out as a result of a change in a building's energy status and work to upgrade the overall energy performance of larger buildings that are being renovated.

Whenever a project involves 'building work', then it must comply with the Building Regulations. This means that the works themselves must meet the relevant technical requirements and they must not make other fabric, services and fittings worse than they previously were.

The Building Regulations may also apply to certain changes of use of an existing building even though the work involved might not seem like 'building work'. This is because the change of use may result in the building as a whole no longer complying with the requirements that will apply to its new type of use, and so having to be upgraded to meet additional requirements. It must always be remembered that a change of use under Building Regulations is usually different to a change of use under planning.

Two systems of building control
If the work amounts to 'building work' it will be subject to, and must comply with, the Building Regulations. To help achieve compliance with the Regulations, developers are required to use one of two types of building control service:

1. Local authority building control service. This can be contacted at the district, borough or city council.
2. An approved inspector's building control service. Approved inspectors are private sector companies or practitioners and are approved to carry out the building control service as an alternative to the local authority. Most approved inspectors belong to the Association of Consultant Approved Inspectors.

Building Control bodies work within a framework of industry set performance standards.

Contravening the Building Regulations
The Building Regulations can be contravened in two ways:

1. By not following the correct procedures; and
2. By carrying out building work that does not comply with the requirements contained in the Building Regulations.

The Local Authority has a general duty to enforce the Building Regulations in its area and will seek to do so by informal means wherever possible.

Where an approved inspector is providing the building control service, the responsibility for checking that the Building Regulations are complied with during the course of building work will lie with that inspector. However, approved inspectors do not have enforcement powers. Instead, in a situation where they consider that building work does not comply with the Building Regulations, they will not provide a final certificate and additionally will notify the Local Authority that they are unable to continue. If no other approved inspector takes on the work, the Local Authority will take on the building control role. From this point the Local Authority will also have enforcement powers to require the work to be altered if it considers this necessary.

If a person carrying out building work contravenes the Building Regulations, the Local Authority may decide to take him to the Magistrates' Court, where he could be fined up to £5,000 for the contravention and £50 for each day the contravention continues (Building Act 1984, section 35).

This action will usually be taken against the builder or main contractor, although proceedings must be taken within six months of the offence (Magistrates' Courts Act 1980, section 127). However this time period is likely to be extended following a governmental review and consultation carried out in 2007.

Alternatively, or in addition, the Local Authority may serve an enforcement notice on the owner requiring alteration or removal of work that contravenes the Regulations (Building Act 1984, section 36). If the owner does not comply with the notice, the Local Authority has the power to undertake the work itself and recover the costs of doing so from the owner.

Current Regulations
- Building Regulations 2000 (SI 2000 No. 2531).
- Building (Amendment) Regulations 2001 (SI 2001 No. 3335).
- Building (Amendment) Regulations 2002 (SI 2002 No. 440).
- Building (Amendment) (No. 2) Regulations 2002 (SI 2002 No. 2871).
- Building (Amendment) Regulations 2003 (SI 2003 No. 2692).
- Building (Amendment) Regulations 2004 (SI 2004 No. 1465).
- Building (Amendment) (No. 3) Regulations 2004 (SI 2004 No. 3210).
- Building (Approved Inspectors etc.) Regulations 2000 (SI 2000 No. 2532).
- Building (Approved Inspectors etc.) (Amendment) Regulations 2001 (SI 2001 No. 3336).
- Building (Approved Inspectors etc.) (Amendment) Regulations 2002 (SI 2002 No. 2872).
- Building (Approved Inspectors etc.) (Amendment) Regulations 2003 (SI 2003 No. 3133).
- Building (Approved Inspectors etc.) (Amendment) Regulations 2004 (SI 2004 No. 1466).
- Building and Approved Inspectors (Amendment) Regulations 2006 (SI 2006 No. 652).
- Building and Approved Inspectors (Amendment) Regulations 2007 (SI 2007 No. 3384).
- Building and Approved Inspectors (Amendment) Regulations 2008 (SI 2008 No.647).
- Building (Amendment) Regulations 2008 (SI 2008 No 671).
- The Building and Approved Inspectors (Amendment) (No.2) Regulations 2006 (SI 2006 No. 3318).
- The Energy Performance of Buildings (Certificates and Inspections)

(England and Wales) Regulations 2007 (SI 2007 No. 991).

Approved Documents
Practical guidance on ways to comply with the functional requirements in the Building Regulations is provided in a series of 14 Approved Documents. Each document contains:

- general guidance on the performance expected of materials and building work in order to comply with each of the requirements of the Building Regulations; and
- practical examples and solutions on how to achieve compliance for some of the more common building situations.

Part A – Structural Stability
(2004 edition)
Part A of the Building Regulations is concerned with the strength and stability of a building. It remained almost unchanged between 1992 and 1 December 2004, when a new edition of the Approved Document came into force.

Part A1 seeks to ensure that a building is constructed in a manner and from materials that ensure all loads are transmitted to the ground:

- safely; and
- without causing deflection or deformation of any part of the building, or movement of the ground, that will impair the stability of any part of another building.

Part A2 deals with ground movement and requires a building to be constructed in such a way that ground movement caused by swelling, shrinkage or freezing of the subsoil, or land-slip or subsidence, will not impair the stability of any part of the building.

Structural safety depends on a successful combination of design and construction, particularly:

- loading;
- properties of materials;
- detailed design;
- safety factors; and
- workmanship.

The Approved Document gives detailed guidance on the construction of certain residential buildings no greater than three storeys in height and other small buildings of traditional construction. All other buildings should be designed to the relevant Code of Practice.

Structural design is heavily dependent on the guidance contained in British Standards and Codes of Practice. These give information on:

- loadings;
- structural work in timber;
- structural work in masonry;
- structural work in reinforced, pre-stressed and plain concrete;
- structural work in steel;
- structural work in aluminium; and
- foundations.

Part A3 requires that a building does not suffer from disproportionate collapse as a result of an accident in a part of the building. It seeks to ensure that, should an accident occur in or around a building, such as a gas explosion or vehicle impact, the building is sufficiently tied together to avoid a catastrophic collapse.

Part B – Fire Safety (2006 edition) – Volume 1: Dwellinghouses, Volume 2: Buildings other than Dwellinghouses
Part B aims to ensure the safety of the occupants and of others who may be affected by a fire in a building, and to provide assistance for firefighters in the saving of lives.

Therefore, buildings must be constructed so that if a fire occurs:

- the occupants are given suitable warning and are able to escape to a safe place away from the effects of the fire;
- fire spread over the internal linings of the walls and ceilings is inhibited;
- the stability is maintained for a sufficient period of time to allow evacuation of the occupants and access for firefighting;
- fire spread within the building and from one building to another is kept to a minimum; and
- satisfactory access and facilities are provided for firefighters.

It is not a function of the Regulations to minimise property damage or insurance losses in the event of fire.

Part B1 applies to all building types (except prisons). In some parts of the country there may be other legislation that imposes additional requirements on the means of escape from a building. In inner London reference needs to be made to the Building (Inner London) Regulations 1987 and elsewhere Local Acts of Parliament (e.g. the Hampshire Act 1983) may apply.

The Approved Documents give specific guidance on means of escape in Vol 1: Dwellinghouses and Vol: 2 Buildings other than Dwellinghouses. Volume Two makes reference to general principles that address fire alarm and fire detection systems and horizontal and vertical escape in flats and other building types.

Guidance is also given on:
- lighting of escape routes;
- provision of exit signs;

- fire protection of lift installations;
- performance of mechanical ventilation and air-conditioning systems in the event of fire; and
- construction and siting of refuse chutes.

Part B2 gives guidance on the choice of lining materials for walls and ceilings. It concentrates on two properties of linings that influence fire spread:

- the rate of fire spread over the surface of a material when it is subject to intense radiant heating; and
- the rate at which the lining material gives off heat when burning.

It also gives guidance on how these properties can be controlled, mainly by restricting the use of certain materials.

Part B3 deals with Internal Fire Spread and includes measures to ensure:

- stability of the load-bearing elements of the structure of a building for an appropriate time in the event of fire;
- subdivision of the building into compartments by fire-resisting construction such as walls and floors;
- sealing and subdivision of concealed spaces in the construction to inhibit the unseen spread of fire and smoke;
- provision of sprinkler protection to high-rise flats;
- protection of openings and fire-stopping in compartment walls and floors including fire damper guidance; and
- provision of special measures to car parks and shopping complexes.

Part B4 seeks to limit the possible spread of fire between buildings. It does this by:

- making provisions for the fire resistance of external walls and by limiting the

susceptibility of their external surfaces to ignition and fire spread;
- limiting the extent of openings and other unprotected areas in external walls in relation to the space separation from the boundary of the site; and
- making provisions for reducing the risk of fire spread between roofs and over roof surfaces.

Part B5 gives guidance on installation of fire mains and hydrants to buildings with further guidance on:

- provision of vehicle access for high reach and pumping appliances;
- access for fire service personnel into and within the building; and
- venting of heat and smoke from basements.

There is interaction between the Building Regulations and other fire safety requirements in England and Wales. It is therefore important for developers and designers to adhere to set procedures to ensure that owners and occupiers do not need to carry out extra building work at the end of a project. The Building Regulations cover means of escape, fire alarms, fire spread, and access and facilities for the fire service, but, for certain buildings, additional requirements are imposed by the Regulatory Reform (Fire Safety) Order 2005. Because of this, there are statutory requirements on the building control body to consult with the fire authority and for fire safety information to be provided to building owners under Regulation 16B. Details of the consultation procedure can be found in *Building Regulations and Fire Safety Procedural Guidance* (4th edition 2007) published by the CLG.

Part C – Site Preparation and Resistance to Contaminants and Moisture (2004 edition)
Part C of the Building Regulations is concerned with site preparation and

resistance to contaminants and moisture. It remained almost unchanged between 1992 and 1 December 2004, when a new edition of the Approved Document came into force.

Part C1 deals with site preparation and the possibility of contaminants.

- Attention needs to be given to the removal of vegetable matter, topsoil and pre-existing foundations.
- Site investigation is recommended as the method for determining how much unsuitable material should be removed.
- Remedial measures are required to deal with land affected by contaminants. These include materials in or on the ground (including faecal or animal matter) and any substance that is, or could become, toxic, corrosive, explosive, flammable or radioactive. Therefore it includes the naturally occurring radioactive gas radon and gases produced by landfill sites, such as carbon dioxide and methane.
- The area of land that is subject to measures to deal with contaminants includes the land around the building.
- Protection from radon includes buildings other than dwellings.
- Guidance is included relating to subsoil drainage and the risk of transportation of water-borne contaminants.

Part C2 deals with resistance to moisture and seeks to ensure that the floors, walls and roof of a building are constructed in such a way that moisture cannot penetrate the building and that nor will condensation occur.

- Guidance recommends that in order to reduce the condensation risk to floors, walls and roofs reference should be made to BS 5250 'Limiting thermal bridging and air leakage:

robust details' and BR 262 'Thermal insulation: avoiding risks'.
- Guidance is now provided on the use of moisture-resistant boards for the flooring in bathrooms, kitchens and other places where water may be spilled from sanitary fittings or fixed appliances.
- Reference is made to BS 8208 for assessing the suitability of cavity walls for filling.
- Where walls interface with doors and windows, checked rebates are now recommended in the most exposed parts of the country.
- Where Part M requires level access, there is a need to pay particular attention to detail in exposed areas to ensure adequate provision is made for resistance to moisture.

Former requirement F2 'Condensation in roofs' has been transferred to Part C as it deals with effects on the building fabric rather than ventilation for the health of occupants.

Part D – Toxic Substances (1985 edition, amended 1992 and 2000)
Part D is probably the least used of the Approved Documents. It was introduced when urea formaldehyde foam was a popular method of providing cavity insulation in buildings. The foam can give off formaldehyde fumes that can be an irritant to occupants.

The Approved Document gives guidance on:

- the type of materials used for the inner leaf of the cavity together with the suitability of walls for filling;
- details of the foam itself; and
- the credentials of the installer.

In recent years the popularity of urea formaldehyde foam has declined.

Part E – Resistance to the Passage of Sound (2003 edition, amended 2004)
Part E1 deals with the protection against sound from other parts of the building and adjoining buildings. It aims to achieve adequate sound insulation to walls and floors between dwelling houses, flats and rooms for residential purposes.

A room for residential purposes means a room, or suite of rooms, which is not a dwelling house or flat and which is used by one or more persons to live and sleep in, including rooms in hotels, hostels, boarding houses, halls of residence and residential homes, but not including rooms in hospitals, or other similar establishments, used for patient accommodation. The requirements for resistance to airborne and impact sound for floors also include stairs where they form part of the separating element between dwellings.

Site testing of sound insulation is intended on a sampling basis. However, as an alternative, robust details have been available to the industry since 1 July 2004. Robust Details Ltd is a non-profit-distributing company, limited by guarantee, set up by the house-building industry. Its objectives are broadly to identify, arrange testing and, if satisfied, approve and publish design details that, if correctly implemented in separating structures, should achieve compliance with requirement E1. It also carries out checks on the performance achieved in practice.

The robust design details are available in a handbook that may be purchased from Robust Details Ltd. The company can be contacted at: PO Box 7289, Milton Keynes MK14 6ZQ; tel. 0870 240 8210; fax 0870 240 8203; email administration@ robustdetails.com. More information can be found at www.robustdetails.com.

Although the design details are in the public domain, their use in building work is not authorised unless the builder has registered the particular use of the relevant design detail or details with Robust Details Ltd to identify a house or flat in which one or more of the design details are being used.

The requirement for appropriate sound insulation testing imposed by the Regulations does not apply to building work consisting of the erection of a new dwelling house (i.e. a semi-detached or terraced house) or a building containing flats where robust details are registered and adhered to.

Part E2 sets standards for the sound insulation of internal walls and floors in dwelling houses, flats and rooms for residential purposes. Site testing is not intended.

Part E3 controls reverberation in the common parts of buildings containing flats or rooms for residential purposes. Site testing is not intended.

All new school buildings are now controlled under the Building Regulations, and Part E4 covers the sound insulation, reverberation time and indoor ambient noise levels. Guidance on meeting the requirement is given in Building Bulletin 93 published by the Department for Education and Skills (DfES).

Part F – Means of Ventilation (2006 edition)
The basic requirements have not been amended by the 2006 changes but the guidance in Approved Document F has been. In order to satisfy Part L, buildings should attain a better standard of airtightness than before. This means that there will be less ventilation due to air flowing into and out of the building through

gaps and cracks in the structure. To take account of this it has been necessary to improve the ventilation requirements that are described in Approved Document F in order to satisfy requirement F1. The new provisions have been designed to ventilate buildings to an air permeability as good as $3m^3/h/m^2$ at 50 pa. Buildings more airtight than this will require additional ventilation provision.

The opportunity has also been taken to improve other aspects of the guidance, and the main changes are listed below:

- A mainly performance-based approach has been adopted to allow designers more flexibility and encourage product innovation.
- Ventilation areas are now described in terms of equivalent area, instead of free area, because equivalent area relates better to air flow.
- More guidance has been given for domestic mechanical and natural ventilation systems.
- Guidance has been given for ventilation of basements in dwellings.
- The recommended air supply rate for offices has been increased from 8l/s per person to 10l/s per person.
- Replacement windows should normally be fitted with trickle ventilators.
- Appendices give guidance on passive stack ventilation; good practice for installing fans in dwellings; and ingress of external pollutants into buildings in urban areas.

Part G – Hygiene (1992 edition, second impression (with amendments) 1992, further amended 2000) (due for Revision 2009)
Part G1 gives guidance on the scale of provision of sanitary conveniences and washing facilities in dwellings (houses, flats and maisonettes) and houses in multiple occupation. For other building

types reference is made to other relevant legislation. The reference to Regulations made under the Offices, Shops and Railway Premises Act 1963 and the Factories Act 1961 can be ignored since both have been replaced by recommendations contained in the Workplace (Health, Safety and Welfare) Regulations 1992. Reference should also be made, as appropriate, to the Food Hygiene (General) Regulations 1970 (amended by the Food Hygiene (Amendment) Regulations 1990), which apply to premises used for the purposes of a food business.

Reference can also be made to BS 6465:2006 Part 1 'Sanitary installations. Code of practice for scale of provision, selection and installation of sanitary appliances'.

Part G2 gives guidance on the provision of bathrooms and recommends that the same provision applies also to a house in multiple occupation.

Part G3 provides guidance on the installation of unvented hot-water storage systems. The Approved Document recommends that such a system should be the subject of an agreed method of approval or assessment and should be installed by a competent person. It must also comply with the Water Supply (Water Fittings) Regulations 1999.

Part H – Drainage and Waste Disposal (2002 edition)
Part H1 gives guidance on the design of above-ground sanitary pipework and below-ground foul drainage. It stresses the need for the drainage system to be designed and constructed to:

- convey foul water to a suitable outfall (a foul or combined sewer, cesspool, septic tank or holding tank);

- minimise the risk of blockage or leakage;
- prevent the entry of foul air into the building under normal working conditions;
- be ventilated;
- be accessible for clearing blockages; and
- not increase the vulnerability of the building to flooding.

Sewers (i.e. a drain serving more than one property) should normally have a minimum diameter of 100 mm when serving no more than ten dwellings. Sewers serving more than ten dwellings should normally have a minimum diameter of 150 mm. Access points to sewers should be in places where they are accessible and apparent for use in an emergency.

Part H2 deals with the siting, construction and capacity of wastewater treatment systems and cesspools so that they:

- are not prejudicial to health or a nuisance;
- do not adversely affect water sources or resources;
- do not pollute controlled waters; and
- are not sited in an area where there is a risk of flooding.

They should be adequately ventilated and should be constructed so that the leakage of the contents and the ingress of subsoil water is prevented.

Wastewater treatment systems should be considered only where the nature of the subsoil indicates that the operation of the system and the quality and method of disposal of the effluent will be satisfactory and where connection to mains drainage is not practicable.

The quality of the discharged effluent is not covered by the Building Regulations, but some installations may require consent for discharge from the Environment Agency.

Additionally, the Environment Agency may take action against any person who knowingly permits pollution of a stream, river, lake, etc., or groundwater, by requiring him to carry out works to prevent the pollution (Water Resources Act 1991 (as amended), section 161A).

Part H2 also contains guidance on:

- the siting and construction of drainage fields; and
- the provision of information regarding the nature and frequency of the maintenance needs of wastewater systems and cesspools.

Part H3 gives guidance on the need for rainwater from roofs and paved areas to be carried away either by a drainage system or by some other means.

Where provided, a rainwater drainage system should:

- carry the flow of rainwater from the roof to a suitable outfall (a surface water or combined sewer, soakaway or watercourse);
- minimise the risk of blockage or leakage; and
- be accessible for clearing blockages.

The Approved Document contains guidance on:

- precautions to be taken where rainwater is permitted to soak into the ground;
- siphonic roof drainage systems;
- eaves drop systems;
- rainwater recovery systems;
- drainage of paved areas;
- the design of soakaways and other infiltration drainage systems; and
- the use of oil separators.

Part H4 gives guidance on the construction, extension or underpinning of a building over or within three metres of the centreline of an existing drain, sewer or disposal main shown on the sewerage undertaker's sewer records.

Building work should be carried out so that it will not:

- cause overloading or damage to the drain, sewer or disposal main; or
- obstruct reasonable access to any manhole or inspection chamber.

Future maintenance works to the drain, sewer or disposal main must be possible without undue obstruction, and the risk of damage to the building must not be excessive due to failure of the drain, sewer or disposal main. The guidance also explains that precautions should be taken if piles are to be placed close to drains.

Part H5 is designed to ensure that:

- rainwater does not enter the public foul sewer system where it may cause overloading and flooding;
- rainwater does not enter a wastewater treatment system or cesspool not designed to take rainwater where it might cause pollution by overloading the capacity of the system or cesspool; and
- foul water, including run-off from soiled or contaminated paved areas, does not enter the rainwater sewer system or an infiltration drainage system intended only for rainwater.

Part H6 gives guidance on the design, siting and capacity of refuse containers and chutes for domestic developments.

For non-domestic developments it is recommended that the collecting authority is consulted regarding:

- the volume and nature of the waste, and the storage capacity required;
- any requirements for segregation of waste for recycling;
- the method of storage, including any proposals for on-site treatment;
- the location of storage areas, treatment areas and waste collection points; and
- the means of access to these, hygiene arrangements, hazards and protection measures.

Part J – Combustion Appliances and Fuel Storage Systems (2002 edition)
Parts J1 to J3 apply only to fixed fuel-burning appliances and incinerators. The Approved Document gives advice on:

- the amount of air supply needed for safe combustion of the fuel;
- the construction of hearths, fireplaces, flues and chimneys;
- the location of boilers; and
- separation of flues and chimneys from structural timbers and thatch.

The guidance also includes ways of demonstrating that the safe performance of combustion installations is not undermined by mechanical extract ventilation systems.

Part J4 calls for a notice providing the performance characteristics of the hearth, fireplace, flue or chimney to be fixed in an appropriate place in the building. The Approved Document gives guidance on the form, content and location of such notices.

Part J5 gives guidance on the protection of oil and LPG fuel storage systems from fire. This includes the positioning and/or shielding so as to protect these systems from fires that might occur in adjacent buildings or on adjacent property.

Part J6 makes provision for protection against leakage from oil storage tanks polluting boreholes and water and drainage courses and for permanent labels containing information on how to respond to oil escapes to be positioned in a prominent position.

Part K – Protection from Falling, Collision and Impact (1998 edition, amended 2000)

Part K1 deals with the design, construction and installation of stairs, ladders and ramps. In a public building the standard of provision may be higher than in a dwelling to reflect the lesser familiarity and number of users.

It deals with:

- the rise and going of stairs (i.e. their steepness);
- provision of handrails; and
- allowing sufficient headroom over a stair.

Parts K2 and K3 cover:

- provision of guards designed to prevent pedestrians from falling;
- provision of vehicle barriers capable of resisting or deflecting the impact of vehicles; and
- measures to protect people in loading bays from being struck or crushed by vehicles by providing adequate numbers of exits or refuges.

Part K4 gives guidance on the installation of windows so that parts that project when the window is open are kept away from people in and around the building and on the provision of features that guide people away from open windows, skylights and ventilators.

The Approved Document also describes measures designed to prevent the opening and closing of doors and gates from presenting a safety hazard. These include vision panels in doors and safety features to prevent people being trapped by doors and gates.

Recommendations for the design of stairs for means of escape included in Approved Document B (Fire Safety) and for the design of stairs and ramps for use by disabled people in Approved Document M (Access to and Use of Buildings) should also be considered.

Compliance with Part K (and where appropriate Part M as it relates to stairs and ramps) would prevent the service of an improvement notice with regard to the relevant requirements of the Workplace (Health, Safety and Welfare) Regulations 1992.

Part L – Conservation of Fuel and Power (2006 edition) (due for revision 2009)

New buildings (Approved Documents L1A and AD L2A)

Compliance involves demonstrating that five separate criteria have been met:

1. The CO_2 performance target has been met.
2. No elements of the design fall outside defined limits of design flexibility. This is to ensure that the performance of the building is not critically dependent on a particular feature that might fail to be maintained in proper working order.
3. The building does not suffer from excessive solar gains. This is to ensure that the building has appropriate passive measures to limit any tendency to retro-fit air conditioning.
4. The building as constructed should deliver the calculated CO_2 performance. This includes mandatory airtightness testing and commissioning to be carried out as detailed in the respective Approved Documents.
5. Appropriate information is provided to the user to enable the building to be operated efficiently.

Dwellings (Approved Document L1A)
The CO_2 target is based on achieving a 20% reduction in CO_2 emissions for heating, hot water and lighting in a gas-heated dwelling. The target for dwellings heated using fuels other than gas is adjusted by the fuel factor, which relates the CO_2 emission factor of the particular fuel to that of gas. This results in an increased CO_2 target, but a reduced energy consumption target. The energy impact of thermal bridging and secondary heating must be included within the estimate of the performance of the proposed building.

Lighting is a non-tradable item in the CO_2 target (i.e. a fixed amount of low energy lighting is assumed in the calculation irrespective of the number of low energy fittings that are installed). The guidance also requires that the fittings be installed with an appropriate shade or diffuser. The existing guidance on the minimum number of fittings is now supplemented by a percentage of light fittings criteria, which means that if a large number of less efficient lamps are specified, then an increased number of low energy lights will be needed to compensate.

The limits on design flexibility mean that the average performance of opaque elements should be no worse than the 2002 elemental standards. Guidance on the minimum efficiency of heating and hot water systems is given in a second tier guidance document. This specifies that all boilers should be rated at least SEDBUK B, although oil boilers are allowed a slightly lower standard in the period to 1 April 2007.

New non-domestic buildings (Approved Document L2A)
The CO_2 target is based on achieving a reduction in CO_2 emissions for heating, hot water, ventilation, cooling and lighting of between 24.5 and 28%, depending on servicing strategy. This overall improvement includes the contribution made from a benchmark provision of LZC technology. Credits can be taken for advanced monitoring and control features, and for power factor correction.

The limits on design flexibility mean that the average performance of opaque elements should be no worse than the 2002 elemental standards. Greater clarity has been achieved through the introduction of definitions for such features as display glazing and high usage entrance doors. Guidance on the minimum efficiency of building services systems is given either in the Approved Document or in a second tier guidance document.

The requirement for testing and commissioning has been widened to include leakage testing of ventilation ductwork.

Work in existing buildings (Approved Documents L1B and L2B)
Most of the changes are concerned with bringing more types of work within the control of the Regulations as described in paragraphs 10 and 11. Particular guidance is given on what would be reasonable provision when renovating a controlled element and the application of consequential improvements to non-domestic properties.

The standards that the building work is expected to achieve are generally more demanding than in 2002, with the exception of replacement windows, where the standard is unchanged (although for dwellings and similar domestic type buildings, compliance can now be demonstrated using a window energy rating). A separate standard has been introduced for doors.

Part M – Access to and Use of Buildings (2004 edition)

Part M covers access to and use of buildings. It used to deal solely with access and facilities for disabled people but is now universally inclusive to encourage the provision of an accessible environment for all.

Parts M1 to M3 cover:

■ the use of access statements;
■ access to the main entrances to the building from the edge of the site and from car parking within the curtilage;
■ access into and within the building and from one building to another on a site;
■ the provision of lifts;
■ access to and use of the building's facilities;
■ design of the building's elements so that they are not a hazard;
■ the provision and design of sanitary accommodation and changing and showering facilities;
■ the provision and design of accommodation for disabled people in audience or spectator seating;
■ aids for communication for people with impaired hearing or sight;
■ accessibility of switches and controls; and
■ visually contrasting surfaces and fittings.

Part M4 covers the provision of reasonably accessible sanitary conveniences in dwellings.

There is interaction between the Building Regulations, the Disability Discrimination (DDA) Act 1995 and the Disability Discrimination (Employment) Regulations 1996. It is therefore important for developers and designers to appreciate how all these pieces of legislation might apply to a particular scheme. This should ensure that owners and occupiers do not need to carry out extra building work at the end of a project.

Part N – Glazing: Safety in Relation to Impact, Opening and Cleaning (1998 edition, amended 2000)

People using buildings may come into contact with glazing in critical locations, such as doors, door side panels and at low level in walls and partitions. Part N1 describes measures to be adopted to reduce the likelihood of cutting and piercing injuries occurring from contact with such glazing by making sure that it will break safely, be robust or be permanently protected.

Part N2 gives guidance on the measures that might be adopted to indicate the presence of large uninterrupted areas of transparent glazing with which people might collide. It does not apply to dwellings.

Part N3 provides guidance on the safe operation of openable windows, skylights and ventilators relating to the location of controls and the prevention of falling. It does not apply to dwellings.

Part N4 gives guidance for the safe means of access for cleaning glazed surfaces where there is danger of falling. Guidance is also given for safe cleaning where the glazed surfaces cannot be reached from the ground, a floor or some other permanent stable surface. Again it does not apply to dwellings.

Parts N3 and N4 contain similar provisions to those in Regulations 15(1) and 16 of the Workplace (Health, Safety and Welfare) Regulations 1992.

Part P – Electrical Safety (2006 edition)

A new section of the Regulations was introduced on 1 January 2005 to control electrical safety in dwellings. Revisions were introduced on 1 April 2006.

Statutory requirements P1 and P2 have been revoked and replaced with a new requirement P1. This requires only that reasonable provision be made in respect of design and installation. There is no longer a statutory requirement to provide information although such provision may be needed for those operating, altering or maintaining installations.

Part P applies in England and Wales to fixed electrical installations in dwellings and in:

- dwellings and business premises that have a common supply;
- common access areas in blocks of flats;
- shared amenities in blocks of flats such as laundries and gymnasia; and
- outbuildings, including sheds, garages and greenhouses, supplied from a consumer unit located in any of the above.

Guidance has been altered to make it clear that installations attached to the outside of dwellings are within the scope of Part P.

The Approved Document includes guidance on a long list of circumstances where work is to be regarded as notifiable or non-notifiable.

The main way of complying is to follow the technical rules in BS 7671:2001 and the guidance given in installation manuals that are consistent with this standard, e.g. IEE On-Site Guide and Guidance Notes Nos 1 to 7.

With certain exceptions, notification of proposals to carry out electrical installation work must be given to a building control body before work begins.

This prior notification is not necessary if:

1. the proposed work is to be undertaken by a competent person, i.e. a firm that has been approved by and certificated by an approved competent person scheme.
2. the proposed work is minor work. This comprises:

- work that is not in a kitchen or special location:
  - adding lighting points to an existing circuit;
  - adding socket outlets and fused spurs to an existing circuit; and
  - installation / upgrading of main and supplementary equipotential bonding;
- work in all locations:
  - replacing accessories such as socket outlets, control switches and ceiling roses;
  - replacement of the cable for a single circuit only;
  - re-fixing or replacing the enclosures of existing components; and
  - providing mechanical protection to existing fixed installations.

See also: Accessible environments, p.50; Disability access and egress, p.204; Disability legislation, p.209; Energy performance, p.290; Fire in non-domestic premises, p.325; Toilets, p.683; Ventilation and temperature, p.704

Sources of further information

Building and planning legislative guidance and downloads of Approved Documents can be obtained at: www.planningportal.gov.uk

Bullying and harassment

Debbie Fellows, Anderson Strathern LLP

Key points

- Ensure that a formal statement or policy exists and is supported by senior management.
- Issue a clear statement that bullying and harassment are totally unacceptable.
- Investigate alleged incidents thoroughly and immediately.
- Provide access to counselling and advice for recipients, where practicable, or consider giving time off for these activities.
- Make appropriate use of grievance and disciplinary procedures, or introduce a harassment procedure.
- Train your managers to increase knowledge and awareness.

Legislation

- Sex Discrimination Act 1975 as amended by the Sex Discrimination Act 1975 (Amendment) Regulations 2008.
- Race Relations Act 1976.
- Disability Discrimination Act 1995.
- Protection from Harassment Act 1997.
- Employment Equality (Sexual Orientation) Regulations 2003.
- Employment Equality (Religion or Belief) Regulations 2003.
- Employment Equality (Age) Regulations 2006.

What is bullying and harassment?

Bullying is an abuse or misuse of power that may be characterised as offensive, intimidating, malicious or insulting behaviour intended to undermine, humiliate, denigrate or injure the recipient.

Harassment, in general terms, is unwanted conduct affecting the dignity of men and women in the workplace. It may be related to age, sex, sexual orientation, disability, religion or similar philosophical belief, nationality, ethnic origin, race or any personal characteristic of the individual and may be persistent or a single incident.

However, if the individual can show that the conduct has created a hostile and degrading environment for them, it will not matter that the harassment related to another individual. An example of this could be where somebody has been offended by sexist remarks made about or to another person.

The key element is that the actions or comments are viewed as demeaning and unacceptable by the recipient.

How can bullying and harassment be recognised?

It is good practice for employers to give examples of what is unacceptable behaviour in their workplace. These may include:

- spreading malicious rumours or insulting someone (particularly on the grounds of race, sex, disability, sexual orientation, religion or belief, or age);
- ridiculing or demeaning someone – setting them up to fail;
- copying memos that are critical about someone to others that do not need to know;
- exclusion or victimisation;

- unfair treatment;
- unwelcome sexual advances –
  touching, standing too close,
  displaying offensive materials even
  generally;
- making threats or comments about job
  security without foundation;
- deliberately undermining a competent
  employee by overloading and constant
  criticism;
- blocking or refusing promotion or
  training opportunities; and
- threatening behaviour, violent gestures
  or physical violence.

Why do employers need to take action?

Not only are bullying and harassment
unacceptable on moral grounds, but they
could cause serious problems for an
organisation, including:

- poor morale and poor employee
  relations;
- loss of respect for managers and
  supervisors;
- poor performance;
- lost productivity;
- absence;
- resignations;
- damage to company reputation;
  and
- tribunal and other court cases and
  awards of unlimited compensation.

The legal position

Employers are generally responsible in
law for the acts of their employees unless
it can be shown that the employer took
such steps as were reasonably practicable
to prevent the employee carrying out the
bullying and harassment ('the reasonable
steps defence'), which has proven to be a
high test to meet.

Since the implementation of the Sex
Discrimination Act 1975 (Amendment)
Regulations 2008, which came into
force on 6 April 2008, employers are

now liable for acts committed by third
parties. An employee who has been
subjected to harassment by a third party
on two or more previous occasions, with
the knowledge of her employer, will be
able to bring a claim against her employer
if the harassment happens again. The
employer will be liable unless they can
successfully rely on the reasonable steps
defence referred to above. The third party
can be different on each occasion but
the employee can only raise a claim if
she herself has been harassed on three
occasions. Therefore employers will not
be able to ignore acts of harassment,
simply because they are due to the actions
of customers or other non-employees. It
remains to be seen whether the liability of
employers for acts done by third parties
contrary to the Sex Discrimination Act
1975 will be extended to the other areas of
discrimination legislation.

Employees who suffer bullying and
harassment in the workplace may bring
a variety of claims against an employer
including:

- A claim of unfair constructive dismissal
  (based on the employer's breach
  of the implied terms of trust and
  confidence).
- A claim for harassment under the
  discrimination legislation (i.e. a claim
  that the harassment is on grounds of
  sex, race, disability, sexual orientation,
  religion or belief, or age).
- In more extreme cases including
  personal injury, a claim can be
  brought in the civil courts based on
  either negligence or a breach of a
  statutory duty such as the duty to
  provide a safe place and system of
  working under the Health and Safety
  Act 1974.
- Employers can be vicariously
  liable under the Protection from
  Harassment Act 1997 for bullying
  by their employees, if it constitutes

harassment under this Act and it satisfies the appropriate tests. In order to bring a successful case under this Act there must be a course of conduct consisting of two or more instances, the conduct must constitute harassment (e.g. cause harm to others) and the perpetrator must have known / ought to have known that the conduct amounted to harassment. In respect of a claim under this legislation there is no 'reasonable steps defence' available.

What should employers do?

- Ensure there are in place up-to-date equal opportunities/harassment policies coupled with commitment from senior management.
- Supplement policies with training for managers and employees.
- Set a good example.
- Maintain fair procedures.
- Ensure complaints are handled confidentially, fairly and sensitively.

Formulating a policy

- Include in the policy a clear statement that bullying and harassment will not be tolerated.
- Give examples of unacceptable behaviour.
- State that bullying and harassment may be treated as disciplinary offences.
- Outline the steps you will take to prevent bullying and harassment.
- Outline the responsibilities of supervisors and managers.
- Give reassurance of confidentiality for any complaint.
- Ensure protection from victimisation.
- Refer to grievance procedures (informal and formal), including timescale for action.
- Refer to disciplinary procedure, including timescale for action.
- Include provisions for counselling and support.

How should employers respond to a complaint?

There are four basic options:

1. *Informal approach.* In some cases people are unaware that their behaviour is unwelcome. Sometimes a 'quiet word' can lead to greater understanding and an agreement that the unwelcome behaviour will stop.
2. *Counselling.* This can provide a vital and confidential path for an informal approach and sometimes the opportunity to resolve the complaint without the need for formal action. Other options include employee assistance programmes funded by the employer.
3. *Grievance procedures.* If the employee does not wish his/her complaint to be dealt with informally (or the informal approach has failed) the complaint should be fully investigated and dealt with in terms of the grievance procedure.
4. *Disciplinary procedures.* Where the outcome of the grievance procedure is that the complaint of bullying and harassment is upheld the employer may consider disciplinary action against the perpetrator in accordance with the disciplinary procedure.

It is important to follow a fair procedure with regard to both the complainant and the person accused. See *'Disciplinary and grievance procedures', p.216* for more information.

What should be considered when imposing a penalty?

Action taken must be reasonable in the circumstances. In some cases, counselling or training may be more appropriate than disciplinary action. When a penalty is imposed, consider the employee's general disciplinary record, action in previous cases, any explanations or mitigating circumstances, and whether the penalty is reasonable.

Written warnings, suspension or transferring the bully or harasser are examples of suitable disciplinary penalties. Suspension or transfer can only be used if permitted in the employee's contract of employment so check it carefully before imposing this.

When gross misconduct has occurred, dismissal without notice may be appropriate. Since October 2004, all employers contemplating dismissal or action short of dismissal (such as loss of seniority or suspension without pay) have had, as a minimum, to follow a three-step statutory procedure (*see 'Disciplinary and grievance procedures', p.216*).

Finally, review your harassment and bullying policy on a regular basis to ensure that it remains effective.

See also: Disciplinary and grievance procedures, p.216; Discrimination, p.222; Employment disputes, p.278; Mental health, p.496

Sources of further information

Equality and Human Rights Commission: www.equalityhumanrights.com

Workplace Law Network provides premium members with unrestricted access to a comprehensive range of online information – factsheets, case reports and daily news items – on employment, health and safety and premises management. Members also benefit from an online advice service and a free subscription to the *Workplace Law Magazine*. For more information email membership@ workplacelaw.net or call our membership services team on 0871 777 8881.

Business Continuity Management

Peter Power, Visor Consultants Ltd

Key points

Business continuity (BC) is now a recognised feature in a great many organisations in both public and private sectors. It has evolved considerably over the past few years from a position where it was little more than just IT disaster recovery by another name, to now being a continuing management process that embraces the vertical needs of the entire organisation (between the furthest points in the entire up/down stream supply chain) to more horizontal issues such as reputation and staff welfare.

BC is fundamentally different from disaster recovery as it focuses on the continuance of key operations, rather than just trying to recover what's left after a disaster. It also differs from insurance, which is chiefly about compensation rather than continuity. It is therefore more realistic to refer to the title of this chapter as BC management (BCM) rather than just BC or planning, albeit a workable plan is a key deliverable of the BC process. When properly applied, BCM embraces, or at least works in complete harmony with, the following business and business support functions, irrespective of private or public sector application:

- Facilities management;
- Risk management;
- Physical security;
- IT security;
- Crisis management;
- Staff welfare;
- Operations; and
- Finance.

Background

In the UK BS 25999 is the definitive standard for Business Continuity Management (BCM). Readers are encouraged to read this standard which is available directly from the BSI website (www.bsi-uk.com). It offers an accepted framework for incident anticipation and response with a series of recommendations for good practice. Some of the following text is therefore taken directly from the BSI standard, as well as the British Government UK Resilience website (which contains advice and links on BCM and many other resilience issues) along with up-to-date information from the Business Continuity Institute and guidance from the author of this chapter who frequently runs BC and Crisis Management workshops.

Although BS 25999 is a most valuable step forward in terms of BC. a growing number of workshops, committees and other research have shown a perceived need to now broaden BC to a new or fourth generation BC (assuming the first generation was basic contingency plans, then disaster recovery followed by the present BC doctrine). The emerging concept of 4GBC™ is intended to much better unite with other discrete 'silos' such as risk management, facilities management, corporate governance and security, probably under a single umbrella of 'resilience' and predicated on a wider acceptance of corporate uncertainty.

It might equally be referred to as Corporate Resilience or a revised approach to Risk Management? However, this chapter will focus more on the existing acceptance of BC, starting with a closer look at the existing BS 25999, which is in two parts:

- BS 25999 Part one. This Standard establishes the process, principles and terminology of BCM, providing a basis for understanding, developing and implementing business continuity within an organisation and to provide confidence in business-to-business and business-to-customer dealings.
- BS 25999 Part two. BS 25999-2 specifies requirements for establishing, implementing, operating, monitoring, reviewing, exercising, maintaining and improving a documented BCM System (BCMS) within the context of managing an organisation's overall business risks.

The requirements specified in BS 25999-2 are generic and intended to be applicable to all organisations (or parts there of), regardless of type, size and nature of business. The extent of application of these requirements depends on the organisation's operating environment and complexity. Therefore the design and implementation of a BCMS to meet the requirements of this standard will be influenced by regulatory, customer and business requirements, the products and services, the processes employed and the size and structure of the organisation. It will not be the intent of this British Standard to imply uniformity in the structure of a BCMS but for an organisation to design a BCMS to be appropriate to its needs and that meets its stakeholder's requirements.

BS 25999-2 can be used by internal and external parties, including certification bodies, to assess an organisation's ability to meet its own business continuity needs, as well as any customer, legal or regulatory needs.

Business continuity management (BCM) is a process that helps manage risks to the smooth running of an organisation or delivery of a service, ensuring continuity of critical functions in the event of a disruption, and effective recovery afterwards. The Government aims to ensure all organisations have a clear understanding of BCM and its importance, and foster discussion of how best to achieve business continuity. This chapter outlines the importance of BCM and how it should be carried out.

Business continuity management
BCM is a generic management framework that is valid across the public, private and voluntary sectors. It is an ongoing process that helps organisations anticipate, prepare for, prevent, respond to and recover from disruptions, whatever their source and whatever aspect of the business they affect. The primary 'business' of private sector organisations is the generation of profit, a process that BCM seeks to protect. Other organisations provide services to the public, and it is equally important that these are protected and resilient.

BCM is a business-owned, business-driven process that establishes a fit-for-purpose strategic and operational framework that:

- proactively improves an organisation's resilience against the disruption of its ability to achieve its key objectives;
- provides a rehearsed method of maintaining or restoring an organisation's ability to supply its critical products and services to an agreed level within an agreed time after a disruption; and
- delivers a proven capability to manage a business disruption and protect the organisation's reputation and brand.

While the individual processes of BCM can change with an organisation's size, structures and responsibilities, the basic principles remain exactly the same for voluntary, private or public sector organisations, regardless of their size, scope or complexity.

BCM linked to mission and strategy
All organisations, whether large or small, have aims and objectives, such as to grow, to provide services and to acquire other businesses. These aims and objectives are generally met via strategic plans to achieve an organisation's short, medium and long-term goals. BCM understanding at an organisation's highest level will ensure that these aims and objectives are not compromised by unexpected disruptions.

The consequences of an incident vary and can be far reaching. These consequences might involve loss of life, loss of assets or income, or the inability to deliver products and services on which the organisation's strategy, reputation or even survival might depend. BCM needs to recognise the strategic importance of perception, welfare and the interest of all stakeholders.

Examples of stakeholders include, but are not restricted to, internal and 'outsourced' employees, customers, suppliers, distributors, investors, insurers and shareholders. Furthermore, consequences

of a disruption unfold, new stakeholders emerge and have a direct impact on the eventual extent of the damage. Examples of these include competitors, environmentalists, regulators and the media.

BCM is complementary to a risk management framework that sets out to understand the risks to operations or business, and the consequences of those risks. Risk management seeks to manage risk around the critical products and services that enable an organisation to survive. Product and service delivery can be disrupted by a wide variety of incidents, many of which are difficult to predict or analyse by cause. However, risk management relates directly to insurance and where a well assembled and audited BCM structure exists it should be possible to explore a reduction in insurance premiums by virtue of now being able to reduce your exposures and demonstrate acceleration in post-crisis business resumption.

By focusing on the impact of disruption, BCM identifies those products and services on which the organisation depends for its survival, and can identify what is required for the organisation to continue to meet its obligations. Through BCM, an organisation can recognise what needs to be done before an incident occurs to protect its people, premises, technology, information, supply chain, stakeholders and above all, reputation. Indeed, a crisis well handled can actually increase the value of the organisation and enhance reputation. Moreover, an organisation with appropriate BCM measures in place might be able to take advantage of opportunities that have a high risk.

BCM forms an important element of good business management, service provision and entrepreneurial prudence within which managers and owners have the responsibility to maintain the ability of the organisation to function without disruption. Organisations constantly make commitments or have a duty to deliver products and services; i.e. they enter into contracts and otherwise raise expectations. All organisations have moral and social responsibilities, particularly where they provide an emergency response or a public or voluntary service. In some cases, organisations have statutory or regulatory duties to undertake BCM.

All business activity is subject to disruptions, such as technology failure, flooding, utility disruption and terrorism. BCM provides the capability to adequately react to operational disruptions while protecting welfare and safety. You should not regard BCM as a costly planning process, but as one that adds value to the organisation. In other words, it should not be thought of as a 'grudge purchase'.

BC plans (BCPs)

Having first established a management framework for BCM, it follows that some form of 'user friendly' plan should be written and be constantly available, plus be regularly updated and exercised.

All organisations should carefully consider the case for BCPs as a systematic basis for managing the continuity of critical functions and recovery of the organisation from disruption. Good BC planning may require both generic and specific plans. A generic plan is a core plan which enables an organisation to respond to a wide range of possible scenarios, setting out the common elements of the response to any disruption (e.g. invocation procedure, command and control, access to financial resources). Within the framework of the generic plan, specific plans may be required in relation to specific risks, sites or services. Specific plans provide a detailed set of

arrangements designed to go beyond the generic arrangements when these are unlikely to prove sufficient.

BCPs should be based on systematic identification and assessment of the significant risks of an emergency occurring in an organisation's area. Identifying the risks threatening the performance of critical functions in the event of an emergency will enable organisations to focus resources in the right areas, and develop appropriate plans.

A BCP cannot be considered reliable until it is exercised and has proved to be workable, understood by all involved and not just a bundle of papers that might be designed to protect the author above informing the reader.

Exercising should involve:

- validating plans;
- rehearsing key staff; and
- testing systems that are relied upon to deliver resilience (e.g. uninterrupted power supply).

The frequency of exercises will depend on the organisation, but should take into account the rate of change (to the organisation or risk profile), and outcomes of previous exercises (if particular weaknesses have been identified and changes made). This is further explored below.

It is important to ensure that relevant people across the organisation – and in other organisations where appropriate – are confident and competent concerning the plan. A training programme should be developed and run for those directly involved in the execution of the BCP, should it be invoked.

Organisations should not only put BCPs in place, but should ensure they are reviewed regularly and kept up to date. Particular attention may need to be paid to staff changes, changes in the organisation's functions or services, changes to the organisational structure, details of suppliers or contractors, changes to risk assessments and business objectives / processes.

Creating BCM in your organisation

The BCM lifecycle comprises six elements explained below. These can be implemented by organisations of all sizes, in all sectors – public, private, non-profit, educational, manufacturing, etc. The scope and structure of a BCM programme can vary, and the effort expended will be tailored to the needs of the individual organisation, but these essential elements still have to be undertaken.

1. *Understanding the organisation.* The activities associated with doing this properly provide information that enables prioritisation of an organisation's products and services, and the urgency of the activities that are required to deliver them. This sets the requirements that will determine the selection of appropriate BCM strategies.
2. *BCM programme management.* This enables the BC capability to be both established and maintained in a manner appropriate to the size and complexity of the organisation – and all its dependencies.
3. *Determining business continuity strategies.* This enables a range of strategies to be evaluated and allows an appropriate response to be chosen for each product or service, such that the organisation can continue to deliver those products and services at an acceptable level of operation and within an acceptable timeframe during and following a disruption. The choice made will take account of the resilience and countermeasure options already present within the organisation.

4. *Developing and implementing a BCM response.* Developing and implementing a BCM response results in the creation of BCPs and crisis management plans that detail the steps to be taken during and after an incident to limit damage to reputation and restore operations.
5. *Exercising, maintaining and reviewing BCM arrangements.* This leads to the organisation being able to demonstrate the extent to which its strategies and plans are complete, current and accurate; and identify opportunities for improvement.
6. *Embedding BCM in the organisation's culture.* This enables BCM to become part of the organisation's core values and instils confidence in all stakeholders in the ability of the organisation to cope with disruptions.

Creating a BCM policy

The BCM policy should, ideally, define the following processes:

- The set-up activities for establishing a BC capability.
- The ongoing management and maintenance of the BC capability.
- The set-up activities incorporating the specification, end-to-end design, build, implementation and initial exercising of the BC capability.
- The ongoing maintenance and management activities include embedding BC within the organisation, exercising plans regularly, and updating and communicating them, particularly when there is significant change in premises, personnel, process, market, technology or organisational structure.

You should ensure that the BCM policy is appropriate to the nature, scale, complexity, geography and criticality of its business activities and that it reflects its culture, dependencies and operating environment. The BCM policy defines the process requirements to ensure that business continuity arrangements continue to meet the needs of the organisation in the event of an incident. This policy should ensure that a business continuity capability is promoted within the organisation's culture and the growth and development of the organisation's products and services. The BCM capability should be integrated into the organisation's change management activity.

You should also develop a BC policy which states the objectives of BCM within the organisation. Initially, this may be a high level statement of intent which is refined and enhanced as the capability is developed.

The BC policy should provide the organisation with documented principles to which it will aspire and against which its business continuity capability should be measured. The BCM policy should be owned at a high level, e.g. a board director or elected representative. You may consider the following useful when developing a BCM policy:

■ Defining the scope of BCM within the organisation.
■ BCM resourcing.
■ Defining the BCM principles, guidelines and minimum standards for the organisation.
■ Referencing any relevant standards, regulations or policies that have to be included or can be used as a benchmark.

Any organisation should maintain and regularly review its BCM policy, strategies, plans and solutions on a regular basis in line with the organisation's needs. The scope of the BCM policy should clearly define any limitations or exclusions that apply, e.g. geographical or product exclusions. But however BCM is resourced, there are key activities that should be carried out both initially and on an ongoing basis. These may include:

■ defining the scope, roles and responsibilities for BCM;
■ appointing an appropriate person or team to manage the ongoing BCM capability;
■ keeping the business continuity programme current through good practice;
■ promoting business continuity across the organisation and wider, where appropriate;
■ administering the exercise programme;
■ coordinating the regular review and update of the BC capability, including reviewing or reworking risk assessments and business impact analyses (BIAs – see below);
■ maintaining documentation appropriate to the size and complexity of the organisation;
■ monitoring performance of the BC capability;
■ managing costs associated with the BC capability; and
■ establishing and monitoring change management and succession management regimes.

Preparing for immediate media interest
A well structured BCM process should recognise that how you are portrayed by TV, radio and the press will, to a very large extent, be decided by how well you have prepared for this and fully understand what the media will expect (sometimes demand) of you during any real or perceived crisis. It follows that your media response should be realistic, exercised and documented, including:

■ an incident communications strategy. A press holding statement might have to be ready in 30 minutes, otherwise speculation will fill in for facts;
■ the organisation's preferred interface with the media. Reporters and

journalists do not want to speak to Spin Doctors or third party agencies. They want a senior figure who can appear honest and make sense of what is going on;

■ a guideline or template for the drafting of a statement to be provided to the media at the earliest practicable opportunity following the initial incident;

■ appropriate numbers of trained, competent spokespeople nominated and authorised to release information to the media. Ideally, a cadre of suitable trained executives should always be contactable – and a decision taken in advance on what any manager might, for example, say if 'door-stepped' by a reporter. Saying 'no comment' is not a good idea; and

■ establishment, where practicable, of a suitable venue to support liaison with the media, or other stakeholder groups.

In some cases, it may be appropriate to provide supporting detail in a separate document, establish an appropriate number of competent, trained people to answer telephone enquiries from the press, prepare background material about the organisation and its operations (this information should be pre-agreed for release) and ensure that all media information is made available without undue delay.

BCM documentation

Individuals tasked with maintaining BC should create and maintain the BC documentation. This may include the following:

■ BCM policy – BCM scope statement and BCM terms of reference.
■ Business impact analysis (BIA – see below).
■ Risk and threat assessment.
■ BCM strategy / strategies.
■ Awareness programme.

■ Training programme.
■ Crisis management plans.
■ BC plans.
■ Exercise schedule and reports.
■ Service level agreements and contracts.
■ Insurance requirements / expectations.

Business impact analysis and determining critical activities

You should determine and document the impact of a disruption to the activities that support critical products and services of your organisation. This process is commonly referred to as a business impact analysis (BIA). For each activity supporting the delivery of critical products and services within the scope of its BCM programme, the organisation should:

■ assess over time the impacts, both in financial and operational terms, that the loss or disruption of the activity would have; and

■ establish the maximum tolerable period of disruption of each activity by identifying the maximum time period after the start of a disruption within which the activity needs to be resumed, taking into account any business cycle implications, the minimum level at which the activity needs to be performed on its resumption, the length of time within which normal levels of operation need to be resumed and identify any inter-dependent activities, assets, supporting infrastructure or resources that have also to be recovered over time.

When assessing impacts, you should consider those that relate to the business aims of your organisation and objectives and its stakeholders. These may include:

■ the impact on staff or public wellbeing;
■ damage to, or loss of, premises, technology or information;

- the impact of breaches of statutory duties or regulatory requirements;
- damage to reputation – yours and your stakeholders;
- damage to financial viability;
- deterioration of product or service quality; and
- environmental damage.

The organisation should document its approach to assessing the impact of disruption and its findings and conclusions.

During a disruption, impacts often increase over time and affect each activity differently. Impacts might also vary depending on the day, month or point in the business lifecycle.

You might assess risk according to (a) likelihood and (b) impact and then categorise activities according to their priority for recovery.

Those activities whose loss, as identified during the BIA, would have the greatest impact in the shortest time and which need to be recovered most rapidly may be termed 'critical activities'. You may then wish to focus your planning activities on critical activities, but should recognise that other activities will also need to be recovered within their maximum tolerable period of disruption and might also require advance arrangements to be in place.

The maximum time period for resuming activities can vary between seconds and several months depending on the nature of the activity. Activities that are time-sensitive might need to be specified with a great degree of accuracy, e.g. to the minute or the hour. Less time-sensitive activities might require less accuracy.

The maximum tolerable period of disruption will influence each activity's

recovery time objective when determining BCM strategies.

Exercising your BCM structure

Nothing correlates to how well your organisation will perform in a real drama as much as how accurately you previously exercised your BCM structure in advance. Not only that, but to have learned the lessons from any exercise so that BC becomes a process that can be moved into at the first opportunity to ensure you are ready to not only react, but predict where any crisis might be heading and take avoidance steps without delay.

Exercises or tests can be either desktop or walk through in style where little or no communications are actually put to the test, but a group of key people sit around a table while a facilitator puts an unfolding scenario to them to explore how things might go if it was real. These sessions normally last just a few hours and might be made much more realistic by showing pre-recorded mock TV news broadcasts, etc. However, the aim is not to put people into a gratuitous pressure test, but to explore in a fairly gentle way where any gaps might exist – and to identify them by leaving enough time to hold a thorough and immediate de-brief.

More complex exercises might follow once obvious problems have been resolved following a desktop walk through. These more structured sessions could involve actual working from home, invocation to IT hot sites and your executive layer facing a simulated TV news camera crew.

Any exercise should be realistic, carefully planned, and agreed with stakeholders, so that there is minimum risk of disruption to business processes. An exercise should also be planned such that the risk of an incident occurring as a direct result of the exercise is minimised.

Every exercise should have clearly defined aims and objectives. A post-exercise debriefing and analysis should be undertaken which considers the achievement of the aims and objectives of the exercise. A post-exercise report should be produced that contains recommendations and a timetable for their implementation.

It follows that where exercises show significant deficiencies or inaccuracies in the BCM structure they should be rerun after corrective actions have been completed.

BC under the Civil Contingencies Act 2004

The Civil Contingencies Act requires Category 1 responders (those on the front line such as the police and fire services, etc.) to maintain BC plans to ensure that they can continue to exercise their functions in the event of an emergency so far as is reasonably practicable.

The BCM duty in the Act relates to all the functions of a Category 1 responder, not just its civil protection functions. Hence the legislation requires Category 1 responders to maintain BC plans to deal with emergencies. But it also requires them to make provision for ensuring that their ordinary functions can be continued to the extent required. The Regulations also require Category 1 responders to put in place a training programme for those directly involved in the execution of the BCP should it be invoked.

The Act also requires local authorities to provide advice and assistance to businesses and voluntary organisations in relation to BCM. This duty is an integral

part of the Act's wider contribution to building the UK's resilience to disruptive challenges.

Category 2 organisations (e.g. HSE, transport and utility companies) are 'cooperating bodies' and are less likely to be involved in the heart of BC planning work but will be heavily involved in incidents that affect their sector. Category 2 responders have a lesser set of duties – cooperating and sharing relevant information with other Category 1 and 2 responders. They should, however, maintain full and workable BC plans.

In the event of any national or regional crisis Category 1 and 2 organisations will come together to form Local Resilience Forums (based on police areas) which will help coordination and cooperation between responders at the local level.

About the BS 25999 standard

The British Standard on BC establishes the process, principles and terminology of BCM. The purpose of this standard is to provide a basis for understanding, developing and implementing business continuity within an organisation and to provide confidence in the organisation's dealings with customers and other organisations. It also enables the organisation to measure its BCM capability in a consistent and recognised manner. The standard is intended for use by anyone with responsibility for business operations or the provision of services, from top management through all levels of the organisation; from those with a single site to those with a global presence; from sole traders and small-to-medium enterprises (SMEs) to organisations employing thousands of people. It is therefore applicable to anybody who holds responsibility for any operation, and thus the continuity of that operation. However, it should be noted that the standard does not cover the actual activities of emergency planning in as much as that topic relates to civil emergencies.

See also: Bomb alerts, p.75; Emergency procedures and crisis management, p.256; Occupational health, p.537; Strikes, p.677

Sources of further information

Business Continuity Institute: www.thebci.org

British Standards Institute: www.bsonline.bsi-global.com

The Institute of Risk Management: www.theirm.org

UK Resilience: www.ukresilience.info

Workplace Law Group's *Guide to Business Continuity 2007* provides a framework for business managers to ensure that their organisation has an action plan in place in the event of an emergency situation arising. The Guide covers issues such as Business continuity management (BCM); BC plans; preparing for immediate media interest; BC under the Civil Contingencies Act 2004; the BS 25999 standard on BC; and crisis management. For more information visit www.workplacelaw.net/Bookshop/GuidesTo.

Buying and selling property

Kevin Boa, Pinsent Masons

Key points

- A buyer will want to ensure it acquires a property with good and marketable title through due diligence.
- A survey and an environmental audit are recommended.
- Until contracts are exchanged, either party can withdraw without penalty. After contracts are exchanged, both parties are legally bound.
- A buyer is generally responsible for insurance as soon as contracts are exchanged.

Overview

This chapter discusses the acquisition and disposal of freehold land and buildings.

A purchase or sale is best described by outlining the various stages involved. This procedure applies in England and Wales. The law and procedure are different in Scotland and are outside the ambit of this chapter.

Legislation

The principal piece of legislation is the Law of Property Act 1925 although there is a significant volume of succeeding legislation.

The pre-contract stage

Firms of chartered surveyors usually deal with the disposal of commercial property. It is not essential to buy or sell through a commercial surveyor, but such firms have knowledge of market conditions.

Surveyors will often agree 'heads of terms' setting out what has been agreed between the seller and the buyer and covering key points including the parties, property, price, timetable and any particular conditions.

A buyer will want to acquire a property which has good and marketable title, as

otherwise the buyer might be concerned about its value and the ability to dispose of the property in the future. Without good and marketable title it might also be difficult to raise finance on the strength of the security of the property. This involves the process of due diligence, i.e. the investigation of the property by the buyer before entering into the contract. There are three possible approaches:

1. A full title investigation is carried out by the buyer's solicitors.
2. A certificate of title is given by the seller's solicitors.
3. Warranties are given by the seller in the contract.

Additionally, there may be a combination of any of these.

Title investigation

This involves the buyer's solicitor investigating the seller's legal title to the property and checking whether there are any restrictive covenants or other matters affecting the property. In addition, pre-contract enquiries will be raised with the seller's solicitors and various searches carried out against the property.

The buyer should also arrange for a survey to be carried out to ensure that the property is sound and that the sale price is not excessive. The buyer will need to consider investigating for contamination, particularly if the property has a history of industrial use.

Certificate of title

Instead of the buyer making a full investigation of the property, the seller's solicitor could produce a certificate of title confirming that the property has good and marketable title and disclosing all information it has in respect of the property.

Unless the seller gives a warranty as to the accuracy of the certificate, the buyer will in essence be relying on the seller's solicitor's professional indemnity policy.

A certificate is useful if there is insufficient time for the buyer to carry out its investigation, if a large number of properties are involved, and where the seller's solicitor acted on the original purchase and so is already in possession of much of the information needed to complete the certificate.

The terms of the certificate will still need to be negotiated and the statements given may be qualified or disclaimers imposed.

Warranties

The seller can give warranties about the property to the buyer which provide the latter with a form of insurance. Ideally they should protect the buyer in respect of the presence of factors relating to the property of which it is unaware and which detrimentally affect the property.

Warranties are vital if the property is acquired as part of a share acquisition to cover the unknown liabilities, actual or contingent, and therefore go beyond matters of pure title.

However, the buyer will need to consider whether the warranties are worth the paper they are written on as it is obviously essential that the seller is financially able to satisfy any claim under the warranties.

The warranties are usually qualified by a separate disclosure letter which will be annexed to the contract. If an item is excluded from the warranties, the risk passes to the buyer. It is therefore essential that there is also an express warranty in the contract that the disclosure letter is accurate.

There may also be some general disclaimers, e.g. that the buyer is aware of all matters apparent from a physical inspection of the property (which means that a survey should be commissioned).

The contract

Most disposals or acquisitions are preceded by exchange of contracts. Until contracts are exchanged, neither party is committed to the transaction and either may withdraw at any time.

A contract is a binding agreement between the buyer and the seller which sets out all the relevant details and the agreed terms. Sometimes completion is conditional, e.g. on planning permission being granted.

Once contracts are exchanged, neither party may withdraw from the transaction without being in breach of contract and facing a possible claim for damages or specific performance. Specific performance is an order by the court requiring the party in default to complete the transaction. It is a discretionary remedy and will normally be awarded only where damages alone are not regarded as being an adequate remedy.

Contracts should not be exchanged until any pre-contract investigations and surveys have been made and the buyer's funding is in place.

If there is a chain of related sales and purchases (common in residential transactions), then all the parties in the chain need to be ready to exchange at the same time. This can lead to delay.

On an exchange of contracts, a deposit is usually paid by the buyer; normally 10% of the purchase price. It is usual for the deposit to be held by the seller's solicitor pending completion, although in certain circumstances the deposit may be used for an onward purchase by the seller. The buyer may lose its deposit if it does not complete the purchase in accordance with the terms of the contract.

Unless the contract says otherwise, the buyer is responsible for insuring the property as soon as contracts are exchanged.

Completion
Completion is when legal ownership is transferred. It is at this stage that the balance of the purchase price is paid over and possession of the property is given to the buyer. The completion date is fixed in the contract and traditionally is four weeks after the exchange, although it can be much earlier or later (depending on what the parties agree).

The transfer
The transfer is the document which formally transfers the property from the seller to the buyer. The transfer describes the property and any rights, restrictive covenants, shared facilities, rights of way and other matters which affect the property and subject to which the buyer will take the property.

Where the property is sold subject to covenants (such as restrictions on the use of the property), the buyer will usually agree in the transfer to observe and perform these covenants and to indemnify the seller for any loss caused to the seller if the buyer fails to comply with them.

Stamp duty land tax
Stamp duty land tax is payable by the buyer on the transaction. A wide range of transactions are subject to SDLT – essentially most dealings with an interest in land. The rate of SDLT varies according to the price paid. Transactions not exceeding a value of £125,000 (for residential property) or £150,000 (for commercial property) are exempt from SDLT. The maximum rate is 4% where the price is more than £500,000.

On commercial property sales, value added tax at 17.5% may be chargeable on the purchase price, and the stamp duty land tax in such cases is charged on the VAT-inclusive figure.

After completion
The transfer must be sent to the Land Registry so that the buyer can be registered as the new owner of the property. A registration fee is payable, which is calculated according to the price paid. The maximum fee is currently £700. Once registration is complete, the Land Registry will issue a title information document which provides that the buyer is the owner of the property and also includes a plan of the property and details of any matters affecting the property such as rights of way and restrictive covenants. It is recommended that older title deeds are retained to assist in resolution of disputes involving rights of way, boundaries or covenants.

Acquisition of a property as part of a business purchase
Sometimes a property is acquired as part of the purchase of a business. This can

happen when a buyer acquires all the shares in a company. The buyer steps into the shoes of the seller so that there is simply a change in control rather than a change in the owner of the business and as a consequence of any property owned by the company). As there is no change in ownership, the buyer will take on all existing liabilities of the company in respect of the property.

Although searches will be carried out, enquiries raised and a contract entered into, there is no need for a transfer to be completed (because there is no change in the name of the owner) and consequently no need for a Land Registry application to be made. There are various tax and other considerations on a share purchase including possible stamp duty savings, as stamp duty on a share purchase is currently fixed at 0.5% of the price. Specialist advice on how to structure the acquisition or disposal of the property is recommended.

See also: Dilapidations, p.193; Landlord and tenant: lease issues, p.448; Landlord and tenant: possession issues, p.444

Sources of further information

Workplace Law Network provides premium members with unrestricted access to a comprehensive range of online information – factsheets, case reports and daily news items – on employment, health and safety and premises management. Members also benefit from an online advice service and a free subscription to the *Workplace Law Magazine*. For more information email membership@ workplacelaw.net or call our membership services team on 0871 777 8881.

Carers

Gemma Cawthray, Martineau Solicitors

Key points
- Caring has an important role in society and workplaces need to accommodate carers.
- Current law does not provide adequate support and assistance to working carers.
- It is in employers' interests to help carer employees.

Legislation
- Disability Discrimination Act 1995.
- Employment Rights Act 1996.
- Employment Relations Act 1999.
- Employment Framework Directive (2000/78/EC).
- Employment Act 2002.
- Work and Families Act 2006.

Definition of a carer

A 'carer' is usually defined as someone who, without pay, looks after and provides help and support to a partner, child, relative, friend or neighbour, who could not manage without their help or support. This caring responsibility could be necessary due to age, physical or mental illness, addiction, sickness or disability.

Facts and statistics

It is estimated that there are approximately six million carers in the UK, of which three million are employees. This equates to one in seven of the workforce having some form of caring responsibilities in addition to their employment. Caring can be difficult and stressful and there is evidence to suggest that one in every five carers has to give up their paid employment to be a full-time carer. Becoming a carer can often happen overnight; for example, if a relative is injured in an accident, or is diagnosed with a serious illness. Therefore, the nature of caring is unpredictable and changeable. It is estimated that over the next three decades the total number of carers in the UK will increase from six million to nine million and this will obviously impact on the workforce.

Providing support for employee carers

It is increasingly important for employers to be aware of the difficulties carers face and provide support to employee carers. Employee carers have to juggle their work commitments with their other responsibilities. Many employers need educating in the issues working carers face and how they can assist them. The question of why employers should work to assist carers is easy to answer. Most carers tend to be over 30 and consequently are in their prime employment years. Employees in this age range are often the most experienced and valuable. Organisations derive benefit from retaining their existing staff, as it reduces the need to recruit and retrain and provide stability. There are many other benefits to providing such support, including lower turnover of staff, reduced absence rates, higher levels of morale and greater productivity.

Carers and the law

Flexible working

The Work and Families Act 2006 extended the right to request flexible working, which was initially introduced in 2003, to carers of adults. However, only certain employees qualify under the legislation. The right applies to employees who have been continuously employed for 26 weeks and who fall into one of the following categories:

- have a child under six or a disabled child under 18 and are responsible for the child as a parent / guardian / foster parent or holder of a residence order, or are the spouse, partner or civil partner of one of the categories listed or are applying to care for the child; or
- are a carer who cares, or expects to be caring, for a spouse, partner, civil partner or relative who lives at the same address and who is over the age of 18.

It is worth noting that the Government is proposing to extend the right to request for those with responsibility for children from six up to 16. Many carers do not fall within the statutory definition of those who are entitled to apply for flexible working. The application to work flexibly must be made in writing. Upon receipt of the application, the employer has a legal duty to consider the request seriously and objectively and it can only object on specified business grounds. The following procedure must be followed.

1. The employer and employee must meet within 28 days of receipt of the application to discuss the matter.
2. The employer must provide the employee with written notification of its decision within 14 days of the meeting.
3. If the employer accepts the request, both parties will need to meet again to consider what arrangements will need to be put in place. An accepted request normally amounts to a permanent variation to the employee's contract of employment.

4. If the request is rejected, the employee has the right to appeal in writing within 14 days.

Within 14 days of receiving the written appeal the parties must again meet and the outcome should be notified to the employee within 14 days of the meeting. This process can take up to 14 weeks. The employee is entitled to be accompanied at all meetings by a workplace colleague. In certain circumstances an employee may lodge a claim in the Employment Tribunal. An employee can only make one request a year under the legislation. Employers should also note that employees have a statutory right not to be subjected to detriment or be dismissed for making, or proposing to make, an application for flexible working.

Emergency time off

The Employment Relations Act 1999 gave employees the right to "reasonable time off" to deal with any unexpected emergencies that arise in relation to 'dependents'. A dependant is classified as a husband, wife, partner, child or parent of the employee. It also includes someone living with the employee as part of the family. In the case of illness or injury, it also includes a person who relies on the employee for assistance. It is unlawful for an employer to penalise an employee for taking time off for genuine reasons. The right is intended to cover genuine emergencies only and is unpaid. There is, as yet, no limit set on the number of times an employee can be absent from work exercising this right. However, it should be noted that this right is generally for unforeseen circumstances. If an employee knows in advance that he/she will need time off, he/she should ask for leave in the usual way. This could involve the employee taking annual leave, or some other type of leave, e.g. compassionate leave, if the employer provides it (*see* 'Leave', p.457).

An employee can make a complaint to the Employment Tribunal if he/she considers that he/she has been unreasonably refused time off, suffered a detriment for taking or seeking to take time off, or been dismissed for taking or seeking to take time off.

Parental leave
Parental leave is available to employees who have one year's continuous service and have, or expect to have, parental responsibility for a child. Employees can take 13 weeks' unpaid leave in total for each child. Parents of disabled children can take up to 18 weeks in total. Leave may be taken in short or long blocks. Employers and employees can agree their own procedures for taking parental leave. However, the legislation provides a fallback scheme which will apply automatically where there is no other agreement in operation. Employees have the right to bring a claim in the Employment Tribunal if their employer prevents or attempts to prevent them from taking parental leave and they are also protected from victimisation, including dismissal, for taking it.

How employers can help
It is evident from the above that only certain employees are entitled, under law, to request certain types of leave and flexible working. Carers who look after friends and families who do not live at the same address are often excluded. Accordingly, employers should consider going beyond the statutory minimum. There are a variety of actions employers can take to help carer employees. An easy first step would be to consult with employees and produce a carer-friendly policy. Employers should investigate a full range of flexible working options, including part-time work, job sharing, flexi-time, homeworking etc. It may be that employees who do not fall within the

statutory definition, or those that do not have any caring responsibilities, become resentful towards those who work flexibly and therefore employers should consider whether it would be appropriate and practical to allow all employees to request to work in a flexible manner.

In particular, employers should try and act promptly in responding to any requests. The use of a trial period may also be a sensible option, to allow both parties to decide if a variation is workable. In addition, some carers may only need to work flexibly at certain times, depending on the circumstances, and employers should aim to be as accommodating as possible. The rights to emergency time off work and parental leave do not carry with them any right to payment, but employers may consider it appropriate for this to be paid. In addition, employers may want to investigate introducing measures such as planned leave for situations where people may need to provide nursing care for a short period, or allow a longer lunch break to enable a worker to visit the person they care for.

Other practical support would be to allow the employee access to a telephone or give him/her parking near work to allow him/her to get in and out of work easier.

National Carers Strategy
In June 2008 the Prime Minister launched the National Carers Strategy. The Strategy sets out a ten-year vision, including a set of commitments on some of the important issues surrounding carers. However, the Strategy does not make clear what precise steps are needed to achieve the goals. Many consider the Strategy to be an important step forward in recognising the needs of carers and it includes a focus upon carers in employment. In relation to employment matters the Government has stated that it will be funding an awareness

campaign to ensure that both employers and employees are aware of their rights. Furthermore, the Government will be undertaking a review of who is entitled to request flexible working rights, due to the fact that many carers do not fall within the statutory definition of a carer and therefore miss out. The Strategy has also committed £38m of additional funding to support carers in returning to work.

Discrimination and *Coleman v. Attridge Law* (2008)

On 17 July 2008 the European Court of Justice handed down a potentially far-reaching decision in *Coleman v. Attridge Law*. Ms Coleman was a secretary at a law firm and the principal carer for her disabled son. She resigned and claimed unfair constructive dismissal and less favourable treatment due to her son's disability. In January 2008 the Advocate General gave his opinion, saying that he considered "discrimination by association" to be illegal. He concluded that subtler forms of discrimination should be caught by the anti-discrimination legislation.

The ECJ followed the Attorney General's opinion and ruled that the ban on employment discrimination is not limited to disabled people but also extends to those responsible, their carers, or those with close connections. This case returns to the Employment Tribunal later in the year for a decision to be made on the facts, but the ECJ's ruling is significant and dramatically strengthens the employment rights of carers. Employers will need to be careful that they do not discriminate against employees who care for either disabled or elderly people, or they could risk facing a disability or age discrimination claim. There is no limit on the amount of compensation that can be awarded if discrimination is proven.

See also: Childcare provisions, p.138; Discrimination, p.222; Family-friendly rights, p.309; Flexible working, p.338; Homeworking, p.406; Leave, p.457; Managing pregnancy, p.484

Sources of further information

National Carers' Strategy: www.carersuk.org

Department for Business, Enterprise and Regulatory Reform: www.berr.gov.uk

Direct Gov: www.directgov.co.uk

Catering: food safety

Jagdeep Tiwana, Berwin Leighton Paisner

Key points

Food should be prepared in accordance with the Food Safety Act 1990 and other legislation. The Act is the principal food-control measure in the UK. It sets out general duties of caterers in respect of food safety and quality together with general consumer protection measures. Subordinate legislation made under the Act fleshes out requirements to be followed by caterers and other food operators and businesses in relation to matters such as claims and advertising. European regulations lay down requirements in respect of hygiene and temperature control.

Legislation

- Food Safety Act 1990.
- Food Labelling Regulations 1996.
- Food Labelling (Amendment) Regulations 1999 and 2003.
- Food Labelling (Amendment) (No 2) Regulations 2004.
- Genetically Modified Food (England) Regulations 2004 implementing Regulation EC 1829/2003.
- Regulation (EC) 852/2004 on the Hygiene of Foodstuffs.
- Regulation (EC) 853/2004 on hygiene rules for foods of animal origin.
- General Food Regulations 2004 implementing Regulation EC 178/2002.
- Food Safety Act 1990 (Amendment) Regulations 2004 implementing Regulation EC 178/2002.
- Regulation (EC) 1924/2006 on Nutrition and Health Claims.
- Food Hygiene (England) Regulations 2006 (SI 2006/14).

Food safety

General duties in relation to safety and quality

It is a criminal offence to render food injurious to health or sell food that is unfit for human consumption. Food can be rendered injurious to health by:

- adding any article or substance to food;
- using any article or substance as an ingredient in the preparation of food – e.g. adding caustic soda instead of baking powder to a product;
- taking out any constituent from a food; and
- subjecting the food to any other process or treatment.

In determining whether a food is injurious to health, regard has to be given to three issues:

1. The probable immediate, short-term and/or long-term effects of that food on the health of consumer *and* subsequent generations;
2. The probable cumulative toxic effects; and
3. Particular sensitivities of certain consumers.

Unless there has been a deliberate act of sabotage, it is rare for proceedings to be brought under this provision.

Proceedings in relation to food safety are more likely to be brought for selling food

Workplace Law Network
www.workplacelaw.net

hat is unsafe. In determining whether food
s unsafe, the following issues have to be
aken into consideration:

- the normal conditions of use by the
  consumer;
- the normal conditions at each stage of
  production processing and distribution;
  and
- the information provided to
  consumers.

n addition, a food will be deemed to
be unfit for human consumption if it is
unacceptable for human consumption. This
could be for reasons of contamination by
extraneous matter, through putrefaction or
deterioration.

Consumer protection provisions
t is also necessary to protect consumers
from food that is safe but of unsatisfactory
quality. It is an offence if the food sold to
the consumer is not:

- of the nature demanded (e.g. the food
  sold is different to that requested,
  such as reformed fish being sold as
  scampi);
- of the substance demanded (this
  applies where the composition differs
  from that requested, e.g. glass in a
  pizza); or
- of the quality demanded (this includes
  mouldy, bad and decomposed food
  as well as food that fails to meet
  commercial quality standards – e.g.
  excess sugar in diet cola).

Consumers are also protected from
false claims in relation to foods as it is
an offence to label, present, display or
advertise food in such a way that it is
falsely described or is likely to mislead as
to the nature, substance or quality of the
food. For example, a menu describing a
cocktail as Red Bull and vodka would be

misleading if the cocktail did not contain
Red Bull but a substitute product. For
further information on menus, see
below.

Other provisions
These are traceability requirements
imposed on all food businesses, including
caterers, requiring them to keep records
of their food suppliers. Internal traceability
is not required. This means that it is not
necessary to state which specific batch
of ingredients went into which meal. The
Regulations also impose an obligation on
caterers to notify the authorities if they
suspect that any food they supply or has
been supplied to them is unsafe.

Labelling and menus
The Food Labelling Regulations set out
requirements for the labelling of food
products. Usually food sold by caterers
does not need to be labelled. However,
there are certain exceptions; for example,
foods that contain irradiated ingredients.

Any food which is supplied to caterers
where there has been an intentional use
of GM ingredients at any level must be
labelled. This is regardless of whether GM
material is detectable in the final product.
But it is not necessary to label small
amounts (e.g. below 0.9% for approved
GM ingredients and 0.5% for unapproved
varieties that have received a favourable
assessment). However, it is less clear
whether caterers should continue to
provide this information to consumers for
foods sold in restaurants, cafés, etc. This
is currently being dealt with at EU level
and, until clarified, it is unlikely that any
action will be taken against caterers that
do not pass this information on.

Food that is pre-packed to sell directly to
customers does not have to be labelled

but where food has been pre-packed by a different supplier, for example where sandwiches have been prepared by another company, the food must be appropriately labelled with an ingredients list and details of allergens such as nuts, milk or fish. In the case of allergens, it may be advisable to provide information to consumers in all circumstances. The Food Standards Agency has issued voluntary Best Practice Guidance for the Provision of Allergen Information for Non Pre-packed Foods.

All this information must be on a label attached to the food, the menu or a notice. Part III of the Regulations requires attention in this context as it applies to claims and descriptions in the labelling and advertising of food products, meaning that it will apply to adverts for food products sold by caterers. It identifies the following:

■ *Prohibited claims.* These are claims that a food has a tonic property or that it has the property of treating, preventing or curing disease. This prohibition prevents caterers from making medicinal claims for products on their menus. For example, although it would be permissible to mention the health maintenance properties of calcium, it would not be permissible to say that calcium could help prevent osteoporosis.
■ *Restricted claims.* These include claims for reduced or low energy, protein, vitamins and minerals.
■ *Misleading descriptions.* Part III sets out when certain wording such as 'ice cream' and 'starch-reduced' can be used.

These prohibitions and restrictions need to be taken into account by caterers when drafting menus. Caterers also need to ensure that all nutrition and health

claims comply with European Regulation 1924/2006.

It is essential that the prices of food and drink sold at the premises are clearly displayed. The easiest way to do this is on a menu. Generally, prices should include VAT when appropriate. There are few rules setting out the composition of food; the exceptions are sausages and burgers, which must contain a prescribed amount of meat.

Care has to be taken when drafting menus to ensure that they are not misleading and that they do not falsely describe the foods in the menus. For example, it would not be acceptable to describe an omelette as freshly cooked if the caterer buys it from frozen and then reheats it. Guidance can be found in the report *Criteria for the Use of the Terms Fresh, Pure, Natural etc. in Food Labelling* published by the Food Standards Agency that sets out terms that should be avoided or used only sparingly. These include the terms 'country-style', 'home-made', 'authentic', 'original' and 'traditional'. It also explains when the words 'fresh', 'natural' and 'pure' should be used.

Hygiene

Regulation 852/2004 on the hygiene of foodstuffs identifies the general obligations on proprietors of food businesses in relation to hygiene. Of particular importance is Annex II, which sets out the rules of hygiene. The Annex is divided into 12 chapters that lay down both general and specific legal requirements relating to the hygienic operation of a food business:

■ Chapter I lays down general requirements for ensuring hygiene of premises including cleaning, maintenance, layout, design, construction and size. It also covers welfare amenity provisions (such as sanitary accommodation, washing and clothing), storage facilities and environmental provisions (including temperature, lighting and ventilation).

- Chapter II lays down more specific requirements for food preparation, treatment areas and rooms. These requirements apply to all rooms where food is prepared, treated or processed except for dining rooms. It covers matters such as floors, walls, ceilings, overhead fixtures, windows, doors and washing facilities for foods.
- Chapter III covers requirements for moveable or temporary premises such as stalls and delivery vehicles.
- Chapter IV sets out the standards that must be maintained in relation to hygiene when transporting food. This would include caterers that make home deliveries.
- Chapter V requires food businesses to keep clean all articles, fittings and equipment with which food comes into contact and is intended to prevent cross-contamination from one foodstuff to another.
- Chapter VI (food waste) lays down requirements to minimise any food safety risk that inevitably arises from working debris and food waste generally. The new Regulation adds the requirements that all waste is to be eliminated in a hygienic and environmentally friendly way.
- Chapter VII prescribes the quality of water to be used in a food business. In particular, it requires an adequate supply of 'potable water', which must be used whenever necessary to ensure foodstuffs are not contaminated.
- Chapter VIII (personal hygiene) sets out the legal requirements designed to achieve 'clean person' strategies. Personnel have two general legal

obligations. First, every person working in the food-handling area must maintain a high degree of personal cleanliness and must wear suitable, clean and where appropriate protective clothing. Second, people working in food-handling areas who are suffering from or carrying a disease likely to be transmitted through food must report the condition immediately to the food business operator. Such persons must not be permitted to handle food or enter a food handling area if there is any likelihood of indirect contamination.

- Chapter IX sets out provisions applicable to foodstuffs. It requires that food businesses must not accept any raw material or ingredients if they are known to be or suspected to be contaminated. Once accepted, raw materials must be stored in appropriate conditions designed to prevent harmful deterioration and protect them from contamination. Food is to be protected against any contamination and adequate procedures must be in place to control pests.
- Chapter X lays down provisions to prevent contamination when wrapping and packaging foodstuffs.
- Chapter XI sets out requirements applicable to food placed on the market in hermetically sealed containers.
- Chapter XII stipulates that caterers must ensure that their food handlers are supervised and trained in relation to food hygiene matters. The training must be commensurate with their work activities.

Food safety management
Regulation (EC) No. 852/2004 requires food business operators to identify critical points for food safety, establish and implement monitoring procedures for critical points, establish corrective actions for critical control points and document

and record the application of these measures. This is commonly referred to as a Hazard Analysis of Critical Controls Points (HACCP) system, or if it is applied to the catering industry, it is referred to as Self-Assured Catering.

Article 5 of the Regulation requires food business operators to put in place, implement and maintain a permanent procedure based on the HACCP principles. An HACCP system requires that a catering operation be analysed step by step. In particular, it requires that stages in preparation at which hazards exist be identified, together with the means by which they can be controlled. These may be as simple as introducing temperature controls, e.g. cooking chicken to a minimum temperature of 75°C or ensuring that it is chilled before cooking.

The critical points that need to be adhered to, to ensure food safety, are summarised below:

- Identify any hazards that must be prevented, eliminated or reduced to acceptable levels.
- Identify the critical control points at the step or steps at which control is essential.
- Establish critical limits that separate acceptability from unacceptability for the prevention, elimination and reduction of identified hazards.
- Establish and implement effective monitoring procedures at critical control points.
- Establish corrective actions when monitoring to indicate that a critical control point is not under control.
- Establish procedures to be carried out regularly to verify whether the measures adopted are working effectively.
- Establish records to demonstrate the effective application of these measures.

Food safety checklist
- Are the premises registered with the competent authority?
- Has a liquor licence been obtained where alcohol is to be sold?
- Does the construction and layout of the premises comply with the hygiene regulations?
- Are suppliers reputable and reliable?
- Have the critical control points been identified and controls put in place and details of the procedure recorded in writing?
- Have the staff been properly trained in all aspects of food safety, hygiene and temperature control?
- Is there a detailed cleaning schedule in place?
- Is waste picked up on a regular basis?
- Are there adequate pest control measures in place?
- Is equipment regularly cleaned and inspected? (This is particularly important for oil filtration systems.)
- Are proper temperature controls in place?
- Are all of the above steps documented?

Temperature controls
Controlling temperatures is one of the most significant ways of ensuring food safety. As of 1 January 2006, this area has been governed by various EC Regulations. The Regulations set out requirements for foods that are likely to support the growth of pathogenic micro-organisms or the formation of toxins at temperatures that would result in a risk to health. In particular, they stipulate when foods must be kept chilled, e.g. dairy products, cooked products containing meat, fish or egg, sandwiches and cooked rice. They also detail temperatures that should be reached during cooking, those that should apply to hot food and cold food displays, and when reheating of food products is acceptable.

Defences

If a breach of food law occurs, it is likely that a prosecution will result. In order to defend proceedings, it is necessary to prove to the court that all reasonable steps had been taken to avoid the offence occurring. This is known as a due diligence defence. What is reasonable will depend on the size of the business and its resources as well as the seriousness of the breach. If steps have been taken to comply with the legislation and controls have been put in place in relation to hygiene, food safety and management, even if an employee has made a mistake that has caused the system to break down, it is likely that the proceedings can be defended.

Penalties

For a conviction under food law, the penalties can range from a fine of up to £20,000 and/or six months' imprisonment in the lower Courts, to an unlimited fine and up to two years' imprisonment in the higher Courts.

See also: Catering: health and safety issues, p.124

Sources of further information

Food Standards Agency: www.food.gov.uk

Chartered Institute of Environmental Health: www.cieh.org.uk

Industry Guide to Good Hygiene Practice: Catering Guide (Chadwick House Group, 1997) ISBN: 0 900 103 00 0.

Catering: health and safety issues

Jagdeep Tiwana, Berwin Leighton Paisner

Key points

Caterers must work in a way that protects the health and safety of employees and those people who could be affected by their activities. The law imposes general duties on caterers as employers to ensure their businesses are run safely and sets out ways in which this can be achieved.

Legislation

- Health and Safety at Work etc. Act 1974.
- Health and Safety (First Aid) Regulations 1981.
- Electricity at Work Regulations 1989.
- Manual Handling Operations Regulations 1992.
- Workplace (Health, Safety and Welfare) Regulations 1992.
- Reporting of Injuries, Diseases and Dangerous Occurrences Regulations 1995 (RIDDOR).
- Health and Safety (Safety Signs and Signals) Regulations 1996.
- Gas Safety (Installation and Use) Regulations 1998.
- Lifting Operations and Lifting Equipment Regulations 1998.
- Provisions for Use of Work Equipment Regulations 1998.
- Management of Health and Safety at Work Regulations 1999.
- Control of Substances Hazardous to Health Regulations 2002.
- Health and Safety (Miscellaneous Amendments) Regulations 2002.
- Management of Health and Safety at Work and Fire Precautions (Workplace) (Amendment) Regulations 2003.
- The Regulatory Reform (Fire Safety) Order 2005.
- The Work at Height Regulations 2005.

Health and Safety at Work etc. Act 1974

The Health and Safety at Work etc. Act 1974 imposes a number of general duties on all employers to ensure their business is conducted in a manner that minimises health and safety risks to its employees, customers and third parties such as contractors.

Employers' general duties to employees include:

- devising and maintaining a safe system of work;
- providing and maintaining equipment;
- ensuring that the use, handling, storage and transport of articles and substances are carried out safely;
- providing training and supervision;
- maintaining the workplace (including entrances and exits) in safe condition; and
- providing a safe working environment which includes adequate facilities.

It is important to note that the general duty to provide safe conditions extends not only to employers but also to people such as landlords who exercise some control over premises or plant and equipment. The way in which an employer fulfils its duties to employees, visitors and third parties is set out in more detail in subordinate legislation.

Risk assessments

The Management of Health and Safety at Work Regulations 1999 set out in broad terms how health and safety should be managed. They provide detailed guidance, and one of the most important issues they address is the requirement to carry out risk assessments. In particular, they require that a suitable and sufficient risk assessment for the activities undertaken by the employer must be carried out.

The purpose of the risk assessment is to identify:

- hazards caused by the procedures in relation to the business' activities;
- risks that arise from those hazards; and
- procedures to eliminate or control those risks.

Where there are more than five employees, significant findings of the risk assessments must be recorded in writing. Guidance issued by the HSE makes it clear that risk assessments should not be over-complicated and should highlight significant hazards that could result in serious harm or affect several people. The assessments should be reviewed from time to time to ensure that the precautions are working effectively. It should be noted that the risk assessment needs only to be suitable and sufficient. This does not mean perfect.

When carrying out the risk assessments, specific consideration should be given to vulnerable employees or third parties such as people under the age of 18 or new and expectant mothers. In relation to people under the age of 18, the risk assessment will need to take into account the young person's inexperience and immaturity and lack of awareness of risks within a workplace.

When employing contractors etc., a copy of a risk assessment for the work they undertake should be provided by their employer. The contractor's employer should also be provided with copies of the risk assessments relating to the premises at which the work will be undertaken.

Once hazards and risks have been identified, safe systems of work should be devised to ensure that employees do not come to harm and procedures should be put in place to ensure the safety of third parties. In this respect, it is particularly important that training and information are provided to employees and appropriate third parties to ensure that they are aware of the risks and the necessary procedure to be taken to avoid them. These procedures should be encapsulated in a company health and safety manual. The manual should also set out an organisation chart detailing the health and safety responsibilities of individuals within the company.

It is also necessary to carry out a risk assessment that deals specifically with the risks arising from fire. This risk assessment must identify the steps that need to be taken to meet fire safety requirements and in particular what procedures must be followed in the event of an emergency. It is important that the risk assessment takes into account the needs of disabled people and children, particularly in the case of schools, in the event of a fire. A detailed assessment is necessary and the rules relating to recording significant findings of the risk assessment apply.

Safety signs

The Health and Safety (Safety Signs and Signals) Regulations 1996 provide details of signage that can be used to help control risks that have been identified in risk assessments. This includes signage to identify corrosive, flammable or explosive substances. The Regulations set out the format that signage should take, including details of the shape, colour and pattern of safety signs. It is necessary to ensure that safety signs are maintained in good condition.

Workplaces

The Workplace (Health, Safety and Welfare) Regulations 1992 aim to ensure adequate welfare facilities are provided for employees. In summary, they cover the following areas:

- The maintenance of the workplace including equipment. In this regard steps should be taken to ensure that equipment and the workplace in general are maintained in good repair and that any problems that may arise are rectified.
- The provision of ventilation, lighting and temperature control.
- The maintenance of cleanliness in the workplace including equipment and furniture.
- Protection from falls and falling objects. This is particularly important for the catering industry as one of the greatest causes of accidents is slips, trips and falls. Employers must ensure that floors and traffic routes are of sound construction and do not present tripping or slipping hazards. These traffic routes and floors should be maintained and kept free from waste, clutter and other objects. Where floors are likely to get wet (e.g. around dishwasher areas), procedures should be put in place to minimise the risks arising from this. These could include the use of matting, a wipe-as-you-go procedure and the provision of non-slip shoes. Physical safeguards should be provided where there is a risk of somebody falling a distance likely to cause personal injury. This calls for the specific consideration of the maintenance and cleaning of windows and roofs. Windows and doors that are made of glass should contain safety glass and should be marked so they are easily visible.

- The provision of sanitary conveniences and washing facilities. When up to five people are at work at the same time, there should be at least one WC and one wash station, two of each for up to 25 workers, three for up to 50 and so on for every 25 extra workers.
- Changing and rest facilities. A rest-room (a rest area) should be provided with adequate seating for employees. There should be the provision of a warm, dry, well-ventilated area to hang personal clothing, and drinking water must be available. Where employees eat meals at work, then the means of preparing a hot drink must also be provided.

Equipment

The Provision and Use of Work Equipment Regulations 1998 set out the safety requirements for the provision and use of equipment at work. In particular, they require that equipment should be of suitable construction and design for the purpose for which it is intended. Work equipment must be used only in relation to work activities for which it is meant and it should be regularly maintained and inspected. Where appropriate, written instructions and training should be provided to enable employees to use the equipment.

Manual handling

The Manual Handling Operations Regulations 1992 prescribe measures that employers must follow to reduce the risk of injury to their employees from manual handling activities. First, employers are required to establish if the manual handling operation that gives rise to risk can be avoided altogether. This could be done by reorganisation or the introduction of mechanical aids. If the operation cannot be avoided, then it is necessary to assess the risk and to try to implement controls to reduce the risk as far as reasonably practicable.

Once a safe system of work has been devised in relation to manual handling, it is important that it is maintained and that there is adequate monitoring to ensure that there are no deviations from these procedures.

Where automated systems are introduced in place of manual handling, then regard has to be given to the Lifting Operations and Lifting Equipment Regulations 1998. Such equipment must be regularly inspected, and, where an employer does not have the requisite competence to do this, he must retain someone who does. For so long as the equipment is in use, it is necessary to keep a copy of the inspection report for two years or until the next report is made.

Working at height

The Working at Height Regulations 2005 which came into force in April 2006 amended the old Regulations which gave a qualifying height threshold of 2.5m. Regulations now cover all work at height where there is a risk of a fall liable to cause personal injury. Employers must now do all that is reasonably practical to prevent anyone falling.

Their responsibilities as duty holders include:

■ avoiding work at height for their employees where they can;
■ using work equipment or other measures to prevent falls where they cannot avoid working at height; and
■ where they cannot eliminate the risk of a fall, use work equipment or other measures to minimise the distance and consequence of a fall, should one occur.

Duty holders must ensure that:

■ all work at height is properly planned and organised;
■ all work takes account of conditions that could endanger health and safety;

■ those involved in work at height are trained and competent;
■ the place where work at height is carried out is safe;
■ equipment for work at height is appropriately inspected;
■ the risks from fragile surfaces are properly controlled; and
■ the risk from falling objects is properly controlled.

See Industry-specific concerns, below, for examples of where the new Regulations may affect the industry.

Control of hazardous substances

It is a necessary part of every caterer's business to deal with hazardous substances. Hazardous substances can come in many shapes and sizes such as liquids, gas, dust and micro-organisms and may occur naturally or be artificially produced. If they create a hazard to health, then it is necessary either to prevent exposure to that substance or, if this is not reasonably practicable, to control employees' and third parties' exposure to the substance. It is particularly important to assess the level, type and duration of exposure. Once this has been done, preventive or control measures can then be introduced.

The most common type of hazardous substance found in the catering industry is cleaning materials. In such cases, because the use of such hazardous substances cannot be avoided, information should be provided to employees stating what action should be taken in the event of an accident or emergency and employees should be trained on how to use the products safely.

Use of electricity

The design, installation and operation of electrical and gas systems are highly regulated. The Electricity at Work Regulations 1989 and the Gas Safety (Installation and Use) Regulations 1998 set out detailed requirements for the health and safety precautions that must be taken when dealing with gas or electricity.

Accident reporting

Employers are under an obligation to report serious work-related health and safety incidents, diseases or deaths.

The Reporting of Injuries, Diseases and Dangerous Occurrences Regulations 1995 (RIDDOR) set out which types of accidents are reportable and how quickly they should be reported. There is now a central reporting system, the Incident Contact Centre at Caerphilly.

There is a distinction between a reportable accident, which is an accident associated with work activities, and reportable diseases, which require to be diagnosed by a doctor. The list of major injuries, dangerous occurrences and diseases that require to be reported are extensive. However, in summary, injuries that should be reported are:

- fractures (except of fingers or toes);
- amputations;
- dislocation of knees, hips, shoulders or spine;
- temporary or permanent loss of sight (including any penetrating injury to the eye);
- injury leading to hypothermia or heat-induced illness;
- unconsciousness;
- admittance to hospital for more than 24 hours; and
- exposure to a harmful substance(s).

Dangerous occurrences that would need to be reported include:

- the collapse, failure or overturning of load-bearing lifting machinery;
- electrical short-circuits leading to a fire explosion;
- the collapse of scaffolding; and

- the escape of any substance that could lead to death or major injury.

Reportable diseases include:

- occupational dermatitis or asthma; and
- repetitive-strain-type injuries.

Incidents that must be reported without delay are:

- dangerous occurrences;
- the death of any person due to an employer's activities;
- a major injury suffered by any person at work; and
- injury to any third party (e.g. contractors, visitors, etc.) that requires their admission to a hospital.

Although it is not specified how incidents should be reported, this must be done by the fastest means practicable, which would normally be by telephone.

Other injuries must be notified within ten days. These include a three-day injury suffered by an employee due to a work-related incident. This means that, where a person is unable to carry out work because of an injury for more than three consecutive days, then the incident must be notified. The day of the accident does not count towards this time period, but non-work days are included. There is a specific form, Form F2508, that must be completed to send to the Incident Contact Centre.

Industry-specific concerns

By way of example, a number of activities that take place specifically within the catering industry are considered to be high risk by the HSE and need to be considered in any health and safety compliance or training session.

In particular:

- Boiling water and splashes from hot fat, especially where the cleaning and emptying of deep fat fryers is concerned;

- Slips, trips and falls, particularly where staff may be working on wet or tiled floors;
- Manual handling, particularly in the brewing industry where items such as large barrels of beer may be moved into and around cellars;
- Working in cellars and confined spaces;
- Working with knives and other sharp implements such as meat slicing machinery;
- Gas saftey in kitchens;
- Looking after hands and skin, particularly in relation to preventing contact dermatitis; and
- Food debris on floors.

Offences

Offences under health and safety legislation can be subject to a fine of up to £20,000 in the Magistrates' Courts and an unlimited fine or imprisonment (although this is unlikely in most cases involving a company) in the higher courts.

Defences

There is no true defence to proceedings brought under health and safety legislation. Where a defendant can show that it did everything that was reasonably practicable (i.e. it did all that it could to prevent an accident), then proceedings may be successfully defended. However, it is notoriously difficult to mount such defences.

See also: Catering: food safety, p.118; Reporting Injuries, Diseases and Dangerous Occurrences (RIDDOR), p.628

Sources of further information

HSE: www.hse.gov.uk

Incident Contact Centre Website: www.riddor.gov.uk

CCTV monitoring

Elizabeth Upton, Bird & Bird

Key points

- Workplace managers should note that most CCTV systems will be covered by the Data Protection Act (the Act). They should therefore familiarise themselves with the Information Commissioner's CCTV Code of Practice.
- Before installing a CCTV system, an impact assessment should be carried out to assess whether the use of CCTV is justified or whether another, less privacy-intrusive solution (e.g. improved lighting in a car park) could achieve the same objectives.
- Workplace managers should put in place a policy regarding use of the CCTV system by camera operators and retention of images.
- Warning signs should usually be posted, and the organisation must ensure it is able to comply with a data subject access request for images.

CCTV in the UK

Increasingly CCTV has become the principal method of carrying out surveillance of areas which may be accessed by the public. In fact, it is believed that Britain has the highest CCTV coverage of public places in the world, with perhaps as many as 4.2 million cameras, equating to one for every 14 people. It is said that a person may be captured on camera as many as 300 times a day. Whilst many members of the public are not concerned, others are troubled by increasing levels of routine surveillance. The main benefit claimed for CCTV is that it provides protection for both the public and property. Whilst many people believe this is true, a Home Office study in 2005 concluded that the CCTV schemes examined had not had any effect on overall crime rates. It should also be acknowledged that it is possible for CCTV to be misused as a means of covert observation. Although many people do not object to the use of CCTV in public places, as they recognise that there are benefits to the community that may override any concerns of a 'Big Brother'

approach to policing, this attitude does not extend to the use of CCTV cameras in the workplace. Employees are suspicious of any form of surveillance by their employers at work. The Information Commissioner has recognised that special considerations apply in the workplace, and has produced guidance to assist employers to comply with the law.

Data Protection Act 1998

The Data Protection Act 1998 is the major legal control over CCTV surveillance. The Data Protection Act requires data controllers to process personal data only in accordance with the principles set out in the Act.

'Personal data' is defined in the Data Protection Act as "Data which relate to a living individual who can be identified (a) from those data, or (b) from those data and other information which is in the possession of, or is likely to come into the possession of, the data controller".

A record of a person's appearance captured on CCTV images is clearly therefore personal data within the meaning of the Data Protection Act, as a person can be identified from his or her appearance. This personal data is processed by automatic means via the CCTV system. Information about people which is derived from CCTV images such as vehicle registration numbers will also be caught by the definition of personal data in the Act. In fact, most uses of CCTV by organisations will be covered by the Act, regardless of the number of cameras or the sophistication of the systems (note that the Information Commissioner has changed his view as to what will be caught by CCTV images. Previous guidance suggested that only the most sophisticated CCTV systems with the ability to zoom in on individuals would be caught by the Act and that very basic CCTV systems would not be covered).

It is also worth noting that 'sensitive personal data' (to which the Data Protection Act applies more stringent processing guidelines) includes information about the commission or alleged commission of any offence, and about any proceedings relating to an offence committed or which is alleged to have been committed. These more stringent processing guidelines will therefore apply to any CCTV footage showing the possible commission of an offence. Workplace managers using CCTV systems should also be aware that they must be able to respond to data subject access requests under the Data Protection Act.

Human Rights Act 1998
Public authorities which use CCTV should be aware that indiscriminate and unjustified use of CCTV surveillance and monitoring could potentially be a breach of the Human Rights Act in relation to the right to respect for privacy. In the case of *Peck v. United Kingdom* (2003), the European Court of Human Rights held

that a man in a public place still had a legitimate expectation of privacy and that the public authority's use of CCTV images breached that right. In the *Peck* case, the public authority had broadcast CCTV images of a man brandishing a knife in a public street on TV. This caused him significant embarrassment as he was recognised by neighbours and friends. He had had mental health problems at the time of the incident and had in fact been attempting suicide. The Human Rights Act also has implications for private organisations using CCTV. In the event that an individual takes a complaint to court or to the Employment Tribunal, as a 'court or tribunal' falls within the definition of a 'public authority' under the Human Rights Act, it will also have a duty to apply European Human Rights Convention principles when adjudicating a dispute. If the litigant establishes a statutory or common law cause of action, he or she may apply a human rights argument. For example, an employee of a private company alleging that his Article 8 privacy rights have been infringed by his employer can argue that the Employment Tribunal must (as a public authority) ensure that it does not act in a way which is incompatible with that right to privacy in deciding the case.

Code of Practice for users of CCTV
The Information Commissioner published a revised CCTV Code of Practice in January 2008 (which replaces the earlier Code issued in 2000 and the supplementary guidance for small users). It sets out the measures which should be adopted in order to ensure that a CCTV scheme complies with the Data Protection Act and provides guidance on good practice. The Code of Practice does not apply to:

■ the covert surveillance activities of the law enforcement community (which are covered by the Regulation of Investigatory Powers Act (RIPA) 2000); or

- the use of conventional cameras (not CCTV) by the news media or for artistic purposes such as for film making.

The code does apply to the passing on of CCTV images to the media. Appendix 3 of the Code is for employers who may use CCTV to monitor their workers. This supplements the Employment Practices Code guidance on monitoring employees. Most uses of CCTV by organisations or businesses will be covered by the Data Protection Act (DPA) and the provisions of the 2008 code, regardless of the size of the system. The Code is available from the Office of the Information Commissioner. The full text should be consulted, but the main practical requirements are summarised in the following paragraphs. Users should conduct an initial impact assessment before installing and using CCTV. They must establish the purposes for which they need CCTV and ensure that a notification which covers these purposes has been lodged with the Office of the Information Commissioner. Cameras should be positioned in such a way that they are only able to monitor areas intended to be covered by the CCTV scheme. The operators of the equipment must be aware that they may only use the equipment in order to achieve the purpose notified to the Information Commissioner. If possible, the movement of the cameras should be restricted so that the operators cannot monitor areas which are not intended to be covered. Clearly visible and legible signs of an appropriate size should be used to inform the public that they are entering a zone which is monitored. The signs should contain the following information:

- the identity of the person or organisation responsible for the scheme;

- the purpose of the scheme; and
- details of whom to contact regarding the scheme.

The contact point should be available to members of the public during office hours, and employees staffing the contact point should be aware of the relevant policies and procedures. Signs may not be appropriate where CCTV is used to obtain evidence of criminal activity. However, the Code sets out tight controls over the use of CCTV in these circumstances. The images captured by CCTV equipment should be as clear as possible, to ensure that they are effective for the purposes intended. Cameras should be properly maintained and serviced, and good-quality tapes should be used. If dates and times are recorded, these should be accurate. Consideration must also be given to the physical conditions in the camera locations (e.g. infrared equipment may need to be used in poorly lit areas). No sound should accompany the images except in limited circumstances. Images should not be retained for longer than necessary. While they are retained, access to and security of the images must be controlled in accordance with the seventh Data Protection Principle of the Act, which sets out security requirements. Disclosure of images from the CCTV system must be controlled and the reasons for disclosure must be compatible with the purposes notified to the Information Commissioner. All access to or disclosure of the images should be documented.

If the purpose of the CCTV is solely to prevent and detect crime, then it should not be used for monitoring the amount of work done or compliance with company procedures. In some cases, it may be appropriate to install CCTV specifically for workforce monitoring. This must be justified under the decision making process outlined in the code. Workers should normally be aware that they are being monitored, but in exceptional circumstances, covert monitoring may be used as part of a specific investigation. Cameras and listening devices should not be installed in private areas such as toilets and private offices, except in the most exceptional circumstances where serious crime is suspected. This should only happen where there is an intention to involve the police, not where it is a purely internal disciplinary matter.

Employment Practices Code

Part 3 of the Information Commissioner's Employment Practices Code on Monitoring at Work sets out the basic 'dos and don'ts' for employers who monitor the activities of their employees. The Information Commissioner has attempted in the Code to strike a balance between the needs of employers and the needs of employees. The Code stresses the need for proportionality – any adverse impact of monitoring must be justified by the benefits to the employer and others. In order to assess whether monitoring is justified, the Code recommends organisations should carry out impact assessments to determine the purpose and likely impact of monitoring, whether there are any alternatives and what obligations will arise. Where possible, CCTV monitoring should be targeted at areas of particular risk and should not take place in areas where employees have a reasonable expectation of privacy; for example, toilets and private offices. Continuous monitoring of particular employees is only likely to be justified where there are particular safety or security concerns that cannot be adequately dealt with in other, less intrusive ways. All employees and visitors should be made aware that CCTV is in operation and of the purposes for which the information will be used. Covert monitoring of employees will only be justified in very limited circumstances; specifically, where

openness would prejudice the prevention or detection of crime or the apprehension of offenders. However, before covert monitoring is used, among other things, employers must identify specific criminal activity and establish that there is a need to use covert monitoring to obtain evidence. Employees and trade unions have resisted the placing of CCTV cameras in the workplace. At Guy's and St Thomas' Hospitals the public sector union UNISON threatened industrial action over the placing of surveillance cameras in locker rooms. However, where employees or their trade unions perceive a benefit in such surveillance techniques, acceptance of the cameras is likely to follow – e.g. where CCTV surveillance at work is for security purposes or is intended solely to detect, and so protect employees from, intruders. The monitoring of construction sites is now commonplace and in an industrial dispute involving workers on the Jubilee line, security data was used in reverse of its usual application to prove that union members could not have been in the vicinity of a suspected act of vandalism.

British Standard

The British Standards Institution has issued Code of Practice BS 7958:2005 *Closed circuit television (CCTV): management and operation*. The Code of Practice assists CCTV operators to comply with the Data Protection Act and to ensure that CCTV evidence can be used by the police to investigate crime. The Code is particularly useful where CCTV systems are used in public places, or have a partial view of a public place, and may therefore be of use to workplace managers.

Conclusion

Workplace managers responsible for CCTV use should familiarise themselves with the Information Commissioner's Code of Practice on CCTV, and the Employment Practices Data Protection

Code and the Employment Practices Code Supplementary Guidance. The main points to be aware of are:

■ An initial assessment should be carried out before installing the CCTV system.
■ Clear guidelines for use should be given to camera operators.

■ Warning signs containing the required information should normally be put in place.
■ CCTV images should be retained in accordance with the requirements of the Data Protection Act.
■ Users should ensure they are able to comply with a data subject access request.

See also: Data protection, p.186; Monitoring employees, p.521; Security licensing, p.646

Sources of further information

Information Commissioner: www.informationcommissioner.gov.uk

CCTV Code of Practice: Revised Edition 2008: www.ico.gov.uk/upload/documents/library/data_protection/detailed_specialist_guides/ico_cctvfinal_2301.pdf

BS 7958:2005 *Closed circuit television (CCTV): management and operation.*

Security Industry Authority: www.the-sia.org.uk

CDM

Raymond Joyce, Freeth Cartwright LLP

Key points

The Construction (Design and Management) Regulations 2007 (CDM 2007 Regulations) came into force on 6 April 2007. The CDM 2007 Regulations revoke the earlier Construction (Design and Management) Regulations 1994 (CDM 1994 Regulations) which had been in force for over 11 years. The CDM 2007 Regulations have already resulted in prosecutions.

Introduction

The CDM 2007 Regulations have been revised and amended to include the requirements that had been included under the Construction (Health, Safety and Welfare) Regulations 1996, which are now revoked. Thus, the CDM 2007 Regulations now give full effect to Council Directive 92/57/EEC. However, any suggestion that the CDM 2007 Regulations are an update or revision to the CDM 1994 Regulations would completely overlook the fact that the amendments and revisions have a radical and far-reaching implication for duty holders, in particular the client.

The CDM 2007 Regulations cover all construction work, no matter how insignificant the construction work may at first appear. The only exception where the CDM 2007 Regulations do not apply is to domestic clients, although the designer and contractor engaged by a domestic client are still obliged to comply with the CDM 2007 Regulations.

The Regulations maintain the distinction of construction work which is notifiable and construction work of a minor nature, which is not. Part 2 of the CDM 2007 Regulations comprising Regulations 4 to 13 inclusive therefore apply to all construction work and Part 3 only applies in respect of notifiable projects.

Demolition is no longer a criterion for imposing a duty of notification, irrespective of the fact that the construction project would not otherwise be notifiable.

Regulations 2 and 3 provide the criteria as to whether a project is notifiable. If the construction phase is likely to involve more than 30 days or 500 person days of construction work, the project is notifiable to the Health and Safety Executive.

The client

The client's fundamental duties are set out in Regulation 9. The client has an overriding duty for any project to ensure that arrangements made for managing the project would be carried out, so far as is reasonably practicable, without risk to the health and safety of any person. Ancillary to the construction work, the client has also to ensure that there are suitable welfare arrangements for the workers and a structure to be used as a workplace after construction will comply with the Workplace (Health, Safety and Welfare) Regulations 1992.

All projects need a designer to a greater or lesser extent even where a project is not notifiable. However, while it is not a primary obligation for a client to appoint a designer, a client must ensure that a designer and every contractor is given all the relevant information in the client's possession which is likely to have a bearing on health and safety; see Regulation 10.

The CDM coordinator

When a project becomes notifiable, a client has an obligation, in accordance with Regulation 14 to appoint a CDM coordinator (replacing the former role of planning supervisor), and principal contractor. A client must be satisfied that all duty holders he appoints to any of the roles are competent.

The CDM coordinator has replaced the role of the planning supervisor under the CDM 1994 Regulations. The CDM coordinator is only appointed on notifiable projects and, once appointed, must advise and assist the client in complying with the Regulations as required by Regulation 20. The CDM coordinator has to ensure that arrangements are in place for planning and coordinating the health and safety measures before and during construction. Although the CDM coordinator does not have the obligation to prepare a construction phase plan, other than liaising with the principal contractor, the CDM coordinator is required to prepare the health and safety file.

The designer

The designer has obligations that apply to all construction work in accordance with Regulation 11. The influential role of the designer on health and safety management in a construction project is underscored by the obligation to satisfy himself that the client is aware of its duties under CDM 2007.

The CDM 2007 Regulations require the designer to have regard to a list of specific risks that covers the full lifecycle of a project including building operational use.

In the case of a notifiable project, the designer should not commence work beyond the initial design stage without the confirmation that the CDM coordinator has been appointed as required by Regulation 18.

The need for the designer to share design information with others, so as to enable them to comply with the CDM 2007 Regulations, is a fundamental requirement.

The principal contractor

The role of the principal contractor only exists in respect of notifiable projects, as set out in Regulation 22, where the obligation to prepare a construction phase plan falls upon the principal contractor.

The principal contractor has the overall responsibility to plan, manage and monitor the construction phase so that the construction work is carried out without risk to health and safety. To assist the principal contractor in undertaking its main tasks, the CDM 2007 Regulations empower and require the principal contractor to manage the activities on site by means of disseminating prescribed information, consulting and giving directions to other contractors.

Contractors other than the principal contractor are required to cooperate with the principal contractor in accordance with Regulation 19. This includes complying with directions given by the principal contractor and providing it with details on the management and prevention of health and safety risks created by the contractor's work on site. On non-notifiable projects contractors are obliged to comply with various duties as set out in Regulation 13.

The construction phase plan

The means by which all the parties to a notifiable project share information and plan for the construction phase is the construction phase plan. The health and safety plan, which was an innovative feature of the CDM 1994 Regulations, has been renamed but maintains its role in linking the duty holders to a project through sharing knowledge, with the objective of improving the exchange and communication of information that affects health and safety.

The construction phase plan is intended to be a dynamic document, subject to continuous review and amendment throughout the construction phase. The construction phase plan also has an important role in fulfilling the general principles of coordination and cooperation that are required by Regulations 5 and 6 of the CDM 2007 Regulations.

On completion of a notifiable construction project, the CDM coordinator is required to prepare a health and safety file that is handed over to the client. The health and safety file is an important record document and should be easily accessible to others who will be responsible for later construction work associated with structure or its maintenance, repair, renovation or demolition.

Approved Code of Practice
The CDM 2007 Regulations should be read together with the Approved Code of Practice (ACoP) which provides practical guidance on compliance with the CDM

2007 Regulations. Failure to comply with the ACoP is not in itself an offence, although such failure may be taken by a court in criminal proceedings as proof that a person has contravened the CDM 2007 Regulations. In those circumstances, it is open to a person to satisfy the court that he has complied with the Regulations in some other way, although that would be very onerous.

The CDM 2007 Regulations are of universal application to construction work in Great Britain. The main reason for the new Regulations was to avoid some of the bureaucracy that became a feature of the CDM 1994 Regulations and to clarify the responsibilities of the parties to a construction project. It would be wrong to assume that the new Regulations create the same duties and obligations.

Any party to a construction project who has responsibility for the design, planning or management of construction work cannot avoid the obligation of becoming familiar with the new CDM 2007 Regulations in making their contribution to the improvement of health and safety in the construction industry.

See also: Construction site health and safety, p.154

Sources of further information

The Construction (Design and Management) Regulations (2007) SI 2007/320: www.opsi.gov.uk/SI/si2007/20070320.htm

HSE: L144 – *Construction (Design and Management) Regulations 2007 Approved Code of Practice* (HSE Books, 2007) ISBN: 978 0 7176 6223 4.

The CDM Regulations 2007 Explained, R. Joyce (2007) ISBN: 978 0 7277 3496 9.

Childcare provisions

Lizzie Mead, Berwin Leighton Paisner

Key points

According to the Government initiative, SureStart (a programme aiming to increase the availability of childcare), an increasing number of employees in UK workplaces have responsibility for the care of children.

A number of family-friendly rights are granted to such individuals of which employers must be aware.

As well as having to comply with the legal and statutory obligations, employers are now increasingly being encouraged, through campaigns such as the Work–Life Balance Campaign, to support government-driven initiatives which assist employees and workers to meet their childcare needs.

Legislation

- Health and safety legislation.
- Family-friendly legislation. The so-called family-friendly legislation now encompasses a wide variety of rights (granted to employees but not workers) which employees may exercise in order to assist them with their childcare needs. By way of summary, these rights currently include:
  - maternity leave and adoption leave of up to 52 weeks (statutory maternity pay and statutory adoption pay are payable (subject to eligibility) for 39 weeks);
  - paternity leave of either one or two consecutive weeks, for which statutory paternity pay is payable;
  - unpaid parental leave of up to 13 weeks for each child up to the child's fifth birthday (or 18 weeks' leave in the case of a disabled child up to the child's 18th birthday) or within five years of placement for an adopted child (or the adopted child's 18th birthday, if sooner);
  - for employees caring for certain adults the right to request a flexible working arrangement;
  - for parents of children under six (or 18 if disabled) who have responsibility for the child's upbringing, the right to request a flexible working arrangement; and
  - the right to take reasonable unpaid time off work to deal with emergencies involving dependants.

Proposed changes will further extend the family-friendly legislation in the near future. In particular, the period for which statutory maternity pay and statutory adoption pay are payable is expected to increase to 52 weeks and the right to request flexible working will be extended to cover children under 16, rather than just under six. Further, new paternity rights are anticipated, entitling eligible employees to additional paternity leave of up to 26 weeks.

Workplace nurseries and employer-supported childcare

Government-driven and trade-union-backed initiatives such as the SureStart Strategy are seeking to encourage greater employer-supported childcare through various voluntary schemes. Under these schemes, employees sacrifice a portion of their salary to be paid towards childcare costs. There are tax incentives available to both employer and employee in respect of that portion of the salary sacrificed. The schemes include the following:

■ *Workplace nurseries*. This is where the employer is wholly or partly responsible for funding and managing the provision of childcare facilities (either a workplace nursery or an in-house / on-site holiday play scheme) on work premises. For small employers, this can be done jointly with other companies. In respect of this cost, the employer is exempt from employer's National Insurance Contributions (NICs) and the employee is exempt from employee's Class 1 NICs and income tax. In April 2005, this exemption was widened so that if you allow another employer's staff who work on your premises to use your childcare facility, they will benefit from the exemption also.

■ *Childcare vouchers*. These are usually paper vouchers issued to employees to pay childcare providers for forms of childcare. There are tax incentives and savings available to both employer and employee, which were extended in April 2005. Currently, the first £55 a week of childcare vouchers paid for by the employer is exempt from NICs for employers, and from income tax and NICs for employees provided that access to the scheme is available to all employees and that the vouchers are used to pay for registered or approved childcare (for eligible children) only.

■ *Enhanced employee rights*. An increasing number of employers are opting to provide enhanced maternity, paternity, adoption and parental leave rights over and above the statutory minimum levels, extra statutory emergency leave to deal with a sick child or problems with childcare, and career breaks or sabbaticals.

Health and safety considerations

In the case of workers who bring their children to work, a number of health and safety considerations must be borne in mind.

In addition to the common law duty of care that an employer owes to provide its workers with a safe place of work, the employer also owes a common law duty of care to visitors while they are on its premises under the concept of occupier's liability. The extent of the duty is defined in legislation and will cover children while they are in the workplace. The legislation states that employers must be "prepared for children to be less careful than adults". It is therefore essential, in any situation where children are present in the workplace, either in a workplace nursery or otherwise, that a full risk assessment is carried out and that health and safety risks are regularly monitored. Employers should also ensure that sufficient insurance arrangements are in place to safeguard against any incidents involving children in the workplace.

Under the Health and Safety at Work Regulations 1999, employers must comply with specific obligations with regard to employees who are pregnant or breast-feeding. An employer must provide suitable rest facilities for such workers which are suitably located (e.g. close to toilet facilities). In addition, employers must carry out assessments of workplace risks to new and expectant mothers and take measures to avoid any risk by altering working conditions or hours of work. In this regard, employers are best advised to speak to the individual concerned to discuss what adjustments or alterations, if any, are necessary. A breach of the health and safety legislation in relation to new and expectant mothers can have serious consequences for an employer, rendering it liable to a claim for sex discrimination or even criminal prosecution following a complaint to the HSE.

See also: Carers, p.114; Children at work, p.141; Family-friendly rights, p.309; Flexible working, p.338

Sources of further information

SureStart: www.surestart.gov.uk

Workplace nurseries capital programme: www.dfes.gov.uk/pns/DisplayPN.cgi? pn_id=2006_0156

Work and Families Bill: www.publications.parliament.uk/pa/cm200506/ cmbills/060/2006060.htm

Right to request flexible working: www.berr.gov.uk

Children at work

Carolyn Haddon, Charles Russell

Key points

A child is a person not over compulsory school age (i.e. up to the last Friday in June in the academic year of his 16th birthday). Note that a young person is a person who has ceased to be a child but is under 18. The employment of children in the UK is subject to limitations regarding the number of hours that they can work. Children also have a number of special rights and protections in the workplace justified on health and safety grounds. It is important for all employers of children to be aware of the legal framework. Any organisation employing a child of compulsory school age must inform the local education authority in order to obtain an employment permit for that child. Without one, the child may not be covered under the terms of the employer's insurance policy. (This does not apply, however, in respect of children who are carrying out work experience arranged by their school.)

Legislation

- Children and Young Persons Act 1933 (as amended).
- Employment Rights Act 1996 (as amended).
- Education Act 1996 (as amended).
- Children (Protection at Work) Regulations 1998 (implementing the provisions of the EC Directive on the Protection of Young People at Work (94/33/EC)).
- Working Time Regulations 1998.
- Management of Health and Safety at Work Regulations 1999.
- Working Time (Amendment) Regulations 2002.

In addition, the United Nations Convention on the Rights of the Child (for these purposes, all persons under 18) provides that Member States have an obligation to protect children at work, set minimum ages for employment and regulate conditions of employment.

Key restrictions on the employment of children

No child may be employed to carry out any work whatsoever (whether paid or unpaid) if he is under the age of 14. This is subject to some specific exceptions, e.g. in relation to children working in television, the theatre or modelling. In the case of a child who is 14 or over, s/he may not:

- do any work other than light work;
- work in any industrial setting such as a factory or industrial site;
- work during school hours on a school day;
- work before seven a.m. or after seven p.m.;
- work for more than two hours on any school day;
- work for more than 12 hours in any week during term time;
- work more than two hours on a Sunday;
- work for more than eight hours on any day s/he is not required to attend

school (other than a Sunday) (or five hours in the case of a child under the age of 15);

■ work for more than 35 hours in any week during school holidays (or 25 hours in the case of a child under the age of 15);

■ work for more than four hours in any day without a rest break of at least one hour; or

■ work without having a two-week break from any work during the school holidays in each calendar year.

Health and safety considerations

The main source of health and safety legislation in relation to the employment of a child or young person is the Management of Health and Safety at Work Regulations 1999. Under these Regulations, the term 'young person' means any person under 18. Before a young person starts work, the employer must carry out a risk assessment taking into account various issues such as the inexperience and immaturity of the young person, the nature of the workstation, the risks in the workplace including the equipment which the young person will use, and the extent of health and safety training provided. Young persons cannot be employed to carry out any work:

■ beyond their physical or psychological capacity (such as heavy manual labour);

■ involving harmful exposure to toxic or carcinogenic agents or radiation;

■ involving the risk of an accident which a young person is more likely to suffer owing to his insufficient attention to safety or lack of experience; or

■ in which there is a risk to health from extreme cold, heat, noise or vibration.

A breach of the Regulations, if sufficiently serious, could lead to criminal prosecution following a complaint to the HSE.

Work experience

In the case of a child engaged on unpaid work experience, the same health and safety considerations apply as set out above. Guidelines were issued by the DTI (now BERR) in 2007 regarding work experience placements in the television industry and these are now regarded as being applicable in various industries. The main points of note in the guidelines are:

■ a written document should detail the framework of the work experience placement;

■ placements should be for a fixed period of time (ideally between two weeks and a month);

■ placements should not entail more than 40 hours work per week;

■ before starting the placement, specific learning objectives should be agreed between the placee and the provider of the placement; and

■ no unpaid volunteer should be under an obligation to comply with an employer's instructions.

Entitlement to holidays and time off

Under the Working Time Regulations 1998, since 1 October 2007, all adult employees are entitled to at least 4.8 weeks' paid annual leave. On 1 April 2009 this will increase to 5.6 weeks. In the case of *Addison v. Ashby* (2003) IRLR 211, however, the Employment Appeal Tribunal ruled that this entitlement does not apply to a child. The Children and Young Persons Act 1933 provides that a child is entitled to two consecutive weeks without employment during a school holiday; however, this period of time is unpaid.

National Minimum Wage and Sick Pay

The National Minimum Wage for young workers, aged under 18 but above the compulsory school age but who are not apprentices, increased to £3.53 on

1 October 2008. There is no National Minimum Wage for children still of the compulsory school age. In England and Wales, a person is no longer of compulsory school age after the last Friday of June of the school year in which their 16th birthday occurs.

The Statutory Sick Pay Regulations specify that workers aged 16 or over are entitled to receive statutory sick pay (SSP). Under 16s are not entitled to SSP.

Age discrimination

As a result of the Employment Equality (Age) Regulations 2006, it is now unlawful to discriminate against any person on the grounds of age. This applies to discrimination against younger individuals as well as older ones The lower age limit of 18 has also now been removed meaning that under 18s have the same rights as older workers and can bring unfair dismissal claims.

> *See also*: Childcare provisions, p.138; Minimum wage, p.504; Young persons, p.778

Sources of further information

Worksmart – children's work rights: www.worksmart.org.uk/rights/viewsubsection.php?sun=75

COMAH: dangerous substances

Jan Burgess, CMS Cameron McKenna

Key points

The growth of industrialisation in the second half of the 20th century brought with it an increasing number of serious accidents, particularly at sites storing dangerous substances. It soon became apparent that greater legal controls were necessary to prevent and mitigate the effects on people and the environment of those incidents involving dangerous substances. The first controls at a European level were a direct result of the Seveso accident in 1976, when dioxin accidentally released from a pesticide-manufacturing plant caused 2,000 people to seek medical attention. Although no immediate fatalities were reported, kilogram quantities of the substance – lethal to man even in microgram doses – were widely dispersed, which resulted in immediate contamination of some ten square miles of land and vegetation.

Legislation

- Control of Major Accident Hazards Regulations 1999 (COMAH 1999).
- Control of Major Accident Hazards (Amendment) Regulations 2005.
- Planning (Control of Major Accident Hazards) Regulations 2005.

The 'Seveso' Directives

The first 'Seveso' Directive (Directive 82/501/EEC) was adopted by the European Commission in 1982. Further incidents in Bhopal, India in 1984 (where a leak of methyl isocyanate caused more than 2,500 deaths) and in Basel, Switzerland in 1986 (where firefighting water contaminated with mercury and other chemicals caused massive pollution of the Rhine) led to the Seveso Directive being amended twice to broaden its scope (Directives 87/216/EEC and 88/610/EEC).

The Seveso Directive was superseded in 1996 by Directive 96/82/EC on the control of major accident hazards – the 'Seveso II' Directive. This was aimed at preventing major accidents at industrial sites storing or using dangerous substances above certain thresholds, and if such an accident did occur, at limiting its consequences for humans and the environment. It introduced new requirements for safety management systems, emergency planning and land-use planning. One of its main aims was to address accidents caused by management failures, a significant factor in over 90% of the accidents in the EU since 1982. The Seveso II Directive also gave more rights to the public in terms of access to information and consultation, with operators and public authorities having certain obligations to inform the public.

The Seveso II Directive was extended in 2003 by Directive 2003/105/EC, as a result of several serious industrial accidents (at Toulouse, Baia Mare and Enschede), and to take into account new studies on carcinogens and substances dangerous to the environment. Major changes included n extension of the Directive to cover sks arising from storage of explosives nd ammonium nitrate, and risks arising om mining operations. Member States vere required to bring into force the aws necessary to comply with Directive 003/105/EC before 1 July 2005.

mplementation of the Seveso II Directive in Great Britain

Vith the exception of the land use lanning requirements, the Seveso II Directive was implemented in Great Britain y the Control of Major Accident Hazards Regulations 1999 (COMAH 1999). These Regulations, which came into force n 1 April 1999, replaced the Control f Industrial Major Accident Hazards Regulations 1984 (CIMAH). The Health nd Safety Executive (HSE) together with he Environment Agency (EA) (in England nd Wales) or the Scottish Environment Protection Agency (SEPA) (in Scotland) act s the Competent Authority and therefore re responsible for enforcing the COMAH Regulations.

Companies regulated under COMAH 999 fall into two categories – either the ower or upper tier – depending on the quantity of dangerous substances present t a site. Lower tier duties apply to all perators covered by the Regulations, and nvolve notification to the HSE and EA (or SEPA) of the presence of any dangerous ubstance. There is also a requirement to repare a written major accident revention policy (MAPP) setting out the verall aims and principles of action for ontrolling major accident hazards.

f the quantity of a substance held at a particular site is above the threshold aid down in the Regulations, it will fall vithin the upper tier. Additional duties hen include an obligation to prepare a safety report, which should include nformation on the safety management system, organisation of the site and its surroundings, and likely causes, probability and consequences of a major accident. Companies falling within the upper tier must also prepare on an on-site emergency plan, and provide information to local authorities to assist them in the preparation of an off-site plan.

Changes to COMAH

The COMAH (Amendment) Regulations 2005 (the 2005 Regulations) implemented the health, safety and environment aspects of Directive 2003/105/EC, amending the Seveso II Directive in Great Britain. Since 30 June 2005, operators who come into the scope of the Regulations due to an increase in the quantity of dangerous substances present must submit a notification prior to any construction or operation. New thresholds and classifications for dangerous substances were introduced, which changed the criteria for triggering the Regulations, with the result that many businesses were brought within the Regulations for the first time.

In response to an explosion at a fertiliser plant in Toulouse, some of the main changes introduced by the 2005 Regulations concern ammonium nitrate. The threshold for the nitrogen content derived from ammonium nitrate was reduced. In addition, two new classes of ammonium nitrate were added – one for fertilisers capable of self-sustaining decomposition and the other for 'off-spec' material.

There are also two new entries for potassium nitrate, to reflect the less-combustible nature of certain fertilisers, which would previously have been categorised as oxidising substances and had threshold quantities of 50 and 200 tonnes.

In addition, seven new carcinogens were added to the existing list. The qualifying quantities for all carcinogens were raised from 0.001 to 0.5 and 2.0 tonnes, and the concentration cut-off increased to 5% by weight. The new COMAH regime also brought in a duty to notify the quantities of petroleum products in disaggregated form. A category for petroleum products includes, specifically, naphthas, kerosenes and diesel fuels. This was introduced so as to enable the competent authority to focus its regulatory activity according to the hazards associated with different types of products. The threshold quantities of 2,500 and 25,000 tonnes for petroleum products that trigger the COMAH Regulations are now half those of the former automotive petrol category.

The definition of 'substances dangerous for the environment' was amended, and qualifying quantities reduced to 100 and 200 tonnes (very toxic to aquatic organisms) and 200 and 500 tonnes (toxic to aquatic organisms). Furthermore, the introduction of the 'summation' or 'aggregation' rules require quantities of all dangerous substances with similar hazards present at an establishment to be added together to determine the application of COMAH.

Changes were also introduced in relation to administrative procedures to be followed under COMAH. Such changes include a duty on operators to notify the competent authority both when a safety report for an upper tier site is revised or reviewed, and to include the EA (or SEPA), employees and members of the public among the consultees on the off-site emergency plan.

Planning regime

Further changes to COMAH were introduced by the Planning (Control of Major Accident Hazards) Regulations 2005 (the Planning Regulations). The Planning Regulations were designed to implement the land use provisions of Directive 2003/105/EC. They are concerned with whether the storage of dangerous substances at a site is an appropriate use of land, taking into account the characteristics of the environment in which it is located. Planning authorities are now obliged to put in place controls on the siting of new establishments, modifications to existing establishments and new developments such as transport links, locations frequented by the public and residential areas in the vicinity of existing establishments. The aim is to ensure that there is an appropriate distance between hazardous establishments and residential areas.

Implications of the new COMAH regime
As a result of the amendments, it is estimated that around 100 additional companies fall within the COMAH regime. A similar number moved from the lower to the upper tier, thereby imposing additional duties such as the obligation to prepare an emergency plan. Companies new to COMAH may have to apply for a hazardous substances consent for the first time. The cost of obtaining a consent is small, but granting it triggers the formation of a consultation zone around the site. This could result in difficulties when trying to expand activities at a COMAH site, as well as limiting any future development near the site. Any proposed new developments in the vicinity of existing establishments now fall under greater scrutiny to assess whether they are likely to increase the risk of a major accident, or whether the consequences of such an accident would be more serious.

Buncefield Incident
On 11 December 2005, a number of explosions occurred at the Hertfordshire Oil Storage Terminal, generally known as

he Buncefield Oil Depot. The explosions were of massive proportions and fire engulfed a high proportion of the site. The fire burned for several days, destroying most of the site and emitting large clouds of black smoke into the atmosphere. In total 43 people were injured, but there were no fatalities. Significant damage occurred to both commercial and residential properties in the vicinity and a large area around the site was evacuated on emergency service advice.

A Government inquiry held jointly by the HSE and the EA is currently taking place. The aim of the inquiry is to identify the immediate causes of the explosion, rather than consider who was to blame for any deficiencies, so as not to prejudice further legal proceedings. An initial progress report by the Major Incident Investigation Board (MIIB) on 13 July 2006 did not examine the causes of the explosion, but looked at the environmental impact. There is still much research to be done in order to deliver sound guidance to the Industry.

The HSE carried out a public consultation from April to July 2007 on the Government proposal that societal risk should be taken into account when assessing safety measures at onshore major hazard installations and for planning applications on the use of land for development in areas around such sites. On 30 January 2008 the HSE published the results of the societal risk consultation. The MIIB is expected to produce its own guidance on land use planning and societal risk in summer 2008.

Although the MIIB's final report is not complete, the Buncefield Standards Task Group (BSTG) issued their final report into safety and environmental standards for fuel storage sites on 24 July 2007. Shortly after the incident, the BSTG was formed, consisting of representatives from the COMAH Competent Authority and Industry. The aim was to translate lessons from the Buncefield incident into effective and practical guidance for industry to implement as rapidly as possible. The purpose of the report is to specify the minimum expected standards of control which should be in place at all establishments storing large volumes of petroleum, and similar products capable of giving rise to a large flammable vapour cloud in the event of a loss of primary containment.

Containment of bulk hazardous liquids at COMAH establishments – Consultation

In response to the accident at the Buncefield fuel storage depot, the Environment Agency published a consultation seeking views on the current containment policy for bulk storage of hazardous liquids. The Consultation closed in September 2007; however the results have not yet been published. The proposed policy sets out ways in which to improve protection of people and the environment, both on and off-site. It applies to sites that are subject to the COMAH Regulations, and which store and use large quantities of petrol and other fuels.

> *See also*: Accident investigations, p.55; Biological hazards, p.72; COSHH / hazardous substances, p.176

Sources of further information

HSE – Control of Major Accidents Hazards: www.hse.gov.uk/comah/index.htm

Competence and the 'Responsible Person'

Raymond Joyce, Freeth Cartwright LLP

Key points

The Corporate Manslaughter and Corporate Homicide Act 2007 provides the latest legislative impetus for employers to ensure that their employees are competent to undertake what is expected of them. Ensuring that employees are competent is the responsibilty of senior management. However, competence is not an absolute concept and senior management may wonder how competence can be recognised and assessed.

The concept of competence in health and safety legislation is so far reaching that the Policy Group of the Health and Safety Executive (HSE) has published an outline map on competence, training and certification, which is regularly updated and available on the HSE website. The outline map is intended to give an overview of requirements for competence and training in health and safety legislation. The concept of competence and its adoption by numerous statutory instruments is such that even the Policy Group has to admit there may be a few omissions. Employers or employees have to assess competence simply by relying on the ordinary definition of 'competent' and the HSE's own guidance.

Competency

The *Oxford English Dictionary*'s definition of the relevant aspects of competent is:

1. suitable, appropriate;
2. sufficient or adequate in amount, or degree;
3. legally authorised or qualified, able to take cognisance (of a witness, evidence), eligible, admissible;
4. having adequate skill, properly qualified, effective.

The definition identifies that competence is based on being suitable and appropriate to undertake a task successfully. The need for suitability and appropriateness is only to the extent that the degree of competence is sufficient or adequate. In considering human factors, competence is defined by the HSE as the ability to undertake responsibilities and perform activities to a recognised standard on a regular basis. Competence is a combination of practical and thinking skills, experience and knowledge. The requirements identified by the HSE for competence are organised under four headings:

1. General health and safety.
2. Health hazards.
3. Safety hazards.
4. Special hazards.

The HSE further identified 37 general goal-setting requirements where there is no precise detail of how the requirement for competence should be met, including five high risk areas as follows:

1. Construction.
2. Major hazards.
3. Off shore.

4. Railways.
5. Nuclear.

Competence has to be assessed with respect to the particular task and associated hazards and risks. The assessment of competence is related to what is necessary to achieve a satisfactory result.

Training and certification are a recognised means of establishing competence in addition to experience. Training and certification alone may not necessarily mean that competence has been achieved. The wider concept of competence and the importance of experience is highlighted by the judgment in the case of *Maloney v. A Cameron Limited* (1961) 2 All ER 934, where the Court of Appeal was prepared to accept without further comment that a competent person required under the Construction (Working Places) Regulations 1966 who was required to be responsible for inspection and supervision of competent workmen meant "possessing adequate experience of such work".

In a decision in *Gibson v. Skibs A/S Marina* (1966) 2 All ER 476 the Judge stated:

"Who is a competent person for the purpose of such an inspection? This phrase is not defined. I think that it is obviously to be taken to have its ordinary meaning of a person who is competent for the task. I think that a competent person for this task is the person who is a practical and reasonable man, who knows what to look for and knows how to recognise it when he sees it."

It is of considerable assistance if a person who is required to be competent can demonstrate that they have had the appropriate and relevant training. Training does not necessarily have to be provided by a recognised training organisation although such organisations have the benefit of demonstrating consistency in the training content and delivery which should be capable of being audited. It is also the case that training organisations can issue certificates of attendance or evidence of having reached an appropriate standard.

Competency should not be considered in isolation and devolved upon one person. All persons involved in activities that affect their own health and safety and that of others should be competent to undertake the role for which they are engaged. The person at the top of the management structure should be able to demonstrate competence for the role they undertake just as much as the 'front line operative' who has to be competent in their activities.

Competence is about obtaining the best performance from the most important resource any organisation has – its people. To ensure that competence is an integral part of an organisation's culture, incompetence should not be tolerated and risk assessments and job descriptions should always refer to objective standards for skills and experience and if necessary formal training and certification.

> *See also*: Construction site health and safety, p.154; Health and safety management, p.386; Risk assessments, p.639; Training, p.691

Sources of further information

Developing and maintaining staff competence, HSE (2002) ISBN: 0 717617 32 7.

Confined spaces

Kathryn Gilbertson, Greenwoods Solicitors LLP

Key points

Entry into confined spaces can be extremely hazardous. An average of 15 people needlessly die each year as a result of lack of oxygen, poisonous gases, fumes or vapours, fire, explosions and excessive heat.

Tragically a large number of people who die are attempting to rescue their colleagues, falling victim to the same conditions that they are attempting to rescue their colleagues from.

The Confined Spaces Regulations 1997 were introduced to put stricter controls on work in confined spaces. They include a definition of confined spaces and the risks associated with working in them.

Legislation

- Health and Safety at Work etc. Act 1974.
- Personal Protective Equipment at Work Regulations 1992.
- Confined Spaces Regulations 1997.
- Provision and Use of Work Equipment Regulations 1998.
- Management of Health and Safety at Work Regulations 1999.
- Control of Substances Hazardous to Health Regulations 1999.

Meaning of 'confined space'

"Any place, including any chamber, tank, vat, silo, pit, trench, pipe, sewer, flue, well or other similar space in which, by virtue of its enclosed nature, there arises a reasonably foreseeable risk."

Under the Regulations a 'confined space' has two defining features:

1. A place which is substantially (though not always entirely) enclosed. Beware; an open-topped tank may be a confined space.
2. There is a reasonably foreseeable risk of serious injury from hazardous substances or conditions within the space or nearby.

The hazards

- Flammable substances and oxygen enrichment.
- Toxic gas, fume or vapour.
- Oxygen deficiency.
- Ingress or presence of liquid.
- Solid materials that can flow.
- Excessive heat.

The above list is not exhaustive. Other hazards may be found which are covered by other Regulations e.g. noise, dust, asbestos.

Risk assessment

The Regulations are quite clear. Can entry be avoided? In some cases you can clean a confined space from the outside using water jetting, steam or chemical cleaning, long-handled tools or in-place cleaning systems. Alternatively, for inspection purposes a CCTV system may be appropriate.

If entry is unavoidable you should assess the general condition of the confined space to identify what may or may not be present. You should consider:

- previous contents;
- residues;
- contamination;
- oxygen deficiency and oxygen enrichment;
- physical dimensions;
- cleaning chemicals;
- sources of ignition; and
- ingress of substances.

Working in confined spaces / safe system of work

It is imperative that a safe system of work is implemented. To be effective it needs to be in writing. The following factors must be considered.

Supervision
Someone must be in charge and be competent for that role.

Competence for confined spaces working
Training is essential before entering a confined space.

Communications
Operatives inside a confined space must be able to communicate with those outside.

Testing / monitoring the atmosphere
Testing and monitoring equipment is not expensive.

Gas purging
Air or an inert gas but it's imperative that if inert gas is used the atmosphere is checked before entry.

Ventilation
Fresh air should be drawn from a point where it is not contaminated. Never introduce additional oxygen to 'sweeten' the air!

Removal of residues
Often the purpose of confined space work. Dangerous substances can be released when residues are disturbed.

Isolation from gases, liquids and other flowing materials
Ideally disconnect pipes, ducting or insert blanks. If this is not possible valves must be locked shut with no possibility of allowing anything to pass through.

Isolation from mechanical and electrical equipment
Ideally the power should be isolated by locking off unless the risk assessment dictates power must be on for vital services e.g. firefighting, lighting, communications.

Selection and use of suitable equipment
Must be suitable for purpose e.g. a lamp certified for use in explosive atmospheres.

Personal protective equipment (PPE) and respiratory protective equipment (RPE)
Always a last resort. May be identified in the risk assessment in which case it needs to be suitable and used by those entering the confined space. PPE and RPE is in addition to engineering controls and safe systems of work.

Portable gas cylinders and internal combustion engines
Do not use a petrol engine within a confined space! Diesel fuelled engines are nearly as dangerous and are inappropriate unless exceptional precautions are taken.

Gas supplied by pipes and hoses
The use of pipes and hoses for conveying oxygen or flammable gasses must be controlled to minimise the risks. For example, at the end of every working

period supply valves are securely closed and pipes and hoses are withdrawn from the confined space.

Access and egress
Needs to be adequate and take into account persons wearing PPE and RPE.

Fire prevention
Wherever possible flammable and combustible materials should not be stored in a confined space.

Lighting
Adequate and suitable lighting, including emergency lighting should be provided. It may need to be specially protected if used where flammable or potentially explosive atmospheres are likely to occur.

Static electricity
Exclude static discharges and all sources of ignition if there is a risk of a flammable or explosive atmosphere.

Smoking
Prohibited in confined spaces. Exclusion area may be required beyond the confined space.

Emergencies and rescue
Procedures need to be suitable and sufficient and in place before any person enters a confined space.

Limited working time
Under extreme conditions of temperature, humidity or the use of respiratory equipment time limits on individuals may be required.

Permits to work
These will be required where there is a reasonably foreseeable risk of serious injury in entering or working in the confined space. The permit to work procedure is an

extension of the safe system of work, not replacement for it!

Health issues
A potential issue for some confined space such as sewers – Leptospirosis (Weil's disease) and Hepatitis.

A doctor should be consulted in the event of flu-like illness or fever, particularly when associated with severe headache and skin infections.

Medical advice should be sought if there are persistent chest symptoms, particularly if consistent with asthma or alveolitis (inflammation of the lung).

Case studies
In July 2004 the HSE issued a warning to the manufacturing industry following the deaths of three employees in a slurry tank. The employees, working on a farm near Thetford, Norfolk, were asphyxiated in the tank after being overcome by carbon dioxide. A fourth worker, who also entered the tank, was fortunate to escape with his life.

The HSE was keen to emphasise the importance not only of assessing the risks but also of ensuring that safe systems of work are implemented:

"This incident highlights the risks common to all industries and everyone ... It's no good managers implementing a safe system of work and assuming employees will follow it. Workers need to be carefully trained and supervised by a competent manager. Senior management must carry out regular checks to be sure the correct procedures are always followed."

In 2002 Workplace Law Network reported on A & P Falmouth Ltd, a ship repair company based in Cornwall, which was fined £10,000 plus £6,627 costs after pleading guilty to the failure to ensure the health and safety of two employees.

During February 2001 John Webb and Desmond Martin were carrying out repair work for the company on a split hopper barge. A little after midnight when they had finished work on the hull of the vessel, the two men climbed into a port void 12.5m × 6m × 4.5m through a small manhole to start painting, using a paint containing xylene and butanone solvents. Although he was in a 'dazed and drunken-like condition', Mr Webb managed to climb out of the tank to get medical help, while Mr Martin lay unconscious. Both men were taken straight to hospital, but

fortunately neither suffered from long-term injury.

The HSE prosecuting inspector, David Corey, said:

"The risks of working in confined spaces like this tank, with solvent-based paints, are well known, as are the precautions that need to be taken. The men should have been trained, informed and supervised to a higher standard than was the case on this occasion. The systems of work and entry procedures should have ensured the full and correct use of the necessary personal protective equipment, there should have been some form of forced ventilation provided, and the provision for raising the alarm should have been made."

> *See also*: Construction site health and safety, p.154; Personal Protective Equipment, p.568; Risk assessments, p.639

Sources of further information

HSE – Confined spaces at work: www.hse.gov.uk/confinedspace/index.htm

HSE – *Safe work in confined spaces*: www.hse.gov.uk/pubns/indg258.pdf

Construction site health and safety

Kathryn Gilbertson, Greenwoods Solicitors LLP

Key points

2.2 million people work in Britain's construction industry, making it the country's biggest industry.

It is also one of the most dangerous. In the last 25 years, 2,800 people have died from injuries they received during construction work. Many more have been injured or made ill.

The main causes of death and injury in the construction industry are:

- falling through fragile roofs and roof lights;
- falling from ladders, scaffolds and other workplaces;
- being struck by excavators, lift trucks or dumpers;
- overturning vehicles; and
- being crushed by collapsing structures.

Legislation

- The Construction (Health, Safety and Welfare) Regulations 1996.
- The Health and Safety (Consultation with Employees) Regulations 1996.
- The Lifting Operations and Lifting Equipment Regulations 1998.
- The Management of Health and Safety at Work Regulations 1999.
- The Control of Substances Hazardous to Health Regulations 2002.
- The Control of Vibration Regulations 2005.
- The Work at Height Regulations 2005.
- The Construction (Design and Management) Regulations 2007.

Key areas to managing construction safety

Correct planning and implementation for safety

- All construction and building work projects have to be managed

under the various parts of the CDM Regulations.

Ladders and towers

- Ladders should not be used without proper justification.
- Where ladders are used they must be used correctly.
- Towers need to be capable of being erected safely.
- Towers need to be erected by properly trained operatives.

Fragile roofs

- No work should be carried out on a fragile roof unless a safe system of work is in place and understood by those carrying out the work.
- It is essential that only trained competent persons are allowed to work on roofs.
- Footwear with a good grip should be worn.
- It is good practice to ensure that a person does not work alone on a roof.

Slips, trips and falls

This is the most common cause of injuries and is largely due to poor site management.

- Housekeeping needs to be actively managed.
- Walkways must be kept clear.
- Work areas should be tidy and free from obstructions e.g. trailing leads.

Construction site transport

- All vehicles should be regularly maintained and records kept.
- Only trained drivers should be allowed to drive.
- Vehicles should be fitted with reversing warning systems.
- Traffic routes and loading/storage areas need to be well designed with enforced speed limits.
- Suitable signs should be erected.
- Good visibility and the separation of vehicles and pedestrians must be used.
- The safety of members of the public must be considered particularly where vehicles cross public footpaths.

Lifting operations

- Must be properly planned by a competent person.
- Must be appropriately supervised.
- Must be carried out in a safe manner.
- Lifting equipment which is designed for lifting people should be appropriately and clearly marked.
- Lifting equipment not designed for lifting people but which might be used in error should be clearly marked to show it is not for lifting people.
- Machinery and accessories for lifting loads shall be clearly marked to indicate their safe working loads (SWL).

Occupational health issues

- Musculoskeletal disorders (MSDs) including back pain, usually from poor

methods of manual handling such as heavy or awkward lifts. Where MSD trends are increasing revision training for manual handling should be considered.

- Contact dermatitis from substances such as cement. Managers should effectively supervise their staff and ensure that gloves are being worn.
- Hand–Arm vibration (HAV) caused by vibrating or poorly managed hand tools.
- Long-term hearing loss caused by excessive noise.
- Asbestos-related illnesses such as mesothelioma.

Other issues

Passport schemes

Passport schemes ensure that workers have basic health and safety awareness training. The HSE is encouraging organisations to work together so that one scheme recognises the core training of other schemes.

Passport schemes are not:

- a way of knowing or identifying that a worker is competent;
- a substitute for risk assessment;
- a way of showing 'approval' of a contractor;
- required by law or regulated by law;
- a reason to ignore giving site specific information; or
- a substitute for effective on-site management.

The HSE and the Environment Agencies do not endorse or approve individual passport training schemes.

Benefits and advantages

- They can help reduce accidents and ill health.
- They can save time and money because workers need less induction training.

- They show a company's commitment to having safe and healthy workers.
- Companies know that workers have been trained to a common, recognised and validated standard.
- Insurance and liability premiums may be reduced if a company can show that all workers have basic health, safety and environmental training.

Case law

A 40-year-old worker fell nine metres to his death from an unprotected edge on top of a partly-constructed operating theatre while a boiler was being lifted into position. The contractors controlling the work failed to identify the risks and communicate with the workers involved. No one on site on the day identified the obvious risks and open edges were left unprotected. Two companies were fined a total of £87,000.

See also: CDM, p.135; COSHH: Hazardous substances, p.176; Working at height, p.395; Lifting equipment, p.466; Reporting Injuries, Diseases and Dangerous Occurrences (RIDDOR), p.628

Sources of further information

HSE: Health and Safety in the construction industry: www.hse.gov.uk/construction

Contract disputes

Rupert Choat, CMS Cameron McKenna

Key points

As disputes are expensive and time-consuming, it is advisable to manage them by:

■ including appropriate dispute resolution provisions in contracts;
■ anticipating disputes in record-keeping practices; and
■ handling disputes effectively.

Legislation

■ Arbitration Act 1996.
■ Housing Grants, Construction and Regeneration Act 1996.

Dispute resolution provisions in contracts

Wherever possible, when drafting any pro-forma contracts and when negotiating contracts, it is advisable to consider the various dispute resolution methods available and to include clauses providing for the chosen method(s). Some 'picking and mixing' of methods is possible.

Negotiation

Discussions invariably occur before any dispute goes to formal proceedings. Even if formal proceedings are commenced, negotiation remains one of the most effective ways of resolving disputes.

It may help to discuss disputes on a 'without prejudice' basis, so that what is said cannot be referred to later in any formal proceedings. This can promote a frank exchange of views.

Some contracts provide for a structured approach to discussions. For instance, a dispute may be required to be considered initially by those at project level. If this is unsuccessful within a specified time, the dispute may go to board or principal level. The contract might make compliance with this procedure a precondition to the commencement of any formal proceedings.

Court proceedings

Generally, unless the contract otherwise provides (e.g. by providing for arbitration), the courts can decide the parties' disputes. Proceedings are started by issuing a claim form.

The Civil Procedure Rules govern court proceedings.

The courts deal with disputes according to their value and complexity. Directions are given to the parties to prepare their dispute for trial. Directions usually provide for the production of statements of case, disclosure of documents, exchange of witness statements and expert reports (if necessary).

Court proceedings are public.

Arbitration

Parties to a contract can agree that their disputes will be resolved by arbitration rather than by the courts. This can be done either in the contract or 'ad hoc' once a dispute arises.

The Arbitration Act 1996 governs arbitration.

Generally the parties decide who the arbitrator(s) will be or, failing that, a nominating body decides. The parties can agree the procedure for the arbitration by which the dispute will be decided. They might agree on a procedure similar to court proceedings or they might opt for the dispute being decided on paper without a hearing.

Arbitration is a confidential process.

One disadvantage of arbitration is that third parties cannot be joined in the arbitration without the consent of all concerned. This is not the case with court proceedings.

Adjudication

The Housing Grants, Construction and Regeneration Act 1996 empowers a party to a written 'construction contract' to refer any dispute arising under the contract to adjudication. The option to go to adjudication exists in addition to the right to go to court or arbitration (whichever is applicable).

Adjudication is rough and ready but usually cheaper than court proceedings or arbitration. The appointed adjudicator is required to reach a decision within 28 days of the dispute being referred to him (subject to extensions). The adjudicator's decision is temporarily binding pending the outcome of any subsequent court proceedings or arbitration.

There is some uncertainty as to the extent to which facilities management contracts are construction contracts. To avoid confusion it is usually sensible to provide expressly for adjudication in such contracts.

Alternative dispute resolution (ADR)

Parties to a contract can agree that their disputes will be resolved by any of a number of forms of ADR. This can be done either in the contract or 'ad hoc' once the dispute arises. The parties may agree that ADR is a precondition to court proceedings or arbitration.

- One method of ADR is mediation. The parties (or an appointing body of the parties' choice) appoint the mediator, whose role is facilitating the resolution of the dispute. The mediator has no decision-making powers, although the parties can empower him to opine on where the merits lie in their dispute. The mediation is held 'without prejudice'. The process is non-binding. Any party can withdraw at any time, and there is no guarantee of a resolution at the end of the mediation.
- Early neutral evaluation involves a third party, who is usually a lawyer, assessing the merits of the dispute and advising the parties of his views in a, usually, non-binding manner. This might help the parties to settle between themselves.
- Another method of ADR is expert determination. It is particularly suited to disputes that turn on technical rather than legal issues. A third-party expert is appointed to reach a decision on the dispute. The parties agree a (usually short) timetable that may allow them to make submissions to the expert. The parties may agree that the expert's decision will be final and binding or that it will be subject to review by the courts or arbitration.

Record keeping

Good documentary records tend to help in resolving disputes and may reduce any legal costs you incur.

Bear in mind that in court and arbitration proceedings you will invariably be directed to disclose to the other party relevant documents under your control (including documents that are prejudicial to your case). Disclosable documents will include emails and other electronic documents. Documents are generally disclosable even if they contain confidential information.

It is advisable to retain documents for between six and 15 years after the matter to which they relate ends (depending upon the nature of the contract).

Handling disputes

When a dispute arises, try to address it early rather than allowing it to escalate. If it is not possible to resolve the dispute by discussion, check the contract to see which dispute resolution method(s)

apply. Consider also whether you want to suggest another method not provided for by the contract (e.g. mediation). In some cases statute may dictate that a certain dispute resolution method applies even if it is not specified in the contract (e.g. adjudication in construction contracts).

It invariably favours a party during any formal proceedings if they have behaved reasonably in conducting the dispute (especially if the other party has not). For instance, if a party unreasonably refuses a proposal to mediate a dispute, that party may later incur a costs penalty.

Remember that even if you win the dispute, you will not recover all of your legal costs and will find it difficult to recover compensation for management time spent in handling the dispute.

See also: Employment contracts, p.273; Employment disputes, p.278

Sources of further information

Civil Procedure Rules: www.justice.gov.uk/civil/procrules_fin/index.htm

Arbitration Act 1996: www.hmso.gov.uk/acts/acts1996/1996023.htm

Housing Grants, Construction and Regeneration Act 1996: www.opsi.gov.uk/acts/acts1996/1996053.htm

Adjudication case summaries: www.law-now.com/law-now/zones/LN_Adjudication.htm

Contractors

Susan Cha, Kennedys

Key points
An employer's undertaking for the purposes of section 3 of the Health and Safety at Work etc. Act 1974 may include the work undertaken by an independent contractor for him.

Legislation
- Health and Safety at Work etc. Act 1974.
- Management of Health and Safety at Work Regulations 1999.
- Construction (Design and Management) Regulations 2007.

Overview
Section 3 of the Health and Safety at Work etc. Act 1974 (HSWA) imposes a duty on employers to non-employees to conduct their business, so far as is reasonably practicable, to ensure that those persons are not exposed to risks to their health and safety. This duty may extend to contractors and those employed by them.

Whether or not this is so will depend on whether the risk forms part of the conduct by the employer of his 'undertaking'.

In the leading case of *R v. Associated Octel* (1996), an employee of a specialist cleaning contractor was badly burned while working at Octel's plant. Like all other contractors on the site, the contractor worked subject to the defendant's 'permit to work system'.

Octel was prosecuted for a breach of section 3(1). It claimed there was no case as the employee was from an independent contractor and not part of its undertaking. The case went to the House of Lords, which held that the key issue of the extent

to which an independent contractor can be left to its own devices will depend on whether the work forms part of the employer's undertaking. If it does form par of the undertaking, then the employer's duty under section 3 extends to ensuring that, so far as is reasonably practicable, the contractor's work is undertaken withou risk.

Where a prosecution is brought and there is a dispute on the facts, it will be for the HSE to prove that a contractor's work formed part of an employer's undertaking.

Practical effect
Work undertaken by a contractor is usuall covered in a contract. It is good practice for health and safety responsibilities to be written into such a contract. However, the duties under HSWA cannot be passed fro one party to another by a contract.

Where CDM Regulations apply, employer and contractor have specific legal responsibilities in relation to duties under HSWA and Management of Health and Safety at Work Regulations 1999 (MHSWR). The principal contractor shoulc plan, manage and coordinate work during the construction phase to make sure that risks are properly controlled.

Thereafter the effect of HSG65 *Successful health and safety management* (see Sources of further information) will apply o the work of independent contractors as does to the employer if the work forms art of the employer's undertaking. It is mportant to remember that both parties will ave duties under health and safety law. The extent of the duties of the parties will epend on the circumstances of each case.

Thus the arrangements for ensuring roper health and safety management nvisaged by HSG65 will apply in these ircumstances to a contractor's work. This means that where an employer uses ontractors it will be expected to have a ealth and safety policy in place together vith an organisation to measure and audit ne contractor's performance and to review regularly.

The first step for the employer will be to dentify the job it wants the contractor to o and that means identifying all aspects f work to be undertaken from initial reparation to final completion so that nere can be no uncertainty over what is equired of the contractor.

An employer should undertake a risk ssessment before using contractors to nsure that the use of contractors generally vill not import risk that is not as low as easonably practicable. This would include pecific checks of the contractor involved o ensure that it is properly licensed, ompetent and qualified to undertake ne role on behalf of the employer. HSE uidance suggests that this would entail ooking at the proposed contractor and etermining matters such as:

■ experience in the type of work concerned;
■ qualifications and skills;
■ the health and safety training and supervision it provides;
■ recent health and safety performance;
■ its recent health and safety policies; and
■ its arrangements for consulting its workforce.

Where an employer uses contractors, he should have systems to ensure that there is proper supply of information, instruction and training to the contractor. There must be proper management and supervision and the employer should undertake monitoring, auditing and sample checking to ensure that the contractor's work, which forms part of its own undertaking, is being conducted in a legally compliant way. Where sub-contractors are used, the employer must satisfy himself that the contractor has an effective procedure for monitoring and auditing the competence of sub-contractors. He must also ensure there are systems in place for the proper supply of information, instruction and training to the sub-contractor.

The greater the risk that operations have on the health and safety of individuals, the greater the requirement for management, supervisory and monitoring responsibilities.

The MHSWR are of particular importance in any employer–contractor relationship. They set out the requirements for a health and safety management system in all workplaces.

See also: CDM, p.135;
Construction site health and safety, p.154; Health and safety at work, p.364; Risk assessments, p.639

Sources of further information

HSE: www.hse.gov.uk and information line (08701 545 500).

L21 *Management of health and safety at work. Management of Health and Safety at Work Regulations 1999. Approved Code of Practice and guidance* (HSE Books, 2000) ISBN: 0 7176 2488 9.

HSG65 *Successful health and safety management* (HSE Books, 1997) ISBN: 0 7176 1276 7.

Workplace Law Group's ***Working with contractors 2008: Special Report*** is essential reading for those involved in the appointment of contractors for work activities. It is designed to provide workplace managers with everything they need to know to ensure they, and the contractors they employ, meet their duties under health and safety and employment law. For more information visit www.workplacelaw.net/Bookshop/SpecialReports.

Corporate manslaughter

Daniel McShee, Kennedys

Key points
The passing of the Corporate Manslaughter and Corporate Homicide Act 2007 to introduce a statutory offence of 'Corporate manslaughter' (called 'Corporate Homicide' in Scotland) followed many years of promises by this and previous Governments to reform the law of corporate manslaughter. The new offence came into force on 6 April 2008. Until then there was a common law offence only, which, in order for a company to be found guilty of it, required the conviction of an individual person for gross negligence manslaughter and for that person to be so senior within the company that he represented its 'directing mind'. This requirement was known as the Identification Principle. The common law offence will remain for any management failure resulting in an incident up to 6 April 2008, but not beyond that date. It is important to emphasise that the Act is an offence-creating statute rather than a duty-setting one. The Act itself imposes no new health and safety duties.

The new offence of Corporate Manslaughter

The Act is designed to make it easier to prosecute organisations where their gross negligence leads to death. As outlined above, under the old law a corporate body could only be prosecuted based on the identification principle. Whilst attempts were made to prosecute big companies under the old law these attempts were all unsuccessful. The new Act abolished the common law offence altogether from 6 April 2008 and replaced it with a statutory offence at section 1 creating a completely new framework for finding an organisation guilty of corporate manslaughter.

The wording of the offence is that an organisation will be guilty of an offence if the way in which its activities are managed or organised:

- causes a person's death; and
- amounts to a gross breach of a relevant duty of care owed by the organisation to the deceased.

An organisation is only guilty if the way in which its activities are managed or organised by its senior management is a substantial element in the breach.

Organisations
Whereas the common law offence only applied to corporate bodies, the new offence applies to a much wider group of organisations including corporations, specified government departments, police forces and partnerships.

Senior management
'Senior Management' is defined in section 1(4)(c) as the persons who play significant roles in:

- the making of decisions about how the whole or a substantial part of its activities are to be managed or organised; or
- the actual managing or organising of the whole or a substantial part of those activities.

Clearly there will be some people, e.g. members of the Board, who will be involved in substantial parts, or arguably the whole, of the company's decision-making process and fulfil the test in 1(4)(c)(i) above. Under the old law those individuals would be identified as representing the directing mind and there does not appear to be any change in respect of people at that level.

However, the definition in section 1(4)(c)(ii) of a person "*actually* managing or organising ... a substantial part of those activities" is a major change. The definition includes two strands; the taking of decisions and actually managing those activities. The term 'significant' is intended to capture those whose role in the relevant management activity is decisive or influential, rather than playing a supporting role.

What amounts to a 'substantial' part of an organisation's activities will be important in determining the level of management responsibility engaging the new offence. The scale of the organisation's activities overall will be a factor and it is stated that the offence is intended to cover, for example, management at regional level within a national organisation. In many big companies there will be managers who manage areas or are responsible for a particular discipline.

The definition in section 1(4)(c)(ii) – "actually managing a substantial part" – would appear to potentially lower the threshold for these types who might become 'senior management' under the new law but who would not be identified as a directing mind under the old common law. As such the definition is bound to catch a layer of management lower in the organisation that would not have been classified as representing the directing mind under the old law. It should also be noted that senior management would cover both those in the direct operational chain of management as well as those in, for example, strategic or regulatory compliance roles.

The other key point about the definition of 'senior management' is that the new offence allows the prosecutor to aggregate the failures of a number of senior managers rather than relying on the conduct of one single 'directing mind' as required by the identification principle under the old common law.

These two points are the key changes from the old law and will undoubtedly increase the potential for the new offence to be investigated against medium-sized and bigger companies. However, as explained below, there are still hurdles to overcome, particularly as the new legal test requires a significant element of 'gross' failure to be at a senior management level.

Meaning of 'Duty of Care'

The new offence only applies in circumstances where an organisation owes a duty of care to the victim. This is no different from the old law. Section 2(1) requires the duty of care to arise out of certain specific functions or activities. The effect is that the offence only applies where an organisation owes a duty of care

- to its employees or other persons working for the organisation;
- as an occupier of premises;
- when the organisation is supplying goods or services;
- when constructing or maintaining buildings, infrastructure or vehicles etc. or when using plant or vehicles etc.; and
- when carrying out other activities on a commercial basis.

Excluded from being a relevant duty of care are public policy decisions made by a public authority.

Gross breach

Section 8 of the new Act requires there to have been a gross breach of the duty of care. The requirement for a breach to be gross is a positive one as it provides a jury with a reminder that the offence should be reserved only for the most serious cases. The notes produced with the draft Bill made it clear that the decision of what is gross is one for the jury. The definition in the Act requires a jury to do the following:

- It *must* consider whether the evidence shows the organisation failed to comply with any health and safety legislation relating to the alleged breach, and if so:
    - how serious that failure was; and
    - how much of a risk of death it posed.

Section 8(3) goes on that in assessing grossness a jury *may also:*

- consider the extent to which the evidence shows that there were attitudes, policies, systems or accepted practices within the organisation that were likely to have encouraged any such failure or to have produced tolerance of it; and
- have regard to any health and safety guidance relating to the alleged breach.

The first part of this definition causes concern. It leaves open to the jury a very subjective assessment of 'corporate culture' which they may not be in a proper position to judge in context, having never been part of the industry concerned.

Causation

The wording of the offence makes it clear that the gross breach must have 'caused' a person's death. Although this is not explained further in the Act, the guidance that went with the Bill is likely to mean that the usual principles of causation in

criminal law will apply, namely that it need not be the *sole* cause but need only be *a* cause. The offence in section 1 specifies that an organisation is only guilty if the way in which its activities are managed or organised by its *senior management* is a substantial element in the breach. Whilst the failure need not be the only cause, the difficulty of proving a causal link between failures by someone classified as senior management and the victim's death will still provide a significant hurdle to the prosecuting authorities similar to the way it did under the old law, albeit to a lesser degree.

Fines

The sanction for a conviction of corporate manslaughter will be a potentially unlimited fine in the Crown Court (section 1(6)), although perhaps the worst sanction that will apply is the stigma of being a 'corporate killer'. The Home Office paper that went with the original Bill stated that the offence would be targeted at the worst cases of management failure causing death. If this is so, it is likely that fines for conviction will be set at a very high level and probably significantly in excess of record fines under HSWA. Fines for offences under HSWA have generally been increasing, particularly for major disasters. The fines imposed on Transco, Balfour Beatty Rail Maintenance and Network Rail in the last few years for HSWA breaches arising out of major disasters heralded a new age in health and safety sentencing, at least in cases at the top end of the scale.

The Sentencing Advisory Panel (SAP) launched a consultation paper in November last year concerning sentencing for the new offence. The SAP's paper highlights a desire for a consistent method of calculating the fine to reflect the seriousness of the offence and the circumstances of the offender. The SAP suggests the fines should be devised to have an equal economic impact on organisations of different sizes and proposes the calculations be based on the company's turnover. The SAP proposes the Courts' consideration of a fine in a successful manslaughter prosecution (following a not guilty plea) might start at 5% of annual turnover averaged over the three years prior to sentencing. It also proposes that the range of fines, taking into account aggravating and mitigating factors, might be between 2.5% and 10% of the averaged turnover figure. The results of the SAP's consultation are not yet known.

Remedial orders

Section 9 of the new Act gives a Court the power to make a remedial order requiring a defendant to take action to put right health and safety breaches. The section states that an order can only be made "on an application by the prosecution specifying the terms of the proposed order". Further, that any such order must be on such terms (whether those proposed or others) as the court considers appropriate having regard to any representations made and any evidence adduced by the prosecution or the accused.

The power is not a new one. The HSWA (section 42) contains a similar power for the Court to make remedial orders and has done so for 30 years. It is rarely used. The potential sanction is fraught with difficulties. Any such orders would need to be consistent with the strategy of improving safety across a whole industry.

Publicity orders

Section 10 of the Act will, once it is rendered effective, allow a Court hearing a Corporate Manslaughter offence to make a publicity order requiring the convicted organisation to publicise the fact hat it has been convicted, particulars of the offence, the level of fine and any remedial order made. The court will have free reign to decide in what manner the convicted company is to publicise its guilt – advertisements, billboards etc. This is a somewhat odd power given the small number of cases that are expected to be prosecuted; one would expect publicity to be given to the case in any event.

DPP Consent

Section 17 of the Act requires the consent of the Director of Public Prosecutions before proceedings are instituted. This is a sensible policy decision to reduce the risk of insufficiently well-founded prosecutions, whether brought by the authorities or private individuals, which would ultimately fail but have an unfair, possibly irreparable effect on an organisation's reputation.

Who will investigate?

The notes to the draft Bill made it clear that only the police and CPS would investigate. Although the Act is silent on this it appears that the HSE, although likely to assist in the police investigation, will not be a prosecuting authority for Corporate Manslaughter.

Individual liability

As stated, the Act imposes no new liability on individuals. The proposals in the earlier drafts to disqualify a manager who had "any influence" on a management failure and to potentially imprison someone who "contributed substantially" were conceptually unsound. They would have lowered the level of possible criminal sanction to an unacceptable and unreasonable level. If an individual's acts or omissions are judged to be sufficiently serious and causative of a death then, regardless of the new law, they can still be liable for an offence of gross negligence manslaughter. It should also be recalled that the enforcing authorities can prosecute senior managers and directors under section 37 of the HSWA where an offence by the organisation is committed with their consent, connivance or neglect. Similarly section 7 creates a duty in the case of employees to take reasonable care for other employees and others affected.

Commencement and extent
The Act applies to the whole of England, Wales, Scotland and Northern Ireland to incidents occurring from 6 April 2008. Section 27 makes it clear that the legislation is not retrospective. Any management failings that pre-date April 2008 will have to be continuing at the time of the death to be a cause of death and will then be caught by the new Act.

What should organisations do?
Although the Act has brought no new duties, it poses a natural reason and opportunity for organisations to review their safety management approach, their organisational framework and the systems underpinning them. Guidance recently published by the HSE/IOD defining what private and public sector directors should do to lead and promote heath and safety should be examined against organisations' existing safety management procedures to establish how they measure up and also to identify any weaknesses. Bearing in mind the reach of the Act beyond the boardroom, organisations should not think that the principles set out in the guidance do not apply lower down the management chain. It would also be prudent for organisations, particularly those in high-hazard industries, to review their liability insurance cover to ensure the legal defence costs for the new offence are covered. Many employers and Public Liability policies will provide such cover but some may not. Dependant on makeup

and size the organisation may wish to explore the possibility of purchasing additional Directors' and Officers' cover or another form of management liability cover. Experienced advice is important in the immediate aftermath of a workplace fatality, particularly as decisions made at this early stage can set the tone for the criminal investigation and can prejudice an organisation's position and that of its directors and employees. In the circumstances, it is sensible to factor this in to the pre-planning of a major accident response.

Conclusion
The new offence created a completely new framework for the prosecution of Corporate Manslaughter. There is no doubt that the new offence will have some impact on the potential criminal liability of companies for manslaughter where there have been serious failures as it is no longer necessary to convict one individual alone. The aggregated failures of a number of senior managers, who form the senior management, will be sufficient.

In addition, the second part of the definition of senior management will catch people lower in the management chain than those who represented the 'directing mind' under the old law, meaning that a much wider part of the workforce is considered by the prosecuting authorities when looking at whether the offence has been committed. Having said that, the new offence continues to have a number of safeguards ensuring that the offence is likely to be restricted for the worst cases. In particular, the requirements for senior management involvement and for any breach to be gross, is likely to mean that the floodgates will not open. It does seem likely, however, that more investigations and prosecutions for corporate manslaughter will result than under the old law based on identification, where it was rare. Whilst there may not be a flood of cases, one can envisage that some of the more serious incidents that may once have been subject to investigations only under the HSWA by the HSE will now be subject to police investigation.

See also: Accident investigations, p.55; Workplace deaths, p.190; Directors' responsibilities, p.198

Sources of further information

IOD/HSE: *Leading Health and Safety at Work*: www.hse.gov.uk/pubns/indg417.pdf

The Corporate Manslaughter and Corporate Homicide Act 2007 is one of the biggest changes to health and safety law since the HSWA. Its influence will affect everyone with responsibility for the health and safety of employees, and will mean greater responsibility is put on the shoulders of managers and directors, to ensure that they are fully compliant, and not at risk of prosecution should an accident occur.

Workplace Law Group's *Corporate Manslaughter and Corporate Homicide Act: Special Report* includes guidance and comment from some of the leading authorities on the subject, and enables directors and managers to identify the risks, put measures in place to safeguard their fortunes and reputations, and to understand the full implications of the Act. For more information visit www.workplacelaw.net/Bookshop/SpecialReports.

Comment...

Corporate Manslaughter cases – what might have been

David Wright is a lawyer at Kennedys, and specialises in advising organisations and individuals who are under investigation or being prosecuted by the authorities in relation to work-related accidents. He has acted for defendants in a number of complex, high profile cases including the Hatfield rail crash case, the trial of which took place over nine months in 2005.

What would have happened in key health and safety cases and failed corporate manslaughter cases had the new law been in force when they were tried? That is a difficult question to answer. Cases of this nature produce a mass of detail and documentation, with weeks and often months of evidence before a jury, and it would be foolhardy to rely fully on summaries or other reports of that evidence. In addition, it is the nature of juries that any attempt to assess whether or not a certain matrix of facts will lead to a conviction is at best an exercise in estimation. Having said this, it is possible to pick out some of the key features of these cases and speculate as to whether or not in broad terms they might fall within the ambit of the new statutory offence of Corporate Manslaughter.

R v. P&O European Ferries (Dover) Ltd (1990)

On 6 March 1987, the roll on / roll off passenger and freight ferry *Herald of free Enterprise* sailed from Zeebrugge. Over 450 passengers were on board, along with 80 crew. There was a light breeze and calm seas. Twenty minutes later the *Herald* capsized. Water rapidly filled the ship with the result that 188 people lost their lives and many more were injured.

Following a formal investigation into the disaster, seven human defendants and P&O European Ferries (Dover) Ltd, owners of the *Herald*, were charged with manslaughter. In 1990, their trial took place in the Central Criminal Court before Mr Justice Turner.

In legal terms, this case has become best known for the principle that a corporate body can, under the current law, be found guilty of manslaughter if an individual so senior within its organisation that he represents the company's 'directing mind' is convicted of manslaughter.

Serious failings were identified on the part of P&O management. There was no proper system to ensure that the vital task of closing the bow doors had been performed, irrespective of the failure of one individual. This was not the first occasion on which such a failure had occurred. In 1983, the assistant bosun of the *Herald*'s sister ship had fallen asleep and neglected to close both bow and stern doors on the sailing of the ship from Dover. A general instruction that it was the duty of the officer loading the main vehicle deck to ensure that the doors were "secure when leaving port" was not enforced.

The formal investigation into the disaster went further still:

"… the underlying or cardinal faults lay higher up in the Company. The Board of Directors did not appreciate their responsibility for the safe management of their ships. They did not apply their minds to the question: What orders should be given for the safety of our ships? The directors did not have any proper comprehension of what their duties were … All concerned in management, from the members of the Board of Directors down … were guilty of fault in that all must be regarded as sharing responsibility for the failure of management. From top to bottom the body corporate was infected with the disease of sloppiness … The failure on the part of the shore management to give proper and clear directions was a contributory cause of the disaster."

With this in mind, it is perhaps surprising that the prosecution of P&O failed. However, it should be recalled that when P&O were prosecuted, the test for corporate manslaughter was largely one of subjective recklessness involving appreciation of an obvious and serious risk by the directing mind of the company, i.e. its directors and very senior managers. One of the reasons the prosecution failed was that there was insufficient evidence to prove that any of the individuals making up the directing mind had sufficient knowledge of the risk that a ferry might sail with its bow doors open to render them legally reckless. The evidence was that none of them were aware that there had been five previous instances of their ferries setting sail with bow doors open.

Had P&O been prosecuted under the new regime there would seem to be every likelihood that it would have found itself convicted of corporate manslaughter.

HMA v. Transco plc (2005)

In August 2005 a record £15m fine was imposed on Transco PLC following its conviction for an offence relating to a breach of section 3 of the Health and Safety at Work etc. Act 1974. This resulted from the death of four members of the same family in a gas explosion in Scotland in 1999.

The company was convicted after a lengthy trial and in passing sentence the judge said that an aspect of Transco's defence had demonstrated that "the corporate mind of Transco has little or no remorse for this tragedy which, they ought at least now to accept was exclusively their own creation".

Whilst the company fine was clearly affected by the fact that it came after a strongly contested trial without corporate expressions of remorse, these should not be seen as the main reasons for the imposition of such a massive penalty. The court clearly had in its mind also the size of the company, which was said to have had a pre-tax profit of over £1bn in 1999 and paid out dividends that year in excess of £300m.

When sentencing, the judge commented that none of the English health and safety cases that had come before involved "such a serious and long term failure".

Applying the new law to the facts of this case is a difficult job. For one thing, there is little to go on in the judge's sentencing statement on the level at which managerial failures took place.

On one reading, one could argue that there is little doubt that Transco's failings were a cause of the deaths. After all, Transco's attempts to argue that the explosion was caused by a leak internal to the Findlay's home (and therefore not Transco's responsibility) were roundly rejected by the judge as having no evidential basis. However, that would be to ignore the fact that Transco's key failure was to settle upon and implement a prioritised replacement scheme. There would probably be a very strong case to argue that, even had such a scheme been adopted, it would not necessarily have led to the identification and replacement of the Larkhall main in time.

A failure over more than ten years to address the serious risk posed by ageing ductile iron mains, a risk which had been brought into sharp contrast by catastrophic incidents in 1988 and 1995 and was well known within Transco, by implementing a reasonable, prioritised replacement scheme could well be considered by a jury the kind of very serious failure to which the term 'gross' should apply. Indeed, in the circumstances a jury might even be expected to conclude that such conduct was of a type for which the term 'gross' was designed.

But was Transco's senior management a substantial element in the arguably gross way in which Transco approached the ductile iron risk? Without a fuller appreciation of the evidence heard at trial and a proper understanding of Transco's managerial and organisational make up and its knowledge of and input in the ductile iron debate, it is impossible to answer this question. The fact that Transco's failure stretched over a decade, and important organisational elements within Transco were aware of the risks and had suggested remedial measures, might suggest that senior management either knew, or should have known, enough to take more action.

R v. BBRM and Railtrack (2005)

Shortly after midday on 17 October 2000 a GNER train, bound from London to Leeds, was taking a bend near Hatfield station at 115 miles per hour when the track beneath it disintegrated. Four passengers were killed and 102 were injured in the ensuing derailment.

After an extensive police investigation, 54 separate charges were laid against two of the companies responsible for the track; Railtrack and Balfour Beatty Rail Maintenance, and 12 of their employees.

Each company was charged with corporate manslaughter of the four passengers who died. Four of Railtrack's managers and two of BBRM's managers were charged with gross negligence manslaughter. There were, in addition, numerous charges relating to alleged breaches of health and safety law.

In September 2004, before the trial started, a number of charges were dismissed, including all charges of corporate manslaughter against Railtrack. In essence, the corporate manslaughter charges against Railtrack fell away because the manslaughter charge against the most senior of its managers charged with manslaughter was dismissed. In effect, there was no longer a human defendant involved in the case who could be argued to constitute Railtrack's 'directing mind'. In July 2005, at the end of the prosecution case, the judge ruled that there was no case to answer against all the remaining charges of manslaughter, including those against BBRM.

The case continued on the basis of health and safety charges and in September 2005 all the individual defendants were acquitted. Railtrack and BBRM were found guilty of a breach of section 3 of the HSWA and were subsequently fined £3.5m and £10m respectively, although BBRM's fine was later reduced on appeal.

Was the way in which matters were managed or organised by BBRM senior management a substantial element in its breach? With an organisation as large and complex as BBRM, senior management might very well have been so removed, justifiably, from the day-to-day goings-on in the Hitchin maintenance team that their managerial or organisational input might have had little impact. Of course,

it depends what level of management 'senior management' descends. The judge certainly considered the Hitchin team to have suffered from a "vacuum of management" and that what he termed "senior management" should have known about the team's serious failings. However, whether he had in mind the kind of elevated management grades seemingly catered for in the new Act, is doubtful.

All things considered, had this case been tried under the new law there would certainly have been a risk to BBRM of conviction.

Corporate Social Responsibility

Sally Goodman, Bureau Veritas

Key points

Corporate Social Responsibility (CSR) is used by a number of leading companies as a strategic framework, through which all company activities are viewed. CSR generally concerns all the impacts that a company has upon society, and the need to deal with those impacts on each group of stakeholders – typically the shareholders, investors, customers, employees, media, suppliers, regulators, communities (global and local) and non-governmental organisations (NGOs).

Key issues will vary according to industry sector but include environmental impacts of products and services; impacts of operations on local communities; human rights and labour conditions in supply chain and companies' own sites; and impacts of products and services upon customers and the public. It can also be considered as a corporate response to sustainable development and builds on Environmental / Health and Safety / Quality systems already in place.

CSR is not a radically new concept, as businesses throughout history have always had to respond to wider societal issues, but increasing concerns about corporate reputation have undermined trust in business and there is growing belief that effective CSR is a sound investment for companies and a civil society. The UK Government believes that mandatory and voluntary disclosures alone are insufficient to generate responses by businesses to legitimate concerns of society. The growing importance of brand and reputation in the corporate sector is acknowledged as being directly related to business success – a recent survey of 350 European CEOs found that 78% agreed that "integrating responsible business practices makes a company more competitive". This is reflected in the investment community which has increasingly adopted CSR criteria for screening investments with considerable success – the FTSE4Good Index is the fastest growing investment index in the UK.

Companies Act 2006

On 28 November 2005, the UK Government announced that it would no longer require quoted companies to prepare an Operating and Financial Review (OFR). Instead, through the Companies Act 2006 companies will need to include a Business Review in line with the EU Accounts Modernisation Directive as part of the Director's Report. The requirement to include a Business Review is enforceable from October 2007 and requires all quoted companies (other than small companies), including subsidiary companies to provide more narrative disclosures in the Directors' Report on the performance of the business consistent with its size and complexity. In addition to information on risks and uncertainties and disclosure of financial key performance indicators, where appropriate, non financial key performance indicators, including information on employment and environmental matters, are required.

Clearly a robust CSR programme will enable the significance of these impacts to be understood and any risk management process to be reported.

First steps

In order to effectively incorporate CSR into a business model, it is common to first evaluate the model as a system of three elements:

1. Principles – the core principles upon which the business operates.
2. Processes – mechanisms by which principles are implemented.
3. Outcomes – the results of applying the principles.

By defining the company dynamics in this way, and considering them alongside a generic CSR template, it becomes clearer how a basic CSR framework might be built. For instance, by understanding principles, facilities managers (FMs) might see how to incorporate a culture of sustainability; by understanding processes, they might outline a plan for ethical procurement; and by understanding outcomes, they might be able to reduce environmental impacts.

Following the adoption of a basic CSR framework, and in order to put the ethos into practice, the next steps would include:

1. Identify key stakeholders;
2. Identify key CSR issues (threats and opportunities);
3. Research best practice in sector and use indicators as benchmarks;
4. Plan CSR programme (set objectives, targets and key performance indicators, or KPIs);
5. Implement communications and meetings with stakeholders.

The FM would then be well placed to put CSR into practice, and attempt to meet or even exceed the relevant objectives, as measured using the KPIs. An important emphasis under this regime is placed upon dialogue between the FM and important stakeholders (who for FMs are likely to be the building owner, its occupants, and suppliers), so as to ensure that appropriate objectives are set and progress is constantly being made, in an interactive and adaptive process.

Putting CSR into practice as an FM

In practice, the adoption of a CSR policy and implementation plan would be made manifest in three main categories:

1. Building management;
2. Procurement; and
3. Travel.

In terms of building management, the objective is to fulfil the three pillars of sustainability (economic, social and environmental considerations) – by increasing the efficiency with which the building is managed so as to make financial savings; by creating an amenable and attractive working environment for users; and by reducing the overall environmental impact of the building respectively. These three strands are closely interrelated, and would be achieved through a number of direct actions; for example, energy and water bills can often be substantially reduced through efficiency gains. Less transparent improvements might be made if, for example, waste streams are carefully organised so that true waste is reduced and reusable waste is sold back to the appropriate sectors (which might reduce waste transport costs besides the clear environmental benefits), or alternatively, if an attractive working environment reduces absenteeism and contributes towards the health of users.

CSR in procurement spans various themes, but largely involves combining ethical and economic considerations in he sourcing of materials and services. Establishing dialogue with suppliers would be essential in ensuring that materials and services are made available without detrimental environmental or social impacts. Despite any moral imperative, in the absence of such considerations it might be the case that various negative externalities are not taken into account, so that true purchasing 'costs' are hidden and poor purchasing choices are made. Consequently, financial gains can often be made in procurement too.

Finally, many environmental gains can be made in fleet management and transport culture. There are increasing numbers of vehicle alternatives available to achieve this end, based upon hybrid, electric and fuel cell technologies, which will probably begin to make long-term economic sense in the face of unstable standard fuel prices and evolving legislation. Equally, but more simply, the incorporation of CSR into the transport culture so as to encourage public and shared transport, or even to reduce use of vehicles altogether, can have similar benefits to those mentioned above.

Many opportunities exist to make gains in each of these three areas that come under sustainability dependant upon the nature of the business, and which are described in widely available publications (see Sources of further information).

Costs and benefits of CSR implementation
The close relationship between CSR and the principle of sustainability demands

that, in incorporating CSR into a business model, a long-term view is taken. As such, costs involved in implementation should be considered alongside all potential benefits, which in the long term would tend to far outweigh costs. These benefits generally originate from four sources:

1. Economic gains;
2. Meeting client demands;
3. Improving public perception; and
4. Adapting to legislation.

As previously alluded to, the absorption of CSR into a business strategy tends to make both direct and indirect economic gains possible. However, in the modern business climate, the demands of clients (be they users, businesses or otherwise) increasingly include ethical consideration to some degree, and as such, a clear and transparent CSR framework can provide a business edge. Equally, the public generally hold a better perception of businesses that demonstrate responsibility to some extent, where this is applicable. Finally, the influence of the sustainability principle upon both European and National policy and legislation continues to increase. In order to strengthen any given business approach for the present and future the inclusion of a robust CSR framework is considered to be one of the most efficient and necessary solutions.

See also: Building Regulations, p.81; Environmental Management Systems, p.296

Sources of further information

The EFQM Framework for Corporate Social Responsibility (2004) – a report by EFQM – www.efqm.org

A manager's introduction to facilities and the environment (1997) – a report by the Environment Council.

COSHH

Chris Streatfeild, Risk Management Consultant

Key points

The Control of Substances Hazardous to Health Regulations 2002 as amended include a number of significant amendments. These include:

- Workplace Exposure Limits (WELs) have replaced the previous two-tier system of limits. WELs are averaged over a specified period of time referred to as a time-weighted average (TWA). Two time periods are used – long term (eight hours) and short term (15 minutes).
- The HSE's publication EH40/2005 *Workplace exposure limits* now includes the list of substances that have been assigned WELs. A revised list came into force on 1 October 2007. This follows the implementation of the 2nd Directive on Indicative Occupational Exposure Limit Values (IOELVs) (2006/15/EC).
- Eight principles have now been introduced which will apply regardless of whether a substance has an Occupational Exposure Limit.

Legislation

- Control of Substances Hazardous to Health Regulations 2002 (as amended) (COSHH).
- Chemicals (Hazard Information and Packaging for Supply) (Amendment Regulations) 2002 (CHIP).
- Registration, Evaluation, Authorisation and Evaluation of Chemicals (REACH) Regulation (EC) No 1907/2006.

There is now a new focus on good practice. This is a radical change which should encourage a significant update of all COSHH assessments. Under the eight principles, employers must:

1. design and operate processes and activities to minimise emission, release and spread of substances hazardous to health;
2. take into account all routes of exposure when developing control measures:
   - inhalation;
   - skin absorption;and
   - ingestion.

3. control exposure by measures that are proportionate to the health risk;
4. choose the most effective and reliable control options which minimise the escape and spread of substances hazardous to health;
5. where adequate control of exposure cannot be achieved by other means, provide, in combination with other control measures, suitable personal protective equipment;
6. check and review regularly all elements of control measures for their continuing effectiveness;
7. inform and train all employees on the hazards and risks from the substances with which they work and the use of control measures developed to minimise the risks; and
8. ensure the introduction of control measures does not increase the overall risk to health and safety.

Substances hazardous to health

COSHH 2002 applies to a very wide range of substances and preparations with the potential to cause harm if they are inhaled, ingested or come into contact with or are absorbed through the skin. COSHH defines a "substance hazardous to health" as anything which:

1. is listed in Part I of the approved supply list as dangerous for supply within the meaning of the CHIP Regulations and for which an indication of danger specified for the substance is very toxic, toxic, harmful, corrosive or irritant;
2. the Health and Safety Commission has approved a workplace exposure limit;
3. is a biological agent;
4. is dust of any kind, except dust which is a substance within paragraph (1) or (2) above, when present at a concentration in air equal to or greater than (i) ten mg/m^3, as a time-weighted average over an eight-hour period, of inhalable dust, or (ii) four mg/m^3, as a time-weighted average over an eight-hour period, of respirable dust; and/or
5. not being a substance falling within sub-paragraphs (1) to (4), because of its chemical or toxicological properties and the way it is used or is present at the workplace creates a risk to health.

Examples would include:

- chemical substances or preparations such as paints;
- cleaning materials;
- metals;
- pesticides and insecticides; and
- biological agents such as pathogens or cell cultures.

Substances hazardous to health can occur in many forms:

- solids;
- liquids;
- vapours;
- gases;
- dust;
- fibres;
- fumes;
- mist; and
- smoke.

Note: The Registration, Evaluation, Authorisation and Evaluation of Chemicals (REACH) Regulation (EC) No 1907/2006 came into effect on 1 June 2007. The Regulations will fundamentally change the format and content of chemical safety information provided by suppliers. For the first time downstream users of chemicals will have specific duties placed on them that was not previously covered by legislation. *(See 'REACH', p.625.)*

To comply with COSHH you need to:

1. *Assess the risks*:
   - Identify the hazardous substances present in your workplace.
   - Consider the risks these substances present to people's health.

2. *Decide what precautions are needed*:
   - If you identify significant risks, decide on the action you need to take to remove or reduce them to acceptable levels. If you have five or more employees you must make and keep a record of the main findings of the assessment either in writing or on a computer.

3. *Prevent or adequately control exposure*. You are required to prevent exposure to substances hazardous to health, if it is reasonably practicable to do so. You might:
   - change the process or activity;
   - replace with a safer alternative; or
   - use it in a safer form, e.g. pellets instead of powder.If prevention is not possible you must

adequately control exposure. You should consider and put in place measures appropriate to the activity and consistent with the risk assessment. COSHH essentials (www.coshh-essentials.org.uk/) can assist in providing advice on the control of chemicals for a range of common tasks, e.g. mixing or drying. It is a practical interactive tool that can assist but not replace the completion of a COSHH assessment. COSHH essentials is supported by a series of general and specific guidance publications aimed at providing practical and informative advice. (www.hse.gov.uk/pubns/guidance/index.htm)

4. *Ensure that control measures are used and maintained.*
Employees are required to make proper use of control measures and to report defects. A common failure with employers is to ignore this point. It is the employer's responsibility to take all reasonable steps to ensure that employees do this.

Some items of equipment such as local exhaust ventilation will have to be regularly checked to make sure that they are still effective. Respiratory protective equipment (RPE) should be examined and where appropriate tested at suitable intervals. The Regulations set out specific intervals between examinations and you must retain records of examininations for at least five years.

5. *Monitoring exposure.*
You must measure the concentration of hazardous substances if your assessment concludes that:

- there could be serious risks to health if control measures failed or deteriorated;
- exposure limits might be exceeded; or
- control measures might not be working properly. Records should be kept for at least five years for general records and for at leat 40 years for personal records.

6. *Carry out appropriate health surveillance.* You are required to carr out health surveillance in the followin circumstances:
- Where an employee is exposed substances listed in Schedule 6 COSHH and is working in one of the related processes and there is a reasonable likelihood that an identifiable disease or adverse health effect will result from that exposure.
- Where employees are exposed t a substance linked to a particula disease or adverse health effect and there is a reasonable likelihood, under the conditions of work, of that disease or effect occurring and it is possible to detect the disease or health effect. Personal records need to be maintained for at least 40 years.

7. *Prepare plans and procedures to deal with accidents, incidents and emergencies.*
This will apply where the work activity goes well beyond the risks associate with normal day-to-day work. If this is the case you must plan your respons to an emergency involving hazardous substances before it happens.

Ensure that employees are properly informed, trained and supervised.
This should include:

- the names of the substances they work with or could be exposed to and the risks created by such exposure, and access to any safety data sheets that apply to those substances;
- the main findings of your risk assessment;
- the precautions they should take to protect themselves and other employees;
- how to use personal protective equipment and clothing provided;
- results of any exposure monitoring and health surveillance (without giving individual employees' names); and
- emergency procedures which need to be followed.

Note: This requirement is regarded as vital by the HSE. Control measures will not be fully effective if employees do not know their purpose, how to use them properly or the importance of reporting faults.

Safety Data Sheets

Collecting manufacturers' or suppliers' data sheets and other information does not in itself meet the COSHH requirements to carry out an assessment. (Note: REACH is likely to see more extended safety datasheets being produced by suppliers.) Gathering the information is only the first stage; the information must then be used to determine the appropriate control measures needed to protect the health of employees. The assessment record has to include the following information:

- The hazardous properties of the substance;
- Information on health effects provided by the supplier, including information

contained in any relevant safety data sheet;
- The level, type and duration of exposure;
- The circumstances of the work, including the amount of the substance involved;
- Activities, such as maintenance, where there is the potential for a high level of exposure;
- Any relevant occupational exposure standard, maximum exposure limit or similar occupational exposure limit;
- The effect of preventive and control measures which have been or will be taken in accordance with Regulation 7;
- The results of relevant health surveillance;
- The results of monitoring of exposure in accordance with Regulation 10;
- In circumstances where the work will involve exposure to more than one substance hazardous to health, the risk presented by exposure to such substances in combination;
- The approved classification of any biological agent; and
- Such additional information as the employer may need in order to complete the risk assessment.

Case law

In the case of *Bilton v. Fastnet Highlands Ltd* (1997) the plaintiff, Bilton, worked in a prawn processing factory, and claimed her occupational asthma, caused by certain substances in the workplace, could have been prevented had appropriate measures been taken.

While employed in this capacity, she developed occupational asthma as a result of exposure to respirable prawn protein. Her condition was aggravated further by contact with certain substances used and produced in the processing of prawns. The appellant contended that these substances, as well as the prawn protein, fell within the definition supplied by the COSHH Regulations, and that her employer was in breach of this duty.

The employer argued that these were insufficient grounds to claim that a breach of COSHH had occurred, and that the appellant also needed to illustrate what measures should have been taken, but were not, in order to comply with the Regulations.

The court referred to the case of *Nimmo v. Alexander Cowan*, where the House of Lords ruled that a plaintiff need only claim that the place in which they had to work was unsafe. It was unnecessary for them to state what they believed was reasonably practicable to actually make and keep it safe.

The court held that an absolute duty lay with the employer to keep the workplace safe. The appellant need do no more than claim she has suffered injury as a result of the employer failing to discharge their duty under COSHH.

Dugmore v. Swansea NHS Trust and another, Court of Appeal (Civil Division) (2002) EWCA Civ 1689 was a further important case on the prevention and control of hazardous substances. It reinforced the authority that:

- the primary duty under COSHH is to prevent exposure altogether where th Regulations apply, unless this is not reasonably practicable;
- if prevention is not reasonably practicable, the secondary duty is to control the exposure. The defence of reasonable practicability qualifies only the primary duty and for purposes of the secondary duty 'adequately' is define without reference to reasonableness;
- the duties under the Regulations are not subject to foreseeability of risk nor is it dependent upon what a risk assessment would have revealed; an
- there is no common law duty to dismiss an employee with a particular sensitivit who is willing to take the risk of carrying on working in what for others is a reasonably safe environment.

See also *Yvonne Mary Naylor v. Volex Group Plc* (2003). In this case, the employer was in breach of its statutory duty by failing to carry out a revised assessment in view of new knowledge of the risks of hazardous substances in use.

See also: Biological hazards, p.72; REACH, p.625; Hazardous waste, p.720

Sources of further information

HSE – Workplace exposure limits: www.hse.gov.uk/coshh/table1.pdf

COSHH – *A brief guide to the Regulations*: www.hse.gov.uk/pubns/indg136.pdf

COSHH essentials: www.coshh-essentials.org.uk

Criminal records

Howard Lewis-Nunn, Howard Kennedy

Key points

Other than in some excepted situations, employees or applicants are not obliged to disclose their past or 'spent' convictions once the appropriate period of time for their conviction has elapsed. The appropriate length of time before the conviction is spent depends on the nature of the sentence.

- Sentences of imprisonment for more than 30 months are never spent.
- Individuals can be required to disclose spent convictions when applying for jobs in certain sectors, where trust is a particular concern.

Legislation

The principal legislation dealing with the disclosure of spent convictions is the Rehabilitation of Offenders Act 1974. Various amendments have been made by Orders in Council, chiefly to identify sectors of work where employers are entitled to know about spent convictions.

Criminal records are also classed as 'sensitive personal data' under the Data Protection Act 1998 and so employers will be required to obtain the individual's explicit consent before making use of such information.

Rehabilitation of Offenders Act 1974

The Act provides that, unless there is an express exception, once a conviction has been spent an individual is a 'rehabilitated person'. The Act sets out a tariff for the timescales before various sentences are classed as spent. Sentences exceeding 30 months, for life or at Her Majesty's Pleasure are never spent.

Once a conviction is spent an individual is not required to give any details and is treated as if he had not been convicted. Any requirement that imposes an obligation (whether legal or contractual) on an individual to disclose information is deemed not to require disclosure of spent convictions or any related matters and he is not required to answer any questions in a way that will reveal his spent convictions. He shall not be prejudiced in law for any failure to disclose his spent convictions. An employer may still ask for disclosure of current (i.e. unspent) convictions.

Consequently, unless an exception applies, an employer has no valid grounds for refusing to employ someone or dismissing him for possessing or failing to disclose a spent conviction. A dismissal on these grounds is likely to be unfair. However, it is not clear what remedy could be pursued for a refusal to employ someone, as an individual must have one year's employment in order to claim unfair dismissal.

Exceptions

A number of occupations have been identified where spent convictions must be disclosed and an individual may therefore be dismissed or excluded from employment because of a spent conviction.

The professions include barristers, solicitors, accountants, teachers, police officers, healthcare professionals, officers of building societies, chartered psychologists, actuaries, registered foreign lawyers, legal executives, and receivers appointed by the Court of Protection. More recently, the exempted occupations have been widened to include anyone who would have access to persons under the age of 18 or vulnerable adults (this includes the elderly and mentally impaired). Organisations employing individuals in any of these occupations are entitled to ask about spent convictions and the potential employee is required to give details.

Criminal Records Bureau

The Government established the Criminal Records Bureau (CRB) as a central point for employers to obtain details of potential employees' or volunteers' criminal convictions. Currently, this system is only available to organisations within the categories of employment that are exempt under the Rehabilitation of Offenders Act 1974, and in particular those working with persons under 18 or vulnerable adults. Two types of disclosure certificates can be obtained at present – Standard and Enhanced Disclosure. Both Standard and Enhanced Disclosure provide details of all convictions including spent convictions as well as cautions, reprimands and warnings held on the police national computer. Where the post involves contact with children the disclosure will also contain any information on lists held by the Department of Health and the Department for Education and Skills. Enhanced disclosure is intended to provide a more thorough check when extensive and unsupervised contact with persons under 18 and particularly vulnerable adults is likely. This is mostly for positions involving social, personal or medical care. It is also available for judicial appointments and for certain positions where licences are required for gaming and lottery. As well as the standard disclosure information, enhanced disclosure includes any information relevant and proportionate to the position applied for held by local police forces that may not necessarily amount to a caution or conviction.

The threshold for what is relevant and proportionate is relatively low. In the case of *R (on the application of John Pinnington) v. Chief Constable of Thames Valley Police* (2008) it was sufficient that the Chief Constable reasonably believed that the allegations disclosed might be true and might be relevant to the post applied for by the applicant. It is therefore up to the employer what it does with the information. Whilst the courts have advised against employers operating a blanket policy of requiring a clean check, employers are likely to be reluctant to take risks if information is disclosed. The result of any check would have to be considered very carefully in the context of the overall application and the post applied for. Detail of the disclosure are provided to the registered body making the application and the individual who is the subject of the application. In limited situations the CRB may provide the employer only with additional information which is not to be disclosed to the individual. There is no legal requirement for employers to make CRB checks on employees or volunteers unless the work is in a 'regulated' setting such as a care home or school.

Even in those situations it is only those who have or are likely to have regular contact with children or vulnerable adults who have to be checked. Even if they are not legally required it may still be advisable to carry out CRB checks. Whether checks should be carried out on volunteers or employees is therefore a matter of risk management for each organisation. In response to criticisms that the CRB regime was discouraging volunteers, the Government's guidance suggests that a risk assessment should be carried out to determine whether checks should be required and they should not be carried out 'just in case'.

CRB checks are free for volunteers although an umbrella body may charge an administration fee for handling an application.

In order to apply for disclosure, employers who are entitled to use the service must either be registered with the CRB or apply through an 'Umbrella body', which is registered. Umbrella bodies can be used by any employer who does not wish to register itself directly with the CRB. Registered bodies are required to abide by the CRB's Code of Practice. Umbrella bodies are required to ensure that their clients abide by the code also. The CRB may audit the user in order to ensure compliance. Disclosure in Scotland is managed by Disclosure Scotland. Both Disclosure Scotland and CRB provide information relating to convictions in the whole of the UK. The location of the position in question will determine which agency to contact.

The Code's key requirements:

■ Registered users should have a written policy on the recruitment of ex offenders to be given to all job applicants. Umbrella bodies must ensure that their clients have a policy in place and provide a model one to the client if necessary.
■ All applicants who will be subject to a CRB request must be informed of the use to which the disclosure information will be put.

■ Where a position will require a CRB check the application form should state that a disclosure request will only be made in the event of a successful application and if a conviction is disclosed this will not necessarily mean that the offer of employment is withdrawn.
■ The contents of the disclosure should be discussed with the individual before any offer is withdrawn. The existence of the code should be brought to their attention and the employer's policy on the treatment of ex-offenders made available.
■ Only authorised personnel should have access to the disclosure, which includes storing it securely. There should be a written policy on secure storage of disclosure records. It is a criminal offence to pass it on to unauthorised persons.
■ Disclosure should not be kept for longer than is necessary and should be securely destroyed.
■ Umbrella bodies are required to ensure that their clients observe the Code and that they are in one of the exempt categories under the Rehabilitation of Offenders Act 1974 who can ask about convictions.

Portability
Some individuals may hold more than one position which requires a CRB check and so organisations may be tempted to accept the disclosure results for a previous position if it is sufficiently recent. This is known as portability. The CRB does not support this and so organisations that re-use disclosure results do so at their own risk. However, as part of a risk assessment, unless there is a legal requirement for the employer to carry out its own check, a check carried out by another organisation may be relied on. One risk to relying on previous CRB checks is that they will not reveal whether

any additional information was provided to the employer which was not disclosed to the individual. In deciding whether to make a fresh check the following factors should be considered:

- Is there a legal requirement to obtain a check?
- Is the existing check at the same level required for the new post?
- Is the position for which the check was obtained similar to the new post?
- Have all the checks the organisation needs been carried out?
- Has the identity of the person holding the check been authenticated?
- Is the applicant still living at the same address as the one to which the check relates?
- Has the applicant given consent to contact the organisation that carried out the previous check?
- Is the check more than six months' old?

Where a previous check is being relied on steps should be taken to confirm the authenticity of the check such as contacting the person who countersigned the certificate for the applying organisation to confirm the registration number and that the details match. The new employer should ask the previous employer if there is any additional information of which they are aware. While they cannot provide the details they can confirm or deny its existence. If there does appear to be further information a new check is advisable; however, there may be difficulties in explaining to the applicant why a fresh application is required.

Overseas applicants

Disclosure from the CRB will have limited information on overseas convictions and so records for anyone who has spent a substantial amount of time outside of the UK may not be complete. It is possible to carry out the equivalent of a CRB check in some countries and the CRB can provide guidance on this. The employer can also ask the individual to obtain the equivalent disclosure where he is resident overseas.

Future changes

The CRB has been proposing to introduce a basic disclosure certificate intended for all types of employment for some time, but this has yet to materialise. This will be issued solely to individuals and cover only unspent convictions. Employers may therefore require this as a matter of course from individuals before offering them employment.

The Government has created the Independent Safeguarding Authority (ISA) to operate a new vetting and barring scheme with the CRB. This is due to start from 12 October 2009. It is intended to be an enhancement of the current disclosure process aimed at preventing individuals who are considered unsuitable from working with children and vulnerable adults from doing so. All employees and volunteers working with these groups will be required to register with authority. This will be phased in over a number of years and the ISA registration will be transferable. This scheme will replace the lists held by the Department of Health and the Department for Education and Skills. Further details are awaited.

See also: Data protection, p.186; Interviewing, p.429; Personnel files – recording information, p.571; Recruitment and selection, p.607

Sources of further information

Information Commissioner: www.informationcommissioner.gov.uk

Criminal Records Bureau: www.crb.gov.uk

Chartered Institute of Personnel and Development: www.cipd.co.uk

Disclosure Scotland: www.disclosurescotland.co.uk

Independent Safeguarding Authority www.isa-gov.org.uk

National Association for the Care and Resettlement of Offenders (Nacro):
www.nacro.org.uk

Data protection

Elizabeth Upton, Bird & Bird

Key points

The Data Protection Act 1998 (the Act) came into force on 1 March 2000, replacing the Data Protection Act 1984. The Act offers more protection to individuals than the 1984 Act and imposes more onerous obligations on organisations which process personal data. The Act also gives individuals certain rights in respect of their personal information.

It is important for companies to know about the Act and whether it applies to them, particularly because of certain criminal offences that may be committed as a result of handling personal data incorrectly.

Does the Act apply to your company?

In short, the Act regulates the processing of personal data which is either held on a computer or intended to be held on a computer or held in paper form in what the Act describes as a relevant filing system. In order to work out if the Act applies to the activities carried out by your company, it is necessary to look at these and other definitions in the Act in further detail.

Personal data

This is defined as information which relates to living individuals who can be identified from it (whether from the data on its own or when used in conjunction with other information in the possession of, or likely to come into the possession of, the data controller). This may therefore include details such as postal address or email address as well as facts and opinions held about an individual. The EU Article 29 Working Party, which helps develop European data protection policy, issued guidance last year (WP136, 20 June 2007) on the meaning of personal data which was followed by guidance on the same topic issued by the Information

Commissioner on 21 August 2007. Both sets of guidance look at all the elements of the definition in greater detail and provide useful examples of what is caught by the definition. However, truly anonymous data such as aggregated statistics will not be regulated by the Act. The Act also recognises that some data is to be regarded as sensitive personal data and can be processed only under strict conditions. Such data is information on racial or ethnic origin, political opinions, religious or other beliefs, trade union membership, health, sex life, and criminal proceedings or convictions.

Processing

Under the Act this means 'obtaining, recording or holding information or data or carrying out any operation or set of operations on the information or data'. This is a very wide definition, and if your company holds personal data then it is likely that any activities carried out by the company in relation to such data will fall within its scope. Processing may only be carried out in accordance with the data protection principles which are outlined below.

Data controller
This is defined as someone who determines how and for what purpose personal data is processed. Obligations in the Act fall mainly on data controllers. This is likely to be the company rather than the individual workplace manager. Lesser obligations fall on data processors who are those people (other than employees of a data controller) who process personal data on behalf of a data controller.

Relevant filing system
The key elements of this definition are that there must be a set of information, e.g. a grouping together of things with a common theme or element. It follows that a mere list of names is unlikely to amount to a set of information about individuals. The set must be structured, by reference either to individuals or to criteria relating to individuals, and specific information relating to an individual must be readily accessible. Recent case law has suggested that this definition is to be interpreted narrowly and that (a) files need to indicate clearly at the outset of the search whether personal data is held within the system and (b) there is a sufficiently sophisticated and detailed means of readily indicating whether and where in an individual file or files specific criteria or information can be readily located.

Data controllers and their responsibilities
Having worked out if the Act applies to the information held by your company, you should then consider what responsibilities lie with the data controller.

Anyone processing personal data as a data controller must comply with the eight enforceable principles of good practice. These say that data must:

1. be fairly and lawfully obtained and processed;
2. be processed for limited purposes and not in any manner incompatible with those purposes;
3. be adequate, relevant and not excessive;
4. be accurate and where necessary kept up to date;
5. not be kept for longer than necessary;
6. be processed in line with the data subject's rights;
7. be secure; and
8. not be transferred to countries outside the EEA without adequate protection.

Most of these points are self-explanatory, but it is worth mentioning the first principle in further detail. This principle requires that the processing of data must be fair and lawful. The Act states that, in order to ensure fairness, data controllers have to ensure that:

- data is obtained in accordance with the fair processing code. This requires data controllers to make certain information readily available to individuals (e.g. the name of the data controller and the purposes for which the data will be processed);
- certain pre-conditions are met to justify the processing of personal data. At least one condition in Schedule 2 of the Act must be met for any processing of personal data and at least one condition in Schedule 3 must be met if sensitive personal data is being processed; and
- the individuals must not be misled or deceived as to the purposes for which their data will be processed.

The data controller also needs to be aware of the data subject's rights when processing personal data. Under the Act, data subjects are granted four key rights:

1. A right of access to personal data held;
2. A right to prevent processing that might cause substantial damage and distress;
3. A right to prevent automated decision-taking; and
4. A right to prevent processing for direct marketing purposes.

In relation to subject access, data controllers should be aware that generally an individual has a right to be provided with copies of all information held about that individual within 40 days of a request being made. Although there are limited grounds for withholding certain information, systems should be structured so that requests can be satisfied as easily as possible.

It should also be noted, in relation to the eighth principle, that 'adequate protection' is legally defined rather than being a matter of judgement for the company intending to transfer the information. Personal data can only be transferred to a third country outside the EEA if:

- the EU Commission has made a finding of adequacy in respect of the third country;
- an assessment of adequacy has been made by the data controller itself following the guidelines set out in the Act;
- there is no adequacy but the parties have put in place adequate safeguards such as the use of Commission authorised standard contracts or binding corporate rules; or
- one of the limited derogations to the eighth principle applies (e.g the individual has consented to the transfer or the transfer is necessary for the performance of a contract between the data controller and the individual).

Notification

Most data controllers will need to notify the Information Commissioner, in broad terms, of the purposes of their processing, the personal data processed, the recipients of the personal data processed and, if relevant, any transfers of data overseas. This information is made publicly available on a register. Under the Act, data controllers must comply with the data protection principles even if they are exempt from the requirement to notify.

Criminal offences

Data controllers can commit criminal offences under the Act. These offences include:

- failing to notify the Information Commissioner either of the processing being undertaken or of any of the changes that have been made to that processing; and
- failing to respond to an information notice or breaching an enforcement notice issued by the Information Commissioner.

Individuals can also commit criminal offences if they obtain, disclose or sell personal data without the consent of the data controller. The Information Commissioner regards this as the most serious of offences which can be committed under the Act and the Criminal Justice and Immigration Act 2008 recently enhanced penalties for those who disclose information for the illegal buying and selling of data. These penalties will be implemented via secondary legislation which will introduce custodial sentences for such sentences of up to 12 months (for magistrates court convictions) or two years (for conviction on indictment).

The Criminal Justice and Immigration Act also provides the Information

Commissioner with a power to impose monetary penalties for certain breaches of the Act. The new power only applies to serious breaches of the Act and will only arise where there have been deliberate breaches of the Act and where the Commissioner thinks that this kind of breach is likely to cause substantial damage or distress. Fines can also be levied for this kind of serious breach if the data controller knew or ought to have known that there was a risk of serious breach which would be likely to cause substantial damage or distress and failed to take reasonable steps to prevent this.

Employment Practices Code

The Information Commissioner has issued a Code of Practice to help companies ensure that they are complying with the data protection legislation with regard to their dealings with their employees. The Code gives employers specific guidance on:

- recruitment and selection processes;
- how best to keep employment records;
- how to monitor their employees at work; and
- issues relating to workers' health.

In addition, the Code provides information about workers' rights under the Act.

Direct marketing

Specific rules apply in relation to direct marketing, whether it is carried out by email, telephone, fax, or SMS messaging.

Freedom of Information Act 2000

Finally, it should also be noted that the Freedom of Information Act gives individuals the right to request information from a public authority. On the receipt of the request, the authority is obliged to:

- tell the individual whether or not it holds the information; and (where applicable)
- to provide the individual with the information requested.

See also: Criminal records, p.181; Medical records, p.491; Personnel files – recording information, p.571; Private life, p.587; Confidential waste, p.716

Sources of further information

Further information on Freedom of Information may be found on the Department of Constitutional Affairs' website: www.foi.gov.uk

Workplace Law Group's *Data Protection Policy and Management Guide, v.3.0* has been published to help employers understand and meet their obligations under data protection legislation and to provide clear guidance for employers on their responsibilities when handling sensitive personal data. For further information see www.workplacelaw.net/Bookshop/PoliciesAndProcedures.

Workplace deaths

Kathryn Gilbertson, Greenwoods Solicitors LLP

Key points
- The police and the HSE have an agreed protocol for investigating work-related deaths.
- The HSE has a policy which requires it to investigate individuals for possible proceedings.
- Prosecution (and conviction) rates are increasing under existing laws.
- On 6 April 2008 the Corporate Manslaughter and Corporate Homicide Act 2007 came into force which introduces an offence of statutory corporate manslaughter.

Legislation
- Corporate Manslaughter and Corporate Homicide Act 2007.

Overview
The police and the HSE jointly investigate workplace deaths, including work-related road traffic accidents. The police will lead the initial investigation and they are often advised in a technical capacity by HSE inspectors. Where either find evidence of culpability, those responsible may be charged:

- with manslaughter, which carries penalties of up to life imprisonment for individuals and an unlimited fine for organisations; or
- under health and safety legislation, which can carry penalties of up to two years' imprisonment for certain specific breaches or an unlimited fine.

Prosecution and conviction rates are increasing.

The effect of the new Corporate Manslaughter and Corporate Homicide Act has still to be seen since no cases have yet been tried in the courts under the statutory offence of corporate manslaughter.

The Centre for Corporate Accountability maintains a database of workplace deaths and legal proceedings as a result of these. They take an active interest in providing accurate data on workplace deaths.

Manslaughter investigations
Currently, workplace deaths are investigated in accordance with a protocol between the Association of Chief Police Officers (ACPO), the British Transport Police (BTP), the HSE, the Local Government Association (LGA) and the CPS. This also covers work-related road traffic accidents (e.g. involving lorry drivers or managers travelling to meetings).

The protocol gives the police primacy in conducting the investigation and allows them to seek assistance from the HSE, thus utilising the HSE's specialist knowledge and effectively allowing the HSE to conduct its own preliminary investigations. In most cases, the HSE investigates with the police, using its greater knowledge of health and safety management systems, and frequently joint interviews take place. A senior police officer then reviews the evidence to decide whether manslaughter charges are possible. The final decision to bring a anslaughter prosecution and/or corporate anslaughter prosecution rests with e CPS. The HSE separately decides n whether to bring proceedings under SWA.

oroner's inquest
he coroner investigates all cases of udden death. The coroner needs to nswer certain questions – to determine ho died, when they died, what was the ause of death, where they died and how ie death came about. Workplace fatalities re normally subject to an early inquest hich convenes in order to allow the eceased to be buried.

he coroner will then adjourn the inquest ntil after the consideration of proceedings or manslaughter or safety offences (or, ı the case of a road-related workplace atality, possible driving offences) is oncluded. This may mean that the inquest oes not resume until several years after ie accident.

the CPS decides that there is insufficient vidence to bring a prosecution for nanslaughter, then the coroner's inquest ill resume, usually following the coroner eceiving the HSE's report into the death.

nquests into work-related deaths are held efore a jury. Several verdicts are available o the jury, including accidental death/ nisadventure, unlawful killing, or an ppen' verdict. Note that if the jury returns verdict of unlawful killing, the coroner nust refer the case back to the CPS for econsideration of manslaughter charges. he CPS must then give its reasons if no uch charges are brought. At this stage the ISE will consider a prosecution for any reach of health and safety law.

f a criminal trial takes place which xamines the facts and considers the

cause of death, then usually only an administrative (paper-based) inquest will be held.

Manslaughter: individuals
An individual may be found guilty of gross negligence manslaughter if a jury is satisfied that:

- the individual owed a duty of care to the deceased;
- the individual breached that duty of care;
- the breach was a substantive cause of death; and
- the individual's conduct was so grossly negligent in all circumstances that the individual deserves criminal sanctions (i.e. imprisonment).

The convicted individual will then face a sentence of up to life imprisonment. To date, there have been few convictions, with most sentences being suspended. However, there have been two recent convictions where the directors of haulage companies have been convicted of manslaughter for tampering with tachograph records, allowing their drivers to drive for excessive periods resulting in fatal road accidents. The maximum sentence to date is seven years' imprisonment, although since this was a combined sentence, it is difficult to gauge the current 'tariff' for the manslaughter charges.

Prosecutions are on the increase. In part this may be because in early 2000 the courts found that the CPS had been using the wrong test when deciding whether to prosecute. Also, the police are now investigating more instances of work-related deaths.

Those individuals most vulnerable to manslaughter charges are those with day-to-day management of work activities, i.e.

directors of small companies, contracts managers, site managers and supervisors.

Manslaughter: organisations

The statutory offence of corporate manslaughter is discussed further in '*Corporate manslaughter*', *p.163.*

Other charges

If manslaughter charges are not brought, the HSE is still likely to prosecute culpable individuals and organisations under separate health and safety legislation for health and safety offences.

Minimising liability

The one certain way of avoiding manslaughter charges is to ensure that no one dies as a result of work activities. Although this may seem obvious, nearly two-thirds of work-related deaths result from just three causes:

1. Falls from height;
2. Being struck by a moving or falling object; and
3. Being struck by a moving vehicle.

By focusing their attention on these hazardous areas, employers can minimise the risks and disruption of both deaths and prosecution.

Other simple measures include:

- promptly informing senior managers of any dangerous circumstances or near misses;
- obtaining specialist legal advice on safety systems and protocols, in particular before any incidents arise, and certainly before any police or HSE interviews; and
- dealing sensitively and appropriately with those involved in the accident and relatives of those killed or injured.

See also: Accident investigations, p.55; Corporate manslaughter, p.163; Health and safety at work, p.364; Reporting of Injuries, Diseases and Dangerous Occurrences (RIDDOR), p.628

Sources of further information

Centre for Corporate Accountability: www.corporateaccountability.org

The Corporate Manslaughter and Corporate Homicide Act 2007 is one of the biggest changes to health and safety law since the HSWA. Its influence will affect everyone with responsibility for the health and safety of employees, and will mean greater responsibility is put on the shoulders of managers and directors, to ensure that they are fully compliant, and not at risk of prosecution should an accident occur.

Workplace Law Group's *Corporate Manslaughter and Corporate Homicide Act: Special Report* includes guidance and comment from some of the leading authorities on the subject, and enables directors and managers to identify the risks, put measures in place to safeguard their fortunes and reputations, and to understand the full implications of the Act. For more information visit www.workplacelaw.net/Bookshop/SpecialReports.

Dilapidations

Catherine Edwards, Chivers Commercial

Key points

- Use the Dilapidations Protocol – it will save time and probably money in the long run.
- Always take advice well in advance of a possible schedule being served.
- Never assume there is or is not a liability.
- Always look at each case on its own merits as no general rule may safely be applied without investigation.
- Tenants should report and pursue defects that they think may be a landlord's responsibility as soon as they occur. Delay could be very expensive.
- Tenants should always read the lease before signing it and consider the repairing liability likely to occur at the end of the lease.
- Landlords should make sure schedules are served having regard to the Protocol.
- Landlords should resist the temptation to exaggerate a claim or serve a schedule for reasons other than maintaining the structure of the building.
- Both parties should weigh up the long-term advantages or disadvantages of the repairing covenants being considered in relation to the type and age of the building and the intended lease length.
- Both parties should try to settle disputes at the earliest opportunity.

Relevant legislation

- Law of Property Act 1925.
- Landlord and Tenant Act 1927, 1954 and 1985.
- Public Health Act 1936 and 1961.
- Housing Act 1936, 1961 and 1985.
- Leasehold Property (Repairs) Act 1938.
- Factories Act 1961.
- Fire Precautions Act 1971.
- Defective Premises Act 1972.
- Health and Safety at Work etc. Act 1974.
- Building Act 1984.
- The Law of Property (Miscellaneous Provisions) Act 1989.

Introduction

'Dilapidations' is the term used to describe the wants of repair because of disrepair, required to a property and sometimes fixtures and fittings under the covenants of a lease or property contract which have not been fulfilled.

This chapter is only applicable to the practice of dilapidations in England and Wales. Dilapidations claims in Scotland and Northern Ireland have a number of significant differences, although many aspects of the procedures and processes described may be relevant to claims in these and other countries.

The remedies that are available will be influenced by the length of lease term that is remaining and the length of the original lease.

It is advisable for landlords and tenants to appoint a suitably qualified surveyor to act for them in any dilapidations issue at the earliest opportunity, which is often well before a schedule is served. Facing dilapidation issues head on well before the end of a lease can save many problems and considerable amounts of money.

Legal framework
The law of dilapidations is not set out in easy-to-find legislation nor based on a single statute but has evolved over time and been influenced by Statute.

The introduction of the Civil Procedure Rules 1998 (CPR) has had a significant impact on how dilapidations claims are processed. A Dilapidations Protocol has been produced which should be used whenever possible. The Protocol encourages parties to exchange full information before proceedings are issued to enable the parties to avoid litigation where possible and support the efficient management of proceedings where litigation cannot be avoided. The protocol also encourages settlement through arbitration or mediation rather than the more rigid route through the courts.

The days of exaggerating claims or being unnecessarily obstructive in defending claims are gone but the price paid for this is in far more expensive initial consultations and schedules being produced at service. It should be remembered that in most leases the cost of the preparation and service of schedules under a Section 146 notice is usually payable by the tenant under the terms of the lease. If the matter is settled by negotiation, the tenant almost always pays, even when in reality there is very little work to be done. Solicitors acting for tenants on entry should look to the possible level of these fees, which can be considerable for a large building, and perhaps consider a more equitable division at the outset.

Under the Protocol, landlords are required to serve any schedule of terminal dilapidations in a prescribed format well before the end of the lease and any claim to be served within 56 days of lease expiry

In addition the schedule should be backed up with copies of relevant invoices, quotes or costings from a professional qualified surveyor and, finally, the surveyor must also include a statement that the works/costs claimed are his/her reasonable and fair opinion. The Diminution Valuation within the Protocol does not have to be done until after negotiations have taken place but it is always worth having an initial assessment carried out early. The total claim will always be capped by the loss to the reversionary interest suffered by the landlord. No loss to the reversion, no claim will succeed however poor the tenant has been at complying with their repairing covenants.

The tenant should respond within 56 days and the parties are encouraged to meet prior to the tenant submitting its response. The Protocol then allows time for negotiations, a stocktake of the position, a formal Diminution Valuation and if necessary issue of court proceedings.

A tenant is, however, well advised to try and settle matters before the end of the lease or very soon afterwards because a landlord who cannot relet because of dilapidations will be able to claim additional monies for rent, insurance and as appropriate service charge after the end of the lease in addition to the amount of the works themselves.

Schedules and when they occur
In the life of a lease there are three particular times when a schedule could occur. It should also be remembered that although schedules of dilapidation are

sually considered in relation to either
eases on commercial premises or long
round leases on residential property,
hey can also occur on periodic or fixed
erm residential agreements with private
andlords and community social housing.
Most of the latter are dealt with under
ifferent legislation but the schedules
hemselves take the same format.

. **At the start of the lease**
At the commencement of a lease on older
property a Schedule of Condition is often
aken to record defects which the tenant
will not take responsibility for at the end of
heir occupation. Tenants should be aware
f three little words that are often in leases
nd which should start alarm bells ringing
rom the outset – 'put and keep'.

f a tenant takes a full repairing liability
or an older building they must be aware
hat if they sign to say they will repair
verything then, without a schedule of
ondition on entry, it matters not at all what
ondition the building was in at the start;
he tenant will be liable to put and keep
nd hand back at the end of the term, the
property in a fully repaired condition with
ery few exceptions.

andlords should be aware that if a tenant
s only repairing to a certain level, no one
s repairing to a level that will maintain the
uilding in the best possible condition. The
andlord who takes this route will have a
uilding that continues to deteriorate over
he years.

andlords should seriously consider either
epairing before reletting, or retaining
esponsibility for external repairs, and put in
lace a regular maintenance programme to
get the best possible life out of the building.

enants should seriously consider the
effect of a continuing deterioration in the
quality and look of the building from which
they are operating their business and what
effect this might have long-term on the
customers' perception of its business.

2. During the lease
A schedule of wants of repair may be
served during the lease if, following
inspection, it is felt that the tenant is not
complying with its covenants. This type
of schedule is usually referred to as an
Interim Schedule and often served as a
Repairs Notice.

There is no legal distinction between an
Interim Schedule and a Terminal Schedule
but these terms are used by surveyors to
distinguish when the schedule has been
served.

An Interim Schedule must contain serious
items of disrepair, served under the Law
of Property Act 1925 Section 146. It is
sometimes used with the intention by
the landlord of gaining possession of the
premises and disposing of the tenant
under a breach of covenant. To avoid this
possibility, tenants should be aware of
the repairing covenants and the recurring
decorating covenants within their lease
and abided by them.

If a schedule of this type is served, a
tenant should always take advice as soon
as possible. Most leases contain a right for
a landlord to enter, following notice, carry
out the work and claim the costs back from
the tenant as a debt. This is sometimes
referred to as the *Jervis v. Harris* remedy.

This is far too involved to discuss here
but suffice it to say that this is a difficult
enterprise and should be done only after
being fully advised. For example, a tenant
may be able to successfully defer such
a notice under the Leasehold Property
(Repairs) Act 1938 if there are more

than three years remaining on a lease with an original term of not less than seven years. To claim this relief, a tenant must serve a counter notice within 28 days of service of the schedule. The matter then goes into the court system and becomes very expensive for all concerned.

3. At the end of the lease

This will be served as a Terminal Schedule of Dilapidations. At this stage a tenant cannot easily avoid the works to be done but again proper advice is required. The overriding factor to consider is under the Landlord and Tenant Act 1927, section 18, which limits the recovery of damages for breach of covenant to the loss to the landlord's reversionary interest. It is up to the landlord to prove any loss he has or might have suffered if the works are not done as in for example, *Simmons v. Dresden* (2004).

Tenants need to be aware that Section 18 does not apply to a covenant to reinstate because reinstatement is not considered to be a situation which makes the tenant keep or leave in repair.

Particularly on older buildings which may be nearing the end of their useful life, either by condition or by lack of demand for that type of building, a tenant should take advice on his dilapidations issues before expending considerable time and money on carrying out work which might not be necessary.

Disrepair

Disrepair is at the heart of dilapidations because if there is no disrepair there is no dilapidation. This may seem clear but in fact is the root of almost all disputes and is extremely complex.

In *Quick v. Taff & Ely Borough Council* (1986), the tenant of a council house failed to obtain an order of specific performance against the landlord where the house suffered from severe condensation. The house lacked insulation around the concrete window lintels, suffered sweating from the single-glazed metal-framed windows and inadequate heating. The windows and lintels were not out of repair and the house was built conforming to the Building Regulations in force at the time. It was held that the landlord could not be forced to replace the windows with warmer materials or insulate the lintels because they were not in disrepair. The ongoing problems caused by the damp and condensation remained the tenant's problem.

Disrepair caused initially by inherent defects, which are usually a landlord's responsibility, may still lie with the tenant for expensive repair, not just inconvenience and higher heating costs a above. Take a situation where a floor has rotted because there is a lack of underfloor ventilation. The landlord would be required to insert air vents to the building but the tenant would almost certainly remain responsible for the replacement of the floor itself at the end of the lease under the full repairing responsibilities.

If a landlord or a tenant decides to take a dilapidations case all the way, either party or both should seriously consider using Alternative Dispute Resolution, which is far better suited to this type of litigation, cheaper, and, if for any reason matters still end up in court, looked upon favourably by the Courts. No party can be forced to mediate or enter into any form of ADR but parties are warned that if the Protocol is not followed and every effort is not made to resolve the dispute other than through the courts, then the Court must have regard to such conduct when determining costs.

See also: Contract disputes, p.157; Landlord and tenant: lease issues, p.448; Landlord and tenant: possession issues, p.444

Sources of further information

Dilapidations claims can be costly and time-consuming for both the landlord and tenant, and a source of grave contention betweeen the two parties. The legislation surrounding dilapidations has evolved over a long period of time and is notoriously complicated. Workplace Law Group's *Guide to Dilapidations* provides a better understanding of this complex issue.

Written by Andrew Olins, this guide is designed to equip the commercial landlord and the business tenant with the necessary knowledge and understanding to resolve a claim for terminal dilapidations. Written in Workplace Law Group's jargon-free, plain-English style, this downloadable guide is an indispensable resource for all users and owners of commercial buildings. For more information visit www.workplacelaw.net/Bookshop/GuidesTo.

Directors' responsibilities

Naomi Branston and Andrew Telling, Taylor Wessing

Key points

Company directors are primarily responsible for the management of their companies and generally, their duties are owed to the company. However, they also owe duties to the owners as a whole. In addition, they have responsibilities in respect of the company's employees and its trading partners, and under statute these duties may be supplemented or modified by a company's memorandum and articles of association. Furthermore, many directors will be subject to service agreements (contracts of employment) which may augment these duties.

Directors are responsible for ensuring that the company complies with the various requirements imposed upon it by law.

Although generally the company is liable for any failure to comply with legal requirements, in certain circumstances the directors can be held personally liable where the default was due to their neglect or connivance.

Legislation

- Health and Safety at Work etc. Act 1974.
- Companies Acts 1985, 1989 and 2006.
- Insolvency Act 1986.
- Company Directors Disqualification Act 1986.
- Value Added Tax Act 1994.
- Management of Health and Safety at Work Regulations 1999.

Directors' duties

Companies Act 2006

The Companies Act 2006 (CA 2006) codifies certain key duties of directors. It introduces a statutory statement of seven general duties:

1. A duty to act in accordance with the company's constitution and only to exercise powers for the purposes for which they are conferred.
2. A duty to act in a way which a director considers, in good faith, would be most likely to promote the success of the company for the benefit of its members as a whole.
3. A duty to exercise independent judgement.
4. A duty to exercise reasonable care, skill and diligence.
5. A duty to avoid conflicts of interest.
6. A duty not to accept benefits from third parties.
7. A duty to declare to the other directors an interest in a proposed transaction or arrangement with the company.

The first four of these duties took effect from 1 October 2007. The remaining three which relate to conflicts of interest, will take effect in October 2008.

These duties are (apart from the duty to exercise reasonable care, skill and diligence) all fiduciary duties. They are expressed to replace the existing common law duties but will continue to be interpreted by reference to the body of case law in this area.

s before, these duties will be owed to the ompany and (subject to the new statutory erivative action enabling shareholders to ring a claim on behalf of the company) nly the company can enforce these uties.

CA 2006 also extends the common law erivative action, making it easier for hareholders to bring a claim on behalf f the company against directors and thers for negligence, default, breach of uty (including the new general duties) or reach of trust, where a prima facie case s disclosed and the court gives permission or the claim to continue.

Duty to act within powers

A director must act in accordance with he company's constitution which, for this urpose, includes resolutions or decisions nade by the company in accordance with ts articles of association of a company, is well as the articles of association hemselves.

Duty to promote the success of the company

n fulfilling this duty, directors must have egard to a statutory non-exhaustive list of actors, namely:

- the likely consequences of any decision in the long term;
- the interests of the company's employees;
- the need to foster the company's business relationships with suppliers, customers and others;
- the impact of the company's operations on the community and the environment;
- the desirability of the company maintaining a reputation for high standards of business conduct; and
- the need to act fairly as between members of the company.

This duty extends and replaces the common law duty on directors to act in good faith and in the best interests of the company.

The decision as to what will promote the success of the company, and what constitutes such success, is one for a director's good faith judgement. For a commercial company, 'success' will usually mean a long-term increase in value.

Duty to exercise independent judgement

This duty is likely to be most relevant where a director wishes to bind himself to a future course of action which might be seen as 'fettering the discretion' of the director to make future decisions. It is not infringed by a director acting in a way authorised by the company's constitution or acting in accordance with an agreement duly entered into by the company that restricts the future exercise of discretion by its directors.

Duty of skill and care

A director of a company must exercise reasonable care, skill and diligence. The standard expected of him is not only the general knowledge, skill and experience he has (for example, a particular expertise in financial matters), but also the general knowledge, skill and experience that may reasonably be expected given his position and responsibilities to the company.

Conflicts of interest

A director must not use information gained by him as a director to further his own interests, nor must he seek to apply company assets for his own gain. For example, a director must not receive commission on a transaction between the company and a third party or offer to take up, on a private basis, work offered to the company.

A director must disclose any direct or indirect personal interests in a contract and will have to account for any profit made unless he complies with the requirement for disclosure before the contract was entered into.

From October 2008, new statutory duties relating to conflicts of interests will come into force under CA 2006. These will include a statutory duty on a director to avoid a situation in which he has, or can have, a direct or indirect interest that conflicts, or may conflict, with the interests of the company, unless the situation cannot reasonably be regarded as likely to give rise to a conflict of interest. This applies, in particular, to the exploitation of any property, information or opportunity (and it is immaterial whether the company could take advantage of the property, information or opportunity).

Directors will also have a duty not to accept benefits from third parties, except where the benefit is not likely to give rise to a conflict of interest (in fact, most directors' service agreements will have an express prohibition on accepting benefits or 'kickbacks' from any third party irrespective of whether or not a conflict of interest might arise). In addition, directors will be subject to a statutory duty to declare the nature and extent of any direct or indirect interest in a proposed transaction or arrangement with the company. No declaration will be needed where:

- the director is not aware of the interest or the transaction in question (unless he ought reasonably to be aware of it);
- it cannot reasonably be regarded as likely to give rise to a conflict of interest;
- the other directors are already aware of it (or ought reasonably to be aware); or

- it concerns terms of his service contract being considered by the board or a board committee.

Directors will also have a statutory obligation (although not a fiduciary duty) to declare any direct or indirect interest in an existing transaction or arrangement with the company.

Duties to employees

While a director owes no common law duty to consider the interests of the workforce, and a director's duties are owed to the company, CA 2006 recognises the principle that the interests of the workforce fall within the wider picture of the interests of the company, as the interests of employees are one of several matters that directors must have regard to when satisfying their duty to act in the way they consider to be most likely to promote the success of the company.

Directors must comply with employment law in dealings with employees. In some circumstances, directors personally can be sued for unfair work practices such as race, sex, disability and other discrimination. Directors must ensure the company complies with any new employment laws.

Health and safety issues

A company has various obligations to fulfil under the Health and Safety at Work etc. Act 1974 (HSWA) and the Management of Health and Safety at Work Regulations 1992 (MHSWR).

The most important of these are as follows:

- A duty to ensure, so far as is reasonably practicable, the health, safety and welfare of its employees. The size of the company and the activities that are carried on by it will be taken into account when assessing what is reasonably practicable.

■ A duty to carry out a risk assessment and implement procedures to minimise any risks that are highlighted.

■ A duty to provide (and periodically revise) a written health and safety policy, to implement it and to bring it to the attention of employees.

These are the company's responsibility, but the directors would be breaching their duties to the company by failing to take the appropriate measures. Furthermore, directors can be prosecuted under section 37 of HSWA where the offence committed by the company occurred with their consent or connivance or through neglect on their part. In addition, the Corporate Manslaughter and Homicide Act 2007 can mean the company is liable where a death is caused as a result of a gross breach of a duty of care and the way in which the company's activities were organised or managed by senior management constitutes a substantial element of that breach.

It is wise for directors to ensure they have health and safety systems in place. The Health and Safety Exective (the HSE) provides comprehensive guidance on this issue.

Financial responsibilities

Accounts

CA 2006 requires directors to maintain accounting records that:

■ show the company's transactions and its financial position;

■ enable the directors to ensure that accounts required under CA 2006 comply with the CA 2006 requirements;

■ contain entries of all receipts and payments, including details of sales and purchases of goods, and a record of assets and liabilities; and

■ show stock held at the end of each year.

Records must be kept at the company's registered office (unless the directors specify a different location) and retained for a period of six years for a public company or three years for a private company.

Annual audited accounts, consisting of a profit and loss account, must be approved by the members of the company (if it is a public company) at a general meeting (usually the AGM) and then filed with the Registrar of Companies within nine months of the end of the company's financial year (six months for a public company). These time periods remain ten months and seven months for private and public companies respectively, for financial years beginning before 6 April 2008. CA 2006 has relaxed the requirement for private companies to have their accounts approved by members. Private companies no longer have a statutory requirement to lay their accounts before the company in general meetings for financial years ending on or after 1 October 2007.

Statutory returns, including the annual report and accounts, the annual return and notice of changes to directors and secretaries, must be filed with the Registrar of Companies on time.

Failure to comply with these requirements renders the company liable to a penalty and directors liable to a fine.

Directors are also responsible for filing tax returns.

Financial management

Directors must exercise prudence in the financial management of the company. In the event of insolvency, directors can find themselves personally liable to creditors where it can be shown that they acted outside of their powers or in breach of their duties or were engaged in wrongful or fraudulent trading. The latter offences will be committed where a director continues to incur liabilities on behalf of the company where he knows or ought to have known that the company was, or inevitably would become, insolvent or there was no reasonable prospect of repaying debts.

CA 2006 also contains new provisions in respect of annual reporting documents and accounts. Directors have a new obligation, since April 2008, not to approve accounts unless they give a true and fair view of the financial position of the company (or of the companies included in the group accounts, to the extent that this concerns members of the company).

Other duties

Directors must maintain various statutory books at the company's registered office including:

- a register of members;
- a register of mortgages and charges;
- a register of debenture holders; and
- a register of directors.

An annual return must be filed with the Registrar of Companies within 28 days of either the anniversary of its incorporation or made-up date of the company's previous annual return.

Directors must ensure that minutes are taken at board meetings, giving a record of all decisions taken.

Checklist: practical steps for directors
All directors should:

- ensure that they are fully aware of their new duties under CA 2006 and

that their board processes reflect these new duties;
- check the company's memorandum and articles of association to establish the scope of their powers;
- ensure that minutes are maintained;
- be alert to conflicts of interest between the company and themselves as individuals;
- always comply with employment law;
- ensure that the company operates a comprehensive system for assessing and minimising health and safety risks;
- keep informed about the company's financial position – ignorance will not save them from facing personal liability in certain circumstances;
- be very clear about what their service agreements require of them – often their obligations in such agreements will be more onerous than their statutory or common law obligations; and
- make sure that the company obtains insurance to protect them in the event of their facing personal liability.

Directors' indemnities
Companies are prohibited from exempting a director from any liability he may incur in connection with any negligence, default, breach of duty or breach of trust by him in relation to the company, unless the provision constitutes a "qualifying third party indemnity provision" (QTPIP). For the indemnity to be a valid QTPIP the director must not be indemnified against:

- liability the director incurs to the company or a group company;
- fines imposed in criminal proceedings or by regulatory bodies such as the FSA;
- legal costs of criminal proceedings where the director is convicted;
- legal costs of civil proceedings brought by the company or a group company, where judgement is given against the director; or

liability the director incurs in connection with applications under sections 144 or 727 CA 1985 (or sections 661 or 1157 CA 2006) for which the court refuses to grant the director relief.

Companies can therefore indemnify directors against liabilities to third parties, except for legal costs of an unsuccessful defence of criminal proceedings or fines imposed in criminal proceedings or by regulatory bodies.

Companies can pay a director's defence costs as they are incurred, even if the action is brought by the company itself against the director. The director will, however, be liable to repay all amounts advanced if he is convicted in criminal proceedings or if judgement is given against him in civil proceedings brought by the company or an associated company.

Companies can now also provide slightly wider indemnities to directors of corporate trustees of occupational pension schemes against liability incurred in connection with the company's activities as trustee of the scheme. This is known as a 'qualifying pension scheme indemnity provision' (QPSIP).

A QTPIP or QPSIP must be disclosed in the directors' report in each year that the indemnity is in force and a copy (or summary of its terms) must be available for inspection by shareholders. The QTPIP or QPSIP must also be retained by the company for at least one year after its expiry. Departing directors may also ask for such policies to be retained after their termination as part of exit negotiations.

See also: Corporate manslaughter, p.163; Health and safety at work, p.364; Insurance, p.416

Sources of further information

Centre for Corporate Accountability: www.corporateaccountability.org

Institute of Directors: www.iod.uk

Disability access and egress

Dave Allen, Butler & Young Group

Key points

Although the Disability Discrimination Act 2005 (DDA) has been in place for some time and the various stages of introduction have provided for gradual change to the built environment, there has always been a need to consider health and safety issues and in particular fire safety and evacuation provision. Unfortunately, guidance on the subject has been slow to keep pace with the need for all buildings to become accessible.

Central to the principle of accessibility to buildings and facilities, and the extent of provision or adaptation necessary is the tenet of 'reasonableness'. This still applies in principle to fire safety provisions for disabled people such as the creation of refuge areas (described below) or installation of evacuation lifts. Clearly the extent and/or nature of use of a building will have a bearing upon what can or should be expected, but this will also impact upon the evacuation strategy and any consequential limitation on access.

Safety has occasionally been stated as a reason for not allowing some disabled people full access to all parts of a building on the basis that the risks cannot be overcome or managed effectively. As a result, there is a potential conflict between the DDA requiring a disabled person to have equal rights and benefits that a non-disabled person enjoys, and the need to assess and prevent any safety risks.

Great emphasis has been placed in the past on management responsibilities and the principles to be adopted. However, practical information on how to go about planning for the safe evacuation of disabled people has, until recent years, been lacking.

Guidance

Guidance can effectively be divided into two elements:

1. Physical provision within the building environment to aid the evacuation process (principally Building Regulations Approved Document B and BS 5588 part 8); and

2. Management and procedural guidance (section 14 of BS 5588 part 12 and *Fire Safety Risk Assessment – Supplementary guide on Means of Escape for Disabled People*).

Approved Document B

Being restricted to new buildings, changes of use, and relevant alterations to buildings, Approved Document B has limited impact. The guidance in paragraph 4.7–4.14 of Approved Document B is essentially an extract of the most relevant sections of BS 5588 Part 8 with respect to the provision of refuge areas and associated communication provision. There is also reference to warnings for people with impaired hearing where others may not be available to make a person aware of an emergency in a room. This could nclude, for example, hotel bedrooms and sanitary accommodation.

BS 5588 Part 8 – Code of Practice for Means of Escape for Disabled People

The Code provides guidance on provision to assist the escape of disabled people including more comprehensive information on the design, location and associated provisions within a refuge area. Commentary on fire alarms is also provided.

Refuges

A refuge is a specified area relatively safe from the effects of a fire where a disabled person (not just a wheelchair user) may travel with or without assistance and await rescue by designated helpers without impeding the escape route of others. In multiple floor buildings it is also beneficial in allowing a place of temporary rest during an evacuation process (see Fig. 1).

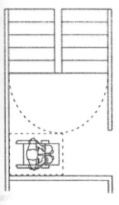

Fig. 1

Within the refuge area there should be a means of achieving two-way communication with a manned control point. The importance of this communication properly used cannot be over-emphasised. The risk that a person

needing assistance may be overlooked is real, and the fire safety consequence and psychological impact on the individual of feeling isolated must be avoided. Most alarms are likely to be false and it is essential that disabled people are made aware of this as soon as an emergency condition is determined. This may then avoid potentially stressful, risky and painful evacuation, which to most would be nothing more than a minor inconvenience.

BS 5588 Part 12 – Fire precautions in the design, construction and use of buildings – Part 12: Managing fire safety

Formerly within Part 8 of the range of codes, section 14 of the document regarding the evacuation of disabled people provides guidance on management procedures and practices which should be implemented and how they interact with the physical provisions in place.

Reference is made to disabled people having a Personal Emergency Evacuation Plan (PEEP); however no guidance is provided of the detail of a plan or any practical information on processes and evacuation techniques.

Fire Safety Risk Assessment Supplementary Guide on Means of escape for Disabled People (DCLG)

An important development with respect to the responsibility and process of evacuation came in 2006 with the introduction of the Fire Safety Order. The Order, made under the Regulatory Reform Act places a duty on a person within a building or organisation to take reasonable steps to reduce the risk from fire and ensure occupants, including disabled people, can safely escape if a fire does occur.

In March 2007 a supplementary guide in association with the Department of

Communities and Local Government (DCLG) publications on fire safety risk assessments was made available (*Fire Safety Risk Assessment – Means of Escape for Disabled People* (Supplementary Guide) – for ease, referred to as the 'guide'). This guide provides important information on the specific issue of planning escape for disabled people and provides the practical guidance missing from BS 5588 Part 12.

A fire risk assessment needs to demonstrate that as far as is reasonable, all 'relevant persons" needs with respect to evacuation have been considered, and this includes disabled people. It is accepted that with respect to people with no mobility or sensory limitations, buildings and procedures are based upon self-evacuation and evacuation times; travel distances, warning systems etc are based upon this principle.

However, step two in the process of producing a fire risk assessment is to identify the people at risk and as a consequence their needs with respect to being aware of and evacuating from a safety risk scenario (step one relates to identifying the hazards).

The production of PEEPs is described within the guide and a matrix is provided to assist in drawing up the plans. The danger, particularly with respect to the evacuation of disabled people, is that it becomes a 'tick box' process without practical understanding of an individual's needs and the risks which exist.

The guide states that all staff should be given the opportunity to have a PEEP. There are a number of hidden disabilities such as heart, respiratory, or stress induced conditions, which may affect a person's escape capability in an evacuation situation. Also, people who are excessively obese may potentially not be considered as disabled under the DDA or consider themselves as such, although any mobility restriction as a consequence may satisfy guidance with respect to the definition of a disability.

An evacuation plan is only of benefit if it is applied effectively and correctly. Information is key; both in that provided by a disabled person, and training and awareness of the Responsible Person and any helpers or persons involved with the implementation of a plan.

Communication and preparation of PEEPs for regular building users will be relatively easy to achieve. However, much of the information in the guide is based upon known and regular building users. Where the visitor is unknown, the system will be more difficult to formulate and a 'broad brush' approach will be necessary to consider all potential situations and disabled persons' needs. General evacuation plans for visitors, based upon range of predicted scenarios, would need to be drawn up. In these instances training of building staff in access awareness and the evacuation procedure contained within the plans is particularly critical.

Standard evacuation plans are described as being offered for people at entry/reception points. Staff awareness of these plans and clear indication to visitors of the plans' existence is paramount.

In uncontrolled visitor situations the general evacuation plans should be broad ranging and flexible. As the guide suggests – "Training for staff is vital … In order to do this they should receive disability etiquette training".

The guide highlights that when it comes to fire safety certain expectations with respect to access, privacy, and dignity may need e compromised. This is not an excuse to reduce standards and the 'reasonableness' consideration with respect to how a disabled person is treated prior to or during an emergency must be a consideration.

The *Supplementary Guide for Means of Escape for Disabled People* provides guidance for the Responsible Person to identify and address the risks to a disabled person and ensure their safe evacuation.

General considerations

It could be contended that, under the DDA, discrimination has not arisen with respect to evacuation until such times as an emergency occurs. However, it is important to appreciate that most disabled people are only too aware of their own safety and vulnerability in an emergency situation. As a consequence, any risks or failings with respect to fire and emergency safety strategies could be deemed to be a failing both under the DDA and the Fire Safety Order, even without an incident occurring.

The guide does acknowledge that when planning for means of escape it is planning for exceptional circumstances". There are many instances where fire safety has been used as an argument for reduced levels of accessibility. Although in limited cases this may be potentially valid, in principle this would only be deemed acceptable when all 'reasonable' options have been exhausted and a 'real' safety risk cannot be ignored.

It must be appreciated that in providing safe evacuation practices there may be a need for the otherwise normally expected dignity and independence of disabled people to be compromised and the nature

of the circumstances of any claim under the DDA in this respect are likely to take this into account. This does not preclude any evacuation plan being drawn up and applied sensitively.

All evacuation practices carry a risk. The guide recognises that unnecessary escapes should be avoided. People using stairs en masse and in haste increase the risk of falls etc. These risks are increased significantly for people with mobility and visual restrictions. It is therefore important that practices and particularly false alarms are kept to a minimum.

This should, however, be without prejudice to the fact that evacuation processes for some disabled people may be complex and involve a number of people. As a result, careful and practiced routines are necessary in order to ensure that safe and successful evacuation occurs.

Good communication systems to keep disabled people informed of the status of an emergency would be of benefit but only if the communication procedures in an emergency are robust. For example, a wheelchair user at a refuge with two-way communication may await confirmation of the need to evacuate prior to making a risky assisted descent down stairs. Early indication as to whether the emergency is a false alarm can avoid a stair descent, which can put the disabled person and potentially their assistant at risk of injury.

Good communication assists in ensuring that the right number of trained helpers reach the point where they are needed, and gives reassurance that the presence is known of a person in need of help and an

assisted evacuation is imminent. Waiting
helplessly whilst a fire alarm sounds is
particularly stressful.

When it comes to evacuating a disabled
person with a mobility difficulty via a
staircase there are four methods advised:

1. Use of proprietary evacuation chairs.
2. Carry down in the person's wheelchair.
3. Carry down using an office chair.
4. Carry down using wheelies.

The evacuation strategy should not only
be determined by individual needs but
will be affected by the building design.
Realistically, carry down strategies are
only possible if the stairs are suitably
wide and not too long (see Fig. 2).

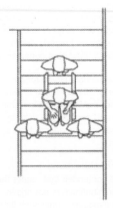

Fig. 2

See also: Accessible environments,
p.50; Building Regulations, p.81;
Disability legislation, p.209;
Discrimination, p.222; Fire, means
of escape, p.322

Sources of further information

The *Fire Safety Risk Assessment Supplementary Guide – Means of Escape for
Disabled People* can be downloaded from www.communities.gov.uk

Planning for inclusion and accessibility is a key aspect of building design and
management, and considering the needs of disabled and less mobile people will
only increase in importance as our working population gets older and in need of
accessible environments. Workplace Law Group's ***Making Buildings Accessible
2009: Special Report*** contains essential guidance and key research on how to
make buildings inclusive and accessible to all.

Covering key legislation, practical examples, case studies and case law, this
informative Special Report has all the information that building managers and
FMs need to ensure their building is inclusive and accessible to all. For more
information visit www.workplacelaw.net/Bookshop/SpecialReports.

Disability legislation

Dave Allen, Butler & Young Group

Key points

The Disability Discrimination Act 1995 (DDA 1995) brought in many rights for disabled people in terms of challenging the discrimination they faced in employment, access to services, transport and education. These rights have subsequently been extended by several measures, including the Special Educational Needs and Disability Act 2001 and the Disability Discrimination Act 2005.

The DDA 1995 imposes separate (but similar) duties on employers, educators, transport providers and organisations that provide services to the public. The overriding duty is not to discriminate against a disabled person. 'Disability' includes any impairment that has a substantial and long-term adverse effect on a person's ability to carry out normal day-to-day activities. Usually, the disability must have lasted for at least 12 months or be likely to last for that period for an individual to be covered by the DDA. However, the definition of disability has been extended by the 2005 Act with respect to the point at which someone with a progressive illness is covered by the DDA 1995, and removal of the need for a mental illness to be clinically well recognised. As such, the provisions of the DDA will cover over ten million people.

To meet the duties imposed by the 1995 Act, employers, educators, transport providers and service providers may be required to make changes to the physical provisions of the buildings they use as well as addressing their organisation's policies, practices and procedures.

Duties and claims

The governing statute is the Disability Discrimination Act 1995 as amended by the Disability Discrimination Act 2005, together with supporting Regulations and Codes of Practice.

The two key duties imposed on employers and service providers by the Act are:

. not treating disabled persons less favourably than persons who are not disabled, for a reason which relates to the disability, without justification. There are only limited grounds which constitute justification and they are set out in the Act; and

2. not breaching certain duties contained in the Act.

Breach of the Act is not a criminal offence. Claims for breach of duty by service providers can be brought by individual disabled people through the civil courts or, for employment issues, through Employment Tribunals. Remedies available include unlimited compensation in the case of employment.

Duties on employers

These duties are contained in Part II of the Act. Duties are owed only to employees or job applicants, not to the public at large.

The number of people employed at the premises is not relevant. The normal definition of an employee can extend to self-employed people who provide personal services or contract workers employed by someone else (e.g. an employment business).

The employer's main duty (other than not to discriminate) is to take reasonable steps to ensure that no arrangements or physical features of the employer's premises place a disabled person at a substantial disadvantage compared to a person who is not disabled. This may involve making one or more adjustments, and include, amongst many others:

- making reasonable adjustments to premises (see Physical adjustments, below);
- acquiring or modifying equipment; and
- modifying instructions or reference manuals,

but only where it is reasonable to do so. There is no obligation for an employer to make physical changes to their premises so that they are accessible to disabled people, on the basis that they may at some time in the future employ a disabled person; unlike Part III of the Act, Part II is not anticipatory. However, the employer cannot use the inaccessibility of a building or facility as a reason for not employing a disabled person unless they can demonstrate, if challenged, that it would be unreasonable for them to make any changes necessary. That will depend on the circumstances of each individual situation.

Examples of good practice are contained in a Code of Practice produced by the Disability Rights Commission. This is not legally binding, although in the case of a dispute the Tribunal is likely to consider whether the employer has complied with its recommendations.

Many of these possible changes involve management responsibilities, but will have knock-on effects on workplace managers. Meeting these duties will involve a discussion with the disabled 'employee' to ascertain his/her requirements and priorities. This is important because it is not a defence for the employer to simply show that the discrimination took place without its knowledge or approval.

It should be recognised that, in the context of disability discrimination, discrimination against an employee who is disabled and who is dismissed on grounds that have no connection with the disability is not unlawful. However, this demands the keeping of meticulous records to minimise the risk of discrimination claims.

In a landmark ruling, the House of Lords decided that the duty to disabled employees can involve positive discrimination. This can entail transferring without competitive interviews, a disabled employee from a post, the duties of which he/she can no longer undertake, to a post within their capabilities.

The Disability Discrimination Act 2005 brings (with some exceptions) the functions of public authorities and some other organisations not already or appropriately covered by the 1995 Act within its scope, and imposes a duty to ensure or promote equal opportunity.

Duties on service providers

These duties are contained in Part III of the Act. They apply to all organisations, of whatever size, that provide services, goods or facilities to the general public or section of it, with or without payment. The are described as 'service providers' in this chapter.

Under the 1995 Act, the only exceptions were:

- clubs which are genuinely private; and
- public transport (but infrastructure such as bus stations is subject to the Act).

However, the provisions of the 2005 Act have now, to some extent, included these areas.

The main duties under Part III of the 1995 Act that are owed to disabled visitors are:

- not to discriminate against disabled people (unless the less favourable treatment can be justified);
- to take reasonable steps to change practices, policies and procedures which make it impossible or unreasonably difficult for disabled people to use the service (this is principally a management issue); and
- to provide auxiliary aids where this is reasonable.

One case has demonstrated that the Courts' view of the standard of service that should be offered to disabled people is that it should be one that is as close as is reasonably possible to the standard normally provided to the public at large.

Physical adjustments under Part III
Service providers are required to take reasonable steps to modify physical features of premises that make it impossible or unreasonably difficult for disabled people to use the service. The term 'physical features' includes the fabric of the building or the environment, its facilities, fittings and furnishings.

Employers have a similar duty in respect of their employees, as noted above.

This duty does not override any requirement to obtain any consent which may be necessary such as planning consent, listed building consent or landlord's consent. Landlords cannot unreasonably withhold consent to make physical adjustments, regardless of what is stated in the lease.

Not all service providers have to make adjustments or at least on the same scale. The Act only requires them to do what is reasonable in the circumstances of each individual situation. To do this, account will be taken of factors such as the size of the business, the organisation and the financial resources available to it. Other factors that may be relevant include what steps the organisation has already taken to improve accessibility, and factors such as the organisation's involvement or association with the environment (in terms of long-, medium- or short-term responsibility).

Where a building met the requirements of Part M of the Building Regulations at the time of its construction, and continues to meet them, no further adjustments will be necessary for up to ten years after the completion of the property – but this exemption applies only to those elements to which the Part M approval related. Therefore, factors such as, for example, the design of signage, taps, lighting, visual contrast, and decorations, etc., which have not previously been covered by Part M, will not be exempt.

Where this has not been previously undertaken, the Disability Rights Commission (DRC) recommends the commissioning of an access audit. Practical examples of adjustments, some of which are relatively inexpensive, include:

- management practices;
- staff training;
- employment practices;
- parking;
- approaches to buildings;
- entrances;
- horizontal and vertical circulation (lifts, stairs, handrails, corridors, doors, etc.);
- visual, contrast, lighting and acoustics;
- wheelchair-accessible and standard toilet facilities;
- signage; and
- emergency egress.

Examples of reasonable steps to take are contained in the DRC's Code of Practice, which will be admissible evidence in a civil claim for compensation.

Possible reasons for treating a disabled visitor less favourably

In limited circumstances, the DDA allows for less favourable treatment of disabled people – providing it can be justified. These circumstances may include, for example:

- when the health and safety of the disabled person or any other person is put at significant risk;
- where the disabled person is incapable of giving informed consent or entering into a legally binding agreement;
- if otherwise the service provider would be unable to provide the service;
- when an adjustment would fundamentally alter the nature of a business or service; and
- if, where a disabled customer is charged more for a service, it would cost more in materials or labour to meet his particular needs.

In the event of a claim, a service provider would need to be able to demonstrate

that he or she had properly addressed the issues that gave rise to the claim. Therefore, for example, claiming that less favourable treatment towards a disabled person was justifiable on health and safety grounds without having undertaken an appropriate risk assessment to demonstrate the legitimacy of that fact is unlikely to be seen as appropriate. Any reasons claiming justification will also be tested against the relevant Code of Practice.

The Disability Discrimination Act 2005 (DDA 2005)

The DDA 2005 makes a number of wide-ranging amendments to the DDA 1995 and extends the scope, range, application and duties imposed by that Act. The 2005 Act addresses a number of issues that were omitted from the DDA 1995, or which had proved to be insufficient, unenforceable, or had not been brought fully into effect.

For example, under the DDA 1995, disabled people were not protected by civil rights legislation with regard to bodies exercising what are referred to as 'public functions'. These included, for example, powers of arrest and other activities that are usually only conducted by public sector bodies. As the public sector is a major employer and the provider of key public services, it was seen by Government as having a vital role in creating and promoting equality for disabled people in the way it conducts its activities, and the 2005 Act addressed this.

What does the 2005 Act cover?

The 2005 Act extends civil rights in areas such as the provision of transport services, letting of premises, the responsibilities and duties of public authorities, membership of private clubs, and the rights of disabled councillors. It also broadens the definition of disability contained in the DDA 1995 to

rovide protection for a broader range of
people.

Some areas of the Act came into effect
n December 2005 and the remainder in
December 2006.

Public authorities and the 2005 Act
Many of the functions carried out by a
public authority appear as being very
similar to the services they provide.
However, under the DDA 1995 there were
a number of areas of public sector activity
where it was unclear as to whether the law
would view them as a 'service' or a 'public
function'. These included, for example,
the provision and management of a public
footpath.

The 2005 Act considers the functions
carried out by public authorities and
outlaws discrimination by them in the way
they do their work – in the same way that
the DDA 1995 does for service providers.
Therefore, in essence, a public body will
be acting unlawfully if it discriminates
against disabled people:

- by treating them less favourably, for
  a reason related to their disability, in
  exercising their public function;
- by adopting practices, policies and
  procedures which, because of the
  person's disability, lead to a less
  favourable outcome (and which could
  have been avoided if the function had
  been carried out differently); and
- in either case, is not able to justify
  that treatment by one of the statutory
  justifications.

In addition, the duties imposed by the
2005 Act require public authorities to have
regard to the need to:

- eliminate unlawful discrimination
  against disabled people;
- eliminate unlawful harassment of
  disabled people; and

- promote equality of opportunity for
  disabled people.

In doing this, public bodies are subject to
a Public Sector Duty (PSD) to eliminate
unlawful discrimination against disabled
people, and to promote and monitor
equality of opportunity.

The 2005 Act also requires public bodies
to promote a 'cycle of performance
improvement', a procedure that should
move the public body towards greater
equality for disabled people and ensure
that the PSD becomes an active,
outcome-based development. A specific
duty imposed by the 2005 Act is for
public bodies to develop a Disability
Equality Scheme (DES) which must set
out how the body will fulfil its duties to
eliminate unlawful discrimination and the
harassment of disabled people, and
how it will promote the equality of
opportunity.

They will also be required to produce an
action plan to identify how and when the
DES will be monitored, reviewed and
updated. The DES should be the subject
of an annual review, and full revision
every three years. The supporting Code of
Practice (from the DRC) provides a list of
those organisations covered by the duty to
produce a DES.

**Justification for discrimination by
Public Bodies**
As with the duties placed on service
providers and employers by the DDA
1995, the 2005 Act allows for public
sector bodies to provide less favourable
treatment, or, in some circumstances, fail
to make a reasonable adjustment, if it can
be justified. In such cases, justification
may be claimed if, for example:

- there are substantiated health and
  safety reasons;

- the cost of undertaking any alterations is unreasonable given all the circumstances of the particular case;
- complying with the duties imposed on the body adversely affects the rights of others; or
- the authority believes that the disabled person is incapable of entering into an enforceable agreement, or of giving informed consent.

Private clubs
Under the DDA 1995, private clubs that offer goods, services or facilities to the general public have duties under Part III not to discriminate against disabled people. However, genuine private clubs were (and in some cases, still are) not covered by the Part III duties for goods or services that are available only to their members.

The 2005 Act now places an 'anticipatory' duty on larger private clubs (more than 25 members) not to discriminate against disabled people and brings them into line with the duties already imposed by the DDA 1995 on service providers such as shops, restaurants, theatres, etc.

Definition of disability
Under the DDA 1995, people with progressive conditions such as, for example, multiple sclerosis (MS), HIV infection and cancer were not covered by the definition of disability until the point at which their impairment has an adverse effect on their ability to carry out normal day-to-day activities. Therefore, someone with a progressive condition, such as those described above, would not have been covered by the definition of disability until they also displayed a symptom associated with that condition. In essence, diagnosis without effect would not, in most cases, have triggered the definition.

However, since December 2005, the 2005 Act provides that people with such progressive conditions will be covered from the point of diagnosis, rather than from when there is an effect. This will afford the protection of the DDA 1995 to the period between the diagnosis of a condition and an effect being apparent; a time when disabled people were liable to experience discrimination.

The 2005 Act also provides that the requirement in the DDA 1995 for a mental illness to be "clinically well diagnosed" before if can be considered as a mental impairment is removed. However, a person with a mental illness will still have to show that their impairment has a long-term and substantial adverse effect on their ability to carry out normal day-to-day activities. This also came into effect in December 2005.

Rental and management of premises
The 2005 Act has increased the duties on landlords and managers to make 'reasonable' adjustments when renting a house or flat to a disabled person. However there is still no duty on them to remove or make changes to physical features that make the property difficult to access, as would be required under Part III of the 1995 Act. Examples of changes that could be made to assist the letting process include, for example, providing forms (paperwork/contracts) in alternative formats, assessing the way the property is managed, and changing, if reasonable to do so, any terms in the letting which might prevent a disabled person renting or using the property.

If requested by a disabled tenant, a landlord or manager will also have to take reasonable steps to provide an auxiliary aid or service if it would assist them in enjoying the premises or any associated benefit or facility. There is no duty on landlords under the 2005 Act to make djustments to physical features of the enant's property, or to any other parts of he landlord's building.

ommonhold associations
4 2004, a new system of freehold wnership was introduced in England nd Wales. The system, known as Commonhold', can be applicable to blocks f flats, shops, offices and other multiple ccupation premises. Where commonhold pplies in multi-occupied premises, there no landlord and tenant relationship, he premises instead consisting of tterdependent freehold properties (known s 'commonhold units') and common parts.

he 2005 Act now has provisions to make iscrimination unlawful against disabled eople who are unit-holders.

dvertising
since October 2004, it has been illegal nder the DDA 1995 for a company to lace a 'discriminating advert'. Under the

2005 Act, it is now also against the law for publishers, for example, newspapers and magazines, to print discriminatory advertisements.

Councillors
Under the 2005 Act, a Local Authority has a duty not to discriminate against a disabled councillor in the opportunities it affords them. These duties apply to the general work undertaken by the councillor, but do not extend to activities brought about by essentially political decisions, such as appointments to serve on committees or to a position on the council's executive.

See also: Accessible environments, p.50; Building Regulations, p.81; Disability access and egress, p.204; Discrimination, p.222

Sources of further information

Disability Discrimination Act 1995: www.opsi.gov.uk/acts/acts1995/ukpga_19950050_en_1

Disability Discrimination Act 2005: www.opsi.gov.uk/acts/acts2005/ukpga_20050013_en_1

Equality and Human Rights Commission: www.equalityhumanrights.com

Planning for inclusion and accessibility is a key aspect of building design and management, and considering the needs of disabled and less mobile people will only increase in importance as our working population gets older and in need of accessible environments. Workplace Law Group's *Making Buildings Accessible 2009: Special Report* contains essential guidance and key research on how to make buildings inclusive and accessible to all. Covering key legislation, practical examples, case studies and case law, this informative Special Report has all the information that building managers and FMs need to ensure their building is inclusive and accessible to all. For more information visit www.workplacelaw.net/Bookshop/SpecialReports.

Disciplinary and grievance procedures

Pinsent Masons Employment Group

Key points

- Contracts and statements of terms must incorporate disciplinary and grievance procedures.
- Statutory disciplinary and grievance procedures must be followed by both employers and employees.
- Written procedures are helpful in this respect. If there are none, then there are certain minimum steps that employers must undertake, as otherwise any decision to dismiss will be automatically unfair. The Advisory, Conciliation and Arbitration Service (ACAS) guidelines form the accepted basis for such procedures.
- Employees have the right to be accompanied at disciplinary and grievance hearings.
- In unfair dismissal cases, an important consideration will be whether the statutory minimum procedure was followed.
- The Government proposes to abolish statutory disciplinary and grievance procedures with effect from April 2009.

Legislation

- Employment Rights Act 1996.
- Employment Act 2002.
- Employment Act 2002 (Dispute Resolution) Regulations 2004.

Written procedures

Procedural fairness in the workplace is essential if employers are to avoid falling foul of employment protection laws.

Best practice, therefore, demands the introduction of fair written procedures to deal with disciplinary issues and to resolve grievances.

Statement of terms and conditions

Every employer is obliged to provide to each employee within two months after the beginning of the employee's employment a written statement of terms and conditions of his employment which specifies:

- any disciplinary rules and any disciplinary or dismissal procedures applicable to the employee (or a reference to a document setting out such rules, which is accessible to the employee);
- a person to whom the employee can apply if dissatisfied with any disciplinary decision;
- a person to whom the employee can apply to seek redress of any grievance; and
- the manner in which any application should be made.

Disciplinary and grievance procedures are generally structured in a tiered system whereby if the grievance is not resolved or there is a recurrence of misconduct the next step of the procedure is taken.

Grievance procedure

A grievance is a complaint by an employee about action which his/her employer has taken or is contemplating taking in relation to him/her.

In a grievance procedure, there will ordinarily be provisions for making several attempts to resolve a grievance. These will start with an informal approach and lead to a requirement for the grievance to be put in writing.

Each attempt to resolve the grievance typically involves a higher level of management for the employee to approach, usually working directly up the line of management responsibilities. On a practical note, when preparing such a procedure, care should be taken to avoid an open-ended series of hearings coming from the one grievance which could lead to very senior managers becoming involved. On the other hand, the procedure should make provision for employees to be sure that their grievance is being considered by the employer and not dismissed at a junior manager level. Employees should also be able to bypass a particular manager if that manager is personally involved in the grievance (e.g. where he is alleged to have harassed an employee).

If an employee raises a grievance and does not follow the minimum statutory procedure, he will not be entitled to make an application to an Employment Tribunal on that grievance (save in very limited circumstances). The minimum procedure is as follows:

- *Step 1*. The employee must inform the employer of the grievance in writing.
- *Step 2*. The employee will be invited by the employer to a meeting to discuss the grievance where the right to be accompanied will apply. The employee must take all reasonable steps to attend this meeting. After the meeting, the employer will notify the employee of its decision in writing.
- *Step 3*. The employee will be given the right to an appeal meeting if he feels the grievance has not been satisfactorily resolved and will be notified of the final decision.

An employee cannot make an application to an Employment Tribunal within 28 days of having lodged the grievance with his employer.

Right to be accompanied

It is perhaps worth looking in more detail at the right of an employee to have a companion attend with him at both grievance and disciplinary hearings. Employees can have a work colleague or trade union official (salaried or voluntary) attend, but this does not extend to include family members or legal representatives unless they have a contractual right to do so; sometimes procedures have been written to include a wide right to be accompanied going beyond the legal requirements.

The companion may have quite an extensive role, including helping the employee put his case, but, while ACAS suggests it is best practice to allow the companion to question witnesses, the employer does not have to agree to this.

An employee does not have the right to request a companion at an investigatory meeting, which sometimes comes before a grievance or disciplinary hearing. However, it is important that the employer recognises that such meetings can turn into hearings and that it may be prudent to allow a companion to be present if the employee wants one to attend.

ACAS Code of Practice on Disciplinary and Grievance Procedures

The ACAS Code of Practice on Disciplinary and Grievance Procedures provides guidelines for employers on what constitutes reasonable behaviour when dealing with disciplinary procedures.

The steps taken by an employer to deal with a disciplinary issue will inevitably be compared by an Employment Tribunal with the ACAS Code when determining whether a fair procedure was followed. If the statutory minimum procedure is not followed, the dismissal will be automatically unfair and the compensation may be increased by between ten and 50%.

- *Step 1*. Write to the employee notifying him/her of the allegations against him/her and the basis of the allegations and invite him/her to a meeting to discuss the matter.
- *Step 2*. Hold a meeting to discuss the allegations – at which the employee has the right to be accompanied – and notify the employee of the decision.
- *Step 3*. If the employee wishes to appeal, hold an appeal meeting at which he/she has the right to be accompanied – and inform him/her of the final decision.

Best practice suggests that an employer should have a written procedure, carefully drafted to take into account the advice set out in the ACAS Code, and the employer should seek to follow the procedure in each case. Each employer is required to have in place a written procedure, which, if not provided to the employee individually, is reasonably accessible.

The written procedure should be incorporated in such a way so as not to be a part of the employment contract, so that it can more easily be changed from time to time. This can be done by making express provision for the employer to amend it. In the case of a contractual policy, the employee may sue the employer or seek to obtain an injunction or interdict for failure to follow it. Remember that if the procedure does not as a minimum

meet the statutory test, following such a procedure will be automatically unfair.

Avoiding unfair dismissal
Section 98(1) of ERA sets out the potentially fair reasons for which an employee may be dismissed. However, even if a fair reason exists, the employer must act reasonably to avoid an unfair dismissal.

An important aspect of this is whether a proper procedure was followed by the employer in arriving at its decision to dismiss the employee.

Employment Tribunals have developed key practical points for employers to follow to avoid unfair dismissals, and guidance is taken from the ACAS Code and from the ACAS handbook, *Discipline and Grievances at Work*.

Disciplinary procedures should be capable of covering a variety of circumstances with implications for the employee ranging from an informal warning to dismissal.

For issues of capability or performance, employers should follow a series of warnings in stages. Typically an employer should issue:

- a verbal warning;
- followed by a written warning;
- followed by a final written warning; and
- finally dismissal.

Very serious matters may merit leapfrogging some of those stages. At each stage of the disciplinary proceedings, the following should take place:

- prior written notice of a meeting or hearing;
- details of how the employee has fallen short of expected performance;
- clarification of how the employee is to improve and in what timescale; and

warning that, if the employee fails to improve, the next disciplinary stage will follow, ultimately up to dismissal.

[I]n cases of misconduct, the key is to follow procedure where the allegations are [p]ut to the employee. The employee must [k]now the allegations against him, but he [i]s not entitled to know the identity of a [f]ellow employee who may have supplied [t]he employer with the information required [t]o make the allegation. It is essential that [t]he employer investigates the matter fully, [t]hat the employee is given full opportunity [t]o explain his actions and given the [o]pportunity to comment on the evidence [a]gainst him, and that decisions are taken [b]ased only on evidence which has been [p]ut to the employee.

[P]rinciples of natural justice always go [h]and in hand with disciplinary procedures. [A]ccordingly:

- employees should know the allegations made against them;
- employees should have an opportunity to state their case; and
- the employer's decision-makers should act in good faith and not be biased.

[D]isciplinary procedures should also list [c]onduct that will be classed as 'gross [m]isconduct' potentially meriting jumping [s]traight to a dismissal hearing stage. [P]rocedures should also include an express [r]ight to suspend the employee pending further investigation. Suspension should be on full pay. This allows the employee to be removed from the workplace while an investigation is carried out, but it should be made clear that this is not a sanction or an indication that the employer has made any decision on the matter.

The procedure should provide for a right to appeal at each stage. Whenever possible this should be to someone not previously involved and preferably should be to a more senior level than the decision-taker.

Abolition of statutory disciplinary and grievance procedures

The Government proposes to abolish statutory disciplinary and grievance procedures with effect from April 2009. At the same time, a new ACAS Code of Practice will replace the existing Code. Whilst a failure to follow the Code will not mean that the dismissal is unfair, Tribunals are obliged to take account of the Code's provisions when assessing fairness. Employment Tribunals will be able to increase / decrease awards by up to 25% if an employer / employee unreasonably fails to comply with the Code.

See also: Dismissal, p.233;
Employment disputes, p.278;
Employment Tribunals, p.285

Sources of further information

Employers should have a clear record of the policy and procedures for disciplinary matters to provide clear guidance to employees on the procedure that will be followed by their employer. Workplace Law Group's ***Non-Contractual Disciplinary and Grievance Policy and Management Guide, v.3.0*** helps employers comply with their obligations, with a view to minimising allegations of unfair treatment. For more information visit www.workplacelaw.net/Bookshop/PoliciesAndProcedures.

Comment...

Statutory dispute resolution procedures – the end is nigh!

Jayn Bond is a Chartered Fellow of the CIPD with over 18 years' experience in HR. She is commercially aware and has a pragmatic approach to her work which is underpinned with an in-depth knowledge of employment legislation and best practice. Jayn is Head of HR at Workplace Law Group and Course Director for our accredited CIPD certificate level courses. Jayn has been advising Chief Executives, Managing Directors and Senior Managers of SMEs, local authorities and not-for-profit organisations at both strategic and operational level for a number of years. Jayn has served as a Lay Member on Stratford Employment Tribunal Panel for the last three years.

This year has seen the completion of the Government (Gibbons) Review and consultation exercise on the future of the Statutory Dispute Resolutions Procedures (SDRPs), as well as the publication of the Employment Bill.

This flurry of activity came about due to realisation that the SDRPs had clearly not achieved the anticipated results. The Government had introduced the measures in 2004 with the aim of both reducing the number of Employment Tribunal claims being lodged and the cost burden to the system.

However, instead of reducing the numbers of cases and associated costs, the procedures in fact resulted in an increase. They also had the added and unwelcome effect of increasing the average cost to employers of defending them.

Where did it all go wrong? Some of the problems were generated by the Grievance Procedures. One of the aims of these procedures was to stop employees lodging claims against employers for issues such as constructive dismissal and discrimination before the employer had received any indication from the employee that there was a problem. By insisting

that employees should initially lodge a grievance it was hoped that the majority of disputes would be settled without the need for a Tribunal hearing. However, due to the lack of guidance as to when a claimant had actually met said requirement of lodging a grievance, in reality a number of extra hearings had to be initiated just to decide that point.

In the course of these procedural hearings the Tribunals have been seen to exercise wide discretion which has led to lawyers having to advise employers that basically almost any reference to a problem could count as a grievance.

The Disciplinary Procedures also produced their own set of hazards. The problems were in the small print as they say. Employers found they could easily fall foul of the system – for example, by failing to adequately spell out in writing the allegations at a disciplinary, or failing to hold a final formal meeting with a redundant employee although they had been in lengthy consultations throughout the process.

As a Tribunal Lay Member, I have sometimes been in the position of having no option but to find against the employer r failing to meet the SDRPs and then aving to add insult to injury by uplifting e compensation to the employee by least 10%. This has led me to advise mployers – "never lose on a technicality!"

o, the Employment Bill has sounded the eath knell for the SDRPs, although the ctual implementation date has yet to be halised. The aim is that the Bill will be in rce from April 2009 but if it is not, then it ill have to wait until October 2009.

is important to note that:

▪ the current legislation will continue to apply until the new implementation date; and
▪ even when the new Bill is in force, the previous legislation will still apply to those cases where the dispute occurred within the life of the SDRPs.

o, what changes will the Employment Bill ring?

Most importantly, the Employment Bill rovides for the complete repeal of the SDRPs.

ollowing the consultation process, the Government has decided that the Polkey Principle should be reinstated. This means hat if an employer fails to comply with a rocedure the dismissal will be found to e unfair even if the employer can show hat the failure did not affect the outcome. However the compensation award can be educed to reflect the likelihood that the dismissal would have gone ahead even if he correct procedure had been followed.

The Tribunals will no longer have the obligation to increase (or decrease) compensation by 10% to 50% but will have new powers to increase or decrease a Tribunal award by between 0% and 25% if either party has acted unreasonably in complying with the relevant statutory code. This will no longer be a duty but will allow Tribunals discretion.

The Bill will also abolish the fixed period for ACAS conciliation and so conciliation will be able to continue throughout the Tribunal proceedings. There are a number of other changes too which will be widely publicised nearer the implementation date.

The Gibbons review did also raise other queries about the overall efficiency of the current Tribunal system, including questioning the role of panel members – a matter closely watched by myself and my fellow 'wingers'.

In 2008 we have seen the Employment Tribunal Chairs re-titled Employment Judges, and the types of cases where Judges will be able to sit alone is likely to be increased in 2009.

However, I was pleased to see that there was strong representation by all parties submitted to the Government supporting the fact that Panel Members add value to the whole process.

As a result of these submissions, I have been able to breathe a sigh of relief that the current structure is to be retained – for the time being at least!

Discrimination

Pinsent Masons Employment Group

Key points

- Employment legislation makes it unlawful to discriminate on the grounds of sex, gender reassignment, marital or civil partner status, pregnancy or maternity leave, race, disability, sexual orientation, religion or belief and age.
- Discrimination will usually be direct or indirect, but can also arise due to harassment and victimisation.
- Workplace managers need to act to avoid discrimination at all stages of employment – recruitment, the provision of benefits, promotion and dismissal – to avoid claims for unlimited compensation being made.

Legislation

- Sex Discrimination Act 1975.
- Race Relations Act 1976.
- Disability Discrimination Act 1995.
- Disability Discrimination Act 2005.
- Race Relations Act 1976 (Amendment) Regulations 2003.
- Disability Discrimination Act 1995 (Amendment) Regulations 2003.
- Employment Equality (Sexual Orientation) Regulations 2003.
- Employment Equality (Religion or Belief) Regulations 2003.
- Employment Equality (Sex Discrimination) Regulations 2005.
- Employment Equality (Age) Regulations 2006.
- Sex Discrimination Act 1975 (Amendment) Regulations 2008.

What is discrimination?

Discrimination laws preclude employers from treating workers differently for reasons that are based on sex, gender reassignment, marital or civil partner status, pregnancy or maternity leave, race, disability, sexual orientation, religion or belief and age.

The law on racial and sexual discrimination is now quite long established and the legislation on discrimination on grounds of sexual orientation, religion or belief and age follows a similar approach, while that on disability discrimination differs in certain respects. Each area of discrimination will be covered in a separate section in this chapter.

Discrimination can be split into four categories – direct, indirect, harassment and victimisation:

1. *Direct.* This is where a decision or action is taken on the sole grounds of the individual's distinctive characteristics – e.g. preferring a male applicant to a female applicant when the female has the better qualifications.
2. *Indirect.* This occurs where an employer's apparently neutral provision, requirement or practice (PCP) has the effect of putting a particular group at a disadvantage. For example, where an employer insists on a wide mobility clause in its contract of employment, this could be interpreted as discriminating against women as they are more likely to be the 'second earner' and therefore less able to relocate. Another example is a requirement for a GCSE in English

for a position that does not require any degree of literacy as this can discriminate against ethnic minorities. Indirect discrimination is often less easy to spot than direct discrimination. Indirect discrimination can be justified if the employer is able to show that its requirement or practice meets a legitimate aim and is a proportionate means of achieving it.

. *Harassment*. This is now a separate form of discrimination in each potential area of discrimination. It is defined as being a person's unwanted conduct which violates another's dignity or creates an intimidating, hostile, degrading, humiliating or offensive environment.

. *Victimisation*. This is where an individual is treated less favourably because he has threatened to bring discrimination proceedings, gives evidence or information in connection with such proceedings, or makes some genuinely held allegation of discrimination.

Discrimination laws are couched in terms where those protected are not only employees but also contractors who are engaged personally to carry out work. An employer is responsible for the discriminatory acts carried out by its employees 'in the course of their employment' (a fairly wide definition) unless the employer has taken reasonable steps to prevent the discriminatory conduct. It is therefore important not only that employers have in place policies to prevent discrimination but also that they take active steps to ensure that staff are aware of their content.

Impact of the Human Rights Act 1998
The Human Rights Act 1998 came into force on 2 October 2000 and requires the courts and tribunals to interpret UK law in a way that is compatible with the European Convention on Human Rights.

It includes a right to freedom of conscience, thought or religion, which could widen the scope of the current laws on discrimination on grounds of racial group / origin or religious group.

Further, other relevant provisions allow the right not to be subjected to inhuman or degrading treatment and the right to respect for private life and freedom of expression (which could include the right to wear certain clothes at work, linked to religion or otherwise).

Moreover, Article 14 of the Convention provides that all of the rights contained within the Convention shall be secured without discrimination on any ground such as sex, race, colour, language, religion, political or other opinion, national or social origin, association with a national minority, property, birth or status. This could potentially widen the concept of discrimination beyond the scope of the discrimination legislation currently in force in the UK. However, the impact of this in the workplace has been fairly limited to date.

One area which may become increasingly contentious is religious observance at work. Article 9 protects freedom of thought, conscience and religion.

Sex discrimination
The Sex Discrimination Act 1975 prevents direct discrimination, indirect discrimination, harassment and victimisation.

Direct sex discrimination, as explained above, is treating a woman less favourably than a man (or vice versa) or a married person less favourably than a non-married person – cases of the latter normally occur where an employer fears that a married woman will want to take time out for a family. The comparison that is used is between the person claiming discrimination and another person with similar skills and qualifications and the test is generally whether the person would have been treated the same but for his or her sex.

It is also unlawful to discriminate against transsexuals, on grounds of civil partner status and on grounds of pregnancy or maternity leave.

If a woman is disadvantaged because she is pregnant or on maternity leave this will be discriminatory. Care should be taken to ensure that during the woman's absence she is kept informed of any new vacancies or promotions that become available and of any other issues that may be of interest that are made available to staff who are not on maternity leave (such as details relating to pay) to avoid any claims that she is being discriminated against.

The definition of indirect discrimination changed in October 2005. Indirect discrimination now occurs where an employer applies a provision, criterion or practice (PCP) which puts persons of the claimant's sex at a particular disadvantage when compared to the other sex, and the individual in question suffers that disadvantage, and the employer cannot show that the PCP is a proportionate means of achieving a legitimate aim.

The concept of a 'provision, criterion or practice' is very broad. For example, it may be broad enough to include informal work practices such as a long-hours culture which would be seen as having a greater impact on women as they tend to have primary childcare responsibilities.

Indirect discrimination has often arisen when fewer or lesser benefits are given to part-time workers than are given to full-time workers, because more women work on a part-time basis (although a part-time

worker would also have a claim under the Part time Workers (Prevention of Less Favourable Treatment) Regulations 2000 in such circumstances. Making decisions on the assumption that women will stay at home and men will go out to work is also liable to lead to claims of discrimination. Indirect discrimination will not be unlawful if the employer is able to show that its PCP meets a legitimate aim and is a proportionate means of achieving that aim. This is the justification test. It requires an objective balance to be struck between the discriminatory effect of the PCP and the reasonable needs of the employer.

So where female employees are refused requests to return part-time or to job-share after a pregnancy, workplace managers will need to be able to justify why the job has to be done a full-time basis or by one person.

Particular danger arises through discriminatory advertisements and descriptions of jobs suggesting that only men or women should apply or requiring qualifications or experience that is weighted towards one sex rather than the other.

Harassment related to a person's sex (or that of another person) and harassment of a sexual nature are now prohibited as a matter of statute. Previously, harassment was not expressly covered by the Sex Discrimination Act, although the courts had held that harassment could constitute direct discrimination.

Employers are able to defend a discrimination claim relating to recruitment/promotion where a 'genuine occupational qualification' necessitates the employment of one sex. Examples are where a man or woman is needed for decency or privacy and where there is a need to live at premises provided by the employer and

e facilities are only for one sex. Further
exceptions exist for institutions such as
all-male hospitals and prisons or care
services.

Employers should also be aware that, after
the employee leaves, any discrimination
against that individual will be unlawful if
the act of discrimination arises out of and
is closely connected to the employment
relationship.

Employment Tribunals have unlimited
scope to compensate affected individuals
not only for pure financial loss but also for
injury to feelings.

Race discrimination

The Race Relations Act 1976
prohibits direct discrimination, indirect
discrimination, harassment and
victimisation. A wide definition of race is
provided in the legislation. Discrimination
is prohibited on grounds of colour, race,
nationality, ethnic or national origins.

As explained at the beginning of this
chapter, direct discrimination is where
one person is treated less favourably than
another. Examples in the context of race
discrimination would be not promoting
someone because he is Indian or not
employing a Sikh because he might not
'fit in' with white workers.

There are two slightly different definitions
of indirect race discrimination. The first
form of indirect discrimination applies
to cases of discrimination on grounds
of colour or nationality. It occurs when
the employer applies a requirement or
condition with which a considerably smaller
proportion in a racial group can comply
compared to those who are not in the
racial group. Also, the person must have
been disadvantaged by the actions. If the
employer can justify the requirement
for a reason other than the race of the

person, this is a defence to the claim. The
second definition of indirect discrimination
applies to cases of discrimination on
grounds of race, ethnic or national origins.
It occurs when the employer applies
a provision, criterion or practice which
is apparently race-neutral (i.e. it would
apply to all races) but puts or would
put persons of the employee's race or
ethnic or national origins at a particular
disadvantage, actually puts the relevant
employee at that disadvantage, and cannot
be shown to be a proportionate means of
achieving a legitimate aim.

If an individual proves a case of indirect
discrimination, the burden of proof shifts
to the employer to prove that it was not
racially discriminatory.

Workplace managers should note that
employers can discriminate if they
segregate racial groups, even if the
facilities given to them are of equal
quality.

A decision to discriminate on racial
grounds may be justified in certain cases
where being of a particular colour, race,
nationality or ethnic or national origin
is an essential qualification for the job
in question – the 'genuine occupational
qualification' defence.

Grounds upon which it may be claimed
there is a genuine occupational
qualification include:

- being a member of a particular
  racial group is a requirement for
  authenticity in a dramatic performance
  or other entertainment, or for
  authenticity purposes as an artist's or
  photographic model;
- the work is in a place where food or
  drink is consumed by the public and
  a particular race of person is required
  for authenticity (e.g. Chinese or Indian
  restaurants); or

■ the job holder provides his or her racial group with personal services promoting their welfare (e.g. an Afro-Caribbean nursery nurse in an Afro-Caribbean area) where those services can be more effectively provided by a person of that racial group.

There is also another defence available but this defence is only available in cases of discrimination on grounds of race, ethnic or national origins (not for discrimination on grounds of colour or nationality). This defence – the 'genuine occupational requirement' defence – applies where being of a particular race, ethnic or national origin is a genuine and determining occupational requirement. Such a requirement must be proportionate in the particular case and the individual who was subject to the discrimination must not be of the race in question. Instructions to or pressure on staff to discriminate is also unlawful (e.g. the owners of a truck rental company instructing staff to tell Asian customers that no trucks are available for hire).

Harassment is now a separate form of discrimination where a person's unwanted conduct has the purpose or effect of violating another's dignity or creates an intimidating, hostile, degrading, humiliating or offensive environment. The test is an objective one and although the Tribunal must take the complainant's perception into account, it must be conduct that could reasonably be considered as having that effect. Therefore, provided there is no intention, there will not be a claim for harassment if the complainant is hypersensitive. Employment Tribunals have unlimited scope to compensate affected individuals not only for pure financial loss but also for injury to feelings.

Disability discrimination
The Disability Discrimination Act 1995 (DDA) prohibits direct discrimination,

disability-related discrimination, victimisation and, since 1 October 2004, harassment has been a separate act wh is regarded as unlawful in its own right. The DDA also provides for a duty to mak reasonable adjustments.

The DDA also prohibits discrimination against people with disabilities in terms of services provided to them as member of the public as well as in the field of employment rights. Since 1 October 200 all employers, regardless of size, can be found guilty of discrimination.

There are five types of disability discrimination. The first is where an employer treats a disabled person less favourably on the grounds of his disabilit than he would a person not having that disability. This is known as direct disabili discrimination.

The second applies where an employer treats a person less favourably for a reason related to his disability than he would treat another person to whom that reason does not or would not apply. This known as disability-related discrimination Unlike direct disability discrimination, disability-related discrimination can be justified, but there must be substantial reasons for the discrimination. Disability-related discrimination cannot be justified in circumstances where the employer wa also under a duty to make reasonable adjustments (see below) and he has not complied with that duty.

Direct disability discrimination differs from disability-related discrimination in that it occurs when the reason for the less favourable treatment is the disability itsel whereas disability-related discrimination occurs where the reason relates to the disability but is not the disability itself. For example, direct discrimination will occur where an employer fails to mploy a person because he has a acial disfigurement (which amounts to disability) solely because he will be ncomfortable working with him.

n example of where disability-related iscrimination will occur is where an mployer dismisses an employee who has een off sick for a long time – in such a ase the reason for the treatment is the ickness (which is related to the disability) ut is not the disability itself. A recent House f Lords decision (*Mayor and Burgess f the London Borough of Lewisham v. Malcolm*) may have reduced the scope for ringing disability-related discrimination laims as a result of a change to the omparator to be used in such cases. *rior to the decision, it was thought that nere were different comparators in cases f direct disability discrimination and isability-related discrimination. For direct iscrimination, the comparison is between ne way the disabled person is treated nd how a non-disabled person would e treated in similar circumstances. For isability-related discrimination purposes, ne case of *Clark v. Novacold* held that the orrect comparator was someone to whom ne reason for the claimant's treatment did ot apply.

io if a person was dismissed for being off ick for too long, the comparison would be vith someone to whom that reason (i.e. ne sickness absence) did not apply – so it vas someone who had not been off work ick at all. Since such a person would ot have been dismissed, less favourable reatment would be made out and vhether the discrimination was unlawful vould depend on whether the employer ould justify its treatment of the disabled mployee.

he recent House of Lords decision uggests that the correct comparator in case of disability-related discrimination is in fact a person without a disability who is otherwise in the same position as the claimant, i.e. the same comparator as for direct disability discrimination. So in the case of the disabled employee dismissed for being off sick for too long, the comparison would be with a non-disabled employee who has been off work for the same length of time. Since such an employee would presumably also have been dismissed, less favourable treatment is not made out and the disability-related discrimination claim fails.

It remains to be seen how Employment Tribunals will approach disability-related discrimination claims as a result of the *Malcolm* case.

The third type of disability discrimination occurs where an employer fails to make 'reasonable adjustments' to the physical nature of its premises or to any 'provision, criterion or practice' to ensure that disabled people are not placed at a disadvantage. Failure to make a reasonable adjustment will constitute discrimination. It is no longer possible to justify a failure to make a reasonable adjustment – the only defence, therefore, is that the adjustment was not a reasonable one to make. Factors that may be taken into account in assessing the reasonableness of the adjustment include:

■ how effective the step will be in ameliorating the disadvantage and the practicability of taking the step;
■ the costs to the employer of making the adjustment and the financial and other resources available to the employer; and/or
■ the nature of the employer's activities and the size of the undertaking.

Examples of what may be regarded as reasonable adjustments are:

■ changing building structure (e.g. by introducing ramps, lowering switches

or panels, moving doors and widening entrances) – but remember most people affected by the DDA are not in a wheelchair;
- permitting different working hours (e.g. to deal with tiredness or medical treatments);
- providing specialist or modified equipment (e.g. computer screens or adapted/different chairs); and
- providing training (e.g. for use of specialist equipment or extra training for someone whose disability may make him/her slower).

The fourth type of disability discrimination is victimisation, i.e. less favourable treatment because a person has threatened to bring disability discrimination proceedings, gives evidence or information in connection with such proceedings, or makes some genuinely held allegation of disability discrimination.

Lastly, it is now also unlawful to harass an employee for a reason relating to that person's disability, by engaging in unwanted conduct which has the purpose or effect of violating the person's dignity or creating an intimidating, hostile, degrading, humiliating or offensive environment for him or her.

A recent decision of the ECJ in the case of *Coleman v. Attridge Law* held that where a person is discriminated against because of their association with a disabled person, rather than because of their own disability, they are protected by the EC Equal Treatment Framework Directive. This means that it may be necessary to interpret the DDA as extending to associative discrimination and if this is not possible, the DDA will need amending to ensure it complies with the Directive.

Meaning of 'disability'
There are no duties or liabilities to an individual if there is no 'disability' as

defined in the legislation. It is therefore important that there is an understanding that not all medical conditions constitute disability.

For a disability to exist, there needs to be a physical or mental impairment which has a substantial and long-term effect (i.e. last or is likely to last 12 months or is likely to recur) on the person's ability to carry out 'normal day-to-day activities'.

Certain provisions of the Disability Discrimination Act 2005 came into force in December 2005. This extended the definition of disability to cover people with cancer, multiple sclerosis and HIV from the date of diagnosis. The 2005 Act also removed the previous requirement that people with a mental illness had to show that it was a 'clinically well-recognised' illness before it counted as a mental impairment.

The Disability Rights Commission Code of Practice: *Employment and Occupation* provides guidance and there is also guidance, issued by the Secretary of State, on matters to be taken into account in determining questions relating to the definition of disability to which workplace managers should refer.

The following examples show the type of physical activities that are regarded as being normal or day-to-day:

- mobility (moving, changing position);
- manual dexterity (use of hands and fingers with precision – e.g. an inability to use a knife and fork may be a disability, but an inability to pick up a tiny item such as a pin may not);
- physical coordination (where again it may be a matter of degree);
- continence;
- ability to lift, carry or move everyday objects;
- speech, hearing or eyesight;

- memory or ability to learn, concentrate or understand; and
- perception of risk or physical danger.

The Guidance indicates that this does not include "activities which are normal only for a particular person or small group of people". However, the courts have been less restrictive in their approach and said that what is normal cannot sensibly depend on whether the majority of people do it. It is necessary to consider what is 'normal' and what is 'abnormal' or 'unusual' as a regular activity, judged by an objective population standard.

Schizophrenia, claustrophobia, epilepsy, back injuries, depression, blindness, arm pains and dyslexia have all been found to constitute 'disabilities'. However, each of these cases has been decided on the level of disability of an individual, and it cannot be taken to be a rule that because someone suffers from arm pains he is disabled in terms of the law.

The legislation is very specific on the subject of substance abuse and excludes alcohol, nicotine or substance dependency as a disability. Again, however, caution is warranted as the effects of the abuse could result in physical disabilities (e.g. liver damage), which would be covered by the law.

Workplace managers should take care in avoiding disability discrimination in terms of advertisements, terms and conditions of employment, benefits provided to staff, dismissals and victimisation.

If an employee is ill, particularly where that illness is long-term and a dismissal is contemplated, the disability discrimination legislation needs to be considered carefully and specialist advice taken as this area is fraught with potential issues.

Discrimination on the grounds of sexual orientation

The EC Equal Treatment Framework Directive sets out an anti-discrimination 'principle of equal treatment' in the context of sexual orientation and this has been implemented through the Employment Equality (Sexual Orientation) Regulations 2003.

The Regulations contain sections dealing with discrimination in employment and vocational training, vicarious liability of employers, exceptions and enforcement.

The law applies to recruitment, terms and conditions, pay, promotion, transfers and dismissals. It applies to all employers regardless of their size.

The Regulations cover:

- direct discrimination (i.e. less favourable treatment on the grounds of sexual orientation);
- indirect discrimination whereby a provision criterion or practice is applied which disadvantages people of particular sexual orientation and which is not objectively justified as a proportionate means of achieving a legitimate aim;
- harassment or conduct which violates dignity or creates an intimidating, hostile, degrading, humiliating or offensive environment; and
- victimisation (i.e. less favourable treatment because of something done in connection with the legislation).

'Sexual orientation' covers orientation towards persons of the same sex (gays and lesbians), the opposite sex (heterosexuals), and the same and opposite sex (bisexuals). The law applies to discrimination on the grounds of perceived as well as actual sexual orientation.

Discrimination on the grounds of religion or belief

The EC Equal Treatment Framework Directive sets out an anti-discrimination 'principle of equal treatment' in the context of religion or belief. The Employment Equality (Religion or Belief) Regulations 2003 came into force in December 2003.

The Regulations contain sections dealing with discrimination in employment and vocational training, the vicarious liability of employers, exceptions and enforcement.

The law applies to recruitment, terms and conditions, pay, promotion, transfers and dismissals. It applies to all employers, regardless of their size.

The Regulations prohibit:

- direct discrimination (i.e. less favourable treatment on the grounds of religion or belief);
- indirect discrimination, whereby a provision or practice is applied which disadvantages people of a particular religion or belief and which is not objectively justified as a proportionate means of achieving a legitimate aim;
- harassment or conduct which violates dignity or creates an intimidating, hostile, degrading, humiliating or offensive environment; and
- victimisation (i.e. less favourable treatment because of something done in connection with the legislation).

The Regulations relating to religion or belief define religion or belief as meaning "any religion, or religious or philosophical belief". Following a change in the law in April 2007, the requirement that a philosophical belief be similar to a religious belief has been abolished. This clearly widens the scope of the protection, though the extent of this has yet to be tested.

Age discrimination

Age legislation is required to comply with the EC Equal Treatment Framework Directive and, on 1 October 2006, the Employment Equality (Age) Regulations 2006 came into force.

There are four main types of unlawful discrimination. These are as follows:

1. *Direct discrimination.* This occurs where a person is treated less favourably on grounds of their age without objective justification. For example, setting an upper and lower age limit for a particular job (whether formally or informally) may be direct discrimination against a person outside the age band.
2. *Indirect discrimination.* This occurs where a provision, criterion or practice has a greater impact on workers in one age group compared to those in another and is not objectively justified. These are not always easy to spot because there is no overt less favourable treatment – everyone appears to be treated the same. However, restricting a post to 'recent graduates' is likely to discriminate indirectly against a worker over 30, since most recent graduates are likely to be in their 20s.
3. *Harassment.* This occurs where, on the grounds of age, the person is subjected to unwanted conduct that has the purpose or effect of violating their dignity or creating an intimidating hostile, degrading, humiliating or offensive environment. Examples of this include intentional bullying, but it can also be unintentional, subtle and insidious, e.g. nicknames, teasing, inappropriate jokes that are not malicious in intent, but which are upsetting. Harassing behaviour may be targeted at an individual or may consist of a general culture that appears to tolerate, for example, the

telling of ageist jokes. Harassment is judged from the perception of the victim, although unintentional harassment is subject to the test of reasonableness.

Victimisation. An employee who complains in good faith of alleged age discrimination or harassment, or who supports another employee in such a complaint, must not be treated less favourably because they have complained/supported a complaint. Employees are protected from acts of victimisation even if the complaint turns out not to be upheld.

is important to remember that, as with ther types of unlawful discrimination at ork, age discrimination can arise not just om what managers do, but also from ow employees behave towards each ther. This may not just be confined to he workplace. For example, if a group f young employees frequently go out r a drink after work, but exclude an lder member of their team, this could some cases amount to discrimination r harassment. Employees should be ncouraged to be as inclusive as ossible.

Jnusually, the new age discrimination law ermits employers to justify objectively oth direct and indirect discrimination.

However, this is not straightforward. It is lifficult to tell what approach the Tribunals vill take to the question of objective ustification. The new law says that an mployer must be pursuing a 'legitimate im' (for example, encouraging loyalty, ewarding experience, or maintaining health and safety) and the means of oursuing the same must be 'proportionate'.

n practice this means that the benefit of a discriminatory practice to an employer must be sufficient to outweigh the discriminatory effect. If there are two ways of achieving a similar aim, the less discriminatory way must be chosen.

Employers also have the option of arguing that there is a genuine occupational requirement for a discriminatory decision although the Department for Business, Enterprise and Regulatory Affairs has indicated that this will only be relevant in very few cases.

Employers can no longer set their normal retirement ages below the age of 65 unless this can be objectively justified. Although the Regulations allow employers to retire employees at a default retirement age of 65, the question of whether a default retirement age is lawful has been referred to the ECJ. Employers who have a retirement age of 65 may therefore wish to consider whether to rely on it.

Employers have to consider an employee's request to continue beyond normal retirement age and will have to inform employees in writing, in advance, of their intended retirement date and their right to request to work after the intended retirement date.

Employers will therefore need to ensure that their recruitment, retirement, promotion and reward practices do not discriminate directly or indirectly on grounds of age.

See also: Carers, p.114; Disability legislation, p.209; Employment Tribunals, p.285; Equal pay, p.300; HIV and AIDS, p.398; Managing pregnancy, p.484; Part-time workers, p.559; Recruitment and selection, p.607; Retirement, p.636; Stress, p.671

Sources of further information

Department for Business, Enterprise and Regulatory Reform: www.berr.gov.uk

Equality and Human Rights Commission: www.equalityhumanrights.com

Equal Opportunities policies are becoming ever more important in today's increasingly multicultural, multiracial society. The purpose of Workplace Law Group's *Equal Opportunities Policy and Management Guide, v.3.0* is to set out the obligations on both the employer and the employee to treat all people with equal dignity and respect within the workplace. The aim is to create a pleasant and harmonious working environment for all.

The Policy sets out and explains the rights of each employee. A well-drafted Equal Opportunities policy combined with good management will ensure your organisation meets its legal obligation to provide a non-discriminatory work environment and persuade employees that an equal opportunities policy at work is for the benefit of the whole workforce. For more information visit www.workplacelaw.net/Bookshop/PoliciesAndProcedures.

Dismissal

Pinsent Masons Employment Group

Key points

Employers must dismiss employees in accordance with contract terms in order not to breach the contract and become liable for wrongful dismissal. Regardless of whether there is a breach of contract, dismissals will be unfair unless:

- the dismissal is for one of a list of potentially fair reasons;
- the employer acts reasonably in dismissing the employee;
- the employer has followed a fair procedure; and
- the employer has followed the statutory dismissal procedure.

Legislation
- Employment Rights Act 1996.
- Employment Act 2002.
- Employment Act 2002 (Dispute Resolution) Regulations 2004.

What is dismissal?
A number of key employment law rights arise when a 'dismissal' takes place. Dismissal is an act of the employer which occasions a termination of the employment relationship. A resignation – although an act of the employee, not the employer – can also constitute a 'constructive dismissal' where it is in response to a breach of contract by the employer.

Dismissal can also include the expiry and non-renewal of a fixed-term contract.

Notice
Dismissal by an employer can be with or without notice. The amount of notice required will usually be set out in the employment contract. If that is silent, 'reasonable' notice must be given, the length of which will vary depending on the employee's circumstances.

In any event, the following statutory minimum notice must be given by an employer:

- An employee who has been continuously employed for one month or more but less than two years is entitled to not less than one week's notice.
- An employee who has been continuously employed for two years or more but less than 12 years is entitled to one week's notice for each year of continuous employment.
- An employee who has been employed for 12 years or more is entitled to not less than 12 weeks' notice.

Generally, once notice has been given it cannot be withdrawn, save by mutual consent.

Failure by an employer to give notice in accordance with the terms of the contract will leave the employer liable to pay damages to the employee in respect of salary and other benefits which would have fallen due in the notice period. If there is a 'pay in lieu of notice' (PILON) clause in the employee's contract, there will be no breach of contract if notice money is paid instead of the employee working out his notice.

The tax treatments of these two types of payment are different. As the latter payment is contractual, the employee will be liable for income tax, whereas the former is treated as damages and may generally be free of tax up to £30,000. An act of gross misconduct or gross negligence on the part of an employee may be expected to justify dismissal without notice, sometimes referred to as 'summary dismissal'.

Unfair dismissal

Save for certain special cases (see below), employees must have one year's continuous service (at the date the dismissal takes effect) in order to have the right to claim that they have been unfairly dismissed. A fair dismissal has two elements:

1. The employer's reason to dismiss must be one of a list of potentially fair reasons (section 98(1), Employment Rights Act 1996 (ERA)).
2. Even if a fair reason exists, it must have been reasonable in all the circumstances for the employer to dismiss the employee (section 94(4), ERA). In other words, the employer must follow a fair procedure.

Potentially fair reasons for dismissal

- *Lack of capability or qualifications.* Capability is skill and ability to do the job. This is most often relevant for poor performance or physical incapability such as injury or sickness. Lack of qualifications could involve a practical qualification necessary to do the job which may be lost during employment (e.g. a driver losing a driving licence).
- *Conduct.* In other words, misconduct on the part of the employee.

- *Redundancy.* For the purposes of the ERA an employee who is dismissed shall be taken to be dismissed by reason of redundancy if the dismissal is wholly or mainly attributable to the fact that his employer has ceased or intends to cease to carry on the business for the purposes of which the employee was employed by him, or to carry on that business in the place where the employee was so employed, or where the requirements of that business for employees to carry out work of a particular kind, or for employees to carry out work of a particular kind in the place where the employee was employed by the employer, have ceased or diminished or are expected to cease or diminish.
- *Retirement.* The Employment Equality (Age) Regulations 2006 introduced retirement as a potentially fair reason for dismissal.
- *Continued employment would breach legislation.* For example where, if the employment continued, either the employer or the employee would be in breach of health and safety laws.
- *'Some other substantial reason'.* In some ways this is a catch-all to allow Tribunals to respond to the circumstances of individual cases. It can cover a multitude of cases including dismissals by reason of a reorganisation and dismissals in order to effect changes in terms and conditions of employment.

Fairness of the dismissal

Having determined that a potentially fair reason exists, one must then ask the question whether the employer has acted reasonably in all the circumstances in dismissing the employee as a consequence of the reason. Has the employer followed a fair and proper procedure?

Tribunals will take account of the size and administrative resources of the employer.

he question of fairness is closely linked
o disciplinary procedures and the need to
ollow a fair procedure in disciplining and
ismissing the employee and meeting the
inimum statutory standards.

What is appropriate in terms of procedure
will vary depending on the reason for the
ismissal. The employer must follow a fair
nd reasonable procedure and the Tribunal
will look at whether the decision to dismiss
he employee and the procedures followed
easure up to the standards expected of
mployers. An employer must also follow
he statutory dismissal procedure before
ismissing an employee (see 'Disciplinary
nd Grievance Procedures', p.216 for
ore information on the statutory dismissal
rocedure). Failure to do so will mean
hat the dismissal will be unfair. Where
n employer has followed the statutory
ismissal procedure but there has been
ome other procedural failing, it may be
ossible to argue that the dismissal was
air on the basis that even if the correct
rocedure had been followed the dismissal
vould still have occurred.

Some key procedural points which
workplace managers should follow for the
most common dismissals are as follows:

Capability

- Tell the employee precisely why his
  performance is poor and what is
  needed to improve it.
- Explain the next stage of disciplinary
  action if there is still no improvement
  (leading up to eventual dismissal).
- Give the employee an opportunity to
  explain his case at each stage.
- Consider whether training is needed
  or if an alternative job can be offered.

Sickness

- Investigate the true medical position
  and prognosis for recovery (usually
  through a medical report).

- Consult with the employee.
- Can the employer be expected to wait
  any longer for recovery?
- The employer should also consider
  the Disability Discrimination Act 1995
  before taking further action.

Conduct

- The question is whether the employer
  has reasonable grounds to believe the
  employee is guilty of misconduct.
- Carry out a full investigation.
- Inform the employee of all the
  allegations in advance of disciplinary
  meetings.
- Put all the evidence of misconduct to
  the employee.
- The employee must have an
  opportunity to put his case on the
  evidence.
- Dismiss only on the evidence put to
  the employee.

Redundancy

Although a potentially fair reason for
dismissal, redundancy can give rise to
unfair dismissals where there is a failure
to follow a fair procedure. Fair and proper
procedures are based on:

- giving the employee advance
  warning of the potential redundancy
  situation;
- consulting with the employee as to the
  selection criteria to be used;
- considering alternative employment;
- the employer taking a decision to
  dismiss for reasons of redundancy
  only after proper consultation has
  taken place;
- allowing the employee time off to look
  for alternative jobs; and
- continuing to look for alternative
  jobs for the employee within the
  organisation.

Retirement

An employer may, although is not obliged
to, retire employees at the employer's

normal retirement age or the default retirement age of 65. However, although retirement is a potentially fair reason for dismissal, employers must follow a 'planned retirement' procedure that includes:

- giving employees at least six months' notice of their retirement date; and
- ensuring employees have the right to request to work past their retirement date and complying with the duty to consider such a request.

If an employer retires an employee before their normal retirement age, or the age of 65, this may amount to unfair dismissal and age discrimination.

Unfair dismissal remedies

Employees have three months after the date of dismissal in which to bring a claim before an Employment Tribunal or, alternatively, employers and employees can decide to place the dispute before an ACAS-appointed arbitrator under the ACAS Arbitration Scheme. The scheme is devised to provide a quicker, cheaper and, where possible, more amicable resolution to this type of dispute. However, very few people have elected to follow this route to date. Remedies available to both the Tribunal and an ACAS arbitrator include re-engagement or reinstatement, both of which are imposed only rarely. More usually, compensation is awarded.

This falls under two heads:

1. The first is the basic award, calculated by reference to salary, age and length of service, subject to a maximum, which was increased on 1 February 2008 to £9,900.
2. The second is the compensatory award, which is designed to reimburse the employee for actual losses and is at the discretion of the Tribunal

subject to a maximum, also increased on 1 February 2008, and now set at £63,000. The overall cap has been increased significantly in recent years and is likely to keep rising in the future.

Automatically unfair reasons

Detailed provisions exist for claims that do not require one year's continuous service and where dismissal for that reason will be automatically unfair.

The most important of these are dismissal for:

- membership of a trade union or for participating in trade union activities;
- taking part in protected industrial action;
- taking action on specified health and safety grounds (including leaving premises due to danger);
- asserting statutory rights against the employer;
- pregnancy or related reasons;
- holding the status of a part-time worker or a fixed-term employee;
- reasons connected with rights under the Working Time Regulations 1998 or National Minimum Wage Act 1998;
- exercising a right to be accompanied by a union representative or fellow worker at a disciplinary or grievance hearing;
- asserting rights under the 'whistleblowers' legislation;
- taking leave for family reasons;
- making a flexible working application;
- refusal of Sunday working by shop and betting employees;
- performing certain functions as a trustee of an occupational pension scheme;
- performing certain functions as an employee representative under TUPE or collective redundancy legislation; and
- selection for redundancy for any of the above reasons.

ismissal for the following reasons will be
utomatically unfair but the employee will still
eed one year's service to bring the claim:

- dismissal because of a spent
conviction;

- certain dismissals in connection with a
TUPE transfer; and
- where the employer has not
completed the statutory dismissal
procedure.

> *See also*: Disciplinary and
> grievance procedures, p.216;
> Discrimination, p.222; Employment
> contracts, p.273; Notice periods,
> p.531; Retirement, p.636

Sources of further information

ACAS: www.acas.org.uk/index.aspx?articleid=871

Employers should have a clear record of the policy and procedures for
disciplinary matters to provide clear guidance to employees on the procedure
that will be followed by their employer. Workplace Law Group's *Non-Contractual
Disciplinary and Dismissal Policy and Management Guide, v.3.0* can also act
as a checklist for managers, in relation to the steps that should be taken, with a
view to minimising procedural irregularities and allegations of unfair treatment.

The draft policy also comes with a nine-page Management Guide containing
helpful notes on the policy and alternative provisions for employers. For more
information visit www.workplacelaw.net/Bookshop/PoliciesAndProcedures.

Display screen equipment

Andrew Richardson, Scott Wilson

Key points

- Use of display screen equipment (DSE) constitutes an adverse health condition.
- Workers using or operating DSE can suffer postural problems, visual problems, and fatigue and stress.
- Employers must identify users or operators – those whose normal work is to habitually use DSE. Laptops and homeworkers are included.
- Employers must carry out a risk assessment of these people's work, using trained personnel.
- Employers must analyse workstations and ensure they meet minimum standards.
- Employers must provide breaks and variety in the DSE users' or operators' work.
- Employers must provide and pay for eye and eyesight tests, and provide spectacles (where needed for screen-viewing distance), if employees request.
- Employers must provide training and information.

Legislation

- Health and Safety at Work etc. Act 1974.
- Health and safety (Display Screen Equipment) Regulations 1992 (as amended by the Health and Safety (Miscellaneous amendments) Regulations 2002).
- Workplace (Health, Safety and Welfare) Regulations 1992.
- Provision and Use of Work Equipment Regulations 1998.
- Management of Health and Safety at Work Regulations 1999.

Display Screen Equipment Regulations

The Regulations define what is deemed to be DSE, who is deemed to be a 'user' or 'operator' and what a workstation comprises. The criteria for determining who can be designated as a user or operator, as updated in 2002, state that it will be generally appropriate to classify people as a user or operator if they:

- normally use DSE for continuous or near-continuous spells of an hour or more at a time; and
- use DSE in this way more or less daily; and
- have to transfer information quickly to or from the DSE; and
- need to apply high levels of attention and concentration; or
- are highly dependent on DSE or have little choice about using it; or
- need special training or skills to use DSE.

The Regulations require that all employers carry out a suitable and sufficient risk assessment on the workstations and it is suggested that a suitable way is to use an ergonomic checklist. Within the appendices of the Regulations is an example of a checklist that can be used. The checklist aids the employer in assessing the following:

Display screen
- Are the characters clear and readable?
- Is the text size adequate?
- Is the image stable?
- Is the screen size suitable?
- Can you adjust the screen brightness and contrast?
- Can the screen swivel and tilt?
- Is it free of glare and reflections?
- Are there window coverings in an adequate condition?

Keyboard
- Is it separate from the screen?
- Does it tilt?
- Is there a comfortable keying position?
- Does the user have a good keyboard technique?
- Are the keys easily readable?

Mouse / trackball
- Is it suitable for the task?
- Is it close to the user?
- Is there wrist/forearm support?
- Does it work smoothly?
- Can the software adjust the pointer speed and accuracy?

Software
- Is the software suitable for the task?

Furniture
- Is the work surface large enough?
- Can the user reach all of the equipment?
- Are the surfaces free from glare?
- Is the chair suitable and stable?
- Does the chair adjust in terms of back height and tilt, seat height, swivel mechanism and castors, etc.?
- Is the back supported, are the arms horizontal and eyes the same height as the top of the VDU?
- Are the user's feet flat on the floor?

Environment
- Is there room to change the position?
- Is the lighting suitable?
- Is the air comfortable?
- Is the heating level comfortable?
- Are the levels of noise comfortable?

The user / operator
- Have they any problems?
- Have they experienced discomfort?
- Do they know of their entitlement to eye and eyesight testing?
- Do they take regular breaks?

Trained personnel, generally meeting the following criteria, must carry out these assessments. They must be familiar with the main requirements of the DSE Regulations and should have the ability to:

- identify hazards and assess risks;
- draw upon additional sources of information on risk as appropriate;
- draw valid and reliable conclusions from assessments and identify steps to reduce risk;
- make a clear record of the assessment and communicate findings to those who need to take action and to the worker concerned; and
- recognise their own limitations as to the assessment so that further expertise can be called upon if necessary.

These assessments must be reviewed whenever:

- a major change occurs to the software, equipment or workstation;
- the workstation is relocated;
- the environment is changed; or
- there is a substantial change to the tasks or amount of time using DSE.

The purpose of the risk assessment is to reduce the risk of the workforce suffering postural problems, visual problems, and fatigue and stress.

Regulation 3 clarifies that the Regulations apply to all workstations, not just those used by users or operators. The Regulations require all employers to ensure their workstations meet the requirements set out in the schedule encompassed within the Regulations. This includes the use of laptop computers and homeworking.

The Regulations set out the criteria for ensuring that the daily work routine of users will not contribute towards any of the risks identified earlier and advises on the nature and timing of breaks. If you are a user or operator, then Regulation 5 places a duty upon the employer to provide eyesight tests and special corrective appliances (normally spectacles) for DSE use. The Regulations require that all users or operators be provided with information on a number of relevant points including:

- the DSE Regulations themselves;
- risk assessment and means of reducing risk;
- breaks and activity changes;
- eye and eyesight tests; and
- to have initial training and training when the workstation is modified (Regulation 6).

Appendices within the Regulations give guidance on the use of laptop computers and compliance with the Regulations and the use of mouse, trackball or other pointing devices.

See also: Eye and eyesight tests, p.305; Health surveillance, p.392; Homeworking, p.406; IT security, p.433; Risk assessments, p.639

Sources of further information

The main source of information in relation to the use of DSE is L26 *Work with Display Screen Equipment – Health and Safety (Display Screen Equipment) Regulations 1992 as amended by the Health and Safety (Miscellaneous Amendments) Regulations 2002 – Guidance on Regulations* (HSE Books 2003) ISBN: 0 7176 2582 6. The document provides all the guidance needed by employers and identifies further documentation that is relevant.

The HSE's recommended guide for most employers is HSG 90 *The law on VDUs: An easy guide: Making sure your office complies with the Health and Safety (Display Screen Equipment) Regulations 1992 (as amended in 2002)* (HSE Books 2003) ISBN: 0 7176 2602 4.

A shorter basic guide, *Working with VDUs,* can be downloaded at www.hse.gov.uk/pubns/indg36.pdf.

Dress codes

Jackie Thomas, Berwin Leighton Paisner

Key points

Employers seek to apply dress codes to their employees for many reasons. In doing so, however, it is important that employers consider any potentially discriminatory implications as dress codes have historically been challenged under both the Sex Discrimination Act 1975 (SDA) and Race Relations Act 1976 (RRA).

Furthermore, since the European Convention on Human Rights has been incorporated into UK law by way of the Human Rights Act 1998 (HRA), it may also be possible to challenge the application of a dress code on the basis that it infringes the employee's human rights.

To avoid potential liability, employers should ensure that the policy applies evenly to both men and women and that any requirements imposed are reasonable when balancing the rights of the employee and the requirements of the employer's business.

Factors that may be relevant include:

- whether the employee has contact with the public;
- whether the dress code is necessary for performance;
- health and safety; and
- illegality.

Legislation

- Sex Discrimination Act 1975.
- Race Relations Act 1976.
- Human Rights Act 1998.
- The Employment Equality (Religion or Belief) Regulations 2003.

In what situations will an employer seek to enforce a dress code?

Dress codes are used in the workplace for a number of reasons. Firstly, dress codes may be applied for reasons of food hygiene. Secondly, employers may require employees to wear a uniform in order to signify their status (for example a ticket inspector). Finally they are also used by many employers merely as a way of ensuring that their employees are dressed appropriately (where the employees concerned come into contact with the employer's clients or customers).

The impact of the SDA on dress codes

The SDA provides that it is discriminatory for an employer to treat an employee less favourably than it would treat an employee of the opposite sex. This amounts to direct discrimination and the employer cannot defend such a claim on the grounds that the treatment is justified.

There are numerous cases of employees claiming that their employer's dress code is directly discriminatory. Examples include provisions of policies that prevented female employees from wearing trousers or that prevented male employees from having long hair. Interestingly, two Tribunals simultaneously considered whether it was discriminatory for a policy to require a male employee to wear a tie; each Tribunal reached conflicting conclusions – in one case finding that such a policy was discriminatory and in the other concluding that the employer's policy was acceptable.

The reasoning for this conflict is that tribunals will not directly compare the treatment of men and women in respect of each requirement of the dress code. The crucial issue will be whether, when viewed as a whole, the policy treats men and women in a generally equivalent manner in order to enforce a "common principle of smartness". In fact, this principle was expressly reaffirmed by the EAT in relation to the appeal of the case in which the Tribunal had found the dress code to be discriminatory. The EAT held that the policy did require women to dress to an equivalent level of smartness (despite the fact that they did not do so in practice) and so the Tribunal should properly have considered whether the requirement for a man to wear a collar and tie with no specific requirements for what a woman should wear was in itself discriminatory. The Tribunal had not considered this point and so the matter was remitted to a fresh Tribunal.

Potential claims under the RRA

It is also possible for claims to arise under the RRA if an employer has a disparate impact on a particular racial group. An example which resulted in a claim was a policy that required a Sikh to shave his beard for health and safety reasons. The employee claimed that this amounted

to indirect discrimination (in that it was more difficult for Sikhs as a racial group to comply). However the Tribunals held that the employer's actions were justifiable as the policy was in place for reasons of food hygiene. To the extent that such a requirement could not be justified it would be discriminatory. Historically, such claims were limited by the fact that the RRA did not prevent discrimination on the grounds of religious belief unless the individual could also be said to fall within a particular racial group; however this loophole has now been closed by the introduction of the Employment Equality (Religion or Belief) Regulations 2003.

This issue also arose in the *Azmi v. Kirklees Metropolitan Council* case, which held that the refusal by a school to permit a Muslim teaching assistant to wear a veil did not amount to either direct or indirect race discrimination. The Tribunal and the EAT both found that this treatment did not amount to direct discrimination (on the basis of the correct comparator being a person who wore a face covering but was not Muslim). They went on to find that it was not indirect discrimination because the treatment could be justified.

Human Rights issues

As well as being potentially discriminatory, is also possible for a dress code to infringe an employee's human rights. The European Convention on Human Rights has now been incorporated into UK law by the HRA. Of the rights it enshrines, Article 10 (the right to freedom of expression), Article 9 (freedom of thought, conscience and religion) and Article 14 (prohibition on discrimination) are all relevant when considering dress codes. In the case of most private sector employers, employees will not be able to bring a claim directly under the HRA but the employees of public authorities may be ble to do so. Further, since the Tribunals re required to construe existing laws in way that is compatible with these rights, ture claims based on discrimination

legislation may also need to take into account these rights when balancing the needs of the employer with the rights of the employee.

See also: Discrimination, p.222; Human rights, p.413; Personal Protective Equipment, p.568

Sources of further information

Equality and Human Rights Commission: www.equalityhumanrights.com

Driving at work

Kathryn Gilbertson, Greenwoods Solicitors LLP

Key points
Employers need to manage the use of both the company car driver and the person using his own vehicle for business, using risk assessments and a car policy.

Legislation
- Health and Safety at Work etc. Act 1974.
- Road Traffic Act 1988.
- Management of Health and Safety at Work Regulations 1999.
- The Road Transport (Working Time) Regulations 2005.
- The Health Act 2006.
- The Smoke-Free (Vehicle Operators and Penalty Notices) Regulations 2007.
- The Highway Code.

Road traffic law and the Highway Code
These lay down certain rules and restrictions (e.g. speed limits) and are normally enforced by the police and the courts. While the driver of the vehicle will primarily be held responsible for any offence, employers may also be liable, for instance in setting timetables or schedules so tight that the driver would be breaking speed limits if he attempted to meet them. The Magistrates Act 1980 may also be relevant to employers in England and Wales who aid, abet, counsel or procure an offence. Employers are responsible for ensuring their company vehicles are properly taxed and insured.

Health and safety legislation
Employers should manage the at-work road journeys and other on-the-road work activities within their usual health and safety protocol. Occupational drivers or people employed to work on or by roads should be offered the same protection as those working within fixed workplaces. Employers also have a responsibility to ensure that others are not put at risk by th work activities of their employees.

Any breach of an employer's statutory or regulatory duties towards its employees giving rise to criminal liability may also be relied upon by a civil claimant as evidence of an employer's breach of duty in a negligence action and indeed in support o a claim for constructive dismissal.

There has been a growing emphasis since the publication of the Work-related Road Safety Task Group's Report recommendations in 2001 (see Sources of further information) towards health and safety legislation and the responsibility of employers to take precedence in any work related vehicle accident.

In light of this it is important that employer implement a health and safety policy for driving at work and keep abreast of the developments affecting workplace driving. The main areas are currently:

- working time;
- mobile phones;
- regulatory compliance;
- risk assessment; and
- smoking.

Workplace Law Networ
www.workplacelaw.ne

Working time

The Road Transport (Working Time) Regulations 2005

The Regulations cover mobile workers who will, in the main, be drivers and accompanying crew involved in road transport activities in a vehicle that is required by EU laws to have a tachograph (Council Regulation 3821/85 on recording equipment in road transport). The new Regulations broadly mirror the provisions of the WTR:

- A mobile worker's working time shall not exceed an average 48-hour working week, typically calculated over a four-month reference period;
- A maximum of 60 hours may be worked in a single week (provided that the average working week does not exceed 48 hours);
- There is a ten-hour limit for night workers over a 24-hour period;
- Workers cannot work more than six consecutive hours without taking a break. If working between six and nine hours, a break of at least 30 minutes is required. If working over nine hours, breaks totalling 45 minutes are required. Each break may be made up of separate periods of not less than 15 minutes each.
- The Regulations will not affect self-employed drivers until 2009. Other drivers who fall outside the scope of the new Regulations, such as drivers of smaller vehicles or drivers exempt from the EU Drivers Hours Rules, have been covered by the WTR; for example, the 48-hour average working week and the need for adequate rest. However, unlike the WTR, employees covered by the new Regulations cannot 'opt out'.
- Employers will monitor working time and should do what they can to ensure the limits are not breached. Records need to be kept for two years. Generally speaking, annual

leave / sick leave cannot be used to reduce the average working time of a mobile worker. For each week of leave that is taken, 48 hours working time must be added to their working time; for each day's leave, eight hours must be added to working time.
- If no employer exists, the agency, employment business or even the worker themselves will monitor working time. The Regulations introduce a new method of calculating average working time. Reference periods are fixed by the calendar, running from April to July; August to November; and December to March for calculating the average 48-hour week. (Other reference periods and other methods of calculating average working time are possible under a relevant agreement.)

For further guidance on working time issues: www.dft.gov.uk/162259/165226/roadtransportworkingtimeguid3241

Mobile phones

Motorists can be prosecuted for driving while using a hand-held mobile phone. Drivers committing this offence will be liable to pay a £60 fixed penalty or a maximum fine on conviction in court of £1,000. (Lorry, bus and coach drivers face a fine of £2,500.) The offence also attracts three penalty points.

The 2003 Regulations apply in all circumstances other than when the vehicle is parked, with the engine off. This means that the prohibition applies even if a vehicle has paused at traffic lights, stopped in a temporary traffic jam, or is in very slow-moving traffic.

The definition of 'hand-held' means a mobile phone or other device which is held at some point during the course of making or receiving a call or fulfilling some other interactive communication function.

An interactive communication function includes sending or receiving oral or written messages, facsimile documents, or still or moving images, or accessing the internet.

The DfT has devised that the pushing of buttons on a phone while, for example, it is in a cradle, on the steering wheel or on the handlebars of a motorbike is allowed, provided that the phone is not held. Hands-free products which do not require drivers to significantly alter their position in relation to the steering wheel in order to use them have not fallen foul of the change in the law.

Employers' liability
The 2003 Regulations also created an offence of "causing or permitting" another person to drive while using a hand-held phone or other similar device. Employers may, therefore, be prosecuted if they require their employees to use their phones when driving.

The DfT has stated that employers cannot expect their employees to make or receive mobile phone calls while driving. This must be reflected in the company's health and safety policy and risk management policy. Information from the DfT indicates that employers will not be liable simply for supplying a telephone or for telephoning an employee who was driving. However, employers must send a clear message to employees that they are forbidden to use their hand-held mobile phones while driving and their employer will not require them to make or receive calls when driving.

Employers should inform their staff that, when driving, hand-held mobile phones should be switched off, or, if switched on, the calls should be left to go through to voicemail, and that a safe place to stop should be found to check messages

and return calls. Company policy should specify that using a hand-held phone or similar device while driving is a criminal offence and will be treated as a disciplinary matter.

If no policy is implemented and employers are shown to have permitted the use of a hand-held mobile phone while driving, they may be:

- liable under the Road Vehicles (Construction and Use) Regulations 2003;
- vicariously liable if an employee causes an accident while driving on business;
- liable under the Health and Safety at Work etc. Act 1974 as employers are obliged to provide a safe system of work and to do what they reasonably can to ensure the safety of staff and others; and
- liable if there is a fatal accident involving the use of a hand-held mobile phone while driving. Where this practice was well known and encouraged throughout the company, there could be the possibility of a criminal corporate manslaughter prosecution against directors, as has been the case with reference to the Working Time Regulations. The Corporate Manslaughter and Corporate Homicide Act 2007 will undoubtedly affect such prosecutions.

Hands-free mobile phones
Hands-free kits are widely available and the use of these kits is still legal. However, employers should be aware that this does not mean that drivers will be exempt from prosecution altogether if they use hands-free kits. Dangerous and careless driving can still be committed as separate offences under the Road Traffic Act 1988.

Research shows that using a hands-free phone while driving distracts the driver nd increases the risk of an accident. Therefore, although it is thought that a hands-free ban would be unenforceable, nevertheless employers should seriously consider if it is safest for them to ban employees using hands-free equipment too. Many businesses have employed an outright ban.

Employers who install hands-free kits should balance the commercial advantage of this with the potential risk of future liability, were an employee to cause an accident while speaking on the phone and driving.

General guidance

- Switch off the phone while driving and let it take messages.
- Alternatively, leave the phone switched on and let the call go into voicemail.
- Alternatively, ask a passenger to deal with the call.
- Find a safe place to stop before turning off the engine and picking up the messages and returning calls.

Regulatory compliance (the vehicle risk assessment)

All vehicles should be taxed, insured, kept in a roadworthy condition and have an up-to-date MOT where necessary.

Employers should check that privately-owned vehicles are not used for work purposes unless they comply with the above and are additionally insured for business use.

Risk assessment

Driving at work requires three types of risk assessment:

1. the driver;
2. the vehicle; and
3. the route.

The driver must be competent. Regular reviews of driving licences will identify those with repeat endorsements which

may suggest that they should no longer be allowed to drive on company business. Equally, receiving a report on someone's medical condition could mean that they are no longer fit to drive.

Full insurance and vehicle safety checks/servicing should be carried out on a regular basis. Documents should be retained. A corporate checklist could be issued covering those frequently required checks – condition of tyres, windows, lights and bulbs, wiper blades, water jets, and the level of essential fluids.

The route needs to be assessed to identify whether drivers:

- can reach the appointment without excessive speeds;
- need to incorporate an overnight stop; and
- whether there is the potential for tiredness as a result of a long drive and long working day.

Managing work pattern, namely the route and driver, effectively can reduce the amount of unnecssary journeys and reduce the potential for a culture of risk-taking through tiredness or unachievable targets.

Smoking

The Health Act 2006 provided that all enclosed public places and workplaces are smoke-free. This includes company, pool and hire vehicles. If a work vehicle is used as a workplace by more than one person it will have to be smoke-free at all times. The legislation does not extend to private vehicles. If a private vehicle is used for work and the employee doesn't ever use it with others, it is permissible to smoke in that vehicle. There is no guidance available at present with regard to vehicles when used for primarily private journeys but sometimes used for business together with others. Owners or managers of smoke-free premises will be guilty of an offence if they fail to prevent people from smoking. 'No smoking' signs must be displayed in all work vehicles. The smoking legislation has some areas that are difficult and will undoubtedly give rise to some form of challenge in the years to come. Managers should as a matter of good practice require that vehicles be smoke-free.

Workplace transport cases
A case which illustrates the combination of working time and dangerous driving and which resulted in a manslaughter conviction for the company director is that of *R v. Melvyn Spree* (Keymark case) of December 2004.

Melvyn Spree, a road haulage director, was jailed for seven years after one of his lorry drivers fell asleep at the wheel and killed three motorists. It was held that Melvyn Spree, a director of Keymark Services, encouraged and enabled his drivers to work dangerously long hours, through fraudulent record-keeping and tachograph tampering. Melvyn Spree's fellow director, Lorraine March, was also jailed for conspiracy offences and Keymark Services was fined £50,000 for manslaughter.

Police investigations had found that the driver, Stephen Law, was part-way through an 18-hour shift when the accident occurred. The police also discovered systematic abuse of working hours restrictions. Drivers were rewarded with a profit-share scheme. Melvyn Spree showed drivers how to jam tachographs and to keep false records of working times that demonstrated legal compliance.

The Keymark case resembled the 2003 conviction of another haulage company owner, Martin Graves of M J Graves International. In that case, Graves was

jailed for four years for the manslaughter of a motorist hit by one of his lorries. The jury accepted that Graves had been grossly negligent in not having a system for controlling his drivers' hours. It also convicted Graves of four offences of falsifying tachograph records, for which he was given four concurrent one-year prison terms.

In December 2005 Raymond Knapman, partner at R&D Drivers, was prosecuted for manslaughter but acquitted after it could not be established that a fatal accident involving the deaths of two lorry drivers was caused by excessive hours or a heart attack by one of the drivers. However, Knapman was subsequently charged with eight counts of obtaining property by deception due to consistently requiring drivers to work excessive hours. Knapman pleaded guilty to the offences and to a breach of section 3(2) of the HSWA for failing to ensure the health and safety of persons not in his employment and was sentenced to two-and-a-half-years' imprisonment in January 2006.

In Criminal Proceedings against Skills Motor Coaches Ltd and others C-297/99 European Court of Justice – 18.01.01 it was held that a driver who went to a specific place, other than the undertaking operating centre, indicated to him by his employer in order to take over and drive a vehicle, was satisfying an obligation towards his employer. During that journey therefore, he did not freely dispose of his time. The court had already held that 'period of work' for the purposes of the Regulations included times at which the driver was actually engaged in activities having a bearing on driving, including driving time (Michielsen C-394/92 (1994) ECR I-2497). Time spent by a driver to reach the place where he took over a tachograph vehicle was liable to have a bearing on his driving, in that it would affect his state of tiredness. In the light of the aim of improving road safety, such time had to be regarded as forming part of all other periods of work within the meaning of Article 15 of Council Regulation 3821/85 on recording equipment in road transport. The question of whether the driver had received precise instructions as to how he should travel was not decisive. By going to a specific place at some distance from his employer's operating centre, the driver was performing a task required of him by virtue of his employment relationship. Therefore, the obligation to record such a period applied regardless of whether it preceded the taking over of a tachograph vehicle. The case of *Eyres v. Atkinson Kitchens and Bathrooms Ltd* (2007) EWCA Civ 365 was before the Court of Appeal in 2007. The circumstances are that the driver (the claimant) was driving on a motorway together with his employer. He lost control of the vehicle and suffered serious injuries. The comments made by the manager received media attention – he told his employee that "sleep was for wimps" when he complained of being tired. The driver also told the court he had been awake for 19 hours before the accident. He said that he had been receiving calls and texting. The original judge awarded his damages with 25% contributory negligence but this was increased to 33% on appeal by the defendant. The case is interesting as it highlighted some unsatisfactory work practices and provided some guidance on the defendant's liability.

Summary

The emphasis has shifted to an investigation of the employer in any workplace accident. It is essential that there is a policy and safety procedure in place so that compliance with health and safety and working time legislation can be seen to be actively implemented and ongoing. This will not only protect against any HSE investigations but will also help to protect against any civil claims.

See also: Corporate manslaughter, p.163; Insurance, p.416; Mobile phones at work, p.510; Smoking, p.660; Vehicles at work, p.701; Working time, p.767

Sources of further information

The HSE web pages on work-related road safety may be found at www.hse.gov.
uk/roadsafety/index.htm

INDG382 *Driving at work: managing work-related road safety* can be downloaded
from www.hse.gov.uk/pubns/indg382.pdf

Managing Occupational Road Risk: The RoSPA Guide is available from RoSPA.
Call 0870 777 2090, or visit www.rospa.org.uk

The Work-related Road Safety Task Group's Report is accessible at www.hse.gov.
uk/roadsafety/traffic1.pdf

Think! Road Safety website: www.thinkroadsafety.gov.uk

Workplace Law Group's *Driving at Work Policy and Management Guide, v.4.0*
helps you cover yourself and your staff and ensure that your employees keep to
the highest standards of safe driving at work. This comprehensive new edition
of the policy and management guide updates several elements of the original
including the implications of recent legislation such as the Health Act 2006, the
Road Safety Act 2007 and the Corporate Manslaughter and Corporate Homicide
Act 2007. If your business hasn't already got a driving at work policy in place, or
your current policy is not up-to-date, this is an essential publication. The policy
highlights the issue of liability should prosecution occur following a driving at work
accident, and who might face prosecution as a result. For more details visit www.
workplacelaw.net/Bookshop/PoliciesAndProcedures

Workplace Law Group has also published the new and revised *Driving at Work
2008: Special Report,* updated from the bestselling first edition. As well as
corporate manslaughter legislation the report considers changes to the Road
Safety Act 2006, the smoking ban, mobile phones and the increasing number
of environmental schemes affecting vehicles. Written by experts in the field, this
new Special Report is packed with extensive, up-to-date, high-level research and
provides a unique insight into practical measures required to comply with the law.
For more information visit www.workplacelaw.net/Bookshop/SpecialReports

NEBOSH National General Certificate

osh
ted Centre
61

New for 2009

NEBOSH National General Certificate by four modes of study:

1. Classroom learning

2. Fast-track learning

3. Blended learning

4. E-learning

The NEBOSH: National General Certificate in Occupational Safety and Ith is specifically designed for facilities nagers and health and safety managers.

Certificate is widely acclaimed as leading accredited health and safety lification in the UK with a deserved utation for excellence. The special -release course run by Workplace Training's expert tutors covers issues in facilities management uded in the core NEBOSH syllabus.

NEBOSH National General Certificate recognised and respected by employers ll sectors and will provide you with a lification that is the benchmark standard inst which others are compared.

benefits to your company

Achieve compliance with UK health and safety law

Cut the health and safety risks that apply in your workplace

Understand the principles involved in managing safety and assess potential hazards

Save your company money by cutting the costs of expensive consultants,

and avoiding costly remedial action

- Protect your organisation's reputation as a professional business

- Learn about the latest case studies including the recent legionella case ruling

Syllabus:

Unit NGC1	Management of health & safety
Element 1:	Foundations in health and safety
Element 2:	Role of health and safety policy
Element 3:	Organising for health and safety
Element 4:	Promoting a positive health and safety culture
Element 5:	Risk assessment
Element 6:	Principles of control
Element 7:	Monitoring review and audit
Element 8:	Incident and accident investigation and reporting
Unit NGC2	Controlling workplace hazards
Element 1:	Movement of people and vehicles – hazards and control
Element 2:	Manual and mechanical handling – hazards and control
Element 3:	Working equipment hazards and control
Element 4:	Electrical hazards and control
Element 5:	Fire hazards and control
Element 6:	Chemical and biological health hazards and control
Element 7:	Physical and psychological health hazards and control
Element 8:	Construction activities hazards and control
Unit NGC3	Practical exam

vork
lace
aw
ealth and safety

For information on courses taking place in 2009 call 0871 777 8881

Electricity and electrical equipment

Mahendra Mistry, Bureau Veritas

Key points

Electricity is invisible, odourless and inaudible. Its presence can be detected by switching on a known load, using voltage-detecting instruments or when someone inadvertently touches it.

Accidents involving electric shock are divided into two categories; direct contact and indirect contact. Direct contact is when someone touches a live conductor, i.e. a bare wire or terminal. Indirect contact is when someone touches a metal part of an appliance when there is an earth fault on the appliance, e.g. the body of a washing machine. Measures have to be taken to prevent persons receiving an electric shock from direct and indirect contact.

Whilst contact with live electrical supplies does not always result in fatal injury, the chances of such an outcome are higher than with other types of accident. In any event, the consequences may still be quite severe, for example deep tissue burns, muscle spasms from the shock, fire and/or explosions. It is also worth noting that an electric shock to someone working at height can result in a serious fall.

The nature of portable appliances is such that they are often subject to mechanical abuse; for example a drill being lowered by dangling it on its cable; tools being accidentally dropped. This probably explains why about 25% of all reportable electrical accidents involve portable electrical equipment. To reduce the risk that damaged or faulty portable equipment might harm someone, the Electricity at Work Regulations 1989 require that portable electrical equipment (or any portable appliance) is tested at appropriate regular intervals. The intervals are not prescribed but are left to the judgement of competent persons. Guidance on suggested intervals can be obtained from the HSE and the Institute of Electrical Engineers (IEE).

Legislation

- Electricity at Work Regulations 1989.
- Provision and Use of Work Equipment Regulations 1998.
- Management of Health and Safety at Work Regulations 1999.

The Electricity at Work Regulations 1989 emphasise the duties and responsibilities of the 'Duty Holder' to ensure that all electrical installations and equipment is selected, installed and maintained at all times in a safe condition to prevent danger. The duty holder is anyone who looks after a premise(s), including an MD, director or manager, or carries out any electrical work.

It also states that only competent persons, who have the technical and practical

nowledge of the electrical equipment and
ave had sufficient training and experience
1 that class of work, should work on such
lectrical equipment and installations.

New guidance document on safe electrical Installations

The 17th edition of the Wiring Regulations,
BS 7671:2008, came into force on 1 July
2008 and applies to all new electrical
installations. Compliance will enable
companies to demonstrate conformity
with the relevant parts of Electricity at
Work regulations, should an incident
occur.

As a result of the changes, Residual
Current Devices that prevent electric
shocks must now be installed on socket
outlets and tested annually. Consideration
must also be given to emergency escape
and warning systems, whilst facilities
provided to ensure life support systems
must have back-up power.

Newly-installed equipment must not emit
dangerous levels of magnetic fields. In
addition, the installation's documentation
must be up-to-date and inspection, and
testing must be undertaken periodically by
a competent person.

A major step forward has been the
reduction of disconnection times to reduce
electric shock exposure and fire risk.
Consideration has also been given to
climate change by enabling the monitoring
and control of energy use.

Causes of electrical faults

All electrical installation deteriorates
over time. Factors affecting the rate of
deterioration include the environment
(dusty, wet, vibration, temperature,
etc.), loading, utilisation of plant (24/7
operations), mechanical damage,
general wear and tear and the level of
maintenance.

The harm caused by faulty electrical
equipment can vary from personal injury to
property damage. Typical causes of such
faults are:

- damaged or worn insulation;
- inadequate or sloppy systems of work;
- over-rated protection (fuses, circuit breakers);
- poor earthing of appliances;
- carelessness and complacency;
- overheated apparatus, e.g. poor ventilation;
- earth leakage;
- loose contacts and connectors;
- inadequate ratings of circuit components;
- unprotected connectors; and
- poor maintenance and testing.

How to avoid accidents involving electricity

The Electricity at Work Regulations 1989
state that "work on or near to an electrical
system shall be carried out in such a
manner as not to give risk, so far as is
reasonably practicable, to danger". In
addition, they require that:

"No person shall be engaged in any work
activity on or so near any live conductor
(other than one suitably covered with
insulating material so as to prevent
danger) that danger may arise
unless:

- it is unreasonable in all the circumstances for it to be dead; and
- it is reasonable in all the circumstances for him to be at work on or near while it is live; and
- suitable precautions (including, where necessary, the provision of suitable protective equipment) are taken to prevent injury."

This latter requirement makes it clear
that working on live equipment is not
something that is ok to do just because

you are an electrician. It prohibits work on live equipment other than in exceptional circumstances, e.g. where other risks to life might exist if the supply were isolated. It should be remembered that testing is also live working and that many faults can be detected safely with the power switched off.

As previously mentioned, many electrical accidents involve the use of portable equipment. The position of the user, for example on a ladder, the tight grip on the equipment, damp conditions, etc. can all conspire to increase the risk of serious or fatal injury. It is therefore important to ensure that:

- the equipment is fit for purpose, e.g. suitable protection from weather conditions;
- low voltage equipment is used where possible, e.g. 110 volt transformers, battery powered tools etc.;
- the proper protective devices are used, i.e. residual current devices for personal protection, fuses/circuit breakers for protection of equipment and wiring;
- staff are adequately trained and competent, e.g. in simple inspection procedures;
- a fault reporting system exists;
- routine inspection and maintenance is undertaken by a competent person; and
- PPE is used where appropriate.

Testing of fixed electrical installations
Fixed electrical installations, i.e. the wiring, distribution (fuse) boards, lighting, etc. also need to be tested periodically. This is because much of what makes up the installation is hidden, perhaps in roof voids, conduits, walls, etc. and thus any developing faults may be overlooked until it is too late. Many fires are caused by cables overheating in attics or between floors. It is therefore

necessary for installations to be tested by a competent person at appropriate intervals, for example at least every five years for commercial premises and three years for industrial locations. Periodic inspection and testing is an essential part of a maintenance programme and assists the duty holder in meeting with parts of the requirements of maintenance as required by the Electricity at Work Regulations 1989.

Portable Appliance Testing (PAT)
Portable equipment is defined by the HSE as equipment that is "not part of a fixed installation but may be connected to a fixed installation by means of a flexible cable and either a socket and plug or a spur box or similar means". Included in the definition are the extension leads that are often used to supply electricity to portable equipment. Testing of portable electrical equipment should be carried out at appropriate regular intervals in order to ensure safety in use.

Since there is no statutory inspection period for such equipment, many employers have set inspection regimes requiring all portable electrical equipment to be tested annually. This may well be inappropriate (and unnecessarily costly), since a personal computer is unlikely to suffer the same rigorous use as an electrically operated disc cutter or power drill. The frequency of PAT therefore should reflect the usage of the equipment and will depend on factors such as nature of the task, frequency of use and environmental conditions (e.g. indoor / outdoor use). It should also be noted that it is highly beneficial to train appliance users to carry out simple visual inspections.

Dealing with electric shocks
It is worth bearing in mind that a few milliamps (one-thousandth of one amp)

s sufficient to cause serious injury
or death. The energy in a 60 W light bulb
s sufficient to electrocute four people
simultaneously.

The critical factor when dealing with a
person receiving an electric shock is to
isolate the victim from the supply. This
of course poses the risk that the person
helping may suffer an electric shock in the
process, e.g. by grabbing the victim whilst
the electricity is still passing through him/
her. It is therefore extremely important
that where there is a significant risk of
electric shock occurring, for example in
switch-rooms, adequate first aid measures
are in place. These would be in addition to
general requirements for first-aid provision

in the workplace. First-aiders should be
trained as a minimum to:

- protect themselves and others;
- adequately assess the situation –
  making sure that it is safe to approach
  the casualty;
- isolate the casualty from the electrical
  supply, either by isolating the electrical
  supply or by pulling the casualty clear
  with a dry insulator, e.g. rubber gloves,
  rope, newspaper, wooden pole;
- stand on an insulating surface, e.g.
  rubber mat, dry wood;
- avoid touching the casualty's bare skin;
- give first-aid treatment for
  electrocution, e.g. cardio-pulmonary
  resuscitation; and
- summon assistance.

> *See also*: First aid, p.333; Health
> and safety at work, p.364; Personal
> Protective Equipment, p.568

Sources of further information

HSE – Electrical safety at work: www.hse.gov.uk/electricity/index.htm

Emergency procedures and crisis management

Peter Power, Visor Consultants Ltd

Key points

This chapter focuses on the important actions to take as soon as a likely crisis starts to unfold. Prompt actions during the acute phase of a catastrophe will considerably determine the amount of damage to reputation, business, and property as well as injuries to people that might otherwise follow. It is important to distinguish between Emergency Procedures (EP) and Crisis Management (CM):

- Emergency proedures differs from crisis Management insofar they are knee-jerk procedures to an event, such as rehearsed fire escape or other evacuation drills. Such reactions are driven more by compliance with health and safety rules than anything else. This includes reference to a range of legislation such as the Management of Health and Safety at Work Regulations.
- CM on the other hand, is much more aligned to Business Continuity (BC) and the need to take immediate and highly flexible steps when any crisis starts to unfold, often without knowing a great deal about the origin of the crisis. For example, a sudden fracture in the supply chain, urgent product recall or terrorist bomb threat.

Readers should note, however, that the existing BSI standard 25999 specifying BC Management refers to 'incident' rather than CM, but with the caveat that the same structure can also be referred to as crisis management. Since the latter is a more commonly accepted term applied to the sudden onset of a calamity it is therefore used in this chapter.

For more details, see *'Business Continuity Management', p.100.*

CM is a multi-level management process, which deals with situations or events that are outside the normal management capability of the organisation at the time of the event. CM encompasses management principles that are non-sector-specific and will include analysis, planning, selection, training, exercising, rehearsing and testing. Four key features confirm the need for all organisations to much better prepare and rehearse CM procedures:

1. *Organisational culture, attitude and ability to respond.* The organisational culture and perception of the event and its impact is likely to determine the way an organisation responds to a crisis. Resources may be invoked to handle a situation, only to find that they have inappropriate levels of skills and/or experience. Consequently, what is an easily managed situation for one organisation may indeed be a 'crisis' for another.

....

Interdependency. More and more organisations have become critically dependent on other separate companies so that a failure at any point in the chain will quickly spread up or downstream. The effect is exacerbated by 'Just in Time' operating procedures applied by almost all organisations. There is therefore, little if any slack in operating systems to absorb the impact of an unchecked crisis, compared to how companies used to operate several years ago.

Complexity. Modern organisations are complex environments, which have multi-layered and multi-dimensional hierarchies of dependencies and interdependencies and as such need proactive strategies to ensure against system failure. It is rare to be dealing with a simple, well-bounded situation. Many situations are, or become, a combination of factors, some of which are ill defined; perhaps involving reputation or potential loss of confidence in the product, service or organisation. Others are of the creeping or rising-tide variety, with consequent unfortunate delays in the invocation of response plans; or events may be external to the organisation and the possible impacts not fully appreciated at first.

Nature of potential impact and consequences. Despite analysis of impact and probability, and decisions made regarding treatment, it is conceivable that planning for a particular impact or consequence may not be justified economically. Such events may still occur to the organisation and the impact may indeed be substantial. Alternatively, an organisation may not have fully analysed or appreciated the possible extent and wider consequences of an event or combination of events (e.g. looking only at the direct economic consequences) and be then

required to take action in unfamiliar circumstances.

Definitions

There are a variety of definitions of 'crisis' that at the time of writing are being considered by the British Standards Institute Crisis Management (CM) Steering Group with a view to publishing a Publicly Available Specification (PAS) later in 2008. This may or may not move to a subsequent stage where a British Standard specifically on CM will be created in identical fashion to BS 25999 mentioned earlier. A review of those definitions so far collated to date has proved that the concept can be controversial. As more research, study and debate will occur while the CM PAS structure and content is developed, the CM PAS Steering Group is not attempting to create a formal defining 'sentence' or 'phrase', but rather work from a list of 'defining features' to use as a starting point for understanding the nature of crises. Therefore, whilst the term 'crisis' still awaits a formal definition, key words and phrases to note may include:

- extraordinary;
- abnormal or unfamiliar situation;
- unanticipated consequences;
- ill-structured problem;
- requires organisation to act;
- requires strategic response;
- may require ad-hoc procedures; and
- decision-making in conditions of uncertainty.

Over the past few years it has become increasingly clear that merely having BC plans in place does not mean an organisation, when suddenly exposed to a catastrophe, can immediately jump to what might be called crisis speed, as opposed to normal speed, and thereby start to operate in what is sometimes referred to as a 'quick time' environment. This is also labelled the acute phase of a crisis where prompt intervention might result in the main BC plans not even being required. However, terms such as emergency and crisis are obviously aligned with each and both shall now be explained.

Legislation
■ Management of Health and Safety at Work Regulations 1999 and associated Regulations.
■ Regulatory Reform (Fire Safety) Order 2005.

The Management of Health and Safety at Work Regulations 1999 require every employer to establish appropriate procedures to be followed in the event of serious and imminent danger to persons at work. This includes the duty of employers or controllers of premises to ensure that any necessary contacts are arranged with external services, particularly with regard to first aid, emergency medical care and rescue work.

Previously the Fire Precautions (Workplace) (Amendment) Regulations 1999 required an employer – or controller of premises – to carry out a fire risk assessment of their premises. This legislation was revoked in April 2006 with the introduction of the Regulatory Reform (Fire Safety) Order 2005 (RRFSO). The duty to carry out fire risk assessments continues to be expressed in the new legislation.

Crisis management
In very serious cases when the build-up of damaging events rapidly passes a certain point normally designated as the border of 'business as usual', a state of chaos often erupts that will need an even more rapid response to counter. This response should focus on the speedy transition from routine to crisis management (CM) styles commensurate with the threat to the business and need to tackle the actual crisis. Equally important is the return to

normality at the earliest opportunity, whic is the second priority for CM.

In any crisis situation there has to be a simple and quickly formed structure to:

■ confirm;
■ control;
■ contain; and
■ communicate,

to then give urgent directions to trigger the correct layer of emergency response, BC or in some cases coordinate the who response without BC (e.g. likely reputatic rather than physical damage).

The place where, conceptually, BC overlaps the actual incident is the point where resources are normally most critical. Where external / market / media perception and pressures overlap the incident will often be the point where the reputation of the target organisation will k in the balance. In the centre of this shoul exist CM.

Very often organisations have not necessarily taken the wrong actions in terms of CM, but probably did the right ones too late, by which time the crisis itself sets the pace and you might end ur following events, rather than getting in front and stopping the spread.

This is the stage where demands for urgent decisions will be at their highest y concomitant with this, accurate informatic about what's going on will be very low. In a nutshell, it's the high risk / low delay in decision-making feature as opposed tc the low risk/high delay in decision-makin, dilemma should a crisis team wait until they get 100% of the facts before making any decision. This will probably result in a good decision being taken too late in whi case it ends up being a bad decision.

Over the past few years there have been signs emerging that the gap between CM and BC is starting to narrow and combine with emergency procedures, especially when we face dramatic threats such as terrorism, flooding, violent protestors, immediate reputation damaged caused by instant media portrayal and so on.

CM should be a process that can be rapidly triggered and should be activated (and often stood down if no further action is needed) whenever a likely crisis starts to become apparent so that:

■ no time is lost identifying the risk and what to do; and
■ you can start pulling the right levers to stimulate reactions at the other non-risk facing end to help you contain and control events. For example, more physical resources, re-routing routes to your building and so on.

The first person or people to act as a crisis manager / CM team probably has to ask themselves five urgent questions to start with:

1. What do we know?
2. What don't we know?
3. What would I like to know?
4. How can I find out?
5. How long have I got?

From the answers to such simple questions a more accurate picture of events should emerge. However, a CM structure needs to be owned, rehearsed and updated as an extension of routine management so it can quickly be called up, but populated only according to anticipated requirements. It also fits comfortably with enterprise risk management to ensure that a uniform approach to risk identification, measurement and treatment is utilised across the whole organisation. By adopting this proactive approach to managing risk

and crises, organisations can move from a 'silo' management approach to a deeper integration of its various businesses to (a) start the alarm ASAP if a crisis approaches and (b) get a pan-company response going without delay. In addition, members of any CM team should:

■ be rehearsed in their roles in advance;
■ have the means to be rapidly contacted;
■ have a set of agreed tools/protocols to help assimilate what is going on;
■ have access to rehearsed decision-making structures / diagrams;
■ have the ability to give accurate and measurable directions;
■ have alternates (not deputies) available if not available;
■ be the supreme executive layer at the commencement of any crisis response;
■ have an agreed quorum;
■ operate in a high risk / no blame culture to encourage rather than deter prompt decision-making;
■ have direct linkage to any BC / emergency procedures plan;
■ have immediate access to legal, HR, welfare, business, finance, IT and media advice (often as core team members); and
■ have the ability to get a Media-holding statement ready in 15-30 minutes.

The CM priorities are derived from the principle that at the very least, two activities need to be dealt with concurrently:

1. *CM* – any crisis needs to be recognised for what it is – and what it might cause. It might easily create other crises that could have a negative impact on reputation. The crisis or incident needs to be addressed and handled effectively since damage to reputation represents one of the most serious impacts of any crisis.

2. *Core business* – the position of all
    core business activities needs to be
    established and a decision taken on
    what to do next. Perhaps to trigger the
    BC plan to continue operations, albeit
    on a reduced scale.

These activities involve three key types
of managerial decisions to separate the
main groups of tasks to reduce overload
risk, whilst a clear decision route is
maximised. As far as possible this should
reflect routine management structure, but
modified since truly routine structures do
not work for non-routine events:

1. Strategic / executive direction.
2. Controlling the incident.
3. Operational tasks.

People not forming the core of any
CM team should not feel obliged to
communicate if they have nothing direct
to contribute, or feel left out if their opinion
is not sought at this stage. CM is about
going through decision-making processes
in minutes rather than hours and avoiding
mere discussions. It is also very much
about action-centred leadership. It's
important that any CM team:

- understands how media awareness
  is a key part of effective crisis
  management;
- appreciates the appetite and
  constraints of the media;
- accepts the ramifications of good or
  bad media handling;
- decides when, or if, to stand in front
  of a camera or microphone and who
  does it (normally the most senior
  person available and as close to the
  'site' as possible);
- understands how to deal with invited
  and uninvited media intrusion; and
- understands how to choose the best
  conditions to face the press, if not ideal.

Emergency procedures

Emergency evacuation plan
Any fire risk assessment (see below)
should enable the employer, or controller
of premises where more than one
business is based, to formulate an
emergency evacuation plan in the event of
fire and most major incidents or accidents.
It should, however, be recognised in
today's climate that potential terrorist
actions may be significant in the premises
you occupy. Plans should, in these
circumstances, be made for action in the
event of a bomb threat or other terrorist
activity. It may well be necessary to carry
out an additional assessment with this in
mind, since the evacuation procedures for
these threats are often different to those
for fire (see Invacuation, below).
An emergency evacuation plan, regardless
of the cause of the evacuation, would
comprise the following four stages:

1. How staff are enabled to recognise an
    emergency (including what to do with
    hoax calls).
2. Communication of the emergency to
    affected staff.
3. Preparation of staff and/or the building
    for the evacuation.
4. Actions of staff and others (e.g.
    visitors) in the emergency evacuation.

The above stages would lead to a plan
that would cover, as a minimum, the
following points:

- What action should be taken by
  persons discovering an emergency;
- Who is responsible for making contact
  with the emergency services and the
  method of doing so;
- Identification of type of warning alarms
  (bells / klaxons / sirens) to be used
  (this is important as confusion can
  arise over what different alarms mean);
- Location of call points, escape routes,
  duties and identities of persons with

special responsibilities and assembly points i.e. places of safety; Procedures for dealing with the emergency services on arrival (including providing information on risks to them, e.g. presence of asbestos, flammables, etc.); and the training that should be provided for all employees or occupiers.

Emergency invacuation plan

Strictly speaking, no such term exists in the English language, but invacuation is progressively becoming obvious to describe in one word the necessity to actually do the opposite of evacuation and keep people inside a building rather than let them to leave. This is especially true in cases of a bomb threat. In such a scenario is quite likely that a knee-jerk evacuation will cause hundreds of people to spill onto the streets and therefore be exposed to greater danger from, for example, a vehicle bomb.

The UK Government's policy for communicating about terrorist threats is to issue a warning if it is the best way to protect any community or venue facing a specific and credible threat. Public safety is the absolute priority. Such advice will be issued immediately if the public need to take specific action. In the event of an incident the message is 'go in, stay in, tune in'.

The 'go in, stay in, tune in' advice is recognised and used around the world. It was developed by the independent National Steering Committee on Warning and Informing the Public as being the best general advice to give people caught up in most emergencies. It follows that creating an invacuation plan makes great sense.

In 2004 the Government published a public information leaflet, *Preparing for Emergencies, What You Need to Know*, which provided common sense advice for a range of different emergency situations, including some information on countering terrorism. With this in mind the key points of invacuation are:

- Before you use a public address system or get line mangers to pass the message to stay in, think about (a) what you are about to say and (b) what you will say. A calm voice in authority works better – especially if you can get hold of the most senior person in the building to make any announcement.
- This is not a time to use words such as 'we would like all staff to consider it a reasonable idea not to leave the building'. If it's necessary to keep everyone inside (and under the umbrella of Duty of Care that includes visitors, contractors and everyone else) it's also necessary to use clear language such as 'this is … speaking. The police have asked us to stay inside … for the time being we have shut all doors, windows … we must all now stay inside … we have plenty of fresh water, clean air here, etc."
- The point above about fresh water, or clean air, warm clothing, ease of communication via the telephone, access to TV sets and so on is very important as a means to attract people to stay inside, rather than risk injury outside.
- If you have an enhanced protection area to minimise the damage of bomb blast, use it.
- Keep all communication lines available to you and be aware that sometimes people inside will take camera images on their mobile phones and they quickly get passed to TV news stations – who will ask for them.
- Make it clear you and/or your team are in command. Give frequent (e.g. every 30 minutes) updates,

even if you have not had any more information. It's vital to reassure people who could easily panic.

Information and training

The plans that have been made will only be successful if properly implemented. It is therefore important that staff and others e.g. occupiers, visitors, etc. are adequately trained or provided with information on what to do in an emergency. When a fire alarm sounds, staff often question whether it is a real emergency or just a drill. Staff should never be in doubt about such matters since delay in evacuation obviously increases the risk to safety.

Information should therefore be available to staff in written form and in a language that they understand. Regular evacuation drills should take place and the performance of these should not only be recorded but should also be reviewed. The frequency of these drills will be determined by the level of risk identified in the assessment.

Use of fire extinguishers

In the workplace, most buildings (and in particular, office blocks) have a number of fire extinguishers. It is not unusual though, to hear staff say "I've never been trained on these," or "I've never had the chance to use one of these". It may be difficult to arrange for staff to actually practice using extinguishers on real fires and thus care needs to be exercised if fire action notices state that persons should tackle the fire with such equipment. Staff can, however, be trained on the choice of, and correct way to use, the proper extinguishers, for example matching the extinguisher to the type of fire. It must be stressed that they should not put themselves at risk in tackling a fire.

Equipment testing

All equipment that could be involved in an emergency evacuation should be tested by competent persons at the required intervals (varying from weekly to annually). This will include:

- detection and alarm system;
- firefighting equipment;
- automatic door release units; and
- emergency lighting.

Records

Although frequency may vary with individual circumstances (i.e. based on the risk assessment), emergency evacuation drills should usually be carried out at least every six months for most buildings. This would usually be every three months if night working at the premises is involved.

The responsibility for ensuring that evacuation drills take place lies with management. The persons appointed to actually coordinate the evacuation; for example, fire wardens, fire marshals, etc., need to report the results of any drill to management in order to identify any shortfalls in the arrangements. Records of drills should be kept by management and should contain such information as:

- exact location of the drill;
- date and time;
- total number of participants;
- the evacuation time;
- any problems identified;
- actions required to be taken; and
- date of next drill.

In addition, records of equipment testing should be maintained.

Fire risk assessment

It is the duty of employers to conduct fire risk assessments of premises under their control. These need not always be complicated exercises but should always involve the following key steps:

Identification of any fire hazards – such as readily combustible materials, highly flammable substances and sources of heat.

Identification of any persons who are especially at risk, and making special provisions for persons with disabilities. Identification of where fire hazards can be reduced or removed.

Recording the findings.

The competent person undertaking the assessment should address the following issues:

- Legal requirements;
- Means of escape;
- Fire alarms / fire detection;
- Special risks e.g. disabled persons, risks to neighbours, etc.;
- Firefighting equipment;
- Emergency lighting;
- Maintenance;
- Housekeeping; and
- Warning / emergency notices.

Emergency procedures and CM combined

Emergency planning should aim, where possible, to prevent emergencies occurring, and when they do occur, good planning and CM should reduce, control or mitigate the effects of the emergency. It is a systematic and ongoing process which should evolve as lessons are learnt and circumstances change.

All emergency and crisis plans should also focus on at least three key groupings of people – the vulnerable, victims (including survivors, family and friends) and responder personnel.

- Vulnerable people may be less able to help themselves in an emergency than self-reliant people. Those who are vulnerable will vary depending on the nature of the emergency, but plans should consider those with mobility difficulties (e.g. those with physical disabilities or pregnant women); those with mental health difficulties; and others who are dependent, such as children.

- Victims of an emergency – which includes not only those directly affected but also those who, as family and friends, suffer bereavement or the anxiety of not knowing what has happened. The impact of such stress / trauma will exist for years if not decades afterwards, so beware of anniversaries, delayed inquests, TV documentaries, etc. that will undoubtedly trigger a recurrence of memories relating to whatever drama initially took place.

- Responder personnel should also be considered. Plans sometimes place unrealistic expectations on management and personnel. Organisations should ensure their plans give due consideration to the welfare of their own personnel. For instance, the emergency services have health and safety procedures that determine shift patterns and check for levels of stress.

Organisations should aim to maintain plans which cover three different areas:

1. *Plans for preventing an emergency.* In some circumstances there will be a short period before an emergency occurs when it might be avoided by prompt or decisive action.

2. *Plans for reducing, controlling or mitigating the effects of an emergency.* The main bulk of planning should consider how to minimise the effects of an emergency, starting with the impact of the event (e.g. alerting procedures) and looking at remedial actions that can be taken to reduce effects. For example, the emergency services may be able to stem the emergency at source by fighting fires, combating the release of toxic chemicals or the extent of floods. The

evacuation of people may be one direct intervention that can mitigate the effects of some emergencies. Recovery plans should also be developed to reduce the effects of the emergency and ensure long-term recovery.

3. *Plans for taking other action in connection with an emergency.* Not all actions to be taken in preparing for an emergency are directly concerned with controlling, reducing or mitigating its effects. Emergency planning should look beyond the immediate response and long-term recovery issues and look also at secondary impacts. For example, the wave of reaction to an emergency can be quite overwhelming in terms of media attention and public response. Plans may need to consider how to handle this increased interest.

As obvious as it sounds, emergency plans should include procedures for determining whether an emergency has occurred, and when to activate the plan in response to an emergency. This should include identifying an appropriately trained person who will take the decision, in consultation with others, on when an emergency has occurred.

The maintenance of plans involves more than just their preparation. Once a plan has been prepared, it must be maintained systematically to ensure it remains up to date and fit for purpose at any time if an emergency occurs.

It may be that multiple organisations can develop a joint emergency plan where the partners agree that, for a successful combined response, they need a formal set of procedures governing them all. For example, in the event that evacuation is required, the police would need carefully pre-planned cooperation from various other organisations such as fire and ambulance services and the local authority, as well as involvement of others such as transport organisations.

UK Government advice

The Civil Contingencies Act 2004 identifies three pieces of legislation pre-dating this Act which were introduced separately in Britain and Northern Ireland under sector-specific legislation operated by the Health and Safety Executive (HSE) and HSE Northern Ireland. These relate to major accident hazards at industrial establishments (Control of Major Accident Hazards Regulations (COMAH)), to hazardous pipelines (Pipelines Safety Regulations) and to radiation hazards (Radiation (Emergency Preparation and Public Information) Regulations (REPPIR). These sector-specific Regulations have established multi-agency emergency planning regimes in cooperation with the operators. To avoid duplication, the Civil Contingencies Act Regulations provide that the duty to maintain plans under the Act does not apply to emergencies that are dealt with by these pieces of legislation.

In the event of a major emergency, whether accidental or deliberate, the Government will start up a central news coordination centre (NCC) to ensure that messages and information to the public, stakeholders and the media are clear, consistent, timely and accurate.

The NCC is on standby at all times and can be activated within 90 minutes of being asked to do so. It works closely to support the central crisis centre, and liaises with communication advisors within the centre, the police strategic coordination centre (SCC) at the scene, and the government liaison team (GLT).

Since 1996 a national Media Emergency Forum (MEF) – a large working group consisting of senior media editors, overnment representatives, local authority mergency planners, emergency services, olice and private industry – has regularly et on a voluntary basis to discuss ommunication issues arising from specific mergencies, and in identifying ways to nprove communications in the future.

he Forum provides a solid framework for leveloping trust and confidence between he media and the authorities through

a growing awareness of each other's responsibilities. In order to recreate this positive formula for progress, separate regional MEFs were established in 2003.

See also: Bomb alerts, p.75; Business Continuity Management, p.100; Occupational health, p.537; Strikes, p.677

Sources of further information

UK Resilience: www.ukresilience.info

Workplace Law Group's *Guide to Business Continuity 2007* provides a framework for business managers to ensure that their organisation has an action plan in place in the event of an emergency situation arising. The Guide covers issues such as Business continuity management (BCM); BC plans; preparing for immediate media interest; BC under the Civil Contingencies Act 2004; the BS: 25999 standard on BC; and crisis management. For more information visit www. workplacelaw.net/Bookshop/GuidesTo.

Employee benefits

Roger Byard, Cripps Harries Hall LLP

Key points

Employers use benefits to attract, retain and provide incentives for employees. Increasingly they are provided as part of an overall strategy designed to achieve defined business objectives. Such benefits take many forms which offer both financial and non-financial rewards and go to make up an employee's total remuneration. The benefits employers make available to employees have seen considerable enlargement in recent years. These now range from traditional occupational pensions and sick pay to flexible working and voluntary arrangements. In this last group the employer offers an amount of cash which employees can use to buy those benefits that reflect their circumstances at the time. However, while offering employees cash to buy their own benefits, employers shift the burden of responsibility to employees, which raises the question of their ability to make an informed choice.

Some benefits have tax advantages, the most obvious being a pension. When determining the value of employee benefits the employer should set targets against which the benefits can be measured. The cost to the employer to administer the benefits should not be underestimated. The impact of the age discrimination legislation (introduced on 1 October 2006) on employee benefits appears to be minimal but has yet to be fully assessed. There are signs that benefits providers are modifying their products to make the level of benefits less age-related.

Legislation

- Equal Pay Act 1970.
- Social Security Contributions and Benefits Act 1992.
- Employment Rights Act 1996.
- Data Protection Act 1998.
- National Minimum Wage Act 1998.
- Income Tax (Earnings and Pensions) Act 2003.
- Finance Act 2003.
- Pensions Act 2004.
- Civil Partnerships Act 2004.
- Work and Families Act 2006.
- Employment Equality (Age) Regulations 2006.

Types of benefit

Financial benefits

These benefits include sick pay, pensions, company cars, bonuses, share option schemes, income protection insurance, medical insurance, life assurance and sports benefits.

Non-financial benefits

Flexitime, home working.

Tax-advantaged benefits

Salary sacrifice, pensions, childcare vouchers, bicycle loans, season ticket loans up to £5,000 and independent financial information worth up to £150 per employee.

Particular benefits

Pensions

Income tax relief is available at an employee's highest marginal rate on their own contributions to a pension

cheme. Employers are able to offset
e contributions they make against
orporation tax. There is also a saving
f both employers' and employees'
ational Insurance contributions. As an
ncouragement to employees to contribute
o their personal pension provision
mployers often offer to match what their
mployees pay in up to certain limits.

alary sacrifice

he employer agrees to provide a benefit
exchange for the employee giving up
art of their gross annual salary. Where for
xample an employee makes a sacrifice
f part of their pay and the employer
nakes an equivalent contribution to their
ension the employee saves on income
ax at their marginal rate. Both employer
nd employee save on National Insurance
ontributions. For lower paid employees
are needs to be exercised as it might
mpact on, for example, the minimum wage.

Healthcare and other risk benefits

These benefits are typically insurance-
based and include occupational sick
pay (where employers pay more than
s provided under the statutory sick pay
scheme), private medical insurance,
critical illness insurance, permanent
health insurance, counselling services
and life assurance. The attraction of these
benefits is the lower cost to employees of
securing the protection which is achieved
through economies of scale. Benefits such
as insurance cover for death in service
and income protection retain a moral or
paternalistic element to them. Recent years
have seen the insurance market harden
and premiums increase substantially. This
s set to continue and prompts questions
about the business rationale for continuing
to provide such benefits.

Company cars and cash allowance

Company cars are commonly provided to
enable an employee to do the job (e.g. a
sales representative) or as a recognition
of status. The Revenue has always taxed
such cars. The basis for taxation is now
referable not only to the make and engine
size but also its environmental impact.
The shift to environmental taxation has
reduced the value of this benefit and as
a result there is a trend for employers to
offer as an alternative a cash sum by way
of an annual allowance to employees who
supply their own vehicle for business use.

Introducing or changing employee
benefits

- Identify the business goals that the
  introduction or modification of benefits
  are intended to support.
- Consult with employees, to learn what
  benefits would be most valued.
- When these have been identified
  thoroughly research the market for the
  best products.
- Promote the introduction of the
  benefits by raising employees'
  awareness of the benefits on offer
  and their value to them according to
  their own circumstances by good and
  effective communication.

Age discrimination

On 1 October 2006 it became unlawful
to discriminate against employees on the
ground of their age. Where decisions are
made or policies applied that are based
on age-related factors there would be
direct discrimination. Employee benefits
are most likely to be affected by indirect
discrimination. This could occur when a
policy, practice or criterion is applied which
disadvantages a group of people who
are defined by their age. This means that
employee benefits that are provided by
reference to length of employment would
be discriminatory as younger workers
are likely to have shorter periods of
employment. For example it is common
for employers to reward employees
with an additional day's holiday after a

number of years of employment. This would be unlawful. Similarly where the amount of an employer's contribution to a pension scheme depends on the length of service of the employee member the practice could be open to challenge for disadvantaging younger people. However, the legislation provides an important exemption for service-related benefits and allows an employer to use a service-related criterion of up to five years.

While an employer may defer providing employee-related benefits to an employee for the first five years of their employment the legislation will not allow an employer to stop providing benefits to an employee reaching a particular age. For example, if an employee works on beyond a retirement age of, say, 65, it will not be possible for an employer to refuse to continue to provide healthcare benefits simply on the ground of cost. An employer who discriminates may try to justify it.

To do so they would need to show on an objective basis that they are pursuing in a proportionate way a legitimate business aim. There have been few cases on the point and it is still thought that employers will find this a difficult test to pass.

Summary
- Employee benefits offer a wide range of financial and non-financial rewards by which employers may attract, retain and incentivise employees.
- It is important that an employer looking to introduce or change benefits has identified clear business goals and analysed how the benefits will relate to their employees.
- For the value of benefits offered to be fully appreciated it is essential that there is effective communication with employees.
- Employers need to be sensitive to anti-discrimination legislation particularly with regard to age.

See also: Flexible working, p.338; Pensions, p.562

Sources of further information

HM Revenue & Customs: www.hmrc.gov.uk

BERR: www.berr.gov.uk

Employee Benefits Research Institute: www.ebri.org

Pension Guide: www.thepensionservice.gov.uk

Pay and Reward Online: www.payandreward.co.uk

CIPD: www.cipd.co.uk

Employee consultation

Kathryn Clapp and Mark McCanney, Taylor Wessing

Key points

- The Information and Consultation of Employees Regulations 2004 (ICER or 'the Regulations') came into force in April 2005. Depending on the number of employees employed in the undertaking the Regulations applied at different stages:
  - undertakings with 150 or more employees from 6 April 2005;
  - undertakings with 100 or more employees from 6 April 2007; and
  - undertakings with 50 or more employees from 6 April 2008.
- Therefore all undertakings with 50 or more employees are now subject to the Regulations.
- The Regulations provide a statutory basis for reaching agreement on the process of keeping employees informed and consulted about matters affecting their employment.
- The request to negotiate an agreement is triggered where either the employer starts the process and wishes to negotiate an existing agreement or introduce a new one or there is a valid employee request. Therefore, there is no automatic obligation on any employer to do anything under the Regulations.
- Where there is a valid pre-existing agreement in place, the employer may ballot the workforce to determine whether they endorse the employee request or whether they are happy with the exisiting agreement.
- If the workforce does not endorse the request, the pre-existing arrangement continues.
- If negotiations fail to lead to agreement, the 'default provisions' will apply.
- If there is no employee request or the employer does not commence negotiations, there is no obligation to establish an information and consultation (I&C) agreement.

Legislation

- Information and Consultation Directive (2002/14/EC).
- Information and Consultation of Employees Regulations 2004.

Introduction

ICER came into force in April 2005 and implemented the EU Information and Consultation Directive. These Regulations are aimed at providing a statutory basis for keeping employees informed and consulted about employment issues which affect them in the workplace. This is a significant piece of legislation which will affect the management of industrial relations in the UK, particularly for employers who are not used to dealing with issues on a collective basis.

The Regulations have been implemented on a phased basis depending on the number of employees in the particular undertaking and the last phase was introduced on 6 April 2008. Now all undertakings in the UK with 50 or more employees are potentially affected by the Regulations.

ICER applies to both public and private undertakings carrying out an economic activity, whether or not operating for gain. It is the number of employees employed by an individual undertaking that is relevant, not those employed by a subsidiary or parent company.

Pre-existing agreements

If there is a valid pre-existing agreement and fewer than 40% of employees in an undertaking make a request for an I&C body, an employer may (but is not obliged to) ballot its workforce to see whether it endorses the request for a new body.

Where a ballot is held, and 40% of the workforce and a majority of those who vote endorse the employee request for a new I&C body, the employer is obliged to negotiate a new agreement (as set out below).

Where fewer than 40% of the workforce or a minority of those voting endorse the employee request for a new agreement, the employer will not be under an obligation to negotiate a new I&C agreement.

ICER sets out the conditions that need to be satisfied to be a valid pre-existing agreement. These include that it must be in writing, cover all the employees of the undertaking, have been approved by them, set out how information is given and how the employees' views on this information will be sought.

The agreement must have been in place before an employee request under ICER was made.

Negotiating an I&C agreement under ICER

There are two ways to trigger negotiations for an I&C agreement:

1. If a valid request under ICER has been made by at least 10% of the employees in an undertaking (subject to a minimum of 15 and a maximum of 2,500 employees); or
2. If the employer initiates the process itself.

Any disputes about the validity of employee requests will be dealt with by the Central Arbitration Committee (CAC).

An employer must initiate negotiations for an agreement as soon as reasonably practicable and within three months at the latest. During this three-month period, the employer must:

- make arrangements for its employees to appoint or elect negotiating representatives; and
- inform employees in writing of the identity of the representatives who have been elected and then invite those representatives to enter into negotiations to reach an ICER agreement.

Negotiations for reaching an agreement may last for up to six months, which is extendable by agreement. If a negotiated agreement is not reached, the 'default model' will apply (see below). There is a further six-month period for an employer to set up the necessary consultation body or reach a negotiated agreement.

Criteria for a negotiated ICER agreement
A negotiated agreement must comply with certain criteria. It must:

- be in writing and dated;
- cover all employees in the undertaking or group of undertakings;
- be signed by or on behalf of the employer;
- set out the circumstances in which employers will inform and consult – ICER gives employers and employees the freedom to agree on the subject matter, method, frequency and timing of information and consultation best

suited to the employer's particular circumstances;

- provide either for the appointment or election of I&C representatives or for information and consultation directly with employees; and
- be approved by the employees.

Duration of agreement

Once a negotiated agreement is in place, there is a three-year moratorium on making further requests.

The 'default model'

If negotiations to reach an agreement fail, the 'default model' will apply. Employers have a further six months to facilitate the election of representatives. This must be via a ballot with one employee representative per 50 employees, subject to a minimum of two and a maximum of 25. If an employer fails to arrange this, it may be subject to a penalty fine of up to £75,000.

Information must be provided to I&C representatives at an appropriate time on:

- the recent and probable development of the undertaking's activities and economic situation;
- the situation, structure and probable development of employment within the undertaking and on any anticipatory measures envisaged, in particular where there is a threat to employment; and
- decisions likely to lead to substantial changes in work organisation or in contractual relations (including those covered by existing legislation in the area of collective consultation on collective redundancies and business transfers).

In respect of the second and third issues, the representatives must be consulted as well as informed.

Other factors

Protection of confidential information

There is a statutory duty of confidentiality on all I&C representatives in respect of information the employer discloses to them. However, they can challenge this duty before the CAC. Employers need not disclose information where to do so would "seriously harm the functioning of the undertaking or be prejudicial to it".

Compliance and enforcement

A complaint may be made to the CAC that an employer has failed to establish a negotiated agreement or has failed to inform and consult with employees in accordance with a negotiated agreement or the default model. This must be done within three months of the failure.

These compliance mechanisms do not apply to pre-existing agreements. The CAC may make a declaration and an order requiring the defaulting party to take such specified steps as are necessary to comply with the I&C agreement within a specific period of time.

There is a maximum penalty of £75,000 for the employer's failure.

Overlapping issues

Where an employer is under information and consultation obligations arising from TUPE or collective redundancy legislation, it is excused from the obligations to consult under ICER, provided it notifies I&C representatives of this.

Protection for I&C representatives

I&C representatives are entitled to reasonable paid time off work during normal working hours and have the right not to be dismissed or suffer any detriment.

Practical steps for employers

Now that the Regulations have come into force for all undertakings with 50 or more employees, employers essentially have the option to either:

- negotiate a voluntary I&C agreement;
- negotiate an I&C agreement with employee representatives once a request has been made; or
- do nothing and allow the default provisions in ICER to apply.

The advantages to an employer of negotiating a voluntary agreement are that it is seen to be proactive, it can seize control of the process and a more flexible agreement may result. The default model is much less flexible with set categories of information and consultation and a predetermined number of representatives.

In preparation and in order to determine which option to follow, employers should:

- carry out an audit of any existing information and consultation processes;
- assess the likelihood of employees making an ICER request or other improvements to existing information and consultation structures;
- develop a strategy for dealing with any request – e.g. how to run internal elections, what the organisation is willing to 'consult' with employee representatives about;
- educate and train management in dealing with employees collectively, particularly where trade unions are likely to be represented on the consultation body;
- consider improving on existing consultation bodies / procedures; and
- consider what competitors are doing.

See also: Redundancy, p.618; Strikes, p.677; TUPE, p.697

Sources of further information

BERR – Information and consultation: www.berr.gov.uk/employment/employment-legislation/ice/index.html

ACAS – Information and consultation: www.acas.org.uk/index.aspx?articleid=1017

Employment contracts

Ian Masson, Anderson Strathern LLP

Key points

A contract of employment can be created very simply. It does not require to
be in writing. However, statutory requirements impose minimum obligations
on employers to issue a written statement confirming the main particulars of
employment. Employers can seek to regulate the employment relationship and
comply with legal obligations by providing a more extensive written contract.
Once contractual terms have been created, they cannot be changed unilaterally.
Whether they are in writing or not, any proposed changes require to be handled
appropriately to avoid claims of breach of contract and constructive unfair
dismissal.

Legislation

Section 1, Equal Pay Act 1970.
Copyright, Designs and Patents Act
1988.
Data Protection Act 1988.
Employment Rights Act 1996.
Working Time Regulations 1998.
Employment Act 2002.
Employment Act 2002 (Dispute
Resolution) Regulations 2004.

Introduction

A contract of employment is created when
one party accepts an offer of employment
from another. Although a written contract
is not required in order to create an
employer–employee relationship, it is a
statutory requirement and good practice
to record the terms of the employment in
writing. This can often be done by issuing
the proposed contract or a statement
of the main contractual terms that will
apply, with the offer of employment. The
employee should be asked to sign a copy
of the written contract to clearly signify
acceptance of its terms.

Certain terms are implied into every
contract by law, such as the implied duty of
trust and confidence, the duty to take care

of health and safety, and the obligation of
equal pay.

**Providing written terms: the compulsory
elements**

Section 1 of the Employment Rights Act
1996 (ERA) places a statutory duty on
employers to provide employees with
particulars in writing of certain fundamental
contractual terms. Since 1 October 2004
employers have been able to provide these
in the form of a written contract, although
they can still be provided in a simple
statement of employment particulars

The main requirements are as follows:

■ Where an employee begins
employment, the employer must give
the employee a written statement of
particulars of employment (section
1(1), ERA).
■ The written statement may be given in
instalments but shall not be given later
than two months after commencement
of employment (section 1(2), ERA).
■ The written statement shall contain
names of the employer and employee,
the date when the employment
commenced and the date when the
period of continuous employment
commenced (section 1(3), ERA).

■ The written statement requires to contain details of all of the following particulars as at a date not more than seven days before the date of the statement (section 1(4), ERA):

■ scale or rate of remuneration, or method of calculating remuneration;
■ the intervals at which remuneration is paid;
■ any terms and conditions relating to normal hours of work;
■ any terms and conditions relating to entitlement to holidays, including public holidays and holiday pay (the latter sufficient to calculate the precise amount payable), incapacity for work due to sickness or injury, and the provision of sick pay;
■ length of notice required to terminate employment;
■ title of the job the employee is employed to do or a brief description of it;
■ the duration of the employment if it is not permanent;
■ the place or places the employee is required to work at;
■ any collective agreements that affect the terms of employment;
■ where the employee is required to work outside the UK, the length of that period and the currency he will be paid in and any additional remuneration or benefits payable to him as a result; and
■ whether there is a contracting-out certificate in force for the purposes of the Pensions Schemes Act 1993, stating that the employment is contracted out.

The written statement must also contain a note specifying any disciplinary rules applicable to the employee or referring the employee to an easily accessible document containing that information (section 3, ERA). The note must contain details of to whom the employee can apply if dissatisfied with a disciplinary decision or for the purposes of seeking redress of any grievance. These requirements apply to all employers. Employers who fail to comply with these requirements now risk financial penalties of between two and four weeks' pay if relevant Employment Tribunal claims are made.

Any changes to the compulsory elements of the statement of terms and conditions should be notified to the employee in writing within one month of the change.

Providing written terms: other important issues

Many employers will employ written contractual terms to exercise control over other important issues. Which issues will be appropriate will always depend on the individual circumstances of the particular contract. Some examples of these additional terms are as follows:

■ Data protection terms, designed to give fair notice of the purposes for which data processing will be carried out, for compliance with the Data Protection Act 1988.
■ Restrictions on acceptance of other work during employment.
■ Flexibility clause (e.g. requirements to work overtime, undertake other duties, mobility clauses).
■ The ability to put employees on lay-off or short-term working.
■ Confidentiality terms, which give the employee notice of the types of information to be regarded as confidential during and after employment.
■ Authority for deductions from wages (e.g. overpayments of holiday pay or expenses).
■ Garden leave terms, designed to allow the employer to require the employee to stay away from work, often used to protect business interests during notice periods.
■ Intellectual property terms, which set out ownership of copyright of work

created during employment and assign rights to it.

Restrictive covenants, which impose restraints post-employment on competition, solicitation of customers and significant employees and the use of trade secrets of the employer. Payment in lieu of notice clause, to allow the employer to dismiss an employee immediately without adhering to the notice period provided for in the contract. If this term is not expressly written into the contract, the employer will be unable to make a payment to the employee in lieu of notice, without being in breach of contract.

Normal retirement age clause, if an employer's normal retirement age is below the deafult age of 65 provided by the Employment Equality (Age) Regulations 2006. Only where a retirement age below 65 can be objectively justified, which in practice will be very rare, will such a retirement age comply with the Employment Equality (Age) Regulations 2006. Many of these clauses will be subject to legal restrictions in relation to

enforceability and it is essential that they are drafted in a manner that will be legally compliant.

Altering terms and conditions of employment

Once established, contractual terms can be varied but only if the consent of both parties to the proposed variation is achieved. This can sometimes involve 'buying out' existing terms with a compensatory financial payment.

If consent is not forthcoming, the only potentially valid alternative is to serve appropriate notice that the contract is being terminated and at the same time, offer a new contract, containing the new terms, to take effect immediately upon termination. However, such an approach can give rise to claims of unfair dismissal, so before taking such action, careful analysis is advised. If the original contract is not brought to an end effectively, breach of contract claims may ensue following any change. If the breach is fundamental, this can lead to a claim that the employee has been constructively unfairly dismissed.

Sources of further information

ACAS: www.acas.org.uk

DBERR: www.berr.gov.uk

All employers are required to issue employees with a written statement of certain terms of employment. Workplace Law Group's draft *Employment Contract and Management Guide, v.4.0* has been published to help employers ensure that they comply with their requirements under law and to provide a clear record of the agreement between employer and employee. The draft policy also comes with a 20-page Management Guide containing helpful notes on the policy and alternative provisions for employers. Visit www.workplacelaw.net/Bookshop/PoliciesAndProcedures for more details.

Comment...

The National Staff Dismissal Register – a step too far?

Sarah Ozanne has specialised in employment since qualifying with CMS Cameron McKenna in 2001. She advises on all areas of employment law, both contentious and non-contentious. Her experience includes advising on employment aspects of mergers, disposals and acquisitions, real estate transactions, outsourcings and PPP and PFI transactions.

The National Staff Dismissal Register (NSDR) went live in May 2008. It is a Register of persons who have been dismissed from their previous employer due to reasons of dishonesty or suspected dishonesty. The categories of dishonesty covered by the Register include theft or attempted theft of money, merchandise or property from the employer, its suppliers or customers; falsification or forgery of documents; fraudulently obtaining money, services or information; and damaging company property.

The Register is an initiative championed by Action Against Business Crime (AABC), the national organisation for Business Crime Reduction Partnerships. AABC is working in partnership with the British Retail Consortium and, so far, mainly retail organisations have signed up to the Register, including Harrods and Selfridges. AABC hopes that the system will be extended to the leisure industry and construction and road haulage groups.

Employers who sign up to use the Register can use it to vet potential employees, as well as to add details of individuals to the database. On the face of it the Register sounds an ideal way for employers to filter out undesirable individuals from their recruitment processes, but its use doesn't come without risks.

One of the most obvious concerns with the Register is the scope for the information appearing on it to be inaccurate, whether through mistake or malice. AABC seeks to resolve this issue by placing the onus on employers using the Register to satisfy themselves that the information they put on the Register is correct. It also requires employers to notify employees during the dismissal process if the employer intends to place their details on the Register. The employee then has a chance to appeal (primarily to the employer, then to the Information Commissioners Office and ultimately to the courts) the decision to put his or her details on the system. Even if such appeal is unsuccessful the employee can record his or her version of events on the Register for users to see.

However, is this enough to protect employers and employees? Employers can dismiss an employee on the reasonable belief that he or she committed an act of dishonesty. Therefore employees could find themselves 'blacklisted' although there has been no involvement by the police or the criminal courts. Further, the Register can include details of employees who resign part-way through an employer investigation into a possible act of dishonesty by them. This could be seen a conviction and sentencing without trial.

Workplace Law Netwo
www.workplacelaw.ne

employees who are able to subsequently establish their innocence and have their details removed from the Register may argue that their reputation has already been ruined. This may lead to increased claims for loss of earnings and injury to feelings in Employment Tribunal claims. Compensation for loss of earnings in unfair dismissal cases is capped, but no such limit applies if employees can establish that their dismissal was discriminatory on the basis of, for example, sex, race, disability, sexual orientation, religion, belief or age. In such cases employees may also claim that the act of putting them on the Register was a separate act of victimisation.

In addition to claims through the Employment Tribunal system, employers who use the NSDR could find themselves the subject of claims of defamation, libel or negligence. There has been a growing tendency for employers to avoid giving expansive written references to employees for fear of exposing themselves to such claims. Why then would an employer run the risk of posting an employee's details on the NSDR? In particular, employers should beware of using previous criminal convictions as a ground for dismissal. The Rehabilitation of Offenders Act 1974 provides that 'spent' convictions should be ignored.

Concerns have also been raised about how the level of personal data on the Register complies with data protection principles. In order to carry out checks using the database employers will be able to search through an encrypted system using criteria including a person's name, address, date of birth, national insurance number and the name of a former employer. AABC states that records will be kept for up to five years and can include an individual's photo to assist with identification. AABC has responded

to the issue of data protection by stating that the system has been developed in coordination with the Information Commissioner and gives reassurance that it complies with data protection principles. AABC also requires that all employers who sign up to use the Register must agree to act in accordance with data protection principles.

However, how has AABC been able to justify processing and disclosing the sensitive personal data that it holds in accordance with the data protection principles? It seems to get round this thorny issue by falling within the exemption that sensitive personal data can be processed without the individual's consent where it is about the commission or alleged commission by a person of a crime. However, it still remains unclear how AABC can justify the disclosure of this type of information as lawful. An answer to this might lie in the proposed amendment to the Data Protection Act 1998 in October this year, which will allow the processing of sensitive personal data on the basis that it is intended to prevent fraud.

These concerns about the NSDR do not seem to have gone unnoticed and may explain the withdrawal of the Home Office's involvement in the development of the Register. The Home Office initially contributed £1m to the development of the system in joint venture with the British Retail Consortium. However, the Home Office has now ceased its funding and its current position is that it has no involvement with the NSDR. In the same vein, some of the retailers who originally indicated they would sign up to the Register have now changed their minds.

Employers who are thinking of using the NSDR should carefully consider whether the advantages outweigh the risks.

Employment disputes

Kathryn Clapp and Mark McCanney, Taylor Wessing

Key points

Most claims brought against a company by job applicants, employees, workers and ex-employees (and also contractors and agency workers) are brought in an Employment Tribunal. Sometimes claims may be brought in the County Court or High Court.

The Employment Tribunal has jurisdiction to hear most employment-related litigation (dismissal, discrimination, working time, TUPE). It is a relatively less expensive forum than other civil courts and is less formal. Historically, each party has met its own legal costs although Tribunals are more frequently making costs awards in particular circumstances.

Breach of contract claims arising or outstanding on termination of employment can be brought in the Employment Tribunal if they are for £25,000 or less. Breach of contract claims where the possible damages are above £25,000 should be brought in the County or High Courts.

The County and High Courts are more formal and expensive. It is possible to get costs awards against the losing party.

Mediation is an increasingly popular option for employers and employees as a means of avoiding having to go to court or to an Employment Tribunal.

ACAS is the Government's conciliation service and is responsible for conciliating between the parties in cases brought in the Employment Tribunal.

It is now also possible to use ACAS as an arbitrator in a dispute if it is an unfair dismissal case.

Legislation
- Employment Tribunal: Employment Tribunals (Constitution and Rules of Procedure) Regulations 2004.
- County / High Court: Civil Procedural Rules.

Proceedings brought in the Employment Tribunal

The Tribunal's procedural regulations are governed by the 'overriding objective', which is to enable Tribunals to deal with cases justly such as ensuring the parties are on an equal footing, saving expense, dealing with the case in ways which are proportionate to the complexity of the issues, and ensuring the case is dealt with expeditiously and fairly.

A case is started when the employee, known as the 'Claimant' presents the Secretary of the Tribunals with a written application in the appropriate form known as the claim form (or ET1).

here are distinctive time limits for lodging
claims in the Employment Tribunal – these
are normally three months from the date
of the termination of the employee's
employment, or the act being complained
of. The time limits are strictly enforced.
However, in certain circumstances relating
to the statutory disciplinary and grievance
procedures, an extension of three months
will be granted in circumstances arising out
of those procedures.

The employer is 'the respondent' and
submits a defence known as 'a Response
Form' (or ET3).

After the response form is received by
the Employment Tribunal, the case will
be prepared for a hearing. To do so, a
number of tasks must be undertaken by
both parties – disclosure of documents,
requests for additional information,
exchanging witness statements.
Sometimes these matters will be
ordered by the Employment Tribunal
in correspondence or following a case
management discussion.

Sometimes there may be issues which
would be dealt with at a pre-hearing
review (e.g. in complex discrimination
cases). After the full hearing, usually
presided over by an employment judge
and two lay wing members, judgment is
made either orally or in writing or both. If
the claimant is successful remedies are
decided by the Employment Tribunal at a
remedies hearing. Either party may appeal
the decision to the Employment Appeal
Tribunal. Again, strict time limits apply.

The Employment Tribunal does not
normally order that the unsuccessful party
pay the costs of the winner. However,
there is an increasing trend towards
the Tribunal making costs orders. The
Employment Tribunal's annual report for
2006–07 demonstrated that in 166 cases

the Tribunals awarded costs in favour
of the Claimant, and in 343 cases the
Tribunal awarded costs in favour of the
Respondent. The maximum award was
£65,000 and the average award was
£2,078. The Tribunal can order costs in
certain circumstances such as where:

- a party or his representative has acted
  vexatiously, abusively, disruptively, or
  otherwise unreasonably in bringing
  or conducting the proceedings or the
  bringing or conducting of proceedings
  has been misconceived;
- the hearing was adjourned at the
  request of one party; or
- a party has not complied with a
  Tribunal's directions order (e.g. to
  supply documents or particulars).

The Employment Tribunal can also make
wasted costs orders and preparation time
orders.

The Tribunal only has the power to award
up to £10,000 in costs without ordering
a detailed assessment. If the costs are
above £10,000 the bill of costs claimed will
then be subject to a detailed assessment
by the county court.

Settlement via the Advisory, Conciliation and Arbitration Service (ACAS)

An ACAS officer is attached to every
claim for unfair dismissal or unlawful
discrimination and has a duty to
conciliate during certain 'conciliation
periods' depending on the type of claim.
In April 2008 ACAS announced that it
would exercise its discretion to extend
conciliation throughout the whole period of
a claim rather than just during those fixed
conciliation periods. This came following
the publication of the Employment Bill
proposing to remove these restrictions on
ACAS. The ACAS officer has no duty to
advise on the merits of the claim and will

not enter into lengthy discussion on legal points.

The ACAS officer will contact each party (by letter or telephone) at the start of proceedings in the Employment Tribunal. He can negotiate between the parties towards a settlement. A settlement agreement reached through ACAS is binding and effective. It is normally recorded on a 'COT3 form'.

ACAS has also set up an arbitration scheme for unfair dismissal cases as a form of alternative dispute resolution (see below). This is different from conciliation in that ACAS provides an independent arbitrator who hears the evidence and decides the case for the employer and employee. As an arbitrator, ACAS can award the same level of payments as a Tribunal against employers.

County Court and High Court

Employment disputes can also give rise to a civil action which is heard in either a County Court (if it is a small claim or if it is not a complex matter) or the High Court. The High Court will not hear a claim whose value is £15,000 or less (or less than £50,000 where personal injury damages are involved). There are three tracks – small claims (under £5,000); fast track, which is for claims between £5,000 and £15,000; and multi-track for claims above £15,000. The main types of civil actions relating to employment are wrongful dismissal/breach of contract or injunctions to stop employees joining a competitor, setting up in competition or disclosing confidential information.

The High Court sits at the Royal Courts of Justice in London as well as at some major court centres around the country. Most employment-related civil actions are heard in the Queen's Bench Division of the High Court.

The parties can appeal a decision of the High Court to the Court of Appeal and in certain rare circumstances on to the House of Lords or European Court of Justice.

Alternative dispute resolution

Alternative dispute resolution encompasses many methods for parties avoiding going to court and settling legal disputes through other means. Mediation is one of those means; arbitration is another.

Mediation is used in employment-related claims very successfully because:

- it can be a cost saving for both parties;
- it is less intimidating than a court or Tribunal;
- it does not involve lengthy trials or hearings; and
- it focuses less on the legal issues and so can be a lot less complex.

Arbitration is used in more complex commercial cases and international cases and is not generally used in domestic employment disputes apart from the new ACAS arbitration scheme mentioned above.

There are a number of bodies that provide alternative dispute resolution such as the Centre for Effective Dispute Resolution (CEDR), the ADR Group and In Place of Strife. Also many barristers' chambers provide mediation services.

Future developments – The Employment Bill

The current employment statutory dispute resolution procedures are due to be repealed with effect from April 2009 under proposals in the current Employment Bill. Instead they will be replaced by a short revised ACAS Code of Practice on discipline and grievance. This was published in draft form in May 2008.

covers the procedure to follow in disciplinary warnings as well as dismissal. Employment Tribunals will be able to take the code into account and increase awards by up to 25% for unreasonable failure of an employer to comply with any part of it. Similiarly an employee's unreasonable failure to comply may result in a decrease of their award by 25%. In June 2008, ACAS published a draft Guide to complement the Code which provides detailed advice to employers on practical aspects of disciplinary and grievance issues in the workplace.

The Employment Bill also proposes to revert to the pre-2004 position whereby a Tribunal may reduce a compensatory award for a procedurally unfair dismissal to relect the likelihood that the dismissal would have occurred anyway even if the correct procedure had been followed.

See also: Disciplinary and grievance procedures, p.216; Dismissal, p.233; Employment Tribunals, p.285

Sources of further information

Centre for Effective Dispute Resolution: www.cedr.co.uk/

ADR Group: www.adrgroup.co.uk

Employment Tribunals Service: www.employmenttribunals.gov.uk

ACAS: www.acas.org.uk/index.aspx?articleid=1461

ACAS – Draft Code of Practice on discipline and grievance: www.acas.org.uk/CHttpHandler.ashx?id=880

Employment status

John Turnbull, BPE Solicitors

Key points

Given that quite distinct rules exist for those who are employees and those who are subcontractors or workers, it is of great importance to be aware of the factors that go towards determining whether an individual is likely to be an employee or a subcontractor. The main issue is to distinguish between a 'Contract of Service' on the one hand, and a 'Contract for Services' on the other.

Under a Contract of Service, a person essentially agrees to serve another, whereas under a Contract for Services, a person agrees to provide services to another. However, it is important to note that what the parties call themselves and how they enable or define the agreement in question is not the decisive factor. If there is a dispute, Employment Tribunals have generally sought to ascertain the true nature of the relationship between the parties. The key element seems to be whether the 'employer' is obliged to provide work for the 'employee' and, in turn, whether the employee is then obliged to personally perform that work. These mutual obligations are a strong indicator that the worker is an employer. Secondly, the worker has to expressly or impliedly agree to be subject to the control of the employer.

Legislation

Although there is a limited amount of legislation in respect of determining 'status' itself, there is a vast amount of legislation that becomes relevant as a knock-on effect of the determination of whether an individual is an employee or a worker or, indeed, a subcontractor. The relevant legislation is listed below:

- Sex Discrimination Act 1975.
- Race Relations Act 1976.
- Transfer of Employment (Protection of Employment) Regulations 1981.
- Social Security Contributions and Benefits Act 1992.
- Disability Discrimination Act 1995.
- Employment Rights Act 1996.
- Public Interest Disclosure Act 1998.
- National Minimum Wage Act 1998.
- Working Time Regulations 1998.
- Employment Relations Act 1999.

- Part-Time Workers (Prevention of Less Favourable Treatment) Regulations 2000.
- Employment Act 2002.
- Fixed Term Employees (Prevention of Less Favourable Treatment) Regulations 2002.
- Employment Equality (Religion or Belief) Regulations 2003.
- Employment Equality (Sexual Orientation) Regulations 2003.
- Conduct of Employment Agencies Employment Businesses Regulations 2003.

Basic categories

Essentially, the basic types of status in employment law are:

- employee; or
- worker / independent contractor – self-employed (note that an independent contractor could mean a separate entity, namely, a company).

Employees

There are three essential elements to a contract of employment, without which such a contract could not be deemed to be a contract of employment:

1. The contract must impose an obligation on a person to provide work personally;
2. There must be a mutuality of obligation between employer and employee; and
3. The worker must expressly and impliedly agree to be subject to the control of the person for whom he works to a sufficient degree, to make that person master.

Similarly, where the terms of the contract express negative mutuality of obligations, there cannot be a contract of employment. Further, if the contract does not require the services in question to be carried out personally by the individual in question, or those in their control, then again, the contract in question cannot be a contract of employment. In saying that, often the Employment Tribunals are required to look at the reality of the situation and go beyond the written contract themselves. Often, individuals are engaged as 'subcontractors' when in fact an Employment Tribunal may deem them to be an employee.

By way of an example, the more personal responsibility that an individual has in relation to his own investment and manager, financial risk and opportunity for profiting, the more likely that person is considered to be an independent contractor, rather than an employee. In contrast, some factors that sometimes go towards demonstrating the existence of a contract of employment are listed below:

■ Remuneration by way of payment of wages or salary;

■ Payment during absence through illness;
■ Paid holiday;
■ Membership of the company pension scheme;
■ Control by a disciplinary code laid down by the employer; and
■ A prohibition on working for other companies or individuals.

By way of a summary in relation to 'employees', if one can say yes to all of the following questions then an individual is likely to be an employee:

■ Do you have to do the work yourself?
■ Can someone tell you at any time, what to do, where to carry out the work, or when and how to do it?
■ Do you work a set amount of hours?
■ Can someone move you from task to task?
■ Are you paid by the hour, week or month?
■ Can you get overtime or bonus payment?

Worker / subcontractor

As mentioned at the start of the chapter, a worker/subcontractor is someone who operates under a 'Contract for Services' as opposed to a 'Contract of Service'.

If one can answer yes to all of the following questions, it will usually mean an individual is self-employed:

■ Can you hire someone to do the work for you or engage help at your own expense?
■ Do you risk your own money?
■ Do you provide the main items of equipment that you need to do your job, not just the small tools which many employees provide themselves?
■ Do you agree to do a job for a fixed price regardless of how long the job may take?

- Can you decide what work to do, how and when to do work, and where to provide the services?
- Do you regularly work for a number of different people?
- Do you have to correct unsatisfactory work at your own time and at your own expense?

Legal consequences of the distinction

An 'employee' enjoys (subject to the satisfaction of relevant qualifying conditions) the following rights (please note this list is not exhaustive):

- Unfair dismissal protection;
- Redundancy payment entitlement;
- Written Particulars of Terms of Employment;
- Statutory minimum period of notice;
- Guaranteed payment;
- Medical suspension payment;
- Protection from discrimination on grounds of race, sex, disability, religious belief and sexual orientation;
- Equal pay;
- Maternity rights;
- Time off for trade union activities;
- The option to be employed for the agreed period or be given the agreed length of notice;
- A safe place of work;
- Statutory sick pay;
- Wages free of any deductions not properly authorised;
- Rights under the Working Time Regulations 1998; and
- In the case of those employed as shop workers or betting workers, the right to object to working on Sundays.

With regard to the self-employed, the following rights are applicable:

- To benefit from all contractual entitlements;
- Protection against discrimination on the grounds of race, sex, disability, sexual orientation or religious belief and equal pay;
- Where applicable, to be provided with a safe place and a safe system of work;
- Wages free of any deductions not properly authorised; and
- Rights under the Working Time Regulations 1998.

Status and the Construction Industry Scheme 2006

As an aside, the Inland Revenue has introduced a new scheme in order to tighten up on the status of employees and subcontractors, given the differences in tax and National Insurance contributions. Under the changes, which came into force in April 2007, subcontractors will no longer supply certificates and registration cards but, rather, will be registered centrally.

There will be an obligation on the 'contractors' to enquire as to whether the individual in question is likely to be an employee or a subcontractor and, once a month, produce a report to the Revenue declaring that 'status' has been properly considered.

See also: Agency and temporary workers, p.58; Contractors, p.160; Self employment, p.648

Sources of further information

Inland Revenue: www.inlandrevenue.co.uk

Employment Tribunals

Anna Youngs, Mills & Reeve

Key points
- Parties do not have to be legally represented, but representation is of assistance in more complex cases, particularly discrimination issues.
- Use only the prescribed forms.
- Follow the Tribunal's Orders.
- Consider settlement via compromise agreement / ACAS conciliation.

Legislation
- Employment Tribunals Rules of Procedure 2004 (which are set out at Schedule 1 of the Employment Tribunals (Constitution and Rules of Procedure) Regulations 2004).

Introduction to proceedings in the Employment Tribunals
The Employment Tribunals are less formal than the other Courts of England and Wales. The idea is that anybody can bring or defend a claim, without necessarily seeking legal advice. That said, employment issues are notoriously complex, particularly where discrimination is alleged and in such cases legal advice is likely to be needed.

The Employment Tribunals Rules of Procedure 2004 (the Rules) set out the way in which proceedings must be lodged and conducted. This chapter will highlight some general practice points for conducting proceedings.

The Overriding Objective
The Overriding Objective is a principle that runs throughout our litigation system. The Objective is to enable the Courts and Tribunal to deal with cases justly. This must be considered when making applications to the Tribunal and when conducting Tribunal proceedings in general, because the Tribunal will make its decisions in accordance with the Overriding Objective.

The Overriding Objective is set out at Regulation 3 of the Employment Tribunals (Constitution and Rules of Procedure) Regulations 2004, which states that dealing with a case justly includes, so far as practicable:

- ensuring that the parties are on an equal footing;
- dealing with the case in ways which are proportionate to the complexity or importance of the issues;
- ensuring that it is dealt with expeditiously and fairly; and
- saving expense.

Using the prescribed form
There are set forms that must be used when bringing (form ET1) and responding (form ET3) to a claim in the Employment Tribunal. If the correct form is not used, the claim or response will not be accepted. The current forms can be downloaded from the Employment Tribunals' website (www.employmenttribunals.gov.uk). There are some sections on the form that are marked with a star (*). These sections must be answered, or the claim or the response can be rejected.

Time limits

Strict time limits apply in the Employment Tribunals. When a claim is sent to the employer, the Tribunal will state on the accompanying letter the date by which they must respond. Failure to respond by that deadline is likely to result in a default judgment being entered in favour of the Claimant, unless the employer has applied for and received an extension of time (which should not be relied upon as a given).

The Claimant also has to comply with time limits. Generally claims must be lodged within three months of either the date of dismissal, or the last act complained of, although if the statutory dispute resolution procedures apply this may be extended by a further three months. It is worthwhile highlighting on your response form if you think the claim may be out of time, or if you think an employee has failed to comply with the statutory grievance procedure (where applicable) but generally due to the various discretions that can be exercised by the Tribunal, it is worth seeking legal advice.

Management of the case

Once the claim has been received and the response has been accepted, the next step is for the Tribunal to set down directions for the future conduct of the case. This is usually done at a Case Management Discussion. These directions will set dates by which the following must have been done:

- *Exchange of documents.* All relevant documents within your possession or control, whether or not they help your case, help your opponent's case, or damage either case.
- *Agree a 'bundle' of documents.* The bundle should contain all documents relevant to the matters in issue. The Claimant is responsible for preparing the bundle, but many Respondents

take on this responsibility as they have more resources and generally have more documents in their possession.
- *Exchange of witness statements.* This is usually done by way of mutual or simultaneous exchange, but may be done by sequential exchange if the Claimant's case is not clear from their claim form or any further particulars of claim.
- *Date and length of the hearing set.*

Parties may also be required to agree a chronology, statement of agreed facts and statement of issues that the Tribunal must determine, although even if the Tribunal does not order a statement of issues, it is important that you know what the issues are so that you can focus your case effectively.

An important document is the schedule of loss. The Tribunal will require the Claimant to serve a schedule setting out what financial losses they have suffered. This is usually ordered at the earliest stage in the hope of promoting settlement. If this is not ordered by the Tribunal employers should certainly ask for one. This will help you assess the cost effectiveness of resisting the claim.

Documents that do not have to be disclosed or included in the Bundle

'Without prejudice' documents, which generally take the form of negotiations between the parties, should not be included in the Bundle.

Documents that attract legal advice or litigation 'privilege' (which is the right not to disclose) do not have to be disclosed:

- Legal advice privilege protects communications passing between lawyer and client created for the purpose of giving or receiving advice. This type of privilege is not confined

Workplace Law Network
www.workplacelaw.net

to advice about legal rights and obligations but it will not arise unless the advice is given in a relevant legal context.

Litigation privilege protects documents created for the dominant purpose of gathering evidence for use in proceedings if they are made:

- confidentially;
- between a lawyer and a client, a lawyer and his agent or a lawyer and a third party; and
- for the dominant purpose of conducting or aiding the conduct of actual litigation or litigation which is reasonably in prospect.

he Tribunal has powers to award costs r even to strike out a claim for failure to :omply with an Order.

he hearing
1 full hearings, where the merits of a claim s to be decided, the Tribunal panel will be nade up of three people:

- A legally qualified Employment Judge (who sits in the middle of the panel and is addressed as 'Sir' or 'Madam').
- Two lay members – one who has an employee background, such as someone from a Union, and one who has an employer background.

The idea is that there is a balanced)anel who will make a balanced decision. \s the Tribunal is a civil court, liability vill be determined on the 'balance of)robabilities', which means, for example, vhether it is more likely than not that the dismissal was unfair.

There are differing rules as to which side goes first, depending on the type of claim. The Tribunal will assist unrepresented parties with procedure as far as possible, but as a rule of thumb, where discrimination is alleged the Claimant's case will be heard first (as the Claimant must prove facts out of which discrimination could be inferred), and in unfair dismissal cases, the Respondent will go first.

Whichever side goes first, the procedure is the same for the witnesses. Using the Claimant's witness as an example:

- the witness may have to read their statement aloud (bear this in mind when drafting statements);
- the Claimant's representative may be able to ask some questions;
- the other side will then cross-examine the witness;
- the Employment Judge or the panel members may ask some questions; and
- the Claimant's representative will have the opportunity to ask further questions to clarify points made by the other side.

After all the evidence from both sides is heard, each side will make 'submissions' about their case. This is an opportunity for each side to put forward their best points, address any damage done to their case by the other side, and highlight the weaknesses in the other side's case.

Top tips for witnesses
- Don't avoid answering a question.
- If you don't know or don't remember, say so (but don't use this as a get out!)
- Don't fill silences by talking (this is where the most damage is commonly done!).
- Familiarise yourself with your witness statement and read documents relevant to your evidence.

The Judgment
The Employment Judge may give an oral Judgment on the day. If s/he does this, s/he will only provide a full written Judgment if you ask for one. A party must have a

written Judgment if you think you have grounds for appeal.

If you win, you may be able to get costs from the other side. Costs are not given automatically in the Tribunal. Refer to the Rules for the circumstances in which you can apply for costs and the time limits for doing so.

The Tribunal has a booklet on Tribunal Judgments that they send out with the written Judgment, which should be of use.

Costs or expenses orders may be made if:

- a hearing or pre-hearing review is postponed;
- in bringing or conducting the proceedings, a party has been misconceived or if the party or his representative has acted vexatiously, abusively, disruptively or otherwise unreasonably; and/or
- a party has not complied with an order or practice direction.

The Tribunal may also make preparation time orders and wasted costs orders as appropriate.

Withdrawal by the Claimant
Please note that if the Claimant withdraws their claim at any stage, this ends the proceedings. However, it does not necessarily prevent them from re-issuing fresh proceedings. Therefore, upon receipt of a notice of withdrawal it is advisable for Respondents to apply to the Tribunal for the claim to be 'dismissed' pursuant to Rule 25(4) of the Rules. This prevents the Claimant from being able to re-issue the proceedings. An application should be made within 28 days from the date that the notice of withdrawal is sent to the parties by the Tribunal. The practice is that the Claimant (or their representative) should be copied in to the application

and given time to object (some Tribunals currently say that the Claimant should be given 14 days to object).

ACAS and conciliation
An ACAS officer is assigned to each case in order to try to assist the parties to conciliate or settle the case. ACAS' services are free and confidential, and therefore settling a claim through ACAS can avoid unwanted costs and publicity.

Litigation risk is avoided if a case settles, and an ACAS settlement can include things that a Tribunal would not be able to consider; for example, an agreed reference can be consideration for a settlement, but the Tribunal cannot order an employer to provide a reference. This is a key negotiation point (but when providing references employers must consider their duty of care to both the employee and to future employers).

Fixed conciliation periods were introduced in October 2004 but have since been abolished.

Judicial mediation
Certain Employment Tribunals (Birmingham London Central and Newcastle) are currently running a Judicial Mediation pilot scheme. The pilot commenced in July 2006 and is still ongoing.

The aim is to encourage resolution of disputes without having a full Employment Tribunal hearing (and therefore will normally be appropriate for cases where there is an ongoing relationship between the parties). The intention is that this will save time and costs.

The pilot scheme is running in relation to cases that include an element of sex, race or disability discrimination.

the parties agree to Judicial Mediation, the Tribunal proceedings will be stayed and the case will be referred to a full time employment Judge who is trained in mediation. The Employment Judge will not make a decision in the case or give what is effectively a Judgment in the case.

The mediation will be in private, and will be confidential. The Employment Judge who mediated the case will not be involved further in the case if the mediation is not successful and it proceeds to a hearing. The mediation files and Tribunal hearing files will be kept completely separate so that the parties can speak freely in mediation.

See also: Contract disputes, p.157; Disability legislation, p.209; Disciplinary and grievance procedures, p.216; Discrimination, p.222; Dismissal, p.233; Employment disputes, p.278

Sources of further information

Tribunals Service: www.employmenttribunals.gov.uk

Tribunals Service – Employment Appeal Tribunal: www.employmentappeals.gov.uk

ACAS: www.acas.org.uk

Energy performance

Mick Dalton, Emaar Properties

Key points

The Building Regulations are made under powers provided in the Building Act 1984, and apply in England and Wales. The current edition of the regulations is the Building Regulations 2000 (as amended) and the majority of building projects are required to comply with them. They exist to ensure the health and safety of people in and around all types of buildings (i.e. domestic, commercial and industrial). They also provide for energy conservation, and access to and use of buildings.

The Energy Performance of Buildings Regulations

The Energy Performance of Buildings Regulations are now in force in England and Wales; Scotland and Northern Ireland are developing similar legislation. These Regulations require buildings to have Energy Performance Certificates which indicate the carbon dioxide emissions and energy efficiency of the building.

Energy Performance Certificate (EPC) for all buildings at construction, sale or rent

To comply with the Regulations, any building in England and Wales with a usable floor area above 500 m² will require an EPC if it or any part of it is sold or let after April 2008; and any building with a floor area of less than 500 m² will require an EPC if it or any part of it is sold or let after October 2008. Separate certificates will be required for any parts of the building designed or altered for separate use; e.g. a shop or residential accommodation in an office block.

The EPC is based on the building construction and assets installed – it is valid for up to ten years and includes an A to G grade. The EPC must be accompanied by an advisory report on measures which could reduce the building's carbon emissions and improve its grade.

Display Energy Certificate (DEC) for larger public buildings

Since April 2008 public buildings with a usable floor area above 1,000 m² have been required to permanently display a Display Energy Certificate, valid for one year and based on metered energy use. The definition of 'public building' includes all public authorities, and also institutions providing face to face public services, e.g. town halls, sports centres and hospitals. An advisory report of energy improvement measures is required with each DEC and this is valid for up to seven years.

Compliance with the Building Regulations

The approved methodology for compliance to Part L comprises the following calculation methods:

- The Standard Assessment Procedure for the Energy Rating of Dwellings (SAP 2005);
- Approved software applications of SAP 2005 as indicated in the notice;

- The Government's Simplified Building Energy Model (SBEM);
- Approved software interfaces to SBEM as indicated in the notice; and
- Approved Dynamic Simulation Model (DSM) software packages as indicated in the notice.

The Building National calculation methods for domestic (SAP) and non-domestic buildings (SBEM – developed by BRE) is used today by the low carbon consultants and Local Authority building control.

There are mandatory pressure tests for non-domestic buildings and sample pressure testing for domestic units.

Airtightness test
- To comply with Building Regulations Part L 2a (2006) it is mandatory to pressure test all buildings with a floor area >500 m².
- Worst acceptable air permeability level of 10 m³/hour/ m² at 50 Pascal.

Types of buildings that will need a pressure test include:

- hospitals;
- airport terminals;
- offices;
- warehouses;
- superstores;
- retail;
- schools and colleges; and
- dwellings.

Very large / complex buildings
When a building is very large (for example Heathrow Terminal 5), or very complex, it may be impractical or impossible to pressure test the building using conventional methods to demonstrate compliance. Building Regulations Part L2a makes provision for these handful of cases.

Design review
Under Part L it becomes very important at design stage to:

- check details crucial to achieving airtight fabric;
- see that this is carried out as early as possible;
- define air barrier;
- identify materials;
- identify trades responsible; and
- check material specification and suitability.

Construction phase inspection
Once construction commences it is essential to ensure the following is carried out:

- Check detailing on site;
- Discuss practical issues/buildability issues; and
- Quality Management.

Since the 2006 Approved Documents for Part L were published on 15 March 2006, DCLG (formerly ODPM) has become aware of inaccuracies in those for each of L1A, L1B, L2A and L2B. These inaccuracies have now been amended and the definitive version was placed on the website on 31 March 2006.

If you downloaded the Approved Documents for L1A, L1B, L2A and L2B between 15 and 31 March 2006, you are encouraged to download the definitive version and refer to marked up versions to view the specific corrections made – www.planningportal.gov.uk/england/professionals/en/.

Issues for building owners or agents
The certification process is complex and time consuming. Owners and managers of large estates are advised to begin to identify buildings most likely to be sold

or let soon after April and October 2008 and ensure that the certification process commences immediately.

Home Information Packs for domestic dwellings
HIPs and EPCs are being introduced on a phased basis to ensure a smooth transition in the housing market, and to begin the process of transforming the home buying and selling process in the interests of consumers and the environment at the earliest opportunity.

HIPs and EPCs will give house buyers energy ratings for homes for the first time, from A to G – similar to consumer friendly ratings for fridges, helping to lower fuel bills and reduce carbon emissions. The packs will also help to cut costs for consumers by increasing transparency and competition in the home buying and selling process.

Since 14 December 2007, properties marketed for sale in England and Wales have needed a Home Information Pack (HIP), which includes a home energy rating.

Energy Performance Certification services for commercial buildings
Companies such as Power Efficiency (www.powerefficiency.co.uk) provide an Energy Performance Certificate service which includes:

- Assisting clients to identify buildings likely to require early certification.
- Establishing which buildings and which parts of the buildings require certificates.
- Developing a certification programme (to include the provision of an agreed number of certificates for April 2008 and October 2008).
- Obtaining and collating relevant data.
- Providing accredited certificates and Asset Ratings.
- Providing advisory reports on energy improvement measures.

Building log books – client / developer role
It is the responsibility of the client / developer to ensure the log book is in place at handover. They may also have to pay for the log book in order to meet the building regulations. It must be included in the client's brief and fee structure so there are resources allotted to develop the log book.

The advantages are:

- The client / developer will know what they are getting as an end product.
- It will hold summary information that might be used in selling / letting the building, thus giving greater confidence to letting agents. Prospective purchasers and tenants will have greater confidence in what they are buying.

See also: Building Regulations, p.81; Environmental Management Systems, p.296

Sources of further information

Carbon Trust: www.thecarbontrust.co.uk

Planning Portal: www.planningportal.gov.uk/england/professionals/en/

Approved Document L2A:
www.planningportal.gov.uk/england/professionals/en/1115314231806.html

Approved Document L1B:
www.planningportal.gov.uk/england/professionals/en/1115314231799.html

Power Efficiency: www.powerefficiency.co.uk

Home Information Packs: www.homeinformationpacks.gov.uk/

Workplace Law Group's *Energy Performance of Buildings: Special Report 2008*
provides in-depth insight into the key requirements of the new legislation and the
practical measures needed to comply with the law. The special report includes
interviews and contributions from leading experts in energy management in the
UK, including the Environmental Industries Commission, the Chartered Institution
of Building Services Engineers, Carbon Trust Enterprises, Energy Services and
Technology Association, and energy management services provider pemXq, as well
as key figures from the facilities management industry. For more information visit
www.workplacelaw.net/Bookshop/SpecialReports.

Comment...

Energy Performance Certificates: impact on the property market

 Fabien Joly de Bresillon leads the Energy Services business in Bureau Veritas, which has extensive experience of working on energy issues with Building and Property owners, managers and occupiers.

On 12 September 2008, the Department for Communities and Local Government announced an additional three-month 'grace' period for the production of Energy Performance Certificates (EPCs) at the time of construction, sale or rental of a commercial property in England and Wales. EPCs are mandatory for all transactions on commercial buildings occurring after 1 October; however, the owner or seller will have until 4 January 2009 to produce retroactively the certificate.

This is an additional delay in the implementation of this requirement of the European Energy Performance of Buildings Directive in the UK, mainly due to the lack of accredited Energy Assessors. However, implementation is happening and commercial property owners should seriously prepare for what some perceive as an additional cost, but what is also an opportunity to improve the value of their portfolio.

EPCs have been designed to ensure prospective buyers or tenants have the necessary information on the energy efficiency of a building and therefore an insight into the energy bills they can expect to pay. An EPC includes an energy rating, on a scale from A+ (carbon passive) to G (least efficient) and a

Recommendation Report. It is valid for up to ten years, in which time the seller or landlord can provide the same EPC to all prospective buyers or tenants. If significant refurbishment works have been carried out to the building, then a new EPC can be required.

EPCs can represent an important cost for owners of large or complex buildings that will require the usage of Dynamic Simulation Modelling. However, even a 'simple' building will require a complex calculation based on a combination of factors. The key factors are:

- the type of construction of the building (including walls, roofs, floors and glazing);
- heating, cooling, ventilation and hot water systems used;
- lighting; and
- whether zones of the building are used for different purposes e.g. office factory etc., and the occupancy profile for each zone.

An approved Energy Assessor has then to input this information in a software package in order to produce the EPC and recommendation report.

he energy performance of a building is shown as a CO_2-based index. This rating depends on the energy used for space heating, water heating, ventilation and lighting, less any energy generated from energy generation technology installed in the building (such as solar water heating, wind turbines etc.). The lower the number (on a scale of 0 to 150+), the lower the typical CO_2 emissions.

The recommendation report that is included with an EPC lists actions to improve the energy rating of the building. The recommendations only include those improvements that are appropriate for the building that has been assessed. For each recommendation indicative paybacks are provided.

To be ready for the new Regulations, it is advised that the following actions are undertaken by property owners:

■ Prioritise buildings within a portfolio: identify those that will need an EPC from April 2008 and those that won't

need any for years. Define a strategy of production for complex buildings like shopping centres or modern office buildings (one EPC for the whole building v. unit-based EPCs).

■ Begin the data gathering exercise. This includes production of plans to scale, preferably in a CAD format that can be easily manipulated to calculate areas for each zone. In addition, an M&E asset register and information on the building fabric will also be required.

■ Commission the production of an EPC by an approved assessor (see www.ndepcregister.com for more information)

Once the EPC is produced, there is no requirement from the property owner to implement any of the recommendations provided in the Recommendation Report.

However, some large portfolio owners have anticipated a premium and increased yields for well-rated buildings. Only time and the market will tell.

Environmental Management Systems

Sally Goodman, Bureau Veritas

Key points

- 'Environmental responsibility' is a term commonly used in boardrooms throughout the UK. This highlights that effective management of environmental issues is an area of concern for many businesses, from large FTSE 100 companies to smaller organisations.
- This interest in environmental responsibility is generated for different reasons within each company. However, they all aim to achieve the same goal – to minimise and control potential negative environmental impacts and risks.
- Many organisations in the UK are achieving this goal by the implementation of an Environmental Management System (EMS).

What is an Environmental Management System?

An EMS is a powerful tool for the identification and management of environmental risks. It also provides a mechanism for delivering performance improvements, effecting resource savings and promoting environmental best practice.

There are two EMS standards to which an organisation can receive external certification: the EU-based Eco-Management and Audit Scheme (EMAS) and the international standard ISO 14001:2004. Both standards represent best practice in environmental management and have been widely accepted by UK businesses with (at the time of writing) nearly 6,000 ISO 14001 certificates and over 300 EMAS registrations currently issued within the UK. More than 129,000 ISO 14001 certificates have been issued worldwide.

ISO 14001 is applicable to any type and size of organisation, anywhere in the world. It can be applied to individual sites, or to entire organisations. Some organisations choose to implement ISO 14001 in a phased manner, site by site, or plant by plant, or subsidiary by subsidiary. Others design the EMS at corporate level and require each site or plant to interpret and implement the EMS accordingly. Which approach is chosen depends very much on resources and the existing company culture.

EMAS is based on an EU Regulation. The main difference between EMAS and ISO 14001 is that EMAS requires the additional production of a periodic public environmental 'statement' (in reality, a detailed report), which describes an organisation's environmental impacts and data, its environmental programme, the involvement of stakeholders and progress in achieving improvement in performance.

Whichever standard is used as the basis for an EMS, there are three underlying

Workplace Law Network
www.workplacelaw.net

inciples that form the backbone of the
ystem:

Compliance with applicable
environmental legislation;
Prevention of pollution; and
Continual improvement.

oth EMAS and ISO 14001 specify that an
ffective EMS should be based around the
ollowing stages:

Planning
Including development of an
environmental policy, the identification
and evaluation of environmental
aspects and impacts, the development
of objectives and targets, and the
preparation of an 'environmental
management programme' (action
plan).

Implementation
Including defining roles and
responsibilities, assessing
competence and delivering training,
communications, documentation and
document control, operational control
and emergency preparedness.

Checking and corrective action
Including monitoring of performance
(including compliance with legislation),
specifying corrective action, record
keeping and internal auditing.

Review
Strategic level review ('management
review').

Why implement an EMS?
The use of EMSs to control environmental
risks is not a new concept. EMSs
have been externally reviewed since
1992, with the number being externally
certified within the UK growing all the
time. This demonstrates that there are
recognised and continued benefits from

implementing an EMS, some of which are
as follows:

- A more systematic approach to
  business management.
- Reduced risk of prosecution and
  improved relationships with regulatory
  authorities.
- The confidence to do business in
  what before may have been viewed
  as high-risk areas or processes.
- Financial benefits in terms of, for
  example, reduced waste and energy
  bills.
- Competitive advantage over
  organisations with less developed risk
  management procedures.
- Improved public profile and better
  relationship with stakeholders.
- Improved staff motivation, retention
  and attraction.

Types of EMS
An EMS can take many forms, from
detailed and prescriptive procedures, to
simple flowcharts. It can also be delivered
and communicated in many different
ways, from paper copies of procedures
to electronic systems held on company
intranets.

The type of EMS that an organisation
chooses depends on the size and
culture of the organisation and the
existing communications process. One
example that a large multi-site organisation
may opt to use is an internet-based
software package. Such packages can
assist an organisation in rapidly
establishing its EMS or to maintain and
keep live its existing system. Alternatively
an SME may opt to install a simple
flowchart-based system to provide clear
instructions which all levels of staff can
understand.

Integration

Although an EMS can be designed as a stand-alone system, it is now best practice to integrate the environmental management requirements with health and safety and quality management systems. It is also increasingly common to find EMS being integrated with systems for improving corporate social responsibility or corporate governance *(see 'Corporate Social Responsibility', p.173)*.

Certification

Certification is a process by which an independent third party audits a management system against a recognised standard.

In the UK, certification bodies are accredited (given a licence to operate) by the United Kingdom Accreditation Service (UKAS). UKAS is the sole national body recognised by government for the accreditation of testing and calibration laboratories and certification and inspection bodies.

There are many certification bodies operating in the UK, among which are the British Standards Institution (BSI), Bureau Veritas, DNV, Lloyd's Register Quality Assurance (LRQA) and SGS.

Links with CSR

Corporate Social Responsibility (CSR), increasingly termed Corporate Responsibility (CR) is a collective term that brings together a company response to social (employee, health and safety and community issues), environmental and ethical issues and risks to deliver greater value to the company. Many companies recognise this with the publication of a CSR report.

CSR confers business benefits to all organisations and stakeholder groups in a number of areas. A coherent CSR strategy based on integrity, sound values and a long-term approach will offer clear business benefits. These cover a better alignment of corporate goals with those of society; maintaining the company's reputation; securing its continued licence to operate; and reducing its exposure to liabilities, risks and associated costs.

A robust CSR strategy should also support reporting against the requirements of the Business Review mandated by the UK Government (under the Companies Act 1985, OFR (Repeal) Regulations). Of importance is how CSR strategy identifies and covers all non-financial risk and opportunities that can affect business performance. The critical aspects to this process are to identify the material non-financial risks, ensure that processes are in place to manage these risks and to explicitly link non-financial risk management to business performance.

As understanding and support for the concept of CSR grows, and consumers become increasingly aware of the issues, more and more companies are building socially responsible elements into marketing and brand identity. Addressing these issues can improve performance whilst also acting as a differentiator to attract customers and corporate partners and create competitive advantage. An EMS is an essential part of a CSR strategy for any sector, although for those sectors with greater environmental impact, the EMS will have greater visibility within the CSR programme.

See also: Corporate Social Responsibility, p.173

Sources of further information

EMAS Helpdesk: europa.eu.int/comm/environment/emas/index.htm

ISO 14000 Information Centre: www.iso14000.com

International Organisation for Standardisation (ISO): www.iso.org/iso/home.htm

UKAS: www.ukas.com

Bureau Veritas UK (consultancy): www.bureauveritas.co.uk

Certification bodies:

British Standards Institution (BSI): www.bsi-global.com

Bureau Veritas Certification: www.bureauveritas.co.uk

DNV: www.dnv.com

Lloyd's Register Quality Assurance (LRQA): www.lrqa.com

SGS: www.uk.sgs.com

Equal pay

Lorna Cowie, MacRoberts Solicitors

Key points

- The principle of equal pay originates from Article 141 of the Treaty of Rome (previously Article 119). Article 141 and, later, the Equal Pay Directive, underpinned the rights in Europe to equal pay between men and women. The UK implemented these EU provisions by the Equal Pay Act 1970 (EPA).
- The EPA gives the right to equal pay to men and women, although for ease of reference the presumption in this article is that a woman is the affected employee.
- The EPA implies an equality clause into any employment contract that does not already include one. This provision applies to all terms and conditions of employment and not only to pay but, for example, sick pay provisions. Any term in a contract which purports to limit or exclude any provision of the EPA is unenforceable (with the exception of a COT3 Agreement or a Compromise Agreement).
- The implied equality clause modifies the contract of employment in any situation where a woman is engaged in like work to a man, on work rated as equivalent to work done by a man, or on work of equal value to that done by a man unless her employer can justify the difference in pay due to a material factor which is not sex.
- Equal pay questionnaires can be served before a claim is issued at the Employment Tribunal to establish facts which are material to a potential claim. If the employer fails to respond to the questionnaire or the employer's response is evasive, the Tribunal is entitled to draw adverse inferences from the employer's failure.

Legislation

- Treaty of Rome, Article 141.
- Equal Pay Directive (75/117/EEC).
- Equal Pay Act 1970.
- Equal Pay Act 1970 (Amendment) Regulations 2003.
- Equal Pay (Questions and Replies) Order 2003.

Like work, work rated as equivalent and work of equal value

Like work

A woman is employed on like work with a man if the woman's and man's work is of the same or a broadly similar nature. Employers need to consider the nature and extent of the differences between the work and the frequency with which such differences occur. For example, a cook in a director's dining room was held to be engaged on like work with the assistant chefs of the company's factory canteen.

Work rated as equivalent

An objective job evaluation study can be carried out in respect of a woman's and man's work, and the woman's job is rated for equivalence on the basis of the demand made in terms of matters such as skill or effort required, or level of responsibility. A woman can compare herself to a man who is rated at the same level or lower than her in the job evaluation study. Where a

oman raises a rated as equivalent claim
ny back pay awarded (see Remedies,
elow) should reflect only the period when
e job evaluation scheme was in place
although the employee could also raise an
qual value claim in respect of the period
rior to the job evaluation study).

Vork of equal value

woman's work may be of equal value
a man's in terms of the demands made
n her, even if it is not like work or rated
s equivalent. A woman may therefore
otentially still claim equal pay with a man
ven if he is doing a different job. For
xample, a female cook employed as a
anteen assistant succeeded in a claim for
qual pay with a male skilled tradesman.
Where work is claimed to be of equal
alue, an independent expert is often
ppointed to determine the issue.

Appropriate comparator

A person making a claim under the
EPA must select a comparator, that is a
erson of the opposite sex whose terms
nd conditions can be compared for the
urpose of determining equality. There is
ne limited exception to the requirement
o cite a comparator and that is in
regnancy-related cases. The comparator
annot be hypothetical. In the recent
ase of *Walter Centre for Neurology v.
3ewley* (UKEAT/0564/07), the EAT held,
verturning previous case law, that a
Claimant cannot compare herself to her
uccessor. The choice of comparator under
he EPA is limited by the requirement for
he comparator to be employed by the
same employer or associated employers.
However, under Article 141 the scope
or comparison is wider and the ECJ has
established that it may not be limited to
he same employer. The important factor
s whether the relationship between the
wo employers is sufficiently close and, in
particular, whether the disparity in terms

and conditions can be attributed to a
'single source'. In the case of *Robertson
v. Defra* (2005) IRLR 363, the Court of
Appeal held that the Crown was not the
'single source' responsible for determining
pay and conditions with the effect that the
Claimants could not compare themselves
with employees in different departments
within the Civil Service.

In the recent case of *North v. Dumfries
and Galloway Council & Others*, a Tribunal
held that a group of claimants who worked
as Classroom Assistants, Support for
Learning Assistants and Nursery Nurses
were in the same employment for the
purposes of the EPA as their comparators
who were Groundsmen, Refuse Collectors,
Refuse Drivers and Leisure Attendants
despite the fact the Claimants were
each based at particular schools and the
comparators (with the exception of leisure
attendants) were based at depots but
worked at a variety of locations across
the geographical area covered by the
Council. The Tribunal relied on the case of
British Coal Corporation v. Smith & Others
(1996) IRLR 404 in which the House of
Lords held that a Claimant can satisfy the
'same employment' test by showing that
male comparators at her establishment
share common terms and conditions with
male comparators at other establishments.
Applying this rule, the Tribunal in *North*
found that, since in this case the Claimants
and comparators were neither employed
under the same terms and conditions
nor at the same establishment, it was
necessary for the Claimants to satisfy the
Tribunal that if their comparators were
employed at their establishment, they
would be employed under broadly similar
terms to those that they were employed
under at present. The Tribunal found that
there was no persuasive evidence that in
the event that the comparators were based
at the same establishment as the Claimant,

their terms and conditions would differ from those under which the comparators were currently employed. Accordingly, the Tribunal found that the Claimants and the comparators were in the same employment for the purposes of the EPA.

A comparison can be made, using the principles of indirect discrimination, between groups of employees where one group is predominantly female and the other group is predominantly male and there is a disparity in the terms and conditions between the groups of employees.

Meaning of 'Pay'

The scope of the EPA is not limited to 'pay' in the usual sense of the word. In this context the word 'pay' can generally be regarded as meaning 'terms and conditions'. For example, the EPA covers ex-gratia perks, redundancy pay and pension contributions.

In one case, the Court of Appeal took the unusual approach of aggregating the employees' basic pay, fixed bonuses and attendance allowances in order to work out an overall hourly rate for the purposes of comparison. The Court of Appeal clarified that an employee cannot pick and choose terms from the comparator's contract for comparison.

Genuine material factor (GMF) defence

An employer can defend an equal pay claim by establishing that the variation between the woman's contract and the man's contract is genuinely due to a material factor which is not the difference of sex; for example, qualifications or performance. The courts, both at a European and national level, have accepted that economic reasons can constitute 'material factors'. An example would be where an employer recruits

a new female employee and offers her more advantageous terms and conditions than an existing male employee carrying out a similar role on the basis that the job market is such that competitive terms and conditions are essential to recruit quality employees. In the case of *Cadman v. Health and Safety Executive* (2006) ICR 1623, the ECJ confirmed that where the difference in pay can be attributed to length of service, it will usually be justifiable unless "the worker provides evidence capable of raising serious doubt in that regard".

There has been confusion surrounding whether it is sufficient for an employer to demonstrate that there is a reason for the disparity in terms and conditions which are not related to gender or whether the employer has to go one step further and objectively justify the difference. Domestic case law has held that the employer will not be required to justify objectively any difference in pay unless the claimant has shown there to be a potentially indirectly discriminatory reason for the difference. The European Court of Justice, however, has held that an employer must objectively justify any difference in pay, even where the claimant has failed to establish that the difference in pay is potentially indirectly discriminatory.

In the case of *Sharp v. Caledonia Group Services* (2005) UKEAT 0041/05/0111, the EAT preferred the ECJ's approach. This decision was appealed to the Court of Appeal, but the case settled before the appeal was heard. However, the recent case of *Middlesbrough Borough Council v. Surtees & Others* (2007) UKEAT 0077/07/1707 adds significant weight to the argument that objective justification is only required where the explanation being put forward for the difference in pay is tainted by sex.

he case of *West Midlands Policy
Blackburn* (UKEAT/0007/07) is
n interesting example of a Tribunal
isunderstanding the purpose of the
MF defence. The Claimants were police
fficers who received less than their
ale comparator who was employed on
e work. The reason for the disparity
pay was that the comparator worked
ifts involving night work and received
special payment (effectively a bonus)
r this but the Claimants did receive
milar special payments because they
d not work at night due to childcare
sponsibilities. The Tribunal held that it
as a legitimate objective to reward night
ork, but that the Chief Constable could
ave paid the Claimants as though they
ad done night work even though they had
ot. It would not have been a significant
xpenditure and would have eliminated
e discrimination. The EAT upheld the
hief Constable's appeal and held that
e Tribunal had misunderstood the nature
f the justification defence and had erred
concluding that the differential was not
asonably justified.

lias P stated that:

The payment of money to compensate for
e economic disadvantages suffered by
ose who have childcare responsibilities
not what the Equal Pay Act requires.
or is the assessment of the employer's
bility to pay sums of this kind a task
hich Parliament could conceivably have
xpected Tribunals to do" (paragraph 46).

mplied equality clause
the employer cannot justify the difference
pay, the implied equality clause operates
o that:

- any contractual term which is less
favourable to a woman is modified
to become as favourable as the
corresponding term in the man's
contract; and

- any beneficial term in a man's contract
which is not included in the woman's
contract is included into the woman's
contract.

To give a simple example, if a man is paid
£500 more per month than a woman for
like work, the equality clause will entitle the
woman to that extra £500 per month.

Remedies
These are:

- back pay (limited to six years, or
five in Scotland from claim date)
representing the difference in pay
between the woman and the 'equal'
or 'equivalent' employee, with interest;
and
- the same level of pay or benefits as
her comparator for the future (if the
complainant remains in the same job).

The EAT has confirmed that a claim
under the EPA cannot include an element
for non-pecuniary losses (e.g. injury to
feelings).

Procedure
As with discrimination claims, cases can
be brought while the employee is still
employed. In the standard case, claims
must be brought at any time during
employment or within six months of leaving
employment (which will be extended to
nine months if the employee raises a
statutory grievance as she requires to do).

An individual may submit equal pay
questionnaires to the employer, either
before a claim is made to the Tribunal
or within 21 days of such a claim being
lodged. Employers are not obliged to
answer these questionnaires, but the
Tribunal may draw an adverse inference
if a questionnaire is not answered
deliberately and without reasonable cause
in an eight-week window from it being

served, or where the reply is evasive or equivocal. This includes an inference that the equality clause has been breached. An employer may be reluctant to disclose certain information when responding to the questionnaire on the basis that it may result in a breach of the Data Protection Act 1998 (DPA). That may be appropriate in some cases; however, if the Tribunal subsequently issues an Order compelling the employer to disclose the information and the processing can be deemed 'fair' then it will have no liability under the DPA.

New legislation

The Equal Pay Act 1970 (Amendment) Regulations 2004 came into force on 1 October 2004, amending the EPA and the tribunal procedural rules. Under the amended EPA, a Tribunal can choose to determine the question of equal value itself rather than appoint an independent expert. Where a job evaluation study ascribes different values to the work of the claimant and the comparator, the Tribunal will be bound to conclude that the work is not

of equal value unless it has reasonable grounds for suspecting that the study discriminated on the ground of sex, or th there are other reasons why it cannot be relied upon.

Schedule 6 of the Employment Tribunals (Constitution and Rules of Procedure) Regulations 2004, which came into force on 1 October 2004, contains procedural rules which apply exclusively to equal pa claims.

The Occupational Pension Schemes (Equal Treatment) (Amendment) Regulations 2005 came into force on 10 October 2005. The Regulations updated the Occupational Pension Schemes (Equal Treatment) Regulations 1995 which were enacted for the purpose of importing an equal treatment rule into the rules of all occupational pensions schemes.

See also: Discrimination, p.222

Sources of further information

Equality and Human Rights Commission: www.equalityhumanrights.com

Equal Opportunities policies are becoming ever more important in today's increasingly multicultural, multiracial society. The purpose of this type of policy is to set out the obligations on both the employer and the employee to treat all people with equal dignity and respect within the workplace. The aim is to create a pleasant and harmonious working environment for all.

Workplace Law Group's *Equal Opportunities Policy and Management Guide, v.3.0* sets out and explains the rights of each employee. A well-drafted Equal Opportunities policy combined with good management will ensure your organisation meets its legal obligation to provide a non-discriminatory work environment and persuade employees that an equal opportunities policy at work is for the benefit of the whole workforce. For more information visit www.workplacelaw.net/Bookshop/PoliciesAndProcedures.

Eye and eyesight tests

Andrew Richardson, Scott Wilson

Key points

- Use of display screen equipment (DSE) constitutes an adverse health condition.
- Users or operators of DSE can suffer visual fatigue or headaches.
- DSE does not cause permanent damage to eyesight, but pre-existing eye conditions may be accentuated.
- Employers must provide and pay for eye and eyesight tests if employees request.
- Tests must be carried out by a registered ophthalmic optician or medical practitioner.
- Employers must provide spectacles where needed for screen-viewing distance if employees request.

Legislation

Health and Safety at Work etc. Act 1974.

Opticians Act 1989 (as amended in 2005).

Health and Safety (Display Screen Equipment) Regulations 1992 as amended by the Health and Safety (Miscellaneous Amendments) Regulations 2002.

Management of Health and Safety at Work Regulations 1999.

Statutory requirements

Regulation 6 of the Management of Health and Safety at Work Regulations requires consideration to be given to carrying out health surveillance of employees where there is a disease or adverse health condition identified in the risk assessments. It has been identified that use of DSE by someone deemed to be a 'user' or 'operator' does constitute an adverse health condition.

The Regulations state that it will be generally appropriate to classify people as a user or operator if they:

- normally use DSE for continuous or near-continuous spells of an hour or more at a time; and
- use DSE in this way more or less daily; and
- have to transfer information quickly to or from the DSE; and
- need to apply high levels of attention and concentration; or
- are highly dependent on DSE or have little choice about using it; or
- need special training or skills to use DSE.

The purpose of the eye test is to improve the comfort and efficiency of the user by identifying and correcting any vision defects specific to DSE use. There is no evidence that DSE usage causes permanent damage to eyesight; what will occur is that pre-existing eye conditions will be accentuated, which can lead to temporary visual fatigue or headaches.

The Regulations require employers to provide users or operators with an appropriate eye and eyesight test if they request it. The employer has a liability to pay for these tests. Note that DSE users are not obliged to have the test.

The employer has a duty to provide tests to employees already designated as a user or operator and to employees who are being recruited or transferred to be users or operators.

The test should include the test of vision and examination of the eye, otherwise known as a sight test in the Opticians Act. The test should take into account the nature of the DSE work carried out. Only a registered ophthalmic optician or registered medical practitioner should carry out the test.

If an employee requests a test for the first time, it must be carried out as soon as practicable. If an employee is to be transferred to a user or operator post, then the test must be carried out before commencement in that post. For people being recruited, once they are definitely going to be an employee, then the test should be carried out before they commence any work that meets the user operator criteria.

After the first test, the employer must be guided by the optician or doctor as to the frequency of subsequent tests.

If the tests show that the employee requires special corrective appliances (normally spectacles) specifically for distances when using DSE, then the employer has the liability to provide a basic special corrective appliance. Normal corrective appliances are those spectacles prescribed for any other purpose, but the employer has no liability for these.

See also: Display screen equipment, p.238; Employee benefits, p.266; Occupational health, p.537

Sources of further information

The main source of information in relation to the use of DSE is L26 *Work with Display Screen Equipment – Health and Safety (Display Screen Equipment) Regulations 1992 as amended by the Health and Safety (Miscellaneous Amendments) Regulations 2002 – Guidance on Regulations* (HSE Books, 2003) ISBN: 0 7176 2582 6. The document provides all the guidance needed by employers and identifies further documentation that is relevant.

Facilities management contracts: essential elements

arc Hanson, Ashurst

Key points

Like all other forms of contract, a facilities management contract is essentially a legally binding and enforceable bargain between two parties.

Each party contributes something to the bargain – the facilities management contractor – the provision of certain services; and the client – payment for those services.

Negotiation

For a contract to be legally binding, there must be an offer from one party, an unconditional acceptance of that offer by the other party, and consideration provided by each party for the promise made by the other party. A client's invitation to tender is not usually an 'offer' – it is usually no more than an offer to negotiate.

A facilities management contractor's tender to carry out the services will, usually, amount to the initial 'offer'.

When the client accepts the facilities management contractor's tender and each party gives consideration, then, provided both parties have an intention to be legally bound, a legally enforceable contract will come into place. Offers and acceptance can be made in writing, orally or by conduct.

It is of course unusual for facilities management contractors' tenders to be accepted without qualification by a client. There may be areas of extensive negotiation, e.g. in relation to scope of services and fees. Every time each party provides any revised proposals, then each revised proposal will take effect as a 'counter-offer'.

When eventually all outstanding points have been agreed, one party will invariably 'accept' the other party's final 'offer'.

When does the contract start?

The process of negotiating a facilities management contract can be protracted. In many cases, services may be provided to the client and payment may be made without any form of contract having been signed. Where relationships subsequently deteriorate, it can be extremely difficult to establish whether there was ever a binding contract in place and, if there was, on what terms it was made.

Whether a binding contract exists in such circumstances will depend on whether the parties managed to agree all the key terms of the contract and whether the terms of the alleged contract included all terms that would be essential for a contract to exist. It would be unlikely that there was a contract agreed if key elements of the contract were still outstanding; for example, if the exact scope of the services was undecided or if a price had not been agreed. However, a contract can still come into effect where certain points in the contract terms are still to be agreed, provided that the key elements have been finalised and agreed.

Scope of contracts

When drafting facilities management contracts, it is important to ensure that they cover the complete understanding and agreement between the parties.
As such, it is necessary to include not only a list of the services to be provided by the supplier but also a mechanism for dealing with changes to the services and also any details as to what equipment or facilities are to be provided to the supplier by the client in relation to the services.

Payment

Careful thought needs to be given as to how payment to the facilities management contractor will be structured. Will it be on the basis of a lump-sum price, by prime cost or by reference to a schedule of rates? If the price is to adjust, then a mechanism needs to be set out allowing for this, detailing the circumstances in which adjustments will be made. Careful consideration also needs to be given to any mechanism to be included in the contract that would allow the contract price to be adjusted to reflect performance or non-performance by the supplier of the services.

Service levels

Service levels should be included in the contract against which the performance by the supplier can be assessed. Consideration needs to be given as to how poor performance is dealt with and whether the liability of the supplier under the contract is to be limited in any way.

Duration

The duration of a facilities management contract is of critical importance, and this should be clearly stated in the contract together with the circumstances in which it can be extended or terminated by either party.

Facilities management contracts should also address other key areas such as compliance with statutory requirements, transfer of undertakings provisions, insurance requirements and provisions dealing with dispute resolution.

See also: Contract disputes, p.157; Contractors, p.160; TUPE, p.697

Sources of further information

Workplace Law Group's *Facilities Management Contracts 2008* follows the success of two editions of the *Guide to Facilities Management Contracts*. Now fully updated, it provides an introduction to contract law as it relates to FM contracts, and a guide to comon contractual law provisions. This extended publication looks at new areas of law including amendments to the Construction Act, amendments to CDM Regulations, revised TUPE Regulations, revised EU Procurement law, dispute resolution procedures, and European standards for facilities management. For more information visit www.workplacelaw.net/Bookshop/Handbooks.

Family-friendly rights

Pinsent Masons Employment Group

Key points

- Pregnant employees, regardless of their length of service, are entitled to 26 weeks' ordinary maternity leave and 26 weeks' additional maternity leave. Additional maternity leave will follow straight on from ordinary maternity leave.
- An employee who is the father of the child or the mother's husband or partner is entitled to take up to two weeks' paid paternity leave on the birth or adoption of a child.
- Eligible employees are now entitled to take 26 weeks' ordinary adoption leave and 26 weeks' additional adoption leave.
- Employees with sufficient continuous service will be entitled to statutory maternity pay or statutory adoption pay for 39 weeks.
- Employees (both male and female) with one year's continuous service are entitled to take up to 13 weeks' unpaid parental leave, or 18 weeks in the case of a disabled child, to care for each of their children.
- Employees who have responsibility for looking after a child can request a variation in their contractual hours.

Legislation

- Social Security Contributions and Benefits Act 1992.
- Employment Rights Act 1996.
- Employment Relations Act 1999.
- Maternity and Parental Leave etc. Regulations 1999.
- Employment Act 2002.
- Maternity and Parental Leave (Amendment) Regulations 2002.
- Paternity and Adoption Leave Regulations 2002.
- Flexible Working (Eligibility, Complaints and Remedies) Regulations 2002.
- Flexible Working (Procedural Requirements) Regulations 2002.
- Work and Families Act 2006.
- Maternity and Parental Leave etc. and the Paternity and Adoption Leave (Amendment) Regulations 2006.
- Statutory Paternity Pay and Statutory Adoption Pay (General) and the Statutory Paternity Pay and Statutory Adoption Pay (Weekly Rates) (Amendment) Regulations 2006.

Employment Act 2002 and Work and Families Act 2006

The Employment Act 2002 contains a number of family-friendly provisions relating to maternity rights, paternity leave and adoption leave. Four new sets of Regulations implemented changes to the previous law and created new rights for pregnant women and parents. The Work and Families Act 2006 extended a number of these rights. Many of these changes have been implemented by the Maternity and Parental Leave etc. and the Paternity and Adoption Leave (Amendment) Regulations 2006 (the 2006 Regulations) which came into force on 1 October 2006.

Maternity rights

The 2006 Regulations amend the Maternity and Parental Leave etc. Regulations 1999 for women whose expected week of childbirth is on or after 1 April 2007. The 2006 Regulations remove the length of service requirement for entitlement to additional maternity leave (AML) and provide that a woman will be entitled to 26 weeks' ordinary maternity leave (OML) and 26 weeks' AML regardless of her length of service.

The employee is required to inform her employer before the end of the 15th week before EWC of the date on which she intends to start her OML.

Employees are entitled not to be unreasonably refused time off with pay to attend antenatal care appointments subject to providing their employer with details about the appointment. Thereafter, women are protected from suffering treatment to their detriment by employers (including dismissal) because they are pregnant.

Pregnancy-related dismissals are automatically unfair, and one year's continuous service is not needed to claim unfair dismissal. Amendments to the Sex Discrimination Act in October 2005 make it clear as a matter of statute that less favourable treatment on grounds of pregnancy or maternity leave will constitute sex discrimination. Previously, this was established as a matter of case law, but the change will make the position clear as a matter of statute.

Employers must not allow women who qualify for maternity leave to work at all in the two weeks immediately following childbirth.

Women entitled to OML have a statutory right to return to their job without giving notice. During OML employment terms continue to apply to the employee except for the right to pay.

During the AML period, only certain terms and conditions of employment continue in force. Care should be taken to ensure that during the woman's absence she is kept informed of any new vacancies or promoted positions or of any other relevant matters (such as details regarding pay rise made available to other employees) which become available to avoid any claims that she is being discriminated against.

Women on maternity leave will now be able to go into work for up to ten mutually agreed 'Keeping in Touch' days without losing entitlement to statutory maternity pay

The notice required from women on maternity leave to return earlier or later than planned has been increased from 28 days to eight weeks.

Maternity pay is often covered in the contract of employment, but must be no less than the statutory maternity pay (SMP) equivalent. Employees will only be entitled to SMP if they have 26 weeks continuous service at the 15th week before the week their baby is due. The SMP pay period is currently 39 weeks. The first six weeks of the maternity pay period are paid at 90% of the employee's average weekly earnings calculated on the basis of earnings during the eight weeks that end with the 15th week before the expected week of childbirth. The remaining 33 weeks are paid at the flat rate which is currently £117.80 per week.

The Work and Families Act 2006 extends the maximum maternity pay period that may be prescribed by regulations to 52 weeks and the Government intends to extend the period to the full 52 weeks by 2009 or 2010.

Paternity leave
The Paternity and Adoption Leave Regulations 2002 came into force on

December 2002 and provide rights for employees who qualify to take paternity leave.

An employee is entitled to take paternity leave when the purpose of the absence is to care for a newborn child or to support the child's mother.

To qualify for paid paternity leave, employees must:

- be the father of the child or the mother's husband or partner (partner is a person of the same or different sex who lives with the mother and the child and is in an enduring family relationship but who is not a relative of the mother);
- have or expect to have responsibilities for the upbringing of the child; and
- have 26 weeks' service.

Statutory paternity pay is paid for two weeks and is £117.80 per week (or 90% of the employee's average weekly earnings if less).

Employees cannot lawfully be subjected to any detriment or dismissed due to taking or requesting paternity leave. Any such dismissal will be automatically unfair.

The Work and Families Act 2006 introduced a new statutory right to additional paternity leave (APL) up to a maximum of 26 weeks and additional paternity pay (APP) for employees during the second six months of the 12-month maternity leave or adoption leave period. The Regulations that will introduce APL and APP have not yet been published. It is expected that they will be introduced at the same time as Regulations to extend maternity and adoption pay to 52 weeks.

Adoption leave

The 2006 Regulations amend the Paternity and Adoption Leave Regulations 2002 to provide that eligible employees now have the statutory right to 26 weeks' ordinary adoption leave and 26 weeks' unpaid additional adoption leave.

To be eligible for adoption leave, an employee needs to be an individual who has been newly matched with a child for adoption by an adoption agency, or be one member of a couple where the couple has jointly been newly matched with a child for adoption by an adoption agency (the couple must choose which partner takes adoption leave) and have completed at least 26 weeks' continuous service with the employer ending with the week (beginning with the Sunday and ending with the Saturday) in which the employee is notified of being matched with the child for adoption.

The partner of an individual who adopts or the other member of a couple who are adopting jointly may be entitled to paternity leave pay (see above).

Adoption leave will not be available in circumstances where a child is not newly matched for adoption (e.g. when a step-parent is adopting a partner's child).

Other changes have also been made which reflect the statutory changes to maternity leave and pay. These include the:

- increase to the statutory adoption pay (SAP) period to 39 weeks (employees entitled to SAP are those with 26 weeks' continuous service leading into the week of notification of an adoption match);
- introduction of ten 'Keeping in Touch' days; and
- increase to the notice period required to return to work earlier or later than planned from 28 days to eight weeks.

The Work and Families Act 2006 also extends the maximum adoption pay period that may be prescribed by Regulations to 52 weeks and the Government currently intends to extend the adoption pay period to the full 52 weeks by 2009 or 2010.

Parental leave

Employees, both mothers and fathers, who have completed one year's service with their current employer are entitled to take 13 weeks' (18 weeks where the child is disabled) unpaid parental leave to care for their child.

Parental leave can usually be taken up to five years from the date of birth or in the case of adoption five years from the date of placement (or up to the child's 18th birthday if that is sooner). In the case of a child entitled to a disability living allowance, parental leave can be taken at any time before the child's 18th birthday. In the case of children born or adopted between 15 December 1994 and 14 December 1999, the employee's right lasts until 31 March 2005 (or in the case of adoption until the child's 18th birthday if that is sooner) and in this case one year's service with a previous employer between 15 December 1998 and 9 January 2002 gives entitlement.

At the end of parental leave an employee is guaranteed the right to return to the same job as before, or, if that is not practicable, a similar job which has the same or better status, terms and conditions as the old job. If, however, the period of parental leave is for a period of four weeks or less, the employee is entitled to go back to the same job.

Wherever possible, employers and employees should make their own arrangements about how parental leave will work, how much notice should be given, arrangements for postponing the leave when the business cannot cope and how it should be taken.

Where employers and employees have not entered into an agreement about these matters, or until they have done so, the fallback scheme set out in the Regulations applies. The fallback scheme provides for employees to take parental leave in blocks or multiples of one week, after giving 21 days' notice, up to a maximum of four weeks' leave in a year and subject to postponement by the employer for up to six months where the business cannot cope. Leave cannot be postponed when the employee gives notice to take it immediately after the time the child is born or is placed with the family for adoption.

Flexible working

Parents and others (as listed in the Flexible Working Regulations) who have responsibility for looking after a child who is under six (or under 18 in the case of a disabled child) can request a variation in their contract of employment to have a more flexible working pattern. However, there is no right to work flexibly. If an employee makes such a request, the employer must follow a set procedure for meeting the employee to discuss the request, making a decision and issuing a decision with reasons. If the employer fails to follow the procedure, the employee may make an application to the Employment Tribunal.

Under the Work and Families Act 2006, from 6 April 2007 the right to request flexible working will extend to those caring for adults. After consultation with various carers groups and business organisations, a carer has been defined as an employee who is or expects to be caring for an adult who:

is married to, or the partner or civil partner of the employee; or

is a near relative of the employee; or

falls into neither category but lives at the same address as the employee.

The 'near relative' definition includes parents, parents-in-law, adult child, adopted adult child, siblings (including those who are in-laws), uncles, aunts or grandparents and step-relatives.

See also: Carers, p.114; Discrimination, p.222; Flexible working, p.338; Managing pregnancy, p.484

Sources of further information

Template adoption, maternity and paternity policies are available as electronic downloads from Workplace Law Group. Visit www.workplacelaw.net/Bookshop/ PoliciesAndProcedures or call 0871 777 8881 for further details.

BERR: Work and Families: www.berr.gov.uk/employment/workandfamilies/work-families-history/index.html.

Fire extinguishers

Andrew Richardson, Scott Wilson

Key points

The legislation covering fire extinguishers is the Regulatory Reform (Fire Safety) Order 2005. The Order requires the Responsible Person to:

- assess the fire risk in the workplace;
- provide reasonable firefighting equipment;
- check that people know what to do in the event of fire; and
- ensure that fire safety equipment is maintained and monitored.

Vehicles carrying dangerous goods are required to be fitted with fire extinguishers, but there is no legal requirement for cars.

Legislation
- Health and Safety at Work etc. Act 1974.
- Management of Health and Safety at Work Regulations 1999.
- Regulatory Reform (Fire Safety) Order 2005.
- The Carriage of Dangerous Goods and Use of Transportable Pressure Equipment Regulations 2007 (CDG 2007).

The Fire Safety Order ('the Order') repealed the Fire Precautions Act 1971 and revoked the Fire Precautions (Workplace) Regulations 1997, as amended in 1999. It came into force on 1 October 2006. The main impact of the Order was to move the emphasis of fire legislation towards prevention – any fire certificate issued under the Fire Precautions Act 1971 has ceased to have effect.

Responsible Person
The Order introduces a new role of Responsible Person. Anyone in full or partial control of a premises may be a Responsible Person. They might be, for instance, an employer for those parts of premises over which they have any control, a managing agent or owner for shared parts of a premises or shared fire safety equipment such as fire detection systems or sprinklers, or an occupier, such as self-employed people or voluntary organisations when they have any control.

It may be clearly evident who is the Responsible Person, but equally several people may have some responsibility. In such cases, the Responsible Persons will need to work together to ensure that the arrangements they make are complete and consistent.

Risk assessments
A Responsible Person has a duty to assess the fire risk in the premises. A fire risk assessment carried out under the Fire Precautions (Workplace) Regulations 1997 would be an excellent start, provided it has been kept up to date; relatively modest revisions would be required to take account of the wider scope of the Order.

The Responsible Person must carry out a fire risk assessment but could get another competent person to do it for them. Even so, the Responsible Person retains the duty to comply with the Order. The objective of the fire risk assessment is to devise arrangements to ensure that all persons on or near the premises can safely escape if there is a fire. Unlike previous legislation, the Order requires consideration of all persons who might be on the premises, whether or not they are employees – visitors, contractors, cleaners, members of the public and so on all need to be thought about. Furthermore, special arrangements may be needed for anyone who has a disability or who may need special help, e.g. persons with mobility impairments or hearing or vision problems.

There are five steps to a fire risk assessment:

1. Identify the potential fire hazards.
2. Identify people at risk.
3. Evaluate the risks, remove or reduce, and protect and decide if existing control measures are adequate.
4. Record findings and actions, plan, inform, instruct and train people.
5. Review and revise those assessments periodically.

The findings and actions from fire risk assessments are usually compiled into a fire action plan.

Classes of fire

In order to fight a fire, you need to determine the following:

- Is the firefighting equipment suitable for the fire risk?
- Is the equipment located correctly?
- Does the equipment have the correct signage?
- Have personnel been trained to use the equipment provided?

In order to determine what firefighting equipment is suitable, you have to identify the classes of fire that may occur in your workplace. There are six classes into which all fires will fall:

- *Class A:* fires involving solids (wood, paper, plastics, etc., usually organic in nature).
- *Class B:* fires involving liquids or liquefiable solids (petrol, oil, paint, wax, etc.).
- *Class C:* fires involving gases (LPG, natural gas, acetylene, etc.).

Type	Colour code	Suitable for
Water	Red	Class A fires only
Foam	Cream	Class B fires but can also be used on class A
Dry powder	Blue	Class B fires but can also be used on class A and electrical
Halon	Green	Do not use*
Carbon dioxide	Black	Electrical fires and small class B fires
Special powder	Blue	Class D fires
Wet chemical	Canary yellow	Class F fires

* Effectively banned after 31 December 2003 under the Montreal Protocol because of their ozone-depleting properties. If you have any of these in your workplace, you should arrange to have a replacement system installed as soon as possible.

- *Class D:* fires involving metals (sodium, magnesium, any metal powders, etc.).
- *Electrical fires:* although not deemed as a class, electrical equipment fires form a separate category.
- *Class F:* fires involving cooking fats / oils.

Once you have determined the class of fire, you can then select the appropriate firefighting equipment. This can include portable extinguishers, hosereels, sprinkler systems, hydrant systems or fixed firefighting systems. Selection should follow the guidance in BS 5306-8: *Fire extinguishing installations and equipment on premises. Selection and installation of portable fire extinguishers. Code of practice.*

Portable firefighting equipment
Portable fire extinguishers come in a variety of types as shown in the table below.

Types of portable fire extinguishers
All are coloured red, but each may have a colour-coded panel to aid in identifying the type.

Fire extinguishers have limitations – they can be used only on the appropriate class of fire, they are of limited duration, and they have a limited range.

The fire extinguishers should be sited:

- conspicuously and readily visible;
- on all escape routes;
- close to specifically identified danger areas;
- close to room exits, inside or outside dependent on risk;
- at the same location on each floor;
- grouped together to form a fire point;
- no further than 30 metres from any person;

- with handle 1.1 metre from floor level and
- away from extreme heat or cold.

Fire extinguishers should be maintained in accordance with BS 5306-3 *Fire extinguishing installations and equipment on premises. Code of practice for the inspection and maintenance of portable fire extinguishers.* This details monthly inspections, annual inspections, and maintenance and discharge test requirements. Those who you entrust to carry out the maintenance must be competent, e.g. ISO9001 certified or BAFE Approved.

Hosereels
Hosereels are primarily utilised on Class A fires. An adjustable nozzle allows the water to be in a jet or spray form: a jet can be used at the base of a fire and a spray allows a larger area of coverage and can be used for protection of personnel. Hosereels obviously have a continuous supply of water, which is provided in greater quantity than from an extinguisher and hence they have a greater range.

Their limitations are:

- greater physical effort is required to operate them;
- they wedge open fire doors allowing possible smoke spread;
- they should be used only on Class A fires;
- they are a trip hazard; and
- there is a tendency to remain fighting the fire for longer periods.

Hosereels should be provided for every 800 square metres of floor area or part thereof and should be in prominent and accessible locations at exits so that they can extend to all parts in all rooms. Hosereels should be inspected monthly and an annual test carried out to check their full functional capability.

raining
he Health and Safety at Work etc.
ct 1974 requires employers to provide
formation, instruction, training and
upervision to ensure the health,
afety and welfare of employees. The
lanagement of Health and Safety at Work
egulations 1999 state that employers
eed to take into account the capabilities
f their employees before entrusting tasks
nd that they should have adequate health
nd safety training and be capable enough
t their jobs to avoid risk.

irefighting is a high-risk activity. If you
s an employer have a fire procedure
hat instructs your employees to tackle
he fire, then you have a legal obligation
o ensure they are adequately trained.
Most instructions to tackle fire usually end
vith 'if it is safe to do so' – unless you
re trained, you will not be able to judge
whether it is safe. Your local fire brigade
vill be able to guide you on the training
vailable, and advise you about any local
ariations to emergency procedures.

Fire extinguishers in vehicles

Vehicles carrying dangerous goods are
required to be fitted with fire extinguishers
under CDG 2007, which came into force
on 1 January 2008. Two extinguishers
are usually required; the level of provision
varies from 2kg to 12kg, depending on the
vehicle weight.

There is no legal requirement to carry
a fire extinguisher in a car, but it is
recommended by RoSPA and other
sources. The extinguisher should be dry
powder or foam type, and manufactured to
BS EN 3 1996. Sizes vary but are typically
in the range of 0.6–1.0kg.

See also: Firefighting, p.330; Fire,
means of escape, p.322; Fire safety
in non-domestic premises, p.325

Sources of further information

The Government has produced a series of 11 guide books to assist the
Responsible Person to carry out a fire risk assessment in different types of
premises. The guides can be purchased through or downloaded from the
Department for Communities and Local Government's website at
www.communities.gov.uk/fire/firesafety/firesafetylaw/aboutguides/. For SMEs with
low risk environments such as offices, there is an Entry Level Guide, which can
be downloaded from the same site:
www.communities.gov.uk/publications/fire/regulatoryreformfire

Legal duties now place a greater emphasis on one person knowing exactly how
their building will be affected by fire, so it is important that Responsible Persons
have accessible information that is easy to understand. Workplace Law Group's
Fire Safety 2009: Special Report provides authoritative, high-level research
that demonstrates the impact of the Regulatory Reform (Fire Safety) Order 2005.
The Report explains fire safety law in detail and provides an analysis of case law
under the new legislation in comparison with the old, using real-life examples to
highlight its importance. For more information visit
www.workplacelaw.net/Bookshop/SpecialReports.

Comment...

The RRO – is it working?

Paul Clarke, Cambridgeshire Fire and Rescue Services, Alan Cox, Fire Consultant, and Clive Raybould, Fire Safety Consultant, each offer their views on the Regulatory Reform (Fire Safety) Order.

The Regulatory Reform (Fire Safety) Order 2005 came into force in October 2006. Why was there a need to bring out another piece of fire safety legislation?

Paul Clarke: "What the RRO did was to bring together around about 80 pieces of fire legislation. Some of those pieces of legislation were only relevant in perhaps one county, so it was important that we brought all those together under one umbrella. Also, it was felt, particularly by business, that the Fire Precautions Act was slightly onerous and a bit too inflexible, so the idea of the RRO is to introduce a piece of legislation that still gives a requirement but there is a flexible approach to meeting those requirements."

Clive Raybould: "There was a need to move away from prescriptive law into more modern risk assessment-style law. This simple approach brings fire safety in line with all modern law and should make it more understandable to business, as the approach should be no different to other issues. More importantly perhaps was the creation of the 'One Stop Shop' for fire safety legislation that the Fire Safety Order creates."

Do you think the RRO has done what the Government intended it to do?

Alan Cox: "It's fairly early days yet to give a definitive answer on this question and whilst there was a lot wrong with the prescriptive approach it's clear to me that owners and occupiers do not understand their responsibilities under the new legislation and as a consequence I am finding some worrying situations. As an example I recently visited a Computer Fair at the National Motorcycle Museum in Birmingham and found obstructed fire exits, fire doors wedged open and obstructed and trailing cables under fire doors – who would have thought that only a few years ago they suffered a multi million pound fire? Clearly, even after such a big loss and the new legislation the message had not reached home here."

Clive Raybould: "Not totally. Where companies have embraced the Fire Safety Order and taken ownership of fire safety management then yes. Unfortunately there are still a large number of organisations that have done very little."

Is the RRO working in practice?

Paul Clarke: "As we are going around undertaking our audits in premises we are ways going to have people who have ... e safety as a top priority and then other ...ople who have fire safety as quite a ...w priority. Because of the flexibility that ...e RRO gives, sometimes people do use ...at to their advantage; that's why we do ...ave to keep going back to do follow-up ...udits on those premises that don't have ...e same interest as others with regards ... fire safety matters. Is it working in ...actice? It is a bit too early to say. It's a ...g shift change for the Fire and Rescue ...ervices to go from the very inflexible ...re Precautions Act to this new method ...ut I think in many ways that flexibility will ...rovide dividends in the end."

...Ian Cox: "I don't believe that it is and ...e reason that I say this is because I am ...till seeing many worrying situations and ...hen I point the problems out to owners ...nd occupiers, many are confused and ...ink that just because they had a Fire ...ertificate and nothing has changed ...verything is still ok. Unfortunately it's ...ot, and it has to be said that many Fire ...ertificates were not worth the paper they ...ere written on. Also many standards ...ave changed and this was one of the ...roblems with Fire Certificates which ...eant the Fire Authorities could not go ...ack to a premises and require changes ...hen new standards were introduced. ...nother example occurred a few months ...go in a 13th century coaching inn in ...hich I was staying – when I did my usual ...uest inspection of the escape routes I ...ound the usual problems of poorly fitting / ...edged-open fire doors, missing fire and ...moke seals, poor housekeeping etc. and ...o I raised these with the management ...who informed me that the Fire Service had ...een in a few weeks prior to my stay and ...ad indicated that everything was ok. I was ...urprised at this because in addition to the ...roblems that I have already listed there ...as an extensive rear fire escape that had ...ardly any fire separation; it should have

been protected with fire-resisting glazing because, as it was, a fire in any of the ground floor rooms – which consisted of a restaurant and bars – could have spread up the stairs and prevented this escape being used.

"I subsequently approached the Fire Service and asked why this situation had been allowed to exist and they indicated that it had been classed as an 'accommodation stair' and they had not seen it as a problem. I went back to the owners and gave them a copy of how an external fire escape should be protected and explained the risk that they were facing and they agreed to carry out the work. Incidentally they had commissioned an independent Fire Risk Assessment and they had also failed to identify this problem."

Do you think general employers and owners of premises understand their duties under the legislation?

Alan Cox: "If you look at the previous examples that I have quoted – and these are not isolated incidents – I think you can see that there is a great amount of confusion and misunderstanding on this subject."

Paul Clarke: "Some do, some don't, and some don't want to, because it's going to cost them money. You'll have some people who prioritise fire safety and some that don't; they think it's a bit of a nuisance; they think it's related to health and safety law, and people sometimes think that health and safety is perhaps going too far. But what price can you put on fire safety? I think that the message from the Government could have perhaps gone out further and wider, because we're still finding people who aren't aware of the legislation, but, having said that, there is a lot of documentation available on the CLG website, if people know how to get to it."

What is the biggest failing in fire safety?

Clive Raybould: "In my opinion the lack of auditing / checking / managing so that fire safety standards are not always in place. For example, on the fire risk assessments I have carried out, I have found approximately 30% of fire exit doors fitted with Redlum bolts do not operate correctly. This type of issue will only be solved by good frequent management checks."

Alan Cox: "This is an easy one to answer as the answer is people – even with the safest building that you can design it's usually people that defeat the safety precautions."

Paul Clarke: "At the moment it's the notion of fire risk assessment; a lot of people just don't understand what a fire risk assessment means and are in actual fact quite afraid of the phrase. The fire risk assessment shouldn't really be any different to any other assessment; you assess your premises, you look at the risks, you look at the people in danger from those risks, and then you look at mitigating those risks to as low as is reasonably practicable. It's a fairly simple process but I think a lot of people are frightened off, and I think that because of the whole of the legislation is based around the notion of risk assessment, that perhaps is its weakest point, because people don't understand the risk assessment process."

What types of premises, in your experience, have the worst fire safety record?

Clive Raybould: "From my experience as an assessor, I would probably say

older factories and, worryingly, housing complexes."

Alan Cox: "Hotels are an area that worry me and with the Penhallow Hotel fire in mind you can easily see why, but generally any premises providing sleeping accommodation are high-risk areas because your safety is usually in someone else's hands."

Do you think, in comparison to the previous legislation, harsher penalties will be given to those that fall foul of the new legislation?

Clive Raybould: "Eventually, yes; we are still in the infancy of this law and the enforcers are still learning. The fact to consider of course is that this law definitely looks more into post-fire investigation and enforcement. Just by being post-fire will potentially make situations appear worse and will probably therefore bring about harsher penalties. Most Fire Services have already seen a large increase in enforcement actions under the Fire Safety Order than they did under previous laws."

Alan Cox: "I certainly think that harsher penalties are the only way to make owners and occupiers realise their responsibilities and maintain fire safety standards to the required standard. Unfortunately, it's not like getting a display screen equipment assessment wrong, where the outcome is very unlikely to be serious – if you get a Fire Risk Assessment wrong the outcome could easily be very serious."

What one measure would you introduce to improve the UK's workplace fire safety record?

Clive Raybould: "I would introduce a formalised monthly audit check of the fire safety standards in the premises."

Ian Cox: "I would like to see a third party rating system for safety where the measures are assessed by an independent organisation that are able to award a premises a rating that people can see before they do business or stay there. The problem now is that if you stay in a hotel, for example, you have no idea if it has carried out a Fire Risk Assessment and if it's credible – under the previous legislation you were fairly sure that the building had applied for and been given a Fire Certificate."

Paul Clarke: "A better knowledge of the fire risk assessment process."

Fire, means of escape

Nicola Cardenas-Blanco, Martineau Solicitors

Key points

- With some limited exceptions, all buildings must have a means of escape from fire.
- At the very least, a place of refuge must be available which must be fire- and smoke-proof for a specified time.
- Previously, a fire certificate used to be issued by the local Fire Authority. Now there is a need for comprehensive risk assessments.
- There are specific requirements as to the means of escape from fire which cover lighting, doors and signage.
- Building occupiers may be required to make specific alterations to enable disabled persons to escape from fire.

Legislation

- Fire Precautions Act 1971.
- Fire Precautions (Workplace) Regulations 1997.
- Regulatory Reform (Fire Safety) Order 2005.

The Regulatory Reform (Fire Safety) Order 2005 requires the 'Responsible Person' to make alterations and to carry out appropriate risk assessments. The Responsible Person is the employer (in workplaces) and the occupier (in other premises). In addition, the employer or occupier must ensure that firefighting equipment inside the premises is maintained and in full working order and also that anyone employed to work in the building is trained on what to do if there is a fire.

If the use of the building changes, a new fire risk assessment will need to be carried out, as the factors affecting the necessary means of escape may change. Employers and occupiers need to be aware that as with any risk assessment, when the circumstances change, the need to assess the risk reappears and the requirement to do risk assessments thoroughly and

carefully in respect of fire are supported well by the law.

A fire risk assessment will normally contain the following information:

- the use of the premises it covers;
- the means of escape in case of fire;
- how the means of escape can be safely and effectively used at all times
- the type, number and location of fire extinguishers and similar equipment the building; and
- how people will be notified if a fire occurs.

Fire risk assessments should be a primary focus for employers and occupiers of buildings. The person responsible for people's safety is required to carry out an appropriate risk assessment which may include at least the above points and more where relevant to those premises.

There is also a statutory duty to provide a means of escape from fire. A breach of this duty could render the occupier liable for a fine under current law. Employers and controllers of premises remain under a duty to provide routes of escape and

mergency exits which are to be kept clear
t all times.

There are also further offences
implemented by the Fire Safety Order,
of which the Responsible Person should
take account. This includes not taking
adequate fire precautions, failure to do
a proper risk assessment or failure to
provide adequate means of escape.
Penalties could include both a fine and
imprisonment.

Codes of practice – means of escape
In addition to the legislative requirements
there are also British Standards or
Approved Codes of Practice (AcoP)
which contain suggested ways of
working towards many safety issues. If
a Responsible Person does not comply
with an AcoP, it will, in the case of a
prosecution, be up to that person, to
demonstrate that the legal standard was
complied with in some other way.

Special considerations
Special regard should be given to
evacuating disabled people or those with
restricted mobility in the event of a fire,
and Responsible Persons should consider
the potential types of disability and how
these may affect any means of escape. The
use of wheelchairs or crutches for
example, or the possibility of dealing
with persons who have impaired senses,
should feature in the fire risk assessment.
In addition there should normally be
alternative means of escape from all parts
of the workplace, particularly in larger
buildings or those housing many people.
For this reason it is also important that any
different escape routes are independent
of one another. The Fire Safety Order has
provided a more appropriate means for
the assessment of risks, in particular for
those with special needs or where there
are children, for example, as is the case
with hospitals, children's homes or hostels,

taking into account any inexperience,
immaturity or lack of awareness of risks.
Risk assessments can therefore be
adjusted appropriately.

The basic considerations for any means of
escape are:

1. the likely time available for escape;
2. the time needed for escape;
3. the number of people to be
   evacuated;
4. the distance required to travel in order
   to get out;
5. the time of day it could be; and
6. whether any assistance is required.

Building design
New buildings are often designed to keep
fires in 'pockets' of the building and, as
such, to contain fires in certain areas
by using fire doors and other similar
equipment. Consideration of the design
of a building, whether old or new, is an
important factor when looking at means
of escape. Architects are also legally
required to consider and eliminate and
then minimise health and safety risks in
building design.

Fire doors are intended to keep out and
contain fire. They should be fitted with
effective self-closing devices, provided
they are kept locked and labelled 'Fire
Door – Keep Locked Shut'. Some doors
may be linked to a fire warning system
and activation of a fire alarm or smoke
detector may trigger the door to shut or
open as appropriate. These should be
labelled 'Automatic Fire Door – Keep
Clear'.

Emergency lighting is another important
consideration. It ensures that people can
get out safely if there is no natural daylight
along escape routes, or if evacuation is at
night. Emergency lighting should function
notwithstanding the failure of normal
lighting, and also if there is a localised

failure which could cause a hazard. In any event, emergency lighting should:

- show escape routes clearly;
- provide light so people can move along the route safely towards final exits; and
- enable fire alarm call points and firefighting equipment to be readily located.

Emergency exit signs should be placed at exits to floors, where stairs begin, at final exits from the premises and should be illuminated if necessary.

There are many precautions that can be taken in building design and used to help reduce the risk of injury from fire, when looking at the means of escape. Regional fire authorities' websites can provide useful advice in carrying out fire risk assessment and there are many simple measures that employers can take in providing adequate means of escape from fire as well as ensuring compliance with relevant legislation.

Effective means of escape can be provided where an appropriate risk assessment has been carried out and acted upon. The five basic steps to always remember are:

1. Identify fire hazards;
2. Identify people at risk;
3. Evaluate the risks;
4. Record the findings; and
5. Review and revise the findings.

See also: Accessible environments, p.50; Disability access and egress, p.204; Fire extinguishers, p.314; Firefighting, p.330; Fire safety in non-domestic premises, p.325

Sources of further information

One important aspect of planning for escape in the event of a fire is protecting those occupants of the building that are disabled. Workplace Law Group's *Fire and Disability 2008: Special Report* provides Responsible Persons with all the information they need to reconcile fire safety and disability. As well as the legal requirements provided by the Regulatory Reform (Fire Safety) Order 2005 and the Disability Discrimination Act (DDA), the report covers guidelines on British standards and Building Regulations; management procedures (evacuation plans, risk assessments, 'buddy' systems); building procedures (refuges, evacuation chairs, emergency lighting); essential information on the range of auxilliary aids available to assist disabled people in an evacuation; and any other specific fire safety considerations arising from different disabilities. For more information visit www.workplacelaw.net/Bookshop/SpecialReports.

Fire safety in non-domestic premises

Nicola Cardenas-Blanco, Martineau Solicitors

Key points

Fire safety reforms have been in place since 1 April 2006, which have simplified, rationalised and consolidated existing fire safety legislation. Historically, fire safety legislation had developed in response to particular tragic fires which resulted in huge casualties. As a result, fire safety provisions were scattered over many pieces of legislation.

The Regulatory Reform (Fire Safety) Order 2005 came into force on 1 April 2006, aiming to make compliance easier, by replacing the existing legislation with a single fire safety regime applying to all workplaces and other non-domestic premises.

Responsible Person

Under the Order, responsibility for fire safety will be placed on the 'Responsible Person' for the building or premises. The 'Responsible Person' means, in relation to a workplace, the employer, if the workplace is to any extent under his control. If the premises are not a workplace the Responsible Person is the person who has control of the premises (e.g. as occupier) in connection with the carrying on of his business. The Resopnsible Person could also be the owner of the premises if the person in control of the premises doesn't have control of the business. The Responsible Person will have to assess the risks of fire and take steps to remove or reduce them. The Order also imposes obligations in respect of firefighting, fire detection, emergency routes and exits, and procedures for serious and imminent danger.

Legislation

- Fire Precautions Act 1971.
- Fire Certificates (Special Premises) Regulations 1976.
- Fire Precautions (Workplace) Regulations 1997.
- Fire Precautions (Workplace) (Amendment) Regulations 1999.
- Management of Health and Safety at Work Regulations 1999.
- Regulatory Reform (Fire Safety) Order 2005.

Previously, the occupier of designated premises (or the owner of a designated multi-occupancy building) was required to apply to the local fire authority for a fire certificate. Before issuing a certificate, the fire authority would inspect the premises to satisfy itself that the following were all reasonable:

- The means of escape in case of fire;
- The means with which the building is provided for securing that the means of escape can be safely used at all times;
- The means for fighting fire; and
- The means for giving warning in the event of fire.

The Fire Precautions (Workplace) Regulations 1997, together with elements of the MHSWR, still require employers to carry out a fire risk assessment, and to provide and maintain such fire precautions as are necessary to safeguard those who use the workplace. They also require the provision to employees of relevant information, instruction and training about fire precautions.

Regulatory Reform (Fire Safety) Order 2005

Background
The focus of this law remains people's safety. However, there is a deliberate shift from the previous prescriptive regime (where the fire authority determines the precautions to be taken) to an approach based on risk assessment, where the Responsible Person decides how to address the risks.

The Order applies to England and Wales only. As fire safety is a matter within the devolved competence of the Scottish Parliament, the Order does not extend to Scotland.

The Order applies to most non-domestic premises used or operated by employers, the self-employed and the voluntary sector; it makes no difference whether the business is operating for profit or not. The Order does not apply to domestic premises, offshore installations, ships, aircraft, locomotive or rolling stock, trailers or semi-trailers, mines or boreholes, or fields, woods or agricultural land (provided the land is situated away from the undertaking's main buildings).

General fire precautions in relation to premises will be covered by the Order. This includes:

- reducing the risk of fire and the risk of fire spread on the premises;
- means of escape from premises;
- ensuring that, at all material times, the means of escape can be safely and effectively used;
- means for fighting fires;
- means for detecting fire and giving warning in the case of fire; and
- arrangements for action to be taken in the event of fire, including measures for the instruction and training of employees and to mitigate the effects of fire.

Relevant persons
People who are owed duties under the Order (e.g employees, tenants) are known as Relevant Persons. A relevant person is any person who may lawfully be on the premises or any person in the immediate vicinity of the premises who is at risk from fire.

General duties
The fire safety regime is based on an assessment of risk, the removal of hazards and the protection of persons from any hazards that remain. Its aim is to promote the avoidance of fires and to mitigate the effect of fire.

In respect of employees, the Responsible Person owes a duty to take such general fire precautions as will ensure (so far as is reasonably practicable) their safety. In respect of relevant persons who are not employees (e.g. visitors, contractors etc.), the duty is to take such general fire precautions as may reasonably be required, in the circumstances, to ensure that the premises are safe.

Risk assessment and specific duties
To comply with the specific obligations imposed by the Order, the Responsible Person must decide what general fire precautions he needs to take. That person must ensure that a suitable and sufficient assessment of risks to relevant persons is undertaken.

azards that are identified should
e removed or reduced, so far as is
easonably practicable, and any residual
sks avoided.

or those premises where a dangerous
ubstance is liable to be present, the risk
ssessment must also address the ten
pecific considerations in Part 1 of
chedule 1 of the Order.

pecial consideration must also be given
) the under 18s. The matters to be taken
to account in any risk assessment in
espect of young persons include their
nexperience, lack of awareness of risks,
nmaturity and the extent of safety training
rovided to the young person.

he purpose of the risk assessment is
) ensure that the risk of fire is either
emoved or reduced as far as possible. It
nay be the case that a risk of fire remains
nd protection is necessary to safeguard
elevant persons due to the features of
ne premises, the activity carried on there,
ny hazard present or any other relevant
ircumstances. In such cases, protection
vill be provided by appropriate fire
recautions in the form of:

- means for detecting and warning of
  fire (Article 13);
- means for fighting fire (Article 13); and
- means of escape through emergency
  routes and exits (Article 14).

he premises – and any facilities,
equipment and devices provided in
connection with general fire precautions –
nust be subject to a suitable system of
naintenance. They must be maintained in
an efficient state, in efficient working order
and in good repair (Article 17).

here must also be procedures (including
safety drills) to be followed in the event
of serious and imminent danger, with a
sufficient number of competent persons

nominated to implement those procedures
(Article 15).

Often, the arrangements for the effective
planning, organisation, control, monitoring
and review of these preventive and
protective measures must be in writing.
This applies where the Responsible
Person employs five or more employees,
a licence required by any enactment is
in force in relation to the premises or an
alterations notice is in force (for a
definition of an alterations notice see
below).

Enforcement
The main enforcing body is the local fire
and rescue authority, although the HSE
will enforce the Order in respect of nuclear
installations, construction sites and ships
under construction or repair.

Enforcement notices
The enforcing authority – through the
service of enforcement notices – will be
able to require work to be carried out to
ensure the safety of persons (Article 30).

Prohibition notices
Where the use of premises involves or
may involve serious risks to relevant
persons, it is possible for the enforcing
authority to prohibit or restrict the use
of the premises, by the service of a
prohibition notice, until such time as they
have been made appropriately safe
(Article 31).

Alterations notices
Certain premises may pose a serious risk
to relevant persons due to their individual
features, such as the purposes for which
they are used and their particular hazards.
A building may also house new practices
as a business changes. In either case,
the enforcing authority may serve an
alterations notice on the Responsible
Person (Article 29).

An alterations notice will require the enforcing authority to be notified, in advance, of:

■ changes to the premises;
■ changes to services, fittings or equipment in or on the premises;
■ an increase in the quantities of dangerous substances that are present in or on the premises; or
■ changes to the use of the premises.

Offences

It is an offence to fail to comply with the requirements of the Order, an enforcement, prohibition or alterations notice. It is also an offence to obstruct an inspector in the exercise of his powers. The level of penalty can be compared with existing fire safety law. For example, in respect of the main duties imposed by the Order, upon summary conviction a fine not exceeding £5,000 may be imposed. Upon conviction on indictment, the penalty is an unlimited fine, or imprisonment for a term not exceeding two years, or both.

Fire risk assessments

The purpose of a fire risk assessment is to identify those measures that need to be taken to comply with Part 2 of the FPWR and the Regulatory Reform (Fire Safety) Order 2005.

There are five steps that a Responsible Person will need to take:

1. *Identify potential fire hazards in the workplace.* This involves identifying potential sources of ignition such as smokers' materials, naked flames, electrical, gas- or oil-fired appliances, machinery, faulty electrical equipment, static electricity, potential arson, etc. The Responsible Person should then identify sources of fuel (combustible materials) including flammable substances, wood, paper and card, plastics, rubber, foam and flammable

gases (such as liquefied petroleum gas). The assessment must consider the workplace as a whole, including all work processes, outdoor locations and areas that are rarely used or visited.

2. *Decide who might be in danger (e.g. employees, visitors, disabled persons).* The assessment must identify who is at risk in the event of fire, how they will be warned and how they will escape. Locate where people may be working (whether at permanent or occasional workstations) and consider who else is at risk such as customers, visiting contractors or disabled people. These individuals may be unfamiliar with your fire precautions and will be at higher risk.

3. *Evaluate the risks arising from the hazards and decide whether you have done enough to reduce the risk or need to do more.* You should consider
   - the likelihood of fire occurring and whether it is possible to reduce the sources of ignition or minimise the potential fuel for a fire;
   - the fire precautions you have in place and whether they are sufficient for the remaining risk and will ensure everyone is warned in case of fire (i.e. fire resistance and structural separation, fire detection and warning systems);
   - the means by which people can make their escape safely or put the fire out if it is safe to do so (i.e. means of escape and means of fighting fire); and
   - maintenance and testing of fire precautions to ensure they remain effective.

4. *Record the findings.* Where you employ five or more employees, you must record the significant findings of your assessment, together with details of any people you identify as being at particular risk.

Keep the assessment under review and revise it when necessary. Changes to the workplace, which have an effect on either fire risks or precautions, should trigger a review of your risk assessment. Examples that may lead to increased risks or new hazards include changes to work processes, furniture, plant, machinery, substances, building layout or the numbers of people likely to be present in the building.

See also: Fire extinguishers, p.314; Firefighting, p.330; Fire, means of escape, p.322

Sources of further information

The Regulatory Reform (Fire Safety) Order 2005: www.uk-legislation.hmso.gov.uk/si/si2005/20051541.htm

Legal duties now place a greater emphasis on one person knowing exactly how their building will be affected by fire, so it is important that Responsible Persons have accessible information that is easy to understand. Workplace Law Group's *Fire Safety 2009: Special Report* provides authoritative, high-level research that demonstrates the impact of the Regulatory Reform (Fire Safety) Order 2005 (RRO). The Report explains fire safety law in detail and provides an analysis of case law under the new legislation in comparison with the old, using real-life examples to highlight its importance. For more information visit www.workplacelaw.net/Bookshop/SpecialReports.

Firefighting

Nicola Cardenas-Blanco, Martineau Solicitors

Key points

Since 1 April 2006, employers or those who have control of non-domestic premises have had a statutory duty under fire safety and health and safety legislation to ensure that there are appropriate means of fighting fires. The employer or controller of the non-domestic premises is known as the 'Responsible Person'. The Responsible Person also has to provide suitably trained people to operate non-automatic firefighting equipment (FFE).

Fire certificates issued by fire authorities under the Fire Precautions Act 1971 have been abolished. Instead, it is up to the Responsible Person to identify the firefighting requirement for its premises.

Legislation

- Disability Discrimination Act 1995.
- Provision and Use of Work Equipment Regulations 1998.
- Fire and Rescue Services Act 2004.
- Regulatory Reform (Fire Safety) Order 2005.

Firefighting systems

FFE can be either active or passive and is designed to extinguish fires by:

- starving the fire of fuel;
- smothering the fire to remove or reduce the concentration of oxygen; or
- cooling the fire to the extent that it cannot support combustion.

Active systems

Active systems are those such as sprinklers, gas floods and portable fire extinguishers, which become active only when a fire occurs, or with human intervention.

Passive systems

Passive systems form part of the structure of the building and involve the division of the building into fire-resisting compartments.

Where compartments are breached to allow movement through the building or the provision of services, 'fire stops' can maintain the integrity of the fire resistance of the compartment.

Breaches in compartment walls for services, etc., should be kept to a minimum and all openings should be protected with intumescent materials (i.e. pipe wraps, seals, etc.) or fire dampers. These should comply with BS 5588-9:1999 (*Fire precautions in the design, construction and use of buildings: code of practice for ventilation and air conditioning*).

Firefighting equipment – statutory requirements

The Regulatory Reform (Fire Safety) Order 2005 abolished fire certificates, which specified minimum FFE requirements in the premises for which they are issued. It is now for the Responsible Person to determine what FFE is required and to provide and maintain appropriate FFE in those premises. Non-automatic equipment must be placed so that it is easily accessible to those who need to use and approved signs must indicate its location.

he introduction of the Fire and Rescue ervices Act 2004 is likely to mean a duction in the number of firefighters d appliances available in certain areas, hich may increase the response times of e Fire and Rescue Services to workplace es (particularly outside normal office urs). As part of its risk assessment, e Responsible Person may have to nsider the provision of additional FFE assist the evacuation of the premises d ensure there are competent people to se it. When assessing its requirements, e Responsible Person could consult his cal Fire and Rescue Service for specific dvice.

FE also falls within the requirements of e Provision and Use of Work Equipment egulations 1998 (PUWER), which rescribe the following:

Equipment should be suitable for the purpose for which it is provided, bearing in mind the risks posed by the activities and people in that work area. The equipment provided should take account of the activities and the number of people working in or using an area, as well as the environmental conditions (e.g. adverse weather conditions or the presence of corrosive chemicals).

Equipment should be capable of being used only for the purpose for which it is provided. It is essential that the correct type of firefighting equipment is provided (e.g. no water-based extinguishers where there is electrical equipment) and if equipment is used correctly it must not increase the risks to the user or others.

Equipment should be regularly inspected and maintained in an effective state (see Maintenance,

below). Inspection procedures should take account of the likelihood of equipment being damaged, moved or abused and the need for more frequent maintenance than that specified by the manufacturer should be considered as part of a risk assessment.

■ People who may have to use the equipment should receive adequate information and instructions in its use (see Training, below). This is particularly important as, unless they are confident in the equipment's capabilities and limitations, people may fail to use it or use it incorrectly in a fire situation, putting themselves and others in danger.

Maintenance
Article 17 of the Fire Safety Order requires the Responsible Person to ensure that a suitable 'system of maintenance' is in place, to maintain FFE in an efficient state, good working order and in good repair. As a minimum, maintenance of FFE should be undertaken in accordance with the manufacturers' instructions.

Training
Article 21 of the Fire Safety Order, Regulation 13 of the Management of Health and Safety at Work Regulations 1999 and Regulation 9 of PUWER require employees (and others who may need it) to be provided with adequate training prior to being entrusted to use FFE.

Disability discrimination
Sections 6 and 21 of the Disability Discrimination Act 1995 require employers to make reasonable adjustments to the workplace to facilitate the use of work equipment, etc., by disabled people.

As part of their risk assessments, employers will have to consider the needs of disabled employees and others with regard to the type, size, location and siting of FFE and, where necessary, they will have to make 'reasonable adjustments' to ensure the safety of their employees and visitors.

Considerations may include re-siting, or reducing the size of, fire extinguishers so that wheelchair users can easily access them.

> *See also*: Fire extinguishers, p.314; Fire, means of escape, p.322; Fire safety in non-domestic premises, p.325

Sources of further information

Workplace Law Group's *Fire Safety Documentation Pack 2007* provides employers with everything they need to meet the requirements of the Fire Safety Order, and to be fully compliant with all fire safety legislation. The pack contains a Fire Safety Policy, which can be tailored to your organisation; a Management Guide, explaining the legislation behind the policy, to ensure you, as the 'Responsible Person', cover all aspects of fire safety; Compliance Documentation, to show that you, as the Responsible Person, have carried out all necessary risk assessments, and have identified the risks of fire relevant to your business; and extensive Risk Assessment Checklists. For more information visit www.workplacelaw.net/Bookshop/Handbooks.

First aid

Andrew Richardson, Scott Wilson

Key points

The Health and Safety (First Aid) Regulations 1981 require employers to provide adequate and appropriate equipment, facilities and personnel so that first aid can be given to their employees if they are injured or become ill at work.

- When people at work are injured or fall ill, they must receive immediate attention.
- An ambulance must be called in serious cases.
- Employees need to assess what their first aid needs are.
- The minimum first-aid provision on any worksite is:
  - a suitably stocked first-aid box; and
  - an appointed person to take charge of first-aid arrangements.
- First aid provision needs to be available at all times people are at work.

Legislation

- Health and Safety at Work etc. Act 1974.
- Health and Safety (First Aid) Regulations 1981.
- Offshore Installations and Pipeline Works (First Aid) Regulations 1989.
- Management of Health and Safety at Work Regulations 1999.

The HSE has been engaged in a lengthy review of the 1981 Regulations and in 2005 announced that the Regulations and Approved Code of Practice should not be changed, but that there should be a new training regime for workplace first aiders. The consultations are continuing about first aid training and approval arrangements; and the latest information (August 2008) is that changes are now expected to be published by April 2009 and to come into force on 1 October 2009.

Requirements and guidance

The aim of first aid is to preserve life and to reduce the effects of injury or illness suffered at work. The Regulations place a duty upon all employers to assess the first aid requirements within their workplace, to appoint competent personnel, and to provide equipment and facilities to enable first aid to be given to their employees if they are injured or become ill at work.

To assess the first aid requirements within each workplace, the employer should consider:

- the hazards and risks in the workplace;
- how many people are located in their premises;
- previous accident/incident history;
- the nature and distribution of the workforce;
- the remoteness of the workplace in relation to emergency medical services;
- the needs of travelling, remote and loneworkers;
- employees working on shared or multi-occupancy sites; and
- annual leave and other absences of first aiders and appointed persons.

It should be noted that the first aid provision for anyone other than employees, including the public, cannot be made under the Health and Safety at Work etc. Act 1974. The HSE strongly recommends employers to consider it, but employers should be aware that employer's liability insurance will not cover litigation as a result of first aid to non-employees; however, public liability insurance may.

The Regulations stipulate that first aid equipment must be provided. The minimum requirement is a first aid container, the contents of which will depend on the risks identified in the risk assessment. The HSE publishes guidance on suitable contents of first aid boxes (see Sources of further information below). First aid rooms must be provided where the risk assessment has identified they are necessary, usually in high-risk working environments. The guidance details what is reasonably expected to be provided in such a room.

When the employer assesses the risk and identifies the need for personnel to give first aid, then sufficient numbers of people of the appropriate competency, in the appropriate locations, need to be arranged.

The guidance offers suggestions as to t competency and numbers of personnel required based on whether the workplac is low, medium or high risk and how ma people are employed at the site.

The competency of personnel falls into two categories – first aiders and appoint persons. The Regulations detail the criteria that each of these positions mus meet, including qualifications and trainir

The Regulations place a duty upon the employer to inform all its employees of arrangements made in connection with aid. The guidance suggests the setting-up of a procedure for informing staff tha would include the details of the first aid provision and how employees are told of the location, equipment, facilities and personnel. It also suggests the provisior of notices that are clear and easily understood to relay all or some of the information. Finally it suggests that first information is included in induction train to ensure all new employees are aware.

See also: Accident investigations, p.55; Health and safety at work, p.364; Slips, trips and falls, p.657

Sources of further information

L74 *First Aid at Work: The Health and Safety (First Aid) Regulations 1981 – Approved Code of Practice and Guidance* (HSE Books, 1997) ISBN: 0 7176 1050 0. This document assists employers in understanding the Regulations and provides practical and realistic advice on how you can ensure compliance.

There is a separate Approved Code of Practice and Guidance foir the offshore industry – L123, ISBN: 0 7176 1851 X, published in 2000.

The HSE website has two useful leaflets available as downloads:
- INDG214 First Aid at Work – Your Questions Answered provides sound basic information: www.hse.gov.uk/pubns/indg214.pdf
- INDG347 Rev 1 Basic Advice on First Aid at Work, gives simple practical advice for use in emergencies: www.hse.gov.uk/pubns/indg347.pdf

Fixed-term workers

Pinsent Masons Employment Group

Key points

- Legislation introduced in 2002 provides statutory protection for fixed-term employees.
- The Regulations state that fixed-term employees have the right not to be treated less favourably than comparable permanent employees because they are employed on a fixed-term basis, unless the different treatment can be objectively justified.
- Employees cannot agree to waive their right to bring a claim for unfair dismissal as part of a fixed-term contract.
- After four years on successive fixed-term contracts, employees will be regarded as permanent.
- Workplace managers should take care in using fixed-term contracts, and should not now assume that they provide employers with any greater protection than they would have in relation to employees on other forms of contracts.

Legislation

- Employment Rights Act 1999.
- Fixed-term Employees (Prevention of Less Favourable Treatment) Regulations 2002.

Who has fixed-term contracts?

In 2002 it was estimated that between 1.1 and 1.3 million workers in the UK were employed on fixed-term contracts, approximately half of whom were public sector employees mainly working in education, healthcare and public administration, while the remainder were employed predominantly by larger businesses.

The Regulations apply only to 'employees' rather than a wider category of workers.

What is a fixed-term contract?

The Regulations define a fixed-term contract as a contract of employment that will terminate:

- on the expiry of a specific term;
- on the completion of a particular task; or
- on the occurrence or non-occurrence of any other specific event other than the attainment by the employee of any normal and bona-fide retiring age in the establishment for an employee holding the position held by him.

Scope of the Regulations

The Regulations came into force on 1 October 2002. They transposed the EC Directive on Fixed-term Work into UK law.

There are a number of categories of employees that are specifically excluded from the scope of the Regulations, namely:

- employees working under contracts of apprenticeship;
- agency workers;
- people employed on training schemes supported by the Government or an EU institution;

- people employed on work experience placements of one year or less that they are required to attend as part of a higher-education course; and
- serving members of the armed forces.

The main provisions of the Regulations can be summarised as follows:

- Fixed-term employees have the right not to be treated less favourably than comparable permanent employees, unless the different treatment can be objectively justified.
- Fixed-term employees are not to be treated less favourably than similar permanent employees as regards the terms of their contract, or by being subjected to any other detriment by an act, or deliberate failure to act, of the employer.
- It is open to an employer to objectively justify any less favourable treatment and where the less favourable treatment concerns the terms of the contract, it can be justified if overall the terms of the fixed-term employee's contract taken as a whole are at least as favourable as those of the permanent employee.
- The right not to be treated less favourably includes a right not to be treated less favourably in relation to the opportunity to secure any permanent position in an organisation. An employer will be required to objectively justify any difference in the availability of internal permanent vacancies between fixed-term and permanent employees.
- An employee who considers that he has been treated by an employer in a manner that infringes a right conferred by the Regulations may submit a request in writing to the employer for a written statement of the reasons for the treatment. Under the Regulations the employer must provide a written statement within 21 days of the request.

- After four years on successive fixed-term contracts (discounting any period before 10 July 2002) an employee shall be regarded as a permanent employee, unless a further fixed-term contract can be objectively justified.
- A waiver of redundancy and unfair dismissal rights in fixed-term contracts is unlawful.
- An employee shall not be subjected to a detriment for relying upon his rights under the Regulations.

Termination of employment

Failure to renew a fixed-term contract on its expiry constitutes a dismissal for the purposes of employment legislation. In such circumstances, workplace managers should take care to avoid the possibility of a claim for unfair dismissal being brought by a fixed-term employee (see 'Dismissal, p.233), remembering the statutory process and steps required to be taken for compliance.

Whether the dismissal was fair or unfair will be determined by whether or not the employer can show that it acted reasonably in not renewing the contract.

Previously, employers have tried to get around this problem by including clauses in the fixed-term contract under which the employee in question agreed to waive his right to bring a claim for unfair dismissal due to the expiry and non-renewal of the contract if it was for one year or longer. Further, employers often engaged in the practice of renewing a fixed-term contract for a further fixed-term period, and still including such an unfair dismissal waiver relating to the end of that further term. However, section 18(1) of the Employment Rights Act 1999 provided that these waivers of unfair dismissal rights would no longer be effective. The waiver of redundancy rights in fixed-term contracts was made unlawful as from 1 October 2002.

y virtue of the Regulations a dismissal
ill be automatically unfair if the reason
or the dismissal is that the employee has
rought proceedings against the employer
nder the Regulations, or requested
om the employer a written statement
f reasons for less favourable treatment
r otherwise done anything under the
egulations in relation to the employer or
ny other person. No qualifying period of
mployment is required for such a claim.

Enforcement
Under the Regulations a fixed-term
employee may bring a complaint to an
Employment Tribunal that he has suffered
less favourable treatment, not been
informed of available vacancies or
suffered a detriment. The complaint will
require to be brought within three months
of the date of the act complained of.

> *See also*: Employee benefits,
> p.266; Employment contracts,
> p.273; Flexible working, p.338;
> Part-time workers, p.559

Sources of further information

BERR – Fixed-term workers: www.berr.gov.uk/employment/employment-
legislation/fixed-term-employees/index.html

Flexible working

Mark Kaye, Berwin Leighton Paisner

Key points
From 6 April 2003 employers have been under a legal obligation to consider applications for flexible working.

Legislation
- Employment Act 2002.

The law
Parents of young children have the right to submit a request to their employer to allow them to work 'flexibly', by changing hours, changing days or working from home. The change, if agreed, will be a permanent change to the employee's terms and conditions. The right applies to parents of children under six (or under the age of 18 if disabled) with more than 26 weeks' service who have responsibility for the child's upbringing and make the request to enable them to care for the child and where the employee is the 'carer' of an adult relative or someone living at the same address.

The procedure is as follows:

- The employee makes a written, signed and dated request, specifying the change requested and proposed date from which it should apply. The request should also state what effect (if any) the employee thinks the change will have on the employer and how any such effect may be dealt with.
- The employer must either agree to the request in writing or hold a meeting to discuss the application with the employee within 28 days of the application being made.
- The employer must notify the employee in writing of its decision within 14 days of the meeting (which

may include detailing any compromise agreed in the meeting).
- Any refusal must specify the grounds (see below) with a sufficient explanation for the refusal.
- The employee has the right of appeal against any refusal within 14 days of receiving the employer's notification.
- The employer must hold a meeting with the employee within 14 days of receiving the notice of appeal in order to discuss the appeal.
- The employer must give the employee notice of its decision in writing within 14 days of the appeal meeting. If the appeal is dismissed, grounds of the dismissal must be provided by the employer.

The following are permitted reasons for refusing a request:

- Burden of additional costs.
- Detrimental effect on ability to meet customer demand.
- Inability to reorganise work among existing staff.
- Inability to recruit additional staff.
- Detrimental impact on quality.
- Detrimental impact on performance.
- Insufficiency of work during the period the employee proposes to work.
- Planned structural changes.

These allow an employer to refuse a request, for example, where the employee wishes to change his days or hours from peak periods to quiet times or where the

Workplace Law Network
www.workplacelaw.ne

perational needs of the business require
aff at a particular time. For example, a
artender who asked to change his hours
work from 11 a.m. to five p.m. could
ave his request turned down on the
rounds that customer demand is highest
the evening.

n employee can complain to a Tribunal
at the ground given did not fall within
he of the permitted reasons or that
e employer's decision was based on
correct facts. However, the Tribunal
annot question the commercial validity
the employer's decision or substitute
s own view on the employer's business
eason. The Tribunal's role is to determine
hether the employer has given serious
onsideration to a request to work flexibly
nd whether the employer has complied
ith the statutory procedure.

the employee's complaint is successful,
e Tribunal can either order that the
mployee's request is reconsidered or
ward up to eight weeks' pay, subject to
e statutory cap, currently £330, making
e maximum award £2,640. It is worth

noting, however, that these rights exist
independently of other employment rights
and that therefore an employee can bring
a sex discrimination claim, for example,
arising out of the same facts as a claim
under the flexible working provisions and
could potentially be successful in one claim
and fail in the other.

Practical guidance for employers
- Treat requests for flexible working
  seriously.
- Follow the statutory procedure.
- If the request cannot be
  accommodated, identify the reason
  and provide an explanation.
- Allow the employee to appeal.
- Consider if a refusal to allow the
  employer's request for flexible working
  could give rise to a claim such as
  indirect sex discrimination.

See also: Carers, p.114;
Employment contracts, p.273;
Family-friendly rights, p.309;
Homeworkers, p.406; Loneworking,
p.476; Managing pregnancy, p.484

Sources of further information

BERR: flexible working – www.berr.gov.uk/employment/workandfamilies/flexible-working/index.html

Workplace Law Group's *Guide to Flexible Working 2008* provides information
on the formal legislative right to request to work flexibly, but also considers flexible
working patterns in a wider sense. It covers the reasons why some employers are
looking to introduce flexible working into their workplace, explores different flexible
working patterns, including their benefits and disadvantages, and provides detail
on the formal legislative right to request. It also looks at the employment and
non-employment legal issues that surround flexible working and the necessary
amendments that need to be made to an employee's contractual terms and
conditions if a flexible working pattern is agreed. Finally, it gives practical advice
in relation to drafting and implementing a flexible working policy. For more
information visit www.workplacelaw.net/Bookshop/GuidesTo.

Foreign nationals

Sue Conlan and Aliya Khan, Tyndallwoods Solicitors

Key points

- It is a criminal offence to employ someone who does not have permission to live and work in the UK.
- A statutory defence is available if employers inspect, take copies of, and keep a record of certain documents.
- Employers apply for a work permit for employees, if one is needed.
- Employers must not discriminate when recruiting foreign nationals.
- Employers must ensure the health and safety of foreign nationals.

Legislation

- Immigration Act 1971.
- Asylum and Immigration Act 1996.
- Nationality and Immigration Asylum Act 2002.
- Immigration (Restrictions on Employment) Order 2004.
- Immigration and Nationality Act 2006.

General principles

Employers may offer employment to Commonwealth Citizens and Foreign Nationals without a permanent right of residence ('indefinite leave to enter or remain') as if they were a British Citizen if they are:

- a Commonwealth Citizen in the UK as a working holiday-maker (a two-year visa given for Commonwealth Citizens between the ages of 17 and 30);
- a Commonwealth Citizen or Foreign National (excluding EEA Nationals) who have been granted permission to enter or remain in the UK on the basis of marriage (two-year visa or extension);
- an EEA National (except 'A8' Nationals within the first 12 months);
- an A8 National within the first 12 months of entry in possession of a registration document and, for each particular employment, a certificate;

- a student who can take employment up to 20 hours term time or full time during vacation;
- those granted 12 months' leave under the International Graduates Scheme;
- those in possession of an Immigration Employment document (IED) from Work Permits (UK), a specialist division of the Immigration and Nationality Directorate (part of the Home Office) which may be given to the individual under Tier 1 or to the company for a specific employee; or
- Asylum Seekers (those waiting for a decision on their claim to refugee status) with Application Registration Card endorsed 'Employment Permitted'.

Passports are not generally endorsed with 'Permission to Work'. It is the absence of a 'prohibition on employment' that demonstrates that a person has permission to work. Students have a 'restriction' on employment endorsed on their passports; in other words limited to 20 hours term time, but they are not required to obtain any form of permit or Immigration Employment Document. Permission to work is not the same as permission to live in the UK. An employer who obtains a Work Permit (see below) for an employee must also ensure that the individual btains permission to enter (by obtaining visa) or remain in the UK (by an pplication for variation of leave). This is process of application that the individual ust go through before their employment ommences.

omeone who has permission to work an continue in their employment (or ke alternative employment) whilst aiting for a decision on their application r an extension of stay providing they plied to extend their leave before their st extension expired. Home Office cknowledgement letters sent in response extension applications contain the tandard wording:

Provided an Applicant has permission be in the UK when an application is nade, he or she is legally entitled to emain here on the same conditions reviously granted until the application as been decided."

esponsibilities under the Asylum and mmigration Act 1996 (the 1996 Act)

he offence
ection 8 of the 1996 Act makes it a riminal offence to employ someone who not entitled to live and work in the UK. mployers and individual managers can ace fines of up to £5,000 per employee.

he Act provides a defence if, before the mployment commences, the employer hecks (Step one), copies (Step two) and etains (Step three) copies of specified ocuments.

tep one – requesting documents
- Before the employment commences, employers must require prospective employees to produce originals of documents from lists drawn up by the Home Office, full details of which can be found on the Home Office website at: www.employingmigrantworkers.org.uk.

- To avoid committing the criminal offence, employers should refuse to employ an applicant if the relevant document or combination of documents cannot be produced.

Step two – checking documents
- Check all details and photos are consistent with the applicant's details and appearance (for example age, gender, race) and that the documents are in date.
- The IND advises that if there are any inconsistencies between the documents, the reason for the difference must be proved by documents showing a valid reason for a change of name.

Step three – record keeping
- Copy the front page and all pages showing any of the employee's details, including photos and signatures.
- Copy pages with an immigration endorsement or stamp.
- The employer must retain the copies.
- If the copies cannot be produced, the defence will not be available.

The defence is not available if the employer knows that the employee is not entitled to live and/or work in the UK – even if they have checked the documents.

Note: these changes apply to employees taken on after 30 April 2004, not for those already in employment at that date. An employer who curtails the employment of Commonwealth Citizens or Foreign Nationals after 1 May 2004 for failure to produce documents specified in the Home Office lists may be liable to a claim for unfair dismissal. Other requirements were in force for employees who were taken on before 1 May 2004.

Work permits

Exempt employees

Some Foreign Nationals or Commonwealth Citizens require Work Permits. The largest group of Foreign Nationals who are exempt from the requirement of having a Work Permit are EEA Nationals.

Some EEA nationals are subject to the Workers Registration Scheme (A8 Nationals). For a full list of EEA Nationals please refer to the website of the Immigration and Nationality Directorate at www.ind.homeoffice.gov.uk/applying/eeaeunationals.

Types of permit

Employers, not employees, must make the application usually whilst the Foreign National is overseas.

Full work permits may last for up to five years. If, after five years, the employer still wishes to employ the employee, the employee can apply for indefinite leave to remain.

Although there are several categories of work permit, most employers will generally apply for a business and commercial work permit until the new Tier 2 roles out in November 2008. The criteria to be met under the work permit scheme are:

either

the employee must be a graduate, have a relevant HND, or have an HND (which is not relevant to the post) plus one year's work experience at National / Scottish Vocational Qualification (N/SVQ) level 3 or above.

or

the job must require three years' full-time experience of the type of job at N/SVQ level 3 or above.

- It must be a genuine vacancy.
- The terms and conditions must be comparable to those of a resident worker.
- Legislation and any licensing requirements must be complied with; for example, the National Minimum Wage and Working Time Regulations
- The potential employee cannot hold a share of more than 10% in the employer or connected business.
- The employer must carry out a sufficient and appropriate search to ensure there are no suitable UK or EEA workers available, or be able to demonstrate that the position and applicant are unique.
- Adverts should include the date of publication, closing date, details of the post, location, and a salary indication At least four weeks should be allowed to receive applications.

For some posts, known as Tier One applications (this is not the same as Tier 1 under the new Points Based System), a recruitment search is not necessary. Examples include:

- 'shortage occupations', such as nursing, where there are generally no enough UK and EEA nationals to fill the vacant roles; and
- intra-company transfers.

Other arrangements

- The Training and Work Experience Scheme (TWES) is available for work-based training for a professional qualification or for work experience. Once this permit expires the employee must usually leave the UK for a set period before making another application. This will be replaced by Tier 5.
- Tier 1 of the Points Based System enables employees to work for themselves or any employer without a permit. Contrast with a work permit / Tier 2 Sponsorship, which is only

applicable to a specific role and employer. Further information on these and other categories is available from Work Permits (UK) at www.workingintheuk.gov.uk.

Applying for the permit

Work permits should be obtained before the employee travels to the UK. The employee must have entry clearance (a visa) before arriving. The issuing of a work permit does not guarantee that a visa will be issued.

Applications should be made on form WP1 no more than six months before the post commences. Employers should enclose:

- the fee, currently £153;
- copies of advertisements and details of responses, with reasons why any resident candidates were not suitable (not necessary for Tier One posts);
- proof of the employee's qualifications / work experience; and
- any information that will help assess the application against the criteria set out above.

If this is the employer's first work permit application, additional documents must be sent to establish that the employer is UK-based, for example, the most recent audited accounts, details of premises, incorporation documents. The forms, and guidance on completing the forms, are available from Work Permits (UK): www.workingintheuk.gov.uk.

Expiry of the permit

If an employee's work permit or visa is due to expire the employer should apply for a new work permit before the expiry of the old permit and the employee should apply for further leave to remain before their current leave expires. This enables an employee to live and work in the UK until a decision is reached by the Home Office – even if in the meantime their permit and/or visa expires.

Health and safety

Employers have health and safety obligations towards all employees. For foreign nationals one additional consideration may be whether they can speak English sufficiently for the role and to recognise any safety notices. Employers should consider whether training or assistance can be provided.

Avoiding race discrimination

All checks must be performed in a non-discriminatory way. The Government has issued a Code of Practice on 'Avoidance of race discrimination in recruitment practice while seeking to prevent illegal working'. The main points are:

- Failure to follow the Code may be considered by an Employment Tribunal.
- All job selections should be based on suitability for the post.
- Make no assumptions based on colour, race, nationality, ethnic or national origins or the length of time someone has been in the UK.
- Identical checks should be performed for all applicants, although employers may decide to only perform checks on candidates who reach a certain stage.
- If someone cannot produce the necessary documents ask them to seek advice.

Proposed changes in 2008

Significant changes are in progress in Managed Migration. Employers are now required to register as Sponsors, prove qualifications for Work Permits through a points system and take active responsibility for employees. The new system is still being rolled out.

Changes to Work Permits

The 2002 Act introduced the concept of Immigration Employment Documents (IEDs) of which Work Permits are one example. Others include certification under the Highly Skilled Migrant Programme

(HSMP) and the Sector Based Scheme (SBS). IEDs in themselves do not constitute residence permits or leave to enter or remain.

The 2006 Act introduced a new system of Managed Migration unifying the process of obtaining IEDs and visas or residence permits. A key feature is the concept of sponsorship in which employers or educational institutions who obtain government registration will be obliged to police the workers or students they have sponsored. The system is being progressively rolled out by the Home Office in 2008/09. It is intended to incorporate 80 current immigration routes in a system of five tiers, only the first of which (broadly equivalent to the existing HSMP innovator and investor categories) will avoid the need for sponsorship. Tier Two will broadly equate to both tiers of the existing Work Permit Scheme; Tier Three to the SBS; Tier Four for students; and Tier Five for youth mobility and temporary workers schemes, including a very wide variety of workers such as previously came under the Seasonal Agricultural Workers scheme (SAWs) but also visiting musicians and working holiday-makers.

On 1 January 2007, the European Union incorporated Romania and Bulgaria (A2 Member States). Bulgarian and Romanian nationals have the right of free movement but are not free to take employment without permission. If a Bulgarian or Romanian national wishes to obtain permission they will generally require an offer of employment, or they, if they are travelling to the UK to seek employment should consider carefully whether they are likely to find work that will meet the requirements of the Work Permit Scheme. In most cases this means skilled employment.

The employer is required to seek approval from Work Permits (UK) under the SBS on form BR1. Once a letter of approval is received the individual will then be able to apply for an Accession Worker Card (AWC). Only when this has been issued will the employee be able to work. The AWC will be issued for a specific job; if the employee wishes to change their job or job description changes, a new AWC will need to be applied for. The posts covered by the SBS are in the Food Manufacturing Sector only. An SBS permit cannot be issued in the food manufacturing sector for posts where the permit holder is required to undertake retail activities such as serving customers. The SBS is issued on a Quota basis. Please refer to Work Permits UK website – workingintheuk.gov.uk – for up-to-date information as the quota may change year to year and may be exhausted in the course of the year. Applications received after the suspension of the quota will not be processed and will be returned to the sender. Anyone who has an AWC for 12 months and in employment will obtain full EU Rights as a worker, business person and all other full EU rights.

The Points Based System

The UK Border Agency has and is in the process of rolling out the new Points Based System. The System is based on an 'Australian style' points system where an applicant wishing to work and reside in the UK will be required to obtain the necessary points before being granted permission to do so. The Points System is broken down into the following Tiers:

- Tier 1 – Highly Skilled Migrants (previously HSMP) – leads to settlement.
- Tier 2 – Skilled Workers requiring a Sponsorship Licence (previously work permits) – leads to settlement.
- Tier 3 – Low Skilled workers – currently suspended until further notice.
- Tier 4 – Students.
- Tier 5 – Sponsorship Licence required – temporary leave.

Certificate of Sponsorship	Points	Qualifications or NARIC equivalent	Points	Prospective Earnings in £ sterling	Points
Shortage Occupation – Check list published by UKBA	50	No qualifications	0	17,000–19,9999	5
Resident Labour Market Test	30	NVQ Level 3	5	20,000–21,999	10
Intra-company transfer	30	Bachelors or Masters PhD	10 or 15	22,000–23,999 or 24,000+	15 or 20
Maintenance Requirement					10
English Language Requirement					10

Therefore the main category affecting employers is Tier 2 and Tier 5. Both Tiers require the employer to apply for a Sponsorship Licence. The main aim of Tier 2 is to enable the UK employer to recruit from outside the European Economic Area (EEA) in jobs that cannot be filled by EEA workers. There must be a genuine vacancy. The employer must apply for a licence to bring in any skilled migrant worker before the Applicant applies for entry clearance. All migrant workers will need to obtain a biometric identity card. The Applicant will require 70 points including ten points for English Language proficiency, ten points for sufficient maintenance and 50 points for the Sponsorship Licence.

How to obtain the 50 points for the licence

As you will note from above, if the job vacancy is a shortage occupation listed by the Migration Advisory Committee (MAC), the full 50 points are awarded. All other occupations must advertise the vacancy. This is known as the Resident Labour Market Test (RLMT). The employer must show there is no suitably qualified worker from the UK or EEA available to fill the vacancy. The employer must have advertised the vacancy in Job Centre Plus or advertised, as agreed in a sector-specific Code of Practice, for two weeks. However, if the prospective earnings for the vacancy are over £40,000 then the vacancy may only be advertised for one week.

Skill level and appropriate rate

The minimum level of skill / education required to obtain a Sponsorship Licence is NVQ Level 3 or equivalent. UKBA will publish a list of occupations that are at or above NVQ Level 3 and those that fall below this standard. If a vacancy requires an NVQ Level 3 applicant, then five points will be awarded. A further 30 points will be awarded for the RLMT being satisfied; however, to obtain the full 50 points, the prospective earnings will have to be £22,000–£23,999. The question to be asked here is, is £22,000–£23,999 the appropriate rate for the job if the skill level is only NVQ Level 3 and not a Bachelors or Masters?

Employers should check the Annual Survey of Hours and Earnings (ASHE), published by the Office for National Statistics for the appropriate rate. If the occupation is not listed, the appropriate rate may be checked on 'Jobs4U' website, a government-maintained website.

Maintenance and English Requirement – 10 points each

Initial applicants must prove they have £800 in their bank account for at least three months. Each dependant must have two thirds of funds available i.e. £533 per dependant.

English Language requirement

The UK Border Agency has a list of countries where they will accept that they are English-speaking countries. All other applicants are required to be assessed at the appropriate level.

Applying for the licence

Applications for licences can only be made electronically on the UK Border Agency website. The employer issues a Certificate of Sponsorship application form on the UKBA Sponsor Management System (SMS). The Sponsor (employer) plays two main roles in the application process:

1. Providing evidence that the migrant is filling a genuine vacancy.
2. Pledges to accept responsibility of sponsorship in respect of the migrant.

The form must be submitted by the employer only. Once the form has been submitted, online certified copies of the documents and the fee must then be forwarded to the UK Border Agency within ten days. Employers must identify key personnel based in the UK. A single individual may play more than one role. The UK Border Agency may make checks

on any of these people before granting the licence. The personnel are as follows.

Authorising Officer (AO)

The Authorising Officer must be an honest and competent member of staff; they are responsible for the activities of anyone acting on the organisation's behalf. They ensure the sponsor meets its duties. A legal representative or an un-discharged bankrupt cannot act as an AO.

Key Contact

The Key Contact is the main point of contact for the Home Office; they will be called upon if there is a problem with the application process. They act as a liaison. If the AO does not wish to be the Key Contact then someone else should be allocated.

Level 1 User

The Level 1 Users will have access to the Sponsorship Management System (SMS). They will operate the sponsor's activities on a day-to-day basis via the sponsor. Their duties include:

- creating and moving others users from the SMS;
- assigning sponsorship certificates to migrants;
- notifying the UK Border Agency of minor changes in the sponsor's details (such as a new telephone number);
- completing the Change of Circumstances screen on the SMS; and
- reporting migrant activity to the UK Border Agency, such as if the migrant does not turn up for his/her job.

Only one Level 1 user may be appointed. The AO or a legal representative may act as a Level 1 User.

Level 2 User

A Level 1 user may appoint one or more Level 2 users. A Level 2 User's duties may include:

- assigning Certificates of sponsorship to migrants; and
- reporting migrant activity to UK Border Agency.

A legal representative may act as a Level 2 user. As the AO is responsible for ALL users then it is sensible to keep Level 2 users to a minimum and only appoint the absolute necessary.

Franchises

If an organisation has a number of franchises that are under its control, each branch may apply for a separate licence or they may apply for one licence covering all the other franchises. If the franchises are separate business not under the control of the parent company each branch will be required to apply separately.

Human Resources Practices

The UK Border Agency will check the Human Resources records of a sponsor. Sponsors must be aware of how many foreign nationals it employs. They must have a system in place to monitor absences from work and inform the UK Border Agency of any absences of more than ten days. The UK Border Agency may arrange for a site visit to the Sponsor's premises to carry out inspections.

Rating A or B

The sponsor will be given an A or B rating. If the sponsor meets all the requirements they will be given an A rating. If the sponsor fails to meet either the compliance check or the Human Resources check they will receive a B rating. If the sponsor does not meet either compliance or Human Resources checks the UK Border Agency will refuse to grant a Certificate of Sponsorship.

Transitional Ratings

B-rated organisations may be given a short period of time (possibly three months) to improve their performance and obtain an A rating. An action plan will be drawn up that will include steps the sponsor should take to improve. This is a joint project; however, the UK Border Agency will have the final say. After three months the UK Border Agency will check to see if genuine attempts were made to meet the requirements. If the sponsor does not improve they will lose their licence. However, if there are circumstances outside of the sponsor's control then the maximum period that a sponsor may be put on probation for is 12 months. The UK Border Agency has the power to cancel a Certificate of Sponsorship and in certain circumstances they will refuse a Certificate. In other situations they may or normally will refuse a licence or award a B rating.

See also: Discrimination, p.222; Migrant workers p.500; Recruitment and selection, p.607

Sources of further information

Home Office: www.employingmigrantworkers.org.uk.

Immigration and Nationality Directorate: www.ind.homeoffice.gov.uk/applying/eeaeunationals

Work Permits (UK): www.workingintheuk.gov.uk

UK Border Agency: www.bia.homeoffice.gov.uk/

Freedom of information

Louise Townsend, Pinsent Masons

Key points

The Freedom of Information Act 2000 (FOIA) came into full force on 1 January 2005, giving individuals a statutory right for the first time to see a huge amount of information held by government departments and public bodies. The Government is currently consulting on whether to extend the duties of disclosure to quasi-public organisations that carry out functions of a public nature and private organisations that enter into contracts to perform such functions on public authorities' behalf. The Data Protection Act has traditionally provided individuals with a right of access to information held about themselves. FOIA extends this right to cover information about third parties as well as any other information that may be held by the public authority or private companies that have public sector contracts.

Under FOIA, anyone of any nationality, and living anywhere in the world, can make a written request for information, and expect a response within 20 working days. The public authority will be obliged to meet that request subject to a number of specified exemptions and certain practical and financial constraints.

FOIA has imposed a substantial burden on those responsible for administering freedom of information (FOI) requests in public authorities. However, it is not only public authorities that have been affected by the Act. Whilst the primary impact of the Act will be on public authorities, it will have a knock-on effect on companies dealing with public authorities.

Public sector employers

The public sector employer is to a large extent caught between a rock and a hard place. Whilst the aim of FOIA is to increase openness in the public sector and disclosing information about decisions and activities of employees may promote this, it is recognised that employees also have legitimate concerns over privacy and rights to have those concerns respected.

With this delicate balancing act, how should the public sector employer deal with requests made by third parties about their employees? They could consider the following factors.

Implement policies

The public sector employer should draw up a policy setting out how it intends to deal with requests for employee information to provide a clear view of how information will be dealt with under the Act. This policy should be made available to all employees and ideally be published on the publication scheme (required under FOIA for all public authorities) for all to see. Policies could cover what types of information and in what circumstances information will or will not generally be disclosed and also what ssues will be considered in determining whether to disclose employee information. Issuing this policy will help the authority to meet its Data Protection Act obligations to employees. Remember, it is not just personal data that may be requested but any information including HR policies and procedures.

Know your information

Records management is important. Try to know what personal data you have. This will also be useful in dealing with subject access requests under the Data Protection Act. Consider separating or flagging information at the point of collection or creation to information which is not exempt from third party requests and other information.

Raise awareness

One potential factor to consider when determining whether information should be disclosed is what the employee was told when the information was collected. With this in mind, the authority could consider alerting new employees to the potential for disclosure of employee information under the Act by including a notice on induction. Including FOIA as part of new employees' training would provide them with a greater understanding of the authority's obligations under the Act and also the relevant exemptions.

Consideration should also be given to alerting employees of their right to object to the processing of personal information (which includes making disclosures) if there is a likelihood of them suffering substantial damage or distress under section 10 of the Data Protection Act 1998.

Give notice of, or consult the employee about, any proposed disclosure and certainly where there is any doubt as to whether the information should be disclosed.

Impact on private sector employers

Although it may seem that FOIA will only be relevant to public authorities, in practice it will also have an effect on the private sector. While there are limited circumstances where a private company may be deemed a public authority for the purposes of the Act (and therefore required to disclose information that it holds), the more concerning effect of the Act relates to information that private sector businesses hand over to the public sector.

Most public authorities contract on a regular basis with private sector companies for the provision of goods and services. Many of these contracts contain sensitive information (about HR, commercial or financial issues), which the private sector company would rather not be disclosed. However, all of this information is held by public authorities and, in theory, is accessible by anyone requesting it.

What can private sector businesses do to protect their interests? They may consider the following factors.

Put in place clear internal policies

Make it clear which individuals are authorised to release information to public authorities and identify individuals to liaise with public authorities with regard to monitoring the information once the authority has it.

Raise awareness within the organisation of the risk that any information disclosed to a public authority may potentially end up being disclosed to a member of the public or a competitor.

Manage information that is provided to public authorities

Identify which customers may be public authorities and review what information is provided to them. Record what information is provided to aid monitoring of this.

If information is particularly sensitive, consider whether it is really necessary to disclose it.

Confidential information
Amend standard terms and conditions used for dealing with public authorities to include drafting to minimise the impact of the Act. Blanket confidentiality clauses are no longer likely to be accepted by public authorities or by the Information Commissioner. Consider segregating confidential and non-confidential material to reduce the risk of inadvertent disclosure and to increase the likelihood of the confidentiality exemption applying.

Consider negotiating a clause in the contract which provides a right to be notified about and make submissions in relation to an information request that may contain employee/commercially sensitive information. This is important as if a decision made by the Information Commissioner is unfavourable to you, it will be the decision of the authority, not you, as to whether to appeal. There is no obligation on the authority to consult any interested third parties.

Be aware that information that is passed to public authorities may contain employee information such as CVs, experience etc. Thought should be given to consulting any affected third parties prior to releasing the information. Consider providing induction training on FOIA, amending your data protection notices and alerting employees when the information may be disclosed.

Use the Act to your advantage
Consider what types of information might be available from the public sector to assist your business and make use of your own rights to access that information. Training employees about the Act will increase your effectiveness in this area.

Conclusion
Both the public and private sectors are increasingly being affected by obligations imposed by the Act, albeit in different ways. What is clear is that it is essential for both sectors to implement policies, training and raise awareness within their organisations as to how the Act should be dealt with within their individual business.

See also: Data protection, p.186; Internet and email policies, p.426

Sources of further information

Freedom of Information Act: www.foi.gov.uk/

Information Commissioner's Office: www.ico.gov.uk

Fuel storage

Ben Shuster, Bureau Veritas

Key points

- Applies to all oil containers in excess of 200 litres situated outside buildings.
- Sets design standards for the tank to minimise risk of leakage and spillage.
- Does not apply to underground tanks, or those situated inside a building.

Legislation

- Control of Pollution (Oil Storage) (England) Regulations 2001.

Guidance

The Environment Agency produces a number of Pollution Prevention Guidance notes (PPGs), each of which is targeted at a particular industrial sector or activity and gives advice on the law and good environmental practice. PPGs are invaluable sources of advice for industry and the public. Those relevant to the Regulations considered here are:

- PPG2: Above Ground Oil Storage Tanks; and
- PPG8: Safe storage and disposal of used oils.

Overview

Every year there are a large number of oil spills, which can potentially result in the contamination of soils, groundwater, rivers, lakes and aquifers. A great deal of money is spent each year on the remediation of spills, which are often caused by inadequate storage facilities and/or poor operating practices. In order to address this problem the Government imposed minimum design standards for fuel tanks via the Control of Pollution (Oil Storage) Regulations 2001, which are now mandatory for all fuel storage facilities, as outlined below. These Regulations are administered by the Environment Agency.

A pollution incident resulting from failure to comply with these Regulations will lead to prosecution. Similar legislation is under consultation in Scotland and is also expected to be implemented in Northern Ireland. Similar legislation exists in Scotland (the Water Environment (Oil Storage) (Scotland) Regulations 2006) and in Northern Ireland (the Building (Amendment) Regulations (Northern Ireland) 2006).

Storage facilities subject to the Regulations

The Regulations apply to all external, above-ground containers of more than 200 litres capacity used for the storage of fuel oil and petrol. The Regulations do not apply to the majority of private dwellings, petrol stations, refineries or farms.
The Regulations do not apply to tanks situated entirely within a building or wholly underground.

Requirements of the Regulations

All storage tanks subject to the Regulations are required to have the following precautions / design features in place:

- The tank must be of adequate strength to store oil without leaking or bursting at full capacity.
- The tank must be surrounded by an impermeable bund of not less than 110% of the tank capacity. Where the bund contains a number of tanks, it

should be able to accommodate 110% of the largest tank's capacity or 25% of the combined capacity, whichever is the greater volume.

- There must be no drain point within the bund.
- Valves, filters, sight points or vent pipes must be located within the bund.
- External fill points must have at least a drip tray.
- All external pipes must be properly supported and positioned to minimise the likelihood of accidental damage from impact or collision.
- Underground fill pipes must have a number of control measures – including a leak detection system, no mechanical joints and a sleeve to prevent damage. If not, they must be tested for leaks every ten years (every five years if they have mechanical joints).
- An automatic overfill prevention device must be present if the filling operation is controlled from a place where it is not reasonably practicable to see the tank and the vent pipe (if present).
- Where mobile bowsers are used:
  - Filling points, pumps and valves must be securely locked.
  - Controls must be in place for flexible pipes.

Exemptions on existing tanks, installed before the Regulations came into force, were in place up to 1 September 2005 but these exemptions no longer apply. This means that many tanks will have only recently become subject to this legislation so companies are encouraged to assess all existing plant, as well as new or recently installed facilities.

Underground tanks

Underground tanks are not subject to the Regulations. However, Defra has published a Code of Practice for the good design, operation and management of underground storage tanks, which would be considered good practice where implemented. In the event of a release from the tank, if a company were following the guidance it would be considered as a mitigating factor during any subsequent litigation.

Measures to control releases from an underground tank might include:

- groundwater-monitoring wells;
- leak detection devices;
- installation of new tanks or other maintenance;
- training; and
- implementation of emergency response procedures.

Careful consideration should be made when installing or removing such tanks. The Environment Agency provides guidance – *PPG27: Installation, Decommissioning and Removal of Underground Storage Tanks* – which should be consulted prior to any such work.

See also: Building Regulations, p.81; Environmental Management Systems, p.296

Sources of further information

Defra: www.defra.gov.uk

Environment Agency: www.environment-agency.gov.uk

Furniture

Phil Reynolds, Furniture Industry Research Association (FIRA)

Key points

Furniture is an unexpectedly complex commodity to specify because it encompasses many different requirements and crosses many different areas. There is more to getting it right than glancing through the pages of a glossy catalogue and basing choice on appearance and price.

First of all, employers have a responsibility to provide a safe working environment with regard to structural stability, fire safety, cabling and, increasingly, the science of ergonomics. Personnel need to know how to adjust furniture to their physique and the tasks they perform. Company image and regulatory compliance apart, a workforce operating in a comfortable environment is likely to be better motivated and less prone to absenteeism than one that has to 'make do and mend'.

So how does the facilities manager or specifier decide which products to choose? The first, and most fundamental, requirement is a test certificate. Has the product been tested to the relevant standards – British, European or international – by an accredited test laboratory?

Legislation

Health and Safety at Work etc. Act 1974.

Furniture and Furnishings (Fire) (Safety) Regulations 1988, amended 1989 and 1993.

Electricity at Work Regulations 1989.

Workplace (Health, Safety and Welfare) Regulations 1992.

Health and Safety (Display Screen Equipment) Regulations 1992 as amended by the Health and Safety (Miscellaneous Amendments) Regulations 2002.

Provision and Use of Work Equipment Regulations 1998.

Management of Health and Safety at Work Regulations 1999.

Regulatory Reform (Fire Safety) Order 2005.

Disability Discrimination Act 2005.

Structural stability

Check that all tables, chairs and storage furniture have been tested to the appropriate standards. This should prove that the item is suitably strong, durable and stable in use to minimise the risk of any accident.

Fire safety

There is no legislation regarding flammability for upholstered office and contract furniture; this is different from the domestic market, where there are strict requirements designed to protect people in their homes. Instead, current legislation demands that the employer / landlord has the responsibility to decide the fire hazard rate of the building based on location and use and carry out suitable risk assessments for the area, which should cover the furniture as well. Once a rating has been set (usually 'low' for offices, rising to 'high' in institutions such as prisons and student accommodation), the upholstered furniture used must meet these requirements. The relevant British Standard is BS 7176:2007 *Specification for resistance to ignition of upholstered furniture for non-domestic seating by testing composites*. In a new or refurbished building it is wise to consult with your local fire officer prior to specification.

Desking and storage items are not normally covered by fire safety requirements; however Clause 12 of BS 5852:2006 *Methods of test for assessment of the ignitability of upholstered seating by smouldering and flaming ignition sources* can be used to assess the fire retardant properties of non-upholstered seating.

Cabling with desks

If a desk is provided with cabling (power or data) or provision for it to be fitted, the item should conform to specification BS 6396:2002 *Electrical systems in office furniture and office screens*. This covers the basic requirements for electrical cabling and should ensure an appropriate degree of safety. It may also fall under the Electricity at Work Regulations.

Ergonomics

The science of ergonomics is fitting equipment and tasks to people, and not the other way around.

The whole installation – desks and chairs used in conjunction with computer equipment – should conform with the Health and Safety (Display Screen Equipment) Regulations 1992. So look for compliance with BS EN ISO 9241:999 Part 5.

Incorrect posture can cause a multitude of long-term health problems including back pain and repetitive strain injury. Personnel should be instructed in how to adjust their furniture correctly so that it meets their specific needs – it is a waste of money to buy expensive, adjustable furniture and then not train people how to operate the controls, but it often happens.

Some forward-looking employers are specifying sit-stand desks that enable the user to alternate between sitting and standing-an approach advocated by many ergonomists including Levent Caglar, senior ergonomist at the Furniture Industry Research Association (FIRA).

The marketplace is flooded with products claiming to be 'ergonomic', many of which fall far short of any decent ergonomic criteria. To give specifiers a reliable measure of true ergonomic performance, FIRA has instigated an Ergonomics Excellence Award. Items must meet, or in some instances exceed, the relevant British and European standards together with ergonomic criteria set by FIRA.

In addition, the Disability Discrimination Act 2005 imposes extra requirements on employers to provide suitable furniture for both disabled visitors and employees. This includes not only work desks and chairs, but also reception counters and visitor areas.

Current standards

Tables and Desking: strength, stability and safety requirements
BS EN 15372:2008 *Furniture. Strength, durability and safety. Requirements for non-domestic tables.*

BS EN 527:2000 Part 1 *Office furniture. Work tables and desks. Dimensions.*

BS EN 527:2002 Part 2 *Office furniture. Work tables and desks. Mechanical.*

BS EN 527:2003 Part 3 *Office furniture. Work tables and desks. Methods of*

st for the determination of the stability of
e mechanical strength of the structure.

**eating: strength, stability and safety
equirements**
S 5459:2000 Part 2 *Office pedestal
eating for use by persons weighing up to
50 kg and for use up to 24 hours a day
icluding type-approval tests for individual
omponents.*

S EN 1335:2000 Part 1 *Office furniture.
Office work chair. Dimensions.*

S EN 1335:2000 Part 2 *Office furniture.
Office work chair. Safety requirements.*

S EN 1335:2000 Part 3 *Office furniture.
Office work chair. Safety test methods.*

S EN 14703:2007 *Furniture. Links for
on-domestic seating linked together in
row. Strength requirements and test
nethods.*

S EN 15373:2007 *Furniture, Strength,
urability and safety. Requirements for
on-domestic seating.*

S EN 13761:2002 *Office furniture.
isitors' chairs.*

**torage: strength, stability and safety
equirements**
S 4875:2007 Part 7 *Strength and stability
f furniture. Methods for determination of
trength and durability of storage furniture.*

S 4875:1998 Part 8 *Strength and stability
f furniture. Methods for determination of
tability of non-domestic storage furniture.*

S EN 14703:2004 Part 2 *Office furniture.
torage furniture. Safety requirements.*

S EN 14703:2004 Part 3 *Office furniture.
torage furniture. Test methods for the
etermination of stability and strength of
he structure.*

BS EN 14704:2004 *Office furniture. Tables
and desks and storage furniture. Test
methods for the determination of strength
and durability of moving parts.*

*Screens: strength, stability and safety
requirements*
BS EN 1023:1997 Part 1 *Office furniture.
Screens. Dimensions.*

BS EN 1023:2000 Part 2 *Office furniture.
Screens. Mechanical safety requirements.*

BS EN 1023:2000 Part 3 *Office furniture.
Screens. Test methods.*

Cable management
BS 6396:2002 *Electrical systems in office
furniture and office screens. Specification.*

Flammability
BS 5852:2006 *Methods of test for
assessment of the ignitability of
upholstered seating by smouldering and
flaming ignition sources.*

BS 7176:2007 *Specification for resistance
to ignition of upholstered furniture
for nondomestic seating by testing
composites.*

Ergonomics
BS EN ISO 9241:1999 Part 5 *Ergonomic
requirements for office work with visual
display terminals (VDTs). Workstation
layout and postural requirements. Office
accessories.*

Other items
FIRA Standard PP045: 2003: *Strength and
durability of VDU platforms and support
arms.*

See also: Display screen
equipment, p.238

Gas safety

Bill Scholes, Chartered Health and Safety Practitioner

Key points

- Persons in control of premises must ensure the safe condition of gas installations and appliances.
- The law requires that nobody should work on gas appliances unless they are CORGI-registered for that particular type of work.
- Annual checks of gas appliances and systems are required where used in residential properties.
- Regular checks must be made of gas appliances and systems used in non-residential properties although the law does not prescribe the inspection interval.

Legislation

- The Gas Safety (Installation and Use) Regulations 1998.

The Regulations apply to the installation, maintenance and use of gas appliances (both portable and fixed), fittings and flues in domestic and commercial premises.

Regulation 3(3) of the Gas Safety (Installation and Use) Regulations 1998, as amended, states:

"No employer shall allow any of his employees to carry out any work in relation to a gas fitting or service pipework and no self-employed person shall carry out any such work, unless the employer or self-employed person, as the case may be, is a member of a class of persons approved for the time being by the Health and Safety Executive for the purposes of this paragraph."

Compliance

Any person in control of premises, either landlord or managing agent, has a duty to make sure that gas appliances, fittings and flues are installed, maintained and repaired in accordance with the appropriate

standards and legislation. By doing this, not only will responsible persons be complying with the law, they will, more importantly, ensure that such equipment can be safely operated.

Failure of the above duty may lead to prosecution of the person responsible for maintenance, with the attendant potential for civil action in the event of an injury or damage to property occurring.

CORGI

In many ways, the name CORGI (Council of Registered Gas Installers) has become synonymous with gas safety. This is largely due to the fact that since 1991, the HSE has used CORGI to maintain a register of competent gas installers in the UK. Since "anyone who has the responsibility for gas maintenance must ensure that they appoint a competent person to undertake work on a gas appliance – installation, servicing, maintenance or repair", this restricts work to persons who are CORGI-registered.

Practical advice for employers

The following points may be useful for employers requiring work to be carried out on gas appliances or systems:

CORGI-registered persons are required to carry an ID card when undertaking work on gas appliances. The card carries photographic ID along with their CORGI registration number.

The ID card shows the type of gas work they can carry out, including whether or not they are allowed to work on commercial gas systems. This is an important point because registration with CORGI does not necessarily mean that person is competent to inspect, repair or maintain every gas appliance.

If there is some doubt about a person's competency, then checks can be made by contacting CORGI on 0870 401 2300.

If you have doubts about the safety of the work undertaken by a CORGI-registered installer, then you can request that such work is inspected by a CORGI Inspector.

For domestic properties, annual safety checks on the appliances, flues and fittings should also be done by a CORGI-registered person. These annual checks should be recorded and held by the landlord or managing agent.

Checks on gas appliances and systems used in non-residential properties need not necessarily be made annually. It is, however, required that the gas plant and equipment is inspected and maintained regularly.

Where a new supply is installed to premises, it must have emergency controls to isolate the supply.

It is good practice to maintain a plan of the premises showing the location of meters, valves, risers, gas appliances, isolation valves, etc.

Uncontrolled gas escapes should be reported to Transco on the emergency number: 0800 111999.

It is illegal to install instantaneous water heaters, which are not room sealed or fitted with a safety device that automatically turns the gas supply off before a dangerous level of poisonous fumes builds up.

Record keeping

- For residential properties, records of safety checks should be held by the landlord or managing agent for at least two years.
- Tenants are entitled to see, upon request, records of safety checks that have been carried out.
- For commercial properties, records must be kept (for an undetermined period) to demonstrate that the systems have been installed and regularly maintained to a suitable standard.

Bad practice

Richard Cartlidge of Limerick Road, Bispham, Blackpool was fined £1,000 and ordered to pay £987 costs at Blackpool Magistrates Court on 30 July 2008. He pleaded guilty to a charge under the Gas Safety (Installation and Use) Regulations 1998 of carrying out work as a gas fitter while not a member of an approved organisation.

The court heard that in March 2003 Richard Cartlidge fitted a gas fire at a flat in Victoria Road East, Thornton. The owner had concerns about the way the fire had been fitted, called in a second gas installer to check the work and found it had been fitted incorrectly and left in a dangerous condition.

HSE Inspector Sheldon Taylor said:

"This prosecution should serve as lesson to anyone having gas work carried out to ensure that the work is carried out by a registered gas fitter. All gas installation businesses, including self-employed gas installers, are required by law to be registered.

"Using a gas installer who is not registered is not only illegal, but can be dangerous, as there is no guarantee of their competence. Registered installers have been trained in gas safety and the standards needed for appliances and installations."

See also: COSHH: Hazardous substances, p.176; Fuel storage, p.351

Sources of further information

L56 *Safety in the installation and use of gas systems and appliances. Gas Safety (Installation and Use) Regulations 1998. Approved Code of Practice and guidance* (HSE Books, 1998) ISBN: 0 7176 0797 6.

HSE: www.hse.gov.uk/gas

HSE gas safety line: 0800 300 363.

CORGI: www.corgi-gas-safety.com

Glass and glazing

Catherine Hogan, Glass and Glazing Federation

Key points
There are a number of Regulations that impact on glazing and glass safety. The Workplace (Health, Safety and Welfare) Regulations 1992 address the issue of glazing in Regulation 14 and window design in Regulations 15 and 16.

Glazing requirements

Regulation 14 requires that, where necessary for reasons of health or safety, doors and low-level glazing in a workplace shall be glazed in a safety or robust material, or shall be protected against breakage. This does not mean that all glass in existing workplaces must be replaced with safety glass. A risk analysis must be carried out to see where there is danger – and that danger must be eliminated.

The HSE's revised Code of Practice, paragraph 147, says that particular attention should be paid to doors, and door side panels, where any part of the glazing is at shoulder height or below, and to windows where any part of the glazing is at waist height or below.

These cases are the same as those referred to in Approved Document N of the Building Regulations as 'critical locations'. Therefore glazing which meets the requirements of Document N (or BS 6262: Part 4) for these critical locations should meet the requirements of Regulation 14.

Regulation 14 also says that glazing in critical locations must be marked, or incorporate appropriate design features, to make its presence apparent – the objective being to avoid breaking the noses of people who might otherwise walk slap into the glazing, not realising it was there.

Reducing the risks

Various options are given in the Approved Code of Practice (ACoP) to Regulation 14 on how to reduce the risk of accidents at critical locations.

They include:

- the use of glazing that is inherently robust, such as polycarbonate or glass blocks;
- the use of glass which, if it breaks, breaks safely – e.g. glass which meets BS EN 12600: *European classification of safety glazing materials*; and
- the use of thick ordinary glass which meets certain thickness criteria.

Window design requirements

Regulation 15 focuses on window design. It requires that the operation of opening, closing or adjusting a window must not expose the operator to any risk. According to the Glass and Glazing Federation (GGF), this means that 'appropriate controls', such as window poles, must be provided where necessary; opening restrictors must be provided if there is a danger of falling out of the window; and the bottom edge of an opening window must be at least 800mm above floor level.

A further refinement is that opening windows must not project into an area where passers-by are likely to collide with them.

Regulation 16 requires that all windows and skylights shall be designed so they can be cleaned in safety. Essentially, this means that, if they cannot be cleaned from floor level or other suitable surfaces, windows must be designed to be cleanable from the inside.

The ACoP to Regulation 16 makes a variety of recommendations about the safe use of ladders, cradles and safety harnesses. It also cross-refers to BS 8213: Part 1 1991 *Windows, doors and rooflights: code of practice for safety in the use and during the cleaning of windows*.

Glazing options

So, what are your options when it comes to ensuring that the regulatory requirements are fulfilled in the most cost-effective way?

Choices include toughened or laminated glass, or the use of safety film.

Toughened glass is a glass that has been modified by thermal treatment to give strength, safety up to BS EN 12600 Classification 1.C1 Class A, and improved resistance to heat. Its light transmission is equal to ordinary glass.

Laminated glass consists of two or more sheets of ordinary or heat-treated glass bonded together under heat and pressure by interlayers of transparent polymer. There are various types of laminated glass, including laminated safety glass, laminated security glass and bullet-resistant glass. Its most significant feature is that if the glass fractures on impact, fragments will remain bonded to the plastic interlayer. This minimises the risk of serious cuts from flying glass and maintains a protective barrier.

Film is a tough sheet of micro-thin high-clarity polyester that can be applied easily *in situ* to the interior or exterior of existing windows, glass doors and partitions. It is available in single-ply and multi-ply formats. The correct application of film on glass can upgrade the original glazing to meet the requirements of Government Regulations on health and safety and British Standards.

Energy efficiency requirements under the Building Regulations

Amendments to Part L of the Building Regulations came into force on 1 April 2002 bringing new requirements for energy efficiency in buildings. The Building Regulations Part L were amended in October 2001, and new approved Documents L1 and L2 – giving approved guidance on how the new Part L can be complied with – were published at the same time. The main changes affect glazing (see below) and some installations of oil-storage tanks, combustion devices and some plumbing.

The new Regulations will apply to new buildings, and to extensions and alterations to existing ones. Local authority building control departments are a traditional source of help on how organisations can meet the Regulations.

Fenestration Self-Assessment Scheme (FENSA)

To assist the effective implementation of the requirements of Part L, a scheme for the self-certification of replacement glazing has been set up by the GGF. This scheme is known as the Fenestration Self-Assessment Scheme (FENSA).

Since 1 April 2002 all replacement glazing has come within the scope of the Building Regulations, so that anyone who installs replacement windows or doors has to comply with strict thermal performance tandards. The Building Regulations have controlled glazing in new buildings for many years, but this represents only a very small percentage of the total building stock.

When the time comes to sell property – says the GGF – the purchaser's solicitors will ask for evidence that any replacement glazing installed after April 2002 complies with the new Building Regulations. There will be two ways to prove compliance:

1. A certificate showing that the work has been done by an installer who is registered under the FENSA Scheme; or

2. A certificate from the local authority saying that the installation has approval under the Building Regulations.

See also: Building Regulations, p.81

Sources of further information

Glass and Glazing Federation: www.ggf.org.uk

Building Regulations Approved Document L:
www.planningportal.gov.uk/england/professionals/en/4000000000563.html

Head protection

Bill Scholes, Chartered Health and Safety Practitioner

Key points

Employers are required to provide head protection for employees who are at risk of sustaining injuries to the head either from things falling on them or by hitting their head against something. This general duty arises under the Personal Protective Equipment (PPE) Regulations 1992 in addition to the specific duty imposed for construction workers under the Construction (Head Protection) Regulations 1989.

Many employees who work at height complain that a safety helmet will not help them if they fall on their head. Whilst it is undoubtedly true that safety helmets will afford little protection in the event of a fall, many such workers are (by nature of the work they are doing), at significant risk of hitting their heads, e.g. scaffolders, steeplejacks, slingers etc. Additionally, the fact should not be overlooked that the construction industry does not have the monopoly on head injuries. In recent times there have been some serious accidents involving the use of quad bikes in agriculture and forestry.

With the exception of Sikhs wearing turbans, all employees must wear such head protection where a risk assessment identifies the need to do so. Employees need to understand where and when the wearing of head protection is a requirement and management need to ensure compliance. Employers can make rules governing the use of head protection and should bring these rules in writing to the attention of all those who may be affected by them.

It is not a requirement under the above Regulations to provide visitors to site (e.g. potential house buyers, deliverers, etc.) with head protection. However, the general duties to others under the Health and Safety at Work etc. Act 1974 apply, and thus where a risk of head injuries might exist it will be necessary to do so.

Legislation

- Health and Safety at Work etc. Act 1974.
- Construction (Head Protection) Regulations 1989.
- Personal Protective Equipment Regulations 1992.
- Management of Health and Safety at Work Regulations 1999.

Selecting the right head protection

Because of the variety of head protection available, it is usually possible to find head protection equipment (e.g. helmets or bump caps), that suit the needs of both the task being undertaken and the wearer. Head protection should fit properly (adjustable), be as comfortable as possible for the wearer (ventilated, possibly cushioned) and compatible with the type of work to be done. For example, a mechanic working under a car in a pit may find that a bump cap is less of a nuisance in such a restricted space than a peaked safety helmet. It is very important that a helmet

oes not interfere with other PPE
e.g. ear defenders or eye protectors),
nd therefore an integrated approach
ay be necessary, such as the
ombinations used by forestry workers
hen operating chainsaws.

Maintenance
s with all PPE, the employer is
esponsible for ensuring that it is
dequately maintained. Users should be
ained to the appropriate level in carrying
ut maintenance and inspection in order to
dentify for themselves any problems with
he equipment. Self-employed persons
ave the same duties in regard to their
wn equipment.

Simple guidelines on use of helmets
Always:

- wear the helmet the right way round;
- wear a chinstrap where necessary;
- wear the helmet so that the brim is
  level when the head is upright; and
- keep a supply of helmets for visitors.

Never:

- use your helmet for carrying materials;
- paint it or use solvents for cleaning;
- store it in direct sunlight;
- modify, cut or drill it; or
- share your head protection.

Risk assessment
If a significant risk of head injuries exists,
then employers are required to adopt a
hierarchy of control measures. As with risk
control in general, the provision of PPE (thus
head protection) is always to be regarded
as a last resort. Measures should be taken
to reduce the risks to as many people as
possible; therefore it may be possible to:

- prevent access to areas where head
  injuries could be caused;
- provide protected routes;
- avoid the movement of loads overhead;
- fit some form of protection (e.g.
  guardrails, toe-boards) to prevent
  falling objects; or
- mark and cushion fixed hazards such
  as pipes and low access points.

See also: Construction site health
and safety, p.154; Health and
safety at work, p.364; Working
at height, p.395; Ladders, p.440;
Personal Protective Equipment,
p.568; Slips, trips and falls, p.657

Sources of further information

INDG174 *A short guide to the Personal Protective Equipment at Work
Regulations 1992*: www.hse.gov.uk/indg174.pdf

Health and safety at work

Nicola Cardenas-Blanco, Martineau Solicitors

Key points

- The Health and Safety at Work etc. Act 1974 (HSWA) imposes general duties on employers, the self-employed, controllers of premises, manufacturers and employees to ensure health, safety and welfare.
- Legislation is supported by Approved Codes of Practice (ACoPs) and guidance notes.
- Employers have a duty to employees in respect of their health and safety and may also be liable for negligent acts committed by fellow employees acting in the course of their employment.
- Occupiers of premises owe a duty of care to lawful visitors and trespassers.

Legislation

- Occupiers' Liability Acts 1957 and 1984.
- Employers' Liability (Compulsory Insurance) Act 1969.
- Health and Safety at Work etc. Act 1974.
- Employers' Liability (Compulsory Insurance) Regulations 1998.
- Management of Health and Safety at Work Regulations 1999.

Overview

The HSWA imposes general duties on all employers and the self-employed to ensure the safety of those who may be affected by their business activities, and on employees to look after their own safety. It also allows outdated, prescriptive legislation to be replaced by objective-setting Regulations, supported by ACoPs and guidance notes.

The European Union has instigated the majority of recent changes in UK health and safety legislation by issuing EU directives that Member States are required to implement by passing their own legislation. The HSWA allows such requirements to be implemented in the UK as Regulations.

Case law has developed alongside legislation, imposing duties of care on employers and the self-employed to look after the health, safety and welfare of their employees and the health and safety of others affected by their business operations.

Breaches of health and safety legislation in the workplace can give rise to criminal liability. Whilst a breach of the HSWA doesn't give an automatic right to a civil claim, in many cases the evidence used against a company in a criminal prosecution may similarly be used in a civil claim.

Health and Safety at Work etc. Act 1974

Before the introduction of the HSWA, health and safety legislation had developed in a piecemeal fashion, providing specified industries and hazardous activities with a set of prescriptive rules to follow. In 1974 this approach was replaced by the HSWA, which is now the cornerstone of modern health and safety legislation.

The HSWA imposes duties on everyone at work – employers, the self-employed, and

mployees. The principal duties it imposes
re as follows.

*Section 2: Duties of employers to
mployees*
mployers must ensure the health,
afety and welfare of their employees
ubject only to the defence of 'so far as is
easonably practicable'.

o discharge its duty an employer must
rovide (so far as reasonably practicable):

- safe plant and safe systems of work;
- arrangements for the safe use,
  handling, storage and transport of
  articles and substances;
- adequate information, instruction,
  training and supervision;
- safe places of work, including safe
  access and egress; and
- a safe working environment with
  adequate welfare facilities.

ll employers must make and review a
uitable and sufficient assessment of
e risks of their activities to employees
Regulation 3 of the Management of
ealth and Safety at Work Regulations
999).

n employer with five or more employees
ust prepare and regularly review a
ritten health and safety policy statement,
he organisational structure and detailed
rrangements for health, safety and
elfare, and bring it to every employee's
ttention.

Employers must also have in place
uch arrangements as are necessary
o effectively plan, organise, control,
nonitor and review any preventive and
rotective measures.

Employers must appoint competent
persons to assist with the measures
necessary for ensuring health and safety
Regulation 7 of MHSWR) and must also

consult with employee representatives
(including trade unions) when making
health and safety arrangements.

*Section 3: Duties of employers to
others*
An employer must conduct his business
so as to ensure that non-employees are
not exposed to health and safety risks.
Again, this duty is subject to the defence
of 'so far as is reasonably practicable'. If
the employer is a self-employed person,
then he must also, so far as is reasonably
practicable, conduct his business to ensure
that he is not exposed to such risks. Non-
employees include contractors, visitors and
members of the public.

An employer must make and review a
suitable and sufficient assessment of the
risks of their activities to persons not in
their employment who may be affected
by the carrying on of their business
(Regulation 3 of MHSWR).

Section 4: Duties relating to premises
Those individuals or organisations with
total or partial control of work premises
must, so far as is reasonably practicable,
ensure the health and safety of all non-
employees who work there, to the extent
of their control.

Therefore, landlords and managing
agents may be responsible for the safety
of those working in the common parts of
buildings (e.g. cleaners, maintenance staff,
etc.), whilst non-domestic tenants will be
responsible for the health and safety of
any person in the areas covered by their
lease.

Section 6: Duty of manufacturers
Anyone who designs, manufactures,
imports or supplies articles or substances
for use at work must ensure, so far as is
reasonably practicable, that those articles
are safe for their intended use and during
cleaning and maintenance.

Section 7: Duties of employees

While at work, employees have a duty:

- not to endanger themselves or others through their acts or omissions; and
- to cooperate with their employer, e.g. by wearing protective equipment.

Section 8: Misuse of health and safety equipment

No person (whether an employee or not) shall misuse anything provided in the interests of health, safety or welfare.

Section 36: Individual liability

Where an offence is committed due to an act or default of some other person (not being an employee), that person shall be guilty of the offence and may be charged and convicted of it whether or not the employer is also charged.

Section 37

Where an offence by the company is proved to have been committed with the consent, connivance or by the neglect on the part of any director, manager or company secretary (or similar person), then he or she will also be guilty of the offence and may be prosecuted personally.

Section 40

An employer who intends to rely on a defence of reasonable practicability in a health and safety prosecution is required to prove that they have done everything reasonably practicable (or everything practicable for some offences) to safeguard the health and safety of employees, non-employees or members of the public. This means that the burden of proof is reversed and is on the employer to prove that adequate prevention methods were in place.

Reasonably practicable

Many health and safety duties require the duty holder to do everything possible to ensure the health and safety of others subject only to a defence of 'so far as is reasonably practicable'. This phrase means doing less than absolutely everything physically possible (i.e. everything 'practicable') and involves a balance to be struck between the risk to health and safety (in terms of the likelihood of harm occurring and the potential consequences of it if it does) and the inconvenience and cost in terms of time, money and other resources of overcoming that risk. If the costs are disproportionate to the risks then the test is satisfied and the employer will be more positively able to seek the defence that it was not reasonably practicable to do more to protect against the risk.

Assistance on what is reasonably practicable comes from ACoPs and guidance documents issued by the HSE. Relevant British Standards industry guidance and common practices should also be relevant considerations.

In practice however, the defence of reasonable practicibility is very difficult to satisfy as it is often the case that when an incident is viewed with hindsight an additional measure with a small resource implication may have been taken in relation to that incident. In addition, the courts have also determined that the standard of care is the same regardless of the size of the company and its available resources.

Employers should record their risk assessments and the decisions to implement or reject certain safety measures. Since safety measures must be proportionate to the risk they are averting, the first step is to identify and assess the risk, after which the available control measures should be identified and assessed. If the time and costs involved in the control measure are disproportionately gh in comparison with the risk involved, en in theory the duty to do everything easonably practicable will be satisfied ven though the measure is not nplemented. In practice, considerable vidence of the reasons for this decision 'ill be required if this defence is to be sed in relation to a health and safety ncident.

he difficulty for many employers in aaking this judgement is that the question f whether the correct balance is reached one that only a court can definitely ecide after looking at all the evidence in ach case.

Regulations

umerous Regulations have been made nder the provisions of section 15 of the SWA that impose detailed obligations n employers and those controlling work ctivities. The most important of these re covered in other chapters of this andbook.

Approved Codes of Practice

CoPs have a 'quasi-legal' status. lthough they do not provide definitive nterpretation of legislation (only the ourts can do that), compliance with the relevant ACoP does provide good

evidence of compliance with the relevant statutory duty, and crucially evidence of doing everything 'reasonably practicable'. Similarly, if an employer cannot show that he has followed an ACoP in relation to a health and safety incident, it must show that he has discharged his relevant health and safety obligations in some other way, or risk prosecution.

Prosecution

Health and safety prosecutions take place in the criminal courts, starting formally with the receipt of a summons to appear at the Magistrates' Court. This is usually issued in a court near to where the accident occurred. Generally, the case may be heard in the Magistrates' Court, where the maximum penalty that can be imposed is a £20,000 fine and/or (for a small number of charges) six months' imprisonment for each charge. Cases that are complex, or result from a more serious outcome, will be committed (referred) by the magistrates to the Crown Court, where the maximum penalty rises to an unlimited fine and/or two years' imprisonment (again for specific charges only).

Maximum penalties under the HSWA and the Regulations are set out in Table 1.

Table 1: Maximum penalties available under HSWA and associated Regulations

Breach	Magistrates' court	Crown court
HSWA	£20,000 fine	Unlimited fine
Regulations	£5,000 fine	Unlimited fine
Certain offences such as failing to comply with an enforcement notice or with the conditions imposed on a licence	Up to six months' imprisonment and/or a fine	Up to two years' imprisonment and/or a fine

Mitigation and aggravation

Sometimes in health and safety investigations the measures that an employer takes may amount to either a complete or partial defence to the charges. However, if a prosecution does follow, the same information may also amount to mitigation of the offence committed. Providing evidence of relevant mitigating factors are likely to result in a reduction in the fine imposed.

The courts have given guidance on the particular factors which amount to mitigating or aggravating features (that result in a higher fine) to an offence.

These include the following.

Mitigating factors
- A prompt admission of guilt.
- The defendant fell only slightly short of meeting the test of reasonable practicability.
- A good safety record.
- Positive steps taken by the company to remedy deficiencies including the cost involved in implementing these.

Aggravating factors
- Failure to heed previous warnings.
- Whether death or a serious injury resulted from the breach.
- Whether profit was put before safety.
- A deliberate breach.

Civil actions

Anyone who suffers injury or ill health as a result of work activities may be entitled to bring a personal injury claim against those responsible for compensation. To be successful, the injured party (the claimant) must prove that:

- the defendant owed him a duty of care;
- the duty was breached; and
- the injury was a foreseeable result of the breach.

The existence of a duty of care is generally easy to prove in an employer–employee relationship, since the employer has a duty to provide under civil law:

- safe plant and equipment;
- safe systems of work;
- safe workplaces with safe access and egress; and
- competent fellow workers.

These civil law duties mirror the duties under section 2 of the HSWA. Comprehensive risk assessments that are up to date will provide good evidence in defence of any claim that the employer has breached any of the above duties.

Occupiers' Liability Acts

Occupiers (those in control) of premises are under duties contained in the Occupiers' Liability Acts 1957 and 1984:

- The 1957 Act imposes a duty to take reasonable steps to ensure that lawful visitors to the premises are safe from dangers due to the state of premises.
- The 1984 Act imposes a duty to take reasonable steps to ensure that trespassers are not injured as a result of dangers arising from the state of premises. This is a slightly lower standard of care than that for lawful visitors.

A breach of these Acts is not a criminal offence and is only actionable in civil law if a claim for compensation.

Vicarious liability

An employer may be responsible for the negligent acts or omissions of employees committed in the course of their employment. A claimant can sue the employer on the basis of vicarious liability, provided he can show that the employee was negligent and this caused his injury. An employer will escape liability if he can show the employee was acting 'on a

olic of his own' outside the course of his
mployment.

amages

uccessful claimants will usually receive
ompensation in the form of a one-off lump
um. This is assessed under a number of
eadings:

Pain and suffering;
Damage to clothing, property, etc.;
Loss of earnings;
Medical or nursing expenses;

- Other out-of-pocket expenses, such as additional travel or medication; and
- Inability to pursue personal / social / sports interests or activities.

Most personal injury claims are paid for out of insurance (employers' liability or public liability), subject to any exclusions or excesses under the policy. The Employers' Liability (Compulsory Insurance) Act 1969 and 1998 Regulations require employers to hold a £5m insurance cover for claims brought by their employees.

> *See also*: Health and safety management, p.386; Health and safety policies, p.390; Insurance, p.416; Mental health, p.496; Risk assessments, p.639; Visitor safety, p.714

Sources of further information

Workplace Law Network provides premium members with unrestricted access to a comprehensive range of online information – factsheets, case reports and daily news items – on employment, health and safety and premises management. Members also benefit from an online advice service and a free subscription to the *Workplace Law Magazine*. For more information email membership@workplacelaw.net or call our membership services team on 0871 777 8881.

Comment...

Dispelling the myths of health and safety

Nattasha Freeman, Director of Health and Safety at Phoenix Beard Property Consultants, is set to become the new president of IOSH in November. Here she speaks about her plans for the year – and IOSH's plans to keep on campaigning for better understanding of risk management.

I first became involved in risk management as a child; we all do as that's how we all learn. As children, we all learn about risk assessment and managing out risk from an early age, doing things like learning the chances of making it from one side of the playground to the other without getting hurt playing British bulldog or whether it's safe to ride your bike down the main road. In the work environment I became involved in Health and Safety about 15 years ago and with that started getting involved with risk assessment and management.

In the work environment we have a more formal approach to risk management and there is now a requirement to document the process. People look more closely at what they need to control and design out if it is recorded for posterity and their name is on it. As the legislation has changed and become more prescriptive in how decisions are recorded – a prime example is the recent change to the CDM Regulations – people have become more aware of their personal liability; particularly where the lines of responsibility and accountability have become clearer. Since I started in the profession, awareness has grown exponentially with regard to those who are owed a duty of care and accordingly those who owe that duty have become more focused on their part in the scheme of things; aware of their own vulnerability an the impact of getting it wrong.

The requirement for risk management still needs to be highlighted. A lot of people decide that the responsibility for this lies with someone else, instead of taking ownership. Once you identify who is responsible, their part in the risk management role becomes clear and the it is easier to get a buy in for their role in the process.

The second stage of the process is gettin people to realise that risk management is shared and that by getting all parties to focus on the highest and most likely of hazards instead of focusing on everything you can allow for the majority of those ris to be managed out to the benefit of all.

One of the ways to bring about change is to do what Ray Hurst (the current IOSH President) is doing, in the rebuttal of media articles. Another way would be to try to force into the open those who are actually fuelling the wrong approach to ris management. Any 'no' to an activity shou be qualified and positive suggestions put forward; I believe this does happen when competent people say "no".

Comment: Dispelling the myths of health and safety

think the press make hard work of risk management because of the associations with liability and blame. In a world where people can be found personally liable, where the culture is still name and shame and where what you *don't* do can bring a company down more quickly than *doing something*, then it is easy to report some but not all of the factors around a 'Health and Safety' story. Qualifying a refusal for something to go ahead isn't really news. If all the facts are not known, and the person who said "no" will not identify themselves all becomes a mystery worthy of news, however accurate the detail that supports the article behind the story.

Outside of the media I think that the penalty for not carrying out robust risk management should be heavier. Where that is your responsibility and you either do not do it, or do it properly and an accident occurs, the penalty awarded should represent the outcome more closely.

IOSH has spent a lot of time this past 12 months on the 'Stop taking the myth' campaign, where we have tried hard to get people to realise that whilst the spotlight is on not playing conkers at school, having lifeguards for paddling pools and banning pancake races, the reality of 241 fatalities in the workplace in the year 2006-07 still gets missed. The accident rate for those in the workplace continues to rise and the impact on those who know the victims – fellow colleagues as well as family – is not appreciated.

If I can help reinforce IOSH's mission to create a safer world of work; if I can help dispel the myth and make people realise that health and safety is positive and those who practice it competently are enablers; if I can underline and facilitate the benefit of health and safety practitioners in assisting those who have a health and safety responsibility and make a positive difference, then this will be my legacy.

Health and safety consultation

David Wright, Kennedys

Key points

There is a general duty on every employer, imposed by section 2(6) of the Health and Safety at Work etc. Act 1974 (HSWA), to consult with safety representatives of trade unions.

For the purposes of discharging that duty, the Safety Representatives and Safety Committees Regulations 1977 (the 1977 Regulations) set out details as to the appointment of safety representatives together with their functions and the employer's duty to consult.

Where employees are not in groups covered by trade union safety representatives, an employer has a duty to consult those employees under the Health and Safety (Consultation with Employees) Regulations 1996 (the 1996 Regulations).

As a consequence an employer might have to consult employees under both sets of Regulations where different employees have different representation in the workplace. A number of other Regulations, such as the Quarries Regulations 1999 and the CDM Regulations 2007, include specific requirements regarding consultation with employees.

Legislation
- Health and Safety at Work etc. Act 1974.
- Safety Representatives and Safety Committees Regulations 1977.
- Health and Safety (Consultation with Employees) Regulations 1996.

Safety representatives and committees

For the purposes of the appointment of safety representatives or committees and the duty to consult, a recognised trade union is one where the employer, or two associated employers, recognises the union for the purpose of collective bargaining.

The recognised trade union may appoint safety representatives from among the employees in all cases where an employer by whom it is recognised employs one or more employees.

A person ceases to be a safety representative for the purposes of these Regulations when:

- the trade union that appointed him notifies the employer in writing that his appointment has been terminated; or
- he ceases to be employed at the workplace; or
- he resigns.

An employer has a duty under section 2(7) of HSWA to establish a safety committee with a function of keeping under review the measures taken to ensure the health and safety at work of its employees where requested in writing by at least two safety representatives. The committee should be established not later than three months after the request is made.

Functions of safety representatives

As well as having a function in relation to the employer's duty to consult in accordance with section 2(6) of HSWA, safety representatives also have other functions set out in the 1977 Regulations. The most important of these are to investigate potential hazards and dangerous occurrences or the causes of any accidents in the workplace. Others include investigating complaints by any employee they represent relating to that employee's health, safety or welfare at work and to make representations to the employer arising out of their investigations or from complaints received or on general matters affecting health and safety at the workplace.

Additional functions are to carry out inspections of the workplace and to receive information from HSE inspectors and consult with those inspectors as the representative of the employees.

Employer's duty to consult safety representatives

In addition to the general duty to consult safety representatives for the purposes of effectively promoting and developing measures to ensure the health and safety at work of employees, the 1977 Regulations state that every employer shall consult safety representatives in 'good time' regarding a number of specified matters. These are as follows:

- The introduction of any measure at the workplace which may substantially affect the health and safety of the employees whom the safety representatives concerned represent.
- Arrangements for appointing or, as the case may be, nominating persons in accordance with the Management of Health and Safety at Work Regulations 1999 or the power to nominate safety representatives under the Regulatory Reform (Fire Safety) Order 2005.
- Any health and safety information that the employer is required to provide.
- The planning and organising of any health and safety training that the employer is required to provide.
- The health and safety consequences for the employees of new technologies into the workplace.

The 1977 Regulations also provide for inspection of the premises and of certain documents by safety representatives on reasonable notice.

Employer's duty to consult employees

The 1977 Regulations apply where there is a recognised trade union. The 1996 Regulations created a duty to consult those employees who did not have the benefit of safety representatives.

The matters on which the employer has to consult are effectively identical to those on which he must consult safety representatives where he recognises a union, and which are set out above.

The persons to be consulted are:

- the employees directly; or
- in respect of any group of employees, one or more persons in that group who were elected, by the employees in that group at the time of the election, to represent the group for the purposes of such consultation (these are referred to as 'representatives of employee safety').

When the employer consults these representatives, he should inform the employees of the names of the representatives and the group of employees represented by them.

An employer shall not consult a person as a representative if:

Health and safety consultation

- that person has notified the employer that he does not intend to represent the group of employees for the purposes of consultation;
- that person has ceased to be employed in the group of employees which he represents;
- the period of his election has expired and that person has not been re-elected; or
- the person has become incapacitated from carrying out his functions under the 1996 Regulations.

If an employer has been consulting representatives and then decides to consult the employees directly, he should inform the representatives and the employees of this.

The 1996 Regulations also impose a duty on the employer to provide employees and representatives with such information as is necessary to enable them to participate fully and effectively in the consultation. Where the employer consults representatives, he should also make available information contained in any records he is required to keep for the purposes of RIDDOR (so long as the records relate to the workplace or group of workers the representatives represent, and any information relating to specific individuals is not shared without their consent).

Functions of representatives of employee safety

These are very similar to those of appointed safety representatives. They are:

- to make representations to the employer on potential hazards and dangerous occurrences at the workplace which either affect, or could affect, the group of employees they represent;

- to make representations to the employer on general matters affecting the health and safety at work of the group of employees they represent and in particular in relation to those matters on which the employer has a duty to consult; and
- to represent the employees they represent in consultations at the workplace with inspectors of the HSE.

Payment for time off and training

Both the 1977 and the 1996 Regulations provide that the employer shall permit safety representatives or representatives of employee safety to take such time off with pay during working hours as is necessary for performing their functions. In reality, employers must adopt a reasonable approach to this issue. Some representatives will try to overstep the mark, and in those circumstance employers will need to be able to demonstrate that their response is reasoned and proportionate.

In relation to training, the 1977 Regulations provide that the employer will permit safety representatives paid time off to undergo training. The situation is more onerous for employers in relation to representatives under the 1996 Regulations. In those circumstances the employer shall ensure that representatives are provided with such training in respect of their functions as is reasonable in all the circumstances and it will be the employer who has to bear the cost connected with that training including travel and subsistence. Again, a good dose of common sense will be the most valuable commodity if there is disagreement over the type and cost of training.

Employer's liability for breaches

A breach of the general duty under section 2(6) of HSWA is a criminal offence punishable by a maximum fine

Workplace Law Network
www.workplacelaw.net

f £20,000 in a Magistrates' Court or an nlimited fine in the Crown Court. In the bsence of other serious failures, it would e surprising were an organisation to be rosecuted for a single, relatively benign reach of its obligations in this area.

breach of the Regulations is punishable y a £5,000 fine in a Magistrates' Court r an unlimited fine in the Crown Court. Again, as the Regulations are principally administrative' in nature, i.e. they do not directly involve risk, prosecution for their breach will be unlikely unless associated with other failings.

A breach of the general duty under section 2(6) or of the 1996 Regulations cannot result in civil liability for a breach. Civil liability can however follow a breach of the 1977 Regulations and both sets of Regulations allow an employee to take action in an Employment Tribunal over an employer's failure to provide paid time off.

See also: Health and safety at work p.364; Health and safety enforcement, p.376; Health and safety management, p.386; Trade unions, p.687

Sources of further information

HSE – Worker involvement: www.hse.gov.uk/involvement/index.htm

HSE – Consulting employees on health and safety: www.hse.gov.uk/pubns/indg232.pdf

Health and safety enforcement

Kathryn Gilbertson, Greenwoods Solicitors LLP

Key points

- Inspectors have wide powers of investigation.
- Enforcement by way of prohibition or improvement notices are a frequent way for inspectors to secure legal compliance.
- A prohibition notice can require work to stop immediately, and will continue to have effect during an appeal against the notice (unless the Tribunal which is hearing the Appeal directs otherwise). The effect of an improvement notice is suspended pending the outcome of any appeal against the notice.
- Criminal prosecutions can be brought for breaches of health and safety legislation.
- Conviction usually results in a fine (which can be substantial) and an order to pay prosecution costs – neither of which are recoverable from insurance.
- Some offences can result in imprisonment (for individuals) for up to two years.
- Directors and managers can also be prosecuted and convicted in connection with offences committed by their company.

Legislation

- Health and Safety at Work etc. Act 1974 (HSWA).
- Police and Criminal Evidence Act 1984 (PACE).
- Health and Safety (Enforcing Authority) Regulations 1998.
- Corporate Manslaughter and Corporate Homicide Act 2007.

Overview

The Health and Safety Executive (HSE) is the body responsible for promoting health and safety at work including enforcement. But for some types of workplace the relevant local authority is the enforcing authority.

HSWA provides powers of investigation, which are in some respects even more stringent than those of the police, since no separate warrant is required to enter premises and persons can be compelled to answer relevant questions and to sign a declaration as to the truth of those answers.

Enforcing authorities regularly serve improvement and prohibition notices to require employers to take remedial action. Contravention of such a notice is a serious criminal offence.

A further sanction for breaching health and safety legislation is criminal prosecution and conviction of the individual or organisation responsible. This could include a company director, secretary or manager being personally culpable.

Although the principal penalty is a fine (which not uncommonly exceeds £100,000 for very serious offences), individuals can be sent to prison for up to two years if convicted of certain offences and an unlimited period if convicted of manslaughter.

Enforcing authorities

The enforcing authority for different workplaces is specified in the Health and Safety (Enforcing Authority)

Regulations 1998. The general rule is that the HSE is the enforcing authority. However, health and safety is enforced by the relevant local authority in certain workplaces, including:

- offices;
- retail outlets;
- catering services;
- exhibitions; and
- sports grounds and theatres.

In this chapter, an 'Inspector' means an officer of the relevant enforcing authority, whether it be the HSE or local authority.

Powers of investigation

Section 20 of HSWA gives inspectors wide powers to investigate suspected health and safety breaches. These include the power to:

- enter and search premises without a warrant;
- direct that the whole premises, or any part of them, be left undisturbed;
- take measurements, photographs, recordings or samples;
- take possession of items for testing or use as evidence;
- interview any person; and
- demand copies of documents as evidence.

Interviews

Section 20

Under section 20, Inspectors can require interviewees to answer questions and sign a declaration that those answers are true. Although there is no right to remain silent, the evidence obtained cannot be used to prosecute interviewees or their spouse. It can, however, be used against any other individual or company, including the interviewee's employer.

PACE

Where an Inspector suspects that a particular individual or a company may

have committed an offence, he should not question or continue to question that individual or company about the matter other than under caution. This will usually result in the individual suspect or a person with authority to speak on behalf of a company (as the case may be) being requested to attend a formal cautioned interview under PACE. Interviewees must be cautioned before the interview begins. The interview is generally tape-recorded and may also be video-recorded. The general form of caution is in the following terms: "You do not have to say anything, but it may harm your defence if you do not mention, when questioned, something you later rely on in Court. Anything you do say may be given in evidence."

Unlike interviews conducted under section 20, answers to questions in PACE interviews may be used to prosecute the interviewee or the company that the interviewee represents.

There is a right in law to refuse a PACE interview or to remain silent but an adverse inference may be drawn by the court at trial where an interviewee declines to answer or incorrectly answers when questioned and at trial gives evidence or different evidence on the subject of questions asked at interview.

Where a prospective interviewee would prefer not to physically attend a PACE interview, and if the enforcing authority is agreeable, then the interview may be conducted in writing. In these circumstances, the answers will have the same legal effect and consequences as if a face-to-face interview had taken place.

Voluntary statements

Inspectors often ask individuals with relevant information to provide a voluntary written signed statement (which may become admissible in court under section 9 of the Criminal Justice Act 1967).

Voluntary statements offer no protection to their makers and can be used against the individual concerned and others, subject in the case of the maker to the discretion of the trial judge or magistrates allowing an uncautioned statement being used against the maker. They are frequently compiled by an Inspector as part of his investigation with a view to the maker of the statement being called at trial as a witness for the prosecution. The maker of the statement is the person who decides what it contains and should not be pressurised into saying something that may not be true.

Informal Enforcement Action
Enforcing authorities have a wide range of tools available to them when considering what type of enforcement action to take.

In instances where there has been a minor breach of the law and the Inspector doesn't consider it serious enough to warrant formal action then the authority may often provide the duty holder with information and advice either in writing or face to face. This will most likely include a warning to the duty holder that in the Inspector's opinion they are in breach of the law.

Enforcement type notices
Inspectors can serve improvement and prohibition notices where service of such a notice(s) is justified.

In summary, an improvement notice is a notice requiring a person to remedy a breach of health and safety law within a specified period. A prohibition notice is a notice prohibiting a person from carrying on certain activities which, in the Inspector's opinion, involve or will involve a risk of serious personal injury until such time as the requisite corrective

action is taken. There is a right of appeal against these notices – the appeal is to an Employment Tribunal and must be exercised within 21 days of service of the notice.

A prohibition notice can and usually will be served to have immediate effect. One important difference between these types of notice is that on appeal the effect of an improvement notice is stayed until the appeal is determined, while a prohibition improvement takes effect even though an appeal is outstanding unless the Employment Tribunal orders to the contrary.

Failure to comply with an improvement or prohibition notice is a criminal offence, punishable by a fine of up to £20,000 and/or up to six months' imprisonment (if the matter is heard in a magistrates' court) or an unlimited fine and/or up to two years' imprisonment (if the matter is heard in the Crown Court).

Formal caution and conditional caution
A caution is a statement made by the Inspector and accepted by the duty holder that there has been a breach of the law. It is an admission by the duty holder that they have committed an offence for which there is a realistic prospect of conviction but the caution is offered as an alternative to court proceedings.

Criminal prosecution
There are two main types of health and safety offence, namely for breach of HSW or safety regulations made under HSWA.

Most offences are triable either in the Magistrates' Court or the Crown Court. The main determining factor as to which court is the seriousness of the offence.

Burden of proof
These are criminal proceedings and so the burden of proof falls on the prosecution

prove beyond all reasonable doubt that the defendant committed the offence charged.

However, for breach of duties under HSWA or safety regulations where the duty is based on what is reasonably practicable (as many are), there is a reverse burden of proof on the defendant who must show, on the balance of probabilities, that what did was reasonably practicable in the circumstances.

Most health and safety offences are offences of strict liability, which means that the prosecutor is not required to prove that the defendant intended to commit the offences or that, through recklessness, committed the offence.

Level of penalty

Until the late 1990s, the average fines or health and safety offences were comparatively low. The Court of Appeal criticised this in October 1998 when providing sentencing guidelines. Since then, fines, particularly for serious offences (for example following fatalities whether single or multiple) have risen sharply, subject to the defendant's genuine means to pay.

The current largest fine against a single company is £15m (against utility company, Transco). It is not uncommon for fines to exceed £100,000 in cases of serious injury and death.

A convicted defendant will generally also be ordered to pay the prosecution's costs, which in substantial cases are usually considerable in amount.

Although insurance policies will sometimes cover the defendant's cost of representation when prosecuted, they do not cover the payment of fines or prosecution costs.

In some instances it is also possible for a court to order the disqualification of individuals from being directors of companies or taking part in the management of a company for up to 15 years.

Personal liability

Section 37 of HSWA provides that, where a company has committed a health and safety offence and the commission of the offence is proved to have occurred with the consent or connivance of, or is attributable to the neglect of a director, company secretary or manager or a person purporting to act in such capacity (for example a shadow director), the individual as well as the company shall be guilty of the offence and liable to be proceeded against and punished accordingly.

The purpose of this offence is to increase the pressure on companies to comply with health and safety law, by putting at risk of prosecution senior officials. It is a provision to which enforcing authorities have had greater recourse in recent times due to increasing public disquiet as to the health and safety performance of many companies.

Enforcement policies

The HSE and Local Authorities publish their own Enforcement Policies. Inspectors refer to these when deciding what health and safety enforcement action to take. The Enforcement Policy provides Inspectors with guidance about the principles to follow and the factors they must take into account when considering prosecutions.

One of the aims of the Enforcement Policy is to hold duty holders, including directors and managers, to account where they have failed to carry out their responsibilities. The policy usually states that Inspectors should identify and prosecute individuals if a prosecution is warranted.

The HSC (now HSE) published a circular regarding its policy on prosecuting individuals. The circular states that, where a body corporate has committed an offence, then there is likely to be some personal failure by directors, managers or employees. In deciding whether to prosecute individuals, enforcing authorities must consider whether there is sufficient evidence to provide 'a realistic prospect of conviction' and whether a prosecution is in the public interest.

In general, prosecuting individuals is stated to be warranted where there have been substantial failings by them, such as where they have shown wilful or reckless disregard for health and safety requirements, or there has been a deliberate act or omission that seriously imperilled their own health or safety or that of others.

In July 2004 the HSE issued a guidance document entitled *Investigating Accidents and Incidents*. The guidance suggests that health and safety investigations form an essential part of compliance with obligations under the Management of Health and Safety at Work Regulations 1999. It also emphasises the importance of identifying 'root causes' of past failures (of which a written record should be kept) and suggests that there are almost always failings at managerial level. However, in practice it is likely that organisations will no doubt be reluctant to produce a document which can later be used as evidence against the organisation or its directors or managers in a health and safety prosecution.

Any business which produces an accident or incident report should consider taking legal advice since it is possible to do so "in contemplation of legal proceedings". This advice should be sought to minimise the likelihood that any report produced can be used against the company involved.

> *See also*: Corporate manslaughter, p.163; Workplace deaths, p.190; Health and safety at work, p.364; Health and safety inspections, p.381; Health and safety management, p.386

Sources of further information

HSE: Enforcement action: www.hse.gov.uk/enforce/index.htm

Health and safety inspections

Chris Platts, Rollits

Key points

There are numerous bodies tasked with enforcing health and safety legislation. In summary, the Health and Safety Executive (HSE) concerns itself with factories, agriculture, mines and quarries, docks and railways to name just four. Local Authorities oversee, amongst others, shops, offices, schools and colleges, and hospitals. A Local Authority Inspector can only exercise his powers within the geographical limit of the Local Authority that employs him. Each enforcing authority appoints suitably qualified individuals to be Health and Safety Inspectors. Each appointment must be in writing and must specify the powers that the Inspector can exercise. You have the right to ask the Inspector to produce evidence of his appointment. These, therefore, are the individuals who both exercise the statutory powers summarised here and who enforce the criminal liability which is envisaged by health and safety legislation. Never underestimate the situation when an Inspector visits.

A Senior HSE Inspector once said to me that the second he walked into a workplace he "put on his enforcement hat". He could not have made a clearer statement of intent, and given the considerable array of powers which he enjoyed it is not surprising. It is the case that those organisations that have sound and compliant health and safety practices are likely to be much better positioned to deal with the Inspector in the exercise of his powers. Nevertheless as the potential for fallout from the exercise of the Inspector's powers can be huge, whether in resources or time, even these organisations should have a good working knowledge of the powers at the disposal of an Inspector. This is particularly important if the visit has been prompted by an accident. This chapter aims to arm you with this knowledge.

Powers of a Health and Safety Inspector

The powers available to an Inspector are set out in Section 20 of the Health and Safety at Work etc. Act 1974 (HSWA). As one Court has observed, the section is "obviously intended to contain wide powers". In summary, they are as follows.

Power to Enter Premises – HSWA 1974 s20(2)(a)

At any reasonable time (or, in a situation which in his opinion is or may be dangerous, at any time) to enter any premises which he has reason to believe *it is necessary for him to enter for the purpose mentioned in sub section (1) above.'*

This is the Inspector's general power to come onto your premises in order to secure compliance with health and safety legislation. He must be exercising his general health and safety powers, and should be in a position to show a reason which would support his subjective belief that it is necessary to enter premises. In reality this is a wide ranging power which permits the Inspector to visit at any reasonable time or at any time where a dangerous situation exists. The Inspector does not need to give you notice of his visit and many visits are unannounced!

Power to examine and investigate – HSWA 1974 s20(2)(d)
'To make such examination and investigation as may in any circumstances be necessary for the purpose mentioned in subsection (1) above.'

This permits the Inspector to make such examination and investigation as he feels is appropriate. The exercise of this power is not necessarily limited to the premises in question. As the words 'examination' and 'investigation' are not defined it is difficult to know what limits there are on this power and it should be regarded as giving the Inspector a wide discretion.

Power to ensure things are left undisturbed – HSWA 1974 s20(2)(e)
'As regards any premises which he has power to enter, to direct that those premises or any part of them, or anything therein, shall be left undisturbed (whether generally or in particular respects) for so long as is reasonably necessary for the purpose of any examination or investigation under paragraph (d) above.'

It is often the case after an accident that a 'no go area' is imposed by the Inspector or a stipulation that an item of equipment has to be left untouched. This section is designed to allow the Inspector to consider the evidence and possibly to bring in another Inspector with specific expertise. The Inspector will serve a written notice indicating the duration of the restriction.

Measurements, photographs and records – HSWA 1974 s20(2)(f)
'To take such measurements and photographs and make such recordings as he considers necessary for the purpose

of any examination or investigation under paragraph (d) above.'

This is a self-explanatory and again wide-ranging power and it should be noted it is not necessarily related to or limited to the premises in question.

Articles and substances – HSWA 1974 s20(2)(g)
'To take samples of any articles or substances found in any premises which he has power to enter, and of the atmosphere in or in the vicinity of any such premises.'

As the word 'articles' is not defined the likely inference is that this power permits an Inspector to consider equipment as well as any substance, but that he can only take away the sample and not the article or substance. The power is intended to cover atmospheric testing. Substance includes any solid or liquid or anything in the form of a gas or vapour. The Inspector must show a clear link to the premises which he has entered. No set procedures are specified and you should demand clear information as to what power is being used.

Power to dismantle or subject to testing – HSWA 1974 s20(2)(h)
'In the case of any article or substance found in any premises which he has power to enter, being an article or substance which appears to him to have caused or be likely to cause danger to health or safety, to cause it to be dismantled or subjected to any process or test (but not so as to damage or destroy it unless this is in the circumstances necessary for the purpose mentioned in sub-section (1) above).'

By virtue of this power the Inspector can carry out relevant tests. The additional stipulation is that if such power is xercised on premises then the person in ontrol of those premises has the right to equire any such testing to be carried out n his presence. This does not mean that ou can demand the Inspector waits for ou to come back from another location!

ake possession of and detain angerous articles or substances – ISWA 1974 s20(2)(i)
n the case of any such article or ubstance as is mentioned in the receding paragraph, to take possession f it and detain it for so long as is ecessary for all or any of the following urposes, namely: (i) to examine it and o to it anything which he has power to 'o under that paragraph; (ii) to ensure 'nat it is not tampered with before his xamination of it is completed; (iii) to nsure that it is available for use as vidence in any proceedings for an ffence under any of the relevant statutory rovisions….'

his power allows the Inspector to remove nd retain any article or substance so 'nat appropriate examination can be arried out or with a view to ensuring it not tampered with so as to retain its uthenticity as evidence for use in any ubsequent proceedings. The Inspector is equired to leave with a responsible person notice detailing the article or substance nd the power he has exercised. He hould also provide a similar sample narked as such.

'ower to require answers – ISWA 1974 s20(2)(j)
To require any person whom he has easonable cause to believe to be able o give any information relevant to any xamination or investigation under 'aragraph (d) above to answer (in the bsence of persons other than a person nominated by him to be present and any 'ersons whom the Inspector may allow

to be present) such questions as the Inspector thinks fit to ask and to sign a declaration of the truth of his answers.'

This wide-ranging power exceeds any power which, for example, the police have. It should be distinguished from the situation where an individual gives a voluntary statement to the Inspector. Here the Inspector has the right to ask questions of individuals about whom there is a reasonably held belief that they can provide relevant information and to compel the individual to answer. That individual is entitled to be accompanied by someone else. He is required to sign a declaration that the answers given are true. It is an offence to supply untrue information or to fail to answer at all. However, any answers given to the Inspector using this power are not then admissible in subsequent legal proceedings against the individual concerned. The Inspector can ask questions in writing as well as conduct a face-to-face meeting. It should be recognised that any answers can still be used in evidence against another individual or an employer.

Power to require production, inspection and take copies – HSWA 1974 s20(2)(k)
'To require the production of, inspect, and take copies of or of any entry in: (i) any books or documents which by virtue of any of the relevant statutory provisions are required to be kept; and (ii) any other books or documents which it is necessary for him to see for the purposes of any examination or investigation under paragraph (d) above.'

Using this power the Inspector can require production of documents. The power does not extend to removing originals but merely taking copies unless copying facilities are unavailable, whereupon the Inspector can take the originals and return them once inspected and copied.

Any documents released and copied in this way should be marked as such by you. The Inspector can specify in quite general terms the type of document he is seeking. This can place an onerous burden on you to search and produce relevant copies of documents which meet the Inspector's criteria. Only documents which are protected by legal privilege are exempt from this requirement. In broad terms these are documents which are prepared during a solicitor/client relationship or with the predominant purpose of dealing with forthcoming litigation.

Power to require facilities – HSWA 1974 s20(2)(l)

'To require any person to afford him such facilities and assistance with respect to any matters or things within that person's control or in relation to which that person has responsibilities as are necessary to enable the Inspector to exercise any of the powers conferred on him by this section.'

This in essence is a general requirement to be helpful and unobstructive. This does not, however, mean that you should shy away from taking any relevant professional advice as to how to react to an Inspector's requests, or considering critically all requests made of you.

Any other power which is necessary – HSWA 1974 s20(2)(m)

'Any other power which is necessary for the purpose mentioned in sub section (1) above.'

This is a very important 'sweeping up power' as one Judge has accurately categorised it. Its practical relevance, in particular in an age of computer information and data, is that the Inspector may well call for production of information that is kept electronically but nowhere else.

Power to deal with cause of imminent danger – HSWA 1974 s25(1)

'Where, in the case of any article or substance found by him in any premises which he has power to enter, an Inspector has reasonable cause to believe that, in the circumstances in which he finds it, the article or substance is a cause of imminent danger of serious personal injury, he may seize it and cause it to be rendered harmless (whether by destruction or otherwise).'

A power which permits the Inspector to deal with causes of imminent danger. There are additional procedural requirements which apply whereby the Inspector should, if practicable, take a sample of any offending substance and provide a portion of that sample to the person responsible for the premises.

Improvement notices – HSWA 1974 s21

If, after using any of his statutory powers and carrying out an investigation, an Inspector feels further action is required (implicitly believing informal action is inappropriate) he can serve an Improvement Notice where there is a suspected, possibly continuing, breach of health and safety legislation. The notice should specify what breaches are alleged to be occurring, and include reasons for the opinion and require the person to remedy the contravention within a set period of time. Where you object to the terms of the notice you have a right of appeal within 21 days. The terms of the notice are suspended until the appeal is disposed of.

Prohibition notices – HSWA 1974 s22

Here the Inspector can bring activities to a halt where he feels that they involve a risk of serious injury by serving a prohibition notice. Again there are procedural requirements whereby the Inspector needs specify his opinion and the matters which give rise to a risk of injury. Ultimately the notice directs that the relevant activities shall not be carried out unless the matters specified in the notice are remedied. A Prohibition Notice can take effect immediately or at the end of a period specified in the notice. Again there is a right to appeal within 21 days of service of the notice.

But beware…

HSE Inspectors, however, do not have a general power of search nor can they obtain a Search Warrant. The police, however, could obtain a Warrant if they are involved in the investigation. It is important not to unwittingly release information and/or documents. In cases where documents are seized unlawfully it may be appropriate to make an immediate application for an injunction.

Help yourself

It can easily be seen that the Inspector has a considerable array of powers. It is an offence to obstruct an Inspector in the exercise of his powers and also to contravene an Improvement or Prohibition Notice. An unlimited fine or two years imprisonment can result from more serious offences. So clearly you should tread carefully. But you can help yourself. An awareness of an Inspector's powers will help you deal with an investigation visit. Forewarned is most definitely forearmed!

See also: Accident investigations, p.55; Health and safety at work, p.364

Sources of further information

HSE – What to expect when a health and safety inspector calls:
www.hse.gov.uk/pubns/hsc14.htm

Health and safety management

Nicola Cardenas-Blanco, Martineau Solicitors

Key points

The Management of Health and Safety at Work Regulations 1999 require employers to manage health and safety by using risk assessments. These risk assessments will include measures for:

- identifying the hazards associated with work activities and workplaces;
- assessing the risks from hazardous work activities and workplaces;
- implementing risk avoidance and risk control measures using standard principles of prevention;
- providing effective systems to plan, organise, control, monitor and review preventive and protective measures in place;
- providing health surveillance where required by specific regulations or by risk assessment;
- appointing competent health and safety advisor(s);
- implementing emergency procedures where appropriate;
- consulting, informing and training employees;
- cooperating with other employers and their employees where appropriate; and
- ensuring the health and safety of young persons and new and expectant mothers.

Legislation

- Health and Safety at Work etc. Act 1974.
- Management of Health and Safety at Work Regulations 1999.

Overview

Historically, legislation provided prescriptive rules to try to prevent injuries and ill health. The Health and Safety at Work etc. Act 1974 (HSWA) imposes a framework of objective-setting legislation on employers, the self-employed and others controlling workplaces or work activities.

This means that employers must manage health and safety in the same way that they manage any other commercial activity (e.g. finance), and increasingly emphasis is being placed on encouraging organisations, through legislation and

otherwise, to integrate health and safety into the organisation's daily activities, rather than being a 'bolt-on' approach.

The general duties imposed by the HSWA are supported by more detailed provisions in the Management of Health and Safety at Work Regulations 1999 (MHSWR).

Many of the general obligations under the MHSWR overlap with other more specific health and safety legislation. Compliance with such specific obligations will usually be sufficient to comply with the MHSWR.

Risk assessments

The MHSWR require employers to make a suitable and sufficient assessment of the risks to the health and safety of their employees and others affected by their activities. As circumstances change, these risk assessments need regular review and revision.

Specific risk assessments

Some health and safety regulations (COSHH and the Regulatory Reform (Fire Safety) Order) require specific risk assessments to be completed in a certain format and to include specific information. Where these risk assessments are required, a separate risk assessment under the MHSWR may not need to be completed.

Preventative measures

Schedule 1 of the MHSWR sets out the general principles of prevention which should be used when considering measures to prevent or control exposure to health and safety risks:

- Eliminate or avoid risks as far as possible;
- Evaluate risks which cannot be avoided;
- Combat risks at source;
- Adapt work to the individual, by reviewing the design of workplaces, choice of work equipment and working methods;
- Adapt to technical progress (through regular reviews of risk assessments);
- Replace the dangerous with non-dangerous or less dangerous (e.g. equipment or substances);
- Develop a coherent overall prevention policy;
- Give priority to collective measures (which protect all those exposed to the risk) over individual protection; and
- Give appropriate instructions to employees.

Health and safety systems

Models of health and safety management systems have existed for a number of years, including BS 8800:1996, HS(G)65 (now HSG 65) and OHSAS 18001:1999.

HSG 65 recommends and Regulation 5 of the MHSWR requires every employer to make and give effect to appropriate arrangements for the effective planning, organisation, control, monitoring and review of preventive and protective measures.

The HSE's guidance entitled *Investigating Accidents and Incidents* (released in July 2004) suggests that effective accident and incident investigation forms an essential part of this process. More advanced health and safety systems may be capable of accreditation to OHSAS 18001. Guidance on how to implement OHSAS 18001 is given in OHSAS 18002:1999.

Health surveillance

Employers must ensure that their employees are provided with such health surveillance as is appropriate having regard to the risks to their health and safety identified by risk assessments. The level, frequency and procedure of the health surveillance should be determined by a competent person acting within the limits of their own training and experience. Health surveillance records should be kept, frequently even after the employee has left the employer's service, and in some instances for over 40 years.

Appointing competent advisors

Every employer must appoint one or more competent persons to assist it in relation to compliance with statutory health and safety requirements. A person is competent if he has sufficient training and experience, or knowledge and other qualities, to enable him to be practical and reasonable and to know what to look for and how to recognise it *(Gibson v. Skibs A/S Marina and Orkla A/B and Smith Coggins Ltd* (1966) 2 All ER 476). There is no specific requirement for formal qualifications. However, the Institution of Occupational Safety and Health (IOSH) recommends a diploma-level qualification associated with full membership of the professional institutions, as does the International Institute of Risk and Safety Management (IIRSM).

The HSE's preference as expressed in the Approved Code of Practice to the MHSWR is for the appointment of a competent person from within the employer's organisation wherever possible, rather than relying solely on external consultants.

Emergency plan

Employers must establish procedures to deal with serious and imminent danger, and appoint competent persons to implement those procedures in so far as they relate to evacuation. Employers must consider all potential dangers, e.g. fire, bomb threats, terrorism and public disorder.

Employers must also arrange contacts with the necessary emergency services (police, fire and ambulance services) as appropriate.

Information and training

Every employer should provide its employees and others working on its premises with comprehensible information on the risks to their health and safety (identified by risk assessments) together with details of the relevant preventive or protective measures.

Employees should be trained upon their induction and whenever working arrangements or conditions change (e.g. following the introduction of new machinery or a revised risk assessment). In some instances there should also be regular refresher training.

However, it is important to note that in dealing with work equipment safety, it is no longer sufficient to select preventative measures which rely solely upon the provision of such information, instruction, training and supervision. Instead employers must use (in this order of priority):

1. the provision of fixed guards;
2. the provision of other guards or protection devices; or
3. the provision of jigs, holders, push-sticks or similar protection appliances.

Cooperation and coordination

Where two or more employers share work premises (e.g. contractors working in the client's premises) they must cooperate with each other to ensure the health and safety (including fire safety) of all persons working on the premises. This may include the appointment of and cooperation with a nominated person appointed to coordinate joint health and safety arrangements.

Employees' duties

- Comply with any requirements or prohibitions imposed by their employer.
- Use machinery, equipment, dangerou substances and safety devices provided in accordance with any training they have received.
- Inform their employer of serious and imminent danger or shortcomings in health or safety arrangements.

New or expectant mothers

Where the employer's activities could pose a risk to pregnant employees (or their babies), the employer must carry out a specific risk assessment, then take preventive or protective action to minimise that risk. If such action would not avoid the risk, then the employer must:

- alter the employee's working conditions or hours of work if it is reasonable to do so to avoid the risk;
- if this is not possible, offer her alternative work in accordance with section 67 of the Employment Rights Act 1996; or
- if this is not possible, suspend the employee from work for as long as necessary to avoid the risk.

Workplace Law Networ
www.workplacelaw.ne

he employer must go through the above rocess if the employee has a certificate om her doctor or midwife indicating at she should not work at night. An mployer is not under any duty to alter a oman's working conditions until informed writing that she is a new or expectant other.

Young persons (under 18)

efore employing any young person, every mployer must carry out a risk assessment hich takes into account:

- the inexperience, lack of awareness of risks and immaturity of young persons;
- the layout of the workplace or workstation;
- the nature, degree and duration of exposure to physical, biological and chemical agents;
- the form, range and use of work equipment and the way in which it is handled;
- the organisation of processes and activities; and
- the extent of health and safety training provided.

n particular, no young person should do vork:

- beyond his physical or psychological capacity;
- involving harmful exposure to toxic, carcinogenic or mutagenic substances, or to radiation;
- involving a risk of accidents which young persons may not recognise or avoid, owing to their lack of attention, experience or training; or
- where there is a risk to health from extreme cold or heat, noise or vibration.

Before employing a child (anyone under 16), the employer must provide a parent of the child with information on the health and safety risks identified by a risk assessment, details of the preventive and protective measures in place, and any information on shared workplaces and measures required for coordinating between two or more employers. A young person who is over 16 may be employed to carry out work in a hazardous environment where the work is necessary for his training, provided that he is properly supervised and any risk is reduced to the lowest level reasonably practicable.

Civil liability

Regulation 22 of the MHSWR was amended in 2002 to allow it to be used to bring some civil claims – in respect of the employer's failure to comply with the duties in the MHSWR – to safely assess and control the risks to young persons or to expectant mothers or women who are breastfeeding.

Other breaches of the MHSWR are not allowed to be used to confer a right to bring a claim for damages. However, it is not only possible for claims to be brought for damages, but also in April 2002 the Court of Appeal ruled in *Peter Nixon v. Chanceoption Developments Limited,* that where there is a breach of the employer's statutory duty there can be no contributory negligence on the part of the employee.

See also: Health and safety at work, p.364; Health and safety consultation, p.372; Health and safety enforcement, p.376

Sources of further information

Investigating Accidents and Incidents (HSE Books) ISBN: 0 7176 2827 2.

Health and safety policies

David Wright, Kennedys

Key points

Section 2(3) of the Health and Safety at Work etc. Act 1974 (HSWA) provides that there is a duty for every employer to prepare, and as often as may be appropriate revise, a written statement of his general policy with respect to the health and safety at work of his employees and the organisation and arrangements for carrying out that policy as well as to bring the statement to the notice of all his employees.

Those employers with fewer than five employees are exempt by virtue of the Health and Safety Policy Statements (Exceptions) Regulations 1975.

What does this mean?

There must be a policy and this should be in writing although employers with fewer than five employees are exempt.

An employer is unlikely to fulfil its duty by the use of a generic non-specific policy. The policy should relate to that particular business and the health and safety issues that are relevant to it.

Regard should also be had to the Management of Health and Safety at Work Regulations 1999, which provide that:

- every employer should make and give effect to such arrangements as are appropriate, having regard to the nature of his activities and the size of his undertaking, for the effective planning, organisation, control, monitoring and review of the preventative and protective measures; and
- where the employer employs five or more employees, he should record the arrangements.

Those Regulations also set out the requirement for every employer to undertake a risk assessment that is 'suitable and sufficient' of the risks to the health and safety of his employees; and the risks to the health and safety of persons not in his employment arising from the conduct by him of his undertaking. Where there are five or more employees the employer is again required to record any significant findings of the assessment.

The undertaking of a risk assessment and the creation of arrangements as set out above together with the putting in place of a health and safety policy can be seen as supplementing one another.

The extent of the policy

If the business is small, perhaps operating in a benign office environment, then the drafting of the policy should be relatively straightforward. This is as compared to a much larger enterprise that uses potentially dangerous machinery or industrial processes, perhaps including chemicals. There the policy would be expected to be far more wide-reaching and detailed to reflect the increased level of risk.

In its publication, *Introduction to Health and Safety – Health and Safety in mall Businesses,* the HSE publishes specimen health and safety policy, ogether with a risk assessment, which vould be suitable for adoption by a small usiness. It should be noted that these o require real input regarding the risks nd the arrangements of the particular usiness.

Review of the policy

is important to note that it is not just a ase of formulating a policy and never ooking at it again – effect must also e given to it in the way a business nanages its health and safety duties and esponsibilities.

he health and safety policy should be, ke other health and safety materials uch as risk assessments and method tatements, a living document. It should e regularly reviewed and this is made lear in section 2(3) of HSWA. This is specially true where the nature or extent f operations change or new relevant egislation is introduced. An example

of this could be a need to review the policy following the introduction of the Work at Height Regulations 2005 and its hierarchical approach to that issue.

Employers' liability for breaches

- A breach of a general duty under section 2 of HSWA is punishable by a £20,000 fine in the Magistrates' Court and an unlimited fine in the Crown Court.
- A breach of the Management of Health and Safety at Work Regulations 1999 is a criminal offence punishable by a £5,000 fine in the Magistrates' Court or an unlimited fine in the Crown Court.
- In reality, it is very rare in the absence of other transgressions for organisations to be prosecuted for a failure to have a health and safety policy in place. However, it can and does happen that such a failure is prosecuted among others or, prior to that, impacts adversely on the decision of whether or not to prosecute in the first place.

See also: Health and safety at work, p.364; Health and safety management, p.386; Risk assessments, p.639

Sources of further information

Under UK law, every employer with five or more employees must have a written health and safety policy. Workplace Law Group's *Health and Safety Policy and Management Guide, v.3.0* is a template for building a customised policy for your organisation. For more information visit www.workplacelaw.net/Bookshop/ PoliciesAndProcedures.

Health surveillance

David Sinclair, Hempsons Solicitors

Key points

Employers who expose their employees to certain chemicals, physical agents, materials or ergonomic risks may be required to undertake systematic, regular and appropriate health surveillance on those employees.

Health surveillance may be either specified in regulations or covered by the umbrella provisions of health and safety legislation.

Where health surveillance is required, it should be undertaken only by competent people, who in many cases must be medically qualified.

Employers are required to provide adequate information to employees on health surveillance provisions, results and the records they keep. Records may have to be kept for up to 50 years.

Legislation

- Health and Safety at Work etc. Act 1974.
- Opticians Act 1989.
- Sight Testing (Examination and Prescription) (No. 2) Regulations 1989.
- Health and Safety (Display Screen Equipment) Regulations 1992.
- Manual Handling Operations Regulations 1992.
- Disability Discrimination Acts 1995 and 2005.
- Data Protection Act 1998.
- Management of Health and Safety at Work Regulations 1999.
- Control of Substances Hazardous to Health Regulations 2002.
- Control of Vibration at Work Regulations 2005.
- Noise at Work Regulations 2005.
- Control of Asbestos Regulations 2006.

Specific and non-specific duties

Health and safety regulations can specify mandatory health surveillance – e.g. Regulation 22(2) of the Control of Asbestos Regulations 2006 and the Noise at Work Regulations 2005 – where employers expose their employees to certain biological hazards, chemicals or physical agents (e.g. asbestos, lead, noise radiation, or vibration).

In such circumstances, the relevant regulations will specify the type, level and frequency of the surveillance to be undertaken, along with details on what records are to be kept by the employer and for how long.

In circumstances where there is no specific duty on the employer to carry out health surveillance, the employer has general duties under section 2 of the Health and Safety at Work etc. Act 1974 and Regulation 6 of the Management of Health and Safety at Work Regulations 1999 to carry out appropriate health surveillance.

This general duty applies where the employer's risk assessments identify that:

there is an identifiable disease or adverse health condition related to the work;

there is a valid technique available to detect indications of the disease or condition;

there is a reasonable likelihood that the disease or condition may occur under the particular conditions of the work; and

health surveillance is likely to further the protection of the health and safety of the employees concerned.

Health surveillance can only be carried out in the above circumstances where the techniques used to undertake the surveillance pose a low risk to the employee.

Employers may need to carry out health surveillance in the following situations:

post-accident (or during long-term illness);

on forklift truck and other machinery operators; and

on drivers to test for colour blindness.

Employers should be extremely careful in undertaking pre-employment health surveillance, so that if, for example, they require candidates to complete pre-employment health questionnaires, they do not discriminate against disabled candidates in breach of the Disability Discrimination Acts 1995 and 2005. Employers should seek expert assistance in deciding what surveillance is needed and who is competent to provide that surveillance.

Objectives
The objectives of health surveillance are to:

protect the health of individual employees by detecting, as early as possible, adverse changes that might

be caused by exposure to hazardous substances;

help to evaluate the measures taken to control exposure to health hazards; and

collect, keep, update and use data and information for determining and evaluating hazards to health.

Procedures
There are a number of health surveillance procedures that employers can use, including:

biological monitoring, i.e. taking samples of blood, urine, breath, etc. to detect the presence of hazardous substances;

biological effect monitoring, i.e. assessing the early biological effects in exposed workers;

clinical examinations by occupational doctors or nurses to measure physiological changes in the body of exposed people, e.g. reduced lung function; and

medical enquiries (often accompanied by a medical examination) by a suitably qualified occupational health practitioner to detect symptoms in people.

Competent people acting within the limits of their training and experience should determine the appropriate level, frequency and procedure to be followed.

For most types of health surveillance the appropriate competent person will be a suitably qualified occupational medical practitioner, occupational health nurse or occupational hygienist.

Once health surveillance has been started, it must be maintained throughout the remainder of the employee's period of employment, unless the risks to which the employee is exposed and the associated health effects are rare and short-term.

Display screen equipment

Regulation 5 of the Health and Safety (Display Screen Equipment) Regulations 1992 (DSE Regulations) places a duty on employers to provide, when requested to do so, an eye or eyesight test to employees who are about to become (or who are already) display screen users.

Eye and eyesight tests are defined in section 36(2) of the Opticians Act 1989 and the Sight Testing Examination and Prescription (No. 2) Regulations 1989, which specify what examinations the doctor or optician should perform as part of the test.

Although the employer only needs to provide the eye or eyesight test when requested to do so, he is under a duty by Regulation 7(3) of the DSE Regulations to provide employees with adequate information about the risks to their health and their entitlement under Regulation 5.

Records

Where health surveillance is undertaken in compliance with particular regulations, those regulations will state what data is to be collected and the minimum period for which information is to be stored. Other health surveillance records should be kept for:

- the period specified in the Regulations; or
- three years after the end of the last date of the individual's employment (the date after which the employee cannot normally bring a claim against the employer); whichever is the longer

Employers will need to provide employees with access to their personal health records and copies of such records may have to be provided to the enforcing authorities.

To comply with the duty to provide information to employees (and others that might be affected), employers should provide the appropriate people with the general results of health surveillance, but keep confidential individuals' data.

Data gathered during health surveillance is regarded as 'sensitive data' within the meaning of section 2 of the Data Protection Act 1998. As such, all health surveillance data must be processed in accordance with the requirements of that Act. Detailed advice should be sought as to these requirements.

See also: Medical records, p.491; Occupational health, p.537

Sources of further information

Understanding health surveillance at work: www.hse.gov.uk/pubns/indg304.pdf

Workplace Law Group's *Occupational Health 2008: Making the business case – Special Report* addresses the issues of health at work, discusses the influence of work on health and highlights the business case for occupational health services at work. Using case studies, examples from professional experience and the findings of the many Government reports and surveys on the subject, the Special Report focuses on the advantages of occupational health services, and the benefits they can provide to a company, in terms of financial savings, increased employee morale, and improved corporate image. For more information visit www.workplacelaw.net/Bookshop/SpecialReports.

Working at height

Jagdeep Tiwana, Berwin Leighton Paisner

Key points

Although the number of accidents whilst working at height has continued to fall year on year, such accidents are still a major cause of workplace deaths and injuries in the UK. In 2005/06, 46 people died (24 of these worked in construction) and over 3,300 suffered serious injuries as a result of a fall from height in the workplace.

What makes these statistics even more of a concern is the fact that the risks from working at height and the procedures to minimise these risks are well-known. For this reason, specific legislation has been introduced. The Work at Height Regulations 2005 (WAH Regulations) governing work at height consolidate previous legislation and implement European Council Directive 2001/45/EC. Unlike previous legislation which was only triggered by work above a height threshold of two metres, the WAH Regulations apply to work at height in any place where a person could be injured falling from it even if it is at or below ground level.

The WAH Regulations require employers to ensure that:

- all work at height is properly planned and organised;
- the work is carried out safely; and
- employees undertaking the work are trained and competent.

The WAH Regulations are broad, covering not only work at height but also falling objects, fragile roofs and equipment. Put simply, the extent of the risk and the wider ranging application of the WAH Regulations mean that employers must consider every aspect of their business which involves working at height, whether it is something as complicated as undertaking building work or as straightforward as changing a light bulb.

Legislation

The WAH Regulations apply to all work at height where there is a risk of fall liable to cause personal injury. Employers, the self-employed and any person who controls the work of third parties (such as contractors) have duties under this legislation. There are certain exemptions for shipping, off-shore installations and docks. It does not apply to the provisions of paid instruction in relation to sports or certain recreational activities. However, the WAH Regulation is not the only applicable legislation. The following legislation also applies:

- The Health and Safety at Work etc. Act 1974.
- Lifting Operations and Lifting Equipment Regulations 1998.
- Management of Health and Safety at Work Regulations 1999.

Duties under the WAH Regulations

Employers are under a duty to do all that is reasonably practical to prevent someone from falling. In fulfilling this duty, the employer must adopt a risk control hierarchy from managing work at height (including the selection of equipment). This hierarchy means that employers must first consider if work at height can be avoided altogether. If not, consideration must be given to the use of equipment and other means which would minimise the causes and consequences of a fall, should one occur.

When planning to undertake work at height, regard must be given to:

- the relevant risk assessments;
- how the work can be carried out safely;
- adverse weather conditions; and
- steps to be taken in the event of an emergency.

In addition, only staff who are trained must undertake the work and even then, when undertaking the work, they must be supervised by a competent person. When considering how the work should be done, thought needs to be given to the place where it is undertaken. For example, if at all possible, access to the elevated area should be from an existing place of work or access. If this is not possible, then the most suitable equipment needs to be determined. This includes equipment to protect workers as well as provide access. To this end, the WAH Regulations emphasise the need to implement collective protection measures as opposed to personal protection measures.

In relation to access equipment, the schedules to the WAH Regulations set out specific requirements which must be applied to equipment such as ladders and scaffolding. So, for example when using ladders, consideration must be given to:

- using the correct type of ladder;
- procedures to ensure that they are used safely, e.g. placed on and against a fixed unmovable surface;
- ensuring employees are trained how to use ladders safely;
- regular maintenance and inspection to ensure that they remain fit for the task
- how to prevent unauthorised and improper use; and
- any ancillary risks that the use of the ladder may give rise to. In particular, they should take into account any risks to employees and third parties using the area in the vicinity of where the work is to take place.

In relation to platforms, rigorous inspection regimes are required for platforms used for or to access construction work from which a person could fall more than two metres. Such platforms will generally be scaffolding. Inspection records should be kept at the construction site until the work is completed and thereafter for a further three months.

The WAH Regulations also regulate fragile surfaces (generally roofs) and require certain safeguard measures to be put in place such as:

- suitable platforms;
- covers and guardrails.

Although not rocket science, it is surprising how often these simple steps are disregarded.

Finally, where work is carried out at height which could result in falling objects, it is necessary to ensure the area adjacent and below where the work is being carried out is clearly cordoned off to ensure that no unauthorised persons can enter this area.

See also: Accident investigations, p.55; Construction site health and safety, p.154; Ladders, p.440; Personal Protective Equipment, p.568; Slips, trips and falls, p.657

Sources of further information

INDG 401 (rev 1) – *The Work at Height Regulations 2005 (as amended) A Brief Guide:* www.hse.gov.uk/pubns/indg401.pdf

HSE: www.hse.gov.uk/falls

HIV and AIDS

Lisa Jinks and Robert Dillarstone, Greenwoods Solicitors LLP

Key points
- Employers and employees need to understand what HIV and AIDS are.
- Employers need to be aware of their liability under various employment-related laws as well as health and safety legislation.
- Specific employment issues include discrimination on grounds of disability and/or sexual orientation, unfair / constructive dismissal and aspects of data protection law.
- Key areas of the employment relationship which need addressing include recruitment, disclosure, medical testing and reasonable adjustments to working conditions.
- Employers should implement an HIV and AIDS policy.

Legislation
- Health and Safety at Work etc. Act 1974.
- Employment Rights Act 1996.
- Data Protection Act 1998.
- Management of Health and Safety at Work Regulations 1999.
- Employment Equality (Sexual Orientation) Regulations 2003.
- Disability Discrimination Act 1995 (DDA), as amended by the Disability Discrimination Act 2005.

What are HIV and AIDS and what are the real risks for the workplace?
It is important for employers and employees to understand what HIV and AIDS are as there are many common misconceptions.

AIDS stands for Acquired Immune Deficiency Syndrome. It is caused by human immunodeficiency virus (HIV) which attacks the body's natural defence system and leaves it open to various infections and cancers.

There are approximately 90,000 adults in the UK living with HIV. It is not known what proportion of those will progress to AIDS and the incubation period between infection and onset of AIDS can be very long. During this time, the individual is unlikely to be ill or even aware of the infection. Although there is no known cure for AIDS, HIV symptoms, such as swollen lymph glands, weight loss and minor infections, can be treated with anti-retroviral drugs and enable HIV positive people to lead healthy lives.

HIV is mainly contained in blood. There is a minimal risk of it being contained in other bodily fluids such as urine, saliva and sweat unless these are contaminated with infected blood.

HIV is not spread through normal social interaction such as sharing cutlery or toilets – it is transmitted through sexual intercourse or direct exposure to infected blood through accidental contamination.

The risk of infection at work is very low for the majority of workplaces. The types of occupation where the risk is higher include healthcare, custodial (e.g. prisons), education, emergency services, hair and beauty and plumbing. N.B. The strict requirements on such specialist occupations are beyond the scope of this chapter.

There is no reason to treat workers with HIV differently from other workers. People who have the virus but have not developed AIDS will not usually be ill and their ability to work will normally be unaffected. Those who develop AIDS will have severe illnesses inevitably affecting performance and should be treated in the same way as anyone with any other life threatening illness.

Discrimination

Protection from discrimination covers the whole of the working relationship – from recruitment, benefits, promotion and training, dismissal and harassment through to post-termination discrimination, such as the giving of references. Unlike unfair dismissal claims, there is no financial cap on awards made for discrimination claims and additional awards can be made for injury to feelings.

Disability discrimination

From December 2005, HIV infected employees have been deemed to have a disability from the point of diagnosis – irrespective of whether they exhibit any symptoms – and are therefore protected from disability discrimination. This contrasts with the previous legal position where an employee was only held to be disabled when he was in the symptomatic stages of HIV or had AIDS.

Reasonable adjustments

One key area of disability discrimination is the duty on employers to make reasonable adjustments to working conditions once they are aware that an employee is HIV infected. In such circumstances, an employer is under a positive duty to take whatever steps are reasonably necessary to prevent the employee from being disadvantaged. For instance, this may require an employer to provide time off for treatment, allocate duties to others and so on.

Note that if an employee requires time off work for an HIV-related reason, the reason for the time off should, as far as possible, be treated in strictest confidence. Managers should not need to know the precise reason for the time off.

Discrimination on grounds of sexual orientation

Dismissal or other detrimental treatment of a worker on the grounds that they are, or are perceived to be, gay is unlawful. This may extend to discrimination or harassment on the basis that a worker is, or is assumed to be, HIV positive. Note that a claim could also be brought on the basis of discriminatory acts against the worker on the basis of association (if, for example, they have gay friends).

Recruitment, disclosure and medical testing

Medical information is protected under the Data Protection Act 1998 and is classified as 'sensitive personal data'. There are various stringent requirements on the 'processing' of medical information, which include obtaining, holding and disclosing such data.

Recruitment

Generally, employers would not be able to justify asking applicants about their HIV status. In addition to a potential claim for disability or sexual orientation discrimination, a claim for indirect sex discrimination might be brought on the basis that more men than women are HIV positive.

However, employers are entitled to ask applicants about any disabilities that may impact upon the job in question so long as they ask all applicants in a consistent way and do not use this information to discriminate. It is also good practice to ask whether the applicant considers that any reasonable adjustments are required to be made to their working conditions, such as time off for treatment. Ideally, employers should have a detachable medical questionnaire which can be given to their HR department.

Disclosure

Applicants do not have to disclose their HIV status although it may be a condition of employment in certain higher risk occupations. However, if the applicant fails to disclose such information, the employer cannot be expected to make reasonable adjustments.

Medical testing

Again, generally, there will be no justification for requiring applicants or employees to take an HIV/AIDS test unless the occupation is high risk or the job requires travel to countries asking for evidence of HIV status.

Employers may ask applicants to undertake a medical test but this is subject to various conditions under data protection principles. Employers must have a legitimate reason as to why they need this information which outweighs any intrusion to the worker, such as a genuine health and safety reason. The worker must be assured that the results will be treated in strictest confidence. Employers should also respect the right to privacy and, wherever possible, obtain the worker's consent. Note in particular, employers are required to obtain an employee's consent before seeking a medical report from the employee's own medical practitioner under the Access to Medical Reports Act 1988.

Employers cannot insist that an applicant undertakes a medical test, but if they

refuse, the employer can refuse to employ them. It is preferable, wherever possible, to use health questionnaires rather than medical tests, as these are less intrusive.

Unfair / constructive dismissal

In extreme cases, workers have been dismissed because of their HIV status. More likely, however, is that an employee with HIV is treated detrimentally, whether by way of harassment, being denied equal benefits and so on. In addition to any claim for discrimination, such treatment could lead an employee to resign, resulting in a claim for constructive dismissal.

Colleagues may refuse to work alongside an employee with HIV or pressurise an employer into dismissing that employee. Employers are also responsible for the actions of their staff and should take steps to deal with such issues, preferably by consulting with and educating such workers but where necessary, by taking disciplinary action. The 'best practice' approach would be to have an effective HIV/AIDS policy already in place.

Health and safety

As part of an employer's legal duty to protect the health and safety of persons at work, an employer is required to carry out a risk assessment to evaluate the risk of infection from HIV and take sufficient steps to minimise such risk. Employers are also required to give adequate information to their workforce on such risks and explain how these are being addressed in line with HSE guidance.

First aiders

There are no reported cases of infection arising from first aid. However, first-aiders will need to be reassured of the low risks of being infected. The best way to do this is to provide up-to-date advice on HIV and review first aid training and procedures.

checklist: policy document and implementation

Employers are advised to draw up a policy on HIV and AIDS so that, if a problem arises, this can be dealt with in accordance with the policy. The policy should be developed in consultation with employee representatives. Once finalised, managers should be provided with appropriate training and an employee awareness programme implemented.

The policy will vary depending upon the type of organisation but could include:

- a brief description of HIV and AIDS and how HIV is transmitted;
- the organisation's position on HIV testing;

- an assurance of confidentiality;
- a guarantee that absenteeism or other AIDS related work issues are to be treated like any other serious illness;
- assurances that colleagues are expected to work normally with such workers and that any refusal to work normally will be dealt with and if appropriate under the disciplinary procedure;
- identifying help available;
- first-aid procedures; and
- provisions for overseas travel – the risks of infection through inadequate medical practices as well as sexual encounters.

It is also advisable to make express reference to HIV/AIDS in anti-discrimination and harassment policies.

See also: Discrimination, p.222; Health and safety at work, p.364; Medical records, p.491; Occupational health, p.537; Recruitment and selection, p.607

Sources of further information

Blood-borne viruses in the workplace – guidance for employers and employees: www.hse.gov.uk/pubns/indg342.pdf

Protection against blood-borne infections in the workplace: HIV and hepatitis (HMSO) ISBN: 978 0 113219 53 7.

Equality and Human Rights Commission: www.equalityhumanrights.com

National AIDS helpline: 0800 567 123

Managing Safely Certificate

Managing safely is for those required to manage safely and effectively in compliance with their organisation's policy and best practice in health and safety.

Assessment is by an end examination comprising of one written paper and a practical assessment. The practical assessment is undertaken after the course within your workplace and consists of conducting your own risk assessments.

Benefits to your company

- Cut the risk of accidents in your workplace
- Get up-to-date with the latest health and safety legislation
- Improve your company's health and safety culture
- Reduce costs from avoidable insurance claims and solicitors' fees
- Raise awareness of the importance of risk assessments and safety management systems

Intended learning outcomes

To ensure that safety requirements are appreciated by people employed as line managers and to enable them to review their own departmental systems for safety, introducing new controls or implementing changes as appropriate to ensure safety in the workplace.

The IOSH syllabus covers the following 8 areas over 4 days. The modules are:

1. Introducing Managing Safely
2. Assessing risks
3. Controlling risks
4. Understanding your responsibilities
5. Identifying hazards
6. Investigating accidents and incidents
7. Measuring performance
8. Protecting our environment

Examination details

There are no academic prerequisites to joining the course. This course is suitable for anyone working in a health and safety environment.

What our delegates say

'We held two IOSH courses with 12 attendees in both, all of whom passed. All attendees have gained the knowledge they require to carry out their roles. They all agreed that the trainers were very knowledgeable in their field and were all easy to approach'

Sarah Chawda, Customer Services Manager, ISS Coflex

2009 courses taking place in London and Cambridge.
Call *0871 777 8881* for more details

Holiday

John Murphy, BPE Solicitors

Key points

The Working Time Regulations 1998 were introduced by Tony Blair's 1997 Government. One of the main parts of the 1998 Regulations sets out a worker's entitlement to four weeks' (20 days') paid leave each holiday year. However employers quickly noticed that the minimum paid holiday they had to provide was 12 days' paid leave in addition to the eight public holidays. In January 2007 it was reported that 22% of the British workforce received 12 paid days' holidays in addition to the eight bank holidays.

The Government held a two stage consultation process in June 2006 and then again in January 2007, during which it received the views of trade unions and employers' representatives with regard to a proposed increase in the holiday entitlement for full time workers from four weeks to 5.6 weeks (28 days).

Legislation

The Work and Families Act was introduced in 2006, in which the Government extended the workers' annual statutory holiday entitlement from four weeks to 4.8 weeks and then to 5.6 weeks by 1 April 2009 (subject to a maximum of 28 days). The increase was enacted by the Working Time (Amendment) Regulations 2007, which took effect on 1 October 2007.

Public holidays

The 2007 Regulations satisfy the political intention to provide an additional eight days' holiday per year for a full-time worker. However, on closer inspection, the 2007 Regulations are careful not to introduce a right to have public holidays as paid leave. If a worker wishes to take paid annual leave on a public holiday, then the worker must make a request to his/her employer in the normal way and the employer is entitled to refuse any such request as long as it is done in accordance with the procedures set out in the 1998 Regulations.

Problems for employers

Following the introduction of the 2007 Regulations employers should review their contracts of employment. Existing contracts may contain holiday clauses along the lines of 'Statutory Entitlement plus Bank / Public Holidays'. At first glance this would appear to provide for 28 days' annual leave for full-time workers (20 days' statutory leave plus eight public holidays).

An employer whose contracts have the above wording might be confronted by an employee who claims that his paid annual leave increased to 32 days in October 2007 and will increase again to 36 days from 1 April 2009.

The 2007 Regulations cater for this potential problem. The new Regulation 26a enables an employer to avoid raising the holiday entitlement of such workers beyond 28 days as long as the following provisions are in place:

- A relevant agreement between the employer and the workforce providing that each worker will receive paid annual leave entitlement of 1.6 weeks / eight days in addition to each worker's current four-week statutory entitlement;
- No provision for payment in lieu of that leave except on termination of employment; and
- Statutory leave cannot be carried over beyond the next leave year.

Carrying over leave entitlement

Employers are often unsure whether or not they are obliged to carry over the remaining annual leave into the next holiday year of a worker who has not exhausted their annual leave.

The 2007 Regulations do allow that the additional entitlement of 1.6 weeks (eight days) can be carried over into the subsequent leave year. This was expressly prohibited by the 1997 Regulations.

The new Regulation 13a(7) provides that the carry-over of 1.6 weeks (eight days) can be done by means of a 'relevant agreement'. This is a document by which an employer agrees with its workers to modify particular aspects of the Working Time Regulations.

Therefore for Regulation 13a(7) to have effect, an employer should ensure that it has specific wording in the relevant agreement to carry over of 1.6 weeks' (eight days') statutory leave.

Small employers will be dismayed by the new Regulation 13a(7) as it will increase their administrative burden. Employers will need to keep track of workers' holiday entitlement past and present and distinguish between holidays taken in the previous holiday year and those taken in the current holiday year. However, this carry forward entitlement is not a right

for the employees. It only comes into effect if it is agreed between a worker and its employer by means of a relevant agreement. An employer can refuse to agree to a request to carry forward annual leave and an employer can insist that the full 28 days' leave is taken in one holiday leave year.

Holiday pay for the long-term sick

The issue of whether or not an employee, on long-term sick, is entitled to receive paid annual leave has vexed the UK courts in recent years. The Advocate General handed down his 'Opinion' on 24 January 2008. His Opinion is often followed by the subsequent European Court of Justice ruling so attention should be paid to the Opinion. The Advocate General stated that:

- entitlement to paid holiday does accrue whilst a worker is absent on sick leave; but
- to take the paid holiday, the worker must return to work to do so; and
- workers should be paid in lieu of their accrued but untaken paid holiday when they are dismissed.

If followed, the Opinion produces a number of issues. Employees on long-term sickness might never be able to take their statutory paid holiday which reduces the cost of holiday for the employer. Equally an employer might be faced with a health and safety dilemma where long-term sick employees return to work, insisting they are fit, in order to take accrued paid holiday. Finally, employers might attempt to time the dismissal of any long-term sick employee for the beginning of the holiday year in order that the accrued holiday payment to the employee is minimised.

The new Regulations are silent. However, in the Government's January 2007 consultation document, the wording from the Government hinted that it could oresee a situation in which the 2007 Regulations were interpreted so that a worker on long-term sickness absence does receive the benefit of paid holiday entitlement.

New contracts of employment

The Working Time Regulations apply to workers. However, under the Employment Rights Act 1996 employers are under a duty to give 'employees' a written statement with particulars of employment detailing such things as rates of pay, hours of work and holiday entitlement. The law states that whenever there is a change in detail, the employer is under a duty to provide a written statement containing particulars of that change.

Employers should ensure that they have already provided amended particulars of employment to their employees to update them regarding the increase to 28 days' paid annual leave from 1 April 2009 and if they have not done so, then they should do so as soon as possible.

> *See also*: Agency and temporary workers, p.58; Employee benefits, p.266; Flexible working, p.338; Leave, p.457; Sickness leave, p.654

Sources of further information

Business Link has an interactive holiday pay calculator that allows you to work out your employees' annual holiday entitlement:
www.businesslink.gov.uk/bdotg/action/layer?r.l1=1073858787&topicId=1079427399&r.l2=1073858926&r.s=tl

BERR – holiday entitlement:
www.berr.gov.uk/employment/holidays/index.html

Homeworking

Dale Collins, Bond Pearce LLP

Key points

The Health and Safety at Work etc. Act 1974 (HSWA) places specific duties of care on the employer, on the self-employed and on employees. Under HSWA employers have a duty to protect the health, safety and welfare of their employees and other staff members working at an employer's workplace. This duty extends to all employees who work either at, or from, their home. As a general guide, therefore, employers should treat both the work area and the equipment used in an employee's own home as though they were in the main office. This approach should be reflected in the employer's employment policies and guidelines as well as in the Home Working Agreement made and signed between the employer and the employee before home working is approved.

Legislation

- Health and Safety (First Aid) Regulations 1981.
- Electricity at Work Regulations 1989.
- Health and Safety (Display Screen Equipment) Regulations 1992.
- Reporting of Injuries, Diseases and Dangerous Occurrences Regulations 1995.
- Data Protection Act 1998.
- The Provision and Use of Work Equipment Regulations 1998.
- Management of Health and Safety at Work Regulations 1999.
- Health and Safety (Miscellaneous Amendments) Regulations 2002.

Health and safety

The Provision and Use of Work Equipment Regulations 1998 cover the use of work equipment in the home. Note that, generally, employers are only responsible for the equipment which they supply to their employees. For employees who work at or from their own homes, it is accepted current best practice that all equipment for use in the home office should be supplied by and remain the property of the employer, largely for reasons of data security and because of the responsibility for health and safety. In some situations it may be appropriate for employees to use their own equipment, but, if this occurs, the equipment should first be assessed from a health and safety viewpoint as well as for its suitability to the work-related task(s) involved. Where computers and any other electrical equipment is used by the employee in the home, these are covered by the provisions of the Electricity at Work Regulations 1989.

Work furniture needs to be adjustable to provide correct and comfortable working heights. A good-quality, comfortable, adjustable chair is especially important. In order to reduce the risks of Repetitive Strain Injury (RSI), Work-Related Upper Limb Disorders, or other injuries due to poor work furniture, the employer is advised to supply all working furniture and any other occupational health equipment for use in the employee's home.

Lighting should be reviewed, especially with regard to glare, as home lighting arrangements are unlikely, on their own, to be fully adequate for office work.

Risk assessments

Health and safety authorities and HSE inspectors have wide powers of inspection and enforcement and can visit employers. They also have the right to visit an employer's homeworkers in their home offices in order to ensure that risks from working at home are being properly managed. In general most HSE legislation includes provisions for workplaces in the home. Under the Management of Health and Safety at Work Regulations 1999 the employer is required to assess the risks and hazards that might be present in the workplace, be this in the office or at a member of staff's home office.

Employers with more than five workers have a legal requirement to carry out and record a conventional health and safety workplace risk assessment on a homeworker's home offices. This can be done either by the employer or by the homeworker himself (e.g. using a self-assessment checklist), if s/he is suitably trained. A hazard is literally anything that may cause harm. A risk is the likelihood that someone will be harmed by the hazard. The risk assessment involves the following five steps:

1. Identifying hazards that may cause harm, however small (such as keeping potentially harmful substances out of children's reach).
2. Deciding who might be harmed and how (e.g. the homeworker, members of the household, visitors).
3. Assessing the risks and taking appropriate action (e.g. deciding what steps must be taken to eliminate or reduce the identified risks).
4. Recording the findings – what steps have been taken to reduce or eliminate risks? Inform the homeworker, or anyone else affected by the work, of the findings.
5. Check the risks from time to time and take steps if needed, especially if there is a change in working procedures.

The HSE produces a free guidance booklet on safety for homeworkers. The Institute of Occupational Safety and Health (IOSH) has an excellent datasheet on its website including a homework premises assessment form stressing the importance of adequate training and of regular reassessment of the risks.

Computer (display) screens

The main legislation relevant to homeworkers (or teleworkers) here is the Display Screen Equipment Directive (90/270/EEC). This is implemented in the UK by the Health and Safety (Display Screen Equipment) Regulations 1992 – as amended by the Health and Safety (Miscellaneous Amendments) Regulations 2002.

This requires that there should be:

■ a clear and stable screen, bright and free from glare, which should swivel and tilt easily;
■ adequate arrangement of keyboard characters, adjustable keyboard with sufficient space to support the hands and arms of the user;
■ sufficient user space to change positions and vary movements, a sufficiently large work desk, a document holder that is adjustable and stable;
■ satisfactory lighting conditions;
■ minimised glare and reflection at the workstation, and minimisation of radiation levels;
■ a work chair that is adjustable in height, including the backrest;
■ a footrest available if required; and
■ provision to reduce environmental factors to a minimum, including the effects of reflection or glare, noise, heat and humidity.

Note that computer users can request an eye examination and an eye test from their employer.

The working environment

Employers should put in place a system for their homeworkers to report accidents or hazards, as there would be in a conventional workplace. Practical experience within the Telework Association suggests that the following areas also often need attention:

- There should be a sufficient number of power sockets, avoiding overuse of extension leads, trailing cables and adaptors. Home offices may need rewiring for more sockets – have the homeworker's installation checked by an electrician.
- The use of IT equipment usually requires an additional two power outlets, and one or two telecoms sockets. Safely stowing cabling is important.
- Electrical equipment needs to be checked for safety (e.g. all cable grips in place, no burn marks on plugs or cracked sockets).
- Shelves should be conveniently situated so that when heavy files are placed and replaced there is no risk of stress on the spine or overbalancing.
- Office chairs and tables should all be of the appropriate height and adjustability for long periods of work.
- If the homeworker wears reading glasses, the prescription should be correct for close work. Anyone working with computers should have their eyes tested, and the optician should be informed of the computer work.
- Spotlights and anglepoise-type lamps are generally less tiring than fluorescents in small spaces. Light levels should be about 350 lux.
- Computer screens should be positioned at right angles to windows. Blinds to prevent sunlight making screens hard to read should be installed where needed.
- Temperatures should be as near as possible to 18.5°C. Small home offices can easily overheat because IT equipment generates heat. Temperatures may become uncomfortably hot in summer unless adequate ventilation can be provided.
- Adequate ventilation is also important where equipment such as laser printers may give off ozone or other fumes.
- Psychologically, most homeworkers prefer to be situated so that they can see out of a window if possible, although, as noted above, it is important to avoid problems with glare and reflection on computer screens.
- Rest breaks are vital. There are now a number of software packages which can be set up to remind homeworkers to take frequent breaks and so interrupt their more concentrated work environment.

First Aid and accidents in the workplace

Under the Health and Safety (First Aid) Regulations 1981, employers are required to ensure that they supply adequate First Aid provisions for their homeworking employees. The exact provisions will depend on the specific nature of the work task(s) being conducted and the hazards and risks involved.

Under the Reporting of Injuries, Diseases and Dangerous Occurrences Regulations 1995 (RIDDOR 1995), employers have a duty to find out about accidents, injuries, dangerous incidents or diseases arising from work-related activities. This might require putting in place procedures for homeworkers to be able to report such events and incidents to their employer.

Planning and Building Regulations

Planning permission

Setting up a home office constitutes a 'change of use' in strict planning terms. However, so far as planning departments are concerned, the average homeworker is unlikely to require planning permission, particularly if he is not creating a nuisance to neighbours.

Surrey County Council provided the following advice to its own homeworking staff, who worked at home under its Surrey Workstyle Programme:

Teleworking at or from home does not represent a significant change of use of a building likely to cause a nuisance or hazard to your neighbours. Unless you intend to make structural alterations to accommodate your working area, or extra noise, pollution etc. is generated because you are working at/from home, there is no requirement for planning permission."

Some other councils differ on whether home offices constitute a 'material' or 'ancillary' change of use (turning an outhouse into a garage and car repair workshop is rather more material than putting a computer into a spare bedroom).

Material changes of use to a property require permission; ancillary changes or temporary changes probably do not. Decisions on whether the change of use is 'material' are based on whether it will cause increased traffic, changes to the visible appearance of the property, nuisance such as noise or smells, or unsocial working hours.

While unfortunately some local authorities have not yet taken into account that homeworking reduces traffic and generally involves no alterations other than provision of electrical sockets and telephone lines, other authorities adopt a sensible approach.

Oldham Borough Council, for example, recognises homeworking formally in its planning guidelines, and regards home offices as ancillary changes of use. The Oldham document is available to other planning authorities, which can use it as a blueprint for their own guidelines if they wish.

Babergh District Council in Suffolk prepared its own leaflet *Working from Home – balancing the issues* because "we often get asked questions about homeworking and we are aware that there are people who don't really want to ask the question".

Business rating

So far as the associated matter of rating is concerned, a number of factors will determine whether the space in your home used as an 'office' will be liable for business rates. These will include the extent and frequency of the business use of the room (or rooms) and any special modifications made to the property. Each case is considered individually, usually through a visit from your local Valuation Office – which you should contact for further details. If your property needs to be assessed for business rates, your Valuation Office will work out a rateable value for the part used for non-domestic purposes, which may lead to a reduction in the council tax figure for the domestic part of the premises.

A Lands Tribunal appeal judgment, *Tully v. Jorgensen* (2003), found in favour of a full-time homeworker who used one room entirely as an office. The impact of this judgment is that if one works from home, uses office equipment, has not made structural alterations and does not employ people from the premises, then business rates will not be levied.

A practical piece of advice for homeworkers is to ensure that their activities do not cause annoyance to neighbours – and hence visits from council officials are much less likely to occur.

Building a workspace

If the establishment of the home office involves any building work, such as conversion of a loft space, there are strict building regulations which must be adhered to, mainly relating to means of escape in case of fire. Loft ladders and space-saver stairs are not favoured because they require familiarity of use for safe passage.

The homeworker may need to upgrade the floor between the loft and the rest of the house to give half an hour of fire resistance.

Another alternative to loft conversion which has been successfully used by a number of homeworkers is a personal office which, depending on specification, can cost around £5,000 and may not need planning permission.

Tax implications for homeworkers

If you set aside part of the house for the sole use of the business, that part of the house is potentially liable for capital gains tax. The precise implications of this will vary from year to year, and so, particularly if the homeworker is self-employed, it is advisable for him to discuss these with an accountant who will also advise on the proportions of household expenses attributable to home-office use that can be legitimately claimed.

'Business' charges by public utilities

There have been rare instances of power utility companies charging a non-domestic rate. The practical situation is that they would have to know that someone is working from home before any change could be made, and that the exact conditions vary from company to company.

For telephone service, BT does not compel people to use the business rate, but points out that the business service has the advantage of Yellow Pages and Business Pages entries. BT also puts business users on a higher priority for fault correction than residential users. In both cases compensation is paid if the fault is not repaired within 24 hours.

Insurance

The insurance market has pretty much caught up with the shift to homeworking. It is still the case that a standard home contents policy is unlikely to cover home office equipment, but specific policies targeted at home offices have been produced to replace the plethora of computer, office and home policies previously designed to confuse the homeworker. These new policies also cover important business issues that can affect homeworkers such as public liability, employee liability and loss of earnings.

Areas particularly to consider include the following:

- Insurance against loss of data (e.g. through virus or malicious attack). Employers should clarify the position on home-stored data with their insurers.
- Public liability or employer's liability insurance if other people work at or visit the homeworker's home office (this is mandatory in the Republic

of Ireland). It is also important for employers to ensure that employees other than the homeworker visiting the home office are covered (e.g. managers or those involved in health and safety checks).

Business interruption insurance, which, in the case of the self-employed or small home-based businesses, would provide compensation for the costs of putting a business back together and other expenditure incurred after an incident.

Computer breakdown insurance – in some situations this can be cheaper than holding a maintenance contract and ensures that expensive part replacements are covered. Employers need to check rather than assume that this insurance applies to computers off site.

Cover off the premises (e.g. for portable computers at the homeworker's home or in transit).

Employment issues

Data protection issues and confidentiality

The importance of this depends on the nature of the work but it is likely that the majority of homeworkers will have at home some confidential information belonging to the employer either on a computer or in another format.

Whilst all employees are subject to an implied duty of confidentiality, most employers will want an express clause on the issue setting out what amounts to confidential information and ensuring that the duty of confidentiality continues post-termination of employment. As ensuring compliance with confidentiality is more difficult for those employees who are not habitually in the office, employers need to address their minds to this issue more closely.

In addition, the Data Protection Act 1998 places additional responsibilities on data controllers, in this instance the employer, to ensure that all personal data is kept in compliance with the data protection principles. Consequently, employers should ensure that homeworkers are trained on the provisions of the Data Protection Act 1998 and what their responsibilities under the Act are. Compliance with any data protection policy should also be stated in the contract.

Competency, supervision and monitoring

As with all employees it is important to ensure that homeworkers are appraised and meet their objectives. Whilst working remotely or at separate times to a supervisor may cause some difficulties, nevertheless a suitable system for appraising such employees is important. It is important not just for employers but also for the employees who may feel more vulnerable than their colleagues whose output is more obvious.

Supervision of employees who do not necessarily work either at the same location or the same time as their supervisor is clearly more complicated. However, there are ways of monitoring employees remotely and supervisors should also be encouraged to spend time working with the homeworker, for example by arranging a regular time to meet with the homeworker to discuss issues. Monitoring of employees should only be done for specific reasons and employees should be made aware of the amount of monitoring that will take place, the methods for monitoring and how the information obtained from monitoring will be used and stored. Any monitoring must be proportionate to the objectives to be met (which in themselves must be reasonable)

and must be the least intrusive method
of achieving those reasonable objectives.

See also: Carers, p.114; Display
screen equipment, p.238; Flexible
working, p.338; IT security, p.433;
Risk assessments, p.639

Sources of further information

The Telework Association: www.telework.org.uk

The datasheet 'Teleworking' can be downloaded free from the Institute of
Occupational Health and Safety's website: www.iosh.co.uk. The datasheet
includes a homework premises assessment form and stresses the importance of
adequate training and regular reassessment of the risks.

Workplace Law Group's *Guide to Flexible Working 2008* provides information
and advice for employers whose employees work from home, and also considers
flexible working patterns in a wider sense. It covers the reasons why some
employers are looking to introduce flexible working into their workplace, explores
different flexible working patterns, including their benefits and disadvantages, and
provides detail on the formal legislative right to request. For more information
visit www.workplacelaw.net/Bookshop/GuidesTo.

An increasing amount of organisations are employing loneworkers, in all areas of
industry and business. Flexible Working Regulations have enabled employees to
enjoy the benefits of working from home; today's 24–7 culture means that more
companies are open around the clock; and greater automation in industry has
meant a shift from the traditional 9–5 working day. Loneworking can be of great
benefit to a business – but it also has its problems. Health and safety issues that
affect traditional employees still apply – in some cases more so. Employment
issues such as data protection and absence management are also paramount,
and must be considered when employing people who work alone.

Workplace Law Group's *Loneworking 2008: Special Report* helps you get
to grips with these issues, to determine whether loneworking is a viable option
for your business. Using practical case studies, checklists and assessments,
the report discusses the pros and cons of loneworking, and what an employer
must do to overcome the dangers, implement healthy and safe working policies,
and ensure their loneworkers are being cared for just as well as those in the
traditional workplace. For more information visit www.workplacelaw.net/Bookshop/
SpecialReports.

Human rights

Susan Thomas, Charles Russell

Key Points

- An employee of a public authority can bring a freestanding claim against their employer directly for a breach of any right provided by the Human Rights Act.
- An employee of a semi-public authority or private employer can only bring a claim under the Human Rights Act which is attached to an existing employment claim.
- All employee policies should be reviewed to ensure any interference with human rights is justifiable.

Legislation

Human Rights Act 1998.
European Convention on Human Rights and Fundamental Freedoms.

Application of the Human Rights Act

The Human Rights Act 1998 (HRA) adopted the European Convention for the Protection of Human Rights and Fundamental Freedoms into UK law on 2 October 2000. Some of the rights and freedoms set out in the Convention relevant to the workplace are:

Prohibition of slavery and forced labour (Article 4);
Right to a fair trial (Article 6);
Right to respect for private and family life (Article 8) *(see 'Private Life', p.587);*
Freedom of expression (Article 10); and
Freedom of assembly and association (Article 11).

The HRA requires public authorities to act in compliance with the Convention. Public authorities include all courts and tribunals, and any person exercising functions of a public nature. This means that the HRA affects different types of employers differently.

Public authorities

Employees can bring a claim against a public authority employer directly for a breach of a right set out in the HRA. Public authority employers include the police, the Government, local authorities, the Advertising Standards Authority, and so on.

Semi-public authorities

Private bodies which carry out public functions are also defined as public authorities, but only insofar as they are carrying out their public function. The relationship between employer and employee would normally be considered to be within the scope of their private function as employer, and any related acts to be outside the scope of their public function. This means that semi-public authority employers are affected by the HRA in the same way as private employers. Semi-public authorities include privatised utility companies, or a private security company exercising public functions in relation to the management of a prison.

Private employers

These are organisations that carry out no public function. The HRA is only indirectly enforceable against such employers, in that an Employment Tribunal's decision about workplace conduct and workplace decisions must be compatible with the HRA. An employee cannot directly bring a claim for breach of the HRA, but may 'attach' a claim that the employer has breached the HRA to an existing employment claim, such as unfair dismissal. Therefore, if an employer were to have unjustifiably breached an employee's human rights in its treatment of the employee in a dismissal situation, a Tribunal might find that the employer's actions made the dismissal unfair. The Act sets out 'justifications' which an employer may be able to rely on, such as the prevention of crime, or the prevention of infringement of rights of others. Whenever a Convention right is breached by an employer, the breach must not only be justified but must also not go beyond what is strictly necessary.

Example

P was employed by the Probation Service, and worked mainly with sex offenders. His employer discovered that he sold bondage and sado-masochism products on the Internet, and dismissed him. P brought a claim for unfair dismissal and breach of his rights under Articles 8 and 10 of the Convention (the right to respect for private life, and the right to freedom of expression). The Employment Appeal Tribunal decided that a probation officer, as a professional, had a reputation to maintain; that P's activities were publicised on a website and in the public domain, and were therefore not part of his private life. This meant that Article 8 was not engaged. There was an interference with P's right to freedom of expression, but this was justified due to the potential damage to the Service's reputation. A recent ECtHR case held that a failure by a hospital to keep a patient's medical record confidential amounted to a violation of her right to respect for private and family life. The case concerned an employee of the hospital whose colleagues had accessed her treatment records relating to treatment she had received at the same hospital. The ECtHR held that the European Convention imposed a positive obligation on public bodies and governments to protect the confidentiality of individuals' personal information as a result of the right to respect for private life.

Equality and Human Rights Commission (EHRC)

The EHRC came into existence on 1 October 2007 and has taken over the functions of the previous equality bodies (such as the Equal Opportunities Commission and the Commission for Racial Equality) and is also responsible for promoting the awareness, understanding and protection of human rights. In early 2008, the EHRC launched an inquiry into the impact of the Human Rights Act in Britain.

Issues for employers

Disciplinary procedures

Disciplinary procedures must now satisfy minimum statutory requirements and are therefore likely to respect the employee's right to a fair trial, incorporating an opportunity to hear and consider the employee's case and a mechanism for appeal. However, once the statutory procedures are repealed in the near future, employers will need to ensure that their procedures maintain compliance with the right to a fair trial.

Dismissal

Any dismissal procedure must also be fair, and any reason given for dismissal must not represent an unreasonable breach of a Convention right. For example, dismissing an employee on the grounds of membership of a political party may lead a Tribunal to find that the dismissal was not fair, since for a Tribunal to uphold such a eason for dismissal would represent an unreasonable breach of the employee's freedom of expression.

Investigating a complaint
The investigation of an employee's complaint or conduct should not involve breach of a Convention right. For example, one individual was awarded £10,000 compensation when her employer tapped her phone without warning during its investigation of her sex discrimination complaint. However, it was also recently held that the actions of a public sector employer who undertook covert surveillance to track an employee's movements were justified as the employer was investigating the suspected submission of fraudulent timesheets, which is a criminal activity.

Codes of Conduct
Codes of Conduct should be reviewed to ensure that they do not unnecessarily restrict an employee's Convention rights. For example, provisions on how an employee wears their hair, or whether they wear a nose ring, could raise issues about the way an individual expresses his or her personality in the workplace.

Employee checks
The right to respect for private life may include matters such as moral or physical integrity, so that 'private' in this context means 'personal'. This means that a security check which collects wide-ranging information about a person's personal affairs may go too far. Also potentially unlawful is the practice of carrying out random drug or alcohol tests, as such testing is likely to entail an invasion of Article 8 – personal privacy. However, such testing could be justified if it was in the interests of public safety, for example, where workers are in high risk situations such as pilots or train drivers. Employers should also ensure that any procedures such as security checks comply with the requirements of UK data protection legislation (*see 'Data Protection', p.186*).

See also: Data protection, p.186; Discrimination, p.222; Employment Tribunals, p.285; Private life, p.587

Sources of further information

Data Protection Act 1998: www.informationcommissioner.gov.ukwww.acas.org.uk

European Court of Human Rights: www.echr.coe.int/echr/

Insurance

Hugh Merritt, Taylor Wessing

Key points

■ Employers are required by law to insure motor vehicles and their own liability to employees.

■ There is a raft of other policies available to insure against the unexpected in the workplace – this chapter summarises some of the most common options.

■ Any business involved in the marketing or sale of insurance or other intermediary services in relation to insurance may be required to obtain authorisation from the Financial Services Authority.

Legislation

■ Employers' Liability (Compulsory Insurance) Act 1969.

■ Road Traffic Acts 1988 and 1991.

■ Insurance Mediation Directive.

■ Motor Vehicles (Compulsory Insurance) (Information Centre and Compensation Body) Regulations 2003.

Compulsory insurances

Employers' liability

With some exceptions, the Employers' Liability (Compulsory Insurance) Act 1969 requires employers to insure their liability to their employees for personal injury, disease or death sustained in the course of their employment in Great Britain. There is currently a penalty of up to £2,500 per day that the employer does not have insurance.

Employers are required to display a certificate of employers' liability insurance at each place of work, and must also retain expired certificates for at least 40 years in case of future claims (although note that the Government has decided to amend the legislation to allow certificates to be displayed electronically and to remove the requirement to retain certificates for 40 years. The amendments are expected

to be made during 2008). Employers are legally required to insure for at least £5m. The Association of British Insurers (ABI) advises that, in practice, most policies offer £10m minimum cover.

Employers' liability insurance must be issued by an authorised insurer; namely an issuer authorised by the Financial Services Authority (FSA). A register of authorised insurers can be found on the FSA website (see below for details).

Employers do not need employers' liability insurance for employees working outside of Great Britain (including where on secondment abroad), but the local law of the relevant jurisdiction should be checked for equivalent regulations.

Since 28 February 2005, employers' liability insurance is no longer compulsory for companies with a single employee who owns 50% or more of the company. Family businesses that only employ close family members are also exempt from the requirement; however, this exemption does not apply to family businesses incorporated as limited companies.

Motor

Third-party motor insurance (as a bare minimum) is compulsory. Employers should also take steps to make sure that employees using private cars for work-related activities are insured to do so. The EU Motor Insurance Directive requires fleet policy-holders to register their vehicles with the Motor Insurance Database. For more information visit www.miic.org.uk.

Other workplace insurances

There are a number of types of insurance policies that businesses should consider to cover a variety of risks. This chapter summarises some of the most common ones.

Buildings and contents

If you own your business premises then you should consider taking out a suitable insurance policy which covers damage from a variety of causes. Standard policies typically cover risks including fire and lightning, explosion, riot, malicious damage, storms and floods. An 'all risks' policy provides cover against other risks, including accidental damage. Insurance policies do not cover wear and tear, electrical or mechanical breakdown or any gradual deterioration specified in the policy. Tenants should ask their landlords who is responsible for insuring the premises. This will normally be the landlord.

The ABI advises that:

- business premises should be insured for the full rebuilding cost (including professional fees and the cost of site clearance) and not just for the market value;
- stock should be insured for its cost price without any addition for profit;
- plant and business equipment can also be insured, on either an 'as-new' or an indemnity basis, in which case wear-and-tear will be taken into account when settling claims; and
- contents are usually covered against theft provided there has been forcible

and violent entry to or exit from the premises. Damage to the building resulting from theft or attempted theft will also normally be covered.

Business interruption

Business interruption insurance should be enough to cover any shortfall in gross profit caused by damage to property (e.g. fire). It should also cover any increase in working costs, and restart costs.

Directors' and officers' liability

Directors' and officers' liability insurance would reimburse the individual director or company officer for personal liability. Alternatively, it can compensate the company itself where the company has reimbursed a director or officer for a personal liability.

Employees

- Employers can take out key-person insurance which would compensate the company in the event of an injury or death preventing a key member of staff from working.
- Fidelity guarantee insurance would cover you for the costs of employee dishonesty (e.g. theft). This would not normally be covered under buildings and contents insurance.
- Make sure that personal assault is covered in your contents insurance. This will provide compensation for you or your employees following injury during theft or attempted theft of money.
- Some employers provide income protection insurance, private medical insurance, life insurance, or personal accident and sickness insurance as an employee benefit.

Legal expenses

Legal expenses insurance would meet the cost of bringing or defending legal action. Most notably, legal expenses insurance is useful in insuring against Employment

Tribunal claims, or court action taken by, for example, HM Revenue & Customs.

Professional indemnity

Professional indemnity insurance protects advisers who give professional advice – e.g. solicitors, accountants, architects and building surveyors.

Public liability

Public liability insurance would pay damages to members of the public for death, personal injury or damage to their property that occurs as a result of your business. It also covers associated legal fees, costs and expenses.

This type of insurance is unlikely to be necessary in the case of, for example, a web design business, but is necessary if the public has access to the business premises. Public liability insurance is compulsory for some businesses.

Product liability

Product liability insurance covers compensation awarded as a result of damage to property or personal injury caused by a product manufactured or (in some circumstances) supplied by a business. Most businesses have cover of between £1m and £5m, although a common level of cover is around £2m.

Important considerations

- Insurance is subject to insurance premium tax, which cannot be set off against VAT. Life insurance, pensions and income protection insurances are exempt.
- It is important for employers to bear in mind that fines as a result of prosecution (e.g. by the HSE for a health and safety offence) cannot be insured against.

Selling insurance

Wide-ranging regulations (under the EU Insurance Mediation Directive) governing the selling and administering of insurance policies by intermediaries came into force on 14 January 2005.

The Regulations apply to any business which purchases or arranges insurance for a third party or assists a third party in the preparation of an insurance claim. The Regulations only apply where the business provides such services by way of business, which in most cases means where remuneration is received for those services.

The following are examples of activities which may fall within the ambit of the Regulations:

- Contractors who obtain insurance on behalf of, or handle claims for, third parties, e.g. developers or funders;
- Employers who obtain project insurance on behalf of the other parties involved with the project;
- Insurance arrangements for joint venture companies or other group companies;
- Landlords who take out insurance in joint names with tenants; and
- Property management service companies that arrange insurance on behalf of clients.

Any businesses carrying out such activities, unless otherwise exempt, are required to obtain authorisation from the FSA or become an appointed representative or introducer-appointed representative of a firm authorised by the FSA. It is a criminal offence to carry out any of the regulated activities without obtaining authorisation or becoming an appointed representative or introducer-appointed representative, even if the business is contractually obliged to provide these services.

The FSA does provide detailed guidance to businesses involved in the marketing

r sales of insurance and other
ntermediary services in the form of
he *FSA Handbook*, which is available
nline (see below for details), though the
subject matter is extremely complex and
professional advice is recommended.
The FSA also provides advice online for
consumers.

> *See also*: Directors' responsibilities,
> p.198; Driving at work, p.244;
> Health and safety at work, p.364;
> Occupiers' liability, p.541

Sources of further information

Association of British Insurers: www.abi.org.uk

Motor Insurers' Information Centre: www.miic.org.uk

Financial Services Authority: www.fsa.gov.uk

FSA Handbook: http://fsahandbook.info/FSA/html/handbook

Intellectual property

Ian De Freitas, Berwin Leighton Paisner

Key points

- Intellectual property can be a valuable asset. Every business will own intellectual property rights of one sort or another. Intellectual property rights should, therefore, be protected and enforced in order to ensure that they retain their value.
- Use of a third party's intellectual property rights (whether knowingly or otherwise) without their permission can be disastrous: infringement is usually very expensive.
- Copyright, unregistered design rights and database rights arise automatically.
- UK patents, registered trade marks and registered designs are granted by the UK Intellectual Property Office based in Newport, Wales.
- Protection is now provided in all 27 Member States of the European Community (EC) for trade marks by the Community Trade Mark and for designs by the Community design right. Applications for these registered rights are made to the Office of Harmonisation for the Internal Market (OHIM) in Alicante, Spain.
- Internet domain names are administered by a network of private non-governmental registries.
- Intellectual property is territorial in scope and an international protection strategy should be considered.

Main legislation

- Registered Designs Act 1949.
- Patents Act 1977.
- Copyright, Designs and Patents Act 1988.
- Trade Marks Act 1994.
- Council Regulation (EC) No. 6/2002 on Community Designs.

Copyright

Copyright arises automatically in any:

- original artistic, literary (which includes computer programs), musical or dramatic works;
- sound recordings, films or broadcasts; and
- typographical arrangements in published works,

which have been recorded in some tangible form. Ideas and concepts are not protected by copyright. It is the way that they are expressed or recorded which is protected. For a work to be original, it must not have been copied from another work and it must involve some skill or judgement (however small). Independent copyrights may therefore subsist in two identical works so long as their respective creators did not copy each other or a third party. In this sense copyright protection does not confer a monopoly.

Broadly speaking, copyright will last for:

- 70 years from the death of the author in the case of literary, dramatic, musical, artistic works (but only 25 years in the case of industrially-exploited artistic works), and films; and
- 50 years in the case of sound recordings and broadcasts.

s copyright arises automatically, there is
need in this country for the owner to
gister it. A UK national's copyright will
so be recognised in all countries that are
gnatories to the Berne Convention 1886,
e WIPO Copyright Treaty 1996, and the
TO Agreement. The copyright owner
ill usually be the person who created the
ork, unless that person was an employee
cting in the course of his/her employment,
which case the employer will own the
opyright. An independent contractor is not
employee, so the independent contractor
ill, generally speaking, own any copyright
the work created for the commissioning
arty. Copyright can be assigned
ransferred) or licensed (a permission is
ven to use it) to a third party.

hen engaging an independent contractor
create a copyright work it is important
at they assign (or at least licence) the
opyright in the work to the commissioning
arty so that the commissioning party
wns the copyright in the work that they
ave paid for (or, in the case of a licence,
ey have express permission to use
). Copyright is infringed by someone
opying the whole or a substantial part of
copyright work without the permission of
e copyright owner. A substantial part can
e quite a small part of the work provided
at it is significant qualitatively. So far as
roving that copying has occurred, the
ourt may assume copying has taken
lace if the similarities are significant
nd it can be shown that there was an
pportunity to copy.

esign rights

esign rights fall into two main categories:
nregistered and registered rights. These
ghts can either be United Kingdom-only
ghts or EC-wide rights.

Unregistered UK design right
esign right protects aspects of the shape
nd configuration of a design, with certain

exclusions for features which are designed
to create an interface with or match the
appearance of other articles. To qualify for
protection, a design must be:

- original (it must be the result of the
  independent skill and labour of the
  designer); and
- not commonplace in the relevant
  design field at the time it was
  designed.

Unregistered design right protection lasts
for ten years, unless the design has not
been commercially exploited. In addition,
anyone can ask for a licence to copy a
design protected by unregistered design
right after the first five years of its being
put into the marketplace. Owing to the
limitations of the UK unregistered design
right, designers are strongly advised to
consider registering their designs in order
to benefit from the greater protection which
a registration offers.

UK and Community registered designs
The owner of a registered design can
prevent a third party from using a design
that is the same as or that creates the
same overall impression as the registered
design, even if the third party can show
that they did not copy the registered
design. A registered design can protect
aspects of:

- shape and configuration of a design;
- contours and lines;
- texture or materials;
- ornamentation;
- colours; and
- packaging, logos, motifs and
  typefaces.

Designs can be registered if they:

- are 'new' (that is, they differ from
  existing designs in the marketplace to
  a material extent); and
- create a different overall impression
  from other designs.

A design can be marketed for up to 12 months in order to test the market before making an application for registration without prejudicing the registrability of the design. Since it is the design itself which is protected, once registered, it can be applied to any number of different products. The duration of a registered design is 25 years, renewable every five years on payment of a fee. The Community registered design allows one registration to be filed for all 27 Member States of the EC. The protection given is the same as for the UK.

Unregistered Community design right
This is based on the Community registered design system. Therefore, the same criteria for protection apply. The period of protection is only three years, however, from the date that the design is first made available to the public. Although the term of protection is less favourable than under United Kingdom unregistered design right, the sort of designs covered by the Community unregistered right are the same as under the Community registered design. The unregistered Community right may therefore be of use where United Kingdom design right fails to protect a design, such as where the shape of a design is commonplace but what makes it new and of individual character is its texture or ornamentation.

Trade marks
A trade mark is any sign capable of being represented graphically and which distinguishes goods or services of one business from those of another business. In theory sounds and smells are registrable as trade marks, although trade marks usually consist of:

- words, designs, letters, numerals (or a combination of these); or
- the shape of goods or their packaging.

Trade marks are territorial in nature and therefore there is a need to seek registration in all countries which may be of interest to the business. Trade marks may be registered through national trade mark applications. An international trade mark application can cover those countries which are signatories to the Madrid Protocol. A Community Trade Mark application (CTM) will automatically cover the countries of the EC. It is advisable to search the relevant trade marks registers prior to filing an application. The searches should reveal the existence of any prior, identical or similar marks in respect of identical or similar goods or services that may be potential obstacles to the use and registration of the proposed mark. Applications are usually examined for 'distinctiveness' of the mark applied for and in some countries there is an examination for conflicts with existing trade marks (no longer the case in the UK). Once the application has been examined, the application is published and, depending upon where the application has been made, third parties may have the opportunity to file an opposition against the registration of the mark. Once registered, trade marks can be renewed indefinitely. However, a trade mark that is not used for a continuous period of five years will be vulnerable to cancellation. A registered trade mark is infringed by someone:

- using an identical sign in respect of identical goods or services; or
- using an identical sign in respect of similar goods or services, where there is a likelihood of confusion by the public; or
- using a similar sign in respect of identical or similar goods or services, where there is a likelihood of confusion by the public; or
- using an identical or similar sign in respect of any goods or services where the trade mark is well known

and the use of the sign takes unfair advantage of, or is detrimental to the distinctive character or the reputation of the trade mark.

Passing off

The identity of a business – its reputation, as well as its name – is generally embodied in its branding. Registering that brand identity as a trade mark (or portfolio of trade marks) will make it easier to protect and enforce its rights in that identity. However, it may be possible for a business to enforce its rights in its unregistered trade marks and associated goodwill by bringing a claim under the law of passing off. Such actions can be costly as substantial evidence needs to be provided to show:

- the extent of the reputation and goodwill that the business has in the unregistered trade mark/branding;
- confusion (or the likelihood of confusion) on the part of the public; and
- the damage suffered by the business as a result of the passing off.

Patents

Patents protect inventions. To be patentable, a patent must:

- be novel;
- involve an inventive step; and
- be capable of industrial application.

A patent will not be granted if the invention is obvious to persons skilled in the field in question or if it has been disclosed to the public prior to the patent application. It is therefore important not to discuss an invention with third parties prior to making an application, unless the discussions are confidential. It is advisable in those circumstances to put a confidentiality agreement in place before such discussions take place. Some things cannot be patented, including some inventions relating to software, business methods, discoveries, and games. To obtain a patent, applications are made to the UK Intellectual Property Office (for a UK patent) with a description of the invention and payment of an application fee.

A separate patent is required for each country where protection is needed, although there is a centralised procedure for making multiple applications within Europe (a European patent application under the European Patent Convention). In the UK, patents last for up to 20 years (sometimes 25 years for pharmaceuticals), with annual renewal fees payable on a rising scale.

- As part of the application process, full details of it are published meaning that some businesses decide not to patent their inventions but instead keep the nature of their invention secret.
- A patent does not give its owner an absolute right to use the invention, if its use infringes someone else's patent, confidential information or design right. Also, it is possible for a patent to be declared invalid following an attack by a third party.
- Like registered design rights, a patent is infringed even if the alleged infringer can prove that their invention was independently developed without copying. In this sense the Patent grants a monopoly to the patent holder.
- In most cases, it is the inventor who has the right to apply for the patent, unless he/she was an employee acting within the course of their employment, in which case it is generally the employer who has the right. In such cases, the employer may have to make a compensatory payment to the employee if the patent is particularly valuable.

Database rights

A database is a collection of independent works, data or other materials which are arranged in a systematic or methodical way and which are individually accessible by electronic or other means. A database may be protected by copyright and/or a database right. To benefit from copyright protection, a database must be original. A database will be original where, by reason of the selection or arrangement of its contents, it constitutes the author's own intellectual creation. The copyright expires after 70 years from the end of the year in which the author dies. Where there is a substantial investment in obtaining, verifying or presenting the contents of a database, the maker will own a separate database right. A database right entitles its owner to take action against a person who extracts or reutilises all or a substantial part of the contents of the database. The database right expires after the later of 15 years from the end of the year in which the database was completed or when the database is made available to the public.

There are exceptions to both rights enabling others to make limited use of the contents of a database, although unauthorised use of a database may also give rise to issues under the Data Protection Act 1998.

Domain names

Domain names are available for registration through a number of registries as a 'private' contractual arrangement. Businesses need to think about not just registering domain names for their trading names and brands, but misspellings as well. They should also ensure that domain names are registered in the company's name, not in the name of an employee (as often happens). Following the inception of the Internet, businesses developed significant internet brands which became a target for third parties to infringe. Cybersquatting (the registration of infringing domain names as a blocking

tactic or to sell on to brand owners for inflated prices) became a particular problem. However, more importantly, infringing domain names were registered and used to point to third parties' websites which often sold goods or offered services similar to those provided by the brand owner. Therefore, right holders were forced to protect their brands by taking legal action (usually registered trade mark infringement or passing off proceedings) against anyone registering domain names similar to their own.

As a result of the increasing number of court actions involving domain names, the bodies that regulate domain names introduced alternative dispute resolution processes solely for domain name disputes. Nominet, the body that regulates co.uk domains, EURid (the regulator of the .eu domain names) and the World Intellectual Property Organisation (WIPO) which regulates other top-level domains, have put in place separate dispute resolution policies and procedures, enabling internet brand owners to bring quick and cheap actions to prevent third parties from using infringing domain names, without having to resort to formal court proceedings.

Confidence

The law of confidence has been developed by the courts to protect confidential or secret information, such as trade secrets or inventions before a patent is granted. To bring a claim for breach of confidence, a person must demonstrate that:

- the information has the necessary quality of confidence;
- the information has been imparted in circumstances importing an obligation of confidence or be obviously confidential; and
- there must have been an unauthorised use of the information.

A claim for breach of confidence can be defeated if the information has already entered the public domain. The law of confidence will not protect immoral information or where there is a public interest in the disclosure of the information. The Human Rights Act 1998 has had a significant impact on the traditional model of breach of confidence, having to strike a balance between the right to respect for private and family life and the contrasting right to freedom of expression. This has been seen in several high-profile cases involving celebrities who have argued that a publication has infringed their right to privacy. The current position is that there is no law of privacy in this country, but instead the law of confidence has been adapted by the courts to cover situations where an individual is aggrieved by an invasion of their privacy. This has led to the development of two distinct new limbs of confidentiality: the right of a celebrity to control the use of their image where they trade on such image; and the right of a person to prevent disclosure or further disclosure of private information, even where they may be public figures.

Remedies for infringement of intellectual property rights

The penalties for infringement of intellectual property rights vary depending upon the right infringed, but typically include:

- court orders to stop infringement, including urgent interim injunctions before a full trial takes place;
- damages (such as loss of sales or a payment equivalent to a licence fee to use the intellectual property right) or an account of the profits made from the infringement (whichever is the greater); and
- delivery up or destruction of infringing goods.

For some intellectual property rights, criminal sanctions apply, including fines and custodial sentences.

Groundless threats

Owners of patents, trade marks and registered and unregistered UK and Community design rights must be wary of making anything amounting to a 'groundless threat' to an alleged infringer. An accusation of particular types of infringement that cannot later be substantiated may result in the accuser being sued.

Sources of further information

Workplace Law Network provides premium members with unrestricted access to a comprehensive range of online information – factsheets, case reports and daily news items – on employment, health and safety and premises management. Members also benefit from an online advice service and a free subscription to the *Workplace Law Magazine*. For more information email membership@workplacelaw.net or call our membership services team on 0871 777 8881.

Internet and email policies

David Browne, Martineau Solicitors

Key points

- Where relevant, employers should have in place a written internet and email policy making employees aware of what, if any, personal usage of the internet and email systems is reasonable.
- This policy needs to be effectively and transparently communicated to employees at the earliest opportunity.
- Employers must take into account the rights of employees (particularly their right to privacy under Article 8 of the European Convention on Human Rights) in assessing how to monitor employees' usage of the internet and email systems and should make employees aware of what monitoring will take place.

Legislation

- Copyright, Designs and Patents Act 1988.
- Defamation Act 1996.
- Protection from Harassment Act 1997.
- Human Rights Act 1998.
- Data Protection Act 1998.
- Regulation of Investigatory Powers Act 2000.
- All discrimination legislation.

The need for a suitable internet and email policy

A survey conducted in 2008 by the Department for Business, Enterprise and Regulatory Reform (BERR) shows that the proportion of UK companies with a broadband connection to the internet stands at 97%, with 16% of UK companies suffering from staff misuse of information systems (which rises to 47% of large businesses suffering from staff misuse).

It is clear that the advantages to businesses of the internet and email systems are undermined by the greater potential for staff to abuse these facilities. The legal issues which an employer may face as a consequence of staff misusing either the internet or email are also surprisingly broad. For example, these may include email harassment or unauthorised use of computer systems, issues surrounding agency law where employees inadvertently form contracts through email correspondence, intellectual property law in disputes over the downloading or dissemination of material subject to copyright, the law of defamation for libel following comments made about individuals or businesses in emails, and criminal law where employees download obscene material or are involved in hacking.

In light of these potential pitfalls for employers, setting out employees' rights, responsibilities and limitations on the use of the internet and email systems will help employers prevent any unauthorised or careless use, which may result in one of the legal risks detailed above. Any such policy should also make clear any monitoring or interception that the employer may lawfully undertake and the reasons for this.

Workplace Law Network
www.workplacelaw.net

Content of the policy

The content of an internet and email policy will largely depend on issues such as the size and nature of the business and there is no one policy which would be appropriate for all businesses. Whilst model policies are useful, they must be tailored to suit the needs of the organisation and its employees.

However, a typical internet and email policy should make provision for the following:

- An indication of the extent to which personal use of the internet and the email is acceptaze conscious of the fact that employees have a reasonable expectation of some privacy in the workplace and if personal use of email is prohibited (or monitored), employers are recommended to provide workers with some means of making personal communications which are not subject to monitoring (by telephone, for example);
- An instruction not to share passwords with other employees and to make appropriate arrangements for relevant staff to access work emails when absent;
- A statement that both internet and email use are intended predominantly for business use;
- Advice on email etiquette, including guidance on when staff should add signatures / disclaimers to emails;
- Guidance on what is deemed 'acceptable use', in particular an outline of the types of websites that are considered inappropriate to access from work, particularly those that contain obscene, offensive or pornographic content. This should include a warning to employees not to access, download or disseminate any material that could be construed as offensive in nature;

- A clear statement informing employees that their email and internet usage may be subject to monitoring; and
- Details of what may happen if employees breach the policy.

In addition, employers should cross reference any internet and email policy with other relevant policies it has in place. Examples include policies relating to the handling of confidential information, use and storage of personal data, consultation and communications at work, training, equal opportunities and harassment, and the employer's disciplinary and grievance policies and procedures.

Monitoring

It is essential that any internet and email policy contains a clear statement about how employees' use of the internet and email systems is to be monitored. A failure to do so may lead to claims from employees that the employer is in breach of Article 8 of the European Convention on Human Rights (right to respect for private and family life). If, however, the employer's policy makes clear that monitoring will take place (and what form this monitoring will take), employees cannot have a reasonable expectation of privacy and this should be sufficient for employers to escape such liability.

It should be noted that by its very nature monitoring of employees' internet and email usage is intrusive. Careful consideration should therefore be given to the impact of such monitoring on workplace relations, as it may be interpreted by employees as a lack of trust in staff. Providing employees with clear reasons as to why the monitoring is taking place, together with assurances that it will only be done within the strict limits set out in the policy, should help to allay any concerns employees have in relation to the monitoring of their internet and email activity. Employers should be aware that monitoring should be proportionate to the legitimate business needs of the organisation. Covert monitoring is likely to be unlawful and should be restricted to circumstances where it is used for the prevention or detection of crime.

The Information Commissioner has provided specific advice on monitoring in relation to data protection issues which can be found at www.ico.gov.uk.

Communicating and enforcing the policy

It is not only essential for employers to have an adequate internet and email policy in place, but also to ensure that the policy's existence is adequately communicated to employees. Tribunals have found employees to be unfairly dismissed in circumstances where the employer did not make them properly aware of its policy, even when employees had clearly carried out acts of misconduct serious enough to be dismissed, such as accessing and distributing pornographic images.

There is no one particular way in which such employees should be made familiar with the contents of the policy, but communication methods may include:

- via email (although employers may require a read receipt to know that employees have opened and read the email);
- a circular sent to all staff, or to incorporate the policy into a staff handbook (which could then be made available to staff either electronically or in hard copy);
- incorporating the policy into the employee's contract of employment;
- a presentation to staff explaining the system and its use; and/or
- holding training sessions on the new policy.

Additionally employers may wish to get employees to 'sign off' that they have read and understand the policy.

See also: Data protection, p.186; Intellectual property, p.420; IT security, p.433; Monitoring employees, p.521; Private life, p.587

Sources of further information

Information Commissioner's guidance on how to comply with obligations under the Data Protection Act 1998, available at www.ico.gov.uk.

2008 Information Breaches Survey, commissioned by BERR, available at www.berr.gov.uk.

Workplace Law Group's *IT and Email Policy and Management Guide, v.2.0* has been designed to alert employers of the potential problems associated with using computer systems, the internet, and email systems within the workplace and to provide certain safeguards. For more information visit www.workplacelaw.net/Bookshop/PoliciesAndProcedures.

Interviewing

Jo Bradbury, Martineau Solicitors

Key points

- Planning and preparation are essential.
- Bear in mind equality and diversity legislation.
- Avoid stereotypical assumptions to minimise the risk of a discrimination claim.
- Be objective: avoid whims or gut instincts.
- Be fair, consistent and transparent.
- Where possible have a mixed interview panel.
- Be organised: plan out questions in advance.
- Focus on the job description and person specification, as the basis for questioning.
- Ask open questions.
- Avoid questions that are not job-related.
- Be able to justify your decisions and record this justification.
- Choose the best person for the job.

Staff are an employer's most important asset and largest investment, but recruitment is a two-way process and is as much about an individual deciding whether he/she wants to work for the employer as it is about the employer deciding which candidate to appoint. The interview is often the first and a very powerful impression for both the candidate and the employer.

In order to recruit and retain the best candidates, an interview selection panel needs to gather all the information it needs during the interview process. Time spent at the beginning of the process, identifying precisely what the role is and what skills and experience are needed to fill it, will aid the decision-making process.

Diversity in recruitment

Diversity should be seen as a positive thing, and something to aspire to. There is often a tendency for employers to look for people who are similar to the person already employed in a particular role, but cloning existing staff is unlikely to add value. Interviewers should therefore bear this in mind from the outset.

Legal perspective

The recruitment and selection process can be a minefield from a legal perspective, particularly in the context of equal opportunities legislation. It is therefore important for the interviewers to understand how employment law can impact on the interview process, what potential liabilities can be incurred and the consequences for getting it wrong.

Equality is not a new concept in employment relationships. The UK is used to the raft of legislation from Europe, including discrimination on the grounds of sex, race, disability, sexual orientation, religion, belief and age. In addition, employers are encouraged to offer flexible working and to address work–life balance issues.

Interview panels should ensure they do not ask questions that expose the employer to potential claims. For example, a panel should not put too much emphasis on the desirability of having qualifications from a UK educational institution, or work experience within the UK, as non-British nationals will find this more difficult to comply with than British nationals.

A panel should use the interview to establish the quality of the qualifications and experience. Similarly, if in an interview situation a non-British candidate's spoken English is not as fluent as that of a British national, an employer may not be justified in using this as a criterion for turning down the non-British candidate from all posts; it will depend on whether fluency in spoken English is an essential requirement for the post.

As a further example, if an interview panel knows in advance that a candidate who is coming for interview is disabled, the panel should consider whether any adjustments need to be made to the physical arrangements for the interview or the interview process itself. From a practical point of view, the panel may want to ask, during the interview, whether the disabled candidate has any particular requirements to help him/her fulfil the role, but should not make any decisions about whether or not to employ him/her based on his/her disability, or the effects, without very good reasons for doing so.

It is imperative to avoid making stereotypical assumptions. If an interview panel gets this wrong, an unsuccessful candidate can bring an Employment Tribunal claim within three months of the act of discrimination (or within such further period as the Employment Tribunal considers just and equitable). The remedies are a declaration of rights, a recommendation and/or potentially unlimited compensation.

The process

As selection is, by its very nature, a subjective process, it is important to consider the process in as objective a way as possible.

The key focuses for the panel during the interview process are:

- to gain all the information needed to decide who is most suitable for the role;
- to ensure that selection is carried out in a fair, objective, consistent and open manner;
- to avoid falling foul of the employment legislation; and
- to appoint the right person.

At the outset, a panel needs to decide how to assess the shortlist of candidates in person. The most common method is interviewing (although alternatives include assessment centres, written testing and psychometric testing).

For interviewing, the following issues need to be considered early on:

- Will there be one stage or two?
- The make-up of the panel. Where possible, the panel should not be potentially gender- or racially-biased. Instead, there should be a mixed panel if this is feasible.
- Is there going to be a Chair? If so, will he/she have a deciding vote?
- What will the structure of the interview be? Be organised and decide beforehand who will ask what.
- How long will the interview last? This is important for both planning and consistency.
- Ensure that the interview takes place in an appropriate setting, without interruptions.
- Be prepared and know what you are asking for. The panel should meet to discuss the interview beforehand and should be familiar with the job description and person specification.

The form

Interviews can take a variety of forms. One suggested format would be to welcome the candidate, introduce the panel and explain the interview format; acquire information by asking relevant questions; supply information by giving the candidate an opportunity to ask questions; make the candidate aware of the next stage, including when he/she will find out the outcome; and thank him/her for attending.

The purpose

The key purpose of the interview is to assess the candidate's suitability for the post. As an interviewer, you should ask yourself if the candidate can do the job; and what he/she would bring to the job.

The job description and person specification should be used as the basis for areas of questioning and the questions should draw out information about the candidate's knowledge, experience and skills. The interviewer needs to be satisfied with the candidate's evidence, whilst considering the relative importance of each of the selection criteria.

It is usually best to ask all candidates the same basic questions, in order to ascertain whether they are right for the role. However, the panel should feel confident about deviating from the basic questions and to probe further to obtain the evidence needed.

Where possible, interviewers should ask open questions which are experience-based, rather than questions which just require a "yes" or "no" answer. Follow-up questions could also include hypothetical situations, to measure thought processes.

As a general rule, questions that are not job-related should not be asked (e.g. questions related to family, marital status, childcare commitments, age and ethnic origin). Also, assumptions about these issues should not be made. These questions or assumptions could cause a panel to inadvertently discriminate against a candidate, which would then be compounded if the decision is based upon the answer to the question.

Subjective judgment

Although gut instincts should be avoided, interview panels will inevitably also take into account the more subjective aspects of a person's character, attitude and confidence. These are likely to be relevant and so, in many cases, the best thing to do is to include these criteria in the scoring grid, together with a space for writing down any comment which an interviewer feels helps to justify the score given. Care should be taken to ensure that any written comments cannot be construed as discriminatory in any form. Where a number of candidates meet the essential criteria for the job, the likelihood is that the successful candidate will be chosen on the basis of how the panel rated his/her more subjective criteria.

In terms of scoring subjective criteria, it is probably prudent to attach less weight to subjective scores than to objective scores. In reality though, where candidates are otherwise equal, the subjective score is likely to tip the balance in any event.

Considerations with internal candidates

Interviewing an internal candidate, or someone you know, presents its own set of challenges. Interviewers should not make assumptions, but should gather evidence of whether he/she satisfies the selection criteria in the same way as with any other candidate. Interview questions should (still) be objective and probing. Interviewers should steer clear of irrelevant points and keep the interview formal, rather than being tempted to adopt a more informal approach.

Written notes

It is a good idea to take brief notes or use an interview form, as this will act as a reminder when the interviewer comes to make a decision. It is also good evidence of why a particular candidate was or was not selected. However, interviewers should avoid making copious notes, as this could make it difficult to establish a rapport with candidates. Also, bear in mind that any notes taken, even on scraps of paper, will be discoverable documents in any subsequent legal proceedings. Therefore, it is important to avoid discriminatory comments or comments that could be interpreted as such.

Where notes are not made during the interview, they should be written up as soon after the interview as is reasonably practicable, in order to ensure that the details are recalled accurately. All notes should be returned to Personnel for storage with the job file and should be kept for at least six months.

Selection

It is crucial to go back to the job description and person specification when deciding which candidate to select for the position. Ideally, each panel member should assess each of the candidates him/herself, where possible immediately after the interview, formulating his/her own view and scoring the candidate before any discussion takes place. It is helpful to have a standard evaluation form to complete, to ensure consistency in ratings. (In practice, the panel will also take into account information from the application process, any references and so on.) These records should be kept for six months.

Each candidate should then be discussed by the panel in turn. Candidates who do not meet the essential criteria can be eliminated. In terms of the remaining candidates, the panel should not come to a premature decision based on personality / who they like best, but should focus on the (essential and preferred) selection criteria.

The panel should then rank the candidates as unappointable and appointable, in order of preference. Again, a record should be kept of this process. The first choice candidate can then be offered the job, ideally with a time limit for acceptance.

Those deemed unappointable can also be informed at this stage. However, it may be prudent to delay informing any reserves of the final decision, in case the first choice declines the offer. It is best practice to keep reserves informed of the situation.

In the long run, it is always better to appoint the right person for the job, even if this means waiting or extending the recruitment process (including any associated costs), so as to avoid ending up with someone who is not suitable for the post.

See also: Criminal records, p.181; Discrimination, p.222; Personnel files – recording information, p.571; Probationary periods, p.592; Recruitment and selection, p.607; References, p.622; Staff handbooks, p.666

Sources of further information

ACAS – Advisory booklet – Recruitment and selection: www.acas.org.uk

IT security

Rhian Hill, Bird & Bird

Key points

Serious breaches of IT security and major losses of customer or employee data regularly feature in the news. Both the public and the private sector have recently suffered high profile losses. Clearly such breaches of security have a major impact on the organisation affected, not least in terms of negative PR. Workplace managers can take a number of steps to protect their organisation against security breaches:

- Put security breach action plans in place;
- Put security policies in place, implement and ensure they are regularly reviewed;
- Update security software regularly; and
- Put effective systems administration procedures in place.

Security breaches in the news

Serious breaches of security have been hitting the headlines with alarming regularity, with the most high profile cases (such as HM Revenue & Customs' data loss in November 2007) leading to a number of government reports on data security. The Information Commissioner has also reacted strongly to these breaches, announcing that he will issue an enforcement notice against HMRC and the MOD (over its loss of data). Serving an Enforcement Notice is the strongest sanction the Commissioner currently has, although the Commissioner's powers are set to increase.

High profile breaches have also been seen in the public sector. Early in 2008, the ICO issued an Enforcement Notice against Marks and Spencer, ordering the company to ensure that all laptop hard drives are fully encrypted by April 2008. This followed the theft of an unencrypted laptop which contained the personal information of 26,000 M&S employees. In light of the nature of the information contained on the laptop, it is the ICO's view that M&S

should have had appropriate encryption measures in place to keep the data secure. Most workplace managers do not need to be convinced of the devastating effect on business of such incidents. A common initial reaction might be to ask how this could happen. No doubt the board / stakeholders / financiers of the business would be asking themselves the same question. If managing a business is seen to be all about managing risk while achieving the highest return on investment, recent cases have shown that the risk of security breaches is really a very serious risk.

The threats

In addition to the threat to an organisation's data, including customer, financial and employee data, there are also a number of possible threats to system integrity and/or availability.

Breach of IT security through human error and organisational failures

Several of the high-profile incidents of Government departments losing data have been blamed either on human error, or on communication and system failures. Security breaches are increasingly occurring as a result of human error or ineffective procedures. Breaches commonly occur as a result of non-encrypted laptops, mislaid disks and a failure to dispose of customer details in a secure way. As many such breaches are not publicised, it is difficult to estimate how many businesses are affected by a physical breach of IT security. Increasingly however, businesses are facing the risk that in the event of a security breach they will suffer adverse publicity and may in some circumstances face sanctions from regulators. The Criminal Justice and Immigration Act creates tough new sanctions for the Information Commissioner's Office, which would give the ICO the power to impose substantial fines on organisations that deliberately or recklessly commit serious breaches of the Data Protection Act. These powers are not yet in force.

Malicious software

It is very likely that malicious software will attempt to attack your network. In April 2008 it was estimated that there are over one million viruses, worms and Trojans in circulation. Just over 711,000 new viruses were identified in 2007-08 – an increase of 468% on the number identified in the previous year. Popular malicious installations include key loggers that spring to life if particular websites are visited or programs, such as online games, are started up. However, it is also believed that malicious software authors are moving away from the mass mailing of viruses and instead are launching targeted attacks. It is believed that malicious software authors will increasingly target social networking sites, where individuals may be less wary of clicking on links. New viruses, worms and Trojan horses are being created all the time. In fact the vast majority of malicious software is

made possible by vulnerabilities in a small number of common operating system services. They count on organisations not fixing the problems, and they often attack indiscriminately, scanning the internet for any vulnerable systems. It is therefore important to ensure your system is always updated with the latest 'patches' released by the software developer. Unfortunately no firewall or scanning of viruses, worms and Trojan horses is capable of eliminating all risk from intrusion by malicious software.

Hacking

Again, no system is foolproof. Any network which has an external connectivity is open to the risk of hacking. Hacking may involve a variety of unacceptable activities, e.g. malicious file destruction, theft of money or intellectual property or a catastrophic denial of service attack.

Hacking is definitely on the increase, but it is difficult to find accurate figures because, like corporate fraud, most activity is not reported due to the embarrassment and damage to business reputation. For example, the Computer Misuse Act 1990 has been in force for 18 years, but, as there have only ever been a handful of successful prosecutions under this Act, it is clearly not providing a deterrent. The Police and Justice Act 2006 has introduced amendments to the Computer Misuse Act 1990 which would allow for tougher sentences. Although these changes are yet to come into force, it is hoped that by broadening the previous offences it will provide more of a deterrent to UK hackers. However, if these laws are to be a true deterrent, more organisations will have to report incidents and the police must be more willing to investigate and take on more cases. The biggest threat of hacking, however, is from inside a large organisation, and businesses should be particularly wary in times of economic lowdown. Unfortunately, staff that are laid off may become disgruntled and present a real security risk. Difficulties may also rise where an ex-supplier has control of the source code, passwords and so on.

Return on investment and risk management

Businesses take on financial risk with a view to making a return on their investment. However investing in IT security and in creating internal controls, does not in itself provide a direct return on investment – it is more about loss avoidance. Reducing the risk of a disastrous system failure will, however, contribute to the bottom line, because in the current climate, doing nothing or nothing much may ensure that the risk of a systems attack is realised.

It would be naïve to suggest that the risk of system intrusion or failure could be eliminated, but it can be properly managed. Indeed, it is worth bearing in mind that every director has a duty to manage serious corporate risk. As with most business risks, a judgement has to be made on:

- which risks can be reduced by using security products or services?
- which risks can be covered by insurance?
- which risks are to be borne by the organisation?

The proportion of risk in the first and last categories is to a large extent determined by the steps an organisation takes to protect its systems and equipment. In any event, it will need to keep its house in order if it is to avoid invalidating its insurance.

What do you need to do to protect your systems and equipment?

Whilst security technology is extremely important, IT security workplace managers should also ensure that they have other security measures in place to prevent or minimise the risk resulting from security breaches through human error, complacency or malice. There are many measures which are common sense and which should form part of your general security policy. Costs range from the minimal, where it is simply a case of more vigorously applying existing procedures, to the highly expensive, where the latest technology is implemented.

Physical security

Physical security measures are important to reduce the risk of intruders and theft of equipment. Some physical measures that should be adopted are as follows:

- Control and monitor access to your building properly using a record of visitors and badging. Also consider installing CCTV systems. Note, however, that CCTV must be used in a proportionate way (see 'CCTV monitoring', p.130).
- Require all staff to take responsibility for security by, for example, challenging 'strangers' out of hours and/or who appear in restricted or non-public areas.
- Make sure that the most important servers are situated in a secure and non-visible part of the premises, or perhaps even at another site.
- If appropriate, consider using biometrics (e.g. retina / iris scans, finger / handprint or facial feature scans, voice pattern scans, keystroke analysis) to identify those authorised to access the most sensitive equipment.
- Keep an inventory of computer equipment and carry out periodical stock checks.
- Staff using laptops and other portable computer equipment should be reminded to ensure that they keep the equipment secure at all times.

- Sensitive information and customer data held on laptops should be encrypted. The ICO expects computers containing personal data to be encrypted.
- Draft and circulate a policy to staff on what to do if their IT equipment is lost or stolen.

Basic system administration

Basic system administration measures include the following:

- Write a system security policy, require staff to apply it and police it. This policy should oblige staff to avoid opening emails and attachments when they do not know their origin. Restrict staff use of hotmail and similar web-based email services as these could increase the risk of virus attacks. Some organisations limit or ban their staff's use of social networking sites such as Facebook and MySpace due to the risk that malicious software may be inadvertently downloaded with video and other files.
- Oblige staff to follow instructions from their IT managers, such as warnings about current virus attacks.
- Segment the network with appropriate authorisation procedures to limit the number of IT support staff that have entire system access.
- Limit system privileges as much as possible and develop a hierarchy of access.
- Implement an effective password policy and require regular password changes.
- Keep the system 'patched' (updated) regularly.
- Warn staff to look out for scams. On the internet this is known as 'phishing' and is where an email is sent to a user claiming to be from the user's bank, for example, and requesting personal details.

Protective software and audit activity

These are some of the software protection and audit measures that can be employed

- Ensure that virus-sweeping software regularly updated across the network
- Carry out regular monitoring of the firewall and general network integrity.
- Use code review software and consider penetration testing (although workplace managers should note that there may be data protection implications if customer or staff data may be accessed during testing).

Staff issues

Whilst difficult to counter, there are a number of measures that businesses can take in order to protect themselves from fraud or malicious acts by staff members. As noted above, good systems administration plays a major part. Passwords should be protected and changed regularly, and access to sensitive systems carefully controlled. It has been found that staff committing fraudulent acts often fail to take time off (presumably for fear that they may be found out in their absence), so it is worth considering checking the leave records of key staff from time to time. Staff access to systems should be carefully controlled from the date of resignation until the person leaves when access should be immediately terminated. Access should be terminated immediately on dismissal.

What can you do to limit the damage if an incident does occur?

The following procedures and precautions are recommended:

- Ensure that your staff know who to contact in the event of a security breach and that the matter is escalated quickly.
- Implement an effective backup policy with secure off-site storage.

Have a contingency plan in place for restoring / recovering / recreating important data in the event of a disaster as well as malicious or negligent damage.

Ensure that forensic evidence is not destroyed in the course of the disaster response as this may deny recourse against the perpetrators or, more importantly, prevent discovery of what went wrong.

Document IP rights and, where relevant, secure software source code (both sensible business practice) to assist fast remedies in preventing unauthorised use by hackers.

■ Ensure that system security obligations are written into staff employment contracts to avoid arguments over what staff were required to do or not do.

Importance of security

Security is not just 'flavour of the month' in the IT world, but has been regarded as a serious issue for a number of years. As regulators' powers in this area are increased by the Information Commissioner, the stability and security of data is likely to be a business priority and an important part of workplace management.

> *See also*: Business Continuity Management, p.100; CCTV monitoring, p.130; Data protection, p.186; Internet and email policies, p.426; Monitoring employees, p.521; Confidential waste, p.716; WEEE: the Waste Electrical and Electronic Equipment Regulations and RoHS, p.744

Sources of further information

Workplace Law Group's *IT and Email Policy and Management Guide, v.2.0,* has been designed to alert employers of the potential problems associated with using computer systems, the Internet, and email systems within the workplace and to provide certain safeguards. For more information visit www.workplacelaw.net/Bookshop/PoliciesAndProcedures.

Jury service

Lisa Jinks and Robert Dillarstone, Greenwoods Solicitors LLP

Key points

- Jury service is a public duty. Those summoned must serve unless disqualified or if they have the right to be excused. There is also a limited right of deferment.
- Explain to the employees their rights in respect of jury service. This can be addressed in the contract of employment or staff handbook.
- Encourage employees to notify you as soon as they have been summoned for service as this will allow time to plan for absences.
- Ask employees to claim compensation for loss of earnings from the court.
- Keep a record of the dates that the employee will be absent from work.
- Provided you have obtained the written consent of the employee in advance, deduct from the employee's salary the allowance for days attended at court.
- If undue hardship would be caused, consider asking the employee to request a deferment.

Legislation

- Juries Act 1974.
- Employment Rights Act 1996.
- Criminal Justice Act 2003.

Jury selection

A jury is made up of 12 people, selected from the electoral roll at random by computer. Any person summoned for service is required by law to serve on the jury unless they are ineligible or disqualified. Jurors tend to be used in trials for serious offences such as murder, fraud and rape. The jury must consider the evidence and decide whether the defendant is innocent or guilty.

Eligibility

Individuals are eligible for jury service if they are aged between 18 and 70, registered on the electoral roll and have lived in the UK, Channel Islands or Isle of Man for at least five years since the age of 13. Many of the original categories of ineligibility have now been removed by legislation. However, an individual may be disqualified from serving if he/she:

- suffers from mental illness;
- knows the defendant, the judge, a solicitor or barrister or a witness involved in the trial;
- is on bail or has been on probation within the last five years; and/or
- has been sentenced to prison or community service within the last ten years.

Deferral

There is a general expectation that anyone summoned for jury service will serve as a juror at the time for which they are summoned. However, it is possible to apply for a deferment by application to the Jury Central Summoning Bureau. An application for deferral is discretionary and service can only be deferred once for up to 12 months from the date of the original summons.

Being excused from jury service

It is very rare for individuals to be excused from jury service. Ordinarily, a deferment will be sought wherever possible, as in the case of pre-arranged holidays. Application r excusal will be granted only in xceptional circumstances. Potential ounds include:

> jury service undertaken or attendance to serve as a juror during the previous two years;
> physical disability or illness;
> religious ideology or beliefs which are incompatible with jury service;
> valid business reason, for example, where a small business would suffer unusual hardship; and
> insufficient understanding of English.

oss of earnings

n average, jury service lasts ten working ays although this can vary considerably om a few days up to several months. ury service is not paid but jurors can ake a claim for their expenses. An mployee who loses earnings whilst erving as a juror can recoup such losses irect from the court, subject to the various urrent daily maximum amounts.

n receipt of a summons, employees hould ask their employer to complete a ertificate of Loss of Earnings (Form 5223) rovided by the court. Employers should eep a record of the dates of service nd arrange for a deduction from salary qual to the allowance for attendance at ourt. Employees are not entitled to their ormal salary payments during the period f jury service, unless their contract of mployment expressly provides otherwise.

Other expenses

Jurors may claim for their travelling expenses although they must obtain permission from the court before using a taxi. An allowance for food and drink can also be claimed. Child-minder or carer fees can be claimed but the court cannot pay more than the maximum allowance, which includes loss of earnings.

Employment rights

Employers are required by law to allow employees (but not workers) to have unpaid time off work to complete jury service. Failure to do so could result in a fine or even imprisonment for the employer. If employees are concerned that jury service will conflict with work commitments, they can apply for a deferral or excusal (employers cannot apply on the employee's behalf).

The employee's continuity of service is preserved during jury service which means that they continue to benefit from existing rights and accrue rights gained by virtue of their length of service. Employees (but not workers) also have a right not to be subjected to any detriment (including dismissal) by their employers on the grounds that they have been summoned for jury service or have been absent from work because they have been summoned. Any dismissal by the employer of an employee who has undertaken jury service will usually be automatically unfair. The employee does not require one year's continuous service to claim unfair dismissal in such circumstances.

Sources of further information

Her Majesty's Court Service: www.hmcourts-service.gov.uk

Criminal Justice System online: www.cjsonline.gov.uk

Jury Central Summoning Bureau: 0845 8038 003 (local rate) 9.00 a.m. to 5.00 p.m. Monday to Friday

Ladders

Jagdeep Tiwana, Berwin Leighton Paisner

Key points

One third of all falls from height involve ladders and stepladders. Such accidents account for 14 deaths and 1,400 injuries each year. The Health and Safety Executive (HSE) considers that misuse of ladders in the workplace is in part due to the way they are used in the home. It has therefore issued a guide for employers on the safe use of ladders and stepladders.

Legislation

- Health and Safety at Work etc. Act 1974.
- Manual Handling Operations Regulations 1992.
- Reporting of Injuries, Diseases and Dangerous Occurrences Regulations 1995 (RIDDOR).
- Provision and Use of Work Equipment Regulations 1998.
- Management of Health and Safety at Work Regulations 1999.
- The Work at Height Regulations 2005 (as amended).

Main legal duties

The Health and Safety at Work etc. Act 1974 imposes a duty on all employers to take steps to ensure the health and safety of all employees and third parties. The duty includes taking steps to control risks to such persons when using ladders or stepladders.

The Work at Height Regulations 2005 (as amended) go further by stating that an employer must ensure that a ladder is used for work at height only where a risk assessment under Regulation 3 of the Management of Health and Safety at Work Regulations 1999 has been carried out. For the use of ladders to be permitted, the risk assessment must show that the use of more suitable work equipment is not

justified because there is a low risk and the work will be of short duration or there are existing features on site which the employer cannot alter.

The hierarchy of control

The HSE advises that the first step in the safe use of ladders or stepladders is to assess whether this is the most suitable access equipment, taking into account the 'hierarchy of control', as set out in the Work at Height Regulations 2005 (as amended). The hierarchy of control requires that:

- work at height is avoided wherever possible;
- where it cannot be avoided, work at height should be carried out using equipment or measures that prevent falls from height; and
- where is it not possible to prevent falls from height, work equipment or other measures should minimise the distance and consequences of a fall should one occur.

Once it has been established that work at height is necessary, an assessment should be carried out as to whether a ladder or stepladder is the most suitable access equipment compared with other options. See *'Working at height', p.395* for further details of what is required under the Work at Height Regulations.

Selection of ladders

Only those ladders and stepladders that have sufficient stability should be used (taking into account the worse case scenario and worst type of surface conditions to be encountered). The HSE recommends Class 1 Industrial or EN131 ladders or stepladders for use at work. Ladders and stepladders should also be stored and maintained in accordance with manufacturer's instructions.

Safe places for using ladders or stepladders

Ladders or stepladders should only be used on firm and level ground or clean, solid non-slippery surfaces, free from oil, moss or loose material so the feet can grip and where:

■ they can be secured;
■ the restraint devices can be fully opened and any locking devices engaged; and
■ they can be put up at the correct angle of 75˚.

Ladders should not be allowed to rest against weak upper surfaces (e.g. glazing or plastic gutters).

Ladders used for access to another level should be tied and stepladders should not be used for this purpose unless designed for such use.

Ladders or stepladders should only be used in areas where they will not be struck by vehicles (and should be protected with suitable barriers or cones if necessary). They should also not be used in locations where they could be pushed over by other hazards such as doors or windows. If this is impractical, the HSE advises that a person should stand guard at the doorway, or inform workers not to open windows until they are told to do so.

Safety checks

It is imperative to establish that the ladder or stepladder is in a safe condition before it is used. A daily pre-use check should be carried out. A ladder or stepladder should only be used if it has no visible defects. Checks should be carried out in accordance with manufacturer's instructions and should include checks to ensure:

■ the ladder or stepladder is suitable for work use. (Class 1 or EN 131 ladders or stepladders. Domestic Class 3 ladders or stepladders are not normally suitable for use at work);
■ ladder stability devices and other accessories are in working order;
■ ladder and stepladder feet are in good repair (not loose, missing, splitting, excessively worn, secure etc.) and clean (as these are essential for preventing the base of the ladder slipping). Ladder feet should also be checked when moving from soft/dirty ground (e.g. dug soil, loose sand/stone, a dirty workshop) to a smooth, solid surface (e.g. paving slabs), to ensure the foot material and not the dirt (e.g. soil or, embedded stones) is making contact with the ground; and
■ the ladder or stepladder has been maintained and stored in accordance with the manufacturer's instructions.

All ladder or stepladder checks should be recorded. Ladders that are part of a scaffold system need to be inspected every seven days.

Use of ladders and stepladders

There are a number of factors which should be taken into account when using ladders or stepladders. These are set out below:

- Ladders or stepladders should only be used for light (not strenuous) work and should be in one position for a maximum of 30 minutes.
- Wherever possible, a handhold should be available. Where this cannot be maintained (either at all or for a brief period of time only), other measures will be required to prevent a fall or reduce the consequence should a fall occur.
- In relation to stepladders, where a handhold is not practicable, a risk assessment will be needed to justify whether use of the stepladder without a handhold is safe or not.
- The user should be able to maintain three points (hands and feet) of contact at the working position.
- The user should never overreach and should keep both feet on the same rung.
- The user should never overload the ladder or stepladder, i.e. the person and whatever they are taking up should not exceed the ladder's maximum load.
- A detailed manual handling assessment will be required where a worker is carrying more than 10kg up the ladder or steps.
- The user should avoid working in a way which imposes a side loading – the steps should face the work activity wherever possible.
- The user should avoid holding items when climbing, for example by using a belt.

Training

Employees should only use a ladder or stepladder if they are competent. Users should be trained and instructed in how to use ladders and stepladders safely. They should also know how to inspect a ladder before using it and should in particular be aware of the following:

- The need to ensure that the ladder or stepladder is long enough.

- In the case of ladders, the top three rungs should not be used and ladders used for access should project at least one metre above the landing point and be tied. Alternatively, a safe and secure handhold should be available.
- In the case of stepladders, the top two steps of a stepladder should not be used unless a suitable handrail is available on the stepladder and the top three steps of swing-back or double-sided stepladders should not be used where a step forms the very top of the stepladder.
- The ladder or stepladder rungs or steps must be level. This can be judged by the naked eye. (Ladders can be levelled using specially designed devices but not by using bits of brick or whatever else is at hand).
- The weather should be suitable – ladders and stepladders should not be used in strong or gusting winds (the manufacturer's safe working practices should be followed).
- Users should wear robust, sensible footwear (e.g. safety shoes / boots or trainers). Shoes should not have the soles hanging off, have long or dangling laces, or slippery contaminants on them.
- Users should be fit – certain medical conditions or medication, alcohol or drug abuse could stop them from using ladders.
- Users should know how to tie a ladder or stepladder properly.

When using a ladder or stepladder, users should not:

- move it while standing on the rungs / steps;
- support it by the rungs or steps at the base;
- slide down the stiles;
- stand it on moveable objects, such as pallets, bricks, tower scaffolds, excavator buckets, vans or mobile elevating work platforms; or

■ extend a ladder while standing on the rungs.

Electricity

Ladders or stepladders should never be used within six metres horizontally of any overhead power lines, unless the line owner has made them dead or protected them with temporary insulation. If this is a regular activity, the employer should ascertain whether the lines can be moved. Non-conductive ladders or steps should always be used for any necessary electrical work.

> *See also*: Construction site health and safety, p.154; Head protection, p.362; Health and safety at work, p.364; Working at height, p.395; Risk assessments, p.639; Slips, trips and falls, p.657; Work equipment, p.761

Sources of further information

INDG402 – *Safe use of ladders and stepladders: An employer's guide*
www.hse.gov.uk/pubns/indg402.pdf

INDG 405 – *Top Tips for ladder and stepladder safety*
www.hse.gov.uk/pubns/indg405.pdf

HSE: www.hse.gov.uk

Landlord and tenant: possession issues

Michael Smith, Pinsent Masons

Key points

- The Landlord and Tenant Act 1954 (as amended by the Regulatory Reform (Business Tenancies) (England and Wales) Order 2003) gives certain tenants of business premises the right to remain in occupation of their premises after the term of their lease expires and to apply to court for a new tenancy of those premises.

- A lease with the protection of the 'security of tenure' provisions in the Act will continue beyond the contractual termination date of the lease until either the landlord or the tenant serves a notice under the Act to bring it to an end (or a surrender of the lease is agreed).

- Following the service of notice under the Act either the landlord or the tenant is entitled to apply to the court for a new lease to be ordered. The tenant will be entitled to a new lease unless the landlord is able successfully to apply to terminate the lease or to oppose an application by the tenant for a new lease on one or more of the grounds set out in the Act (see below).

- The Act does not protect a tenant who does not continue to occupy the premises for business purposes. Failure by a tenant to observe its lease covenants could also entitle a landlord to oppose the renewal of the tenant's lease.

Legislation

- Landlord and Tenant Act 1954 (as amended by the Regulatory Reform (Business Tenancies) (England and Wales) Order 2003) (the Act).

Landlord's notice (section 25)

A landlord of business premises can take steps to terminate a business tenancy by serving on the tenant a notice under section 25 of the Landlord and Tenant Act. The landlord must give between six and 12 months' notice to the tenant and stipulate in the notice a termination date not earlier than the contractual termination date of the lease.

A landlord must use the appropriate form of notice or a 'form substantially to the same effect' and the landlord should take care to use the correct version of the form depending on whether the landlord does or does not oppose the grant of a new tenancy to the tenant.

If the landlord does not oppose the grant of a new tenancy to the tenant, he must set out his proposals for the terms of the new tenancy including the property to be demised, the new rent, and other terms in the schedule attached to the notice itself. If the landlord does oppose the tenant's right to a new lease, the ground(s) of opposition must be stated in the notice (see below).

Tenant's notice (section 26)

It is also possible for a tenant to start the lease renewal process by serving on the landlord a request for a new tenancy under section 26 of the Act.

The request must state the date on which the new tenancy is to begin, which must be between six and 12 months after the making of the request and not earlier than the contractual expiry date of the lease. If the landlord wishes to oppose any application by the tenant for a new lease lease of the Premises, he must serve a counter-notice within two months, stating the ground(s) of opposition on which the landlord intends to rely.

Applications to Court

At any time after the service of the landlord's section 25 notice and up until the termination date stipulated in the notice itself (or where the tenant has served a section 26 request, any time after the landlord has served a valid counter-notice and up to the date immediately before the date specified in the section 26 request) the tenant is able to make an application to court for a new tenancy of the premises.

Alternatively, if the tenant has not made an application to court and the landlord does not oppose the grant of a new tenancy to the tenant, the landlord can make an application to court itself for the grant of a new tenancy to the tenant.

Where there has been no application by the tenant or the landlord to renew the lease and the landlord has served a section 25 notice (or counter-notice to a section 26 request) stating that he is opposed to the grant of a new tenancy the landlord may apply to court for a termination order.' This is an order by the court that the lease be terminated.

The Act specifies that the deadline for making any of these applications is the date specified in the landlord's section 25 notice or the tenant's section 26 request.

This 'statutory period' can, however, be extended by written agreement between the landlord and tenant before the current deadline expires. There is no limit in the Act on the length of the extensions to the statutory period that can be agreed between landlord and tenant or the number of extensions that can be agreed.

Grounds of opposition

The seven grounds of opposition, which entitle the landlord to oppose the grant of a new lease if he can prove one or more of them, are:

1. tenant's failure to repair;
2. tenant's persistent delay in paying rent;
3. substantial breaches of other covenants by tenant;
4. landlord willing to provide suitable alternative accommodation;
5. tenancy is of part only and the landlord wishes to let property as a whole;
6. landlord intends to demolish or reconstruct the premises; and/or
7. landlord intends to occupy premises for his own business.

Grounds (1), (2), (3) and (5) confer a discretion on the court whether or not to order a new tenancy even if the ground is made out.

Grounds (4), (6) and (7) are not discretionary. If the landlord proves the requirements of the ground, the court must refuse to order a new tenancy.

If the landlord successfully opposes the grant of a new lease on grounds (5), (6) or (7), it is required to pay compensation to the tenant equivalent to one times or two times the rateable value of the premises as at the date of service of the landlord's section 25 notice or the tenant's section 26 request.

Excluding security of tenure

It is possible for the landlord and tenant of business premises to agree to exclude the security of tenure provisions of the Act in respect of a business lease by following the exclusion procedure described in the Act.

In summary, the landlord must serve a prescribed form of notice on the tenant not less than 14 days before the tenant enters into the tenancy, or becomes contractually bound to do so. The tenant (or a person authorised by the tenant) must then make a declaration in the prescribed form (or substantially in that form) before he enters into the tenancy or becomes contractually obliged to do so.

If the landlord's notice is given less than 14 days before the tenant enters the tenancy or becomes contractually obliged to do so, the tenant (or a person authorised on his behalf) must make a statutory declaration in a prescribed form which must be sworn before a solicitor or commissioner for oaths.

Once the 'security of tenure' provisions of the Act have been excluded in this way, the procedures described above concerning the service of notices and the making of an application to court will not apply and the tenant must leave the premises when the contractual term of the lease expires.

Forfeiture

The 'security of tenure' provided by the Act does not protect a tenant who commits breaches of the lease and leases invariably contain a forfeiture clause which allows the landlord to terminate the lease in the event of certain acts of default by the tenant.

There are two ways in which a landlord can forfeit a lease, either by:

1. issuing and serving court proceedings on the tenant for possession of the premises; or
2. by 'peaceable re-entry' whereby the landlord re-enters the premises and takes back possession by changing the locks.

Where the breach involves a failure to pay rent, the landlord will ordinarily have a contractual right under the lease to forfeit (by peaceable re-entry) after a period of usually 14 or 21 days from when the rent fell due.

Where the breach involves something other than non-payment of rent, the landlord must serve a notice on the tenant under section 146 of the Law of Property Act 1925, which notifies the tenant of the breach; requires it to be remedied within a reasonable time (if the breach is capable of remedy); and requires the tenant to pay compensation for the breach. If the tenant still fails to remedy the breach within a reasonable time, the landlord can at that stage proceed to forfeit the lease, either by peaceable re-entry or the service of proceedings at the landlord's election.

Following forfeiture, the tenant (or any sub-tenant) does have the right to apply to court to ask for 'relief from forfeiture', which is effectively an order that the lease be reinstated. This is a discretionary remedy of the court which will normally be granted provided that the tenant's breaches are remedied and the landlord's costs are paid. The court does, however, have a very wide discretion to impose, as a condition of granting relief, whatever other conditions it considers appropriate in the circumstances.

Peaceable re-entry / waiver

Peaceable re-entry can be perceived as an aggressive and sometimes risky step for a landlord to take. Before taking this

Workplace Law Network
www.workplacelaw.net

step (or serving a section 146 notice), a landlord must ensure he has not 'waived' the right to forfeit a lease, for instance, by demanding or accepting rent after a breach has been committed by the landlord.

f a landlord does attempt to re-enter the premises once the right to forfeit has been waived, the re-entry will be unlawful and the landlord may be sued for damages by the tenant who has been unlawfully

excluded from the premises. A landlord also has a duty of care in respect of any items belonging to the tenant which remain in the premises after a re-entry.

It is a criminal offence for a landlord to re-enter if he is aware that someone is in the premises who is resisting the landlord's re-entry. The landlord cannot peaceably re-enter residential premises and must obtain an order from the court to recover possession.

See also: Landlord and tenant: lease issues, p.448

Sources of further information

Workplace Law Network provides premium members with unrestricted access to a comprehensive range of online information – factsheets, case reports and daily news items – on employment, health and safety and premises management. Members also benefit from an online advice service and a free subscription to the *Workplace Law Magazine*. For more information email membership@ workplacelaw.net or call our membership services team on 0871 777 8881.

Landlord and tenant: lease issues

Kevin Boa, Pinsent Masons

Key points

- Leases are documents which pass exclusive legal possession / control or exclusive occupation of land or premises for an agreed period in return for rent, usually paid monthly or quarterly.
- The landlord (who is not necessarily the freeholder) retains his title and receives the rent.
- The tenant pays the rent and enters into covenants (obligations) restricting and regulating his use of the premises, and other aspects as well as positive obligations including repairs and decoration.
- A lease may be transferred to a new tenant subject to restrictions within the lease. Usually the landlord's consent is required but is not to be unreasonably withheld.

Legislation

- Law of Property Act 1925.
- Landlord and Tenant Act 1927.
- Leasehold Property (Repairs) Act 1938.
- Landlord and Tenant Act 1954.
- Landlord and Tenant Act 1985.
- Landlord and Tenant Act 1988.
- Landlord and Tenant (Covenants) Act 1995.
- Land Registration Act 2002.
- Commonhold and Leasehold Reform Act 2002.

Advantages of leases

The granting or taking of a lease is an alternative to holding a freehold interest in property. There may be the following advantages to both parties:

- The landlord retains an interest in the property.
- The landlord can enforce both positive and negative obligations against the tenant.
- The lease may have investment value to the landlord, with the payment of rent creating an income stream.

- Payment of rent at regular intervals may be a more manageable cost to the tenant than raising finance to acquire the freehold.
- The tenant can have flexibility as to the duration of his interest in the property.
- Leases are an effective means of splitting up the disposal of a multi-occupied building.

Heads of terms

- Heads of terms may be agreed by the parties before a lease or agreement for lease is entered into.
- Heads of terms represent agreement in principle as to the basic matters to be contained within the lease and any other related documents. The more detailed the heads of terms, the less argument there will be in agreeing the terms of the lease.
- Heads of terms will generally not be legally binding between the parties, although, at a practical level, they may be difficult to renegotiate once specific principles have been agreed.

Workplace Law Network
www.workplacelaw.net

It is therefore important for a landlord or tenant to involve surveyors and lawyers at an early stage.

The surveyor

Commercial property surveyors will generally represent each party's interest, and each party will usually pay his own surveyor's fees on the grant of a lease.

The surveyors will advise their clients on and negotiate such matters as:

the premises to be let;
amount of the rent;
length of the lease;
options to break the lease early;
whether the tenant has statutory security of tenure;
rent reviews;
rights over common parts;
management of the building;
parking;
use of the premises;
restrictions on assignment;
who is responsible for repairs;
insurance responsibilities; and
tenant's guarantee.

These should all be covered in the heads of terms.

Agreement for lease

The parties may enter into an agreement for lease in advance of the lease itself being granted. An agreement for lease is simply a contract between the parties for the landlord to grant and the tenant to accept a lease at a future date or following certain agreed conditions being satisfied within a set period.

The form of the lease has to be agreed and attached to the agreement for lease. Once an agreement for lease has been exchanged, neither party may unilaterally withdraw from the transaction without being in breach of contract (see *'Buying and selling property'*, p.110).

Leases for three years or less taking immediate effect do not have to be in writing. However, oral leases are highly undesirable.

An agreement for lease can have advantages to both parties:

■ It creates certainty that the lease will be granted, on the given date or on satisfaction of any relevant conditions. This assists both parties in forward planning.
■ The agreement for lease represents a tangible asset for the landlord from an investment perspective, and the tenant will be able to prepare for his future occupation of the property.
■ A landlord may wish to be sure he has a tenant for his premises before acquiring them or carrying out works to them.

Conditional agreement

An agreement for lease may be made conditional on any matters which either party requires to be satisfied before being obliged to complete the lease. Examples include:

■ obtaining planning permission;
■ carrying out of works by one of the parties;
■ obtaining consents needed under a superior lease; and
■ obtaining a licence to carry out the tenant's business (e.g. sale of alcohol).

Where an agreement for lease is conditional, the terms of the conditions are of fundamental importance. It is important that surveyors' and legal advice is obtained.

Principal issues in the lease

Parties
The lease will be granted by the landlord (or lessor) to the tenant (or lessee). The

landlord will want to be satisfied that the proposed tenant has the financial status to pay the rent and other sums due under the lease and to perform the various tenant's covenants.

Generally speaking, from an investment standpoint, the stronger the tenant the more valuable the lease will be to the landlord.

The landlord will usually want to see evidence of the tenant's financial status. This may include, for instance, providing copies of accounts and references. If the tenant is a new company without a proven track record, or is not perceived to be financially strong, the landlord may require additional security, such as third-party guarantees or a rent deposit.

Property to be leased
The lease will need to clearly define the extent of the premises. This is particularly the case where the letting is only part of a building. Relevant issues include the extent to which parts of the exterior, roof, foundations and other structural parts are to be included or excluded. This will also affect the tenant's repairing obligations, which will generally be by reference to the extent of the premises that are leased. Access and parking must also be agreed.

Term
The length of the term is a basic issue which is likely to affect the other terms of the lease. From the tenant's standpoint, the length of term will be influenced by the tenant's need for the premises in question, and any plans that the tenant may have for the future. New lease accounting standards may have an impact on the length of the term and the tenant's obligation to pay stamp duty land tax, which can be considerable in the case of longer leases (e.g. SDLT for commercial premises with a rent of £100,000 a year

plus VAT will cost the tenant over £15,000 for a 20-year lease, under £4,000 for a five-year lease and zero for a one-year lease). Break rights do not reduce the tax.

From the landlord's perspective, a longer lease, with regular upwards-only rent reviews, will be more valuable from an investment standpoint, creating greater certainty as to the landlord's future income stream and an enhanced capital value.

Security of tenure
Subject to specific exclusions, business leases granted for more than six months benefit from security of tenure under the Landlord and Tenant Act 1954. This entitles the tenant to the grant of a new lease at the end of the original agreed term, unless the landlord has specific grounds to resist this right. The landlord can, subject to restrictions, override the tenant's rights on various grounds including showing an intention to demolish or reconstruct the property and requiring possession for its own business.

Subject to these and other exceptions and to the tenant complying with various procedural requirements, the courts have power to intervene if the parties cannot agree on a new lease.

As the procedures for invoking these rights are both complex and prescriptive, it is important that you seek legal advice on any proposed renewal at the relevant time.

Contracting out
It is possible for the parties to contract out of the security of tenure provisions in the lease. To do so, the landlord must send a notice to the tenant which is in a prescribed form. The notice explains the effect of contracting out of the security of tenure provisions. Two weeks later the tenant must sign a declaration to the effect that he has understood the terms

f the notice and has agreed to contract
ut of security of tenure. The two-week
eriod can be waived if the tenant
igns a statutory declaration before an
idependent solicitor.

Contracting out of security of tenure
s an important issue in negotiating a
ew lease and obtaining legal advice is
ecommended.

Licences

t is sometimes suggested that the landlord
an prevent the Landlord and Tenant
\ct 1954 from applying by granting an
ccupation licence instead of a lease, so
hat the tenant does not have exclusive
ossession of the property which he
ccupies. Licences are to be treated with
aution as such arrangements cannot
e guaranteed to be legally effective.
lowever, they are often used for short-
erm arrangements in business centres.

Break options

ither the landlord or the tenant may be
ranted a right to terminate the lease
efore the expiry of the agreed term.
From a landlord's standpoint, break
ptions granted to a tenant may reduce
he investment value of the lease.

\ tenant may, nevertheless, want the
lexibility to terminate the lease early,
ither at a fixed date or dates, or possibly
hrough a rolling break on or after a given
eriod during the term.

he landlord may expect some incentive to
agree to this, in the form of a higher rent
or a compensation payment if the tenant
subsequently exercises the break right.

Many landlords seek to impose conditions
on the exercise of tenants' break rights,
.g. performance of tenant's covenants.
These are strictly construed and constitute
a trap for the unwary tenant as they can
ender the break right illusory.

Superior leases

If the landlord does not own the freehold
to the property, but instead occupies the
premises under an existing lease, then
it will be necessary for a tenant to take
account of the terms of any superior
leases. This will be important for the
following reasons:

- He must ensure that the superior lease lasts longer than the new underlease.
- The superior lease(s) may require that consents are obtained from the superior landlord(s), in order to permit the underlease to the undertenant, or to permit other matters such as changing the use or carrying out alterations.
- The landlord may want to pass on obligations under the superior lease by requiring the undertenant to perform these. From an undertenant's standpoint this may not be acceptable or reasonable. For example, repairing or service charge obligations in a superior lease may be geared to a much longer term than the sublease.
- Where the superior lease contains restrictions affecting the use or occupation of the premises, the undertenant will generally be subject to these same restrictions. It is important, therefore, that an undertenant knows what these are and that it is able to comply with them.
- An undertenant will want to ensure that its intermediate landlord does not breach its obligations to its superior landlord(s), as this could give rise to a potential forfeiture action by the superior landlord, which in turn could prejudice the undertenant's position.

Rent

Rent is important for both the landlord and
the tenant. It affects the affordability of the
premises to the tenant and the income
stream received by the landlord.

It is common for rents of commercial properties to be calculated by reference to a rate per square foot. In addition to the rate itself, the basis of measurement will need to be agreed. Surveyors commonly measure a premises on either a net or gross basis. Your surveyor or solicitor will be able to advise you further on these issues. Other issues to consider include the following:

- Is the tenant to receive an initial rent-free period? This is particularly common where the tenant needs to carry out fitting-out works.
- Is the rent exclusive or inclusive of other payments, such as insurance premiums or service charges? Exclusive rents are most common in commercial leases, but a rent that is inclusive of insurance premiums and service charges may be appropriate for both parties on a short-term letting or where the premises are a small part of a much larger building.
- Will value-added tax be payable on the rent?

Rent reviews

If the lease is for more than five years, it is common for the landlord to require the rent to be reviewed at periodic intervals. The most common review cycle in today's market is for five-yearly reviews, although other cycles as frequent as three-yearly are sometimes agreed. It should be noted, however, that cycles more frequently than every five years can increase the tenant's stamp duty land tax costs.

Rents can be reviewed by reference to a fixed percentage increase or to an index such as the Retail Price Index. The most common system, however, remains upward-only review to the open market rent at the relevant review date. On each review date the rent becomes the rent which a new tenant would pay for those premises.

'Upward only' means that the rent will be increased to the open market rent, but, if rental values stay the same or fall during the review period, the rent will remain the same and will not fall. This means that the landlord's income stream is protected against falls in rental value in the future. Although the Government is keen to promote flexibility in the letting market, including 'upward or downward' reviews, this has yet to receive general acceptance. However, for the time being the threat of legislation in this area has receded.

Tenant's covenants

The issues of most frequent concern are as follows:

Permitted use

The landlord will generally want to restrict the use of the premises to a given category of use or uses (such as retail or office), to allow him to retain some control. If the permitted use is too restrictive, then this could have adverse rent review consequences for the landlord. The tenant needs to check that the permitted use gives sufficient flexibility for its present purposes and for any changes which might be needed in the future or for an assignee.

Alterations

The degree of control over alterations required by the landlord is likely to be influenced by the nature of the building and the length of the term. A landlord will not want the tenant to have the ability to carry out alterations which may adversely affect the future letting of the premises, and may also require the tenant to reinstate any alterations at the end of the term. The tenant will, again, need to ensure there is sufficient flexibility for any changes which may be needed, either now or in the future.

A distinction may be drawn, for instance, between alterations affecting either

e structure or the exterior (which are
generally barred) and those, such as the
erection of internal partitioning, that affect
only the interior and are non-structural
which are generally permitted with the
landlord's consent).

epairs

The lease will govern the extent to which
the parties are liable for repairs. An
institutional landlord will frequently want
the lease to be on a full repairing and
insuring basis (known as an FRI lease).
The tenant would be responsible for any
repairs which arise during the term, and
the landlord would be entitled to have the
premises back at the end of the term –
sometimes these would be in a better state
of repair and condition than they were at
the start. Conversely, a tenant may look to
limit his repairing obligations, particularly if
the lease is for a relatively short term and
the tenant's interest is therefore limited.

Other issues to consider include the
following:

- Should there be a schedule of
  condition attached to the lease,
  providing evidence of the premises'
  condition at the start of the lease,
  and for the tenant's obligations to be
  limited accordingly?
- With new or recently constructed
  premises, will the tenant have the
  benefit of warranties from the building
  contractor, services subcontractor
  and professionals responsible for
  the design of the premises and
  supervision of the work?
- The tenant may seek to avoid
  liability for inherent defects, covering
  defects arising from deficiencies
  in the building's initial design or
  construction.

When considering repairing obligations,
it is important to bear in mind not only

the tenant's obligations to repair the
premises themselves, but also its liability
to contribute to the cost of repairs to other
parts of the building through the service
charge.

Assignment and subletting

Unless there are special circumstances,
such as a very short term or very generous
break rights, a tenant will generally want
the ability to assign the remaining period
of the lease to a third party, or possibly to
underlet either the whole or part. When the
lease is assigned, the assignee becomes
the landlord's tenant. A landlord will wish
to keep control over who can occupy the
premises in the future and to know that
any substituted tenant will be able to pay
the rent. The landlord will always require
the right to approve any new tenant or
undertenant, but most leases stipulate that
such approval cannot be unreasonably
withheld.

Insurance

The lease should state who is responsible
for insuring the premises and who pays
the premiums. The landlord will frequently
want to retain control for insuring the
building but to pass on the premium, or
an appropriate proportion of it, to the
tenant. This is particularly the case in
a multi-occupied building or where the
landlord has a portfolio of properties
which are insured on a block policy. If
there is a superior lease, this may also
specify insurance requirements. A landlord
will also want there to be loss-of-rent
insurance so that the landlord's income
stream is maintained if the premises are
damaged or destroyed so as to be unfit for
occupation. The tenant normally pays the
cost of this.

In recent years there has been a debate
with regard to uninsurable risks, in
particular terrorism or flooding in a flood

plain area. Currently most leases do not permit suspension of rent or termination by the tenant in such circumstances. Unless leases are amended, there is considerable risk to the tenant.

Position following destruction or damage

The parties need to consider whether either the landlord or the tenant (or both) should have any rights to terminate the lease if the premises are destroyed by an insured risk. If the lease is not terminated, the tenant will want to ensure that rent due is suspended and that the landlord has an obligation to reinstate the premises as quickly as possible so that the tenant can resume occupation.

Service charge

The lease may require the tenant to pay a 'service charge'. This is particularly common in the case of a multi-occupied building, which may include common parts, or where there are services such as security, reception facilities or cleaning. The service charge may also cover repairs and maintenance to the building as a whole, so that each of the tenants contributes an appropriate proportion of these costs. Service charge provisions are also common where premises are part of a larger estate, such as a retail or industrial park. In those instances, where there are other services such as car parking facilities, additional security and landscaped areas, the service charge payable by each tenant can be a considerable sum.

Particular issues include:

- the services that the landlord is required to provide;
- the basis of calculation of the cost and the likely amount of each payment;
- the method of payment;

- the ability of the landlord to vary, add to or suspend services;
- the ability of the landlord to set up a fund for anticipated capital expenditure;
- the tenant's right to check the landlord's expenditure; and
- any cap on the level of the service charge.

With commercial property, there are no statutory restrictions limiting the level of service charge which can be imposed, or requiring the landlord to undertake services at the most competitive cost. Issues such as these need to be dealt with in the drafting of the lease. The landlord's ability to pass on particular costs needs to be examined carefully against the length of the lease and the condition of the building (and sometimes the estate) of which it forms part.

Assignment of an existing lease

The lease may be sold or transferred, possibly at a price according to its value, to a new tenant (known as the 'assignee'). It is likely that consents will be needed from the landlord, in relation both to the assignment itself and to any changes that the new tenant wishes to make, such as changing the use of the property, or making alterations. The landlord will usually want his fees paid by the tenant, who may try to pass the cost on to the assignee.

The terms of the assignment need to be agreed between the assignor and the assignee – this is similar to the arrangements outlined in *'Buying and selling property', p.110.*

The tenant will usually have no right to renegotiate the terms of the lease itself at this stage to accommodate the assignee.

In leases granted before 1996 the tenant will remain liable to the landlord for performance of the covenants in the lease

ven after the lease is assigned. Generally
is is not the case for leases granted
ter 1995, but the tenant may still have
 guarantee the immediate assignee's
erformance of the covenants in the lease.
his is a complex area of law on which
gal advice should be taken.

and registration

eases of seven or more years must
e registered at the Land Registry.
xceptionally shorter leases must also
e registered where there are express
ghts within them over other property (e.g.
ommon parts or services) as otherwise
ese rights are not enforceable. From
id-2006 registered leases have been
equired to contain certain prescribed
lauses otherwise the Land Registry will
efuse to deal with them.

Key questions

. Preliminary issues

- Is a new lease to be granted or will
  the tenant acquire an existing one? If
  it is an existing lease:
  - Is there a superior lease?
  - Are any consents required from
    the freeholder or from superior
    landlords?
  - What professional advice will be
    needed to assist in the negotiation
    of the heads of terms and the
    lease documentation?
- Generally, has the proposed landlord
  or assignor a proper title?

2. Is an agreement for lease necessary or desirable?

- When does the tenant want to
  occupy?
- Are there any conditions which need
  to be satisfied before the lease can be
  granted or assigned?

- Are any works required prior to the
  grant or assignment of the lease?
- If works are required, who will carry
  them out, and at whose cost?

3. What are the costs?

- Surveyor's fees.
- Legal costs.
- Search fees.
- Survey / valuation fees.
- Stamp duty land tax.

4. Rent and other payments

- What is the initial rent? Will there be a
  rent-free period?
- Are there to be rent reviews? If so, at
  what intervals and on what basis?
- Are there any other expenses such
  as service charges and insurance
  premiums?
- Is there a premium?
- Is VAT payable? Can the tenant
  recover this?

5. Terms of the lease

- Who will be the landlord and the tenant?
- Does the landlord require guarantors
  or other security?
- What will be the contractual term?
- Will the tenant have security of
  tenure?
- Will either party get break rights?
- What is the extent of the property to
  be let?
- Does the lease provide sufficient
  control for the landlord, and sufficient
  flexibility to the tenant, as to issues
  such as permitted use, alterations and
  alienation?
- What are the arrangements
  concerning insurance and following
  events of damage or destruction?
- What services will the landlord be
  responsible for carrying out?
- What will the tenant have to contribute
  by way of service charge?

See also: Buying and selling property, p.110; Dilapidations, p.193; Landlord and tenant: possession issues p.444

Sources of further information

Workplace Law Network provides premium members with unrestricted access to a comprehensive range of online information – factsheets, case reports and daily news items – on employment, health and safety and premises management. Members also benefit from an online advice service and a free subscription to the *Workplace Law Magazine*. For more information email membership@workplacelaw.net or call our membership services team on 0871 777 8881.

Leave

Michelle Billingsley, Martineau Solicitors

Key points

- Adopting carefully defined policies that formalise practices on compassionate leave, time off for dependants and sabbatical leave can help employers promote fair and consistent treatment of their employees.
- Preparing a written policy is also a good opportunity for employers to clarify their attitudes and approach to sensitive issues which, in turn, should help to increase staff morale and wellbeing.
- Employers should avoid the implication of a contractual right to compassionate leave, sabbatical leave and time off for dependants, unless this is clearly intended.

Legislation

- Section 57A(1)(C) of the Employment Rights Act 1996.
- Employment Equality (Religion or Belief) Regulations 2003.

Case law

Forster v. Cartwright Black (2004) IRLR 781

What is compassionate leave?

Compassionate leave is a term used to describe a period of time off work (either paid or unpaid) that an employer allows an employee who is faced with difficult personal circumstances, such as the death of a family member.

Whilst employees are not legally entitled to compassionate leave as a result of a bereavement, employers should take a serious and sympathetic view of requests for time off following the death of a dependant or family member.

Practical tips

- Ensure that policies are applied consistently and fairly to all employees.
- Set out a clear reporting structure in the event that compassionate leave is needed (i.e. supervisor / Head of HR).
- Ensure that bad news affecting an employee is communicated promptly but sensitively to the rest of the team or department and that workloads are delegated effectively.
- Recognise that employees affected by bereavement may not be able to comply rigidly with a policy (i.e. often death and emergencies will be unexpected and employees will not be able to report his/her absence straight away or may not feel emotionally able to make the call to HR personally).
- Arrange a 'return to work interview' with the affected employee.
- Employees who develop psychological illness following a bereavement may find themselves needing to extend their periods of compassionate leave with sickness absence. Employers may therefore wish to offer return to work interviews to affected employees to assess their ability to cope with the stresses and strains of the workplace. They may also wish to offer employees a period of free bereavement counselling via Occupational Health.

Time off for dependants

Compassionate leave should be distinguished from an employee's statutory right to take a reasonable amount of unpaid time off during the employee's working hours to deal with certain unexpected or sudden emergencies, such as the death of a dependant (see section 57A(1)(C) of the Employment Rights Act 1996). The right is to "take action which is necessary" such as to organise or to attend a funeral.

In *Forster v. Cartwright Black*, the Employment Appeals Tribunal (EAT) considered the scope of qualifying actions for time off work taken in consequence of the death of a dependant. Following the death of her mother, Forster had taken five days' bereavement leave followed by two consecutive periods of sick leave (each lasting two weeks), which her doctor had certified as 'bereavement reaction'. Following receipt of the second sick note, she was dismissed due to her period of absence following her mother's death and her general absence record. The EAT held that the right to time off in consequence of the death of a dependant covered time off to make funeral arrangements, to attend a dependant's funeral and to make necessary practical arrangements, such as registering a death and applying for probate. However, it stated that section 57A(1)(c) did not cover time off as a result of the emotional consequences and grief associated with the death of a dependant. To avoid any doubt arising, employers should therefore refer to time taken off to grieve the psychological effects of a bereavement in a separate compassionate leave policy.

Who can exercise this right?

The right to take emergency time off applies to all employees, namely any individual (male or female, full time or part time) who has entered into or works under a contract of employment (whether that is an express or implied, written or oral contract). There is no minimum period of qualifying service required.

As well as having the right to time off to deal with the death of a dependant, an employee is entitled to take unpaid time off under the following circumstances:

- Where a dependant falls ill or has been injured or assaulted;
- When a dependant is having a baby (please note that this does not include taking time off after the birth to care for the child, but an employee may be entitled to take maternity, paternity or parental leave for this purpose);
- To make longer term care arrangements for a dependant who is ill or injured;
- To deal with a death of a dependant – this enables an employee to take time off to make funeral arrangements and attend the funeral;
- To deal with an unexpected disruption or breakdown of care arrangements for a dependant; and/or
- To deal with an unexpected incident involving the employee's child during school hours.

Who counts as a dependant?

A dependant is defined as the employee's spouse, civil partner, child or parent; or a person living in the same household other than by reason of being a tenant, lodger, boarder or employee. This could include a partner or an elderly aunt or grandparent.

Additional issues to be considered by the employer

Although the statutory right to time off work is unpaid, an employer may want to consider offering its employees paid leave to organise or to attend a funeral. This could improve staff loyalty and retention and help achieve a better work–life balance.

Depending on the composition of an employer's workforce, it may wish to consider extending the application of its policy beyond employees to include

Workplace Law Network
www.workplacelaw.net

...ther types of worker or to include other emergency situations; such as house fire or flood etc.

The right to time off for dependants is intended to cover genuine emergencies, so the employer should not set a limit on the number of times that an employee can be absent from work under this right. However, employers who are concerned that abuse of the right to time off to care for dependants may become an issue, should consider stating that abuse of the right is a specific disciplinary offence that could lead to disciplinary action under its disciplinary procedures.

If a funeral is taking place overseas, an employer should agree a length of absence which is reasonable and fair in all the circumstances. This may mean the employer striking a balance between its own business needs and the needs of the individual employee.

The right to emergency leave does not apply unless the employee tells the employer the reason for his/her absence "as soon as reasonably practicable" (unless it is not reasonable for the employee to tell the employer the reason for his/her absence until after his/her return to work). Any policy should therefore set out expected time scales for receipt of this information.

An employee who exercises the right to time off for dependants is protected against dismissal or victimisation. This means that it would be unfair to dismiss an employee or to select him/her for redundancy for taking, or seeking to take, time off to exercise this right. Similarly, an employee who is not offered a promotion or an appraisal because he/she has exercised this right would be able to complain that he/she has suffered a detriment. If the dismissed employee

is also female, the employer may also be at risk of a claim of indirect sex discrimination.

In order to comply with the requirements of the Employment Equality (Religion or Belief) Regulations 2003, employers should, where reasonably practicable, accommodate the requirements of their employees' religions or beliefs when a death occurs. This may mean creating less rigid compassionate leave policies to cater for specific bereavement customs. For example, Hindus believe that cremation must take place as soon as possible following death and it is usual for close relatives of the deceased to remain at home and observe a 13-day mourning period.

Sabbatical leave

Sabbatical leave is a period of leave (usually unpaid), typically lasting between three and six months, which employers allow employees to take in order to spend more time with family or to merely recharge their batteries.

Sabbatical breaks are not officially recognised by law. However, more and more employers are recognising that it is in their best interests to implement well thought out sabbatical schemes.

So what are the advantages to employers of offering these schemes?

- Adopting a flexible 'can do' approach to sabbatical leave can be an effective way of recruiting and retaining the best talent.
- In demonstrating a sensitivity to the work–life balance, employees often return to their former roles feeling more refreshed, motivated and productive.
- Staff can acquire new skills and bring valuable knowledge to the workplace.
- Encouraging a culture of flexibility amongst employees can have a

positive effect on staff retention and turnover.

■ Can be used by employers to prevent burnout of employees and to assert a progressive approach towards work.

To formalise requests for sabbatical leave, employers are advised to have a formal policy in place. However, no matter how the policy is worded, the period of sabbatical leave is technically a resignation in the hope of a later re-engagement. This means the employer has no certainty as to whether the employee will return to the organisation at the end of his/her break.

Additional concerns for the employer
Problems may arise when a returning employee seeks to establish that continuity of employment was not broken by virtue of the sabbatical leave. Whilst some employers may allow re-engaged employees to count their period of employment prior to the sabbatical leave for the purposes of accruing contractual rights (such as entitlement to holiday and sick pay), a returning employee is likely to have lost any entitlement to statutory rights that depend on accrued length of service (such as the right to claim unfair dismissal after a year's service).

Employers should word policies carefully to ensure that the employee has no automatic right to return to the same job or on the same terms and conditions at the end of the sabbatical leave period.

A sabbatical leave package requires careful planning and good communication, so that each party fully understands the implications of any commitments made. It may be useful for individuals to have an obligation to inform employers, by a particular date, of whether they intend to return to the organisation.

The needs of the business should determine the length of any period of sabbatical leave granted. However, a limit of three months may be reasonable, on the basis that it is not long enough for the employee to forget know-how or technical skills, but long enough to have a meaningful break.

> *See also*: Absence management, p.46; Holiday, p.403; Jury service, p.438; Managing pregnancy, p.484; Restrictive covenants and garden leave, p.633; Sickness leave, p.654

Sources of further information

Workplace Law Network provides premium members with unrestricted access to a comprehensive range of online information – factsheets, case reports and daily news items – on employment, health and safety and premises management. Members also benefit from an online advice service and a free subscription to the *Workplace Law Magazine*. For more information email membership@ workplacelaw.net or call our membership services team on 0871 777 8881.

Legionella

Kathryn Gilbertson, Greenwoods Solicitors LLP

Key points

- The Regulations require anyone in charge of premises, including providers of residential accommodation, to undertake a risk assessment with regard to legionella.
- L8 applies to both hot and cold water systems as well as air conditioning plant.
- Notification to the local authority is required for cooling towers and evaporative condensers.

Legislation

- Health and Safety at Work etc. Act 1974.
- Notification of Cooling Towers and Evaporative Condensers Regulations 1992.
- Reporting of Injuries, Diseases and Dangerous Occurrences Regulations 1995.
- Management of Health and Safety at Work Regulations 1999.
- Control of Substances Hazardous to Health Regulations 2002.
- L8 Approved Code of Practice (ACoP) – *The Control of Legionella Bacteria in Water Systems.*

What is legionella?

Legionella bacteria is common in ponds and rivers and may contaminate and grow in water systems such as cooling towers and hot and cold water services. It survives low temperatures and thrives between 20°C and 45°C if a supply of nutrients is present, such as:

- sediment;
- sludge;
- scale;
- algae; and
- other bacteria.

Infection is caused by breathing in small droplets of water contaminated by the bacteria. Symptoms are flu-like with high fever and headache. The disease cannot be passed from one person to another and everyone is susceptible to infection, particularly:

- people over 45 years old;
- smokers;
- heavy drinkers;
- diabetics;
- sufferers of a chronic respiratory or kidney disease; and
- people whose immune system is impaired.

Assessing the risk

- Is the water temperature between 20°C and 45°C, creating the conditions for the bacteria to multiply?
- Are there any areas where stagnant water occurs (dead legs)?
- Are the showers and taps used frequently?
- Is there debris such as rust, sludge or scale in the system?
- Is it likely any employees, residents or visitors are susceptible?

Controlling the risk

Careful planning, competent staff and attention to control strategies are essential in managing the risk. A written scheme setting out how you intend to control the risk from legionella must be in place. The scheme should detail:

- an up-to-date plan or schematic diagrams of your system;
- who is responsible for carrying out the assessment and managing its implementation;
- the safe and correct operation of the system;
- what control methods and other precautions will be used; and
- what checks will be carried out on the control scheme and how often these will be carried out.

Control measures fall into four categories.

1. Physical aspect of the system
- Water storage containers should be the right size to ensure uniform heating and to prevent stagnation.
- Where possible, tanks should be horizontal rather than vertical.
- Cisterns and storage tanks should have properly fitting covers.
- Cold water tanks should not be sited in warm areas of buildings.
- All pipe runs should be as short and direct as possible.
- Redundant pipework or tanks should be isolated from the system.
- Vermin traps should be fitted where appropriate.
- Insulation should be adequate.
- Ideally, it should be possible to drain or pump out the system completely.
- If possible, wet cooling towers should be replaced by dry cooling systems.
- Drift eliminators should be fitted in cooling towers to reduce spray.

2. Water temperature
- Cold water should be below 20°C.
- Hot water should be stored above 60°C. Caution: temperatures above 43°C pose a risk of scalding. Ideally, water should be circulated at 50°C with thermostatic control valves fitted to prevent scalding.

3. Maintenance and cleanliness
This aspect is considered crucial in the prevention of legionnaires' disease.

A competent person should make regular inspections, carrying out preventive maintenance as required by the written schedule. Records must be kept.

4. Water testing and treatment
Water testing and treatment carried out should either comply with L8 or exceed the perimeters specified in the ACoP. The sampling, analysis and treatment of the water system must be carried out by a competent person, preferably someone who is a member of a recognised professional body, and the records kept for a minimum of two years.

It is usual for HSE inspectors to ask to see these documents as part of any planned audit or during an investigation into a suspected outbreak.

Next steps
Consider the L8 and identify the maintenance regime necessary for your premises. Appoint a competent contractor to undertake any specialist work required – having selected that organisation using your usual procurement protocol. Have an ongoing dialogue with your water treatment contractor to ensure your policies and risk assessments are appropriate for your site and plant. Seek legal advice where necessary.

Interesting cases
In 2008 HP Bulmers and its water treatment contractor NALCO were jointly prosecuted following a legionella outbreak in Hereford in 2002 in which two people died and more than 30 contracted the illness. During the investigation, legionella was found flourishing in two cooling towers. The towers had been inadequately cleaned; the risk assessments were

nadequate; the water treatment policy was out of date and staff had not been properly rained.

The companies both pleaded guilty to health and safety offences and were fined £300,000 each and ordered to pay costs. No company director was prosecuted.

n 2002, the largest outbreak of the disease struck the North West of England. Five people died and over 170 people contracted legionnaires' disease following an outbreak at the Forum 28 arts centre in Barrow. The premises were owned and operated by Barrow Borough Council. Both the council and their in-house architect were charged with manslaughter and safety offences. They were acquitted of manslaughter following trials but were found guilty of offences under section 3(1) and section 7 of HSW respectively.

The Council were fined £125,000 and ordered to pay £90,000 in costs, whilst the architect was fined £15,000.

See also: Water quality, p.738

Sources of further information

L8 Legionnaires' Disease: the control of legionella bacteria in water systems (HSE Books, 2000) ISBN: 0 7176 1772 6.

Research and investigation indicates that most outbreaks of legionnaires' disease in the UK have been attributed to building water services, in particular hot and cold water supplies, cooling towers, water spray humidifiers, spa baths and pools, industrial plant and machinery utilising water storage with potential to create airborne droplets or particles. Every employer has a duty to ensure, so far as is reasonably practicable, the health, safety and welfare of their employees and members of the general public. The importance of a sound Legionella policy has been clearly highlighted over the last few years by the high profile Gillian Beckingham case.

Workplace Law Group's *Legionella Policy and Management Guide, v.3.0* has been published to help employers in England and Wales ensure that they comply with their duties under law, and to provide a clear record of the policy and procedure. For more information visit www.workplacelaw.net/Bookshop/PoliciesAndProcedures.

Lift safety

Kathryn Gilbertson, Greenwoods Solicitors LLP

Key points

- Lifts must be examined at statutory intervals – at least every six months if the lift is used at any time to carry people or every 12 months if it only carries loads.
- All passenger lifts supplied after 30 June 1999 should be fitted with safety features to assist trapped occupants in the event of a mechanical breakdown.
- Building managers have a responsibility under the Lifts Regulations 1997 to keep records relating to the operation, maintenance and repair of passenger lifts in premises under their control.
- The safety of lifting equipment in general (including machinery for lifting loads, as well as people) is covered under the Lifting Operations and Lifting Equipment Regulations 1998.
- The greatest risk relates to the maintenance – rather than use – of lifts.

Legislation

- Health and Safety at Work etc. Act 1974.
- Lifts Regulations 1997.
- Lifting Operations and Lifting Equipment Regulations 1998.
- Management of Health and Safety at Work Regulations 1999.

Lift Regulations 1997

While the Regulations mainly govern the manufacture of passenger lifts and lift components, they are of interest to building managers who are responsible for the safe use of lifts and lift maintenance. The Regulations were introduced to ensure manufacturers designed enhanced safety features into lifts, including:

- a means of two-way communication in the event of a breakdown;
- adequate ventilation during a prolonged stoppage; and
- the operation of emergency lighting systems during a power failure.

The Regulations require building managers to keep documentation such as:

- an instruction manual containing the plans and diagrams necessary for use;
- a set of guidelines relating to maintenance, inspection, repair, periodic checks and rescue operations; and
- a log book in which repairs can be recorded.

Lifting Operations and Lifting Equipment Regulations 1998 (LOLER)

If you are a lift owner or someone responsible for the safe operation of a lift used at work you are a 'dutyholder' under LOLER. You have a legal responsibility to ensure that the lift is thoroughly examined and safe to use.

A thorough examination is a systematic and detailed examination of the lift and all of its associated equipment by a competent person.

Competent person

It is unlikely you will have the necessary competence in-house to undertake the test examination. Accreditation by the United Kingdom Accreditation Service to BS EN 45004 is an indication of competence. Most insurance companies can recommend accredited inspecting organisations.

Examination should take into account the condition and operation of:

- landing and car doors and their interlocks;
- worm and other gearing;
- main drive system components;
- governors;
- safety gear;
- suspension ropes;
- suspension chains;
- overload detection devices;
- electrical devices (including earthing, earth bonding, safety devices, selection of fuses, etc.);
- braking systems (including buffers and overspeed devices); and
- hydraulics.

Notification of defects

You should receive a written and signed report of the examination within 28 days but if there is a serious defect that needs to be addressed you should expect to receive it much sooner. Notification of a serious and significant defect will necessitate the lift being taken out of service until the fault has been addressed. The competent person is also legally required to send a copy of the report to the enforcing authority.

Risk assessment

Apart from the safety and health of people using the lifts, it is the ongoing maintenance of lifts that poses the greatest hazard. Regulation 5 of LOLER covers the safety of people working on lifting equipment, including provisions to prevent falling. A risk assessment should be undertaken before maintenance work on lifts is carried out, and the maintenance instructions provided by the manufacturers and installers should be given careful consideration.

Permit to work

The person responsible for the building should ensure that a permit to work system is in place to control access to the lift shaft and to dictate a safe system of work.

Emergency procedures

Action on what to do in the event of people being trapped in lifts should be clearly documented. Nominated competent employees must be trained and regularly practice any procedures.

A note on signage

Lifts should not be used in the event of a fire unless they have been designed to do so, and signs should be displayed to this effect. Many lifts are only supported by two-way communication in the event of breakdown during normal office hours. In order to avoid people becoming trapped in lifts outside these times, signage to this effect can also be displayed.

See also: Work equipment, p.761

Sources of further information

BS 7255:2001 Code of Practice for safe working on lifts.

Lift and Escalator Industry Association: www.leia.co.uk

Lifting equipment

Kevin McFahn, Bureau Veritas

Key points

- Equipment comes under the Lifting Operations Lifting Equipment Regulations 1998 (LOLER).
- Lifting equipment is work equipment for lifting or lowering loads and includes its attachments used for anchoring, fixing or supporting it.
- A lifting operation is an operation concerned with the lifting or lowering of a load. A load in this context also includes people.
- Accessories for lifting are work equipment for attaching loads to machinery for lifting. Examples include single items such as a shackle, slings, eyebolts, swivels, clamps and lifting magnets. It could also be an assembly of items such as a lifting beam and multiple slings.

Legislation

- Supply of Machinery (Safety) Regulations 1992 and Amendment Regulations 1994.
- Health and Safety (Safety Signs and Signals) Regulations 1996.
- Lifting Operations and Lifting Equipment Regulations 1998.
- Provision and Use of Work Equipment Regulations 1998.
- Supply of Machinery (Safety) Regulations 2008 (with effect from 29 December 2009).

It should be noted that the new Supply of Machinery Regulations are the implementation of the revised Machinery Directive 2006/42/EC within the UK. They replace the previous Regulations and come into force on 29 December 2009. These clarify relevant machinery and excluded machinery but also give the manufacturer the option to use an approved Quality Assurance module for specific types of machinery consistent with the Lift and Pressure Equipment Directives.

Equipment marking

Items must be distinctly marked with the safe working load (SWL) / the working load limit (WLL). Where the SWL/WLL varies, dependant on the configuration, then it must be marked to indicate its SWL/WLL at each configuration. Where it may be possible to mistake similar items then they should be marked with individual unique identification numbers. Relevant machinery and lifting accessories manufactured after 1995 should exhibit a 'CE' marking.

Inspection criteria

- All employers must have lifting equipment examined when it is first put into service.
- Where the safety of the equipment depends upon the installation conditions it must be examined after installation and before being put into use for the first time and after reassembly at a new site or in a new location.
- Lifting equipment must be examined during its lifetime when it is exposed to conditions that cause deterioration

Lifting equipment must be examined each time that exceptional circumstances that are laible to jeopardise the safety of the lifting equipment have occurred.

Inspection frequency

- Lifting equipment used for lifting persons – at least every six months.
- Lifting accessories – at least every six months.
- Other lifting equipment – at least every 12 months.
- In either case, in accordance with an examination scheme.
- Each time that exceptional circumstances that are liable to jeopardise the safety of the lifting equipment have occurred.
- The user should have enough knowledge to examine the equipment for obvious defects each time it is used.

Employers' duties

- Lifting equipment must be of adequate strength and stability for each load, particularly when stress may be induced at mounting or fixing points.
- A load including anything attached to it and used in lifting must be of adequate strength.
- All lifting operations must be properly planned by a competent person.
- Lifting operations must be appropriately supervised and safe.

Users' duties

The user must:

- ascertain the centre of gravity and arrange each lifting operation;
- identify the weight of loads to be lifted; and
- only use the correct rated equipment for lifting.

Competent person

The competent person carrying out the thorough examination must have such appropriate practical and theoretical knowledge and experience of the lifting equipment to be thoroughly examined as will enable them to detect weaknesses and to assess their importance in relation to the safety and continued use of the lifting equipment.

In order to undertake thorough examinations the competent person must have sight of either:

- the Declaration of Conformity; or
- the original test certificate; or
- the last thorough examination report.

If paperwork is not available it is the responsibility of the competent person to decide whether a test is required or not, or if a thorough examination will be sufficient.

Proof load testing

A proof load must not be applied without reference to the manufacturer or the relevant British Standard.

Reporting of defects

The competent person must:

- report all defects immediately to the owner of the equipment;
- advise the employer immediately if a severe defect is found. This should be in writing and contain relevant information about the faulty equipment and the repairs that are required to be effected; and
- send a copy of the defect report to the relevant enforcing authority within a 28-day timetable or as soon as is practicable. This is limited to cases where there would be an existing or imminent risk of serious personal injury arising from failure of the equipment should anyone attempt to use it.

Thorough examination report

The report should contain:

- name and address of employer for whom the examination was made;
- premises address where the examination was undertaken;
- identification marks or number of the equipment examined;
- date of the last thorough examination;
- SWL/WLL;
- whether it is a report after first installation, a report within six or 12 months, in accordance with a written scheme or after the occurrence of exceptional circumstances;
- date of the next thorough examination;
- any parts that are found to be defective or in need of attention, the required repairs and the date by which they should be repaired;

- details of test required or undertaken
- name of competent person making the report and address of their employer; and
- date of the report.

Hired lifting equipment

Both the hirer and the hire company have responsibilities when lifting equipment is brought onto premises:

- The hire company must ensure that adequate evidence is transferred with the lifting equipment to show that the last thorough examination has been carried out. The Responsible Person hiring the equipment must ensure that he has selected suitable equipment and that evidence has been obtained that the last thorough examination has been carried out.

See also: Work equipment, p.761

Sources of further information

INDG290 *Simple guide to the Lifting Operations and Lifting Equipment Regulations 1998* (HSE Books, 1999) ISBN: 0 7176 2430 7.

HSG6 *Safety in working with lift trucks* (HSE Books, 2000) ISBN: 0 7176 1781 5.

GS6 *Avoidance of danger from overhead electrical power lines* (HSE Books, 1997) ISBN: 0 7176 1348 8.

PM28 *Working platforms on fork-lift trucks* (HSE Books, 2000) ISBN: 0 7176 0935 9.

GA700/04/D3 *Lifting equipment and accessories for lifting* (Construction Industries Training Board, 2004).

Lighting

Liz Peck, Society of Light and Lighting

Key points

In general there is little by way of legislation governing lighting in the workplace, and what the law does require is mostly qualitative (sufficient and suitable) rather than quantitative.

The major provisions are found in the Health and Safety at Work etc. Act 1974 and the Health and Safety (Display Screen Equipment) Regulations 1992, but other legislation such as the Disability Discrimination Act 2005 also has to be complied with.

The Building Regulations, and in particular Part L on conservation of fuel and power, have provisions regarding the energy efficiency and carbon emissions of lighting in new and refurbished premises, but do not prescribe lighting standards. As part of the implementation of the Energy Performance of Buildings Directive and in fulfilment of Government policy to make buildings more efficient, a new edition of Part L came into force during 2006.

Legislation

Health and Safety at Work etc. Act 1974

The primary requirement in the Act is that lighting should be 'sufficient and suitable'; only the courts can define what that is, and there are very few reported cases. The HSE publishes the guide *Lighting at work* (HSG38, ISBN: 0 7176 1232 5), which indicates what it believes to be the minimum acceptable standards. However, these cover only very general work types, defined in terms of the visual difficulty of the task. Note that these levels are for safety, not effective or efficient performance of the task.

Emergency lighting is now required by various provisions of the Act and it should be assumed that it is required in all workplaces and most other buildings used by the public. The detailed requirements are in British Standards (see Best practice guidance below). Note that the 2005 Regulatory Reform (Fire Safety) Order replaced many existing references to fire in legislation with one consolidated document (see below).

Health and Safety (Display Screen Equipment) Regulations 1992

These Regulations include provisions for lighting of workplaces where display screen equipment (DSE) is used. Note that this covers far more than just offices. DSE is found in many environments including factory equipment controls and on forklift trucks in warehouses. Again, the requirements of the Regulations are general, but are supplemented by an HSE guidance document, *Display screen equipment work. Guidance on regulations* (L26, ISBN: 0 7176 0410 1). This covers far more than just lighting, but provides useful practical guidance on issues which the HSE expects to see addressed.

Disability Discrimination Act 2005

Lighting is one of the areas to which 'reasonable adjustments' need to be made if otherwise disabled people are likely to be disadvantaged (see also Building Regulations and Best practice guidance, below).

Regulatory Reform (Fire Safety) Order 2005

Over the years, legislation on fire safety had grown enormously and been included in many Acts and Regulations. The decision was therefore taken to bring it all together in one place. The Regulatory Reform (Fire Safety) Order 2005 does this. There is little change to the legislation other than the significant issue of transfer of responsibility from the fire service to the building owner. This means that all building owners and users (e.g. those who rent or lease buildings or occupy them under other agreements) have to carry out a risk assessment and implement appropriate measures. This work can be carried out in-house or subcontracted to consultants.

Other legislative provisions

There are many small references to lighting in legislation covering specific industries, especially foodstuffs and catering, and heavy industry involving hazardous processes. These are too numerous to discuss in this chapter.

Building Regulations

Lighting is covered in the Building Regulations, Part L Conservation of fuel and power, a new version of which came into force in England and Wales on 6 April 2006. Supporting the Regulations are four Approved Documents:

1. L1A: Conservation of fuel and power in new dwellings.
2. L1B: Conservation of fuel and power in existing dwellings.
3. L2A: Conservation of fuel and power in new buildings other than dwellings.
4. L2B: Conservation of fuel and power in existing buildings other than dwellings.

The revised Building Regulations are also being used to provide the means for implementing the EU Energy Performance of Buildings Directive, which will require energy labelling of buildings.

Scotland and Northern Ireland have separate legislation dealing with building control.

The Building Regulations (Northern Ireland) 2006 Part F is similar to Part L for England and Wales. The Department of Finance and personnel (DFP) has produced two technical booklets:

1. F1: 2006 – Conservation of fuel and power in dwellings; and
2. F2: 2006 – Conservation of fuel and power in buildings other than dwellings.

Domestic premises in England and Wales put on the market must have Home Information Packs (HIPs) provided by the vendor. An HIP includes an Energy Performance Certificate for the property and identifies the potential for improved efficiency of the building services. Lighting is specifically listed and it is expected that the recommendations given by the certificate assessors will allow the owner to apply for improvement grants where appropriate. HIPs are not currently required in Northern Ireland. Simpler Purchasers Information Packs (PIPs) were introduced in Scotland in early 2008.

Part L requires proper commissioning of new lighting installations and their controls, and this requirement has been strengthened in the new Approved Documents. At the request of the Office of the Deputy Prime Minister (ODPM), the Society of Light and Lighting and the Chartered Institution of Building Services Engineers (of which the SLL is part) published Commissioning Code L: Lighting

2003 (ISBN: 1 903287 32 4) to give guidance on acceptable procedures.

art M of the Building Regulations and the Disability Discrimination Act are also relevant although neither says a great deal specifically about lighting. However, lighting should be suitable for the visually impaired and where appropriate the hearing impaired. This normally means careful control of glare, adequate luminances, good colour rendering and good modelling (e.g. to enable the deaf to lip-read). It is not recommended that lighting levels be increased above those in published guidance, except where a building is being specifically designed for the use of the partially sighted and the type of vision problem is known. It is normally appropriate instead to provide supplementary local lighting to meet the needs of the individual. This legislation should be read in conjunction with *BS: 8300 Design of buildings* and their approaches to meet the needs of disabled people, recently revised (see below).

Environmental issues

In September 2007, the Department for Environment, Food and Rural Affairs (DEFRA) announced the Government's plan for the phased withdrawal of energy-inefficient light bulbs by 2012. The proposed timetable for this voluntary scheme is outlined below:

- January 2009: All inefficient GLS A-shaped lamps of energy rating higher than 60W (predominantly 150W, 100W plus some 75W lamps).
- January 2010: All GLS A-shaped lamps of efficacy of energy rating higher than 40W (predominantly 60W lamps).
- January 2012: All remaining inefficient GLS A-shaped lamps and 60W 'candle' and 'golfball' lamps (predominantly 40W and 25W A-shaped GLS bulbs, and 60W candles and golfballs).

Some special interest charity organisations have expressed concern about health risks of the 'energy saving' alternatives. Anyone who has queries in this regard can contact the Radiation Protection Division of the Health Protection Agency (optical@hpa.org.uk). As a form of fluorescent lamp, these contain a very small amount of mercury (typically around 3-5mg) and as such should not be disposed of with household waste but should be recycled (see WEEE directive below).

WEEE

The Waste Electrical and Electronic Equipment Regulations came into force on 2 January 2007. There are specific requirements for recycling lamps and luminaires, and restrictions on dumping lamps containing mercury or sodium in the Landfill Regulations. The lighting industry has developed a recycling management framework to deal with the specific issues raised by discharge lamps (including fluorescent and compact fluorescent) and luminaires. Further information can be obtained from Lumicom (www.lumicom.co.uk) on recycling of luminaires and Recolight (www.recolight.co.uk) for recycling of lamps.

It is worth noting that it has been suggested that current UK office specification practice may have to change as a result of the WEEE Directive. It will no longer be acceptable for almost unused luminaires installed as part of the landlord's scheme to be replaced when a tenant arrives. This may drive developers towards a shell and core approach, with no lighting installed until the tenant's needs are known. Developers wishing to promote themselves as having environmentally conscious credentials will particularly have to take this into account.

The Restriction of the Use of Certain Hazardous Substances (RoHS) in Electrical and Electronic Equipment Regulations 2005 include mercury which is widely used in discharge lamps and fluorescent tubes. Schedule 2 lists exemptions for lamps where the amount of mercury is less than defined quantities.

However, the EA has determined that fluorescent tubes are hazardous waste in England and Wales and as such should be recycled or disposed of at the limited number of landfill sites that can cater for mercury-bearing waste. The Scottish Environmental Protection Agency has similarly designated fluorescent tubes as special waste. Practical procedures associated with domestic waste of fluorescent tubes and compact fluorescent lamps have yet to be implemented.

Best practice guidance

Since the only British Standard covering lighting of buildings (BS: 8206-2 on daylighting) is very out of date and due to be revised to take account of new ways of measuring daylight in buildings, the major relevant standard is BS EN 12464-1: *Light and lighting. Lighting of workplaces. Part 1: Indoor workplaces* (2002). However, the general reference document, which incorporates the relevant information from BS EN 12464-1, is the SLL's Code for Lighting 2006 available as a CD-ROM (ISBN: 1 903287 47 2) or as printed extracts (ISBN: 0 7506 5637 9). This provides extensive guidance on the lighting of all types of building and associated spaces. Equivalent information appears in separate ISO/CIE standards for the lighting of indoor and outdoor workplaces. The Code for Lighting and other Society of Light and Lighting recommendations have already been updated to take account of its recommendations.

The European Commission has asked CEN (the European Standards Organisation) to draft a number of standards covering aspects of the Energy Performance of Buildings Directive; these are currently in draft. Two are directly relevant to lighting and others will have secondary impacts. Details can be found from the BSI (www.bsi-global.com).

Neither British Standards nor the recommendations of professional bodies such as the SLL have any legal status except as best current practice, but mandated European standards currently have to be followed for projects coming within the scope of the Public Procurement Directives, unless a specific reason is given why they are not appropriate.

The SLL also publishes a series of Lighting Guides covering specific building types. *Lighting Guide 7: office lighting* includes recommendations on ensuring the lighting is suitable for offices containing display screen equipment. The essential change from previous versions of Society recommendations on this topic is relaxation of the luminaire luminance limits when modern screens and software are in use, and a recommendation for ensuring that there is adequate light on the walls and ceiling. The former Luminaire Category Rating system has now been withdrawn as it is no longer relevant.

The current guidance on emergency lighting is in BS 5266 *Emergency lighting*. Part 1 of this standard implements EN 50172 and is the code of practice; Part 7 is the UK implementation of EN 1838. Other parts of the standard cover specific issues such as wayfinding. Further parts are in preparation. Especially important is regular planned maintenance and testing of emergency lighting, and this is provided for in the standards. Note that emergency lighting should include luminaires outside the final exit to the building to assist adaptation to outside night-time lighting evels. This is particularly important for the elderly and the visually impaired.

The SLL's *Lighting Guide 12: Emergency lighting design guide* (ISBN: 1 903287 51 0) covers all aspects of emergency lighting from design to maintenance.

Exterior lighting of areas such as public car parks and access roads, including those in shopping centres, is covered by BS 5489-1 *Code of practice for the design of road lighting. Lighting of roads and public amenity areas* (2003). However, this document is difficult to apply in many cases as it is intended for use by road lighting engineers. Guidance on practical aspects of car park lighting is in preparation to supplement the standard.

BS 8300 *Design of buildings and their approaches to meet the needs of disabled people* has few recommendations directly related to lighting, but many of its provisions have indirect relevance, e.g. requirements for appropriate visual contrast between doors and door furniture.

Frequently asked questions

1. *Is it mandatory to provide daylight in offices?* The answer is yes, if it is reasonably practicable – unlike the situation in countries such as Germany where it is mandatory. However, the interpretation of 'reasonably practicable' is open to wide variation, and in practice the provision has no force.

2. *Do employers have to provide the recommended illuminance if the employee requests a lower level?* There is no authoritative answer to this question as it has not been tested in court, but it would be unwise to let the illuminance in the space drop below 200 lux since this is the minimum in the European Standard for continuously occupied spaces and is also the level recommended for office tasks in the HSE's guide, *Lighting at work.*

3. *Must I provide emergency lighting in schools?* Because most users of schools will be familiar with the layout and use in hours of darkness by school pupils is very limited, it is not generally necessary to provide emergency lighting. However, if the building will be used out of hours or by individuals who are not familiar with the building, e.g. evening classes, parents' evenings, escape lighting should be provided in those parts of the building so used.

Note, however, that the recommendations in the Schedule of the SLL's Code for Lighting are for the task area, and that lower levels of lighting are suggested for surrounding areas. In offices, the task area will normally be only the area of the desk.

See also: Building Regulations, p.81; Display screen equipment, p.238; WEEE and RoHS, p.744

Sources of further information

HSE – *Lighting at work* (HSG38) ISBN: 0 7176 1232 5.

Society of Light and Lighting and the Chartered Institution of Building Services Engineers – *Commissioning Code L: Lighting* in 2003. ISBN: 1 903287 32 4.

SLL's Code for Lighting 2006: available as a CD-ROM (ISBN: 1 903287 47 2) or as printed extracts (ISBN: 0 7506 5637 9).

Lightning conductors

Jonathan Riley, Pinsent Masons

Key points

- A lightning protector system protects buildings by providing a low-resistance alternative between the highest point of the building and the earth.
- Various consents may be needed for the installation of a lightning conductor. Planning consent will probably not be required, but listed building consent, conservation area consent or scheduled monument consent may be required.

Purpose of lightning conductors

In certain atmospheric conditions a build-up of static electricity results in a discharge between the sky and the earth and the 'strike' may hit the earth at its highest point. A lightning conductor channels the strike and directs it towards buildings or structures along the path of least resistance to earth.

A lightning protection system can reduce the amount of damage that may be caused to buildings by providing a low-resistance alternative between the highest point of the building and the earth. In its basic form, it usually takes the form of a metal rod installed at the pinnacle of the building and connects via a rod to the earth.

Standards and specifications

Benjamin Franklin invented lightning rods in 1747 when he realised that attaching a conductor to a rod could divert the 'strike' of lightning harmlessly to earth. His concept remains the basis of lightning-rod designs today.

Evidently, the lightning protection system has been improved and modified since Franklin's time and the relevant specifications are found in BS 6651:1999 *Code of practice for the Protection of Structures against Lightning*.

BS 6651 clearly advises strict adherence to the provision of a conventional lightning protection system – to the total exclusion of any other device or system which may enhance protection – is made.

The principal components of a conventional structural lightning protection system, in accordance with BS: 6651, are as follows:

- *Air termination network*. This network is the point of connection with a lightning strike. It typically consists of a meshed conductor made of copper or aluminium tapes covering the roof of the structure, designed to intercept the lightning.
- *Down conductors*. These carry the current from the lightning strike safely to the earth termination network. Rods are attached to the external façade of the structure.
- *Earth termination network*. This is the means of dissipating the current to the general mass of earth. They can take the form of earth electrodes in the form of rods and plates or earth rod clamps, all of which serve the purpose of establishing a low-resistance contact with the earth.

However, there are other lightning protection systems available, outside the scope of BS 6651 including the 'early streamer emission' device, which is a modern alternative to the rod. The device emits a stream of charged particles upwards which helps to attract the 'strike'. The lightning is then safely passed to the earth through the rest of the system. However, not everyone in the industry supports the use of this system.

The effect of a lightning conductor had been improved by using an isotope named americium-241 (a sealed source of ionising radiation) coating to the spike. However, because all radioactive material is subject to control by the Environment Agency, its use on lightning conductors has not been permitted since February 2000. Any remaining sealed conductors should be removed with expert advice and guidance. Great care must be taken in particular in handling the sealed conductors and ensuring appropriate disposal.

The British Standards Institution (BSI) provides advice on other British Standards relating to electrical installations and good earthing practice. There are also various international standards that provide useful guidance. The European International Electrotechnical Commission (IEC) prepares standards that serve as a basis for national standardisation. The UK is a member of the IEC through the BSI and BS 6651 reflects the standards of the IEC. The IEC standard 61024: *Protection of structures against lightning* is an internationally recognised standard, as is IEC 61312: *Protection against lightning electromagnetic impulse*.

Planning consents

Planning permission is not normally required to erect a conductor on most buildings since it is not a 'development' for the purposes of the Town and Country Planning Act 1990. However, if a lightning protection system is sufficiently complex and has a degree of permanence as well as affecting the external appearance of a building, it may require planning permission. If the building concerned is listed, a scheduled ancient monument or within a conservation area, care needs to be taken as it will be subject to special controls.

Listed building consent from the appropriate local planning authority is required. Any works that affect the character of a building of special architectural or historic interest must be authorised. It would depend on each individual case whether the erection of a lightning conductor would have this effect as location and materials are relevant factors. While compliance with BS 6651 ensures that technical issues are adequately addressed, it does not necessarily ensure that aesthetic criteria are met. Placing the conductor behind a buttress or otherwise out of sight could avoid affecting the character of the building.

If the building is an ancient monument, it could be damaged by the attachment of a conductor or a lightning protection scheme. Any addition to a scheduled monument needs prior consent and this includes any machinery attached to a monument (if it cannot be detached without being dismantled). In all the above cases reference should be made to English Heritage or Cadw (as appropriate) or the local planning authority before erecting a conductor on an ancient monument or a listed building since unauthorised works to either are a criminal offence.

If the building is in a conservation area, there may also be controls affecting the erection of a lightning conductor and a preliminary check should be made with the conservation officer of the relevant planning authority before proceeding with any work.

See also: Building Regulations, p.81

Loneworking

Kathryn Gilbertson, Greenwoods Solicitors LLP

Key points

Loneworkers are those who work by themselves without close or direct supervision. Risk assessment is, therefore, essential.

There are a number of legal provisions that specify systems of working that require more than one person. These include:

- Electricity at Work Regulations 1989.
- Work in Compressed Air Regulations 1996.
- Diving at Work Regulations 1997.
- Confined Spaces Regulations 1997.
- Control of COSHH Regulations 2002.

There are other provisions that require work to be done "under the immediate supervision of a competent person" or similar wording which would suggest that the work, although carried out by one person, must be done in the presence of another.

Legislation
- Health and Safety at Work etc. Act 1974.
- Electricity at Work Regulations 1989.
- Work in Compressed Air Regulations 1996.
- Diving at Work Regulations 1997.
- Confined Spaces Regulations 1997.
- Management of Health and Safety at Work Regulations 1999.
- Control of COSHH Regulations 2002.

Who is at risk?
- People who work separately from others in factories, warehouses, shopping centres etc.
- People working on their own in petrol stations, shops, small workshops, homeworkers, security guards.
- Mobile workers working away from their fixed base e.g. engineers, sales representatives, breakdown mechanics, social workers, estate agents; the list is not exhaustive.

Remember that loneworking is not a formal categorisation of work – anyone who stays late at the office to finish off a report, or who pops in at the weekend to prepare for the coming week, is a loneworker.

Risk assessment

As an employer, you need to be fully aware of all loneworking that is going on in your organisation, whether it is undertaken by people who are employed by you directly (such as your sales force) or by people who work on your premises (such as your cleaners). A risk assessment should be carried out for loneworking as with other areas of risk in the workplace. A risk assessment for loneworking needs to take particular account of the specific hazards associated with the work task, and of the people who are carrying it out. Every loneworking situation will be different, but some common issues to consider are:

Access to and egress from the place of work. Can the loneworker get to and from the workplace safely? Is the work being carried out in a confined space?

Nature of the work. What sort of work is being undertaken? Are loneworkers dealing with the public, where they might face aggressive or violent behaviour? Do they have to carry heavy items, or work in outdoor weather conditions?

Location of work. Where does the work take place? Where work is carried out by mobile workers or off site, the employer will have little control over first aid provision and emergency procedures. Does work take place at height?

Time of work. When does the work take place? We are all naturally tired first thing in the morning and last thing at night. Are there any increased risks related to the time of day, such as pub closing time or rush hour? According to recent research tired drivers are the cause of one in ten accidents.

Use of work equipment. What, if any, work equipment do they need to use? Use of electrical equipment or machinery will increase the risk. Don't forget that drivers will be using very complex pieces of work equipment – a car, van or truck – to carry out their work. Check that they have been trained how to use it.

People. Who are the people who are working alone? You will need to consider their age, maturity, experience, health and fitness, and general state of mind. Where young people or new and expectant mothers are concerned, the risks will be increased.

An evaluation of the risks should highlight the control measures that are required to ensure work is carried out in a suitably safe manner. Some common control measures for loneworkers are the following:

- *Redesign of the task to eliminate the need for loneworking* – for example, by changing shift patterns to implement a buddy system where two people work together at all times.

- *Provision of information, instruction and training.* This might include training in the safe use of work equipment, or how to handle aggressive behaviour when dealing with the public.

- *Establishment of communication and supervision procedures.* To ensure that a manager is able to contact the worker at regular intervals; to make sure that arrangements in the case of an emergency have been put in place; and to check that a loneworker has arrived back safely once work has been completed.

- *Provision of mobile first aid facilities.* To ensure that loneworkers can deal with minor injuries themselves.

- *Health surveillance of loneworkers.* At regular intervals, to ensure that workers are fit and healthy to carry out the tasks required of them.

See also: Health surveillance, p.392; Night working, p.527; Work equipment, p.761; Working time, p.767

Sources of further information

An increasing amount of organisations are employing loneworkers, in all areas of industry and business. Flexible Working Regulations have enabled employees to enjoy the benefits of working from home; today's 24–7 culture means that more companies are open around the clock; and greater automation in industry has meant a shift from the traditional 9–5 working day. Loneworking can be of great benefit to a business – but it also has its problems. Health and safety issues that affect traditional employees still apply – in some cases more so. Employment issues such as data protection and absence management are also paramount, and must be considered when employing people who work alone.

Workplace Law Group's *Loneworking 2008: Special Report* helps you get to grips with these issues, to determine whether loneworking is a viable option for your business. Using practical case studies, checklists and assessments, the report discusses the pros and cons of loneworking, and what an employer must do to overcome the dangers, implement healthy and safe working policies, and ensure their loneworkers are being cared for just as well as those in the traditional workplace. For more information visit www.workplacelaw.net/Bookshop/SpecialReports.

Comment...

Why loneworker safety should be high on the agenda

suzy lamplugh
trust

Personal safety charity, Suzy Lamplugh Trust, says demand for loneworker training, resources and consultancy services has grown considerably this year. Jo Walker, Campaigns and Communications Officer for Suzy Lamplugh Trust, explains why.

The Corporate Manslaughter and Corporate Homicide Act 2007 means that, for the first time, companies and organisations can be found guilty of corporate manslaughter as a result of management failures that result in a gross breach of duty of care. The Act clarifies the criminal liability where serious failures in the management of health and safety – including personal safety – result in a fatality. A serious breach in management's duty of care, which leads to the death of an employee, could now result in the organisation facing a criminal conviction and possible unlimited fines.

Since the new legislation came into force earlier this year, we have seen a marked increase in demand for the Trust's services. We believe this indicates that senior management in a wide range of companies and organisations of all sizes are now sitting up, asking some probing questions about their health and safety management systems, and finding the drive and money to ensure their personal safety systems are robust and their staff suitably trained and equipped where necessary.

Unfortunately, in the past, many organisations did not properly assess the personal safety risks to their employees – either they hadn't thought enough about

the tasks involved in the job and therefore didn't recognise there were risks; or they carried out a risk assessment based on what they assumed their loneworkers did, but without consulting the workers themselves; or they had carried out an assessment of risk years before and assumed it still worked for their current staff. Since the cost of getting this wrong is now so high, more and more organisations are putting the money and effort into getting it right.

One common, but mistaken, approach to getting this right is for a company to spend a great deal of money on loneworker technology – e.g. tracing systems – in order to be able to tell where staff are at all times in case they need help – and think their job is then done. This approach is common because being able to tell where each member of staff is if there is a problem makes a lot of sense and some of the technology on the market is excellent. However, where they are mistaken is in thinking that this is sufficient. This technology should only be used as part of cohesive personal safety strategy, which includes policies and procedures that have been discussed and formulated with the assistance of the loneworkers themselves, as well as suitable training for staff in how to handle a difficult situation. This is vital because the technology might tell you they are in trouble and where they are, but it will still take time to get help to them and in the meantime being able to handle a potentially violent situation in the correct way could save their lives.

The Trust certainly believes that the new loneworker technology can play an important part in a good personal safety strategy and in fact we have just added a new Loneworking Technological Solutions directory to our website. This is a list of companies that can provide such technology and has been included in order to help the many organisations that approach us each month looking for technological solutions to complement their loneworking personal safety policies.

Another factor we believe is making a difference to the awareness of personal safety in the workplace is National Personal Safety Day (13 October). This was established ten years ago and as more and more individuals, schools, workplaces and councils are becoming aware of it, they appear to be using it as a prompt to re-visit their personal safety measures and highlight various personal safety issues to staff. Every year the Trust is seeing a greater increase in demand for services during the month of October and we are delighted at this ever growing response to this national awareness day.

Finally, Suzy Lamplugh Trust believes part of the increase in demand could also be attributed to the high number of attacks and tragic murders of boys and young men, which have been highlighted in the media during the last few years. It appears that more and more people are waking up to the fact that males are as in need of personal safety training and systems as females. Over the last 12 months the Trust has been encouraged to see a marked increase in enquiries from companies who employ a large percentage of male loneworkers.

The Trust has worked for over 20 years to bring personal safety to the workplace and whilst we believe we have had considerable success, there is still a long way to go, so we have been particularly heartened by the significant advances in awareness we have seen this year.

Machine guards and safety devices

Kathryn Gilbertson, Greenwoods Solicitors LLP

Key points
- Operation of dangerous work equipment requires the use of machine guards and other safety devices, as specified under the Provision and Use of Work Equipment Regulations 1998.
- Failure to ensure that machine guards are used properly is harder for employers to defend under health and safety legislation because the duty to comply is more stringent and does not allow them to take into account mitigating factors such as time, cost and inconvenience.

Legislation
- Lifting Operations and Lifting Equipment Regulations 1998 (LOLER).
- Provision and Use of Work Equipment Regulations 1998 (PUWER).
- Health and Safety (Miscellaneous Amendments) Regulations 2002.

Statutory requirements
Guards are fitted on machinery as a control measure to prevent the risk of accident or injury caused by contact with moving parts. Machine guarding is covered by the Provision and Use of Work Equipment Regulations 1998 (PUWER). Regulation 11 states that measures must be taken which:

- "prevent access to any dangerous part of machinery or to any rotating stock-bar"; or
- "stop the movement of any dangerous part of machinery or rotating stock-bar before any part of a person enters a danger zone".

It is worth noting that this requirement under health and safety law is to do what is 'practicable' – not 'reasonably practicable' – to comply. What this means is that, unlike many of the employer's duties under health and safety law, there can be no argument about the time, cost or inconvenience it takes to make sure guards are used. The only justification can be whether there is no technical solution to protect workers from the dangerous machinery in question – an unlikely argument to win in the event of an accident.

Types of guard and safety device
There are a number of types of guard and control device to protect from dangerous machine parts, including the following:

- *Fixed guards.* These are always in position, and difficult to tamper with, but can restrict access and make cleaning difficult.
- *Adjustable guards.* These can be adjusted by the user, or automatically by the machine as work is passed through them. They allow better access, but increase accidental risk of contact with dangerous parts.
- *Interlocking guards.* These ensure that equipment can only be operated when a moveable part connects to

the power source, so that they default to safe. A good example here is the door of a photocopier machine, which disconnects the power when opened.

- *Trip devices.* These detect the presence of an operator within a danger zone to shut off power, using trip switches, pressure pads or laser sensors.
- *Other measures.* These include two-handed control devices and hold-to-run controls, which default to safe (for example by isolating the equipment from its power source) if the operator releases them.

Risk control measures

One of the most common areas of risk with the use of machine guards is human intervention by the operator. This can be as a result of human error, in that guards have not been properly reinstated following cleaning or maintenance; or it can be as a result of overconfidence or negligence, where an operator thinks he can work faster or better without the guard in place. For these reasons, it is imperative that employers monitor work with dangerous machine parts closely and at regular intervals, carry out regular inspections to ensure the safe operation of guards and safety devices, and ensure that operators are provided with all the information, instruction, training and supervision that is necessary.

Recent and proposed changes

While PUWER remains substantially in force, some amendments were introduced under the Health and Safety (Miscellaneous Amendments) Regulations 2002 which affect the employer's approach to work with dangerous machine parts. The HSE had been concerned under the original Regulations that there was too much leeway for employers to simply provide training and instruction

to workers as a control measure when using dangerous machinery, instead of starting with the safest option of fitting fixed guards. Under the 2002 amending Regulations, "information, instruction, training and supervision" are now seen as an additional requirement, but not as one of the principal control measures to manage risk when working with dangerous machine parts.

The UK is required by the European Commission to report on the introduction of national legislation brought in to comply with European Directives.

Recent cases

In 2005 Company Director Paul White was jailed for 12 months following the death of an employee at his paper recycling business, M W White Ltd of Ketteringham, Norwich in December 2003. The custodial sentence followed Mr White's earlier guilty plea to manslaughter and health and safety charges. His company was also fined £30,000 with costs of £55,000.

The sentencing followed a full investigation jointly carried between detectives from Norfolk Constabulary CID and inspectors from the HSE into the death of Kevin Arnup. Mr Arnup climbed into a paper-shredding machine to clear blockages when the machine started, fatally injuring him. The machine contained a series of hammers projecting 15 cm from a shaft, which revolved at high speed.

The extensive investigation revealed that the machine was not securely isolated whilst the unblocking work was being carried out (there was no local electrical isolator provided for the machinery), there was no safe system for such work and the electrical controls for the machine were contaminated with dust.

Commenting on the case, HSE investigating Principal Inspector Paul Carter said:

This was a horrific incident that was entirely foreseeable. Isolating the machinery, a safe system of work for clearing blockages, together with adequate instruction, training and supervision of Paul White's staff would have prevented this incident. Evidence showed that Paul White chose not to follow the advice of his health and safety consultant and instead adopted a complacent attitude allowing the standards in his paper recycling business to fall."

> *See also*: Health and safety at work, p.364; Work equipment, p.761

Sources of further information

INDG291 *Simple Guide to the Provision and Use of Work Equipment Regulations 1998* (HSE Books, 1999) ISBN: 0 7176 2429 3.

Managing pregnancy

Mandy Laurie, Dundas & Wilson

Key points
- Employment legislation provides new and expectant mothers with special rights and protection, including the right to take time off for antenatal care; maternity leave and pay; return to work to the same job; request flexible working; and protection from suffering a detriment or dismissal on pregnancy grounds.
- Health and safety legislation protects new and expectant mothers from certain risks in the workplace.
- This chapter applies to mothers whose expected week of childbirth (EWC) is on or after 5 October 2008.

Legislation
- Workplace (Health, Safety and Welfare Regulations) 1992.
- Employment Rights Act 1996.
- Maternity and Parental Leave etc. Regulations 1999.
- Management of Health and Safety at Work Regulations 1999.
- Work and Families Act 2006.
- The Statutory Pay, Social Security (Maternity Allowance) and Security (Overlapping Benefits) (Amendment) Regulations 2006.
- The Maternity and Parental Leave etc. and Paternity and Adoption Leave (Amendment) Regulations 2006.

Key employment issues

Time off for antenatal care
Expectant mothers are entitled to paid time off to attend antenatal appointments (where the appointment has been made by their doctor, midwife or a registered nurse). The right to time off:

- is during working hours;
- includes not just the appointment time but traveling and waiting time; and
- should be paid.

If an employer unreasonably refuses time off, or allows time off but does not pay for it (either in whole or in part), the employee can make a complaint to an Employment Tribunal within three months of the date of the antenatal appointment concerned. If the complaint is justified, the Employment Tribunal must make a declaration to that effect and if the refusal to allow time off is unreasonable, the employer will be ordered to pay the expectant mother an amount of pay equal to the pay she would have received for the period of time off requested.

Maternity leave
There are three different types of maternity leave, which are as follows:

1. *Compulsory* – all new mothers (irrespective of length of service) must take two weeks' maternity leave (four if they work in a factory) after the birth of their baby. For mothers whose expected EWC starts on or after 5 October 2008 it is prohibited to deduct the two week period of compulsory maternity leave from any calculation of a discretionary bonus.

- *Ordinary* – all new mothers may take 26 weeks' maternity leave, providing they inform their employer in writing (no later than the end of the 15th week before their EWC) that they are pregnant, the date of their EWC and the date they intend their ordinary maternity leave (OML) to start.
- *Additional* – since 1 April 2007 new mothers, irrespective of how long they have worked for their employer, are entitled to a further 26 weeks' additional maternity leave (AML), which begins at the end of OML. Mothers on AML whose EWC starts on or after 5 October 2008 will be entitled to the same benefits available to mothers on OML, with the exception of remuneration.

Maternity pay

A new mother is entitled to Statutory Maternity Pay (SMP) if, by the end of the 5th week before the EWC:

- she has been continuously employed for 26 weeks; and
- her normal weekly earnings for the previous eight weeks were not less than the lower earnings limit for the payment of primary class I National Insurance contributions.

Since 1 April 2007 new mothers are entitled to SMP during all of their OML and for 13 weeks of their AML, meaning that they are now entitled to 39 weeks' statutory maternity pay.

The Government has noted its intentions to extend SMP from 39 weeks to 52 weeks for babies due on or after April 2010.

SMP will start on any day of the week, concurrently with OML.

Keeping in Touch Days

New mothers can return to work for up to ten days during their maternity leave

without losing their right to leave or SMP, provided both parties agree.

Return to work
Following OML and AML, new mothers are entitled to return to the same job as if they had not been absent. If this is not reasonably practicable, following return from AML, the new mother should return to another suitable and appropriate job within the employer's organisation. If a new mother wants to return early from either OML or AML she must notify her employer eight weeks in advance.

Right to request flexible working
A mother who has been continuously employed for 26 weeks has the right to formally apply in writing to her employer to request a change in hours, times or location of work for the purpose of enabling her to care for her child. An employer may refuse such a request, but only if they are justified by certain business reasons. Any request should follow the formal statutory flexible working process *(see 'Flexible working', p.338)*.

Unfair dismissal
Dismissals relating to the right to take time off for antenatal care, maternity leave and pay, return to work, detrimental treatment and pregnancy-related dismissals will be automatically unfair, irrespective of the new or expectant mother's length of service. These are covered in *'Family-friendly rights', p.309*.

Fertility treatment
In February 2008, the ECJ ruled that women who have had their ova fertilised but not yet implanted will not be considered pregnant and thus are not protected from dismissal by the EC Pregnant Workers Directive. However dismissal of a woman, if related to her IVF Treatment, may amount to discrimination

on the grounds of sex, as IVF Treatment is for women only.

Health and safety legislation

Risk assessments

The Management of Health and Safety at Work Regulations 1999 require employers to carry out a risk assessment for new or expectant mothers and their babies.

A new or expectant mother is an employee who is pregnant, who has given birth within the previous six months (which includes a stillborn birth after 24 weeks of pregnancy) or who is breastfeeding.

Provided the new or expectant mother has notified the employer (in writing) of these circumstances, the employer must:

■ provide the new or expectant mother with information on any identified risks to her or her baby's health; and

■ take reasonable actions to avoid identified risks.

If reasonable actions cannot be taken to avoid identified risks, the employer must alter the new or expectant mother's work, or hours of work, if it is reasonable to do so and it would avoid identified risks. If it is not reasonable to alter a new or expectant mother's work, or hours of work, or, if in doing so, it would not reduce identified risks, the employer should offer the employee suitable alternative work. If this is not possible the employee should be suspended on full pay for as long as is necessary to avoid risks.

Night work

New or expectant mothers may be exempted from night work by a medical certificate from a doctor or midwife. In these circumstances, the employer should offer the new or expectant mother suitable alternative work before considering suspending (on full pay).

Rest facilities

The Workplace (Health, Safety and Welfare Regulations) 1992 require the

Risk assessment flowchart

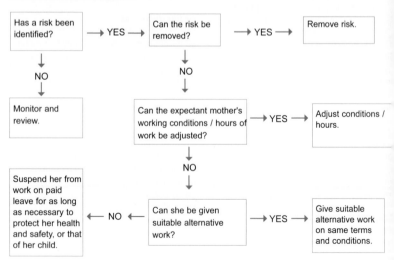

Workplace Law Network
www.workplacelaw.net

mployer to provide suitable rest facilities
or new and expectant mothers. Any
est facilities must be equipped with an
dequate number of tables and seating
vith backs for the number of persons
t work likely to use them at any one
me.

Risk assessment flowchart
On notification of pregnancy, birth or
breastfeeding, employers are required
to carry out specific risk assessments as
shown on the risk assessment flowchart on
the previous page.

> *See also*: Dismissal, p.233; Family-
> friendly rights, p.309; Flexible
> working, p.338; Leave, p.457

Sources of further information

Electronic template maternity, paternity and adoption policies and
management guides are downloadable from www.workplacelaw.net/Bookshop/
PoliciesAndProcedures.

HSE – Expectant mothers: www.hse.gov.uk/mothers/faqs.htm

Workplace Law Group's *Guide to Flexible Working 2008* provides information
on the formal legislative right to request flexible working, but also considers
flexible working patterns in a wider sense. It covers the reasons why some
employers are looking to introduce flexible working into their workplace, explores
different flexible working patterns, including their benefits and disadvantages, and
provides detail on the formal legislative right to request. For further details visit
www.workplacelaw.net/Bookshop/GuidesTo.

Manual handling

Bill Scholes, Chartered Health and Safety Practitioner

Key points
Manual handling has been defined as "any handling task involving the human body as the power source".

Manual handling thus includes lifting, lowering, pushing, pulling, carrying and holding. The most common injuries that occur as a result of manual handling are strains, sprains and slipped discs, i.e. musculo-skeletal disorders (MSDs). It shouldn't be overlooked, though, that other injuries such as cuts, burns and bruises may also occur when handling items or equipment.

The HSE suggests that in 2007 some ten million working days were lost through MSDs. One frequently asked question is "what weight am I legally permitted to lift?" The simple answer is that there are only guidelines, and no limits. For example, a sack of potatoes weighing 25 kg may be lifted safely by an individual who is properly trained and physically fit. By contrast, however, we have all heard of people who injured their back by just picking up a pen from the floor. The HSE produces a simple guide to manual handling, *Getting to Grips with Manual Handling*, INDG143.

It is therefore very important that employers look at their manual handling activities and try to ensure that employees are not put at unreasonable risk. Such prudent measures as manual handling training (which must be appropriate to the type of work) should be used. It is especially important to record the training and to provide refresher training at appropriate intervals.

Legislation

- Manual Handling Operations Regulations 1992.
- Health and Safety at Work etc. Act 1974.

Under the key legislation, both employers and employees have duties.

The employer's duties are to:

- avoid, so far as is reasonably practicable, the need for its employees to undertake any manual handling operations at work which involve a risk of their being injured; this can be either by elimination of the activity or by mechanisation; and

- where it is not reasonably practicable to avoid the need for manual handling which involves the risk of injury, assess the risk of all such manual handling operations;

- take appropriate steps to reduce the risk of injury to the lowest level reasonably practicable;

- provide information, instruction and training as necessary to reduce the risks to their employees;

- take appropriate steps to provide employees with general indications of the weight of each load and, so far

Workplace Law Network
www.workplacelaw.net

Factors affecting the risk of injury from manual handling	Questions to ask in the assessment
What task is being undertaken?	Does the task involve: ■ Holding or manipulating loads at distance from trunk? ■ Unsatisfactory bodily movement or posture? ■ Twisting or stooping? ■ Reaching upwards? ■ Excessive movement of loads, especially: - excessive lifting or lowering distances? - excessive carrying distances? - excessive pushing or pulling or loads? ■ Risk of sudden movement of loads? ■ Frequent or prolonged physical effort ■ Insufficient rest or recovery periods? ■ A rate of work imposed by a process?
How well suited is the individual to the task?	Does the job: ■ Require unusual strength or height? ■ Create a risk to those who might reasonably be considered to be pregnant? ■ Create a risk to those who are known to have a health problem e.g. returned from relevant sickness absence? ■ Require special information or training for its safe performance?
What are the properties of the load itself?	Is the load: ■ Heavy, bulky or unwieldy? ■ Difficult to grasp, unstable, or with contents likely to shift? ■ Sharp, hot or in some other way potentially damaging?
Does the environment increase the risk?	Are there workplace limitations such as: ■ Space constraints preventing good posture? ■ Uneven, slippery or unstable floors? ■ Variations in level of floors or work surfaces? ■ Poor lighting conditions? ■ Weather conditions?
Other factors affecting the risk	■ Is movement or posture of the individual hindered by clothing or personal protective equipment?

as is reasonably practicable, precise information on the weight of each load and the heaviest side of any load; and

■ ensure that any risk assessment shall be reviewed if:
  - there is reason to suspect it is no longer valid; or
  - there has been a significant change in the manual handling operations to which it relates.

If the review shows that changes are necessary, the employer should make them. The employer's obligations under the Regulations are thus ongoing.

The employee's duties are to:

■ take reasonable care of his own health and safety and those affected by his activities;

■ cooperate with his employer in health and safety issues;

■ make use of appropriate equipment in accordance with the training provided; and

■ follow appropriate systems of work laid down by his employer with regard to manual handling.

The risks presented by manual handling activities are affected by a variety of factors, not least the physical condition of the individual concerned. Hence in fulfilling the above duty, employees could reasonably be expected to advise their employers of any significant medical condition that might put them at greater risk, for example previous or current MSDs, injuries as a result of sporting activities etc.

See also: Construction site health and safety, p.154; Health surveillance, p.392; Lifting equipment, p.466; Occupational health, p.537; Risk assessments, p.639; Training, p.691.

Sources of further information

HSE: Better Backs Campaign: www.hse.gov.uk/msd/campaigns/whybetterbacks.htm

INDG143 REV2 *Getting to grips with manual handling: a short guide* (HSE Books, 2004) ISBN: 0 7176 2828 0.

Workplace Law Training provides a half-day manual handling course to train your employees in manual handling tasks.
Programme:

■ The legal requirements and the duties of the employer and employee;
■ The harm that poor manual handling causes;
■ Safe lifting techniques;
■ Safe handling techniques;
■ The relevant personal protective equipment requirements; and
■ Team lifts.

For more information visit www.workplacelaw.net/training/course/id/18.

Medical records

Lisa Jinks and John Macaulay, Greenwoods Solicitors LLP

Key points

- 'Medical records' encompass any records which may contain information about workers' medical conditions.
- Employers need to be aware of the legal procedure under the Access to Medical Reports Act 1988.
- Employers should be aware of data protection principles as they apply to medical records and establish who in the organisation is responsible for ensuring compliance.
- Employment contracts should contain a provision allowing employers access to medical information.
- Employers should always bear in mind the principles of the Disability Discrimination Act 1995 as amended by the Disability Discrimination Act 2005.
- Employers also need to be aware of the right to privacy.

Legislation

- Access to Medical Reports Act 1988.
- Disability Discrimination Act 1995 as amended by the Disability Discrimination Act 2005.
- Data Protection Act 1998.
- Human Rights Act 1998.

Background

A major issue for employers is how they can access and use information on workers' medical conditions. This may arise in a variety of situations, for example, where an employee is off on long-term sickness absence, where employers wish to use pre-employment medical questionnaires or carry out drugs and alcohol testing etc. They may also need to collate information for insurance schemes such as private medical insurance or permanent health insurance. Employers need to understand what information they may have access to, and how they may process such information once received.

In addition, employers always need to be careful not to discriminate against employees on grounds of disability.

Access to medical reports

Employers may obtain access to employees' medical records, subject to certain conditions. If they wish to obtain a report from a medical practitioner who has been responsible for the employee's clinical care, they need to comply with the Access to Medical Reports Act 1988 (the Act). Such practitioners include the employee's GP but also others who have such responsibility such as the employee's physiotherapist, psychiatrist or other specialist.

The Act requires that the employer must:

- obtain the employee's express consent in writing before applying to the medical practitioner for a report; and
- notify the employee of their rights under the Act. These include the

right to withhold permission from the employer obtaining the report, the right to have access to the report either before it is sent to the employer or afterwards and, on seeing the report, the right to withdraw consent or request amendment of the report.

The medical practitioner will normally have to provide the report within 21 days. One frustration for an employer is that an employee who has stated that they do not want to see the report may subsequently write to their doctor and request to see the report, without informing the employer. If this happens within 21 days of the employer's request, the doctor may not release the report until the patient gives consent. In this situation it may be sensible for the employer to contact the employee directly to discuss the issue.

The requirements of the Act do not apply if an employer wishes to refer the employee to a medical practitioner who has not been responsible for the employee's clinical care. This means that employers can, subject to having the contractual right to do so, request an employee to be examined by a company-appointed doctor whether from within the organisation or externally. In these circumstances, the employee does not have the same rights to see or challenge the report before the employer sees it. Hence the importance of an express provision in the contract of employment stating that the employee consents to be referred to a medical practitioner of the employer's choice at any time.

However, even if such a provision exists, it is always advisable to obtain an employee's written consent before carrying out any medical assessment. The issue of consent and the right to privacy are considered below. It is also recommended that any in-house medical adviser should inform the employee of any advice that will be passed to management following a health assessment.

Data protection

Medical records amount to 'sensitive personal data' under the Data Protection Act 1998 (DPA). If sickness records are to be 'processed' under the DPA (e.g. obtained, retained, disclosed or disposed of), then employers must comply with the sensitive personal data rules. It is worth noting that the DPA only comes into play when such information is held on a computer system or in a 'relevant filing system' (which may include certain structured personnel files).

Under the Data Protection Employment Practices Code, some core principles are set out regarding the processing of information about workers' health. These include:

- the intrusiveness to workers of obtaining information about their health;
- a worker's right to privacy;
- the need for employers to be clear about the purpose of processing such information and whether this is justified by real benefits; and
- the requirement for one of the sensitive data conditions to be satisfied (see below).

Workers should be made aware of the extent information about their health is held and the reasons for this. Decisions on workers' suitability for particular jobs are management decisions but the interpretation of medical information should be left to qualified health professionals.

With regard to the sensitive personal data rules which must be satisfied

to process medical information, the
following are likely to be the most relevant:

1. *Processing is necessary by law.*
   This condition has quite a wide
   application in the employment
   context. Typical examples would be
   maintaining records of statutory sick
   pay, maternity pay, ensuring health
   and safety and preventing disability
   discrimination.
2. *The processing is necessary to protect
   the vital interests of the worker / some
   other person.* This would occur when
   it is vital to access medical records
   where consent cannot be given. An
   example would be if an employee was
   involved in a medical emergency and
   the employee or another person was
   at risk of harm.
3. *The processing is necessary in
   connection with actual or prospective
   legal proceedings.* This is most likely
   to occur when an employer is trying
   to rely upon medical information to
   defend a claim for unfair dismissal or
   unlawful discrimination.
4. *Worker's 'explicit' consent.* There are
   limitations on how far consent can
   be relied upon. To be valid, consent
   must be explicit and freely given.
   'Explicit' means the worker must have
   been clearly told what personal data
   is involved and informed about the
   use of this information. The worker
   must give a positive indication of their
   agreement, e.g. a signature. 'Freely
   given' means the worker must have a
   real choice whether to consent or not
   and there must be no penalty imposed
   for refusing to give consent.

'Processing' of medical records

The processing of medical records (e.g.
obtaining, holding, disclosing, disposing
of etc.) must comply with data protection
principles. Before processing medical
information, employers should carry out
an impact assessment, i.e. identifying the

purpose for which the medical information
is required and the likely benefits of this,
identifying any adverse impact on the
worker, considering alternative options and
judging whether the processing of such
information is justified.

It is also advisable that employers
identify who within their organisation is
authorised to process workers' medical
information. In addition, access to medical
information by managers / colleagues
should be undertaken no more than is
necessary. For example, managers should
not access information about a worker's
medical condition when information is
only needed about length of absence. It is
recommended further that medical records
(giving details of the medical condition)
are separated from absence records
(which do not have such details) and that
medical records are subject to enhanced
security, perhaps being password-
protected.

Workers' access to records

Workers have a right to access information
held about them. This is known as subject
access and covers sickness or absence
records held about an individual, whether
on computerised files or as part of a
'relevant filing system'.

An employer can charge a fee of £10 to
provide this information and must respond
to a request within 40 days of receipt. The
employer must provide the information
in a hard copy or other readily readable,
permanent electronic form, making clear
any codes used and the sources of
information. Note, however, that access
does not have to be granted where it is
likely to cause serious harm to the health
/ condition of the worker or any other
person. In this situation, the employer
should consult with an appropriate health
professional.

Refusal to consent / right to privacy

Although an employee may refuse to give consent for their employer to access their medical records, the Courts will balance the right to privacy against the rights of the employer. For example, it is possible that a sick employee who claims a right to privacy by consistently refusing access to medical information could still be fairly dismissed on grounds of incapability where it is considered that the employer has followed the appropriate procedures and otherwise done all it could to resolve the matter.

> *See also*: Employment status, p.282; Fixed-term workers, p.335; Occupational health, p.537; Self employment, p.648

Sources of further information

The Employment Practices Code can be downloaded from www.ico.gov.uk

Mental health

Robert Males, Underwoods

Key points

Employers are subject to legal obligations in respect of their employees' health and wellbeing. These obligations arise from health and safety legislation, the breach of which is a criminal offence and also from the law of negligence, contract and discrimination. Injury to an employee's mental health is treated by the law in the same way as injury to physical health. The Health and Safety Executive defines 'workplace stress' as 'the adverse reaction people have to excessive pressure or other types of demand placed on them'. The Health and Safety Executive draws a distinction between pressure, which can be a positive state if managed correctly, and stress, which can be detrimental to health. The Health and Safety Executive has urged employers, in order to comply with their legal obligations, to carry out risk assessments and implement measures to eliminate or control workplace stress or risk criminal prosecution.

Employers are not under a duty to eliminate all stress in the workplace, but once an employee has raised the issue of stress, an employer is under a duty to investigate the matter fully and to protect the employee as far as is reasonably practicable.

Legislation

- Health and Safety at Work etc. Act 1974.
- Management of Health and Safety at Work Regulations 1999.
- EC Working Time Directive.

Main cases

- *Stokes v. Guest, Keen and Nettlefold (Bolts and Nuts) Ltd* (1968) 1 WLR 1776.
- *Sutherland (Chairman of the Governors of St Thomas Beckett RC High School) v. Hatton and others* (2002) IRLR 262.
- *Barber v. Somerset County Council* (2004) ICR 457.
- *Intel Corporation (UK) Ltd v. Daw* (2007) EWCA Civ 70.
- *Hone v. Six Continents Retail Ltd* (2006) IRLR 49 CA.
- *Sayers v. Cambridgeshire County Council* (2006) EWHC 2029.
- *Hartman v. South Essex Mental Health and Community Care NHS Trust and other cases* (2005) ICR 782.
- *Essa v. Laing Ltd* (2004) ICR 746.
- *McAdie v. Royal Bank of Scotland plc* (2007) IRLR 895.

Health and safety legislation

The Health and Safety at Work etc. Act 1974 requires employers to ensure the health, safety and welfare of their employees as far as is reasonably practicable. This includes taking steps to prevent stress-induced illnesses. Under the Management of Health and Safety at Work Regulations 1999 employers are obliged to carry out an assessment of the risks to employees' health, and this includes employees' mental health. If after completing an assessment an employer believes there is a potential risk they should take all reasonable steps to limit this risk and to monitor the situation. Non-compliance of this duty is a criminal offence as well as creating a civil liability for damages as a result of losses.

Workplace Law Network
www.workplacelaw.net

Working Time Regulations

The EC Working Time Directive was implemented as a health and safety measure and therefore the Working Time Regulations, which implement the Directive, should be interpreted in this manner. Employers have a duty to take all reasonable steps to ensure that the limits contained in the Working Time Regulations are complied with. This includes a maximum 48 hour week (which the employee can contract out of) and limits on night working.

Common law duties

There is a duty implied into all contracts of employment that the employer will take reasonable care to ensure the employee's safety. A breach of this duty is a breach of contract. If an employer breaches this duty, an employee can alternatively bring a negligence claim against them. To do this the employee must show that they have suffered reasonably foreseeable psychiatric injury as a result of the employer's breach of duty. In deciding whether an employer is negligent an important point will be whether the employee's psychiatric injury was reasonably foreseeable.

Reasonable forseeability

Sutherland (Chairman of the Governors of St Thomas Beckett RC High School) v Hatton and others (2002) – Guiding principles

Key guidance was given in this case regarding reasonable foreseeability. The main points are as follows:

- The threshold question is whether this kind of harm to this particular employee was reasonably foreseeable. This test has two limbs:
  - an injury to health, as distinct from occupational stress which,

  - is attributable at least in part to stress at work, as distinct from other factors.

- Forseeability depends upon what the employer knows, or ought reasonably to know, about the individual employee. An employer is usually entitled to assume that an employee can withstand the usual pressures of the job unless he knows of a particular problem or vulnerability.

- No occupation should be regarded as intrinsically dangerous to mental health.

- An employer is generally entitled to take what he is told by his employee at face value, unless he has a good reason to think to the contrary.

- To trigger a duty on the employer to take steps, the indications of impending harm to health arising from stress at work must be plain enough for any reasonable employer to realise that he should do something about it.

- The employer will only breach the duty of care if he has failed to take the steps that are reasonable in the circumstances, bearing in mind the magnitude of the risk of harm occurring, the gravity of the harm that may occur, the costs and practicability of preventing it, and the justifications for running the risk.

- The size resources and scope of the employer's operation, and the need to treat other employees fairly, can all be taken into account when deciding what is reasonable.

- An employer can only reasonably be expected to take steps that are likely to do some good.

- An employer who offers a confidential advice service, with referral to appropriate counselling or treatment services, is unlikely to be found in breach of duty.

- If the only reasonable and effective step would have been to dismiss or demote the employee, the employer will not be in breach of duty in allowing a willing employee to continue in the job.

Barber v. Somerset County Council (2004)
On appeal from the Court's decision in Sutherland v. Hatton the House of Lords stated that the above guidance was useful, but nevertheless was only guidance and that the statement of Mr Justice Swanwick in *Stokes v. Guest, Keen and Nettlefold (Bolts and Nuts) Ltd* (1968) remained the guiding principle which is as follows:

"The overall test is still the conduct of the reasonable and prudent employer, taking positive thought for the safety of his workers in the light of what he knows or ought to know … where there is developing knowledge, he must keep reasonably abreast of it and not be too slow to apply it."

Provision of counselling services

Intel Corporation (UK) Ltd v. Daw (2007)
In this case the Court of Appeal held that an employee's email to her manager stating that she was 'stressed out' and 'demoralised' and including two references to previous episodes of post-natal depression, was crucial to the issue of reasonable foreseeability. In the circumstances, urgent action should have been taken to reduce the employee's workload and the court rejected Intel Corporation's submission that its provision of a counselling and medical assistance service was sufficient to discharge its duty of care. This shows that although the guidance in *Sutherland v. Hatton* (2002) states that an employer who offers a confidential advice service is unlikely to be found in breach of the duty of care, each case will turn on its facts.

Relevance of the Working Time Regulations

Hone v. Six Continents Retail Ltd (2006)
The claimant in this case consistently worked around 90 hours per week despite not opting out of the Working Time Regulations. He successfully used the breach of the Regulations as part of his argument that his psychiatric injury had been reasonably foreseeable.

Sayers v. Cambridgeshire County Council (2006)
This case made clear that the fact that an employee is working in excess of the 48 hour per week limit will not in itself render any resulting injury reasonably foreseeable.

Intrinsically stressful jobs

Hartman v. South Essex Mental Health and Community Care NHS Trust and other cases (2005)
One of the appeals considered in this case was *Melville v. Home Office*. The employee in this case was a prison officer whose duties included the recovery of bodies of prisoners who had committed suicide. After helping to cut down a body and attempting revival in May 1998, Mr Melville developed a stress-related illness and retired in 1999 on the grounds of ill health.

Before the Court of Appeal the defendants argued that since it knew of no particular vulnerability of Mr Melville that it was entitled to assume that he was up to the normal pressures of the job. The defendants were not successful in this argument and the Court of Appeal held that the employer had foreseen that such an injury may have occurred to employees exposed to traumatic incidents, given that Home Office documents noted that persons whose duties involved dealing with suicide might sustain injuries to their health.

iscriminatory harassment

iscrimination legislation outlaws
arassment on the grounds of sex, race,
sability, sexual orientation, religion or
elief and age. The legislation provides
at an employer will be liable for
orkplace harassment on one of the above
rounds, carried out by his employees,
nless he has taken reasonable steps to
revent this from occurring.

ssa v. Laing Ltd (2004)

 this case the Court of Appeal
onfirmed that personal injury, which
cludes psychiatric injury, arising from
cts of discrimination does not need to
e reasonably foreseeable in order for
mployees to recover damages. The
mployee only needs to prove that the
'scrimination caused the injury to occur.

nfair dismissal

 health is a potentially fair reason for
smissing an employee as it relates to
eir capability to do a job.

cAdie v. Royal Bank of Scotland plc
2007)

 the case of *McAdie v. Royal Bank
f Scotland plc* the employee's stress
roblems were due to the fault of the
mployer and this was taken into account
y the Tribunal. However, the Court of
ppeal held that it was reasonable to
ake into account whether the dismissal
vas reasonable. The employee had no
rospect of recovery from the illness and
ad expressly stated she would not return
o work; the dismissal was therefore fair.

owever, the Court of Appeal also
pproved of the EAT's suggestion that
mployers should 'go the extra mile' in
finding alternative employment for an
employee who is incapacitated by the
employer's own conduct, or they should
put up with a longer period of absence
than they would in other circumstances.

Disability discrimination

If an employer is considering dismissing an
employee who is suffering from a stress-
related illness they must consider whether
the illness may constitute a disability
under the Disability Discrimination Act. If
an employer dismisses an employee for a
reason related to their disability they may
be guilty of disability discrimination unless
they can show the dismissal was justified.

Conclusion

To protect themselves against enforcement
action and employee claims employers
should consider the following:

- Organise risk assessments of
  potential stressors.
- Make counselling facilities available to
  employees.
- Show a receptive and flexible
  response to complaints.
- Comply with the HSE Management
  Standards / Guidance.
- Consider pre-employment health
  checks.
- Provide a written health and safety
  policy to employees which includes a
  section on how to deal with stress.
- Put a bullying and harassment policy
  in place.

See also: Bullying and harassment,
p.95; Discrimination, p.222;
Occupational health, p.537; Medical
records, p.491; Stress, p.671

Sources of further information

HSE – Work-related stress: www.hse.gov.uk/stress/research.htm

Migrant workers

David Browne, Martineau Solicitors

Key points

- Under the Asylum and Immigration Act 1996, it has been an offence since January 1997 for employers to employ any person who is not entitled to work in the UK.

- There is a distinction between the rights to work in the UK of individuals of Member States of the European Economic Area (EEA) (and Switzerland), the new 'A8' EU Member States (Czech Republic, Estonia, Hungary, Latvia, Lithuania, Poland, Slovakia, Slovenia) and countries outside the EEA.

- Employers must be conscious of the Race Relations Act 1976 in considering employing migrant workers to ensure they do not discriminate against them.

- The Government has introduced an 'Australian style' points-based system, which consolidates more than 80 existing work and study routes into the UK into a five tier system. The first tier, for Highly Skilled Migrant Workers, was introduced in March 2008. Tiers 2 and 5 are expected to be implemented in the third quarter of 2008, and Tier 4 in early 2009. At this time Tier 3 has been suspended indefinitely, largely due to the fact that these jobs are currently filled by EEA nationals.

- The new law on the prevention of illegal migrant working is set out in the Immigration, Asylum and Nationality Act 2006, which came into force on 29 February 2008.

Legislation

- Race Relations Act 1976.
- Asylum and Immigration Act 1996.
- Nationality, Immigration and Asylum Act 2002.
- Immigration (Restrictions on Employment) Order 2004 (SI 2004/755).
- Immigration, Asylum and Nationality Act 2006.

The law

Sections 15-25 of the Immigration, Asylum and Nationality Act 2006 (the 'Act') detail the law preventing illegal migrant working. In particular, employers must be aware of the following:

- Employing someone who has no right to work in the UK (or to do the work an employer is offering) is a criminal offence.

- Employers have a statutory defence for employing an illegal worker by checking and copying certain original documentation belonging to the employee. What documents are required depends on the individual circumstances of each worker. Guidance for this is available on the Home Office website.

- Employers are obliged to ensure that recruitment practices do not discriminate against individuals on racial grounds.

Under section 15 of the Act, employers found to be employing migrant workers illegally will be subject to a fine, payable for each person found to have been employed illegally. There is a sliding scale of penalties, principally determined by the number of times an employer has been und to be employing illegal migrants. The Border and Immigration Agency has published a Code of Practice on these civil penalties, and this can be found at www.ukba.homeoffice.gov.uk.

Under section 21 of the Act there is a specific offence of knowingly employing an illegal migrant worker, which carries a maximum penalty of a two-year custodial sentence and an unlimited fine.

Nationals of the EEA

Article 39 of the Treaty of Rome introduced the principle of free movement of labour and this now applies to all members of the EEA (and Switzerland). Under the legislation the family of an EEA worker may also move to the UK without restrictions on their right of entry. In particular, EEA nationals are entitled to the same treatment as UK nationals on:

- pay;
- working conditions;
- housing;
- training;
- social security; and
- trade union representation.

Furthermore, under the Immigration (European Economic Area) Regulations 2006, EEA Nationals (together with their Swiss counterparts) may reside in the UK for an initial period of three months provided they have a valid passport or identity card. Once this period has expired the individual may continue to reside in the UK provided they continue to be a 'qualified person', namely:

- a job seeker;
- a worker;
- a self-employed person;
- a self-sufficient person; or
- a student.

If an EEA / Swiss National has worked and resided in this country for more than five years they will acquire a permanent right of residence.

'A8' Nationals

Workers from these new Member States must register with the Home Office under the 'Worker Registration Scheme' as soon as they find work. They are not, however, subject to worker registration if they are self employed or provide services in the UK on behalf of an employer who is not established in the UK. Romanian and Bulgarian Nationals require authorisation from the Home Office *before* commencing employment in the UK.

Employers may continue to employ an unregistered worker whilst their application is processed, provided copies of their registration application are retained for the duration of the application process. If, however, an unregistered A8 worker is employed after one month and a copy of the Home Office application form has not been retained by the employer (or a certificate of registration has not been received), an employer may commit a criminal offence, facing a maximum penalty on conviction of £5,000. Employing a worker whose application has been refused may also constitute a criminal offence.

The law determining whether a worker is an employee or self employed is complex and outside the scope of this chapter (see *'Self-employment', p.648*). Guidance on A8 nationals is available at the Border and Immigration Agency website.

Non-EEA Nationals

Non-EEA Nationals who are subject to immigration control must obtain work permits prior to taking up employment in the UK. There are, however, certain persons who do not require permits, including business visitors, Gibraltarians, Commonwealth citizens given leave to reside in the UK because at least one of their grandparents was born in the UK, and persons wishing to engage in certain specified occupations, for example ministers of religion.

A points-based system for immigration
The Government has announced a new points-based system for immigrants that is expected to come into effect in phases between 2008 and 2010. This is the start of a five-year plan announced by previous Home Secretary Charles Clarke. The Home Office defines these immigration routes as follows:

- *Tier 1* – designed to bring into the UK those migrants with "the very highest skills". They do not need a job offer and will have unrestricted access to the labour market. A migrant who enters under tier 1 will not need a sponsor under the new system.
- *Tier 2* – for those skilled workers who have received a job offer from a UK employer. Their attractiveness to the UK is demonstrated by the fact that a UK employer wants to take them on.
- *Tier 3* – for low-skilled migration. The expectation is that low-skilled migration from outside the EU will be phased out following the enlargement of the EU. The only low-skilled routes that remain will be quota-based, operator-led, time-limited, subject to review, and only from countries that have effective return arrangements. Any new routes will be based on identifications of temporary shortages by the Skills Advisory Body.
- *Tier 4* – for students. There will be more objectivity and transparency to the decision-making process and a greater role for sponsors in vouching for the students they want the Home Office to allow into the UK.
- *Tier 5* – for youth mobility and temporary workers. People coming to the UK under this tier are principally here to satisfy non-economic objectives. Youth mobility schemes can play an important role in promoting the UK abroad, as Nationals return home and encourage further trade and tourism.

Under this system it is now the responsibility of the employee to lodge and complete the application. Consequently employers with experience of the requirements of immigration applications will be limited as to the influence they can exercise. It remains unclear as to whether the Border & Immigration Agency (which operates in the same time zone as the employer) will become obsolete, to be replaced by an entry clearance officer who could potentially be on a twelve-hour time difference to them. As there has not yet been full detail as to how or when the points based system will be fully introduced it remains to be seen whether the proposed 'one stop shop' application process, where the work permit and visa applications are filed as one, will be effective in practice.

Migrant workers and race discrimination
Whilst employers should be aware of the potential pitfalls in employing illegal immigrants, they must not discriminate against migrant workers when seeking to avoid conviction under Section 8. Under the Race Relations Act 1976, it is unlawful for an employer to discriminate on grounds of race, colour, ethnic or national origin or nationality.

The Home Office advises that the best way for employers to ensure they do not discriminate in considering migrant workers is to treat all applicants the same at each stage of the recruitment process. Particularly, employers should not ask people who look or sound foreign for their passports in the first instance if, in other circumstances, they would ask people who ok and sound British for a document hich includes their National Insurance umber.

imilarly, if employers only carry out hecks on potential employees who by heir appearance or accent seem to be ther than British this may also constitute nlawful racial discrimination. Employers re advised to remember that the opulation of the UK is ethnically diverse and that most people in the UK from ethnic minorities are British citizens. Moreover, most non-British citizens from ethnic minorities are entitled to work in the UK.

Note: The new system for immigration is not completely finalised and the above is accurate at the time of writing (September 2008). For more on this subject, see '*Foreign nationals*', *p.340*.

See also: Discrimination, p.222; Dress codes, p.241; Foreign nationals, p.340; Human rights, p.413

Sources of further information

Border and Immigration Agency: www.ukba.homeoffice.gov.uk

Minimum wage

Pinsent Masons Employment Group

Key points

- The National Minimum Wage Act 1998 came into force on 1 April 1999. It provides for a single national minimum wage with no variations by region, occupation or size of company. It covers all relevant workers employed under a contract of employment or any other contract.
- The detailed rules of the national minimum wage (NMW) are contained in the National Minimum Wage Regulations 1999. These are updated annually with new minimum rates.
- All relevant workers must be paid the minimum hourly wage averaged across a 'relevant pay period'. The hourly rate was increased for workers aged 22 and over to £5.73 from October 2008.
- Rules exist to say what is relevant pay, and how relevant hours are calculated for different types of workers.
- The NMW applies to gross earnings and is calculated before tax, National Insurance contributions and any other deductions.
- Employers must keep records.
- Employment Tribunals and HM Revenue and Customs inspectors can enforce the duties of employers.
- Not all workers qualify for the NMW. For example, workers attending work experience as part of a course of higher education are excluded.

Legislation

Both the Act and the Regulations came into force on 1 April 1999.

Together, they introduced the concept of a national minimum wage together with employers' obligations and the mechanisms by which workers can enforce these obligations.

Hourly rates and other rules

The present hourly rate (which has been effective from October 2008) is £5.73 per hour for workers aged 22 and over. The rate is reviewed annually and changes in October each year. However:

- from October 2008, there is a minimum rate of £3.53 per hour for those under 18 but above the school minimum leaving age;

- there is no minimum wage for apprentices under the age of 19 and for apprentices between 19 and 25 in the first 12 months of an apprenticeship contract. Apprentices aged 26 or over are entitled to the national minimum wage; and
- the minimum wage for workers between the ages of 18 and 21 inclusive is (from October 2008) £4.77 per hour.

According to the Act, the term 'worker' has a specific meaning. It is wider than the term 'employee' and covers a contractor carrying out services personally, unless the employer is the client or customer of the person involved. Truly self-employed people are not 'workers'.

Whether a worker has been paid the requisite minimum wage is determined by reference to his total pay over a relevant period. It is necessary to determine a worker's average minimum pay over a 'pay reference period'. This period is specified in the Act as one month unless the worker is specifically paid by reference to a shorter period (e.g. weekly or fortnightly).

In basic terms the calculation to determine if the minimum wage has been paid is the total relevant remuneration divided by hours worked in the pay reference period.

The Regulations contain detailed and complicated rules relating to pay reference periods, as well as how to calculate what remuneration actually counts towards assessing whether a worker is being paid the required amount. Further, only certain time will count in the calculation of hours worked – only 'working time' counts.

For example:

- travelling to and from home is not working time, but travelling for the purposes of duties during work is;
- time spent training at a different location from a worker's normal place of work is working time; and
- deductions from wages due to an advance or overpayment of wages are not subtracted from the total remuneration.

Generally commission, bonuses and tips paid through payroll systems are included in relevant pay to calculate the hourly pay. However, the current position is likely to change, as the Government announced in July 2008 that it intends to change the law so that tips, gratuities and service charges can no longer be taken into account when calculating a worker's remuneration. Consultation on the proposed changes will commence in the autumn of 2008.

Benefits in kind such as uniforms, meals and private health insurance do not count. The only benefit in kind which counts is accommodation. Gross pay figures should be used. Also, different types of workers will demand different consideration, particularly where hours vary from week to week. Those types of workers are:

- time workers (paid by reference to the time that a worker works, e.g. hourly paid workers);
- salaried hours (paid an annual salary in instalments for a set number of hours each year);
- output workers (paid according to the productivity of the worker); and
- unmeasured work (no specified hours – all hours worked should be paid for, but the employer and worker can enter into a 'daily average agreement' to clarify the position, although sometimes as with agricultural workers there are specific legal requirements as to what must be included).

Records

Employers are obliged to keep records that are sufficient to show that they have paid their workers the appropriate minimum wage. It is important that employers maintain sufficient records as they may be asked to prove that they are paying the NMW. A worker has the right to inspect these records if he believes he is being paid less than the required amount. An employer must respond to this request within 14 days (or a later date if one has been agreed between the employer and the worker).

Enforcement

If the employer fails to produce the relevant records, the worker is entitled to complain to an Employment Tribunal, which can impose a fine on the employer up to 80 times the relevant hourly national minimum wage.

The Act implies a right to the NMW into contracts of employment, so a worker who has been underpaid can commence proceedings in an Employment Tribunal to recover the difference between the wages paid and the NMW. It is presumed that the worker has been underpaid unless the employer can prove otherwise.

The Home Secretary can appoint public officers, who have a variety of enforcement powers. These include powers to require employers to produce records to evidence compliance with the NMW, to require any relevant person to furnish them with additional information, and to gain access to premises for the carrying out of these powers.

Inspections and enforcement can be carried out by HM Revenue and Customs inspectors.

The Act also creates a number of criminal offences, based on obligations under the Act.

These include:

- refusing to pay the required minimum wage;
- failing to keep records proving that the minimum wage has been paid for three years;
- entering false information into these records;
- obstructing a public officer; and
- refusing to answer questions or provide information to a public officer.

The Employment Bill will make changes to the methods of enforcement of the minimum wage and is intended to come into force in April 2009. The proposed changes include:

- a new method of calculating arrears for workers who have been underpaid;
- a penalty payment for employers not paying the minimum wage;
- enhanced inspection powers for public officers; and
- enhanced criminal sanctions for minimum wage offences.

See also: Discrimination, p.222; Employment contracts, p.273; Equal pay, p.300; Young persons, p.778

Sources of further information

Guidance on minimum wage:
www.berr.gov.uk/employment/pay/national-minimum-wage/index.html

Low Pay Commission: www.lowpay.gov.uk

National Minimum Wage helpline: 0845 6000 678.

Mobile phone masts

Siobhan Cross, Pinsent Masons

Key points

- There are many opportunities for property owners to obtain revenue from the siting of mobile phone masts on buildings, and joint ventures between building owners and mobile network operators are becoming more common.

- There are also other opportunities for building owners to work with telecommunications companies to increase the services that are offered both to tenants of their buildings and to visitors, often sharing the resulting income with the operator.

- You should ensure that the documentation is suitable for your needs. Operators will proffer a standard document, but you should take professional advice to ensure that the document represents the terms that have been agreed and does not prejudice your property interests.

Mobile phone masts

The first opportunity relates to GSM mobile network operators. Almost all commercial property owners will have received requests from time to time from the four GSM mobile network operators; namely O2, Orange, T-Mobile and Vodafone, to permit installations of mobile network apparatus forming part of their networks on rooftops or other such structures. The apparatus typically consists of a base transceiver station (BTS), normally housed in a small cabin or equipment room, together with an array of antennae used for receiving and transmitting signals both from subscribers and between cells forming the operator's network.

The arrangements in each case will also include a power supply for the BTS, and an arrangement for the connection of the BTS to the fixed-wire network. This is usually achieved by way of a fibre-optic connection from the BTS direct to a fixed-wire network (usually BT), or by use of a microwave dish which sends the signal to the nearest convenient point where it can be connected to the fixed network.

Third-generation networks

A second opportunity available for property owners is to work with the five third-generation (3G) licensees (the four GSM licensees plus Hutchison 3G) in connection with the construction of their 3G networks. The technology involves cells of a much smaller size than is the case with GSM traffic. It follows that there will be a need for many more base stations, and these are required quickly as the operators are keen to recover the substantial sums that they have already paid to the Government for the spectrum licences. As a result of encouragement from OFCOM and the European Commission, and also for cost saving purposes, certain mobile network operators and third-generation licensees are entering into site- and network-sharing agreements with each other. Accordingly, requests to install electronic communications apparatus on rooftops or other structures may be made in joint names on occasion.

Tower companies

A third opportunity for property owners is to deal with a set of new intermediary players, known as 'tower companies', which instead of building one base station tower for one operator, build larger towers and rent the antenna space out to multiple operators. The property owner can either enter into a partnership agreement with a tower company in respect of the rights to site towers on its buildings or other property, or appoint the tower company as a managing agent.

Other opportunities

Other opportunities for joint ventures between property owners and telecoms companies include the following:

- *Installation of in-building systems.* These will permit users within a limited area, for example, shopping centres, airports, holiday camps, to receive services without interference. The necessary infrastructure is expensive to install (the equipment for a regional shopping centre might cost in the region of £500,000) and therefore tends to be shared between operators. The landowner benefits from receiving a share of the revenue and making the property more attractive to visitors, tenants and other users of the property.
- *Installation of high-speed connections, to allow organisations to have permanent connections to the internet.* Larger organisations can afford their own connections, but it is also possible for smaller organisations to obtain such facilities by joining forces. Landlords of office buildings are in an ideal position to provide such services to their tenants, in partnership with so-called building local exchange carriers (BLECs). Once again, the landlord can expect to share the revenues while the BLEC bears the installation costs. Such a system can be expected to make a building more attractive to potential tenants.

Typical contents of a telecommunications agreement

The contents of telecoms agreements vary according to the circumstances, but typically will include provisions regulating:

- the type of arrangement to be created (lease, licence and so on) and how long it is to last for;
- the exact location of the site;
- the amount of the rent, whether it is subject to review and, if so, on what basis;
- any rights of way (or other rights – e.g. power or fibre) that the operator will need;
- the obligations to be undertaken by each party;
- whose responsibility it is to obtain planning permission if this is required;
- the type and amount of equipment to be installed;
- whether sub-letting or sharing is to be permitted and, if so, on what terms; and
- if the arrangement is by lease, whether it should be excluded from the security-of-tenure provisions of the Landlord and Tenant Act 1954.

Operators have standard agreements that they proffer, but they may not be suitable for every transaction and will need to be checked carefully with the help of professional advice.

Electronic Communications Code

Telecoms operators may enjoy various rights under the Electronic Communications Code, which is part of the Telecommunications Act 1984 (as amended by the Communications Act 2003). Those rights can make it difficult to remove masts from property at the end of an agreement. Professional advice will be needed on the implications of these rights in connection with the particular building as well as the terms of the agreement itself.

Health concerns

There have been some well-publicised health and safety issues recently in relation to mobile phones network equipment. Research is continuing, but for the present the perceived risks arising from the equipment will need to be managed and apportioned between the parties within the agreement.

Sources of further information

Workplace Law Network provides premium members with unrestricted access to a comprehensive range of online information – factsheets, case reports and daily news items – on employment, health and safety and premises management. Members also benefit from an online advice service and a free subscription to the *Workplace Law Magazine*. For more information email membership@workplacelaw.net or call our membership services team on 0871 777 8881.

Use of mobile phones at work

John Turnbull, BPE Solicitors

Key points

The Road Vehicles (Construction and Use) (Amendment) (No. 4) Regulations 2003 (the Regulations) came into force on 1 December 2003 and render it unlawful for individuals to drive a motor vehicle on the road if using a handheld mobile telephone, including any device that performs an interactive communication function by transmitting and receiving data, other than a two-way radio.

Practical implications

The law has important implications for both employers and employees. Employers should have a detailed and practical policy that explains the law in clear and unambiguous language. Employers are strongly advised against purely paying 'lip service' to a mobile phone policy given that employers will be liable if they encourage, pressure or require staff to use a handheld phone whilst driving. As such, it is not enough to simply issue the policy. Employers need to ensure it is being adhered to.

There has been some debate over what exactly is meant by 'hand-held'. The Regulations define a mobile telephone or other device to be hand-held if it "is, or must be, held at some point during the course of making or receiving a call or performing any other interactive communication function". Therefore, logically, not only would this include making or receiving calls but it would also include receiving or responding to text messages, other messages including video imagery or photographs or accessing the internet.

In terms of what constitutes holding a phone, perhaps not surprisingly, this would include positioning the phone between an individual's shoulder and ear! The law in this area does not allow for what some people may consider to be 'clever little loopholes'.

The Regulations apply to vehicles whether they be public service vehicles such as buses or taxis, private hire vehicles such as airport cars and coaches, together with all other vehicles that are used on the road including cars, vans, goods vehicles, heavy goods vehicles and motorcycles.

Therefore, in terms of producing a mobile phone policy employers should make it clear to employees that they are not required to make or receive telephone calls whilst driving, even if they have a hands-free kit. In any case, the policy should make it absolutely clear that employees should never use handheld mobile phones whilst driving and that they will never be required to do so.

Exemptions

Again, there is little in respect of loopholes and the Regulations apply even when vehicles are stopped at traffic lights or level crossings, including traffic jams and the like. The only real exemption to using a hand-held phone is for genuine emergency calls to 999 and this is only when it is not practical or it is unsafe to pull over and stop the vehicle.

In order to operate a phone whilst driving and not be in contravention of the Regulations the individual is required to use hands-free equipment. This involves using a bona fide cradle, which can also be placed on the handlebars of a motorcycle. The key point is that the person in question does not hold or attempt to cradle the phone themselves.

Health and safety
Employers need to be aware that the Regulations state clearly that no person shall "cause or permit" any other person to drive a motor vehicle on the road whilst that person is using a hand-held mobile phone or device. However, obligations under the Regulations are not all that needs to be considered.

In light of the clear health and safety obligations that employers are under to manage risks relevant to their employees, the advice has to be that staff should be told, by way of a contractual document, where relevant, or a non-contractual policy, that they are strictly prohibited from using hand-held mobile phones whilst driving and that to do so is likely to result in disciplinary action. In any event, prudent advice would be that staff are recommended not to use a mobile phone even if there is a hands-free kit in the vehicle. The reason being that even though the Regulations may not be contravened, health and safety laws may well be. Telephone conversations between employer and employee can often be very detailed in nature, requiring thought and

analysis on behalf of the employee which invariably is likely to reduce the amount of concentration to which that employee is turning to the road.

To reiterate, employers should go further to protect themselves by being aware of their duty to provide a safe working environment under the Health and Safety at Work etc. Act 1974 and be aware that both employer and employee can be prosecuted for careless or dangerous driving if causation shows that the person in control of the vehicle was distracted and not showing due care and attention.

Mobile phones in the office
Leaving the issues of mobile phones and driving to one side, the other important point to consider is the effect, and perhaps more importantly, the disruption, that can be caused by mobile phones in the office.

Ring tones can be loud and irritating. Further, if employees are allowed to keep mobile phones on in the office they may embark on conversations with friends and family which may not be appropriate. Employees who have casual conversations with their friends about what they may be doing at the weekend could arguably, in some circumstances, cause offence to other members of staff.

Several employers have had to deal with grievances raised by other members of staff following inappropriate conversations that have taken place in the office, often sparked by supposedly 'light hearted' conversation with friends.

Thinking logically, a mobile telephone connects people to pretty much everything in their personal life from parents, husbands, wives and also dealing with issues such as paying gas bills and ordering new ring tones!

Practically, it is advisable for employers to have a policy that mobile phones should be switched off or on silent during office hours, albeit this policy should be exercised sensibly if an employee informs you that they are expecting an urgent call.

Conclusion

In summary, it would be sensible to promote a policy within the company that phone calls, dealing with text messages, emails and the like should only be dealt with when employees are parked away from the road in a safe place. The policy should further promote that mobile phones be switched off or turned to voicemail during journeys so that messages can be picked up safely at the end of any particular journey.

Employees should further note, as should anyone else, that since 27 February 2007 three penalty points are applicable for using a hand-held mobile phone whilst driving, together with a £60 fine.

See also: Driving at work, p.244; Vehicles at work, p.701

Sources of further information

Workplace Law Group's fully-revised ***Driving at Work Policy and Management Guide, v.4.0*** helps you cover yourself and your staff and ensure that your employees keep to the highest standards of safe driving at work. The work has already been done for you – simply download and customise our comprehensive user-friendly MS Word formatted documentation and insert your company's details where highlighted, saving you time and money on tedious research and drafting.

As with all policy documentation from Workplace Law Group, this policy has been fully reviewed by our qualified lawyers to provide expert guidance that you can trust. For more information visit www.workplacelaw.net/Bookshop/PoliciesAndProcedures.

Money laundering

Anna Odby and Claire Lipworth, Peters & Peters

Key points

- The regulation of money laundering and terrorist financing remains highly topical.
- Imposing a range of compliance obligations on key participants in the financial system is intended to safeguard the integrity of the market and to assist in the global fight against crime and terrorism.
- Financial transactions are frequently borderless, and financial crime equally so. It is therefore imperative that efforts to combat money laundering and terrorist financing are coordinated at an international level.
- The UK derives its standards from the EU Money Laundering Directive, as amended, and from the recommendations of the Financial Action Task Force.
- Both the size of the 'regulated sector' subject to anti-money laundering and counter-terrorist financing obligations, as well as the scope of those obligations themselves, have been repeatedly expanded to reflect reported shifts in trends and techniques.
- The UK regime was most recently revised on 15 December 2007, when the Money Laundering Regulations 2007 came into force; and shortly thereafter on 26 December 2007 when the statutory tipping off offence was amended.

Legislation

- Terrorism Act 2000, Part 3 (as amended by the Anti-terrorism, Crime and Security Act 2001 and by the Terrorism Act 2000 and Proceeds of Crime Act 2002 (Amendment) Regulations 2007).
- Proceeds of Crime Act 2002, Part 7 (as amended by the Serious Organised Crime and Police Act 2005 and by the Terrorism Act 2000 and Proceeds of Crime Act 2002 (Amendment) Regulations 2007) and the Proceedings of Crime Act 2002 (Money Laundering: Exceptions to Overseas Conduct Defence) Order 2006.
- Directive 2005/60/EC of the European Parliament and of the Council of 26 October 2005 on the prevention of the use of the financial system for the purpose of money laundering and terrorist financing.

- Financial Action Task Force (FATF) 40 Recommendations and 9 Special Recommendations on Terrorist Financing.
- Money Laundering Regulations 2007.

Relevant cases

- *R (on the application of UMBS Online Ltd) v. Serious Organised Crime Agency & HM Revenue and Customs* (2007) EWCA Civ 406.
- *Hogan v. DPP* (2007) EWHC 978.
- *R v. Gabriel* (2006) EWCA Crim 229.
- *K Ltd v.* National Westminster Bank Plc (2006) EWCA Civ 1039.
- *R v. Da Silva* (2006) EWCA Crim 1654.
- *Bowman v. Fels* (2005) EWCA Civ 226.

Supporting material

- FSA: Handbook, Senior Management Arrangements, Systems and Controls (SYSC) *Sourcebook*, 6.3 Financial crime

- HM Revenue and Customs, Notice MLR8 – *Preventing money laundering and terrorist financing* (effective from 15 December 2007), *MLR8 At a glance – a quick guide to the prevention of money laundering and terrorist financing* and *MLR9 – Guide to Registration* (effective from 15 December 2007).
- Office of Fair Trading, *Money Laundering Regulations 2007: Core guidance* (November 2007) and *Money Laundering Regulations 2007: Information for estate agents and consumer credit licence holders* (June 2008).
- Joint Money Laundering Steering Group (JMLSG): *Prevention of money laundering / combating the financing of terrorism: Guidance for the UK Financial Sector*, Part I (generic) and Part II (sectoral) (13 November 2007 edition, approved 18 December 2007).
- HM Treasury: Press Notice 20/08, *HM Treasury warns of higher risk of money laundering and terrorist financing*, 29 February 2008; Statement on equivalence, 12 May 2008.

The Proceeds of Crime Act 2002
The Proceeds of Crime Act (POCA) 2002 (in force from 24 February 2003) consolidated and strengthened the previously fragmented UK anti-money laundering regime. The terrorist financing regime had already been separately revised under the Terrorism Act (TA) 2000 (see below). A money laundering offence can be committed in the following three different ways:

1. By concealing, disguising, converting, transferring or removing criminal property (section 327 POCA).
2. By entering into, or becoming concerned with, an arrangement that you know or suspect facilitates the acquisition, retention, use or control of criminal property (section 328 POCA).
3. By acquiring, using or possessing criminal property (section 329 POCA).

The maximum punishment for each offence is 14 years' imprisonment. 'Criminal property' is defined as the known or suspected proceeds of any criminal conduct, however small the amount and in whatever form. In the case of tax evasion for example, the 'criminal property' would be the pecuniary advantage obtained by cheating the Revenue, i.e. that which would have been payable on a proper declaration (*R v. Gabriel* (2006) EWCA Crim 229). Conduct committed abroad can also give rise to 'criminal property' in the UK for the purpose of the money laundering offences, unless it is known or believed on reasonable grounds that the overseas conduct in question was lawful in the place that it occurred (not being an offence specifically excluded by Order of the Secretary of State, such offences currently including any offences punishable in the UK by more than 12 months). No offence will be committed by a person who does not know about or suspect that the property with which they are dealing is 'criminal property'.

'Suspicion' for these purposes has been widely interpreted by the courts and will be found to exist where someone thinks that there is a possibility, which is more than fanciful, that another person is, or has been, engaged in or has benefited from a crime (*R v. Da Silva* (2006) EWCA Crim 1654). There must be some evidence on which a suspicion can be based, but those grounds need not be reasonable.

A limited defence is available where someone acquires, uses or possesses criminal property in return for 'adequate' consideration, unless they know or suspect that the consideration in question is helping to carry out criminal conduct. This defence can apply, for example, to he provision of professional services, provided the fee charged is reasonable in relation to the work carried out. It is for the prosecution to prove the reasonableness of any such consideration, to the criminal standard of 'beyond reasonable doubt' Hogan v. DPP (2007) EWHC 978).

A general defence to all three money laundering offences is obtained by making a disclosure of your knowledge or suspicion of money laundering, and the information on which it is based, to the Money Laundering Reporting Officer (MLRO) or to the Serious Organised Crime Agency (SOCA). This disclosure is also known as a 'suspicious activity report' or SAR. The disclosure can be made either before or during or, in exceptional circumstances, after an otherwise prohibited act' occurs, provided that it is made on your own initiative and as soon as reasonably practicable. Continuing with what would otherwise be a prohibited act after a disclosure has been made will, however, require SOCA's express or implicit consent to proceed. If SOCA does not respond to a request within seven working days, consent can be presumed. f SOCA refuses permission, however, a moratorium' period of 31 working days is imposed during which time no action can be taken.

The Home Office has recently consulted on reported practical problems created by the need to obtain consent to transact Obligations to Report Money Laundering: The Consent Regime, 13 December 2007). At present, disclosures may need to be repeated despite the content of such reports being largely identical. Yet the only concession in recognition of the repetitive nature of much of financial services work s limited to deposit-taking bodies. They are exempted from the scope of the money laundering offences themselves, and therefore also from the need to make

multiple requests for consent in respect of the same accounts, wherever transactions do not exceed £250 or such higher threshold amount as is specified by an officer of HM Revenue and Customs or by a constable (sections 327(2C), 328(5) and 329(2C) and 339A POCA).

Even where a voluntary disclosure and a request for consent to proceed is not necessary to avoid committing a money laundering offence, such a disclosure can nevertheless be required by law. The obligation arises if you acquire information as a result of carrying on a business in the 'regulated sector' which you know or suspect, or reasonably believe, reveals – or it is reasonable to expect that the information will assist to reveal – the identity of a money launderer or the location of laundered property. The offence is committed even by someone who does not in fact know of or suspect any money laundering, as long as there are 'reasonable grounds' which should have given rise to knowledge or suspicion on the part of a reasonable person (the so-called 'objective' test). The 'regulated sector' for the purpose of the POCA disclosure regime has gradually expanded since POCA first came into force, and currently consists of the following types of business:

- Credit and financial institutions;
- Auditors, insolvency practitioners, external accountants and tax advisers (so-called 'relevant professional advisers');
- Independent legal professionals;
- Trust or company service providers;
- Estate agents;
- High value dealers receiving total payments over €15,000 in cash;
- Casinos.

The disclosure obligation imposed on businesses in the 'regulated sector' frequently gives rise to problems when applied to professionals, who may owe duties of confidentiality to their clients. SOCA has undertaken to preserve the confidentiality of reports as far as possible, and concerns about breaches of confidentiality by both the person making the disclosure and the end user of the disclosure can be reported to a SAR Confidentiality Hotline. Whereas confidential information may often need to be disclosed, information protected by legal professional privilege should not be as it is expressly excluded from the disclosure obligation. The protection afforded by legal professional privilege extends for these purposes to any information passing between a legal adviser and a client, or between an appropriately regulated relevant professional adviser and their clients, for the purpose of seeking or providing legal advice (known as 'advice privilege').

Privilege also extends to the wider category of information passing between such professional advisers and anyone, be it a client or a third party, in connection with legal proceedings (known as 'litigation privilege'). Persons employed by or in partnership with such professional advisers are equally bound by the privileged nature of any information that is passed to them, for example support staff or experts. Nor is an MLRO obliged to pass on any privileged information he receives. By contrast a constable or an officer of HM Revenue and Customs must forward to SOCA any disclosures made to them, in full, as soon as practicable (new section 339ZA POCA).The courts have recently confirmed the importance of preserving legal professional privilege in the context of the operation of the anti-money laundering regime as a whole, by stating that no money laundering offence can be committed by any steps taken by legal advisers in the ordinary course of litigation (unless of course such litigation is itself a

sham) (see *Bowman v. Fels* (2005) EWCA Civ 226).

In respect of non-privileged information, a failure to make a required disclosure in the regulated sector is punishable by a maximum of five years' imprisonment (section 334 POCA). A limited defence applies to employees who have not received appropriate anti-money laundering training from their employer. A more general, but as of yet untested, defence is available on a showing of a 'reasonable excuse' for failing to report. Separate offences, punishable by the same sentence, are committed by an MLRO who fails to pass on to SOCA information received both within and outside the regulated sectors (sections 331 and 332 POCA). There is as of yet no prescribed form for disclosures, but once introduced a failure to use them will be an offence punishable by a fine (section 339 POCA) subject to a defence of reasonable excuse (section 339(1B) POCA). In the meantime, SOCA encourages electronic disclosure.

A new 'tipping off' offence applies only to the regulated sector under new section 333A of POCA, replacing the now repealed tipping off offence which previously applied in the regulated and non-regulated sectors alike. Where you learn, in the course of a business in the regulated sector, that an authorised or required disclosure has been made, it is an offence to tell someone (other than your supervisory authority) about the fact of the disclosure if you know or suspect that this would be likely to prejudice any investigation. It is similarly an offence for someone who learns, as a result of carrying out a business in the regulated sector, of the existence of any money laundering investigation that is or may be conducted to pass on this information if it is known or suspected that doing so would be likely to prejudice at investigation. The punishment for breach of the prohibition on 'tipping off' has been reduced from a maximum of five to two years' imprisonment. The restrictions on 'tipping off' have reportedly caused problems in practice, where regulated persons and institutions have found it difficult to provide their clients with a credible reason for any delay in performing their instructions. You cannot, for example, tell a client that a transaction is being delayed because you are awaiting consent, that you have received consent to transact (unless you have express permission from SOCA to do so, or a court order to the same effect) or that an investigation is being or may be conducted.

Professional advisers continue, however, to benefit from an exemption, albeit now much reduced in scope, which permits them to discuss the fact of a disclosure or an investigation with their clients but only for the purpose of dissuading them from engaging in conduct amounting to an offence (new section 333D(2) POCA). A range of further exemptions have been introduced to permit tipping off, either of the fact that an authorised or relevant disclosure has been made or that a money laundering investigation is or may be underway, as between:

- Members of the same undertaking;
- Credit or financial institutions in an EEA State, or elsewhere if subject to equivalent anti-money laundering obligations, who are members of the same group;
- Credit institutions, financial institutions, professional legal advisers and relevant legal advisers of the same kind, and subject to equivalent duties of professional confidentiality and the protection of personal data, if situated in an EEA State, or elsewhere if subject to equivalent anti-money laundering obligations, but only as regards common clients, transactions or services, and only for the purpose of preventing a money laundering offence.

For the purpose of applying these provisions, as well as the risk-based elements of the Money Laundering Regulations (see below), the Treasury on 12 May 2008 published a 'statement on equivalence' agreed by the EU Committee on the Prevention of Money Laundering and Terrorist financing. The Home Office is also in the process of agreeing a form of wording to explain the reason for delays to transactions to clients.

Practical concerns have been further alleviated by the confirmation by the courts that any delay in performing instructions will not expose the disclosing party to any risk of legal action for breach of contract, in circumstances where it would be a criminal offence to honour a customer's mandate (*K Ltd v. National Westminster Bank Plc* (2006) EWCA Civ 1039). Also the problems experienced by customers and clients affected by disclosures have been somewhat alleviated by the confirmation that SOCA is obliged to reconsider a decision to refuse consent to proceed with a transaction, not only at the request of the disclosing party but also at the request of the affected customer or client (*R (on the application of UMBS Online Ltd) v. Serious Organised Crime Agency & HM Revenue and Customs* (2007) EWCA Civ 406).

The Terrorism Act 2000

The three separate terrorist financing offences of fund-raising, use and possession and funding arrangements (sections 15–17 TA) criminalise any involvement with property likely to be used for the purposes of terrorism and with property representing the proceeds of terrorism or the proceeds of other acts carried out for the purposes of terrorism.

There is also a separate offence of laundering terrorist property (section 18 TA). The maximum penalty for both terrorist financing and terrorist laundering is 14 years' imprisonment.

Like the 'authorised disclosure' defence to the money laundering offences under POCA, it is a defence to the terrorist financing and terrorist laundering offences to disclose any suspicion or belief that property is terrorist property, as long as it is made on the discloser's own initiative and as soon as reasonably practicable. There is now also the opportunity of obtaining consent to proceed from SOCA, either before or after the act (new sections 21ZA and 21ZB TA). Like under POCA, consent can be presumed if not expressly refused within seven working days of a request. The defence will also apply where the intention was to disclose, but there is a reasonable excuse for the failure to do so (new section 21ZC TA). The consent defence is similar to the pre-existing separate defence of acting with the express consent of a constable, or intending to obtain such consent but having a reasonable excuse for failing to do so (section 21 TA).

A belief or suspicion that a terrorist financing or terrorist laundering offence has been committed must be disclosed in any event, where it is based on information gained in the course of a trade, profession, business or employment (section 19 TA). This is wider in scope than the disclosure obligation under section 330 POCA, which is limited to the regulated sector. A similar but separate obligation to disclose knowledge or suspicion of a terrorist financing or terrorist laundering offence applies within the regulated sector, triggered not only by actual knowledge or suspicion but also by reasonable grounds for knowledge or suspicion (amended section 21A TA). The offence now also

extends to attempted as well as actual incidents (new section 21ZC(2) TA). The regulated sector for this purpose is defined exactly the same as for the purposes of POCA. Both offences of failing to disclose are punishable by a maximum of five years' imprisonment. The same defences are available as those for the analogous POCA offence (information protected by legal professional privilege and reasonable excuse), except for the limited defence of lack of training. Finally, as under POCA, it is similarly an offence under the TA to 'tip off' someone about a disclosure relating to, or an actual or potential investigation into, terrorist financing or terrorist money laundering, where such information has been obtained in the course of a business in the regulated sector (new section 21D TA). The same exceptions to the new tipping off offence apply as to the analogous offence under section 333A POCA discussed above (lack of the requisite knowledge or suspicion of likely prejudice, or a disclosure in permitted circumstances).

The Money Laundering Regulations

The Money Laundering Regulations (the Regulations) implement the EU Money Laundering Directive in the UK, which in turn implements the Recommendations of the FATF. The first set of Regulations came into force in 1993, and have thereafter been amended in 2001 and again in 2003. They were replaced by the Money Laundering Regulations 2007 on 15 December 2007, implementing the most recent third Directive adopted by the EU institutions in October 2005.

The aim of the Regulations is to make money laundering and terrorist financing more difficult to carry out, and easier to detect, by requiring the financial sector to be more vigilant. The obligations they impose only apply to 'business in the regulated sector', as defined for ne purpose of the POCA and the TA bove, with the exception of persons vho engage in financial activity only on n occasional or very limited basis. The ecent expansion of the regulated sector as been accompanied by a requirement or previously unregulated businesses to egister with their relevant supervisory uthority – consumer credit institutions nd estate agents with the Office of Fair rading (OFT), and high value dealers, noney service businesses and trust r company service providers with HM Revenue and Customs. A 'fit and proper' est has also been introduced for money ervice businesses and for trust or company service providers.

he obligations imposed on the regulated sector by the Regulations fall into hree broad categories: obligations o conduct 'due diligence' on clients and their instructions; obligations to establish internal reporting procedures; and obligations to adopt appropriate compliance systems. The due diligence obligations ensure that information about clients and their instructions is obtained and recorded. Clients must be identified, and their identities must be verified, wherever possible at the outset of a relationship or a 'one-off' transaction. The new Regulations now require due diligence to be performed also on existing customers. Further information needs to be obtained to support the stated purpose and intended nature of a business relationship. Due diligence is an ongoing obligation, and must be monitored throughout the duration of the transaction or relationship.

The extent of the due diligence required will, however, vary according to the nature of the client and the transaction in question. The intention is that the degree of due diligence is tailored to the risk. Additional 'enhanced' due diligence measures must be applied to clients who

are 'Politically Exposed Persons' (PEPs) or close business associates or family members of such persons, as well as to clients who are not physically present when due diligence is performed. Enhanced Due Diligence (EDD) will also be necessary in circumstances covered by advice from the Treasury, for example for transactions associated with the jurisdictions identified in the advice issued by the Treasury on 29 February 2008 following a warning by the FATF on 28 February 2008 to the same effect (Uzbekistan, Iran, Pakistan, Turkmenistan, São Tomé and Principe and northern Cyprus). Less extensive 'simplified' due diligence measures may be applied to certain low risk categories of clients and products.

As part of this new focus in the Regulations on risk-based regulation, due diligence can also be outsourced to appropriate third parties in certain circumstances. However, ultimate responsibility for compliance can never be delegated. If due diligence cannot be performed properly you cannot act, and you may as a result of the failure to perform due diligence also have sufficient knowledge or suspicion to trigger disclosure obligations under POCA or TA. The second category of obligation imposed by the Regulations relates to the establishment of internal reporting procedures, in order to enable compliance with the disclosure requirements under POCA and TA above. In accordance with the internal procedure, disclosures are to be forwarded to the MLRO.

The final set of obligations relate to the adoption of appropriate compliance systems. A range of procedures and policies are required to ensure compliance with the obligations, and more broadly to prevent money laundering and terrorist financing. Internal systems must be established to ensure that employees are regularly provided with appropriate training. Internal compliance systems must also be established to retain any records generated as a result of compliance for a period of five years from the end of business relationship or the completion of a one-off transaction. These records may potentially be of assistance to law enforcement in the investigation and prosecution of money laundering and terrorist financing. Compliance with the Regulations is monitored by the supervisory authorities, who have been provided with powers to request information and to enter and search premises in order to assist enforcement. A breach of the Regulations is a criminal offence punishable by a maximum of two years' imprisonment, regardless of whether any money laundering or terrorist financing has actually taken place. In addition, the supervisory authorities can impose civil penalties for breach as well as de-registration. A defence is available to a person who took all reasonable steps and exercised all due diligence to avoid committing the offence.

Practical implications

The combined effect of the POCA, the TA and the Regulations is to create a comprehensive anti-money laundering and counter-terrorist financing regime which aims more at preventing crime in the first place than punishing it after the event. The obligations imposed on the financial sector for this purpose are extensive and often onerous, and their breach is severely punished.

A range of industry bodies have produced 'best practice' guidance to help with compliance, including the Joint Money Laundering Steering Group (JMLSG). Court and regulators alike may take compliance with relevant guidance into account when deciding whether an offence has been committed under POCA or the Regulations, and are obliged to do so where the guidance has been approved by the Treasury.

The role played by the MLRO in securing compliance within an organisation is crucial. The MLRO must not be impeded in his functions by reason of a lack of independence, failure to cooperate or inability to access information. For firms authorised by the FSA the position of MLRO is a 'controlled function' for which FSA approval of appointments must be sought. Firms regulated by the FSA should also be aware of the responsibility imposed by the FSA Handbook on senior management to ensure that appropriate anti-money laundering policies and procedures are in place.

The new risk-based approach adopted in the Regulations will require considerable attention to be spent on identifying and assessing money laundering and terrorist financing risk specific to individual businesses. As a result, obligations and compliance procedures are likely to vary considerably as between different industries, sizes of business and types of clientele. Careful notes should be made of any compliance-related decisions and the reasons for them. These records can be relied on to demonstrate compliance if necessary. Businesses should undertake risk assessments on a regular basis and should revise their anti-money laundering policies and training materials accordingly.

Sources of further information

HM Revenue and Customes – Money laundering Regulations 2007: www.hmrc.gov.uk/mlr/

Monitoring employees

Elizabeth Upton, Bird & Bird

Key points

The monitoring of emails, internet use and telephone calls by both public and private organisations has become a highly discussed topic. Many organisations have a legitimate need to record commercial transactions, to monitor the quality of service being provided and in some circumstances to monitor their employees' activities. Increasingly, organisations have at their disposal a range of technologies and methods for carrying out employee monitoring. These technologies enable organisations to log their employees' keystrokes, sent and received emails, internet usage, use of software applications and access to documents. There are also a range of technologies with application outside the office. For example, businesses in the transport or services sectors (e.g. delivery or plumbing companies) may be using Global Satellite Positioning (GPS) technologies to track their vehicles and drivers.

Organisations that undertake such monitoring should be aware of the rights of monitored employees and of any third party (e.g. customers) who might be caught by such monitoring. Organisations should also be aware of their obligations under the law and any best practice guidance available. The consequences of implementing monitoring incorrectly include:

- breaches of human rights and other legislation;
- damage to employment and public relations;
- complaints to the Information Commissioner's Office; and
- claims by employees in court or in the Employment Tribunal.

This chapter should be read in conjunction with those on *'CCTV monitoring'*, *p.130*, *'Data protection'*, *p.186*, and *Internet and email policies*, *p.426*.

Human Rights Act 1998

The Human Rights Act 1998 (HRA) requires UK courts and tribunals to give effect to the rights of individuals under the European Convention for the Protection of Human Rights and Fundamental Freedoms. Under the HRA, it is unlawful for a public authority to act in a way which is incompatible with a Convention right, and therefore actions can certainly be brought against public authorities for Convention violations.

However, case law since its implementation has shown that the HRA may also be used in a dispute between private parties. Although the Human Rights Act cannot be enforced directly against private individuals or companies, it may still be relevant. Since a court or tribunal falls within the definition of a 'public authority' it has a duty to apply Convention principles when adjudicating a dispute. As long as a private individual or company can establish an existing cause of action they may bring in a human rights argument. Therefore, when considering any monitoring activity, organisations should be aware of and understand the impact of Article 8 of the

HRA, which provides that "everyone has the right to respect for his private and family life, his home and correspondence". The right of an employee to keep personal matters personal, even when these intrude into the workplace has been confirmed before the European Court of Human Rights *(Copland v. United Kingdom,* 3 April 2007), in which it was held that Ms Copland's email traffic, internet activity and telephone usage were all monitored by her employer in a manner which did not comply with the law.

Regulation of Investigatory Powers Act 2000

The Regulation of Investigatory Powers Act 2000 (RIPA) lays down the legal basis for monitoring. RIPA sets out provisions for authorising surveillance and specifically addressing the legality of surveillance over some private networks.

RIPA makes it an offence to intercept a communication in the course of its transmission by means of a public telecommunications system or postal service. Therefore in the same way as it is an offence to open an individual's letter before it is delivered to them, an email sent from an internet service provider cannot be intercepted.

RIPA also makes it a criminal offence to intercept a communication made over certain private telecommunications systems which are attached to a public telecommunications system. For the interception to be caught by this provision, it must be intentional, made without lawful authority and made without the authority of the person who controls the operation or use of the system. As an organisation will have the right to control the use of its own private telecommunications system, its subsequent decisions to intercept communications would clearly not amount to a criminal offence. This provision will

not therefore restrict organisations from carrying out monitoring over their own networks.

Section 1(3) of RIPA does, however, restrict monitoring by organisations. This provides that anyone who intercepts a communication over a private network may be liable to the sender or the recipient, or intended recipient, of the communication that is intercepted. However, as there are many legitimate occasions in which an organisation would wish to monitor communications, RIPA sets out some broad exceptions to this principle.

Section 4(2) of RIPA also gives the Secretary of State the power to implement Regulations to authorise conduct which appears to him to constitute a legitimate practice required by a business in order to monitor or keep a record of business communications. It is under this authority that the Telecommunications (Lawful Business Practice) (Interception of Communication) Regulations 2000 (LBP Regulations) were introduced.

The LBP Regulations only authorise the interception of communications wholly or partly in connection with an organisation's business and only if such interception is effected solely for the purpose of monitoring or keeping a record of communications relevant to the organisation's business. This would mean, for example, that if an organisation makes available an internet terminal or a telephone in the staff canteen solely for the employees' private use and not in connection with the employer's business, then the organisation would not be entitled to intercept any such communications under the LBP Regulations.

The LBP Regulations do authorise employers to intercept communication without consent in order to:

- establish the existence of facts relevant to the business;
- ascertain compliance with relevant regulatory or self-regulatory practices and procedures;
- ascertain the standards achieved by employees (i.e. quality checking);
- prevent or detect crime;
- investigate or detect unauthorised use of the telecommunications system; and
- ensure the system's security and effective operation.

In order to obtain the benefit of the LBP Regulations, the organisation must also make all reasonable efforts to inform users of the system that communications may be intercepted. 'Users' has been interpreted by the DTI to mean employees and others using the organisation's system for the purposes of receiving and making outbound calls (but not people calling into the system).

For employers who are public authorities, RIPA also imposes supplemental restrictions on their ability to carry out covert monitoring. Surveillance is covert if it is carried out in a manner that is calculated to ensure that persons who are subject to the surveillance are unaware that it is or may be taking place.

Data Protection Act 1998
Where monitoring of employees involves the processing of personal data, the Data Protection Act 1998 (DPA) also applies (see 'Data protection', p.186) and employers will need to comply with any relevant obligations under the DPA. This will be the case particularly where monitoring is automatic (e.g. the automatic recording and monitoring of telephone calls, emails and internet access), but may also apply where staff are recorded on CCTV or where their GPS position is monitored. Monitoring which is not done automatically but which creates

paper records that are then entered into a computer system or are filed in a structured filing system will also be covered. However, if an organisation arranges for a supervisor to listen into a call but no record of the call is made, then the DPA is not relevant – although other legislation such as RIPA may still need to be considered.

There are two key provisions in the DPA that affect monitoring:

1. transparency; and
2. proportionality / necessity.

In order to establish transparency, the fair processing code in the DPA obliges organisations to inform individuals about whom they collect personal data as to the purpose of the processing – including, in this case, monitoring. The individuals should not be misled as to the purposes for which the information was obtained and are also entitled to know the identity of the party controlling the information.

The data protection principles further provide that personal data may only be collected where it is necessary for one of the lawful bases for processing, and where it is relevant and not excessive for the purpose for which it is collected. It must not be retained longer than is necessary.

These tests of transparency, necessity and proportionality are, in broad terms, consistent with the principle stated at a high level in Article 8(2) of the European Convention of Human Rights.

It is important to remember that the Information Commissioner, as a public authority, is bound to act in a way which is consistent with Convention rights. This will extend to interpreting the DPA so as to promote these principles.

Organisations should be particularly careful if it is possible that sensitive personal data, such as information about an individual's health, could be captured by monitoring as there are stricter requirements for the processing of such data.

The DPA grants the individual's rights to compensation and rectification, blocking, erasure and destruction of personal data. A monitored individual will also have the right to be provided with copies of all information held about him. The Information Commissioner may be able to take action against organisations that do not comply with their obligations under the DPA.

Employment Practices Code
The Information Commissioner has issued an Employment Practices Code for the use of personal data in employer–employee relationships. The Code has no specific legal status and there are no specific sanctions for failing to comply with this Code. However, it provides an indication as to how the Commissioner will apply the DPA and it is possible that Employment Tribunals may have regard to the Code.

It is in the interests of both the employer and employees to comply with the Code. The Code encourages transparency about monitoring, which increases trust in the workplace, and it helps the employer to meet its legal requirements under the DPA and RIPA, protecting it from legal action.

Part 3 of the Code is concerned with processing, which the Information Commissioner classifies as 'monitoring'. The Code suggests that this means "Activities that set out to collect information about workers by keeping them under some form of observation, normally with a view to checking their performance or conduct. This could be done either directly, indirectly, perhaps by examining their work output, or by electronic means."

Some of the examples of monitoring are exactly the kinds of activity that one would expect to be covered. For example:

- using automated software to check whether a worker is sending or receiving inappropriate emails;
- randomly checking emails to detect evidence of malpractice;
- examining logs of websites or telephone numbers to check for inappropriate use; and
- use of CCTV cameras – to ensure compliance with health and safety rules, for example.

The Code also covers some activities that one may not have expected to be covered. So, for example, it would also apply to electronic point of sale information gathered through checkout terminals used to monitor the efficiency of checkout operators and videoing workers to collect evidence of malingering. The Code is also intended to cover information obtained through credit reference agencies to check that workers are not in financial difficulty.

The key message in the Code is that monitoring must be proportionate. In the Commissioner's view monitoring is an interference with workers' privacy which is permissible only where "any adverse impact of monitoring on workers (can) be justified by its benefit to the employer and/or others".

The Code provides employers with detailed guidance to help organisations ensure that monitoring is proportionate. Employers are encouraged to carry out impact assessments. This involves considering:

- the purpose of the monitoring arrangement and the benefit likely to result;
- whether it would have an adverse impact;
- whether there are any alternatives to achieve the identified purpose;
- the obligations arising from the monitoring; and
- whether it can be justified.

Other recommendations cover:

- notifying employees with a sufficient level of detail that monitoring is being carried out;
- ensuring that information collected through monitoring is only used for the purpose for which it was collected;
- ensuring that information collected through monitoring is stored in a secure way and access is limited;
- ensuring that individuals can gain access to monitoring information if requested in a subject access request;
- providing monitored individuals with an opportunity to make representations; and
- having a person responsible for checking that the organisation's policies and procedures comply with the DPA.

It is important to remember that different people in a company will have a role in monitoring, and they should all be given training. These people include management at different levels, IT staff and human resources.

The Code contains guidance concerning specific types of monitoring, such as the monitoring of electronic communications, video and audio monitoring, and covert monitoring. The Code suggests that organisations adopt a policy in relation to electronic communications, setting out acceptable and unacceptable use of email, internet and telephone and the monitoring that will be carried out of such use.

The Advisory Conciliation Arbitration Service (ACAS) is an independent statutory body that provides guidelines on good practice in developing effective workplaces with good employment relations. By following the recommendations of ACAS, an employer can show that it has followed reasonable guidelines to help it stay within the law, and this would be taken into account in any subsequent court or tribunal hearing. ACAS has produced an advice leaflet on internet and email policies, which is available in printed form and on the internet, setting out the advantages of adopting a policy and providing guidance as to the content of a policy.

The Code also provides guidance on how an organisation can meet the requirements of, and come within the exemptions of, RIPA and the LBP Regulations. It should be noted that, if an organisation is making use of an exemption under RIPA and the LBP Regulations, it still needs to comply with the requirements of the DPA regarding the collection, storage and use of the information involved in the monitoring.

Regulation of Investigatory Powers Orders

The Enterprise Act 2002 gave new powers of surveillance to the Office of Fair Trading (OFT) for the purposes of investigating cartel activities. Sections 199 and 200 of the Enterprise Act 2002 amended the Regulation of Investigatory Powers Act 2000 to grant the OFT the powers of intrusive surveillance and property interference.

In addition to the Enterprise Act powers, the Regulation of Investigatory Powers (Directed Surveillance and Covert Human Intelligence Sources) Order 2003 has added the OFT to a list of bodies given certain powers under RIPA.

The legislation allows:

- authorised OFT officers access to communications data such as telephone records;
- authorised OFT officers to conduct directed surveillance (e.g. watching a person's office); and
- the use of covert human intelligence sources (i.e. the use of informants).

The OFT can only exercise these powers after authorisation by a senior OFT official (currently the chairman) and following the Home Office Codes of Practice. It has also published its own Code of Practice setting out how it will exercise its powers. The OFT is subject to regular inspection by the Interception of Communications Commissioner and the Surveillance Commissioners to ensure the powers are used appropriately.

The power of access to communications data is only available to the OFT in the investigation of criminal cartel cases under the Enterprise Act 2002. The powers do not enable the OFT to obtain details about the content of the calls or other communications, but only details of the times, duration and recipients of communications.

Authorisations to use the power can only be given when they are necessary and proportionate in order to investigate a cartel. The OFT officers can also carry out directed surveillance, i.e. to observe a person with the objective of gathering private information to obtain a detailed picture of the person's life, activities and associations.

Summary

The recording and monitoring of phone calls, emails and internet access is legally and politically sensitive. If organisations intend to record or monitor communications, they should first establish a coherent policy that meets all relevant legislative requirements. Part 3 of the Employment Practices Code should assist organisations to adopt monitoring policies that are likely to be successful and that avoid the legal pitfalls outlined above.

See also: CCTV monitoring, p.130; Data protection, p.186; Human rights, p.413; Internet and email policies, p.426; IT security, p.433; Personnel files – recording information, p.571

Sources of further information

The Employment Practices Code: www.informationcommissioner.gov.uk

Information about the OFT's powers can be found at www.oft.gov.uk

Information about RIPA can be found at www.homeoffice.gov.uk

ACAS – internet and email policies: www.acas.org.uk/media/pdf/d/b/AL06_1.pdf

Workplace Law Group's *IT and Email Policy and Management Guide, v.3.0* has been designed to alert employers of the potential problems associated with using computer systems, the internet and email systems within the workplace and to provide certain safeguards. For more information visit www.workplacelaw.net/Bookshop/PoliciesAndProcedures.

Night working

Pinsent Masons Employment Group

Key points

Employers should ascertain whether they employ workers who would be classified as night workers. If so, they should check:

- how much working time night workers normally work;
- if night workers work more than eight hours per day on average, whether the amount of hours can be reduced and if any exceptions apply;
- how to conduct a health assessment and how often health checks should be carried out;
- that proper records of night workers are maintained, including details of health assessments; and
- that night workers are not involved in work that is particularly hazardous.

Legislation
- Working Time Regulations 1998.

The Working Time Regulations provide basic rights for workers in terms of maximum hours of work, rest periods and holidays. Night workers are afforded special protection by the Regulations. Depending on when they work, workers can be labelled 'night workers'.

Once that label is applied, an employer must take all reasonable steps to ensure that the normal hours of a night worker do not exceed an average of eight hours for each 24 hours over a 17-week reference period (which can be extended in certain circumstances). In addition, an employer must offer night workers a free health assessment before they start working nights and on a regular basis thereafter. The other provisions in the Regulations relating to rest breaks and holidays apply equally to night workers.

What is night-time?
In the absence of any contrary agreement night-time is defined as the period between 11 p.m. and six a.m. Night-time hours can be determined through particular forms of agreement provided it lasts at least seven hours and includes hours between midnight and five a.m. A 'night worker' is any worker whose daily working time includes at least three hours of night-time:

- on the majority of days he works;
- on such a proportion of days he works as is agreed between employers and workers in a collective or workforce agreement; or
- sufficiently often that he may be said to work such hours as a normal course, i.e. on a regular basis.

If workers work fewer than 48 hours on average per week, they will not exceed the night work limits.

Special hazards
Where a night worker's work involves special hazards or heavy physical or mental strain, there is an absolute limit of eight hours on any of the worker's working days. No average is allowed. Work involves a 'special hazard' if either:

- it is identified as such between an employer and workers in a collective agreement or workforce agreement; or
- it poses a significant risk as identified by a risk assessment that an employer has conducted under the Management of Health and Safety at Work Regulations 1999.

Health assessment
All employers must offer night workers a free health assessment before they begin working nights and thereafter on a regular basis. Workers do not have to undergo a health assessment, but they must be offered one.

All employers should maintain up-to-date records of health assessments. A health assessment can comprise two parts – a medical questionnaire and a medical examination. It should take into account the type of work that the worker will do and any restrictions on the worker's working time under the Working Time Regulations. Employers are advised to take medical advice on the contents of a medical questionnaire.

New and expectant mothers
New and expectant mothers have certain special rights in relation to night work. See 'Managing pregnancy', p.484.

> See also: Loneworking, p.476;
> Managing pregnancy, p.484;
> Occupational health, p.537;
> Working time, p.767

Sources of further information

Guidance on night working is available from the DirectGov site:
www.direct.gov.uk/en/Employment/Employees/WorkingHoursAndTimeOff/
DG_10028519

Noise at work

Andrew Richardson, Scott Wilson

Key points

- Employers have a legal duty to safeguard their employees' hearing.
- Employers must assess the risks of hearing loss and implement risk control measures.
- There are three action levels of daily personal noise exposure.
- Employers must take at least the stated measures to reduce noise exposure, from providing ear protection or installing soundproof enclosures to using quieter processes or equipment.
- Control measures may include health surveillance, where noise exposure levels are significant.

Legislation

- Health and Safety at Work etc. Act 1974.
- Provision and Use of Work Equipment Regulations 1998.
- Management of Health and Safety at Work Regulations 1999.
- The Control of Noise at Work Regulations 2005.

The 2005 Regulations replaced the 1989 Regulations and introduced new action requirements on employers, e.g. action to protect workers must now be taken at levels of noise five decibels lower than in the 1989 Regulations and hearing checks are now required for workers regularly exposed above 85 decibels. The Regulations only came into force in the music and entertainment sectors on 6 April 2008 and seagoing ships have until 6 April 2011.

Statutory requirements

Hearing loss can be greatly reduced if machinery manufactured is quieter, if employers introduce policies and risk control measures to reduce exposure to noise, and if employees utilise risk control measures.

Under the Health and Safety at Work etc. Act 1974 an employer has a legal duty to safeguard its employees. Under the Management of Health and Safety at Work Regulations 1999 there is a duty to carry out risk assessments, implement risk control measures and where necessary carry out health surveillance.

The Control of Noise at Work Regulations 2005 require the employer to carry out noise assessments using the following five basic steps:

1. Identify where there is likely to be a noise hazard.
2. Identify all workers likely to be exposed to the hazard.
3. Evaluate the risks arising from the hazard and establish the noise exposure.
4. Record the findings.
5. Review the assessments and revise as necessary.

Employers have an overriding duty to eliminate exposure to noise of their employees and others affected – ideally by combating the noise at source. Where elimination is not reasonably practicable, the employer's duty is to reduce the risk of damage to their employees' hearing from exposure to the noise to the lowest level reasonably practicable. The Regulations identify action levels at which various actions need to be taken by the employer. These levels include reference to daily personal noise exposure, which is defined as the personal exposure to noise at work (over an eight-hour day), taking account of the average levels of noise in working areas and the time spent in them but not including the wearing of any ear defenders or protectors. The 2005 Regulations have reduced the exposure action levels of the 1989 Regulations by 5dB(A). This is a significant change, since a drop of 3dB(A) represents a halving of the sound pressure level ('loudness') of the noise. The current action levels are as follows:

- First action level – a daily personal noise exposure of 80dB(A) and a peak value of 112 pascals.
- Second action level – a daily personal noise exposure of 85dB(A) and 140 pascals.
- Limit value – a peak sound pressure of 87dB(A) and 200 pascals. The limit value will take into account the reduction afforded by hearing protection.

If an employee is exposed to the first action level or above, but below the second action level, then the employer must provide suitable and sufficient personal ear protection. However, it is not compulsory for workers to use it.

If an employee is exposed to the second action level or above or to the peak action level or above, then the exposure to the noise must be reduced so far as is reasonably practicable (excluding the provision of ear protection). An example would be the provision of a soundproof enclosure.

If it is not reasonably practicable to reduce the noise, then an ear protection zone must be demarcated and identified; ear protection must be provided to all workers likely to be exposed, the employer must ensure it is being worn and the employer must provide information on how to obtain that protection.

With the exception of ear defenders issued because of exposure between the first and second action levels, the employer has to ensure that all other equipment and ear protection is utilised and maintained in a suitable manner. This will mean regular checks on their use and condition, and health surveillance.

Employees have a duty to comply with and use the measures the employer introduces and to report any defects or difficulties in complying with the Regulations. Information, instruction and training have to be provided for all employees likely to be exposed to the first action level or above.

See also: Construction site health and safety, p.154; Occupational health, p.537

Sources of further information

Basic HSE advice – *Noise at Work – Guidance for employers on the Control of Noise at Work Regulations 2005* – can be downloaded at www.hse.gov.uk/pubns/indg362.pdf.

L108 *Controlling Noise at Work – The Control of Noise at Work Regulations 2005 – Guidance on Regulations* (ISBN: 0 717661 64 4) is the Approved Code of Practice for the 2005 Regulations.

Notice periods

Vanessa di Cuffa, Freeth Cartwright LLP

Key points

- In an employment law context a contract (whether express of implied) will have a period of notice to end the relationship.
- There is a statutory minimum level of notice which has to be given but the parties can contract to give greater period of notice.
- The notice period will be determined either by law or by the terms of the contract, but it can be varied in some circumstances.
- Employees intending to take maternity, paternity, adoption or parental leave must give notice to the employer.
- An employee wishing to take adoption leave will also need to give notice.
- Employees close to retirement have legal rights to notice.

Legislation

- Section 86 of the Employment Rights Act 1996.
- Section 4, section 11, Maternity and Parental Leave Regulations 1999.
- Schedule 2, Regulation 16(2) Maternity and Parental Leave Regulations 1999.
- Maternity and Parental Leave Regulations 1999 and the Paternity and Adoption Leave (Amendment) Regulations 2006.
- Work and Families Act 2006.
- Employment Equality (Age) Regulations 2006.

Contractual and statutory notice

In employment law, when the parties to an employment relationship want to bring the relationship to an end, they will have to serve notice.

Section 86 of the Employment Rights Act 1996 provides that employees with between one month and two years' continuous service are entitled to at least one week's statutory notice and, thereafter, to a further one week's notice for each complete year of continuous employment, up to a maximum of 12 weeks notice after 12 years. The minimum period of notice given by an employee after one month's employment is one week. A longer period of notice may be expressly agreed.

Garden leave

Many contracts of employment provide an employer with the option of not allowing an employee to attend the workplace during the notice period. The employee is paid and receives the same benefits. This is known as 'garden leave'. It means that an employee is unable to commence any new role.

The reason behind such a clause is clear. It allows an employer to keep an employee on notice, out of circulation and away from confidential information and/or trade secrets in the business. The clause has to be inserted into the contract in order that the employer is not acting in breach of the contract. See 'Restrictive covenants and garden leave', p.633 for more information.

Payment in lieu of notice (PILON)

A PILON clause gives the employer the right to terminate an employee's contract of employment with immediate effect and to pay in lieu of the notice period that would have been worked. This means that the employer is not terminating the employee's contract in breach of contract and can still enforce post-termination restrictive covenants if applicable.

The inclusion of PILON in a contract of employment means that the payment will be fully taxable.

If a PILON clause is included in the contract and is not discretionary, an employee does not have an obligation to mitigate their loss in the event that they are dismissed without notice or pay in lieu in the circumstances where the employer is not entitled summarily to terminate the contract. Therefore the employee will have a claim as a debt for pay in lieu of notice in relation to the notice period, even if the employee succeeds in finding another job on identical terms and conditions of employment immediately.

Fixed term contracts (FTC)
Statutory notice periods do not apply to a contract of employment for a specific task which is not expected to last more than 13 weeks unless, due to circumstances, the employment extends to 13 weeks or more. You can, however, include a notice period that allows for earlier termination.

If an FTC is for a period of four weeks or less, but owing to circumstances the employer allows the employee to continue in post for 13 weeks or more, the contract stops being an FTC and in a sense becomes a permanent contract with statutory notice periods applying.

If an employee has been employed on an FTC that has expired and then enters into a further FTC with the same employer, provided the gap between the two contracts is not more than 26 weeks, the

interval between the two contracts will not break the continuity of the contract.

Subject to the above, statutory notice periods do not apply to an FTC. There is nothing to prevent an employer from including a notice period in an FTC that allows earlier termination of employment as a contractual term, if the employer wishes to have this facility. It is actually considered sensible to do this as, without an early termination clause, an employer may be committed to pay for the full term of the FTC, even if circumstances change such that the employee is no longer required. The reason why the employer ends a contract early should, in any event be a fair reason and be reasonable in all the circumstances.

Notice periods of maternity, paternity, adoption or parental leave
An employee intending to take maternity or paternity leave must give notice before the end of the 15th week before the expected date of birth. They must state the expected week of childbirth and the date of the start of the leave. An employee taking paternity leave should also state how much leave is being taken. An employee taking maternity or paternity leave is able to change their mind albeit when they want to start maternity / paternity leave providing they inform the employer at least 28 days in advance.

For an employee intending to take adoption leave, employees must notify the employer within seven days of confirmation that they have been matched for adoption the date the child is expected and the date leave will commence.

Employees, unless it is otherwise collectively agreed, must provide their employer within 21 days' notice of when they will take parental leave.

Employees returning from maternity or adoption leave do not have to give any notice to their employer if they are returning at the end of their entitled leave. The employer is responsible for informing the employee of when the leave expires.

In the event that an employee wants to return early, eight weeks' notice must be given to the employer. Failure to do this means an employer can postpone the return until this has run out or until the date when the leave would have ended. Should the employee not wish to return at the end of a period of leave, normal contractual notice must be given to the employer. There is no requirement for an employee to state in advance whether she intends to return after maternity or adoption leave.

Retirement

If an employer wishes to compulsory retire an employee, the starting point is that the employer will need to formally notify the employee in writing of their intended retirement date, and of their statutory right to request not to retire, at least six months, but not more than twelve months, before their intended retirement date.

Once an employer has properly notified an employee of their intended retirement date and of their right to request to continue working beyond that date, if they wish to make a request they must do so in writing at least three months, but not more than six months, before their intended retirement date.

Where an employer has failed to comply (either at all or within the prescribed time limits) with their duty to notify the employee of their intended retirement date and of their right to request, the employee can still make their request at any time in the six months up to the intended retirement date. Where an employer has completely failed to notify, the employee's request should identify what they believe to be their intended retirement date.

See also: Dismissal, p.233; Employment contracts, p.273; Fixed-term workers, p.335; Leave, p.457; Managing pregnancy, p.484; Restrictive covenants and garden leave, p.633; Retirement, p.636

Sources of further information

Workplace Law Network provides premium members with unrestricted access to a comprehensive range of online information – factsheets, case reports and daily news items – on employment, health and safety and premises management. Members also benefit from an online advice service and a free subscription to the *Workplace Law Magazine*. For more information email membership@workplacelaw.net or call our membership services team on 0871 777 8881.

Nuisance

Kevin Boa, Pinsent Masons

Key points
- A nuisance may arise by reason of unjustified acts or omissions in the occupation or use of land or property.
- Some nuisances can be the subject of private civil law claims whereas others constitute criminal offences or are enforced by local authorities.

Private nuisance

Private nuisance is an unlawful interference with a person's use or enjoyment of land, or some right over, or in connection with it. Private nuisance is historically concerned with the regulation of land use between neighbours. You may encounter a nuisance either when you are adversely affected by a situation or when another party claims that a nuisance has been committed by you.

Private nuisance problems may lead to litigation or be settled by some form of mediation. Specialist legal advice is usually necessary. Evidence for or against the nuisance is always crucial, so formal records and other evidence should be kept. Certain defences are allowable to specific nuisances.

Generally only a person or organisation who has an interest in the affected land may take legal action. There must be provable damage, whether direct damage to land, interference or encroachment. Normally the damage caused must have been reasonably foreseeable by the person who caused the damage.

Liability may lie with more than one party at the same time.

A number of specialist defences can be raised by a defendant including

prescription, which means that the nuisance has been actionable for a period of 20 years and the claimant has been aware of this during that time.

Certain types of 'damage' may not be claimed. For example, personal injury claims cannot be made in private nuisance.

Examples of private nuisance
- Structural damage as a result of pile-driving.
- Resurfacing of a driveway so that water flows onto a neighbour's land causing damage.
- Allowing a building to become so dilapidated or infested that the building, or part of it, falls onto neighbouring land or the claimant's property is affected by vermin or damp.
- Encroachments, e.g. tree branches overgrowing neighbouring property or tree roots growing into neighbouring land. Tree problems are very often the cause of private nuisance actions. They are also often encountered in boundary disputes.
- Noise nuisance, e.g. from persistent loud music. This is a very commonly encountered nuisance and one where the local authority can be involved (see Statutory nuisance, below).
- Loss of amenity caused by smoke, fumes, vibration, smells or dust. In regard to this type of private nuisance

and noise nuisance, the locality must be considered as well as the conduct. While conduct may be a nuisance in one area, it may be tolerated in another. Compare (a) a residential estate with (b) an industrial estate.

Adopted nuisance

A nuisance need not have been originally created by a defendant if, with knowledge, he has adopted or acquiesced in it – e.g. a new occupier does nothing to prevent damage caused by encroaching tree roots.

Rylands v. Fletcher

The rule in *Rylands v. Fletcher* arises from an 1865 court case. This established a tort (civil wrong) whereby a defendant would be strictly liable for all foreseeable consequences where damage was caused by the escape of something dangerous which had accumulated on the land for some 'non-natural' purpose. The original case concerned a leak of water from a reservoir. The following principles apply:

- The absence of wilful default or negligence by the defendant is irrelevant.
- The substance that 'escapes' must as a result be likely to do mischief.
- The substance must have accumulated on the land and escaped from the land.
- Damages can only be claimed in respect of damage to the land or to objects on the land.
- The damage must have been foreseeable by the defendant as a result of the escape.
- Certain defences to strict liability are recognised – e.g. Act of God or acts by trespassers or strangers that result in the damage.

Examples of the application of *Rylands v. Fletcher*

- An electric current discharging into the ground.
- Explosives.

However, the escape of water from a sewer serving a block of flats was recently held to be non-actionable on the basis that the sewer was an ordinary incident of domestic activity.

Anti-social behaviour orders

Anti-social behaviour orders (ASBOs) have come into force under the Crime and Disorder Act 1998 (CDA 98) to prohibit a person from acting in an 'anti-social' manner. In December 2005 the Home Office announced the Environment Agency will have the power to issues ASBOs to tackle environmental crime such as nuisance.

Public nuisance

Every public nuisance is a criminal offence.

An individual claimant who wishes to pursue a civil claim in public nuisance must prove that the nuisance affects a widespread class of people as opposed to an individual alone.

The class of people affected can be broad, e.g. all the staff of a building or a group of neighbours.

A civil claimant must prove special damage, which goes beyond damage suffered by others affected by the same circumstances. For that reason private claims in public nuisance areas are rare. Any sort of damage can be the subject of compensation.

Many public nuisance cases are concerned with the highway:

- Highway nuisance such as obstructions on the highway.
- Dangerous premises abutting the highway.
- Impeding rights of access to and from property adjoining the highway.

Statutory nuisance

Certain types of nuisance are governed by statute. The Environmental Protection Act 1990 (EPA) covers many statutory nuisances and provides a procedure for enforcement. Almost all statutory nuisances are enforced by local authorities. They do not depend on a complainant having occupation rights (although usually he/she will).

The EPA covers a wide range of nuisances such as condition of premises, smoke emissions, emissions of fumes, gases, dust, steam and smells, problems due to the keeping of animals, and noise problems, both from premises and from vehicles and equipment.

If a nuisance falls under the provisions of a statute, enforcement by a local authority is likely to be more efficient and certainly less costly than pursuing a claim in private nuisance.

The local authority will require good evidence of the nuisance. It will usually inspect and, in cases of noise, will employ decibel meters.

Enforcement is by way of abatement notices. You may encounter these either by asking the local authority to take action to serve one or by having one served on you. There are specific procedures for service of notices, appealing against notices and offences in connection with them. Specialist advice will be needed. Failure to comply with an abatement notice (which is not successfully appealed) will constitute a criminal offence.

Examples of statutory nuisance

- Emission of smoke, fumes or gases to residential premises.
- Premises that are so dilapidated or neglected as to be prejudicial to health or a nuisance.
- Loud music being played several nights each week after 11 p.m.
- Nuisance from animals.

See also: Occupiers' liability, p.541

Sources of further information

The Environment Agency: www.environment-agency.gov.uk

Occupational health

Greta Thornbory, Occupational Health Consultant

Key points

'Work is generally good for your health and wellbeing.' The authors of this statement, Waddell and Burton, added several provisos in that there are various physical and psychological aspects of work that are hazardous and can pose a risk to health and work should do the worker no harm. Conversely, employers want to employ people who will give them good service, who have the knowledge, skills and understanding to take on the roles and tasks required of them. Occupational health (OH) services are designed to support and help employers meet these requirements.

This chapter will cover:

■   What is Occupational health (OH)?
■   How OH can help employers to fulfil their legal requirements.
■   The financial implications of health and safety at work whilst ensuring business viability.

What is OH?

In 1950 the Joint ILO (International Labour Organisation) / WHO (World Health Organisation) issued the first definition of OH, which was updated in 1995 to the following three objectives:

1. The maintenance and promotion of workers' health and working capacity;
2. The improvement of working environment and work to become conducive to health and safety; and
3. The development of work organisation and working cultures in a direction which supports health and safety at work and in doing so promotes a positive social climate and smooth operation and may enhance the productivity of the undertaking.

Defining 'health'

The most accepted definition is from the World Health Organisation, which defines health as 'a state of complete physical, mental and social wellbeing and not merely the absence of disease or infirmity'.

Why occupational health?

OH has been and is promoted on all levels; the international perspective is supported by the WHO/ILO. In turn OH has been, and is, supported at a national level by all UK governments to a greater or lesser extent, although to date there is no legal requirement for employers or employees to have access to OH it is strongly recommended in much of the guidance issued from government departments.

OH also figures clearly in the Government strategies for health at the beginning of the 21st century. Various government departments, together with the HSE, have produced a plethora of strategies and plans. The first of these was 'Securing health together' as a long term strategy for Great Britain. 'Securing health together' is the Government's ten-year occupational health strategy. It aims to tackle the high levels of work-related ill heath and to reduce the personal suffering, family hardship and costs to individuals, employers and society.

With the motto 'Healthy work; healthy at work and healthy for life,' the strategy encompasses all aspects of health and work combined. The 'Securing Health Together' document states in its introduction that better occupational health will benefit everyone; that if an individual's health at work is improved they will have more fulfilled lives and that the benefits to organisations are that people will work more effectively.

Since then there have been a number of new initiatives including www.workingforhealth.gov.uk. 'Health, work and wellbeing – caring for our future' seeks to pull together all the different strands of work that is going on in this area of government and to address the high rate of sickness absence and the need for proper rehabilitation procedures. The most significant aspect of this strategy has been the appointment of a national Director for OH, Professor Dame Carol Black, who acts as a link between the DWP, DoH and the HSE.

At the moment 'Investors in People' are incorporating a 'Wellbeing at Work' Framework and a free online assessment is available; there are many health promotion programmes ongoing such as Well@Work managed by the British Heart Foundation and funded by Sport England and the Big Lottery Fund.

In 2000, the Government and the HSC launched their 'Revitalising Health and Safety' initiative, 26 years after the Health and Safety at Work etc. Act 1974 became

law. The aim of the strategy was to inject new impetus into the health and safety agenda and to gain maximum benefit from links between OH, safety and other government programmes. The programme highlighted the importance of promoting better working environments. In 2004 the White Paper, *Choosing health; making healthy choices easier*, concluded in its executive summary that this was the start, not the end of a journey and that the Government was serious about engaging everyone in choosing health.

In the same year the Better Regulation Task Force produced its report, *Better Routes to Redress*. The report recommends better management of OH. It recommends that companies use the HSE research evidence-based health and safety performance index known as the Corporate Health and Safety Performance Index or CHaSPI. CHaSPI aims to help in the assessment of how well organisations manage their risks and responsibilities; it helps employers to measure, benchmark and report their health and safety performance – see www.chaspi.info-exchange.com

Legal aspects

There is a great deal of legislation that employers are required to consider and comply with regarding the health, safety and welfare of employees; not only health and safety legislation but also the legislation that comes under employment law, all of which affects the health of the employee.

The Health and Safety at Work etc. Act 1974 (HSWA) is an overarching piece of legislation in that it sets out the duty of the employer to take care of the health, safety and welfare of their employees, and of others who may be affected by his work undertaking – so far as is reasonably practicable. It is from this main Act that most secondary health and safety legislation is derived and singularly the most important regulation is the Management of Health and Safety at Work Regulations, which charge employers with the duty to undertake a risk assessment in relation to the health and safety of employees.

Employers will take a calculated risk of not getting caught by the enforcing bodies, be it the HSE or local councils, by not complying with the law. However, if they want to attract business then they may be compelled to do so. Comments have also been made that to be profitable means that companies have to operate very closely to what is legally acceptable, otherwise they would not remain in business and to succeed in business you have to be prepared to take risks – this is particularly so for small and medium-sized enterprises (i.e. enterprises with fewer than 250 employees).

One legal requirement for employers is Employer Liability Compulsory Insurance (ELCI) and this is often quoted when challenging employers about their health, safety and wellbeing provision for employees. However, there are many costs not covered by the insurance. The issue here is that it is the cost of the insurance that is the problem, not that it is a compulsory legal requirement.

OH professionals offer sound advice on how to comply with applicable legislation to reduce the adverse effects of work on health and to reduce the risk of prosecution and legal liability. This is particularly relevant where health surveillance is required or where health is likely to be affected resulting in costly long term sickness absence. It is known that work-related stress related conditions and

MSDs are the two main causes of long term sickness absence.

At an Employment Tribunal, when Dundee City Council was found in breach of the Management of Health and Safety Regulations, the personnel manager admitted that he did not understand the meaning of OH and the Tribunal itself struggled to define it during the course of the hearing. It would probably have been better if they had asked for an OH expert from one of the OH bodies to give an explanation and to demonstrate the business case. According to reports, the HSE has said that the appropriate use of OH expertise and resources is necessary to comply with statutory duties and will help with reducing work-related sickness absence.

Financial aspects

If employers want 'maximum output for minimum outlay' then they need to appreciate the financial benefits of considering the health and wellbeing of employees, particularly the occupational health or the ill health that is caused or made worse by work. OH advises organisations on pre-employment health assessment, health surveillance and monitoring, managing absence and general health and lifestyle issues.

Every employer pays a premium for ELCI. This is to cover injuries and ill heath experienced by employees whilst at work. It does not cover the whole scenario. For every £1 of insured costs of an accident or ill health there will be another £10 of uninsured costs. The HSE describes ELCI as the tip of the iceberg. As the founder of easyJet said after being cleared of the death of five people in a tanker accident and a subsequent 11 year lawsuit: "If you think safety is expensive, try an accident".

See also: Absence management, p.46; Asbestos, p.66; Eye and eyesight tests, p.305; Health surveillance, p.392; HIV and AIDS, p.398; Managing pregnancy, p.484; Manual handling, p.488; Medical records, p.491; Mental health, p.496; Noise at work, p.529; Smoking, p.660; Stress, p.671

Sources of further information

Workplace Law Group's *Occupational Health 2008: Making the business case – Special Report* addresses the issues of health at work, discusses the influence of work on health and highlights the business case for occupational health services at work.

Using case studies, examples from professional experience and the findings of the many Government reports and surveys on the subject, the Special Report focuses on the advantages of occupational health services, and the benefits they can provide to a company, in terms of financial savings, increased employee morale, and improved corporate image. For more information visit www.workplacelaw.net/Bookshop/SpecialReports.

World Health Organisation (WHO): www.who.int/en/

Working for Health: www.workingforhealth.gov.uk

HSE: *Securing health together* (2000): www.hse.gov.uk/sh2/sh2strategy.pdf

Health and wellbeing at work project: www.investorsinpeople.co.uk

DETR *Revitalising Health and safety: a strategy statement* (2000) www.hse.gov.uk/revitalising/strategy.pdf

Occupiers' liability

Kevin Boa, Pinsent Masons

Key points
Occupiers of premises owe a duty to take reasonable precautions to protect visitors or those who trespass on their premises under the Occupiers' Liability Acts and under health and safety legislation. A higher duty will be owed to disabled people and children.

Legislation
- Occupiers' Liability Act 1957.
- Defective Premises Act 1972.
- Health and Safety at Work etc. Act 1974.
- Occupiers' Liability Act 1984.

Visitors
'Visitors' includes all lawful visitors including invitees, licensees and those who have a contractual right to enter. Occupiers' liability to visitors is governed by the Occupiers' Liability Act 1957 (OLA 1957) which requires occupiers of premises to take such care as is reasonable in the circumstances to ensure that any visitor is safe when using the premises for the purposes for which he/she is invited or permitted to be there.

In the event of an accident and a subsequent claim, the court, in determining whether the occupier has kept the visitor reasonably safe, is likely to consider:

- lighting;
- any warnings given;
- the purpose of the visit;
- the conduct of the visitor;
- the occupier's knowledge of any hazards and any warning the occupier gave about those hazards; and
- the state of the premises.

Occupiers will owe a higher duty of care towards disabled people and children, and extra care will be required in assessing the risks and on deciding what controls are needed to ensure these groups are not harmed. Occupiers should, as a minimum, be able to provide, on demand, suitable risk assessments, disability access audits and access statements.

The occupier
The 'occupier' for the purposes of OLA 1957, will depend largely (but not solely) on the degree of control the individual or company exercises over the premises. It is possible for the landlord and his tenants to be the occupiers of the same premises (i.e. where the tenants control the let areas and the landlord retains control of the common areas).

Is there a danger?
When an accident occurs, the court has to consider whether the cause of the accident was a source of real danger. A danger to a visitor is likely to produce liability unless the occupier can demonstrate it has taken reasonable care to avoid or warn people of the danger. It is essential therefore that occupiers can provide evidence of adequate risk assessments, inspections and maintenance. The courts are unlikely, however, to find that there is a duty on an occupier to warn visitors of obvious matters, nor will the courts look at matters with the benefit of hindsight. This duty under OLA 1957 is therefore not absolute and is subject to reasonable limits.

Organised events

Organisers of events will of course owe a duty to visitors who attend their event. However, they may also owe an occupier's duty to others who, for example, may help to organise the event or to those who participate in the event, i.e. exhibitors or bands. It is important to consider the insurance arrangements for those organisers and any participants, otherwise there may be unlikely and unforeseen consequences.

Those participating in organised events (i.e. as exhibitors) should make reasonable enquiries into, for example, the organiser's insurance cover and require it to highlight any hazards that might pose a danger to people.

Contributory negligence

A visitor who has failed to use reasonable care for their own safety and that failure was a cause of their damage will have their damages reduced.

Trespassers

Not all visitors, however, are invited or welcome, nor do they do what was perhaps intended. As one judge observed in a 1927 case, "when you invite a person into your house to use the staircase you do not invite him to slide down the banisters". That may not stop an occupier being liable in such circumstances.

A 'trespasser' is a person who goes on to land without an invitation of any sort and whose presence is unknown to the occupier, or if known, is objected to. The Occupiers' Liability Act 1984 imposes a duty on occupiers in relation to trespassers. If an occupier is aware of a danger or has reasonable grounds to believe that a danger exists, and he/she knows or has reasonable grounds to believe that a trespasser is in the vicinity of such danger, then he/she may be found liable to the trespasser for injuries caused. The risk has to be one against which in all the circumstances of the case the occupier may reasonably be expected to offer some protection.

To balance the situation, there will be no liability on an occupier if he/she is unaware of the existence of any hazard or he/she has no reasonable grounds for suspecting that such a hazard could exist. Nor will there be liability if there is no reason to assume that a trespasser would be in the vicinity of a hazard at a particular time of night.

Particular care needs to be taken where children are liable to trespass onto premises. Damaged or lack of fencing, access to roofs, or the presence of equipment on which children can play can easily entice them and they are unlikely to heed warnings. Many years of case law has held that the content of the duty may vary according to whether the trespasser was a child or an adult. However, while this still stands, recent case law has tightened up this area of law, stating that there is a difference between being dangerous and children 'finding danger'. An occupier cannot be held liable for someone, of any age, indulging in dangerous activity on safe premises.

Occupiers should therefore consider the possibility of children and others gaining access to their premises as part of their risk assessments and, where necessary, implement reasonable controls to prevent this happening. See *'Trespassers and squatters', p.694.*

Health and Safety at Work etc. Act 1974

Sections 2 and 3 of the Health and Safety at Work etc. Act 1974 (HSWA) place general duties on employers (who can also be occupiers) with regard to the health and safety of their employees and others.

Section 4 of HSWA also places a duty on any person who has to any extent control of premises to take reasonable steps to ensure the health and safety of any person entering or using those premises.

A breach of this Act does not in itself form the basis for a claim for damages, but it could form a basis for a prosecution by an enforcing authority.

Conclusion

Unless occupiers take all reasonable precautions to ensure the safety of people entering their premises, they could face the unwelcome prospect of a claim and/or a prosecution. Taking all possible precautions to ensure the safety of all visitors is a matter of common sense. Trespassers, you might be tempted to think, are another matter, but this may not be the case. Generally, a sensible approach to safety is to consider not only those people who are invited onto your premises, but also to consider the circumstances in which others might gain access to implement reasonable measures to protect invitees and avoid trespassers gaining access.

> See also: Insurance, p.416; Nuisance, p.534; Property disputes, p.595; Trespassers and squatters, p.694

Sources of further information

Workplace Law Network provides premium members with unrestricted access to a comprehensive range of online information – factsheets, case reports and daily news items – on employment, health and safety and premises management. Members also benefit from an online advice service and a free subscription to the *Workplace Law Magazine*. For more information email membership@ workplacelaw.net or call our membership services team on 0871 777 8881.

Outdoor workers

Kathryn Gilbertson, Greenwoods Solicitors LLP

Key points

- Employees whose work requires them to be outside for long periods of time could be exposed to excessive amounts of sun.
- Too much sun is harmful to the skin. A tan is a sign that the skin has been damaged. The damage is caused by ultraviolet (UV) rays in sunlight.

Legislation

- Health and Safety at Work etc. Act 1974.

Employers are responsible for the health and safety of their staff under the Health and Safety at Work etc. Act 1974. Employees who contract skin cancer could potentially launch a claim in negligence against their employers years after their job has ended, in a similar way to asbestos-related illnesses.

There are over 1,500 deaths from skin cancer in the UK every year and that number is rising. Up to 90% (1,350) of these deaths are preventable and many can be dealt with if diagnosed in time.

In 2005 the European Parliament ruled that members' governments must decide themselves whether businesses would be required to ensure their workers are protected from exposure to the sun.

The proposed EU Directive required employers to carry out daily risk assessments for the strength of the sun and could have made firms liable for any skin cancers suffered by their workers.

However, in September 2005 MEPs voted against the EU-wide standards for the protection of workers against sunlight. Voting on the Optical Radiation Directive, which was aimed at protecting workers from damage to their eyes at the workplace, MEPs rejected a proposal that the measures included in the Directive should cover natural sources of radiation (including sunlight) as well as artificial radiation (e.g. from lasers). Therefore, the Directive only relates to health and safety requirements regarding the exposure of workers to the risks from artificial optical radiation only. The Directive has to be implemented in all member states by 27 April 2010.

The HSE offers the following guidance for employers on the subject of workers and sun protection in its leaflet, *Sun Protection: advice for employers of outdoor workers:*

- Include sun protection advice in routine health and safety training. Inform workers that a tan is not healthy – it is a sign that skin has already been damaged by the sun.
- Encourage workers to keep covered up during the summer months – especially at lunchtime when the sun is at its hottest. They can cover up with a long-sleeved shirt, and a hat with a brim or flap that protects the ears and neck.
- Encourage workers to use a sunscreen of at least SPF 15 on any part of the body they can't cover up and to apply it as directed on the product.

Workplace Law Network
www.workplacelaw.net

- Encourage workers to take their breaks in the shade, if possible, rather then staying out in the sun.
- Consider scheduling work to minimise exposure.
- Site water points and rest areas in the shade.
- Encourage workers to drink plenty of water to avoid dehydration.

- Keep workers informed about the dangers of sun exposure.
- Encourage workers to check their skin regularly for unusual spots or moles that change size, shape or colour and to seek medical advice promptly if they find anything that causes them concern.

See also: Personal Protective Equipment, p.568; Radiation, p.598; Weather, p.741

Sources of further information

HSE – *Sun Protection: advice for employers of outdoor workers*: http://hse.gov.uk/pubns/indg337.pdf

Cancer research: Sunsmart: http://info.cancerresearchuk.org/healthyliving/sunsmart/

Overseas workers

Jan Burgess, CMS Cameron McKenna

Key points

- All employers who send employees to work overseas or who are responsible for hiring labour must have management systems and support services in place to assess and minimise the risks associated with working abroad.
- Risk assessments must consider both UK law and local law. These should take into account the environment where the work is to be performed, the worksite itself, travel to and from the worksite and medical risks associated with the area.
- A failure to carry out appropriate risk assessments may result in prosecution under UK law if an employee is exposed to unnecessary risk, due to the fact that the initial breach (failure to risk assess) would have occurred in the UK, and not overseas. Breaches under the local law may also result in prosecution in the local country. There may also be a civil claim for compensation for an injury or a fatality.
- Employers' liability insurance must cover overseas accidents.

Legislation

Key legislation and regulations include:

- Health and Safety at Work etc. Act 1974.
- Management of Health and Safety at Work Regulations 1999.

Employers should also follow the guidance in the relevant Approved Code of Practice issued by the HSE.

Criminal liability

If employees are sent to work overseas, or if an employer has responsibility for contract staff working on their overseas worksite, it is important to know that if an employee or contractor is injured, killed or is put in a position which could have resulted in injury or death, that employer could be prosecuted in the UK, as well as in the country where the incident happened. Whilst the Health and Safety at Work etc. Act 1974 and associated legislation only applies to Great Britain, an employer could still be prosecuted for an overseas accident / incident if that employer failed to properly assess the risks associated with the work and did not take reasonably practicable steps to minimise the risk. The employer would have to have broken the law in Great Britain – for example, at the planning stage, when it decided to send an employee to work overseas. All employers sending staff to, or employing staff in, overseas countries must be aware of their responsibilities and liabilities, along with potential penalties, under health and safety law in that local country. It is very common for overseas countries to deal with health and safety issues in an entirely different manner from the way it is dealt with in the UK and – in particular – the liabilities of directors and individual managers may be far more prominent (since in many foreign jurisdictions, there is no possibility for prosecution of a corporate entity).

Steps to reduce the risk of prosecution:

- *Maintain records* – you should ensure that all plans and decisions to send workers abroad are documented and records retained to ensure evidence is available to show the basis of the decision.
- *Risk assessments* – you should ensure that risk assessments are performed in relation to any individual selected for work abroad. Ensure that all systems for assessing those risks are regularly reviewed and updated.

Civil liability

It is often the case that if an employer is based in the UK and there is an accident overseas, it can be sued in a UK court, even though the accident happened in a foreign country. The employer may also be sued in the courts of the country where the accident happened. In order to hear the case in the UK, the court must have jurisdiction. In most cases, jurisdiction will be accepted if the employer's registered office or place of business is in the UK. If the employer is based in England, the English courts will hear the case. Likewise, if the employer is based in Scotland, the Scottish courts will hear the case.

Assuming the court is prepared to hear the case, it will also need to apply the relevant law, which may be set out in the employee's contract of employment. There are special rules for determining which law governs the contract in the absence of an express choice of law (but see latest case law on this subject below). In those circumstances, whilst the court is prepared to hear the claim, it may be required to apply the law of the jurisdiction where the accident occurred to establish liability and compensation payable.

Prosecution of directors / officers

Death or injury of an overseas worker or member of the public in a foreign jurisdiction

In terms of the main item of legislation – the Health and Safety at Work etc. Act 1974, section 37 – individual directors, officers, and company secretaries may be prosecuted for conniving, consenting or neglecting in the offence committed by the company of exposing those in its employ of risk of injury. If the decision making process took place in the UK, and individual directors or managers were neglectful in the decisions they took in sending workers abroad, who were subsequently injured, it is possible that the company and individuals could be prosecuted under UK legislation.

The Corporate Manslaughter and Corporate Manslaughter Act 2007 makes specific provision for fatalities in the workplace; however, there is no provision for prosecution of any individuals (who could nonetheless still be prosecuted for common law manslaughter). The fatality must take place on UK territory (or an offshore platform in the North Sea, or a UK registered ship or aircraft) and therefore should a worker be killed overseas, this particular piece of legislation would not operate. Prosecution under the law of the foreign territory for the fatality would, however, be highly likely.

Insurance

In the UK all employers are legally obliged to carry employers' liability insurance. However, this requirement does not extend to employees working abroad. There have been tragic cases of employees involved in serious accidents overseas, only to discover that their employers' insurance did not cover overseas incidents. It is therefore vital that employers ensure that their policy is endorsed to cover overseas risks. Employers should also check what is required by way of compulsory insurance in the country where they are sending the employee to work.

Checklists

Practical considerations for the risk assessment

In order to show that proper risk assessments were conducted the following should be considered:

- Do you have a documented audit trail in relation to a particular decision showing managerial involvement?
- Did you ask to be briefed in local arrangements and particular circumstances that could adversely affect safety?
- Did you conduct a site inspection?
- Are there weekly reports submitted from the local area of operation detailing incidents, injuries, near misses, etc?
- Were you shown, or at least briefed, on the relevant contractual provisions relating to the scope of work with particular regard to safety management requirements?
- Do you keep training records for all team members? Are these reviewed and is training updated?
- Have you been briefed on the environmental, political and medical risks associated with the locale? This would include taking advice from the Foreign and Commonwealth Office, and taking medical advice on matters such as vaccination requirements etc.
- Do you keep written work instructions and/or operate a permit to work system? Are you satisfied that this is adequate for the work and that the system has been implemented and followed?
- Do you prescribe minimum language requirements for your teams to

overcome any linguistic problems posed by having a mixed expatriate/ local workforce? Are you satisfied that this has been complied with and is regularly monitored?

- Have you performed a safety audit in relation to local legal requirements? What steps were taken to remedy any deficiencies identified by that audit?
- If relevant, do you insist that team members perform toolbox talks? Do you keep written records of those toolbox talks?
- Do you spot-check individual team members returning to the UK to debrief them on health and safety matters overseas?
- Do you have a whistleblowing scheme in place? If you do, are employees encouraged to use it if they believe that there are health and safety issues that need to be addressed in the locale?
- Have you adequate insurance in place to cover the risks of overseas work?
- Are you fully aware of your health and safety liabilities and duties in the overseas country?

Travel risk assessment factors

The role of the country region manager or locally appointed agent will be important in dealing with the following questions:

- What is the country of destination?
- Where will the worker be staying? What type of accommodation will he/ she be occupying?
- What occupational work activities will the worker be performing?
- What medication will the worker require?
- How much travel experience does the worker have?
- What access to medical services will the worker have in the country of destination?
- How will the worker be travelling to the country of destination? What type of travel will he/she be using in the country of destination?

- How long will the worker be staying in the country of destination? Will his/her family accompany him?
- What is the worker's medical and psychiatric history?
- What is the worker's lifestyle / behaviour? Will he/she require coaching and assistance on this prior to departure? (e.g. alcohol consumption in certain countries).
- Is the worker covered by insurance?
- What arrangements are in place for emergencies and for emergency evacuation?
- Is necessary security in place?
- How will contact be maintained at all times?

Case summaries

McDermid v. Nash Dredging and Reclamation Co Ltd

Accident whilst working on employers premises – delegation of duty of care

The claimant was asked to work on a tug in Sweden owned by the defendant's parent company. The claimant was seriously injured and sued his employer claiming that they had breached their duty of care by delegating their responsibility to the parent company. The House of Lords held that the duty could not be delegated.

Square D Ltd v. Cooke

Accident whilst working on someone else's premises

The claimant was sent to work in Saudi Arabia on premises occupied by another company. He had an accident whilst working there. He sued his employer. The Court of Appeal held that the UK employer was not responsible for the injuries whilst working in Saudi Arabia on premises occupied by another company. It would be too much to ask the employer to assume responsibility for daily events in relation to premises occupied by a third party abroad. However, the UK employer would be expected to consider matters such as the place where the work was to be done, the type of work, the employee's suitability to do the work. The level of control that the UK employer would be expected to exercise would depend upon what was reasonable under the circumstances.

Palfrey v. Ark Offshore Ltd

Dealing with overseas health hazards

The claimant was sent to work for a contractor in West Africa by his UK employer. He did not receive the necessary vaccinations for the country in question, contracted malaria and died. In between trips he had been to a UK travel clinic for a yellow fever vaccination but did not ask for any anti-malarial tablets. His widow sued his employer and the clinic. The court held that the employer was required to ascertain publicly available information in respect of health hazards that the employee would face, draw these to the employee's attention and give advice on appropriate medical steps to be taken. However the employer did not do that and the widow won the case.

See also: Health and safety at work, p.368; Insurance, p.416

Sources of further information

Foreign and Commonwealth Office: www.fco.gov.uk

Parking

Kelvin Reynolds, British Parking Association

Key points

Parking and traffic management is a growing sector and this will continue to increase as there are more cars on the roads, greater issues with congestion and concern about pollution. The Government has introduced a number of initiatives to constrain the use of the motor car, especially where those drivers contribute to the daily rush-hour. In Central London, exceptional circumstances have attracted the introduction of Congestion Charging, with a significant and positive impact upon the reduction of, principally, private motor car traffic. In 2006 the London Scheme was extended west to increase the controlled area by over 50%. A similar solution is not necessarily justifiable in all towns and cities, but it is being considered by some, including Manchester for example, as part of an overall transport strategy.

Greener travel and driving

Road charging

During the summer of 2005, then-Transport Secretary Alistair Darling gave the firmest indication yet that the road tax regime will in the future be replaced by a system of 'pay as you drive' road charging. The latest proposals on road charging could see the introduction of metered usage costs ranging from 2p per mile up to £1.34 per mile, calculated using GPS tracking software fitted in the vehicle. As far as parking is concerned, road charging could have the effect of reducing the number of vehicles actively used on journeys to and from work or in the course of work, and hence may actually reduce the burden on employers to provide parking in future. With six new bands being added to the Vehicle Excise Duty Bill next year and a first-year road duty for high-emitting cars being introduced in 2010, coupled with increasing fuel prices, drivers are becoming much more aware of car usage and are exploring alternative transport options. The year

2006 also saw the introduction in London of Residents Parking Schemes where charges were based upon the energy efficiency and emissions ratings for vehicles. Hybrid fuel and efficient vehicles enjoy significant discounts in these schemes as well as in Congestion Charging. More Councils are now adopting this approach in Resident Parking Schemes.

Car Sharing Schemes and Car Clubs

There is also now significant emphasis being placed on these schemes and many web-based services are now available to help find people who might be able to share a journey to work. Additionally multi-occupancy lanes are being created as part of two motorway widening schemes on the M1 and M606/M62. The West Yorkshire Scheme will allow vehicles carrying more than one person to bypass congestion at M62 J26 and gain priority entry on to the eastbound M62. Other vehicles on the M606 and M62 will not suffer from additional delays and should also benefit from improved journey times.

Workplace parking levy

Every one of Britain's towns and cities should have an effective strategy for parking management which should always be considered as part of an overall transport policy; indeed the Traffic Management Acts endorse this approach. With over 30 million cars registered for use in the UK, proper and effective management parking is absolutely necessary for our towns and cities. For some the car is the most appropriate form of transport and the Workplace Parking Levy is just one of a number of measures available to Councils to combat rush-hour congestion subject to improved local public transport and enhanced on-street parking controls One such scheme is being mooted in Nottingham at present. Certain organisations and businesses out of town, or whose staff and customers do not contribute to the rush-hour, are at present exempt.

The levy is charged as a supplement to the standard annual business rates and based upon an application for a licence for a declared number of parking spaces. Enforcement is carried out by the random visits of authority inspectors. Financial penalties will apply where it can be shown that the licensed number of parking spaces has been exceeded.

It can be assumed that some employers will prefer to give up spaces to gain relief from the levy. In such cases, it may also be assumed that, with increased on-street parking controls, those displaced employees who cannot be persuaded to use public transport will seek alternative off-street parking places, especially where there may be no parking charges. It is recommended that employers and their associations involve themselves from the outset in any public consultation process.

If the levy becomes inevitable, it should be a priority to protect against unauthorised use of private parking places, if necessary by barriers that can be controlled by pass-card or similar systems. Visitors' and delivery vehicles cannot always be anticipated, but simple add-on systems and voice communications exist to enable barriers to be safely opened from a remote reception or office to allow authorised access and egress. For transparency and legitimacy of purpose it is important that any surplus raised through such levies are invested in improved transport and parking systems and not used simply as revenue-raising opportunities. If the Nottingham scheme goes ahead and is successful, it is likely other City Councils may follow suit.

Civil Parking Enforcement

On 31 March 2008 new Regulations, under the Traffic Management Act 2004, were introduced in England that saw the first changes to on-street parking since 1993. The policies provide motorists with a fair and consistent service across the country, helping raise industry standards in parking. Under the new proposals, DPE has become Civil Parking Enforcement (CPE), and Parking Attendants are now known officially as Civil Enforcement Officers (CEOs), although many will still be seen operating as Parking Attendants in our towns and cities. Councils now need to be more transparent about their parking management policies. Under the regulations they have to provide better training for everyone involved in parking enforcement; undertake regular reviews of policies through consultation with stakeholders; and communicate these policies effectively to the public. They must make clear that enforcement is based on compliance with local parking regulations and not the number of tickets issued. The new regulations give greater authority to independent adjudicators. They now have the power to refer cases back to local authorities where a parking contravention has taken place, and can, in mitigating circumstances, ask the local authority to consider cancelling the penalty charge. Enforcement will now also be 'proportional' to the contravention's seriousness, providing for differential charges, with penalties for such matters as parking on a double yellow line being higher than those for, say, overstaying on a meter. These measures can only benefit drivers, and will help to reassure the public that everyone is working towards making parking management and enforcement a fair and consistent service. As these new regulations apply to all areas where local councils undertake parking control, regulation and enforcement, and most of our towns and cities do this now, almost everyone should see the benefits that are intended with the new regulations.

Approved Operators Scheme
As a part of raising operating standards in the private parking industry, in October 2007, the Driver and Vehicle Licensing Agency (DVLA) began releasing vehicle registration information electronically only to those companies which are members of an Accredited Trade Association (ATA). The British Parking Association (BPA) is the DVLA's first ATA and currently the only one in the parking sector. As part of its aim to standardise the industry's approach to ticketing on private land and encourage fairness for the consumer, the BPA has launched its own Approved Operator Scheme (AOS), backed by a Code of Practice for Parking Enforcement on Private Land and Unregulated Car Parks. Members that do not comply with the terms of this Code will be subject to a stringent compliance audit, and could have their BPA membership initially suspended, and possibly terminated.

The AOS is designed specifically for BPA members that operate parking enforcement services on private land and unregulated public car parks. Operators

may conduct a range of services in this sector, including but not limited to, vehicle immobilisation and/or removal, ticketing, or services such as back office functions, data management and debt recovery. The Code is designed to ensure that motorists are treated firmly but fairly and will mean an end to rogue companies issuing parking tickets on private land. Landowners and businesses, especially those that provide public parking, are encouraged to employ only companies that are members of the BPA's AOS to manage their parking. This will ensure high standards plus fair and reasonable enforcements and should mitigate the number of complaints and media coverage for poor parking management. Where a Local Authority or a hospital, for example, contracts out off-street enforcement, that third party will be required to become a member of the AOS in order to maintain electronic access to vehicle keeper data, even if the contractor uses the Local Authority gateway to the DVLA data. The Approved Operators Scheme Code is being fully revised and updated and will be published in early 2009. It will provide Guidance on the management and enforcement of privately controlled parking areas and related activities.

Protect your parking rights and resources
Parking on private land is a much misunderstood area and significant press coverage is a result of some of the enforcement methods used. See below for information on the BPA's Approved Operators Scheme (AOS) for enforcement of parking on private land which became effective on 1 October 2007 and is being developed with the DVLA. As an additional means of safeguarding the use of spaces, it is recommended that the rights of entry to and use of the property by car drivers be governed by a 'contract to enter / wait / park'. This should be displayed as

a conspicuous sign at the entrance to the property. In this way, the contract is an offer that may be refused and so drivers can turn away before entering. However, f drivers pass the sign and by entering the land, it may be deemed that they have given their consent to the posted terms and conditions of entry and will be bound by any sanction for non-compliance that has been published; in effect a contract has been established. Good practice suggests that the wording of these signs should be periodically reviewed, as usually, once written, they are rarely revisited, even if circumstances change.

For the avoidance of doubt, your contract signs should ideally include all relevant terms and conditions of entry to the land and be repeated in conspicuous locations where drivers can see them after leaving their vehicles. The BPA Code of Practice for its AOS makes recommendations about best practice for this kind of signage. A new updated version will be published in early 2009. Similarly, while a property owner cannot be held responsible for the autonomous criminal actions of third parties, it is common to display a disclaimer notice to that effect. Vehicle crime is prevalent and people should be encouraged to take care of themselves and their property. Motorists using car parks should be reminded not to leave valuables on display and to remove then if practical – windscreen-mounted Sat Navs should always be taken out of the car and the 'tell-tale' ring marks on screen should be wiped off. Cars should always be securely locked.

Automatic Number Plate Recognition – a growing trend
For any business that operates off-street parking as a private Landlord / Landowner, they will have two main concerns:

1. Protect his property from unwanted trespass.

2. Ensure that in protecting his property, legitimate users of his facilities are able to park unhindered in his private car park.

There are a number of methods by which this can be enforced, but the newest of these is Automatic Number Plate Recognition technology (ANPR). As with all methods of enforcement of unregulated private land, charges enforced by ANPR are subject to the law of Contract. They are also self regulated through the BPA's Code of Practice for parking enforcement on private land and unregulated private car parks (a revised edition will be published in early 2009), and voluntary membership to the BPA's Approved Operator Scheme.

The principle is as follows:

1. CCTV style cameras are placed at the entrance and exit to a car park.
2. Timed photographs are taken of the vehicle itself entering and leaving the car park, and also close-ups of the vehicle's number plate.
3. The duration of the stay of the vehicle is calculated from the times registered on the two sets of photographs.
4. If a vehicle has exceeded the duration of stay either mentioned on the parking ticket or on car park signage (e.g. 'Maximum 2 hour stay for customers only'), then the driver of the vehicle will be required to pay an excess parking charge (which will also be mentioned in the car park's signage).
5. If a driver does contravene any of the terms and conditions laid out in the signage, they should be aware that they will not receive a ticket at the car park site. Using the vehicle's registration number, the operator will access the DVLA's Vehicle Keepers' details database (with the Reasonable Cause of pursuing a broken contract for parking on private land) and send a charge certificate to the keeper of

the vehicle. Proper enforcement on private land is dependant on clear signage that is visible from all points of the car park.

The BPA's revised Code of Practice contains recommendations for the size, placement and information for private car park signage, including the fact that the car park is monitored by ANPR technology and that DVLA with be contacted to obtain keeper details in the event of a parking contravention occurring. As with all new technology, there are issues associated with its use:

Repeat users of a car park inside a 24 hour period sometimes find that their first entry is paired with their last exit, resulting in an 'overstay'. Operators are becoming aware of this and should now be checking all ANPR transactions to ensure that this does not occur.

Some 'drive in / drive out' motorists that have activated the system receive a charge certificate even though they have not parked or taken a ticket. Reputable operators tend not to uphold charge certificates issued in this manner (unless advised differently by the Landowner / Landlord), but operators should also now be factoring in a small 'grace period' to allow a driver time either to find a parking space (and to leave if there is not one) or make a decision whether the tariff is appropriate for their use or not. This 'grace period' is however at the discretion of the Landlord/Landowner and will also vary in duration, dependant on the size/layout/ circumstances of the car park.

The BPA has published a *Parking Practice Note of Grace Periods and Observation Periods* (to confirm that a breach of contract or contravention has occurred) and it is important to understand the difference. Copies may be obtained from BPA.

Safer Parking Scheme

Large or long-term car parks used by employers, staff and customers can all benefit from being a member of the Safer Parking Scheme (SPS). The scheme is run by the British Parking Association (BPA) for the Association of Chief Police Officers and is aimed at reducing crime and the fear of crime in parking areas. The Park Mark® Award has been designed to create a benchmark standard for parking across the UK, establishing safer parking, for drivers and vehicles. The Safer Parking Scheme (SPS), instantly recognisable by the ParkMark® logo, is designed to create a benchmark standard for all parking areas across the UK, to create safer parking areas both for the public and their vehicles. National statistics show that around 22% of vehicle crimes occur in car parks. When using a Park Mark® car park people can be confident in the knowledge that the area has been thoroughly vetted by a Police Accredited Assessor and they are parking in a safe and non-threatening environment. Many parking facilities with the award have experienced a dramatic reduction in crime or, where facilities do not experience vehicle related crime, have been able to create an environment where motorists feel safer. The scheme has nearly 4,000 member car parks in the UK and is increasing weekly. To find out where your nearest Park Mark® accredited car park is visit www.parkmark.co.uk. Driving directions are also available on this website and further useful information and links will be added during 2009.

Life-Care Plans and Asset Management for Parking Structures

The owner or operator of any car parking facility has a duty under law to provide and maintain them in such a manner that it does not endanger persons whilst in use – this may include employees, maintenance workers, visitors (lawful or otherwise) and children. There are no exceptions, and failure to comply with the legal obligations may give rise to prosecution. The law in this area is complex and advice should be taken on best practice. If a car park structure is left unchecked, or has reduced levels of safety, problems can easily occur. This can be avoided by adopting a Life-Care plan, which is a strategic and managed approach to the inspection, maintenance and management of parking structures. It is also a requirement to confirm that a Life-Care Plan exists where appropriate when considering entering a parking facility into the Safer Parking Scheme. The BPA has published a Parking Practice Note on Life Care Plans and Asset Management and copies may be obtained from the Association.

Nuisance vehicles – abandoned vehicles and trailers

Public perception of an area with abandoned and other nuisance vehicles is of deprivation and neglect and is regarded by the police as 'signal crime'. From the perspective of running car parking services, the principal points to be considered are that abandoned and nuisance vehicles are usually untaxed, unregistered and not roadworthy.

The legislation

There is little doubt that many of the problems with the fast removal of abandoned and other nuisance vehicles revolve around the very complicated set of legislation which governs them. No fewer than five acts of parliament or regulations directly affect how they are to be classified, removed and restored to the owner, and when they can be destroyed. This does not include the human rights requirements or the European End of Life Vehicle Directive. The main piece of legislation on vehicle abandonment is the Refuse Disposal (Amenity) Act 1978. This provides a clear 'duty' on the local authority for removing vehicles that they believe to be abandoned

in their area. The local authority must delegate the removal of the vehicle to what are referred to as 'authorised officers'. These officers should be well trained and experts in the field; they should understand the legislation and be able to offer themselves as 'expert witnesses' in cases of vehicle abandonment in courts. In legal terms, it is their decision alone as to whether a vehicle is abandoned or not. The local authority duty extends to all vehicles believed to be abandoned in the 'open air', which by definition means a car park facility with at least one side being open. There are different routes for dealing with the vehicle if it has been abandoned on a road or private land. The BPA has published a Parking Practice Note on Abandoned and Nuisance Vehicles and copies may be obtained from the Association.

Requirement to meet the needs of the disabled

Since 1 October 2004 owners or operators are required by The Disability Discrimination Act 1995 (DDA) to have taken all 'reasonable' steps to meet the needs of motorists and passengers with a disability including any changes to their car parks to ensure that there is no disadvantage to disabled people when using the service. The Act covers the widest spectrum, including those with auditory and visual impairments as well as those with specific mobility difficulties. Remember, not everyone who is disabled is a wheelchair user – these are just the obvious ones and employers should positively give consideration and take action to meet the varying needs of disabled people wherever change may be necessary, through consultation, education and constant review at every level.

When assessing the area needed for staff and customer parking, it should be noted that the current UK 'norm' for parking spaces is 2.4 metres wide by 4.8 metres long. The space for manoeuvring (roadways) between bays is six metres. These dimensions are neither minimum nor written in tablets of stone, and may be revised to suit your particular needs but remember that good access and wider bays aids efficient use of the parking area.

Government Guidelines (*Inclusive Mobility* published by DfT) recommends that 6% of parking should be allocated to disabled people unless otherwise covered by local planning regulations. The Guidance also recommends how to identify these spaces, with special markings and signage. It is recommended that parking spaces for disabled people are 3.6 metres width, where the difference (1.2 metres) is yellow hatched to enable sufficient access for wheelchair users. These spaces should carry the 'wheelchair' logo on the surface of the bay and display the appropriate sign at a driver's eye level. Advice on how to ensure that you cater for the needs of people with disabilities can be obtained from organisations such as Mobilise and RADAR whom the BPA works closely with.

Blue Badge Scheme

Since its introduction in 1971, the Blue Badge Scheme has played an important part in traffic management for those with mobility impairment. Its aim is to ensure that these people are more mobile and have access to adequate and fair parking provision. However, the growing abuse and fraudulent use of the badges, over the past five years, has threatened the integrity of the system. Accessibility is a key concern for local authorities, but at the same time, misuse of the scheme cannot be left unchallenged. There are no standard processes in place for the issue of badges – different departments within different Local Authorities are responsible

for their issue and administration. Enforcement is difficult, as the badge is issued to the holder and not to the vehicle and this, coupled with the fact that there is no central database for Blue Badge information, creates problems. It is estimated that currently 500,000 motorists are abusing the scheme across the UK, meaning that there is less space for eligible badge holders. Blue Badge fraud is a growing and widespread problem, from the use of fake badges; theft of genuine badges from cars; and non-disabled people using Blue Badge parking spaces. The introduction of the powers for enforcement officers to inspect Blue Badges is a good first step in combating the issue of Blue Badge fraud but it doesn't go far enough.

Current legislation, in England, Wales and Scotland does not recognise on-street investigators, therefore their powers are limited, especially with regard to inspection and seizure of blue badges. In Scotland, Section 73 of the Transport (Scotland) Act 2001 empowers the police, police traffic wardens and Council Parking Attendants to inspect blue badges. Only a uniformed police officer can seize a blue badge. Some Local Authorities in England deploy on-street investigators who do not necessarily involve the police when conducting investigations and reporting individuals for prosecution. This is based on the fact that they are in possession of sufficient evidence to prove the case and that the prosecution is in the public interest. Investigations into Blue Badge Fraud must be done at all times in accordance with a number of Acts and Regulations including:

■ the Regulation of Investigatory Powers Act 2000 (RIPA) (with associated relevance to the Human Rights Act);
■ Data Protection Act 1998; and
■ Freedom of Information Act.

The legislation differs for England and Scotland. As abuse of the Blue Badge Scheme takes varying forms, different legislation comes into enforce for prosecuting offenders. The laws relating to this differ for England and Scotland.

England
- Theft Act 1968.
- Forgery and Counterfeiting Act 1981.
- Road Traffic Regulation Act 1984.
- Road Traffic Act 1991.
- Proceeds of Crime Act 2002.
- Traffic Management Act 2004.
- Fraud Act 2006.

Prosecutions in Scotland have been successful using the Road Traffic Regulation Act 1984. The Blue Badge Scheme currently only affects on-street parking. In the UK, there are currently no statutory concessions available to blue badge holders in off-street parking places. The blue badge system is designed to provide convenient access for disabled motorists to reserved, accessible parking, rather than to provide free parking. Many parking providers, such as private landowners, do charge – particularly where there is a barrier system for entry to the car park. Others do not – but this is purely discretionary and is up to the individual landowner. The BPA has commissioned a study in conjunction with the DfT, *Mobilise and the British Council of Shopping Centres,* looking at the provision of Blue Badge parking off-street. The findings and recommendations will be published later this year. In Scotland, changes are being proposed by a Private Members Bill that would mean the same concessions would be available off-street as on-street. If this goes ahead, England may well decide to go down the same route. The House of Commons Transport Committee has also undertaken a review of the Blue Badge Scheme. The findings were published in June 2008 and covered areas such as eligibility, time limit concessions and enforcement, with the proposition of setting up a single national database for sharing information. The consultation has just been completed and it will be the end of the year before any developments are seen. Any legal changes would only affect England and decisions would be made separately by Scottish Government and Welsh Assembly about the scheme. The Blue Badge Scheme is invaluable to people with mobility difficulties and managing it correctly is vital to ensure that only the right people benefit from it.

The scheme needs to be pro-actively managed, have consistent standards and the ability to share information and best practice. The latest consultations seem to be taking the scheme in the right direction.

Hospital car park charging
With the recent decision by the Welsh Assembly Government to abolish charging for hospital car parking spaces, the subject is very much under debate. NHS Trusts are increasingly under pressure to ensure that health funding is used to provide health care services. Parking at some hospitals is often very busy, with competing demands which cannot all be met. Staff, patients and their visitors have different needs and it is necessary to manage the parking to ensure that it is used effectively and efficiently, and priority is given to those most in need of it. Pressure on spaces is the main reason behind many hospitals introducing parking charges. Hospitals in town centres and near other facilities have to ensure that their parking is protected against use by others, such as commuters, shoppers and local residents, and effective parking management is important in these circumstances. The last ten years have seen a rise in the number of hospitals introducing some form of controlled

parking, and with this there has been an increase in parking operators being brought in to manage and run the facilities. Many hospitals and operators take a joint venture approach which allows them to project what the scheme will cost and the potential for any surplus. Where NHS Trusts do make a surplus income from parking operations, this is usually diverted to enhance patient care facilities or to support the parking charges for people with disabilities or with life-threatening illnesses who make frequent and regular visits to the hospital.

It doesn't always have to be a case of charging for parking. One option is to offer free parking for up to two hours, similar to the schemes run by supermarkets and retail parks. This can work well with smaller hospitals, and tickets can be made available if someone needs to stay longer. Problems with this system can arise if parking in the areas around the hospital are Pay and Display – people will then take advantage of the free parking at the hospital. For larger and city centre hospitals, the most common option is Pay and Display. With this system, hospitals have the flexibility to issue permits to staff or provide a reduced rate for parking. They can also offer permits to patients who are terminally ill or those visiting patients in the hospital for a long-term stay for the time they need. In Wales, free charging will be available at almost every hospital by 2011. In England, the Government has given the decision to local health chiefs to make on policy and charges are common. This is similar to Northern Ireland, but a review of this policy is currently being undertaken. In Scotland, the Government has introduced a maximum of £3 a day for parking, although many hospitals charge less. The jury is still out for what, if any, changes Government and Local Government will make to hospital car park charging policies.

> *See also*: Disability access and egress, p.204; Driving at work, p.244; Vehicles at work, p.701

Sources of further information

The BPA, on behalf of the Parking Forum, produces a number of Parking Forum Position Papers, which describe various aspects of parking and the associated benefits and challenges. These are available as free PDF documents from the BPA website: www.britishparking.co.uk. Additionally BPA Parking Practice Notes which provide guidance on a range of parking matters are available to purchase. For more information contact Emily McCunn at emily.m@britishparking.co.uk

British Parking Association: www.britishparking.co.uk

Association of Chief Police Officers: www.acpo.police.uk/

Inclusive mobility: www.dft.gov.uk/transportforyou/access/tipws/inclusivemobility

ParkMark®: www.parkmark.co.uk

Part-time workers

Pinsent Masons Employment Group

Key points

- It has always been risky to treat part-time workers less favourably than comparable full-time workers, owing to the potential for a claim of sex discrimination.
- Regulations introduced in 2000 now provide protection for part-time 'workers' (wider than the term 'employees') irrespective of sex discrimination.
- Part-time workers can request a written statement from their employers if they suspect discrimination requiring their employer to provide an explanation for their treatment.
- Employers should review their practices and procedures to ensure that they are compliant with current legislation.

Legislation

- Part-time Workers (Prevention of Less Favourable Treatment) Regulations 2000.
- Part-time Workers (Prevention of Less Favourable Treatment) Regulations 2000 (Amendment) Regulations 2002.

Overview

The Part-time Workers (Prevention of Less Favourable Treatment) Regulations 2000 (the Regulations) came into force on 1 July 2000 to provide a basic right for part-time workers not to be treated less favourably on the grounds of their part-time status than comparable full-time workers unless this can be justified on objective grounds. This means part-time workers are entitled, for example, to:

- the same hourly rate of pay;
- the same access to company pension schemes;
- the same entitlements to annual leave and to maternity and parental leave on a pro rata basis;
- the same entitlement to contractual sick pay; and
- no less favourable treatment in access to training.

Definitions

The Regulations apply to 'workers' and not just to 'employees'. The wider definition will include part-time workers who may not be employees, such as homeworkers and agency workers.

A part-time worker is someone who is "paid wholly or partly by reference to the time he works and, having regard to the custom and practice of the employer in relation to workers employed by the worker's employer under the same type of contract, is not identifiable as a full-time worker".

A part-time worker must therefore be identified by reference to the particular circumstances of each employer.

'Less favourable treatment'

To assert less favourable treatment, a comparison must be made with a particular full-time worker. However, the Regulations only allow part-time workers to compare themselves with full-time workers working for the same employer in the same or similar work and with a similar level of qualifications and experience. They must also be employed under the same type of contract.

By virtue of the Amendment Regulations, which came into force on 1 October 2002, a part-time worker can compare himself to a full-time worker regardless of whether either of the contracts is permanent or for a fixed term.

Where they believe they are being treated less favourably than comparable full-timers, part-time workers may request a written statement of the reasons for their treatment from their employer, to be provided within 21 days.

Discrimination at all stages of employment – recruitment, promotion, terms of employment and dismissal – is potentially unlawful. Promotion is an area where employers have often in the past favoured full-time staff over part-timers. Previous or current part-time status should now not form a barrier to promotion to a post, whether the post itself is full-time or part-time.

Part-time employees must not receive a lower basic rate of pay than comparable full-time employees, unless this can be 'objectively justified' (e.g. by a performance-related pay scheme).

The same hourly rate of overtime pay should be paid to part-timers as to comparable full-time employees, once they have worked more than the normal full-time hours. The Regulations do not provide part-time workers with an automatic right to overtime payments once they work beyond their normal hours. However, part-timers working beyond their contracted hours should be paid the same as a full-timer would be paid for working the same number of hours, otherwise there is a risk of an equal pay claim.

The Regulations allow part-time workers to participate in the full range of benefits available to full-timers such as profit-sharing schemes, unless there are objective grounds for excluding them. Any benefits should be pro rata to those received by comparable full-time workers.

Employers must not exclude part-time workers from training schemes as a matter of principle. They should take great care to ensure that part-timers get the same access to training as full-time workers.

Part-time workers must be given the same treatment in relation to maternity leave, parental leave and time off for dependants as their full-time colleagues, on a pro rata basis where this is appropriate. Similarly, career break schemes should be made available to part-time workers in the same way, unless their exclusion is objectively justified.

Less favourable treatment will only be justified on objective grounds if it can be shown that the less favourable treatment is to achieve a legitimate objective (e.g. a genuine business objective), that it is necessary to achieve that objective and that it is an appropriate way to achieve the objective.

Dismissal

There are certain situations in which a dismissal by an employer for a specific reason will be treated as being automatically unfair. For example, where someone is dismissed for bringing proceedings against the employer under the Regulations, this will be deemed automatically unfair. No qualifying period of employment is required for such a claim. Where someone is dismissed as a result of his part-time status and a comparable full-time worker was not dismissed, this will be a form of less favourable treatment and the employee may make a complaint to a

Tribunal under the Regulations, as well as bringing an ordinary unfair dismissal claim.

If there is a redundancy situation, then part-time workers should be treated just as favourably as full-timers, unless this difference in treatment can be objectively justified. Part-time status should not be a criterion for selection for redundancy.

Practical points

Government guidance has been published with the Regulations and may be accessed at www.berr.gov.uk/employment/workandfamilies/part-time/page12080.html.

Employers will find it useful to take note of the following points:

- They should review periodically when they can offer posts on a part-time basis. If an applicant wishes to work part-time, the employer should ascertain whether a part-time worker could fulfil the requirements of the job.
- Employers should look seriously at requests to change to part-time working and, where possible, explore how this can be carried out.
- They should review how individuals are provided with information on the availability of part-time and full-time positions.
- Employers are encouraged to keep representative bodies informed about certain aspects of the business' use of part-time workers.
- Managers should amend their handbooks to include a section on part-time workers and the consequences of breaching the Regulations.
- Disciplinary procedures should be amended to make it a disciplinary offence to discriminate against part-time workers.
- Awareness of the rights of part-time workers may need to be raised and training provided on the subject.

Enforcement

Employees are able to present a claim to an Employment Tribunal within three months seeking compensation if they believe that their rights have been infringed.

See also: Discrimination, p.222; Employee benefits, p.266; Family-friendly rights, p.309; Fixed-term workers, p.335

Sources of further information

Workplace Law Group's *Guide to Flexible Working 2008* provides information on the formal legislative right to request flexible working, but also considers flexible working patterns in a wider sense. It covers the reasons why some employers are looking to introduce flexible working into their workplace, explores different flexible working patterns, including their benefits and disadvantages, and provides detail on the formal legislative right to request.

It also looks at the employment and non-employment legal issues that surround flexible working and the necessary amendments that need to be made to an employee's contractual terms and conditions if a flexible working pattern is agreed. Finally, it gives practical advice in relation to drafting and implementing a flexible working policy. For more information visit www.workplacelaw.net/Bookshop/GuidesTo.

Pensions

Dana Shunmoogum and Emma Tracey, Taylor Wessing

Key points

- Pension provision in the UK falls into two categories – state benefits and private arrangements.
- State pensions comprise of basic state pensions and state second pensions (S2P). Contributions are collected from employees and employers via National Insurance Contributions (NICs). The amount of state pension that an individual will receive will depend on the NICs paid or credited over an individual's work life.
- Private pension arrangements may take the form of either occupational pension schemes or personal pensions.
- Occupational pensions schemes are schemes established by an employer, for the benefit of the employees. Different occupational pension schemes operate different arrangements. These are commonly known as defined benefit schemes or defined contribution schemes.
- Employers with more than five relevant employees who do not offer an occupational or personal pension scheme must provide employees with access to a stakeholder pension. This is a type of personal pension to which both employers and employees may contribute.

Legislation

- Income and Corporation Taxes Act 1988 (as amended by the Income Tax (Earnings and Pensions) Act 2003).
- Social Security Contributions and Benefits Act 1992.
- Pension Schemes Act 1993.
- Pensions Act 1995.
- Welfare Reform and Pensions Act 1999.
- Child Support, Pensions and Social Security Act 2000.
- Pensions Act 2004.
- Finance Act 2004.
- Civil Partnership Act 2004.

State benefits

State pensions are provided by the Government on the basis of contributions made or credited to the National Insurance Fund over an individual's work life. These contributions are compulsory and are effectively part of the general taxation and benefits system.

There are two tiers of state benefits – the basic state pension and the state second pension (S2P).

Basic state pension

An individual is entitled to receive the basic state pension if they meet the following criteria:

- they are aged 60 for females (this is gradually being increased to age 65 between April 2010 and 2020) or 65 years for men; and
- they (or their husband, wife or civil partner) have enough qualifying years employment based on NICs.

If NICs have been paid for less than 25% of an individual's working life, they may not be entitled to a State Pension. The Government has recently sought to overhaul this system to the extent that from 6 April 2010 the number of years that will be required in order to qualify for a full State Pension will be reduced to 30 years and any number of qualifying years will give entitlement to at least some basic State Pension.

There will also be NIC credits available for individuals who care for children or severely disabled people. An employee with a full NIC record is currently (2008/09) entitled to receive £90.70 a week if they are a single person and £145.05 a week if part of a pensioner couple.

State Second Pension (S2P)

Until April 2002, the additional state pension for employees was called the State Earnings-Related Pension Scheme (SERPS). The amount of SERPS pension that an employee received was based on a combination of the amount of NICs that they had paid and their salary.

In April 2002 SERPS was reformed and the additional state pension is now known as the State Second Pension (S2P). This provides a more generous additional pension than SERPS for low and moderate earners, and certain carers and people with long-term illness or disability.

Employees may choose to 'contract-out' of S2P. This means that employees can divert their NIC payments to a private pension scheme but will receive a smaller benefit from the State as a result.

Private pension arrangements

Private pension provision in the UK is highly regulated, both by the Government and other regulatory bodies. In recent years there has been much reform of the pensions industry and this has served to increase the powers of regulatory

authorities, including the Pensions Regulator.

Other than in respect of stakeholder pensions (see below for further details) employers and employees are not compelled to set up or contribute to private pensions. The Government is aware that this is likely to result in long-term problems for individuals who have failed to provide sufficiently for their retirement. They have therefore proposed to introduce a new regime whereby employees who are not already enrolled with a recognised occupational pension scheme will automatically be enrolled into the Personal Accounts scheme (although they will have the option to opt out) and employers will be compelled to contribute to the scheme. The proposal is in the very first stages of consultation and, if implemented, will not be established before 2012.

Although there is currently no element of compulsion for employers or employees to contribute to a private pension there are significant tax benefits if they choose to do so. In return for complying with specific requirements laid down by legislation, private schemes registered with HMRC can enjoy generous tax relief, both for employees and employers.

Under the current pensions regime, implemented from 6 April 2006, an individual contributing to a private pension scheme is only able to accumulate tax-advantaged benefits from pension saving up to £1.65m (the 'Lifetime Allowance'). This Lifetime Allowance was capped at £1.65m for the year 2008/09 but is subject to change.

Tax relief is further restricted by reference to the amount by which pensions savings increase in any one year (other than the year of retirement). This is known as the 'Annual Allowance' and is limited to

£235,000. Again, this sum was set for the year 2008/09 and is subject to review.

The amount of contributions that can be made by an individual, whether employed or self-employed, is restricted to the greater of 100% of UK earnings (subject to the £235,000 limit mentioned above) or £3,600 per annum. A number of further tax limits were imposed under the new pensions regime but these are outside the scope of this summary.

There are two types of private pension arrangement – occupational pension schemes and personal pension schemes.

Occupational pensions schemes
Occupational pension schemes are established under trust and operated in accordance with the scheme's trust deed and rules. A group of people will be appointed as trustees of the scheme and are responsible for running the scheme. Legislation requires that at least one third of the scheme's trustee board must be nominated by the members (and pensioners) but it is possible that this fraction may be increased to one half in the future. Previously employers were able to suggest alternative arrangements, which meant they could opt-out of the member-nominated trustee requirements but this is no longer possible. The trustee board must also consult advisers such as actuaries, administrators and solicitors when reaching its decisions.

Traditionally most occupational pension schemes were established on a defined benefit (DB) basis, meaning that the pension payable at retirement was calculated by reference to a salary-related formula set out in the scheme's rules. DB schemes involve employees making contributions during their working life and the employer guaranteeing that the final pension will be at a specific level. The advantage of this type of arrangement for employees is that, in the absence of employer insolvency, it provides certainty. The problem for employers is that they bear the risk of poor investment returns and expensive annuity rates.

Owing to the risks outlined above many employers have chosen to close their DB schemes and now offer employees admission to a defined contribution scheme (DC). DC schemes do not guarantee members a specific level of final pension but instead provide a promise to contribute a given percentage of employee salary and invest this, together with any employee contributions. The actual pension payable at retirement is dependent upon the investment return achieved during the period of membership of the scheme and the cost of securing a pension on the annuity market on retirement.

When an employee leaves a company that operates an occupational pension scheme they may leave their benefits in the scheme until they reach retirement age (during this time they will be referred to as 'deferred members') or they may transfer the benefits they have built up under the scheme to:

■ a new pension scheme operated by their new employer;
■ a personal pension scheme; or
■ an insurance company by way of a deferred annuity (i.e. a promise to pay a pension when the employer reaches a specific age).

Personal pension schemes
Personal pensions are a contract between an individual and a provider other than the employer, usually an insurance company or a bank. All personal pensions operate on a DC basis. Personal pensions are often used by individuals without access to an occupational scheme, employees who do not wish to join their

occupational scheme, the self-employed or employees who have access to an employer's group personal pension scheme (a GPP).

Employers frequently offer GPPs as an alternative to an occupational pension scheme. GPPs are simply a collection of personal pension schemes provided by one provider, with each employee having his own personal pension operating within this arrangement. The employer is not obliged to make contributions, although most do. Because a personal pension scheme is provided by an organisation other than the employer this should not affect the employees' ability to continue to contribute to the pension in the event that they leave the employer's employment (although any reduced commissions / charges negotiated by his previous employer may not continue).

Stakeholder pensions
The stakeholder pension is a particular type of personal pension scheme and was an initiative introduced by the Government in 2001, realising that the basic state pension and S2P was unlikely to provide sufficient benefits for people who were not also contributing to an occupational or personal pension. There is no compulsion on employees to join a stakeholder pension but employers are obliged to make it available in certain circumstances.

Employers' obligations are:

- to designate a stakeholder pension for their staff (having consulted with

employees about the introduction of the stakeholder); and
- to allow employees to have their contributions to the stakeholder deducted from their salaries and passed directly to the insurance company operating the stakeholder.

There is no obligation upon employers to contribute anything towards employees' stakeholder pensions, although this option is available to them. Employers who fail to comply with their obligations risk civil penalties of up to £50,000 from the Pensions Regulator.

Some employers are exempt from the legislation governing stakeholder pensions. In particular it does not apply to:

- employers with fewer than five 'relevant' employees (this is broadly dependent on the number of employees and whether the employer is based in the UK or overseas); or
- employers who operate an alternative occupational or personal pension scheme for their employees which meets certain criteria.

Life assurance
Both occupational pension schemes and GPPs are often linked to a life assurance scheme providing a tax-free lump sum defined as a multiple of salary in respect of employees who die while in the employer's service.

See also: Discrimination, p.222; Employee benefits, p.266; Retirement, p.636

Sources of further information

HMR&C pension schemes: www.hmrc.gov.uk/pensionschemes

The Pensions Regulator: www.thepensionsregulator.gov.uk

Permits to work

Kathryn Gilbertson, Greenwoods Solicitors LLP

Key points

- A formal written system used to control certain types of work that are potentially hazardous.
- A permit is issued by an authorised person (AP) who understands the risks and the control measures required to be put in place.
- It is issued to a competent person (CP) in charge of the work stating that it is safe to work in the plant/area specified.
- The permit will detail precautions that must be observed by persons carrying out that work.
- The permit will have a specified time limit.
- Only the person who issued the permit should amend or cancel it.
- The competent person is responsible for the safe conduct of the work and must not break the conditions specified on the permit.
- The competent person must fully understand the requirements of the permit and inform everyone what they may or may not do.
- The competent person must return the permit to the authorised person for cancellation when the work is completed or when he has withdrawn from site. A permit is not a replacement for risk assessments and method statements.
- Permits should be retained for at least three years by the authorised person.

Legislation

- Health and Safety at Work etc. Act 1974.
- Electricity at Work Regulations 1989.
- Construction (Health, Safety and Welfare) Regulations 1996.
- Confined Spaces Regulations 1997.
- Management of Health and Safety at Work Regulations 1999.
- Control of Substances Hazardous to Health Regulations 2002.

Where permits apply

These are used to control high-risk activities and areas where specific hazards could be present. As such, permits are usually issued on the following occasions:

- Electrical work including high-voltage electrical work;
- Lift works;
- Asbestos;
- Roof works;

- Work on scaffold towers and Mobile Elevated Working Platforms (MEWPs);
- Confined spaces;
- Demolition works;
- Excavation works;
- Pressure systems;
- Hot works; and
- Work which can be carried out only by removing normal control measures (e.g. live working on a supply to a critical piece of equipment).

Contents of permits

There are four stages in the process of permits to work, namely issue, receipt, withdrawal and cancellation. Thus, the following process should take place:

1. *Issue* – detail safety precautions that have been taken. Authorised person gives declaration that it is safe to proceed with the job within specified limits.

2. *Receipt* – declaration by competent person in charge of the work that he fully understands the requirements, and has informed everyone what they may or may not do.

3. *Withdrawal* – declaration by the CP that the work has been done or discontinued and the staff under his control have withdrawn. A declaration that the work area is in a safe condition.

4. *Cancellation* – The AP signs to cancel the permit to work. AP makes the plant / area operations.

Why should I issue a permit to work?

A higher degree of safety is achieved through using a permit to work rather than verbal instructions. Verbal instructions can be misheard or misinterpreted. Thus, a permit to work system provides an additional level of safety for the authorising person / company.

Examples of control measures

Roof works

- Adequate means of access, either temporary or permanent (the use of crawling boards, roof ladders etc.).
- Testing of the roof's fragility.
- Edge protection.
- Preventing the hauling of materials or objects.
- Personal protective equipment.

Confined spaces

- Atmospheric monitoring.
- Emergency rescue procedures.
- Isolation of fluid or energy sources.
- Personal Protective Equipment e.g. breathing apparatus.
- Additional supervision and monitoring.

Hot works

- Ensuring that sprinklers (if installed) are isolated and re-activated after the works.

- Housekeeping – removal of combustible materials from the area, e.g. paper, cardboard, flammable liquids etc.
- Use of protective non-combustible curtains to protect property and person.
- Provision of suitable fire extinguishers.
- Fire trained person to re-visit area 30 to 60 minutes after the hot works have finished ensuring no smouldering embers or hot surfaces remain.
- Ensure hot work equipment is maintained and inspected.

What do I need to do?

You should review your existing system and clarify how it works, the types of jobs permits are used for and check that it is in operation. In particular the responsibility and training of those involved in authorising and overseeing work undertaken under a permit should be reviewed. Only designated individuals should authorise work permits and should clarify who is responsible for specifying the precautions, making sure that these also cover contractors. The precautions need to specify requirements while the work is in progress as well as requirements needed to cover the work itself, such as welding fumes, vapour from cleaning solvents etc. It is usual to have plans and diagrams along with detailed work and method statements attached to permits to work.

A first aid kit and, if appropriate, emergency breathing apparatus, should be kept close at hand to the area in which the work is being carried out. For confined spaces, this could include a rescue harness and lifting equipment to retrieve the worker if an incident occurs.

Sources of further information
HSE: www.hse.gov.uk/comah/sragtech/techmeaspermit.htm

Personal Protective Equipment

Andrew Richardson, Scott Wilson

Key points

- Personal protective equipment (PPE) is worn or held by persons at work to protect them from risks to their health and safety.
- Waterproof and weatherproof clothing only falls within the Regulations if it is necessary to protect the wearer from health and safety risks due to adverse climatic conditions.
- The Personal Protective Equipment at Work Regulations 1992 apply in most instances; there are six other sets of Regulations which include their own particular PPE requirements.
- PPE is at the bottom of the hierarchy of risk control measures; PPE should therefore be used only as a last resort.
- Employers must decide if PPE is necessary and, if so, must select suitable PPE, provide it free of charge, and maintain it and replace it as necessary.
- In addition, employers must provide accommodation for PPE; information, instruction and training about it and how to use it; and a system for employees to report defects and losses.

Legislation

- Health and Safety at Work etc. Act 1974.
- Personal Protective Equipment at Work Regulations 1992 as amended by the Ionising Radiations Regulations 1999, the Police (Health and Safety) Regulations 1999 and the Health and Safety (Miscellaneous Amendments) Regulations 2002.
- Management of Health and Safety at Work Regulations 1999.
- Personal Protective Equipment Regulations 2002.
- Work at Height Regulations 2005.

Personal Protective Equipment Regulations 2002

The PPE Regulations deal with the suitability of PPE brought to market. The Regulations place a duty on Responsible Persons who put PPE on the market to ensure that the PPE satisfies the basic health and safety requirements that are applicable to that type or class of PPE, and

that the appropriate conformity assessment procedure is carried out. All new PPE should have the CE mark identifying that the equipment satisfies certain safety requirements and has been tested and certified by an independent organisation.

Personal Protective Equipment at Work Regulations 1992

The PPEW Regulations exist to ensure that certain fundamental duties covering the provision and use of PPE are applied whenever PPE is required.

The Regulations define PPE as "all equipment (including clothing affording protection against the weather) which is intended to be worn or held by a person at work which protects him against one or more risks to his health and safety".

Protective clothing includes aprons, clothing for adverse weather conditions, gloves, safety footwear, safety helmets, high-visibility waistcoats, etc. Protective equipment includes eye protectors, life jackets, respirators, underwater breathing apparatus and safety harnesses.

The guidance identifies items including uniforms, food hygiene protective clothing, cycle helmets, motorcycle leathers, shin guards, etc., which are not covered. Waterproof, weatherproof or insulated clothing improves the comfort of the wearer, but is only subject to the Regulations if employees must wear it to protect themselves against adverse climatic conditions that would affect their health and safety.

The Regulations do not apply to PPE provided under the following Regulations, which have their own specific requirements:

- Construction (Head Protection) Regulations 1989.
- Ionising Radiations Regulations 1999.
- Control of Substances Hazardous to Health Regulations 2002.
- Control of Lead at Work Regulations 2002.
- Control of Noise at Work Regulations 2005.
- Control of Asbestos Regulations 2006.

However, if a task requires an employer to provide PPE under PPEW and one of the above specific requirements, the PPE items must be compatible.

The Management of Health and Safety at Work Regulations 1999 require employers to carry out a suitable and sufficient risk assessment to enable the most appropriate means of reducing the risks to acceptable levels. When determining the most suitable risk-control measures, there is a risk-control hierarchy. PPE is the final category, and, in effect, PPE should not be used unless the risks to health and safety cannot be adequately controlled in any other way.

The Regulations place the following responsibilities on the employer, who must:

- assess the risk and determine if PPE is needed;
- select suitable PPE;
- provide the PPE;
- maintain all PPE and replace as necessary;
- provide accommodation for the PPE;
- provide information, instruction and training on the PPE provided; and
- provide a system to allow employees to report defects or loss of PPE.

Employers are not allowed to charge for PPE.

The Regulations require the employee to take reasonable care of the PPE provided, and, under the Health and Safety at Work etc. Act, the employee has a duty to use the PPE.

Fall arrest equipment

When carrying out work at height, the Work at Height Regulations 2005 apply in addition to the PPEW Regulations. Specific items of PPE for this class of work include fall arrest equipment such as safety harnesses and energy-absorbing lanyards. There are additional PPE-related requirements under the Work at Height Regulations:

- Inspections by a competent person at suitable intervals where the PPE has been exposed to conditions which may have caused a dangerous deterioration in its condition; and
- Inspection by a competent person every time PPE has been exposed to conditions that might jeopardise safety.

There is also a British Standard, BS EN 365:2004, which gives general requirements for instructions for the use, maintenance, periodic examination, repair etc. of such PPE.

See also: Construction site health and safety, p.154; Head protection, p.362; Health and safety at work, p.364; Ladders, p.440; Slips, trips and falls, p.657.

Sources of further information

L25 *Personal Protective Equipment at Work (second edition) – Personal Protective Equipment at Work Regulations 1992 (as amended) Guidance on Regulations* (HSE Books, 2005) ISBN: 0 7176 6139 3, provides authoritative guidance on all aspects.

Basic information is also available free from HSE. *A Short Guide to the Personal Protective Equipment at Work Regulations 1992 – Rev 1,* can be downloaded at www.hse.gov.uk/pubns/indg174.pdf

Further advice on inspection and deterioration of lanyards made from webbing or rope can be downloaded at www.hse.gov.uk/pubns/indg367.pdf

Personnel files – recording information

Amy Thickett, CMS Cameron McKenna

Key points

Accurate and easily accessible personnel records assist employers in many ways. They improve the efficiency of recruitment, training and promotion of staff, help identify problems such as performance, sickness absence or labour turnover, provide information for the purposes of equal opportunity monitoring and assist in compliance with legal requirements.

Data protection principles are likely to apply to information recorded in personnel files.

What information should be held in personnel files?

Operating a business involves keeping information about each of the organisation's workers. Employers collect, record and maintain information about their workers during every stage of the employment relationship; for example, during recruitment and through appraisals, training records, sick notes, disciplinary records and the administering of benefits. There is no definitive list of what information should be contained in a personnel file. However, examples of information that are likely to be held in personnel files are:

- personal details, such as name, date of birth, address, telephone number, emergency contact details, qualifications, national insurance number, details of any disability;
- details of employment within the organisation, such as job description(s), job application(s), date employment commenced, job title, promotions, shift allocations, pay reviews, secondments;
- terms and conditions of employment, such as statement of employment particulars, remuneration, notice period, hours of work, holiday entitlement;
- benefits, such as insurances, private medical cover, share options, company cars, loans, nursery care schemes;
- training and development activities;
- performance reviews or appraisals;
- sickness or injury records;
- absences, such as holiday, lateness, maternity / paternity / adoption / dependents' leave, compassionate leave, sabbatical;
- work-related accidents;
- disciplinary action;
- grievances raised; and/or
- record of termination of employment, such as garden leave, post-termination restrictive covenants, payments made on termination, reasons for leaving.

Why do employers keep personnel files?

Some information is required to fulfil legal requirements. For example, employers need to keep records of:

- their workers' pay (including payments of Statutory Sick Pay, statutory maternity, paternity and adoption pay) for the purposes of complying with tax and national insurance obligations and to meet the requirements of the National Minimum Wage Act 1998;
- hours worked by most workers and holidays taken, to comply with the requirements of the Working Time Regulations 1998;
- accidents, injuries and diseases, to comply with health and safety rules and regulations; and
- disciplinary action taken and grievances raised to provide evidence of compliance with the statutory disciplinary and dismissal procedures and statutory grievance procedures.

Keeping accurate personnel files also helps organisations to operate efficiently and remain competitive. Good personnel records can help organisations:

- treat staff fairly and properly, for example in accordance with legislation (see above);
- use their staff resources effectively, for example, appraisals or details of a worker's qualifications and experience can help an employer to assess whether a worker would be suitable for promotion;
- develop or amend employment policies and procedures and implement such policies and procedures fairly and consistently. For example, records of disciplinary action can help employers to ensure consistency in the application of the disciplinary procedure;
- improve the efficiency of their recruitment, training and development of staff. For example, a record of a worker's qualifications and experience can help an employer to assess whether a worker has any training needs. Performance reviews or appraisals can help to assess a

worker's performance and decide whether there are needs for training;
- more accurately detect, monitor and control problems, such as in relation to performance, discipline, sickness, lateness, absenteeism and high turnover of staff. For example, individual absence records can be used to monitor an individual's absence levels. Statistics on absence levels across the organisation may help employers to detect and monitor problems across the workforce and take corrective action. Exit interviews can provide information to help employers deal with high labour turnover;
- reduce the risk of discrimination on the grounds of, for example, sex, race, disability or age, by providing the information necessary to implement and monitor equal opportunity policies. For example, sickness records can be useful when considering making reasonable adjustments to the job or the workplace for the purpose of complying with the Disability Discrimination Act 1995; and
- provide important evidence if an employee makes a claim to an Employment Tribunal. For example, Employment Tribunals would expect organisations to hold records of an employee's termination to show what payments have been made to the employee (e.g. notice pay, redundancy pay, outstanding holiday pay, etc.). Records of disciplinary action and dismissal are vital if an organisation is faced with complaints about, for example, unfair dismissal or discrimination.

What considerations do employers need to think about when recording information?

Employers need to understand that the personnel files they keep contain information that is personal and can be sensitive. The Data Protection Act 1998 the DPA) lays down both legal obligations and standards that aim to balance an employer's need to keep information about its workers against a worker's right to respect for his or her private life.

The DPA places legal responsibilities on organisations to register under the DPA and process (e.g. obtain, record, retain, use, disclose or dispose of) personal data in a fair and proper way. The DPA is concerned with personal data that can be processed by equipment operating automatically or which is recorded, or intended to be recorded, in a 'relevant filing system' (see below for further information). Everything from workers' personnel files to customer lists may be covered by the DPA. The DPA gives special protection to personal data that is 'sensitive'. Sensitive personal data is information concerning an individual's racial or ethnic origin, political opinions, religious or other beliefs, trade union membership, health, sexual life and any actual or alleged criminal offence. Sensitive data can only be processed under strict conditions.

The DPA – personal data

Personal data is any information that relates to an identified or identifiable living individual. An individual's name and address can be personal data and other information about an individual, for example, an individual's employment history or job title would also be personal data if the individual could be identified from that information and/or from other information in the possession of the person controlling the processing of that information. Personal data also includes any expression of opinion about an individual and any indication of the intentions of the person controlling the processing of the information, or any other person, in respect of that individual. In August 2007 the Information Commissioner, who is responsible for the enforcement of the DPA, issued a guidance note on what constitutes personal data for the purposes of the DPA. The guidance includes a flowchart, comprising a series of questions together with illustrative examples, to assist in determining what is personal data.

The DPA – relevant filing systems

A relevant filing system contains information within a system that is structured and/or indexed by reference to either individuals, or to criteria relating to individuals, that is readily accessible (i.e. the information is stored in a similar way to a computerised filing system). The Information Commissioner has given guidance on when manual files will be deemed to be a relevant filing system and has indicated that such files will only be covered if they are sufficiently structured so that the searcher can retrieve the personal information without leafing through the contents. To help identify whether a relevant filing system is in place, the Commissioner has devised the 'temp test':

"If you employed a temporary administrative assistant (a temp), would they be able to extract specific information about an individual without any particular knowledge of your type of work or the documents you hold?"

If the temp could easily locate the relevant information, the information will be held in a relevant filing system.

A paper personnel file, relating to an individual and indexed internally by subject matter, for example, by reference to personal details, sickness, absence, disciplinary record, etc. is likely to be organised in a relevant filing system for the purposes of the DPA. Similarly, name dividers within a file on a particular topic are likely to be deemed to be a relevant filing system. However, files that are organised chronologically are unlikely to be covered by the DPA.

The DPA – data protection principles
Anyone who processes personal information must comply with the eight data protection principles. In summary, these principles state that data must be:

1. fairly and lawfully processed;
2. processed for limited purposes;
3. adequate, relevant and not excessive;
4. accurate and up to date;
5. not kept for longer than is necessary;
6. processed in accordance with the data subject's (e.g. the employee's) rights;
7. secure; and
8. not transferred to other countries without adequate protection.

For more information about the DPA, see *'Data protection', p.186.*

How to establish and operate an effective personnel records system
It is important to ensure that the system operates effectively for the needs of the organisation, and, where relevant, complies with the DPA. The employer should take into account the following points when setting up and managing a personnel records system:

- *Be clear about the purpose(s) for which any personal information is collected about workers.* The information collected should meet the needs of the organisation.
- *Keep staff informed.* It is not necessary to seek workers' prior consent to keep most employment records about them; however, employers should explain to staff the purposes for which they intend to process personal data. Employers could include this information in a staff handbook, intranet site or employment

contract, or draft a separate data protection policy, to inform workers about the records that are being or are likely to be kept about them and why, the uses to which they are likely to be put, where the records will be kept and for how long, who will have access to the records and the circumstances in which they might be disclosed.

- *Keep personal information stored securely.* Employers are responsible for the security of personal information collected and must take appropriate measures to prevent unauthorised access or unlawful processing, accidental loss, destruction or damage to the employment records. Records may be kept:
  - electronically (on a computer) – there are a number of advantages to storing records electronically, for example, the speed of the provision of information and the flexibility of the information available makes updating and analysing data easier. Password protection, or similar security measures, should be implemented to limit unauthorised access to computerised records.
  - manually – a simple and effective approach for smaller organisations might be to keep paper personnel records using a card index system. Manual files that contain personal information should be securely locked and only those who should have access retain the key
  - in a combination of the above systems. Employers should restrict information which is taken outside the workplace to what is necessary and put in place rules and procedures, which deal with, for example, the information that may be taken off-site and keeping that information secure. In November 2007, following the

loss of child benefit records by HM Revenue and Customs, the Information Commissioner's Office issued a recommendation that, amongst other things, portable and mobile devices used to store or transmit personal information, should be protected by encryption software designed to safeguard against unauthorised access to the information stored on the device. In April 2008 the Information Commissioner published two Good Practice Notes on management and notification of breaches of data security, which give guidance on some of the things that an organisation needs to consider where a security breach occurs and on the notification of breaches to the Information Commissioner's Office.

- *Consider which staff should have access to which records.* In July 2008 the European Court of Human Rights ruled that the European Convention on Human Rights imposes an obligation on public bodies and governments to implement measures to keep private data confidential.

- *Ensure that information is easily accessible.* It is useful if the system (whether computerised or manual) is designed so that important information on each subject is easily accessible (e.g. visible on one screen or one side of a card) as this makes locating and updating information easier. However, structuring personnel files in this way is likely to be deemed to be a relevant filing system and thus within the scope of the DPA.

- *Differentiate between sickness or injury records and absence records.* Because sickness and injury records contain sensitive personal data (details of the illness, condition or injury responsible for a worker's absence) they should be kept separately from absence records (which note the incidence of absence but do not include details of the illness or specific medical condition), where possible. For example, sickness and injury records could be kept in a sealed envelope or subject to additional password protection on an electronic system. This helps to ensure that information on workers' health is not accessed when only information regarding a worker's absence is required. For more information about health information, see *'Medical records', p.491.*

- *Keep personal data accurate and up to date.* Workers should be asked to check for accuracy and to update information held on their personnel files that is likely to be subject to change, such as their home address, for example on a yearly basis. It is important that the personnel records system is set up to limit access to individuals' records, so that each worker can only access his or her own record, before asking workers to check and update their records. It is also useful for organisations to review personnel records regularly to check that all the information stored is useful and necessary and that there is no unnecessary duplication of records. Information that is not relevant, out of date or for which there is no genuine business need or legal duty to keep should be destroyed.

- *Comply with the provisions of the DPA when passing data to third parties or across national borders.* Unless certain conditions are satisfied, personal data should not be transferred to a third party outside the European Economic Area unless contractual or other guarantees have been put in place to ensure an adequate level of data protection for workers.

- *Check the effectiveness of the personnel records system regularly.*

It is useful for organisations to know whether the system is providing the information it requires quickly and accurately and to determine whether any improvements can be made.

How long should records be retained for?
It is up to each employer to decide how long to retain their personnel records as there are no specific document retention periods specified in the DPA. Employers should decide how long to retain information based on:

■ the business needs of the organisation; and
■ any relevant professional guidelines or statutory requirements (for example, three to six months for Employment Tribunal claims and six years for county court claims; six years for wage / salary records).

Employers must therefore strike a balance between ensuring that employment records are not kept for longer than is necessary but are not destroyed where there are business needs to retain them.

When deciding which records should be retained, it is advisable to:

■ treat pieces of information individually, or in logical groupings, to prevent all the information in a record being retained just because there is a need to keep part of it; and
■ consider the principle of proportionality; i.e. records about many workers should not be kept for a long time on the basis that one of the workers might possibly query some aspect of his employment in the future.

Where records are to be disposed of, they should be effectively destroyed; for example, by shredding information recorded on paper and completely and permanently deleting information stored in a computerised format.

See also: Data protection, p.186; Medical records, p.491

Sources of further information

The Data Protection Act 1998 contains a number of important principles regulating the way in which information relating to individuals is held and used. The Act sets out eight Data Protection principles which employers are obliged to follow. The Act also creates a number of offences that employers may commit if the provisions of the Act are breached, some of which impose personal liability on company directors and other officers.

It is vital that employers familiarise themselves with their obligations under the Act and ensure that the appropriate procedures are put in place to ensure compliance. Workplace Law Group's *Data Protection Policy and Management Guide, v.3.0* has been published to help employers understand and meet those obligations and to provide clear guidance for employees on their responsibilities when handling sensitive personal data. For more information visit www.workplacelaw.net/Bookshop/PoliciesAndProcedures.

Pest control

avid Cross, Igrox Ltd

Key points

Put simply, pest management or control is the destruction or prevention of unwanted pests.

Many differing techniques are used, but the basic principles are common to most situations. These involve environmental management to exclude pests from sites, restrict access to food, water and harbourage, and, as a last resort, physical or chemical control.

Legislation

- Protection of Animals Act 1911.
- Prevention of Damage by Pests Act 1949.
- Health and Safety at Work etc. Act 1974.
- Food Safety Act 1990.
- Wildlife and Countryside Act 1981.
- Food and Environmental Protection Act 1985.
- Control of Pesticide Regulations 1986.
- Wild Mammals Protection Act 1996.
- Biocidal Products Directive (98/8/EC).
- Control of Substances Hazardous to Health (COSHH) Regulations 2002.
- Food Hygiene (England) Regulations 2006 (there are similar regulations in Wales, Scotland and Northern Ireland).

What is a pest?

A pest is any animal that is found in the wrong place at the wrong time and whose presence could result in damage, contamination and/or transmission of disease.

The most common pest species include those shown in the table below.

Types of service available

- Contracted pest control services monitoring entire sites on a regular

Common pest species	
Commensal Rodents Birds	Brown rat, black rat, house mouse. Feral pigeon, woodpigeon, Collard dove, jackdaw, jay, magpie, carrion/hooded crow, rook, herring gull, lesser black-backed gull, great black-backed gull and Canada Goose.
Textile pests	Including: varied carpet beetle, fur beetle, common clothes moth, case-bearing clothes moth and many more.
Stored product Insects	Grain weevil and beetle, flour beetle, book lice, warehouse moth, mediterranean mill moth.
Public health Insects Vertebrate pests	Files, fleas, cockroaches, bed bugs, wasps, ants. Rabbit, grey squirrel, mole, feral cat.

basis against specific pests, to ensure that the site remains pest free.

- Employment of a pest control company to eradicate a localised pest problem such as a wasps' nest or mouse infestation.
- Preventive proofing to buildings to deter pests from entering or roosting on sites.
- Supply of insect control devices such as fly killers.
- Supply of insect-monitoring devices, such as moth pheromone pots and flea traps, which are used to establish the presence and scale of an infestation.
- Fumigation of containers, commodities and entire buildings to eradicate deep-seated infestations.
- Localised heat treatments for the control of insects such as bed bugs in bedroom furniture.

Categories of legislation

Legislation covering pest control can be split into three categories.

1. Species protection legislation

Protection of Animals Act 1911
This Act provides general protection for domestic and captive animals and makes it an offence to do or omit to do anything likely to cause unnecessary suffering. This would include not providing food and water to animals confined in a cage or live capture traps.

Amendments to this Act include the prohibition of the use of poisons on any land or building except for the purpose of destroying insects, rats, mice and other small ground vermin.

Wildlife and Countryside Act 1981
This Act provides protection for certain animals and the environment. From a pest control point of view, the Act covers most of the legislation affecting birds and lists birds that may be taken by authorised

persons. (Refer to the list of pest birds in the table.) An authorised person is the owner or occupier of the land on which the birds are to be controlled, or any person authorised by the owner or occupier.

Birds from this list may be controlled using live capture traps or by shooting (excluding weapons with a muzzle diameter greater than 1.25 inches) under a general licence which is updated and issued by the Department for Environment, Food and Rural Affairs (Defra). Certain species of bird from this list may also be controlled using stupefying baits under a specific, one-off licence which is applied for and issued under the discretion of Defra Wildlife Administration Unit.

Birds can only be controlled in order to:

- prevent spread of disease;
- protect public health and safety; and
- protect crops, livestock, forestry, fisheries and water.

Wild Mammals Protection Act 1996
This Act is designed to protect wild mammals against abuse and cruel treatment.

It makes it an offence to mutilate, kick, beat, impale, stab, burn, stone, crush, drown, drag or asphyxiate any wild mammal with intent to inflict unnecessary suffering.

2. Environmental health legislation

Prevention of Damage by Pests Act 1949
This Act requires, as far as is practicable, that districts are kept free from rats and mice.

It requires local authorities to carry out periodic inspections, to destroy rats and mice on their land, and to enforce the same duties onto owners and occupiers.

Food Safety Act 1990

This Act makes it an offence to sell food for human consumption that fails to comply with food safety requirements. This would be the case if the food was contaminated with droppings or pest bodies.

The defence under the Food Safety Act is due diligence, which means that everything reasonably practicable must have been done to avoid contamination.

Food Hygiene (England) Regulations 2006 (similar Regulations exist in Wales, Scotland and Northern Ireland)

New EU food hygiene regulations have consolidated 17 EU measures in the food hygiene area into just two; the Food Hygiene (England) Regulations 2006 provide the framework for these measures to be enforced. This legislation is structured so that it can be applied flexibly in all food businesses regardless of their type and size. It is now required that microbiological hazards along with other foreign body contamination should be considered as part of a Hazard Analysis Critical Control Point (HACCP) system. The control and prevention of pests should be a prerequisite of any HACCP system because of the risk of them carrying and spreading microbiological hazards.

The Food Safety (General Food Hygiene) Regulations 1995 and the Food Safety (Temperature Control) Regulations 1995 have both been superseded by these Regulations.

3. Legislation on pesticide use

The following legislation covers the duties placed on pesticide users and their employers.

Food and Environment Protection Act 1985

Part III of this Act is of direct concern to pest control as it provides for the making of Regulations concerned with the control of pesticides with a view to protecting the health of human beings, creatures and plants, safeguarding the environment and securing safe, efficient and humane methods of controlling pests.

Control of Pesticide Regulations 1986

These Regulations were introduced under the Food and Environmental Protection Act 1985 and stipulate that only approved pesticides may be advertised, supplied, stored or used in the UK and that only those with provisional or full approval may be sold.

Health and Safety at Work etc. Act 1974

This Act provides a comprehensive system of law covering the health and safety of people at work and members of the public who may be affected by activity at work.

Biocidal Products Directive (98/8/EC)

The Directive is intended to harmonise arrangements for the authorisation of pesticides used in public health pest control, wood preservatives, industrial preservatives, disinfectants and certain germicidal chemicals.

The Directive was implemented in March 2000, but full harmonisation could take as long as ten years to complete.

Control of Substances Hazardous to Health (COSHH) Regulations 2002

These Regulations were originally introduced under the Health and Safety at Work etc. Act 1974 and make it necessary to assess the risk to health arising from work involving a hazardous substance and, if a risk is identified, to determine what precautions are required either to eliminate or to reduce the risk. This may involve the use of personal protective equipment for people working with the substance, or the exclusion of personnel from an area while a substance is being applied.

Recent and forthcoming developments

There are some major developments that will affect, or will be likely to affect, the pest control industry:

- Methyl bromide gas has been phased out and is only available for use if a critical use exemption has been granted.
- Sulfuryl Fluoride is available for use as a fumigant gas in empty flourmills, food and feed manufacturing units and stores in the UK.
- Hazardous waste Regulations – the Regulation for the disposal of hazardous waste came into force on 16 July 2005. These Regulations change the way in which waste can be categorised and disposed of. For further details consult www.environment-agency.gov.uk.
- Electrical waste – WEEE Regulations. These came fully into force during July 2007. Additional costs will be associated with the disposal/recycling of fluorescent tubes and waste electrical goods. This is most relevant to the pest control industry in terms of the disposal of spent UV tubes from electronic fly control units.
- Work at Height Regulations – the Work at Height Regulations 2005

apply to all work at heights where there is a risk of a fall liable to cause personal injury. The Regulation places duties on employers, the self-employed and any person controlling the work of others. This is most significant to the pest control industry when applying anti-roosting and perching devices to building ledges to deter nuisance birds. The Regulations came into force on 6 April 2005; guidance notes are available from www.hse.gov.uk.

- Workplace exposure limits – changes are being made to the way that exposure to a variety of chemicals is measured. Previously two principal measures of exposure were the Occupational Exposure Standard (OES) and the Maximum Exposure Limit (MEL), both of these have been replaced by a new measure, the Workplace Exposure Limit (WEL). Ultimately all documentation, including Material Safety Data Sheets (MSDSs) will be changed to show WELs rather than OESs and MELs. The HSE does not consider that this change merits the destruction and replacement of MSDSs for pesticide use and the change will be gradual.

See also: Catering: health and safety issues, p.124; Hazardous waste, p.720

Sources of further information

Environment Agency: www.environment-agency.gov.uk

Planning procedures

Jonathan Riley, Pinsent Masons

Key points

- Planning permission (subject to a number of exceptions) is required for material changes of use of land and operational development.
- An application for planning permission will be made to the local planning authority (LPA).
- Failure to secure planning permission, or comply with planning conditions, may entitle the LPA to take enforcement action.
- There is a right of appeal to the Planning Inspectorate.

When is planning permission required?

Planning permission is required for development, which means:

- operational development (which includes building, engineering or mining operations); or
- material changes in the use of any buildings or other land.

Operational development

Building operations include the demolition of buildings, the rebuilding of buildings, structural alterations of, or additions to, buildings and any other operations normally undertaken by a person carrying on business as a builder.

A building includes any structure or erection, and any part of the building, structure or erection, but does not include plant or machinery.

Not all structures are considered by the law to be buildings. The three primary factors are size, degree of permanence and physical attachment.

Material changes of use

In order to assess whether planning permission is required for a material change of use, it is necessary to look at the primary use of a piece of land or building and the extent of any ancillary uses. Ancillary uses do not require planning permission. For example, the primary use of a building may be for office purposes, but there may be ancillary storage uses within that building.

In addition, a slight or trivial change of use will not require planning permission. For example, a small amount of storage use in an office building would not require planning permission.

Demolition

Although demolition constitutes development, currently planning permission is only required for demolition of dwelling houses and adjoining buildings. No planning permission is required for demolition of other buildings, provided they are not in a conservation area, are not listed buildings and are not scheduled ancient monuments.

Exceptions

Legislation provides that certain operations or material changes of use are exempted from the need for planning permission. For example, internal or external improvements, alterations or maintenance work, none of which materially affect the external appearance of buildings, may not require planning permission. Some of these concessions are removed in respect of certain sensitive areas, such as conservation areas or national parks. Also, the Government has introduced a requirement for planning permission for mezzanine floors over a certain size threshold in retail premises.

The Town and Country Planning (General Permitted Development) Order 1995 grants an automatic planning permission for certain operational development and material changes of use including certain industrial and warehouse developments subject to a series of complicated conditions and restrictions. Government directions and planning conditions can withdraw these rights.

Securing a grant of planning permission

If a particular proposal requires planning permission, a formal planning application needs to be made to the relevant LPA. If the proposal is acceptable in planning terms, planning permission should be granted either conditionally or unconditionally.

Usually the permission will automatically run with the land. A person who buys a piece of land which has the benefit of a planning permission can implement that planning permission and build in accordance with any approved plans. It may be necessary to secure the copyright in any approved plans.

Only two types of planning permission can be obtained:

1. Detailed planning permission; and
2. Outline planning permission, which establishes the principle of development. Any such permission would include a condition requiring

reserved matters (e.g. layout, scale, appearance, access and landscaping) to be submitted to the LPA within three years of the date of the outline permission.

Environmental impact assessment

In respect of certain types of development or activity, an environmental impact assessment will need to be submitted. The assessment is required to ensure that the effect of development on the environment, in particular of certain specified public and private projects, is taken into account as part of the decision-making process and before permission is granted. Following recent European case law, the need for environmental assessment must be considered both on the initial outline planning application and any subsequent reserved matters application.

Keeping permissions alive

All permissions are subject to strict time limits. If development is not begun within those time limits, the permission will lapse. In the case of a detailed permission, the usual time limit condition requires development to be started within three years from the date of the detailed permission.

In the case of an outline planning permission, the usual time limit condition requires development to start no later than three years from the date of the outline planning permission or, if later, two years from the final approval of reserved matters. To keep the permission alive, work must commence within the time limits.

Breach of planning control

A breach of planning control can take one of three forms:

1. The carrying out of operational development without the benefit of planning permission;

2. The carrying out of a material change of use of any building or land without the benefit of planning permission; or
3. The breach of a condition attached to a permission.

LPAs have wide powers of enforcement (including criminal sanctions), should development be carried out without any necessary planning permission or failing to comply with planning conditions.

Listed buildings and conservation areas
Buildings may be 'listed' as being of special historic or architectural interest. Any works that affect the character of a listed building require a listed building consent. Non-compliance with the listed building legislation can lead to enforcement action and criminal sanctions.

LPAs must determine, after consultation, whether any part of their area should be designated as a conservation area. Such designation has the following consequences:

■ building design has to be of a high quality;
■ restrictions are placed on demolition; and
■ trees are protected.

Planning appeals
If the LPA refuses to grant planning permission, listed building consent or the modification of a planning condition, the applicant has the right to appeal to the Planning Inspectorate. An appeal can be pursued through written representations, a hearing or a public inquiry.

The appeal is determined by a planning inspector appointed by the Secretary of State for the Department of Communities and Local Government. He will be independent from the local planning authority. The process may take many months or even years. In respect of certain more complex sites, the decision is made by the Secretary of State following receipt of a report by an appointed planning inspector.

Note that an LPA's decision to grant planning permission is open to challenge by means of an application for judicial review within three months calculated from the date of the Decision Notice. The judicial review procedure is commonly used where a third party seeks to quash the decision of the LPA. Only certain types of person have the right to make such an application, and only if there are grounds for a challenge.

See also: Building Regulations, p.81

Sources of further information

Workplace Law Network provides premium members with unrestricted access to a comprehensive range of online information – factsheets, case reports and daily news items – on employment, health and safety and premises management. Members also benefit from an online advice service and a free subscription to the *Workplace Law Magazine*. For more information email membership@workplacelaw.net or call our membership services team on 0871 777 8881.

Power lines

Martin Damms, Pinsent Masons

Key points

- Power companies can negotiate rights to install power lines and equipment with landowners, or may use compulsory powers. In either case compensation will be payable to the landowner.
- Power companies have the right to fell or lop trees if they present a danger to the power lines.

Legislation

- Electricity Act 1989.
- Town and Country Planning Act 1990.
- Utilities Act 2000.

Overview

This chapter concentrates on who can install power lines, what agreements they enter into and how they can compulsorily acquire rights where landowners refuse to grant them voluntarily.

Who can install power lines?

The generation, supply and transmission of electricity are activities regulated by section 6 of the Electricity Act 1989 as substituted by section 30 of the Utilities Act 2000. No person (which includes companies) may carry out these activities without a licence issued by the Secretary of State. It is only such licence holders that are permitted to install electricity lines on or above land.

However, before installing any power lines, licence holders must also obtain the Secretary of State's consent pursuant to section 37 of the Electricity Act 1989 and this consent may be subject to any conditions the Secretary of State considers appropriate. The most common licence holders are the regional electricity companies which took over the supply of electricity from the area boards following the changes introduced by the Electricity Act 1989. These include, for example, London Electricity plc, Powergen plc, National Power plc and other such well-known companies.

Agreements relating to power lines

Before a licence holder can install a power line it also needs the consent of all landowners whose land will be subject to the installation of the power line. The most common forms of agreement giving effect to the licence holder's right to install a power line are as follows.

Easements

Easements are rights in land that can be granted permanently or for a set number of years. An easement is a legal right attached to the land. Therefore it binds any future owner of the land upon which the power line has been installed and will benefit any successor to the licence holder who has installed the power line. Where an easement is granted it will give the licence holder the right to install the line and to retain it permanently and will generally include such ancillary rights as are reasonably necessary for the exercise or enjoyment of the rights granted.

Workplace Law Network
www.workplacelaw.net

Wayleaves

Wayleaves are access to property granted by a landowner for payment. They are very common, especially where licence holders require rights over residential properties. They are of a less permanent nature than easements and are personal to the parties to the agreement. It is important to note, however, that wayleaves can only be terminated in one of three ways; namely when the period of the wayleave expires; or if the landowner gives notice under the termination provisions of the wayleave; or if the ownership of the land changes and the wayleave ceases to be binding on the new landowner. Even in these circumstances notice must be properly served on the licence holder and the right to keep the power lines on the land can be obtained compulsorily (see below).

Following the proper service of a notice, if the licence holder does not make an application to compulsorily acquire the right or does not negotiate a new wayleave, it must remove the power lines within three months of the service of the notice.

Compulsory powers

Where a licence holder requires power lines and the consent of the landowner cannot be obtained, the Electricity Act 1989 provides a mechanism for the compulsory acquisition, on payment of compensation, of the necessary rights.

The Electricity Act 1989 provides two routes for the acquisition of such rights.

Compulsory purchase

Schedule 3 to the Electricity Act 1989 permits the Secretary of State to authorise the compulsory acquisition of land by a licence holder where that land is required for any purpose connected with the activities it is authorised to carry out. This extends to both the transfer of any existing right or the creation of any new right in the land, as well as the compulsory purchase of the land itself. This would include, for example, an easement. Before making an order for compulsory purchase, any interested party is afforded the opportunity to make objections. This can result in an inquiry being held to determine whether the order will be beneficial.

Necessary wayleaves

Paragraph Six of Schedule 4 to the Electricity Act 1989 allows a licence holder to apply to the Secretary of State for a necessary wayleave where:

- the licence holder has given the landowner 21 days' notice to grant the wayleave and the landowner has failed to do so;
- the licence holder has given the landowner 21 days' notice to grant the wayleave and the landowner has made it subject to conditions to which the licence holder objects; or
- the landowner has given notice to the licence holder requiring the licence holder to remove an existing power line in place under a wayleave.

Before making any order in relation to a necessary wayleave, the Secretary of State must give both parties the opportunity of stating their case.

Compensation

Whether land is acquired compulsorily or by agreement, the licence holder must pay compensation to the landowner for the rights it has acquired in the land. The compensation, based on the provisions of the Land Compensation Act 1961, should take into account:

- the value of land taken, applying normal market rules;
- injurious effect on land such as dangers associated with electromagnetic fields;
- the visual impact of the power lines;

- loss of development value;
- loss of use of the land and the effect on quiet enjoyment of it; and
- the landowner's legal and surveyor's costs.

The rule-of-thumb guide is that the landowner should be in no worse a position than before the acquisition of the right. The compensation may be payable as a lump sum or as a periodic payment.

Other rights for licence holders

The Electricity Act 1989 provides other rights for licence holders including the right to fell or lop trees causing or likely to cause an unreasonable source of danger due to their proximity to the power lines and the right to enter property to carry out such felling or lopping. Licence holders also have the right to disconnect other services to property if required to allow maintenance works, together with the right to break up streets (private or public) in order to repair and maintain electricity cables and power lines.

Practical issues

Unless the grounds for objection are very strong, it is sensible to deal with the licence holder's request by way of agreement. This also enables the landowner to negotiate on a level playing field, although the compulsory powers will always be in the background should negotiations break down.

Aside from the property issues, appropriate indemnities should be sought from licence holders to cover eventualities such as the death or injury caused to any person on the land and any potential nuisance caused by the existence of the power lines. Landowners should also ensure that the licence holder makes good any damage caused to the land in the process of installing or maintaining the power lines.

Finally, landowners should be aware of Schedule 6 (as amended by the Utilities Act 2000) to the Electricity Act 1989, which contains the Public Electricity Supply Code. This provides that any person intentionally or by culpable negligence damaging or allowing any power line to be damaged is liable on summary conviction to a fine.

See also: Electricity and electrical equipment, p.252; Mobile phone masts, p.507

Sources of further information

Workplace Law Network provides premium members with unrestricted access to a comprehensive range of online information – factsheets, case reports and daily news items – on employment, health and safety and premises management. Members also benefit from an online advice service and a free subscription to the *Workplace Law Magazine*. For more information email membership@workplacelaw.net or call our membership services team on 0871 777 8881.

Private life

Mark Kaye, Berwin Leighton Paisner

Key points

- It is reasonable for workers to have a legitimate expectation that they can keep their personal lives private and workers are entitled to a degree of privacy in the workplace.
- Interference in a worker's private life is justifiable in certain circumstances. However, disciplining or dismissing without proper justification could give rise to an unfair dismissal claim and special protections are in place to ensure that workers are not discriminated against because of issues in their home life.
- Employers have an obligation to take into account a worker's human rights. The use of personal data by an employer, in particular 'sensitive data', is strictly regulated in the UK, principally under the Data Protection Act 1998.

Legislation

- Access to Medical Reports Act 1988.
- Employment Rights Act 1996.
- Data Protection Act 1998.
- Human Rights Act 1998, Schedule 1.
- Employment Equality (Sexual Orientation) Regulations 2003.
- Employment Equality (Religion or Belief) Regulations 2003.

General rules

Most employees would have an expectation that what they do in private or in their own time is their own affair. It is reasonable for workers to assume that they can keep their personal lives private, and workers are entitled to a degree of privacy in the workplace.

However, the right to respect for privacy is not absolute. Sometimes it is fair and reasonable, because of the impact that the individual's private activities have on either his work or the workplace, for the employer to interfere.

Generally, dismissal for outside conduct will only be fair if it has a material impact on either the employee's suitability to continue in his role or the employee's business (e.g. reputation or adverse customer reaction etc). Before dismissal, alternative positions might have to be considered (e.g. an employee-driver facing a temporary driving ban might be able to undertake alternative work in the short term or perform his driving duties by alternative means).

Where an employer is, in principle, justified in probing into an employee's private life, the law protects an employee in a number of respects. The employer must ensure that it is not contravening these protections if any disciplinary action or dismissal is going to be fair.

Where disciplinary action or dismissal for outside conduct is contemplated, general principles of fairness require an investigation, and a proper disciplinary process should be followed.

Relying on a criminal conviction to justify dismissal will not necessarily be fair. The employer must generally conduct its own investigation and satisfy itself that dismissal is reasonable and appropriate.

Care needs to be taken with regards to respect for private life not just during employment but at the recruitment stage as well.

Principal protections for workers are given in the legislation discussed below.

Human Rights Act 1998
The relevant parts of the Human Rights Act 1998 (HRA) for these purposes are the right to respect for private and family life (Article Eight) and the right to freedom of expression (Article Ten). It is possible to interfere with a worker's human rights where this can be justified in a work context.

While the rights of employees under the HRA are only directly enforceable against a public sector employer, all employers must be aware of these rights to ensure that their treatment of employees is fair. As Tribunals have to take account of the HRA, if an employee's human rights have been disregarded in a disciplinary investigation leading to dismissal, for example, it could result in the Tribunal finding the dismissal unfair.

Data Protection Act 1998
Information about a worker's private life will involve personal data and, in many cases, sensitive personal data. The Data Protection Act 1998 (DPA) regulates the use of personal data by an employer and covers data contained in some manual records as well as all computerised records.

The Employment Practices Code issued by the regulatory body, the Information Commissioner, assists employers in complying with the DPA. It emphasises the need, when intruding into a worker's privacy, to carry out an impact assessment, which balances the employer's objectives against any adverse impact of the intrusion for the employee. An area where impact assessments are especially relevant is workplace monitoring.

Sensitive personal data includes information about a person's ethnic or racial origins, political opinions, religious or other beliefs, trade union membership, health and criminal record. Before using 'sensitive personal data', it may be necessary to obtain explicit consent from the employee. Consent is not necessary where the data is to be used for, among other things:

- ensuring a safe system at work or otherwise to comply with health and safety rules; or
- preventing or detecting crime.

Therefore, where an employer suspects that an employee has been involved in a criminal offence outside work which is relevant to the job that he performs, or within the workplace, intrusion into the employee's privacy may well be justified under the DPA.

Discrimination legislation
The rules governing discrimination most likely to be relevant to a worker's private life are the Employment Equality (Sexual Orientation) Regulations 2003 and the Employment Equality (Religion or Belief) Regulations 2003. They make it unlawful for employers to discriminate on grounds of actual or perceived sexual orientation, religion or belief.

Sexual orientation covers orientation towards persons of the same sex, of the opposite sex, and of the same sex and the opposite sex. Religion or belief covers religion, religious belief or similar philosophical belief.

he Regulations prohibit:

direct discrimination – e.g. dismissing
someone because he frequents gay
clubs or bars;

direct discrimination – e.g. inviting
ly spouses of employees to a work
ial event, or holding all social
ts on a Friday, or catering only for
yees of a Christian belief;
sation – e.g. not promoting
e because he has made (or
o make) a complaint about
criminated against on sexual
or religious grounds; and
' – being unwanted
has the purpose or
ting a person's dignity
intimidating, hostile,
ensive environment.

Care ı ȵ at the recruitment
stage a employment.
Question pective worker's
private life itment
stage coulc er forms of
discriminatio mination
on the ground bility.
For example, a licant or
existing employe lans to
have children cou ı sex
discrimination clair ut
serious medical ailn ı
interview could creat a
disability discrimination

Tribunal cases

As noted above, the gene t
off-duty conduct can be a v or
dismissal if it is relevant to th person's
employment and makes that employee
unsuitable for the job or risks damaging
the employer's business.

Examples of past Tribunal cases include
the following:

■ A teacher of teenage pupils fairly
dismissed after having allowed others

to grow cannabis in his garden, in
view of the position of responsibility
and influence that he held.

■ A manager fairly dismissed after
having smoked cannabis in front of
subordinates at a work party, because
the employer decided that her conduct
had undermined her authority at
work.

■ A teacher fairly dismissed after his
conviction for an offence of gross
indecency with a man.

■ An air traffic controller fairly dismissed
for use of drugs outside work,
because of a need to maintain public
confidence in the safety of the air
traffic control system. While there
were no signs of the employee being
anything other than fully capable at
work, dismissal was a proportionate
response in the circumstances.

■ A probation officer (whose duties
included supervising sex offenders)
fairly dismissed for participation
outside work in activities involving
bondage and sado-masochism. The
court decided that the individual's
human right to respect for his private
life had not been infringed because his
activities were public knowledge (via a
website on the internet), and although
his right to freedom of expression was
infringed, the employer was entitled
to protect its reputation and maintain
public confidence in the probation
service.

■ An employee unfairly dismissed when
banned from driving, because he had
offered to perform his duties using
public transport, at his own expense,
which was, in the circumstances, a
workable alternative.

■ A postman unfairly dismissed after a
conviction for football hooliganism,
because the Post Office could not
show that its reputation had been
damaged by the conduct.

■ An employee fairly dismissed after
his employer discovered he had been
cautioned by the police for engaging

in sexual activity with another man in a public toilet. The Court of Appeal found that as the activity had taken place in a public place the employee's right to respect for his private life had not been engaged.

- An employee fairly dismissed for falsifying timesheets where the employer had obtained evidence through covert surveillance of the employee's home. The employer was found not to be in breach of Article Eight and its actions were justified as it was investigating criminal activity.

Recruitment considerations

Employers often ask prospective workers questions which relate to their private life, particularly during the interview process. Recording the answers gives rise to data protection principles. Employers do not have complete freedom to ask any question they like about a job applicant's private life as this could result in potentially damaging evidence against them (e.g. asking a woman about whether she is pregnant or has children).

Drug / alcohol testing

The extent to which employers have the right to require workers to undertake random drug or alcohol testing is limited, as such testing is likely to entail an invasion of personal privacy which breaches Article Eight. However testing is justified where it is in the interests of, among other things, ensuring safety at work and public safety. The Information Commissioner's Employment Practices Code provides helpful guidance on alcohol and drug testing.

Workplace relationships

Although workplace relationships are commonplace, many employers are uneasy about relationships formed between work colleagues – especially if one is the direct report of the other. The risks include claims by other employees of favouritism and fallout when the relationship ends (e.g. sexual harassment claims).

Some employers require the employees to make a 'relationship declaration' (at the beginning and the end of the relationship). Others introduce a complete ban or a ban on relationships between a supervisor and his/her direct or indirect report. Such bans can risk infringing the right to privacy under Article Eight.

An employer needs to be very careful if it seeks to resolve the issue by dismissing an employee for breaking a rule on workplace relationships or asking one of the employees to leave. Such action carries a high risk of exposure to unfair dismissal, and possibly discrimination, claims.

Practical steps for employers

Have clear rules on what amounts to acceptable conduct both in and outside work.

- Communicate the rules to employees.
- Ensure that the rules are followed, consistently, in practice.
- Ensure that any allegations of inappropriate off-duty conduct are properly investigated and that, where relevant, the requirements of the HRA and the DPA are taken into account.
- Be satisfied that the off-duty conduct makes the employee unsuitable for the job.
- Check whether there is any alternative to dismissal.
- Do not automatically assume that a criminal conviction will justify an employee being dismissed.

See also: CCTV monitoring,
p.130; Data protection, p.186;
Discrimination, p.222; Dismissal,
p.233; Human rights, p.413;
Monitoring employees, p.521;
Personnel files – recording
information, p.571

Sources of further information

The Employment Practices Data Protection Code can be found at the Information
Commissioner's Office: www.ico.gov.uk/

Probationary periods

Gemma Cawthray, Martineau Solicitors

Key points
- A probationary period is a trial period at the beginning of a new employment relationship which usually lasts for a few months.
- The employee should be subject to assessments and reviews throughout the probationary period, in order to assess whether he/she is capable of undertaking the role to which he/she was appointed.
- At the end of the probationary period, the employee may be confirmed as a permanent employee if he/she has successfully completed the period, or if his/her performance is considered unsatisfactory he/she may then be dismissed, or if his/her employment is unsatisfactory but there is hope of some improvement the probationary period may be extended for a short period to continue to assess suitability.

Legislation
- Employment Act 2002.

Introduction
A probationary period is a trial period of normally about three to six months, sometimes longer, at the beginning of an employment relationship. During the probationary period the employer will assess the employee's suitability for the position and at the end of the period decide whether or not the individual should be confirmed as a permanent employee.

When should a probationary period be used?
It is usually sensible and advisable for employers to use a probationary period when appointing a new employee. Although interviews and assessments are a useful way of assessing applicants they cannot fully reveal whether an employee is suitable for the position. Usually this can only be done by observing the employee in the role. Accordingly a probationary period allows an employer to assess whether the employee is capable of performing the job and whether he/she fits into the team. However, there may, of course, be circumstances where a probationary period may not be appropriate – for example, if an employee is going to be employed on a short, temporary contract, or if the employee is an existing employee who has simply moved to a different post.

Length of period
Normally, a probationary period will last for between three and six months. However, the length of the period should be determined by the industry sector and how long the employer needs to assess the employee's suitability for the specific role. Some roles may require a longer probationary period in order to properly assess an employee's capabilities. However, it should be borne in mind that, generally speaking, an employee cannot bring a claim for unfair dismissal until he/she has 12 months' continuous service. This is the reason why most employers choose to set probationary periods of fewer than 12 months, as it enables them to dismiss the employee during or at the end of the probationary period without the risk of the employee

bringing a claim for unfair dismissal. There is persuasive case law that implies that a failure to confirm an appointment at the end of a probationary period, even if it is over 12 months, is not a dismissal, but this is untested in England and Wales and is uncharted waters which most employers would prefer to avoid.

It is usually prudent to include a provision allowing for the extension of the probationary period if the employer considers that this is appropriate in the circumstances. However, before deciding whether or not to extend the probationary period, consideration should be given to whether an extension is likely to lead to an improvement in performance or whether there are specific issues to be addressed. If performance has generally been poor and there is no further training or guidance that could be offered which would be of benefit and lead to a significant improvement, then it may not be worthwhile extending the period. Consideration should also be given to whether the employee has been unable to work during some of the period, for example due to sickness. As mentioned above, when considering extending the period the employer should bear in mind the date upon which the employee will acquire one year's service.

During the probationary period

During the probationary period employees have the same statutory entitlements as permanent employees, such as entitlements to minimum wage and holiday pay and the benefit of the health and safety regulations and working time regulations. However, during the probationary period most employees only have limited contractual rights. In particular there is usually a reduced notice period. The terms of the probationary period should be set out in the employee's contract of employment. It is also prudent

for employers to have a probationary policy that clearly sets out the purpose of the period and the details relating to the governance of the employment relationship during the probationary period. The main purpose of the probationary period is to assess the employee's suitability by monitoring and reviewing performance regularly. Such reviews allow the employer to assess the employee's performance to date and consider if further supervision or training is required, or whether steps should be taken to dismiss the employee prior to the end of the probationary period. Any concerns with the employee's performance or capability should be brought to the attention of the employee as soon as possible, in order to give him/her the opportunity to rectify the situation. Employers should ensure that all employees who have similar roles, or who undertake substantially the same role, are subject to the same length of probationary period and the same rules.

Expiration of the probationary period

At the end of the period (whether or not extended) the employer must decide whether to dismiss the employee, or confirm the employee in post. If it is the latter situation, the employer should clearly notify the employee that he/she has successfully passed his/her probationary period and that he/she is now a permanent employee on permanent contractual terms. If the employee is dismissed, it is good practice for the dismissal to be in accordance with the three-step statutory dismissal procedure. There is no free standing right to complain of breach of the statutory dismissal procedure and although many employees will not have one year's service at the end of their probationary period and therefore will be unable to bring a claim for unfair dismissal, they may still be able to bring claims that do not require a year's service, such as unlawful discrimination. Best practice, regardless of length of service, would be for the employer to set out in writing that it is considering dismissal and inviting the employee to a meeting to which he/she has the right to be accompanied by a work colleague or trade union representative. The meeting should be held and the employee given the opportunity to make representations. The employee should be informed of his/her right to appeal.

See also: Dismissal, p.233;
Employment contracts, p.273;
Notice periods, p.531

Sources of further information

Workplace Law Network provides premium members with unrestricted access to a comprehensive range of online information – factsheets, case reports and daily news items – on employment, health and safety and premises management. Members also benefit from an online advice service and a free subscription to the *Workplace Law Magazine*. For more information email membership@ workplacelaw.net or call our membership services team on 0871 777 8881.

Property disputes

Michael Brandman, Blake Lapthorn Tarlo Lyons

Key points

- Keep copies of documents and records of telephone calls and other conversations.
- Act quickly. Some remedies are available only if you act without delay.
- Take professional advice at an early stage.
- Consider mediation as a means of resolving disputes. It is often quicker and cheaper than litigation. The courts encourage mediation, and successful litigants have in some cases been refused costs against their opponents in circumstances where mediation has been offered and rejected. However, the Court of Appeal recently ruled that litigants cannot be forced into mediation against their will.

Strategy

Always verify your rights before tackling the problem. Start by assembling and checking the relevant documents. They will often tell you what your position is.

In a landlord and tenant dispute, consider:

- the lease;
- rent review documents;
- licences for alterations;
- licences for change of use; and
- guarantees.

In a neighbour dispute, consider:

- title deeds; and
- planning documents.

In disputes with the previous owner, consider:

- the contract;
- pre-contract enquiries and replies;
- the transfer or conveyance; and
- relevant correspondence.

Gather your evidence

You may need to be able to prove your case in court or in some other kind of dispute resolution process. Good-quality evidence will help you.

It is important that you always do the following:

- Keep a written record of relevant events. Keep a log setting out times, dates and people involved as events unfold. This is essential where the events complained of are changing. Where there are, for example, building works, or where conduct of individuals is the problem, make a careful note of things that happen from day to day.
- Take photographs before and after any alterations are made.
- Keep an accurate written record of telephone calls and other conversations.

Act quickly

Remember that property disputes rarely just go away. The property does not move and the value of property makes it likely that disputes will continue until they are resolved by some sort of process.

Delay in reacting to circumstances may result in some emergency remedies being unavailable. Injunctions or restraining orders preventing further building works or demolition works, for example, can be obtained only where prompt action is taken.

Delay may result in a change in the balance of power. It is almost always easier to prevent a building from being constructed, or from being demolished, than it is to obtain an order for the removal or reconstruction of such a building.

Take professional advice
The value of the property as an asset usually warrants good professional involvement. Surveyors are necessary in many disputes (e.g. repair and boundaries). A planning expert will help to win arguments about the right to construct or alter a building, even before an application for planning permission is made.

Expert evidence will often be necessary if a dispute goes to court. Early involvement of expert professionals ensures that case preparation is carried out along the right lines from the beginning.

Solicitors should be asked to provide an early assessment of the strengths and weaknesses of any case as soon as a problem arises. Weaknesses can then be addressed and strengths shown to the opponent in the best possible light. The aim is always to find an early resolution.

Resolving disputes
The best strategy for dealing with the particular dispute needs to be identified as quickly as possible. The documents, evidence and expert advice will assist in this respect.

If an injunction or restraining order is necessary to prevent a problem from becoming entrenched or to avoid a major change in the position on the ground, then court action will be necessary.

Lawyers will assist in the preparation of witness statements and expert evidence. Subject to Claimant undertaking being given, restraining orders can be obtained on the same day where the matter is extremely urgent, or more usually within three to seven days from the commencement of action.

Many disputes are settled by mediation, rather than through the courts. This allows the parties to remain in control of the procedure and to create a solution that may be more flexible than possibilities available through the courts. Mediation is a form of facilitated negotiation and is voluntary – in a mediation, no one can be forced into a solution against their will. It is almost always quicker and cheaper than litigation.

Statutory time limits
In some cases (e.g. applications for renewal of business leases and applications for judicial review of planning decisions) there are strict and very short time limits within which to bring proceedings. In such cases obtaining prompt legal advice can be crucial. Mediation must not be allowed to delay the issue of proceedings when time is critical.

See also: Buying and selling property, p.110; Dilapidations, p.193; Landlord and tenant: lease issues, p.448; Landlord and tenant: possession issues, p.444

Sources of further information

Centre for Effective Dispute Resolution: www.cedr.co.uk/

Dilapidations claims are a common form of property dispute, and can be costly and time-consuming for both the landlord and tenant, and a source of grave contention between the two parties. The legislation surrounding dilapidations has evolved over a long period of time and is notoriously complicated. Workplace Law Group's *Guide to Dilapidations* provides a better understanding of this complex issue. The reader is offered practical advice on what to do if faced with a claim for dilapidations, whether from the point of view of a landlord or tenant, and a sample Schedule of Dilapidations is included to highlight the process of a dilapidations claim. Discussion of a real-life dilapidations case is also included, to show how theory is put into practice. For more information visit www.workplacelaw.net/Bookshop/GuidesTo.

Radiation

Stephen Day, Bureau Veritas

Key points

- There are two types of radiation – ionising and non-ionising.
- Specific regulations require employers to protect employees from the adverse effects of ionising radiation, either from irradiation or from radioactive contamination.
- Employers also have a general duty to protect employees from non-ionising radiation (e.g. over-exposure to the sun).

Legislation

- Radioactive Substances Act 1993.
- Ionising Radiations Regulations 1999.
- Management of Health and Safety at Work Regulations 1999.
- Radiation (Emergency Preparedness and Public Information) Regulations 2001.
- The Transport of Dangerous Goods and Use of Transportable Pressure Equipment Regulations 2007.

Types of radiation

Radiation may be classified as either ionising or non-ionising:

- Non-ionising electromagnetic radiation (e.g. ultraviolet and radio waves) does not change the structure of atoms.
- Ionising electromagnetic radiation has enough energy to ionise or electrically charge atoms. Ionising radiation has sufficient energy to cause changes within the DNA molecule and can therefore be a cause of cancer.

Non-ionising radiation

Non-ionising radiation (NIR) is the term used to describe the part of the electromagnetic spectrum covering two main regions, namely optical radiation (ultraviolet (UV), visible and infrared) and electromagnetic fields (EMFs) (power frequencies, microwaves and radio frequencies).

Optical radiation

Optical radiation is another term for light, covering ultraviolet (UV) radiation, visible light, and infrared radiation. The greatest risks to health are probably posed by:

- *UV radiation from the sun.* Exposure of the eyes to UV radiation can damage the cornea and produce pain and symptoms similar to that of sand in the eye. The effects on the skin range from redness, burning and accelerated ageing through to various types of skin cancer. Protective measures include minimising time of exposure, use of sun screen lotions, wearing clothes, including a hat, which cover the skin, and use of sunglasses.
- *The misuse of powerful lasers.* High-power lasers can cause serious damage to the eye (including blindness) as well as producing skin burns. The main method of protection is to use engineering controls that prevent intra beam viewing.

Electromagnetic fields

Electromagnetic fields (EMFs) arise whenever electrical energy is used.

So for example, EMFs arise in our home from electrical appliances in the kitchen, from work processes such as radiofrequency heating and drying and in the world at large from radio, TV and Telecoms broadcasting masts and security detection devices. It has been known for a long time that exposure of people to high levels of EMFs can give rise to acute effects. The effects that can occur depend on the frequency of the radiation. At low frequencies the effects will be on the central nervous system of the body whilst at high frequencies, heating effects can occur, leading to a rise in body temperature. In reality, these effects are extremely rare and will not occur in most day-to-day work situations.

Employers should conduct a risk assessment, as required by the Management of Health and Safety at Work Regulations 1999. The effects from these electromagnetic frequencies can be controlled by compliance with guidelines published by the Health Protection Agency (HPA).

Ionising radiation
Ionising radiation occurs as either electromagnetic rays (such as X-rays and gamma rays) or particles (such as alpha and beta particles). It occurs naturally (e.g. from the radioactive decay of natural radioactive substances such as radon gas and its decay products) but can also be produced artificially. People can be exposed externally, to radiation from a radioactive material or a generator such as an X-ray set, or internally, by inhaling or ingesting radioactive substances. Wounds that become contaminated by radioactive material can also cause radioactive exposure.

The Ionising Radiations Regulations 1999 apply to a large range of workplaces where radioactive substances and electrical equipment emitting ionising radiation (X-rays) are used. They require employers to keep exposure to ionising radiation as low as reasonably practicable and to not exceed annual dose limits. Employers should bear in mind that two distinct types of hazard may exist – irradiation; i.e. the emission of penetrating radiation (gamma- or X-rays), and contamination; i.e. the presence of radioactive powders, liquids or gases which could be inhaled, ingested or absorbed into the body. The following hierarchy of control measures is recommended:

1. Engineering controls, including shielding and ventilation.
2. Procedural controls, e.g. restricted access and safe systems of work.
3. Personal protective equipment – this should be used as a last resort.

The Regulations contain specific requirements that may apply depending on the nature of the work. They include the following:

■   Employers must notify enforcing authorities before starting work.
■   Employers must appoint a suitably qualified Radiation Protection Adviser and a local Radiation Protection Superviser.
■   Employers must set up either controlled or supervised areas where radiation hazards exist.
■   Employers must assess whether any of their employees will fall into the category of classified workers in which case arrangements must be made with an Approved Dosimetry Service and for annual medical examinations.
■   Employers must produce a set of local rules that describe the safe operating procedure for working with the radiation source(s).

The Radioactive Substances Act includes the following requirements for users of radioactive materials:

■ Registration of holdings. The user must be in posession of a Registration that specifies the type and amount of radioactive material under their control.

■ Authorisation for the accumulation and disposal of waste. The user must be granted an authorisation by the Environment Agency which specifies the disposal route, the physical form and the limit / frequency of disposals.

See also: Occupational health, p.537; Outdoor workers, p.544; Personal protective equipment, p.568; Weather, p.741

Sources of further information

HSE: www.hse.gov.uk/radiation.

INDG337 *Sun protection: advice for employers of outdoor workers* (HSE Books, 2001) ISBN: 0 7176 1982 6.

Health protection Agency Centre for Radiation Hazards: www.hpa.org.uk/radiation

Non-domestic Rates and the 2005 revaluation

Catherine Edwards, Chivers Commercial

Key points

Non-domestic Rateable Values have been reassessed on a five-yearly cycle since 1990, the latest being as from 1 April 2005. The Rateable Value is the figure along with the multiplier, known as the Uniform Business Rate (UBR), which is used to calculate the rates liability on all non-domestic properties in England and Wales. The Scottish system is different to that of England and Wales. Further information on Scottish Non Domestic Rates can be found at www.saa.gov.uk.

The biggest change to come into operation, as of April 2008, is the abolition of Empty Property Rates Relief. The budget announcement in 2007 slashed the rates relief for vacant property and since then the Government has made unheard of haste to force through legislation in the form of the Rating (Empty Properties) Act 2007.

The Act applies in England and Wales although the devolved assembly in Wales could reverse or amend its provisions but at the time of writing has so far not done so. The Scottish administration has given no indication that it intends to change the Scottish empty property rules.

Empty non-domestic properties received 100% relief for the first three months of vacancy and 50% relief ongoing but with industrial premises and listed buildings continuing to receive 100%. The new legislation imposes a 100% relief period of just three months for almost all property except factories and warehouses, which will have six months but thereafter full liability becomes payable. This has created a huge liability for both owners and tenants of empty property and in the current poor climate there is little chance of much of this property being occupied. The legislation has also been written to make sure that no small measures are taken to avoid this liability such as removing the roof. Unless the building is demolished, the liability with very few exceptions remains.

The following Properties remain excempt from the empty property charge:

- any small property with a rateable value below £2,200;
- where liability falls on a charity or community amateur sports club, if the property's next use is likely to be wholly or mainly for charitable or sports club purposes; and
- any listed buildings and properties subject to insolvency / administration.

Workplace Law Network
www.workplacelaw.net

What is the Rateable Value and how is it calculated?

Under sections 43(4) and 54(4) of the Local Government Finance Act 1988 the rate bill of the property is its rateable value multiplied by the national rate multiplier.

The RV is the figure that represents broadly the rental value of the occupied property as at the relevant date, which for the 2005 list is 1 April 2003. All non-domestic property is assessed as at this date to ensure as far as possible fairness across the spectrum. New property is also assessed as if it had been in existence at the relevant date. If there is a new lease or a rent review at or close to 1 April 2003 which is based on full repairing terms without premiums or incentives then the rateable value should not be dissimilar to the rent payable.

For the first time in the 2005 list, the Valuation Office Agency (VOA) responsible for the preparation of all the rateable values across England and Wales produced a summary valuation for every non-domestic property. The summary valuation was sent to the occupier by 1 April 2005 and they are also all available on the VOA website (www.voa.gov.uk). The valuation gives a breakdown of how the VOA has arrived at the RV.

These summary valuations should be viewed with caution as many contain inaccurate information which has been held historically, and perhaps does not include subsequent alterations to buildings which have been made, particularly if there has been no previous appeal against a rateable value. An appeal against a factual inaccuracy can be made fairly easily but be cautious; only one appeal for each type of reason can be made during the lifetime of the list. Unless you are sure of the dimensions of your property it is advisable to seek professional help with measurement. Different types of property are measured in different ways, shops are zoned with the most valuable space being the front, Zone A, and then apportioned backwards becoming less valuable the deeper the shop, whereas factories are measured on a gross internal basis.

How much is paid?

For a number of years, there has been a dual calculation which involves the multiplier (UBR) and transitional relief. For the 2008/09 year there continues the further complicated use of two UBRs, a sliding scale and additional relief in some – although very few – cases.

The basic multipliers are:

- the small business multiplier at 45.8p in the pound for properties with RVs below £15,000, up from 44.1p in 2007/08; and
- the standard multiplier at 46.2p in the pound for properties with RVs above £15,000 up from 44.4p in 2007/08.

In London the small business multiplier is used where the RV of the property is under £21,500.

The standard multiplier is used for all other RV and continues to include a supplement to pay for those properties eligible for the additional small business relief.

What additional relief is available?

Small business relief is available if the RV is between £5,000 and £10,000, and an occupier can claim up to 50% relief on a sliding scale. This relief must be applied for by the ratepayer each year.

A small business eligible for additional relief is classed as one with a combined rateable value for all of its premises being below £10,000 and providing additional properties do not have individual RV of more than £2,200. So if a company operates from, say, three outlets, all with an RV of £3,000 making a total of £9,000 RV, it will not qualify for the small business relief nor for the small business rate even if the outlets are in different towns.

Finally, there continues the transitional relief which limits the actual amount payable each year to ensure that the increased liability due to an increase in the RV does not rise to a level which might put great pressure on the occupying company. The phasing helps those whose bills should increase substantially due to the revaluation but penalises those with a decrease in the RV by phasing reductions also.

Transitional relief will depend upon individual circumstances for continuing occupiers only. New occupiers will automatically pay the full liability based on the RV, the multiplier and any small business relief that might be available. Phasing is set to be abolished altogether from 2009/10 at which time all ratepayers will pay their full liability. There have been some adjustments to bills due to the phasing which has seen some bills come down this year from last year but in the main the trend is relentlessly upwards. The phasing provisions for transitional relief are as follows.

There are also some specific reliefs available depending on individual circumstances as follows:

- Charities and non-profit making organisations;
- Rural village populations under 3,000;

Table 1. Proposed limits by which a rates bill can increase in a single year before transitional arrangements apply

Year	Small business	Large business
2005/6	5%	12.5%
2006/7	7.5%	17.5%
2007/8	10%	20%
2008/9	15%	25%
2009/10	n/a	n/a

Table 2. Proposed limits by which a rates bill can decrease in a single year

Year	Small business	Large business
2005/6	30%	12.5%
2006/7	30%	12.5%
2007/8	35%	14%
2008/9	60%	25%
2009/10	n/a	n/a

- Non agricultural businesses on former agricultural buildings or land; and
- Some severe hardship cases.

There are also individual arrangements for such things as:

- working from home; and
- renting out a holiday home or providing bed and breakfast.

Can the rateable value be appealed?

The short answer is yes. The rateable values in the 2005 list can be appealed at any time during the lifetime of the list and for various reasons such as:

- factual inaccuracies in the calculations which might be too large an area or the addition of car parking spaces which do not exist;
- combining more than one RV to reduce the overall RV;
- taking part of the property out of the RV, perhaps because upper floors are to be used for residential purposes and should be included in the Council Tax listings, or some space is now fully vacant and should be excluded; or
- as a result of other appeal decisions.

However, be aware that only one appeal can be made by the same occupier for the same reason during the lifetime of the list but an appeal, if appropriate, can be backdated to the start of the list at 1 April 2005.

Appeals have been made considerably easier with the introduction of the appeal system online. Initially, the appeal form is completed which includes a concise and calculated reason for the appeal.

The appeals are then programmed in batches and notification of the dates of these batched appeals, which will often involve a number of properties within a 'scheme' (similar type properties in similar areas), will be held at the same time.

As with the 2000 list, the appeal timetable is long and appeals may not occur for several years after the appeal has been made. Until the appeal is agreed and the RV altered, the ratepayer is obliged to continue paying at the original billed rate and will then receive a refund if the RV reduces. However, professional advice should always be taken if in any doubt about the reasons for appeal, and always if there is a question of rental value or measurement.

An appeal can also result in an increase in an RV if the VOA finds the property has been extended or reorganised internally. In this list occupier items such as central heating and in particular air conditioning are being given assessments and car parking spaces are also being individually separated out and assessed. It seems very unjust that an occupier improves the working environment for staff and is immediately slapped with an increased rating liability.

The new list due to be published in 2010 is starting to be put together. The RVs will be based upon the rental value of the property as at 1 April 2008 – so if you have a review around that date be aware it may not just impact on your rental payments but on your non domestic rates bill from 1 April 2010.

What should the ratepayer look out for?

- It is wise to take a few moments to look at the rates bill and check the calculations.
- Remember, if the RV is less than £15,000 (£21,500 in London and subject to the comments above) you should be eligible for the lower UBR multiplier.
- If your RV is less than £10,000 remember to apply annually for the small business relief.
- Consider the RV assessment in line with the rent payable in 2003 if

appropriate. If these wildly differ you might have grounds for a successful appeal.

- If the RV is close to either the £15,000 (£21,500 in London) limit for eligibility for the small business multiplier, or the £10,000 or below RV which might give eligibility for the small business relief as well, it is worth reviewing the summary valuation and taking professional advice to see if an appeal might move the RV into the relief area.
- Be aware that the VOA under the Local Government Finance Act 1988, as amended, now issue form VO6003 called *Non Domestic Rating Rent Return* and form VO 6004 called *Non Domestic Rating Request for Rent Review Information*. Completion of these within 56 days of issue is now a statutory requirement and penalties or even prosecution can result if these forms are not completed and returned. Almost all of the VOs are taking

a hard line on this and some are issuing fines without delay and adding punitive interest rates and penalties in addition. The advice must be – if you get one of these fill it in and send it back immediately.

- Take care if approached by anyone suggesting they make an appeal on your behalf. Remember that in this list, only one appeal for each type of eligible appeal can be made for the lifetime of the list to 31 March 2010 and the RV can go up as well as down. Never pay 'up front' for an appeal to be lodged.
- If a refurbishment is planned of the property, consider making any appeal before refurbishment rather than after. Remember that improving your property, installing air conditioning and laying out parking spaces will increase your annual liability and may be backdated within the life of the list to the date you did the work.
- If in doubt seek professional help.

See also: Landlord and tenant: possession issues, p.444; Landlord and tenant: lease issues, p.448

Sources of further information

The Valuation Office Agency (VOA): www.voa.gov.uk

Recruitment and selection

Kathryn Haigh, Mills & Reeve

Key points

- Carefully and clearly define the job description of the vacant post(s).
- Carefully draft the advertisement for the job vacancy and consider where the advertisement is to be placed.
- Limit the information requested on the application form to information relevant to the post.
- Prepare questions to be asked at interview in advance and keep score sheets to record answers given during the interview.
- Data collected during the recruitment process must be used in accordance with the Data Protection Act 1998.
- Confirm any offer of employment in writing and clearly set out any attached conditions.

Legislation

- Equal Pay Act 1970.
- Rehabilitation of Offenders Act 1974.
- Sex Discrimination Act 1975.
- Race Relations Act 1976.
- Disability Discrimination Act 1995.
- Data Protection Act 1998.
- Employment Equality (Religion or Belief) Regulations 2003.
- Employment Equality (Sexual Orientation) Regulations 2003.
- Employment Equality (Age) Regulations 2006.

Some employment rights start on the first day of employment. However, all discrimination legislation offers protection throughout the recruitment process starting when the job advertisement is placed. Equally, an employer must ensure that all documentation relating to a job is accurate to ensure that misrepresentations are not made.

Job description

Once a vacancy has arisen and there is a need to recruit, the initial step should be to clarify the role and the employer's requirements within a job description. The vacancy may be a new role within an organisation or a vacancy caused by a person leaving or reducing their working hours (for example working part-time); in any case careful consideration should be given to the job description, including necessary skills, expertise and qualifications.

The job description will become an important document because it can be used to identify the duties of the job but also build in some flexibility. This will be useful if there are any disputes over the nature and requirements of the job but should be flexible enough to allow changes to duties for, say, operational reasons. Also, it will give focus to those involved in the recruitment process, making them aware of the requirements of the organisation.

Therefore it is not necessary to list every task the employee would be required to carry out within the job description. The job description should contain the main duties and responsibilities, reporting structure, place of work, and objectives. Other details such as pay and working hours do not need to be included as these will be contained within the contract of employment. The job description should say something to the effect that it describes the main duties but the role generally encompasses all duties that might be undertaken in connection with the advertised job so the job holder will be expected to be flexible in undertaking the role.

In addition to the job description, a person specification can be used to detail the type of person and competencies required to perform the job. The document would list those qualifications, training, skills, experience, knowledge and personal skills that are either essential or desirable criteria. Like the job description these should be relevant to the job, such as the ability to manage a team. Consideration should be given to how necessary these criteria are and whether any alternatives are equally as acceptable, such as equivalent qualifications to GCSEs.

Advertising
The next step in the recruitment process is to advertise the vacant post. Not only must the advert be accurately drafted so as to not misrepresent the job vacancy, but also an employer must be aware of discrimination legislation.

When drafting the advertisement certain phrases should be avoided which may be perceived as discriminatory, such as gender-specific words like 'salesman' and the use of phrases such as 'young and dynamic' or 'fit and healthy'. It is advisable to state within the advert that the organisation is an Equal Opportunities Employer.

Not only must care be taken over the wording of the advert but also where the

advert is placed. If adverts are publicised in limited places, it could be argued that it limits the types of people who will be aware of the vacancy; for example, only placing the advert on the internet could be considered to discriminate against older people who are less likely to have access to the internet, or if a job is only advertised internally or by word of mouth, there is a risk that an employer will continue to recruit people of a certain race, sex, religion etc.

Application forms
Certain questions should be avoided on the application form and placed on a separate equal opportunities monitoring form, which should then only be used by Human Resources / Senior Management and not those directly involved in selecting applicants.

The following questions should not be placed on the application form:

- The applicant's marital status or previous names;
- The applicant's race or religion;
- The applicant's national insurance number or passport number;
- The applicant's nationality;
- The applicant's sexual orientation;
- The applicant's date of birth;
- The level of sickness absence taken by the applicant; and
- Whether the applicant has a particular health condition.

It is legitimate to ask questions about the applicant's health, but again these should be kept to a document other than the application form. If questions are asked about an applicant's health, reasons for such questions should be given. For example, asking whether any adjustments need to be made to the recruitment process or to assist the applicant when they attend interview. A blanket request for answers to health-related questions may lead to an inference of discrimination (for example on the grounds of age or discrimination) so you must have a good reason for asking.

It is legitimate for an employer to ask whether or not an applicant requires a work permit.

It is also permissible to ask about past criminal convictions. However, an applicant is not required and should not be asked to provide details of spent convictions unless an exemption applies under the Rehabilitation of Offenders Act 1974. In certain cases where an employee will be working with a vulnerable group of people an employer is entitled to information about spent convictions.

Shortlisting

When considering which applicants to shortlist for interview, only the information provided on the application forms should be considered (as well as any accompanying documents provided by the applicant such as their CV). The equal opportunities monitoring form should not be considered by those carrying out the shortlisting exercise.

Applicants should be selected for the next stage of the recruitment process after a comparison of the details provided on the application form with the job description and person specification. If an applicant is to be rejected, the reason should be recorded and kept for a maximum of six months to assist in providing feedback to unsuccessful applicants and to explain any decisions, should a claim be brought at an Employment Tribunal.

Some employers may choose to use selection and aptitude tests as part of their selection process. Any such tests should be carefully considered to ensure that the

tests are evaluating skills relevant to the post. Adjustments should be made to any such tests if an employer is aware that an applicant has a certain condition(s) which may hinder their ability to perform in the test.

Interviews

It is important that those employees who are to carry out interviews should be trained in equal opportunities and aware of their employer's equal opportunities policy.

At the interview, questions should centre around the needs of the job, as identified in the job description and the candidate's suitability on a personal level as identified in the person specification. To ensure consistency, questions on key topic areas should be prepared prior to the interview and asked of each candidate. It is accepted that an interview process will be discursive and non-scripted supplementary questions may be asked, but you should endeavour to maintain consistency throughout. Some written form of scoring or assessing candidates should be used and retained.

If, during the interview, the applicant discloses information about themselves, such as they have children under the age of five or require certain adjustments to be made to their workplace, the information should be noted as well as the response given by those conducting the interview. Notes of the interview should be kept for a maximum of six months after the interview, again to provide feedback and to allow any decision not to offer the job to be justified.

There are certain questions that should not be asked of an applicant during the interview and are the same as set out above in the section on Application Forms. It is legitimate to ask during the interview if an applicant has a disability and discuss any adjustments that need to be made to the role.

Retention of recruitment records

Throughout the recruitment process an organisation will collect a great deal of personal data about an applicant and the Data Protection Act 1998 will apply to these records. The Information Commissioner has issued the Employment Practices Code. Part 1 of the Code provides guidance on how to remain within the remit of the Data Protection Act during recruitment and selection.

The Code does not specify how long an organisation should retain information obtained during the recruitment process, but states that it should only be retained for such periods as are necessary to complete the recruitment process and suggests that any data obtained during a recruitment process should be retained for no more than six months, although as the time limits for bringing claims can be extended by three months under the Statutory Dispute Resolution Procedures, a period of nine to 12 months may be justifiable. Any information obtained during the recruitment process must be stored securely until it is destroyed.

In relation to the successful applicant, an employer should only retain information that is relevant to the continuing employment relationship.

Making a job offer

Once the successful applicant has been identified, an offer of employment should be made in writing and should set out comprehensively the terms of employment to avoid any uncertainty at a later stage, such as salary, job description and start date.

The letter should state a date by which the offer of employment is to be accepted.

It is most important to remember that if you are making an offer subject to a medical, references, CRB checks, immigration status check etc. the offer must clearly state that it is conditional upon satisfactory completion of such checks and may want to advise the candidate not to resign from their current post unless and until the checks have been confirmed as satisfactory.

See also: Criminal records, p.181; Data protection, p.186; Disability legislation, p.209; Discrimination, p.222; Equal pay, p.300; Foreign nationals, p.340; Interviewing, p.429; Personnel files – recording information, p.571

Sources of further information

ACAS: Advisory booklet – *Recruitment and induction*: www.acas.org.uk

Information Commissioner: The Employment Practices Code – Part 1 www.ico.gov.uk/Home/what_we_cover/data_protection/guidance/codes_of_prac-tice.aspx

Age Concern: www.ageconcern.org.uk

Equality and Human Rights Commission: www.equalityhumanrights.com

Comment...

The Apprentice – lessons to learn

Alan Nicholson is a Senior Associate with McGrigors LLP. He advises a broad range of clients on all aspects of employment law, including disciplinary and grievance issues, discrimination and TUPE. He regularly represents clients at Employment Tribunals and the EAT both north and south of the border.

The BBC Series *The Apprentice* describes itself as 'the job interview from hell'. As far as employment lawyers are concerned, the issues it raises are manna from heaven.

In 2008, Sir Alan Sugar spent 12 weeks grilling 16 aspiring tycoons in the search for his latest protégé. Flanked by PR expert, Nick Hewer, and ex-lawyer, Margaret Mountford, Sir Alan put the candidates through their paces, and gave us all lots to think about when it comes to workplace law.

As with any employer, Sir Alan's quest for the perfect hire started long before the pointy-finger-bit in his boardroom. It's difficult to imagine quite what he must have said in the job advert and which publications he placed it in, but these are factors every employer should give careful consideration to if claims are to be avoided. In a judgment issued in July 2008, the European Court of Justice went against the prevailing opinion of UK courts by deciding that discriminatory job adverts can in themselves form the basis of discrimination claims by individuals, even those who never go on to apply for the job. Such adverts can raise a presumption that the employer's recruitment process is directly discriminatory, forcing the employer

to prove that the actual selection process is not.

It seems unlikely that *The Apprentice* excluded any groups with the wording of its advert, as it apparently received 20,000 applications via its website. Reports that 15,000 of those were submitted by Michael Sophocles are unconfirmed. Regional interviews whittled the number down to 75, and of that group, 20-30 had their references checked, before being assessed by a psychologist.

Not many employers invest in psychological assessments of candidates before interview, and judging by the 'issues' some of Sir Alan's 16 seemed to have, one wonders if it's worth it. Still, vetting procedures and short-listing techniques have come a long way in the last few years. Employers who take on staff to work with children or vulnerable adults are required to carry out fairly stringent criminal record checks. Other employers need to give careful thought to how much detail is actually necessary at the short-listing stage, and to when vetting perhaps goes too far.

If you thought Bebo was one of the Teletubbies, the web-based social networking phenomenon has probably passed you by. But if you are an employer who checks Facebook to see what job candidates get up to on weekends, you might want to think about what relevance that really has to their application. Mind you, if you catch someone doing a reverse pterodactyl impression on YouTube, you can't say you weren't warned.

One of the most talked-about employment law issues thrown up by this year's *Apprentice* was series-winner Lee McQueen's economy with the truth on his CV. Lee embellished his qualifications to mask what he saw as a weakness in his claim to be the next Apprentice. Unluckily for him, his interviewer had contacted the college and found out the truth. Sir Alan wasn't too worried about what he called 'over-flowering' of the CV, but most employers would be bloomin' furious.

Whether it pays to check every detail on a candidate's CV will depend on what stage has been reached in the recruitment process, and how important the information is to the role. If qualifications are required, or where there is reason to suspect a candidate's honesty, it makes sense to test the information supplied and seek original documents. Any job offer should be expressly conditional upon the employer being satisfied that all criteria are met, which may include appropriate references and in some cases work permits, criminal record checks and medical assessments.

Lee's dressing-down at interview and indeed Sir Alan's own forthright style of hiring and firing serve as interesting case studies in the field of interviewing techniques. If you watched the series you probably jotted down a few pointers yourself:

1. If sceptical about a candidate's claim to be Jewish, do not ask them to drop their trousers as a means of clarification; and

2. When attempting to build a rapport with an applicant, avoid phrases such as "this is the most boring CV I have ever read" etc.

Bearing in mind that the interviewing process might later be scrutinised by an Employment Tribunal, it is advisable to plan in detail how it will work. Who will be doing the interviewing? What are the common questions they will ask? What criteria will be applied when assessing the answers? What feedback will be given and how? How will this all be documented?

Of course, the legal assault course that is *The Apprentice* bears little resemblance to the average interview process (I hope). Its participants are to all intents and purposes employees of the Sugar empire for however much of the 12 week stint they or Sir Alan can endure. From that perspective, the series does perhaps provide a window into some of the problems arising in workplaces across the UK. Across the three-month run, we dipped our collective toes into most of the UK's discriminatory waters, and hopefully learned a lesson or two along the way.

A sojourn to Morocco highlighted a concerning lack of awareness among the wannabes of the basic underlying principles of major faiths. Thankfully in our case it was a solitary chicken that was offended, but with laws prohibiting discrimination on the grounds of religion or belief now firmly rooted, perhaps employers and employees alike should seek to educate themselves about the religions or beliefs of others.

Second-choice-Claire proclaimed that behind every successful man is a very successful woman". With the gender pay gap in London reported to be around 25%, and only 11% of the capital's company directors being female, perhaps she has a point, and maybe the law should do more to help those women step in front. Norway has taken a bold step in this direction, with laws enabling the dissolution of any publicly-listed company whose board was not at least 40% female by the start of 2008.

And didn't we all age by about 20 years after hearing Alex go on and on about him only being 24? Michael also used his youth as a reason for keeping him on, with Helene forced to argue she was not past her best at 32. These attitudes perhaps reflect a common view that age discrimination laws are aimed only at protecting older workers. In fact, the Employment Equality (Age) Regulations 2006 target all discrimination on the grounds of age, whomever it is directed at.

Meanwhile, with Sir Alan arriving at the UK's default retirement age in under four years' time, he may well be keeping one eye on the *Heyday* challenge in the European Court of Justice. The Advocate General's opinion on the lawfulness of compulsory retirement at 65 is expected very soon, with the Court's decision to follow, probably in 2009.

Add to that all the undertones of bullying and harassment, questionable performance management techniques and potential breaches of the Working Time Regulations, Sir Alan should be grateful he's ended up with another willing Apprentice, and not 16 Employment Tribunal claims from hell.

Recycling

Bethan Herbert and Mark Webster, Bureau Veritas

Key points

Article 1(a) of the Waste Framework Directive defines waste as "... any substance or object ... which the holder discards or intends or is required to discard". Collaborative studies conducted by the Environment Agency and the Department for Environment, Food and Rural Affairs (Defra) indicate that on average, the UK produces approximately 330 million tonnes of waste per annum. A quarter of the waste is attributable to common household and business activities.

Although the UK Government recognises the importance of a robust waste management strategy, our businesses display a more lenient attitude towards their responsibilities as very few businesses are aware of the true cost of waste. Studies conducted by Envirowise have consistently shown that the true cost of waste is ten times that of the cost of disposal to the business. Good waste management including reduction, reuse and recycling has the potential to improve the bottom line performance of any business.

Business waste

The generation of waste arising from business activities, and subsequently its route to the next stage use or disposal should be undertaken in a responsible manner, adopting best practice – the waste hierarchical system to determine the best waste minimisation option. It represents a chain of priority for waste management, citing the prevention of waste as the most favourable option. If not possible, waste prevention is succeeded by minimisation, reuse, recycling, energy recovery then disposal, which is considered the least favourable. Although waste recycling is prominent, heavily publicised and promoted in businesses, there is no overriding legislation that enforces recycling in the UK. Specific requirements to recycle are, however, embedded in European Union (EU) legislation relating to certain industries and activities.

Demonstrating compliance with current regulations will protect your business from prosecution. The overriding Directive which focuses on recycling and waste management throughout the EU is the Framework Directive on Waste (Council Directive 75/442/EEC as amended by Council Directive 91/156/EEC and adapted by Council Directive 96/350/EC). The contents of the Framework Directive are implemented in the UK through the Environmental Protection Act 1990, amended by the Environment Act 1995 and also by various principal regulations.

End of Life Vehicles (Producer Responsibility) Regulations 2005

Car manufacturers now have an obligation to take back old/scrap cars from consumers and ensure that more of the waste from scrap cars and light vans is recycled rather than landfilled. The Regulations establish responsibilities for vehicle manufacturers and professional importers to:

■ put in place collection networks to take back their own brands of vehicles, when those vehicles reach the end of their lives;
■ from 2006, ensure that value reused or recovered is at least 85% of the weight of their end of life vehicles (95% from 2015); and
■ from 2007, provide 'free take-back' to last owners, who present their end of life vehicles for scrapping at collection networks.

The Regulations apply to passenger cars and light vans.

End of Life Vehicles Regulations 2003
The End of Life Vehicle Regulations 2003 apply to vehicles, end of life vehicles, their components and their materials. It places the main responsibilities for recycling and collection on dismantlers and scrap metal recyclers, outlines materials and components that manufacturers cannot use in vehicle manufacture as well as the requirement on manufacturers to provide material coding to facilitate identification of materials and components suitable for reuse and recovery.

The Packaging (Essential Requirements) Regulations 2003 (amended 2006)
This Regulation implements Articles 9 and 11 of Directive 94/62/EC of the European Parliament and the Council on packaging and packaging waste. Companies must ensure that any packaging placed on the market by the organisation meets the minimum national standards necessary for safety, hygiene and consumer 'acceptance' purposes and that it is reusable,

biodegradable or recoverable by recycling, energy recovery or composting.

The Producer Responsibility Obligations (Packaging Waste) (England and Wales) Regulations 1997 (amended 2008)
The Producer Responsibility Regulations 1997 implement the 1994 European Directive on packaging and packaging waste. The UK was required to recover a minimum 50% by weight of packaging material and to recycle a minimum of 25% by weight of the total waste flow by 2001. These Regulations differ from most other environmental legislation to date, as they require collaboration between a wide range of players throughout the packaging chain. The obligations are broad and affect not only producers of packaging and packaging materials, but also those who use the packaging around their products and those who sell packaging to the final user.

The Regulations, last updated in 2008, are designed to encourage more sustainable use of packaging by promoting recovery / recycling / minimisation – thus reducing the amount of packaging waste going to landfill and minimising resource wastage. A company is obligated if its turnover in the previous financial year was more than £2m per year and it handles (in aggregate) more than 50 tonnes of packaging material and/or packaging in a year. It is then required to ensure that a proportion of the packaging is diverted from the waste stream and recovered for reuse, recycling or incinerated with energy recovery. The exact nature of a company's obligation depends on the amount of packaging the organisation supplies, the materials it comprises and its role in the packaging chain. Recycling and recovery targets are set for raw material manufacturers, converters, packers or sellers.

Waste Electrical and Electronic Equipment (England and Wales) Regulations 2006 (amended 2007) and The Waste Management Licensing Amendment (Waste Electrical and Electronic Equipment) (Scotland) Regulations 2007

These Regulations transpose the main provisions of Council Directive 2002/96/EC on waste electrical and electronic equipment as amended by Council Directive 2003/108/EC. The Waste Electrical and Electronic Equipment (WEEE) Directive has recently been by far the most widely publicised legislation as WEEE is currently the fastest growing waste stream in the UK. Volumes for business WEEE in London alone are estimated to be around 100,000 tonnes per annum. Producers who put electrical and electronic equipment (EEE) on the market in the UK, must set up systems for the treatment of WEEE and are responsible for financing the costs of the collection, treatment, recovery and environmentally sound disposal of the EEE items. In respect of any WEEE cited under these Regulations, the operator of a scheme must ensure that systems are set up to provide for the treatment of WEEE using the best available treatment, recovery and recycling techniques. The WEEE Directive and Regulations will affect every business that uses electrical equipment in the workplace. The Directive places responsibility on business users along with producers for ensuring WEEE is correctly treated and reprocessed, encouraging the reuse of equipment over recycling.

Restriction on the Use of Certain Hazardous Substances in Electrical and Electronic Equipment Directive (RoHS)

Complementary to the WEEE Directive is the Restriction on the Use of Certain Hazardous Substances in Electrical and Electronic Equipment Directive (RoHS). This Directive aims to harmonise legislation controlling the use of hazardous substances in EEE across the EU and also seeks to reduce the environmental impact of WEEE by restricting the use of certain hazardous substances during manufacture. The ROHS Directive covers all products mentioned in the WEEE Directive except medical, monitoring and control equipment. The Directive requires the substitution of lead, cadmium, hexavalent chromium, polybrominated biphenyls (PBBs) and polybrominated diphenylethers (PDBEs) by 1 July 2006. Manufacturers need to understand the requirements of the RoHS Directive to ensure that their products, and their components, comply.

The Landfill (England & Wales) Regulations 2002 (amended 2005)

These Regulations set out a pollution control regime for landfills for the purpose of implementing Council Directive 99/31/EC on the landfill of waste ('the Landfill Directive') in England and Wales. The obligation to meet the requirements of the Regulations is mainly on landfill operators, but there are provisions that waste producers need to be aware of such as:

- granting of permits for landfill;
- prohibition of certain wastes; and
- duty of care / waste transfer notes.

The Landfill Directive is helping to bring about a change in the way we dispose of waste in this country. It aims to reduce the pollution potential from landfilled waste that can impact on surface water, groundwater, soil, air, and also contribute to climate change. In England and Wales the Directive is applied under the Landfill (England and Wales) Regulations 2002 and must be fully implemented by July 2009. The Directive sets demanding targets to reduce the amount of biodegradable municipal landfilled waste.

Since 30 October 2007, new rules apply for non-hazardous waste. Liquid wastes are banned from landfill and all waste must be treated before it can be landfilled, factors which will force businesses to review their waste management strategies. 'Treatment'

of non-hazardous waste is defined as either a physical, thermal, chemical or biological process including sorting. To comply with these Regulations businesses could either collect waste as individual waste streams or send to separate waste streams to be recycled, or make a request with its waste management contractor to sort the waste for recycling.

See also: Waste management, p.725; WEEE – the Waste Electronic and Electrical Equipment Regulations and RoHS, p.744

Sources of further information

A considerable amount of information on waste management can be found on the website for the Department for Environment Food and Rural Affairs (Defra), which offers information on environmental topics at www.defra.gov.uk/.
Envirowise: www.envirowise.gov.uk

WRAP works in partnership to encourage and enable businesses and consumers to be more efficient in their use of materials and recycling at www.wrap.org.uk/ or contact the helpline on 0808 100 2040.

NetRegs is a partnership between the UK environmental regulators – the Environment Agency in England and Wales, SEPA in Scotland and the Environment and Heritage Service in Northern Ireland – which provides free environmental guidance for small and medium-sized businesses throughout the UK. Help and advice is available by business type, environmental legislation and environmental topic and has useful links to other websites. www.netregs.gov.uk/ netregs/ or telephone the EA National Customer Contact Centre on 08708 506 506.

The National Industrial Symbiosis Programme (NISP) works directly with businesses of all sizes and sectors with the aim of improving cross industry resource efficiency via commercial trading of materials, energy and water and sharing assets, logistics and expertise. It engages traditionally separate industries and other organisations in a collective approach to competitive advantage involving physical exchange of materials, energy, water and/or by-products together with the shared use of assets, logistics and expertise. NISP is delivered at regional level across the UK. www.nisp.org.uk or telephone 0121 433 2650.

Redundancy

John Turnbull, BPE Solicitors

Key points

Section 139 of the Employment Rights Act 1996 defines redundancy as the dismissal of an employee from employment wholly or mainly due to:

- his employer ceasing or intending to cease carrying on business for the purposes for which the employee was employed, either completely or in the place that the employee was employed (known as the place of work redundancy) ;or
- the requirements of the employer's business to carry out work of a particular kind having ceased or diminished or are expected to cease or diminish whether that is across the business or where the employee is employed (known as type of work redundancy).

Section 195 of the Trade Union and Labour Relations (Consolidation) Act 1992 (TULRCA) also includes a definition of redundancy when used for assessing eligibility for redundancy payments. Section 195 defines redundancy as a dismissal for a reason not related to the individual concerned.

Collective consultation must take place where an employee intends to make 20 or more employees redundant in any 90-day period. As a result of the Dispute Resolution Regulations 2004 employers should follow a basic procedure for consultation regardless of the number of employees involved.

Legislation

- Trade Union and Labour Relations (Consolidation) Act 1992 (TULRCA).
- Employment Rights Act 1996 (ERA).
- Employment Act 2002.
- Employment Act 2002 (Dispute Resolution Regulations 2004).

Redundancy payments

To be eligible for a statutory redundancy payment an employee must have at least two years' continuous service. The lower and upper age limits (18 and 65) on the right to claim redundancy payments no longer apply as a result of age discrimination legislation which came into force on 1 October 2006. Statutory redundancy payments are calculated in accordance with the employee's age, length of service and the rate of the employee's weekly pay (subject to a statutory cap which is currently £330 per week but traditionally increases on 1 February each year). The employee's weekly pay is multiplied by their complete year's service and age multiplies as follows:

- By 1.5 for every year in which the employee was 41 years old or older;
- By 1 for every year in which the employee was aged between 22 and 40; and
- By 0.5 for every year in which the employee was between 18 and 21.

Workplace Law Network
www.workplacelaw.net

The maximum payment is 30 weeks' pay or £9,900. A redundancy ready reckoner is available on the BERR website to calculate statutory redundancy payments due.

Penalties
Failure to carry out a proper procedure (whether the statutory dispute resolution procedure or collective consultation procedure) may result in substantial claims. Getting the collective consultation wrong can result in claims for protective awards in the value of 90 days' pay per employee.

Claims for unfair dismissal in relation to any aspect of the redundancy process can also be brought if there is a fault in the process. Employees usually need one year's continuous employment to make such a claim unless they link it to discrimination. The current statutory maximum compensatory award for unfair dismissal is £63,000. There is also potential liability for a basic award, which is calculated on the same basis as the redundancy payments. Therefore, if they are paid the redundancy pay, only the compensatory award will be made. Failure to follow the statutory Dispute Resolution procedures will allow an Employment Tribunal to increase a compensatory award by between 10% and 50% depending on the circumstances and will also make the dismissal automatically unfair. Any uplift will not take an award beyond the statutory maximum.

Redundancy process checklist
Below is a checklist of the most important issues to be considered in a redundancy process. Please note it is not a comprehensive guide and individual circumstances may vary. It is not intended to be a substitute for legal advice, which

should be sought regarding individual circumstances.

Step 1 – Planning
As soon as the possibility of redundancy has been identified as an option, document the reason for the proposed redundancies and plan the redundancy process.

Step 2 – Redundancy Policy
Does your company have a redundancy policy in place, which has been communicated to the employees, or is there an implied policy in place through custom or practice? If so, check that those policies are compatible with the statutory procedures and then follow your own policy. If you have no policy or it does not follow the statutory Dispute Resolution procedures the following steps should be taken.

Step 3 – Collective Consultation
If you are proposing to dismiss 20 or more employees from one establishment over a 90-day period, you are required to enter into collective consultation with appropriate representatives. This may be a Trade Union representative or an elected employee representative. Your collective consultation should set out the framework for redundancy selection and who will be in the pool of selection. You will also have to carry out individual consultation after the collective consultation.

If you are proposing to make 100 or more employees redundant at one establishment within a 90-day period, consultation must take place in 'good time' and at least 90 days before the first of the dismissals.

If you are proposing to dismiss at least 20 but fewer than 100 employees at one establishment within a 90-day period, collective consultations must begin in 'good time' and at least 30 days before the first dismissal.

Collective consultation should start as soon as redundancies are proposed. The employee representatives can assist in the planning stage of the selection process and reduce the risk of claims being brought for failure to follow proper procedure.

There is an obligation for employers to inform the Secretary of State for Trade and Industry of proposed large-scale redundancies using form HR1. A copy of the form should be sent to the appropriate representatives.

Collective consultations should include discussions about avoiding dismissals, reducing the number of employees to be dismissed and mitigating the consequences of dismissal. Consultation should also be undertaken with a view to reaching agreement. Regardless of whether or not agreement is possible, the next step is individual consultation.

Step 4 – Individual Consultation
To follow a fair procedure in accordance with the statutory Dispute Resolution procedures, all employees should be invited to a meeting in writing informing them of the potential redundancy situation.

Employees are entitled to attend meetings with a fellow employee or a Trade Union representative of their choice.

Inform each employee of the reason for the redundancy and the selection process which is going to take place. Inform them of the reason why they are potentially

at risk of redundancy and ask them to consider whether they are in the correct pool for selection. If they do not consider they are in the correct pool, consider their reasons for this.

After the meeting confirm whether or not the employee is in the pool of selection and provide them with details of the redundancy selection criteria (e.g. length of service, skills and qualifications, disciplinary record) taking care not to unlawfully discriminate against the affected employees.

Hold a second meeting where you discuss the selection criteria and any alternatives to redundancy you or the employee may have including alternative employment or job sharing.

Confirm the options in writing
If appropriate, apply the selection criteria and provisionally select the redundant employees. Write to those selected employees to confirm this. Do not state that they will be made redundant but do inform them that a possibility of the full and final meeting will be their dismissal.

Inform the employee at the final meeting the reason why they have been selected for redundancy and explain the consequences of this. Invite the employee to comment on the selection. After the meeting consider any points raised by the employee and then confirm to them in writing their selection for redundancy. Be sure to offer the employees the opportunity to appeal to a higher level of management.

Consider whether there is any suitable alternative employment within the company or group of companies which can be offered to the employees, and if they accept it decide whether a trial period should be given in their new role.

Redundant employees will be entitled to notice payments, redundancy payments and payment of accrued but untaken holiday pay.

Statutory dismissal procedure
Write to the affected employees and invite them to a final meeting. Inform them of their dismissal and then write to them offering them an appeal against their dismissal on grounds by reason of redundancy.

See also: Disciplinary and grievance procedures, p.216; Discrimination, p.222; Dismissal, p.233; Employment disputes, p.266; Employee consultation, p.269; Employment Tribunals, p.285; Notice periods, p.531

Sources of further information

BERR's Redundancy Ready Reckoner: www.berr.gov.uk/employment/employment-legislation/employment-guidance/page33157.html

Workplace Law Group's *Redundancy Policy and Management Guide, v.3.0* can help employers in England and Wales ensure that they comply with their requirements under law, and to provide a clear record of the policy and procedure. For more information visit www.workplacelaw.net/Bookshop/PoliciesAndProcedures.

References

Pinsent Masons Employment Group

Key points

The subject of employee references will usually arise when offering a prospective employee a contract of employment or when providing a reference for a current or former employee.

An employer is under no obligation to provide a reference for a current or former employee, unless a term in the contract of employment compels it, or, as in some regulated industries such as financial services, it is obliged to provide a reference under the regulations of a relevant body.

If a reference is given, the referee must take great care in compiling it and must use all reasonable skill and care to ensure the accuracy of the facts contained in the reference and the reasonableness of the opinions contained within the reference as the referee may be liable as a consequence of a defective reference.

Employers should be aware that if the reference results in the former employee suffering a loss or failing to be employed by the new employer then the content of the reference will be made known to the individual.

Offering a prospective employee a contract of employment

When recruiting new staff it is common for a prospective employer to make a job offer expressly conditional on receiving satisfactory references from the prospective employee's previous employer.

If the prospective employer's decision to employ is conditional upon receipt of a satisfactory reference, this must be made clear in the offer letter. To avoid dispute, it should be made clear that it is for the employer to determine what is satisfactory.

Providing a reference for a current or former employee

An employer is under no obligation to provide a reference for a current or former employee, unless a term in the contract of employment compels it, or, as in

some regulated industries such as financial services, it is obliged to provide a reference under the regulations of a relevant body.

However, if a reference is given, the referee must take great care in compiling it, for he may be liable as a consequence of a defective reference.

Duties are owed by the employer to recipients of references and to the subject of those references.

When giving a reference about an existing employee who is seeking employment with another employer, there are a number of points that an employer must consider:

- An employer must use all reasonable skill and care to ensure the accuracy of the facts contained in the reference and the reasonableness of the opinions contained within the reference. Failure to do so may amount to a breach of the implied term of trust and confidence, entitling the employee to resign and claim constructive dismissal.

- Even if the reference is factually accurate, the employer must be careful not to give an unfair impression of the employee concerned. Therefore the employer should not include a disproportionate amount of negative facts and exclude those that are to the credit of the employee (e.g. stating that he always took long lunches, but not stating that he always worked late in the evening).

- Where an employee has been the subject of disciplinary action, this should only be referred to in the reference being provided where the employer:
  - genuinely believes the statement being made to be true;
  - has reasonable grounds for believing that the statement is true; and
  - has carried out as much investigation into the matters referred to in the statement as is reasonable in the circumstances.

- It would accordingly not be appropriate for an employer to refer to a disciplinary incident where the employment is terminated before a full investigation was conducted.

- Other than in certain circumstances (e.g. where industry rules or practice require full and frank references), references do not have to be full and comprehensive. The employer's obligation is to provide a true, accurate and fair reference that does not give a misleading impression overall. Some employers will limit the reference to basic facts such as the dates of employment and the position held. Employers are entitled to set parameters within which the reference is given, e.g. by stressing their limited knowledge of the individual employee.

A practical danger

References could be used in evidence where the dismissal of an employee is the subject of litigation, so employers should take care in giving a reference in such circumstances. It is not unusual for employers to give positive references to employees who have been sacked for poor performance, as part of a negotiated settlement in such circumstances. Should they choose to do so in terms which are misleadingly favourable to the employee, the referee may find himself liable to a subsequent employer who relies on the references.

Employees' claims

The most common action for an employee who is the subject of an inaccurate reference is a damages action in respect of any economic loss which may flow from a carelessly or negligently prepared reference.

In order to establish that an employer is in breach of its duty to take reasonable care in the preparation of a reference, the employee must show that:

- the information contained in the reference was misleading;
- by virtue of the misleading information, the reference was likely to have a material effect upon the mind of a reasonable recipient of the reference to the detriment of the employee;
- the employee suffered loss as a result; and
- the employer was negligent in providing such a reference.

See also: Employment contracts, p.273; Interviewing, p.429; Recruitment and selection, p.607

Sources of further information

Workplace Law Network provides premium members with unrestricted access to a comprehensive range of online information – factsheets, case reports and daily news items – on employment, health and safety and premises management. Members also benefit from an online advice service and a free subscription to the *Workplace Law Magazine*. For more information email membership@ workplacelaw.net or call our membership services team on 0871 777 8881.

Registration, Evaluation, and Authorisation of Chemicals (REACH)

Chris Streatfeild, Risk Management Consultant

Key points

REACH is a fundamental change in chemical safety regulation impacting across the EU. REACH stands for Registration, Evaluation, and Authorisation of Chemicals. It is an EU Regulation which means that the Regulations (Regulation (EC) No 1907/2006 and Directive 2006/121/EC Amending Directive 67/548/EEC) apply directly to duty holders in each member state.

The Regulations took effect on 1 June 2007. According to the EU, REACH "aims to improve the protection of human health and the environment while maintaining competitiveness, and enhancing the innovative capability of the EU chemicals industry. REACH will furthermore give greater responsibility to industry to manage the risks from chemicals and to provide safety information that will be passed down the supply chain."

REACH puts a responsibility on those who place chemicals on the market (mainly manufacturers and importers) responsible for understanding and managing the risks associated with their use. REACH replaces a complex framework of European Directives with a single system.

Overview of REACH

- REACH is a new Regulation that applies to the registration, evaluation and authorisation of chemicals and other substances.
- It entered into force on 1 June 2007.
- It aims to ensure a balance improving human health protection and the environment, alongside business competitiveness.
- It transfers responsibility for data gathering and carrying out initial risk assessments from state agencies to industry.

Key elements

- *Registration.* Manufacturers or importers will need to register any substance supplied into the EU market above one tonne per year.
- *Evaluation.* Competent authorities will carry out annual in-depth evaluations of substances flagged as being of potential high risk.
- *Authorisation.* Substances of very high concern – CMRs (carcinogens, mutagens, and toxic) and PBTs (persistent, bioaccumulative, and toxic) – will require authorisation.

Registration

All substances that are manufactured or imported above one tone per company must be registered. It is estimated that will cover at least 30,000 substances. Industry will be required to submit the relevant chemical data to the European Chemicals Agency (ECHA) on the hazardous properties of these substances. Registration will be phased in over an 11-year period:

- Substances supplied above 1,000 tonnes a year, or substances of highest concern, must be registered in the first three years;
- Substances supplied between 100 and 1,000 tonnes a year must be registered in the first six years; and
- Substances supplied between one and 100 tonnes a year must be registered in the first 11 years.

Industry will also be required to prepare risk assessments and provide information on suitable control measures for using the substance safely to downstream users.

Evaluation

Two evaluation processes will be conducted under the Regulations. These are a Dossier evaluation and a Substance evaluation. Under the Dossier evaluation the European Chemicals Agency will scrutinise all testing proposals submitted with a registration dossier. In addition 5% of all registration dossiers will be subject to a full compliance audit by the Agency. Under the Substance evaluation, Member States and the European Commission will agree on an annual list of substances to be assessed in-depth. Competent Authorities (e.g. HSE) will carry out substance evaluations that may lead to new control measures or to no further action.

Authorisation

Due to its high risk, industry will be required to obtain Community-wide authorisations for the use of substances considered to be of very high concern. This will apply to substances identified as carcinogenic, mutagenic or toxic to reproduction (CMRs); persistent,

bioaccumulative and toxic substances (PBTs); substances that are very persistent and very bioaccumulative (vPvBs); and substances demonstrated to be of equivalent concern, such as endocrine disruptors. Authorisation will only be granted if the risks of the substance are 'under control'. If adequate control is not possible, authorisation could still be granted on socio-economic grounds.

Downstream users

REACH in general places no substantial duties on downstream users of chemicals. However there are commercial, supply chain and operational risk reasons for downstream users to familiarise themselves fully with REACH. Downstream users should provide detail of their uses of the chemicals to their suppliers. In certain cases downstream users may need to produce their own Chemical Safety Report (CSR).

Downstream users have a right to join a Substance Information Exchange Forum during the registration process. In addition downstream users have a right to request that the suppliers' chemical safety assessment covers their specific use. Duties under REACH also extend to those who produce or import articles. These are defined as "an object which during production is given a special shape, surface or design which determines its function to a greater degree than does its chemical composition". The key duties relate to the provision of information where the article contains over 0.1% (w/w) of substances deemed of very high concern.

Competent Authority

The HSE is appointed as the UK Competent Authority for REACH. Its responsibilities are far reaching and include:

- providing advice to manufacturers, importers, downstream users and other interested parties on their respective responsibilities and obligations under REACH;

- conducting substance evaluation of prioritised substances and preparing draft decisions;
- proposing harmonised Classification and Labelling for CMRs and respiratory sensitisers; and
- identifying substances of very high concern for authorisation.

The HSE has provided a help desk that can be contacted at 0845 408 9575 or via email at ukreachca@hse.gsi.gov.uk.

Enforcement

Member states are responsible for the enforcement of REACH in their jurisdiction. The Government has proposed a best practice approach which encourages duty holders to comply. However enforcement activity is more likely in situations where:

- manufacture, import, sale, supply or use of substances is conducted without the appropriate registration;
- a hazardous substance is used outside the terms of an authorisation or contrary to a restriction;
- there has been a failure to provide required information up and down the supply chain;
- there has been a failure to comply with other duties regarding information;
- there has been a failure to comply with the duty to apply recommendations such as in safety assessments; and
- there has been a failure to comply with the duties to cooperate and supply information.

See also: Hazardous waste, p.720

Sources of further information

DEFRA (UK responsible department): www.defra.gov.uk/environment/chemicals/reach/

HSE (UK Competent Authority): www.hse.gov.uk/reach/index.htm

HSE guidance: www.hse.gov.uk/reach/resources/guidance.pdf

European Chemical Bureau: http://ecb.jrc.it/REACH/

European Chemicals Agency: http://ec.europa.eu/echa/home_en.html

CEFIC: www.cefic.be/

DG Enterprise: http://ec.europa.eu/enterprise/reach

DG Environment: http://ec.europa.eu/environment/chemicals/reach/reach_intro.htm

CIA 'REACH Ready': www.reachready.co.uk/

Reporting of Injuries, Diseases and Dangerous Occurrences (RIDDOR)

Kathryn Gilbertson, Greenwoods Solicitors LLP

Key points

In addition to the obligations under Social Security legislation to keep records of accidents at work, employers are legally obliged to report certain work-related injuries or illnesses. These obligations fall under the Reporting of Injuries, Diseases and Dangerous Occurrences Regulations 1995 (RIDDOR).

For recording accidents, employers have, since January 2004, been required to use a version of B1510 (Yellow) Accident Book that complies with the needs of the Data Protection Act 1998, i.e. limiting access to confidential information of a personal nature. The HSE and Department for Work and Pensions (DWP) combined their efforts to produce the current version of B1510 which enables compliance with legislation. This book also contains guidance on the Reporting of Injuries, Diseases and Dangerous Occurrences Regulations 1995 and the Health and Safety (First Aid) Regulations 1981.

Legislation

- Reporting of Injuries, Diseases and Dangerous Occurrences Regulations 1995.

What needs to be reported

Certain categories of incidents need to be reported. These are shown below.

You need to report:

- deaths;
- major injuries;
- accidents resulting in over three days' lost time;
- injuries sustained by a visitor or third party who is taken from your premises to hospital;
- diseases;
- dangerous occurrences; and
- gas incidents.

When it needs to be reported

If any of the above instances occur, the Responsible Person (as designated in the RIDDOR Regulations) shall notify the relevant enforcing authority by the quickest practical means, usually a telephone call, and within ten days send a report to the relevant enforcing authority.

Death or major injury

If there is an accident connected with work and:

- your employee, or a self-employed person working on your premises is killed or suffers a major injury (including as a result of physical violence); or
- a member of the public is killed or taken to hospital;

you must notify the enforcing authority without delay. You can either telephone or complete the appropriate form on the website: www.riddor.gov.uk.

Reportable major injuries are:

- fracture other than to fingers, thumbs or toes;
- amputation;
- dislocation of the shoulder, hip, knee or spine;
- loss of sight (temporary or permanent);
- chemical or hot metal burn to the eye or any penetrating injury to the eye;
- injury resulting from an electric shock or electrical burn leading to unconsciousness or requiring resuscitation or admittance to hospital for more than 24 hours;
- any other injury leading to hypothermia, heat-induced illness or unconsciousness; or requiring resuscitation; or requiring admittance to hospital for more than 24 hours;
- unconsciousness caused by asphyxia or exposure to harmful substance or biological agent;
- acute illness requiring medical treatment, or loss of consciousness arising from absorption of any substance by inhalation, ingestion or through the skin; and
- acute illness requiring medical treatment where there is reason to believe that this resulted from exposure to a biological agent or its toxins or infected material.

Over-three-day injury
- If there is an accident connected with work (including an act of physical violence) and your employee, or a self-employed person working on your premises, suffers an over-three-day injury you must report it to the enforcing authority within ten days.
- An over-three-day injury is one which is not 'major' but results in the injured

person being away from work or unable to do the full range of their normal duties for more than three days.

Diseases
If a doctor notifies you that your employee suffers from a reportable work-related disease then you must report it to the enforcing authority.

Reportable diseases include:

- certain poisonings;
- some skin diseases such as occupational dermatitis, skin cancer, chrome ulcer, oil folliculitis/acne;
- lung diseases including occupational asthma, farmer's lung, pneumoconiosis, asbestosis, Mesothelioma;
- infections such as leptospirosis; hepatitis; tuberculosis; anthrax; legionnellosis and tetanus;
- other conditions such as occupational cancer; certain musculoskeletal disorders; decompression illness and Hand–Arm vibration syndrome;
- Bursitis of the knee or elbow (Beat knee or Beat elbow);
- traumatic inflammation of the tendons of the hand or forearm or of the associated tendon sheaths, e.g. Tenosynovitis or Tennis elbow;
- carpal tunnel syndrome; and
- Hand–Arm vibration syndrome.

The above list is not exhaustive and if in doubt, employers should check on the RIDDOR website to see if a condition is reportable.

It should be noted that a disease only needs to be reported if its occurrence has been caused by a work-related activity as specified in column two of schedule three of RIDDOR. For example, carpal tunnel syndrome is only reportable if it has been caused by hand-held vibrating tools, not by working at a desk.

Dangerous occurrences

Certain types of incident are designated as dangerous occurrences. This is more than a 'near miss', and the Regulations clearly define the type of dangerous occurrences that should be reported. These include:

- Collapse, overturning or failure of load-bearing parts of lifts and lifting equipment;
- Explosion, collapse or bursting of any closed vessel or associated pipework;
- Failure of any freight container in any of its load-bearing parts;
- Plant or equipment coming into contact with overhead power lines;
- Electrical short circuit or overload causing fire or explosion;
- Any unintentional explosion, misfire, failure of demolition to cause the intended collapse, projection of material beyond a site boundary, injury caused by an explosion;
- Accidental release of a biological agent likely to cause severe human illness;
- Failure of industrial radiography or irradiation equipment to de-energise or return to its safe position after the intended exposure period;
- Malfunction of breathing apparatus while in use or during testing immediately before use;
- Failure or endangering of diving equipment, the trapping of a diver, an explosion near a diver, or an uncontrolled ascent;
- Collapse or partial collapse of a scaffold over five metres high, or erected near water where there could be a risk of drowning after a fall;
- Unintended collision of a train with any vehicle;
- Dangerous occurrence at a well (other than a water well);
- Dangerous occurrence at a pipeline;
- Failure of any load-bearing fairground equipment, or derailment or unintended collision of cars or trains;

- A road tanker carrying a dangerous substance overturns, suffers serious damage, catches fire or the substance is released; and
- A dangerous substance being conveyed by road is involved in a fire or released.

The following dangerous occurrences are reportable except in relation to offshore workplaces:

- Unintended collapse of any building or structure under construction, alteration or demolition where over five tonnes of material falls; a wall or floor in a place of work; any false-work.
- Explosion or fire causing suspension of normal work for over 24 hours.
- Sudden, uncontrolled release in a building of 100 kg or more of flammable liquid; 10 kg of flammable liquid above its boiling point; 10 kg or more of flammable gas; or of 500 kg of these substances if the release is in the open air.
- Accidental release of any substance that may damage health.

Note: additional categories of dangerous occurrences apply to mines, quarries, relevant transport systems (railways etc.) and offshore workplaces. These categories can be found at schedule two of RIDDOR.

If any injury occurs and is reportable under one of the other categories in Regulation 3 then a dangerous occurrence should not be reported separately. If, however, the injury is not reportable under Regulation 3 then the dangerous occurrence must be reported.

Gas incidents

If you are a distributor, filler, importer or supplier of flammable gas and you learn, either directly or indirectly that someone has died or suffered a 'major injury' in connection with the gas you distributed, filled, imported or supplied, then this must be reported immediately.

If you are an installer of gas appliances registered with the Council for Registered Gas Installers (CORGI), you must provide details (using form F2508G2 – *Report of a Dangerous Gas Fitting*) of any gas appliances or fittings that you consider to be dangerous, to such an extent that people could die or suffer a 'major injury', because the design, construction, installation, modification or servicing could result in:

- an accidental leakage of gas;
- inadequate combustion of gas; or
- inadequate removal of products of the combustion of gas.

How to report incidents

All accidents, diseases and dangerous occurrences may be reported to the Incident Contact Centre (ICC). The Contact Centre was established on 1 April 2001 as a single point of contact for reporting all incidents in the UK.

You can still report directly to your local HSE office or Local Authority by completing and sending them the relevant hard copy form. These are:

- F2508 – Report of an injury or dangerous occurrence.
- F2508A – Report of a case of disease.
- F2508G1 – Report of a flammable gas incident.
- F2508G2 – Report of a dangerous gas fitting.
- F2508OIR9b – Report of an injury or dangerous occurrence offshore.

These reports will be processed by the ICC and forwarded to the relevant enforcing authority. Employers will receive a copy acknowledgement and incident

number for each report. In the case of internet reports, they will receive a PDF version of the completed report.

Certain incidents (e.g. fatality, major injuries) require the report to be made by the quickest practicable means (normally by telephone). Also bear in mind that fatalities will be treated as a scene of crime. If it is necessary to report an incident out of hours, you may need to contact the local enforcing authority, who will, if required, involve the police.

Record keeping

Records may be kept in any form, i.e. paper or electronically and must be kept either where the work to which they relate is carried out or at the usual place of business of a Responsible Person. For accidents, records should be kept for a minimum of three years. Details kept must include the following:

- date and method of reporting;
- date, time and place of event;
- personal details of those involved; and
- a brief description of the nature of the event or disease.

All workplace accidents should be recorded in an accident book (B1510). This applies to organisations employing ten or more employees and is in addition to any requirement to report to the HSE or other enforcing authority.

Future developments

The RIDDOR procedure was reviewed and the outcome of the first stage of the review was reported to the HSC in July 2006. The outcome of this review was that the RIDDOR legislation would not be changed but awareness would be raised on the simpler and quicker methods of reporting.

See also: Accident investigations, p.55; Health and safety at work, p.364; Health and safety inspections, p.381; Slips, trips and falls, p.657

Sources of further information

L73 A guide to the Reporting of Injuries, Diseases and Dangerous Occurrences Regulations 1995 (HSE Books, 1999) ISBN: 0 7176 2431 5.

Restrictive covenants and garden leave

Anna Youngs, Mills & Reeve

Key points
- Restrictive covenants operate to protect the employer's business after an employee has left employment.
- They are prima facie void as a restraint of trade.
- To enforce a covenant, the terms must be no wider than necessary to protect a legitimate business interest.
- Restrictive covenants are enforced by the Courts.

Introduction

An employee must observe certain restrictions that are implied by law into a contract of employment (e.g. fidelity, obedience, working with due diligence and care, not to use or disclose the employer's trade secrets or confidential information during employment). However, these implied terms are of a limited nature and, save in respect of highly confidential information, do not apply after termination of the contract.

Restrictions that apply to employees after the employment relationship ends either take the form of a garden leave clause or a restrictive covenant.

What are restrictive covenants and when do employers need them?

Restrictive covenants are contractual post-termination obligations (commonly incorporated into an employee's contract of employment) that seek to prevent employees from doing certain things when they leave the employment that may be damaging to the employer's business.

The main types of restrictive covenants are:

- Non-solicitation of staff (to prevent ex-employees from recruiting key employees of the business).

- Non-solicitation of customers and non-dealing covenants (to protect the client base of the business by preventing employees from dealing with and soliciting customers).
- Non-competition (to prevent the ex-employee from taking up employment in competition with the business).
- Protecting confidential information acquired by the ex-employee during the course of employment.

These covenants can be used in isolation, or together in order to bolster the protection provided to the employer.

However, the employer's need to protect its business must be balanced against the employee's right to earn a living and take up work in their area of expertise.

The legal approach to restrictive covenants

The starting point in law is that restrictive covenants are void as being a restraint of trade and are therefore unenforceable unless the employer can show that it is a justifiable covenant, which will only be the case where:

- the employer has a legitimate interest to protect which will vary depending on the nature of the business (examples include business connections, stability of the workforce, confidential information etc.); and

■ the covenant goes no further than is reasonably necessary for the protection of the legitimate interest.

There can never be any certainty as to the enforceability of restrictive covenants because to enforce any restriction the employer has to obtain a court order, which is granted at the discretion of the court by reference to what it regards as reasonable in the circumstances.

When will a restrictive covenant be enforceable?

Even if there is a legitimate interest to protect, the restriction can be no wider than reasonably necessary to protect that interest. This is achieved by limiting the scope of the covenant by reference to the restricted activities, the length of the period of restraint and where appropriate the geographical area to which it applies (e.g. the duration of the restricted period should be no longer than necessary to protect the business interest). The following factors are useful pointers:

■ *Non-solicitation of staff* – consider which groups of employees need to be protected and the time period necessary for the influence over these staff to diminish.

■ *Non-solicitation of customers* – in respect of current customers, the covenant should be limited to customers with whom the employee had contact, and the time period should be limited by considering the amount of time it would take for the employee's successor to build up a relationship with these customers. The general customer base and prospective customers can also be protected in certain circumstances.

■ *Non-dealing covenants* – a blanket ban on dealing with any customer should be avoided, and therefore consideration should be given to which key contacts are at risk because of the relationship with the employee.

■ *Non-competition* – the restriction must be for a limited time and may need to be limited in terms of geographical area. Consider how long it will be until competitive activities by the individual are no longer a material threat to the legitimate business interest, as well as the area of activities of the employee and the size of the restricted area.

■ *Protecting confidential information* – the key to confidentiality clauses is to carefully define what is 'confidential information'.

As well as considering what the legitimate business interest is, the employer must consider what level of protection is reasonably necessary in respect of any given employee. What is enforceable against one employee may not be against another. For example, a senior employee would have very different contacts to someone at a trainee level, and even employees at the same level may have different access to customers and confidential information.

In almost all cases, the length of the restrictive period will be a key factor.

What if the clause is too wide-ranging?

If a clause is too wide-ranging, it will not be enforceable. The court will not re-write the clause, but they may sever unenforceable clauses and 'blue pencil' restrictions, leaving enforceable restrictions intact.

The court, in deciding whether unlawful provisions may be severed from the rest of the terms, will consider whether:

🎧 **Workplace Law Network**
www.workplacelaw.net

- the provisions can be removed without needing to amend the remaining wording;
- the remaining terms are supported by adequate consideration; and
- deleting the unenforceable wording changes the character of the contract.

Note that if an employer commits a repudiatory breach of contract, or terminates the employment in breach of contract, it is highly unlikely that any restrictive covenants will be enforced.

Garden leave

The need for garden leave normally arises where employees hand in their notice in order to work for a competitor, although they can still work where the employer gives the employee notice of termination. The aim of garden leave is to keep the employee away from confidential information long enough for the information to become out of date, and from customers long enough to enable customer relationships to be forged with an alternative contact. This can be done either by changing the employee's duties during their notice period, or by requiring the employee to stay at home (whilst enjoying normal pay and benefits) on 'garden leave' during all or part of their notice period.

Putting an employee on garden leave is still a restraint of trade, and therefore the same principles as with restrictive covenants apply, such as having a period no longer than is reasonably necessary to protect a legitimate business interest. Therefore, even where, for example, 12 months' notice is required, in the first six months the employee could be assigned alternative duties (provided the contract allows for this) and then only the latter six months would be garden leave.

Enforcing restrictive covenants

Restrictive covenants are enforced by the courts. An employer may seek an injunction to prevent an employee from breaching the terms of the covenant. If this is not possible, there is a claim for damages from the employee for breach of the covenants, provided that the covenant is enforceable (i.e. not an illegal restraint of trade) and provided that any breach of the covenant has caused the employer loss.

Enforcing breaches of restrictive covenants is difficult and expensive, so employers need to think carefully about whether their 'legitimate business interest' warrants the time and expense of litigation. Perhaps negotiation and persuasion is a sensible first step, but bear in mind that litigation must be commenced swiftly if there is to be any hope of enforcing a restrictive covenant.

See also: Dismissal, p.233; Employment contracts, p.273; Leave, p.457; Redundancy, p.618

Sources of further information

Workplace Law Network provides premium members with unrestricted access to a comprehensive range of online information – factsheets, case reports and daily news items – on employment, health and safety and premises management. Members also benefit from an online advice service and a free subscription to the *Workplace Law Magazine*. For more information email membership@workplacelaw.net or call our membership services team on 0871 777 8881.

Retirement

Lizzie Mead, Berwin Leighton Paisner

Key points

The law on retirement in the UK has been revised radically by the implementation of legislation preventing age discrimination.

The Employment Equality (Age) Regulations 2006 (the Regulations) provide that retirement at the age of 65 or over is not unlawful provided that the correct statutory retirement procedure is adhered to.

Retirement ages of less than 65 are directly discriminatory on the grounds of age unless they can be justified. However, in most industries, lower retirement ages are unlikely to be justifiable.

Legislation

- The Employment Equality (Age) Regulations 2006.
- The Employment Rights Act 1996.

The position pre-October 2006

Prior to 1 October 2006, it was lawful to retire an employee at normal retirement age. Employees who were over the employer's normal retirement age (or 65 if there was no default age) were not entitled to bring an unfair dismissal claim if their employment was terminated for any reason. The entitlement to a statutory redundancy payment also ceased at the age of 65 (or at normal retirement age if this was lower).

The impact of the Age Discrimination Regulations

This position has been changed by the introduction of the Regulations. The Regulations give effect in the UK to the EU Employment Directive 2000/78/EC. Less favourable treatment on the grounds of age, whether direct or indirect, is now unlawful unless it can be justified. This applies throughout the sphere of employment, from recruitment through to retirement. One of the most significant

consequences is that it is now potentially unlawful for an employer to seek to enforce a retirement age for its employees.

Seeking to force an employee to stop working merely because they have reached a certain age is less favourable treatment on the grounds of age. Before the implementation of the Regulations, there was a significant amount of discussion and consultation as to whether enforced retirement ages would become entirely unlawful or, if not, at what age they should be permitted. Although it is perhaps the clearest example of age discrimination, the counter arguments are that preventing employers from retiring employees at all would hinder legitimate business succession planning and put an added strain on pensions arrangements.

Eventually, the legislation has settled on a default retirement age of 65. This means that the Regulations allow employers to retire employees once they reach the age of 65 (or another default retirement age set by the employer if it is higher than 65). There is, however, a proviso. Retirement at the default retirement age is only exempted from being age discrimination if the employer follows the statutory retirement procedure. The obligation to follow the procedure applies notwithstanding any express term in the employee's contract of employment.

If an employer seeks to apply a retirement age of less than 65, they will need to show that this can be objectively justified and then follow the statutory retirement procedure. Justification means showing that the employer had a legitimate aim for introducing a lower retirement age and also showing that the policy was a proportionate means of achieving this aim. In reality, it will seldom be possible to do so. For example, in a safety-critical industry it may be legitimate not to employ individuals over the age of 60 if there is a concern about their physical ability to do the job. However, it may be possible to address this concern by asking employees over the age of 60 to undergo medical examinations to confirm their continued fitness. If a medical would address the issue, a blanket retirement age of 60 will not be proportionate and will not therefore be justifiable.

The statutory retirement procedure
The Regulations amend the Employment Rights Act 1996 (the Act) so that retirement is now a potentially fair reason for dismissal. Instead of employees over normal retirement age or 65 being exempted, however, the crucial issue is whether the statutory procedure as set out in the Act has been followed. This process is as follows:

- *Stage One*. The employer must notify the employee of the date on which it is intended that they will retire and of their right to request not to be retired. This notification must be given no fewer than six and no more than 12 months before the retirement date.
  If the employer fails to give this notice within six months of retirement, the employee may be awarded up to eight

weeks' capped pay. The employer still has an ongoing duty to give this notification up to two weeks before the retirement date. Whether or not this is complied with is important when considering unfair dismissal issues.

- *Stage Two*. The employee may make a written request not to be retired. The request may be made between three and six months before the retirement age (or at any time less than six months if the employer has not complied with stage one). The request must be in writing, set out the details of how the employee wishes their employment to be extended (whether indefinitely, for a set period or until a set date) and should state that it is made under paragraph five of Schedule Six of the Regulations.
- *Stage Three*. The employer must hold a meeting to consider the request within a reasonable period (unless the request is agreed to immediately) at which the employee has the right to be accompanied and respond in writing as soon as is reasonably practicable. The response must set out details of the outcome. If it is refused or granted for a shorter period, the employee must be given the right to appeal. There is no duty for the employer to give reasons or to consider the request in good faith.
- *Stage Four*. If the employee appeals, the appeal meeting takes the same form as the initial meeting. An appeal does not extend the employee's employment which will terminate no later than the date that the original decision is notified in accordance with Stage Three.

Employers should ensure that any requests to work beyond the normal retirement age (NRA) are considered on a case by case basis. If the employer has a blanket policy of allowing all employees to work beyond its contractual retirement age (to the same later age) this may have the effect of raising the NRA.

In what circumstances will a retirement amount to an unfair dismissal or age discrimination?

The Regulations have significantly amended the unfair dismissal provisions in the Act. There is no longer an age cap for unfair dismissal claims but, if the above procedure is followed correctly, the employee cannot challenge the reason for dismissal. It is deemed to be on the grounds of retirement and to be fair. The employee could potentially raise another discrimination claim, for example sex discrimination, if only women are not permitted to work past retirement.

If the retirement takes place at or after a retirement age of 65 or over and notice was given in accordance with Stage One, the retirement is deemed to be fair and cannot be challenged by the employee. If the employer has not given notice in accordance with Stage One and/or the retirement is before the normal retirement age, retirement shall not be the reason for dismissal. Although the employer can seek to rely on another reason, it is unlikely to be able to demonstrate a fair dismissal in these circumstances and so it is likely to be both unfair dismissal and age discrimination.

Alternatively, in cases where the employer has failed to give the appropriate Stage One notification within six months of the retirement date but there is an intended date of retirement and the employee's employment terminates on or after that date, retirement may be the reason for dismissal and this is to be determined by a Tribunal giving consideration to the extent that the employer did comply with the ongoing duty to give notice and with

Stage Three of the duty to consider procedure.

While this process is technical, the crucial issue is that it is extremely important for employers to follow the correct procedure. Failing to do so leaves companies vulnerable to findings of unfair dismissal, age discrimination and potentially an uplift for breach of the statutory dismissal procedure (this does not apply to retirement dismissals but if the dismissal was not on the grounds of retirement, there is a risk that the procedure applied and was not followed).

Future developments

The Government has pledged to review the concept of retirement ages again in 2011. There is a possibility that the default age of 65 may be raised or it may be removed altogether, meaning that all retirements will need to be capable of justification. At the time of writing, the retirement age is also potentially the subject of a judicial review, as there is an argument being raised by age charities that it does not comply with the EU Directive and is therefore unlawful. In July 2007 the application was referred to the ECJ. Employers should be alive to the possibility that employees who bring age discrimination tribunal proceedings in the UK may request a stay of the proceedings until a decision is made on this subject by the ECJ.

See also: Discrimination, p.222; Dismissal, p.233; Health surveillance, p.392; Redundancy, p.618

Sources of further information

BERR: www.berr.gov.uk/employment/discrimination/age-discrimination/index.html

---

Risk assessments

Kathryn Gilbertson, Greenwoods Solicitors LLP

Key points

The process of risk assessment is to many people an unnecessarily complicated exercise. However, this need not be the case since all that is really involved is looking at what can go wrong and trying to prevent it. For most risks then, risk assessment is quite straightforward.

Probably the most significant factor in producing a suitable and sufficient risk assessment is involving the right people in the process. That means people who understand the risk assessment process as well as those who are involved in the work or area being assessed. The output of the process should be the controls necessary (e.g. safe systems, precautions) to lower risks to as low a level as is reasonably practicable.

Legislation

- Health and Safety at Work etc. Act 1974.
- Management of Health and Safety at Work Regulations 1999.

Management of Health and Safety at Work Regulations 1999

The Management of Health and Safety at Work Regulations 1999 (MHSWR) introduced the need for employers to make a suitable and sufficient assessment of health and safety risks to employees and other persons affected by work activities. These, therefore, are the Regulations that require employers to conduct risk assessments in order to identify and manage their workplace risks.

Employers' duties under MHSWR include the requirement to carry out specific risk assessments when employing young persons (i.e. 16- and 17-year-olds), and where employing women of childbearing age to take into account any risks to such persons arising from their work.

In addition to duties under MHSWR, many regulations impose specific duties

to conduct as necessary, additional risk assessments, e.g. COSHH, Manual Handling Operations, Fire, Noise, and Display Screen Equipment Regulations.

Risk assessments, as with other duties in health and safety legislation, should be carried out by competent persons.

Why do we need risk assessments?

The main reason for conducting risk assessments is to ensure that we have adequately considered the things that can go wrong in the workplace and their likely effects. By so doing we can implement measures that will either reduce the likelihood of such events occurring, or if the worst should happen, limit the severity of injuries that occur.

Adequate risk assessments are therefore fundamental to ensuring the effective management of health and safety risks at work. They should take into account:

- people;
- premises;
- plant; and
- procedures.

Since risk assessments are an absolute requirement under health and safety legislation, failure to conduct them is an offence that can be easily prosecuted. Such a failure often comes to light as a result of inspections or investigations by the relevant enforcement authorities. In addition, the competence of those persons conducting risk assessments may be called into question.

Approach to risk assessment

The HSE suggests that risk assessments should follow five simple steps, notably:

- *Step 1:* Identify the hazards.
- *Step 2:* Decide who might be harmed and how.
- *Step 3*: Evaluate the risks and decide on precautions.
- *Step 4:* Record your findings and implement them.
- *Step 5*: Review your assessment and update if necessary.

Principles of prevention

The best way to avoid risks is of course to remove the hazard completely. Unfortunately, that is not often an option but nonetheless the law requires that, as an initial step, that's what we should try to do. In other words we should apply a hierarchy of risk controls to a situation in order to arrive at the reasonably practicable measures we need. MHSWR suggests the following:

- Avoid the risk completely – e.g. change the design or the process.
- Substitute – use less hazardous materials e.g. different chemicals.
- Minimise – e.g. limit exposure to individuals perhaps by job rotation.
- General control measures – guarding, barriers or warning systems.
- PPE – the last resort because it protects only the individual.

Two general principle risk control measures should be applied:

- controls should give priority to protecting collective groups rather than individuals; and
- in general terms, the more that human behaviour is involved in the control measure, the more likely it is to go wrong at some point. This explains why PPE is often a weak control measure, since it depends on correct usage by the individual.

Categories of risk assessment

Generic and site- / location-specific assessments

In many workplaces the risks that exist may be considered to be low or trivial and few if any additional control measures would be necessary to protect people. This is often the case with repetitive work tasks. It may well be that one office environment is pretty much the same as another and therefore a generic risk assessment may well suffice for most of the activities. Caution should be exercised however, in adopting this approach because incorrect assumptions can be made. It may therefore be necessary to conduct a site- or location-specific risk assessment in order to take into account differing hazards such as:

- differing work conditions;
- differences in work location e.g. difficult access; or
- time constraints, e.g. pressure of work at different times of the year.

Generic risk assessments at times may result in forgetting that other risks exist. They should not be used as a basis for assuming that common sense will always be applied by employees. As with all risk control measures it is necessary to maintain an appropriate level of monitoring in the workplace to ensure their continued effectiveness.

Qualitative versus quantitative assessments

Risk assessments may be *qualitative* in nature e.g. a written report describing identified hazards and the recommended means of controlling related risks, or *quantitative*, where some form of numerical rating is applied to identify the level of risk. Some objective quantitative elements exist in risk assessments that involve measurement such as noise, hazardous substances etc. but risk assessment is not usually an exact science. The choice of qualitative versus quantitative is often a matter of personal or organisational preference.

For a quantitative assessment, a matrix is often used, e.g. low / medium / high or 1–5 scales for likelihood and severity of an accident occurring. The drawback with a numeric approach is that often people are persuaded that the numbers are scientific and thus the risk assessment process becomes driven by the need to achieve a certain score rather than to effectively identify and control risks.

The key to successful risk assessment therefore lies largely in the competence of those involved. Whatever choice is made regarding type or method of risk assessment, the results should always be consistent as well as being simple to understand and action.

Conducting risk assessments

The law doesn't define the term 'risk assessment' and neither does it suggest any given template for conducting them. Whilst that may not seem much help to those conducting them, there is much guidance available regarding the type

of control measures that are necessary in order to achieve the usually required standard of 'reasonably practicable'. Therefore, when conducting risk assessments, it is wise for the assessor to be aware of the information that is available for the type(s) of risks involved. Sources of such information include:

■ Regulations, e.g. Work at Height Regulations 2005.
■ Regulations usually have an associated Approved Code of Practice (ACoP) which provides practical interpretation of the legislation for employers.
■ Good practice guidance notes from the HSE, special interest groups and trade associations.
■ Company's own health and safety policy and arrangements document (sometimes more exacting than the law itself).
■ The people doing the job are invaluable; you need to know how things are actually done rather than just how they should be done.
■ External consultants, e.g. asbestos specialists.

With regard to the cost of the control measures deemed necessary, a common definition of the term reasonably practicable is "the cost in time, trouble, effort and money versus the level of risk that exists". The cost bears no relation to the size of the business, it is purely dependant on the level of risk that exists.

If an accident occurs, it may well be necessary for the employer and by extension the assessor, to show that it was not reasonably practicable to have done more to prevent it. To do this, a minimum requirement would be to consult relevant information sources (particularly ACoP), and expertise and thus employ good practice.

Don't just file them away
Employers with five or more employees have a legal duty to record risk assessments in writing. That, however, should not be the end of the matter since the exercise has little value if the people affected are not aware of the key findings and control measures. These have to be communicated whether by memos, training, team briefs etc. The method of communication must reflect the needs of the audience and the seriousness of the risk that exists.

When conducting a risk assessment, it is also important to set a date for review to check whether or not it is still adequate. Review would also be necessary as a result of changes in working practices, new plant, changes in legislation and especially as a result of an accident.

Finally, it is necessary to get out into the workplace and make sure that not only are the risk control measures in place, but they are also working.

See also: Health and safety at work, p.364; Ladders, p.440; Slips, trips and falls, p.657

Sources of further information

INDG 163 REV1 *Five steps to risk assessment* (HSE Books, 1998) ISBN: 0 7176 1565

Risk Assessments are an essential part of a successful health and safety management system. Under the Health and Safety at Work etc. Act 1974 there is an express duty on employers to ensure that risks to their employees and others affected are as low as is reasonably practicable. As a planning aid risk assessments assist in defining what hazards exist around your undertakings, the risks represented by these hazards and the precautions or controls that need to be taken to protect against those risks. Workplace Law Group's *Draft Risk Assessment Policy and Management Guide, v.3.0* deals with the most common safety issues found at the majority of workplaces to help you ensure a safe working environment and comply with legislation. For more information visit www.workplacelaw.net/Bookshop/PoliciesAndProcedures.

Safety signage

Nicola Cardenas-Blanco, Martineau Solicitors

Key points

- The purpose of safety signs is to warn and/or instruct people of the nature of certain risks and the measures to be taken to protect against them.
- Employers have a duty to display safety signage where some risk is still present after all other appropriate steps to avoid or control risks have been taken.
- Employers must provide and maintain any such safety sign.
- Employees must receive suitable and sufficient instruction as to the meaning of safety signs and what they need to do to comply with them.

Legislation

- Health and Safety (Safety Signs and Signals) Regulations 1996 (SI 1996/341).
- Management of Health and Safety at Work Regulations 1999 (SI 1999/3242).

Statutory requirements

Employers are required to make a suitable and sufficient assessment of the risks to health and safety of employees which they are exposed to whilst at work. In addition employers have the same duty to non-employees involved in the workplace. This duty also extends to the self-employed in relation to their own wellbeing. These assessments must be reviewed if any matter affecting the work changes or if the employer has any other reason to suspect that the assessment is no longer valid.

If, after assessing a certain risk, the employer believes there is some residual risk, which cannot be avoided or reduced by other means, safety signage to warn of the hazard should be provided.

Signs have the purpose of either warning, instructing, or both as to the nature of the risk, and how the risk should be protected against. This is a decision to be taken by the employer and should only be taken where there is no significant risk of harm remaining, having considered the nature and magnitude of the risks arising from the work concerned.

A safety sign is information or instruction about health and safety at work and may comprise a sign board, a safety colour, an illuminated sign, an acoustic signal, a verbal communication or hand signal. Where the risk relates to traffic control on an employer's premises, traffic signs of the same colour and style used on public roads should be put up where appropriate. Traffic routes are recommended to take the form of continuous white or yellow lines. There are separate regulations which relate to the supply of substances, equipment and products and to the transport of dangerous goods.

The 1996 Regulations on safety signs implement European law, which is an attempt to standardise safety signage across Europe, so that wherever in the EC the signs are placed, they have broadly the same meaning.

Employers have a further legal duty to provide information, instruction and training to employees on the safety signs used in the workplace. This should involve the measures to be taken in connection with safety signs, for example wearing safety footwear beyond a certain point.

Employers are also required to label pipes that contain dangerous substances

MEANING	EXAMPLE	SIGN TYPE
Toxic material		Warning sign
Dangerous location		
No pedestrian access		Mandatory safety sign
Safety helmets must be worn		Mandatory safety sign
Emergency exit		Fire exit and equipment sign
Explosive material		Dangerous substance sign

where, for example, there is a discharge or sample point and therefore a risk of leakage. These are similar to those seen on receptacles containing dangerous substances.

Safety signs that the employer uses in the place of work must be large enough to be seen and understood and of the types specified in the table opposite, depending upon the type of risk.

See also: Construction site health and safety, p.154; Health and safety at work, p.364

Sources of further information

How well do you know your safety signs? Could you decipher the meaning of every safety sign without the aid of the accompanying written warning? Images alone can be unclear and confusing – creating a potential hazard for those whose first language is not English, who have a visual impairment or learning difficulties. Workplace Law Group has created a quick quiz for members to take part in. We've displayed 20 regularly used safety images in an interactive quiz, which you can find at www.workplacelaw.net/news/display/id/15609. Take part to find out how much you really know!

Security licensing

Robert Buxton, Security Industry Authority

Key points

In these times of heightened security, it is essential that businesses and public bodies take a closer look at how their premises and staff can be better protected, and they should be demanding higher quality and greater accountability from their security provider. From the security providers' point of view, they need to be able to demonstrate to their customers that they are responsible, act within the law and can provide a quality service.

At licensed premises, or places of regulated entertainment, changes to the Licensing Act 2003 created an increased need, and a market, for professional door staff; men and women who are trained, qualified and fit and proper for their role – and who have a recognised licence to prove it.

To address these needs and to raise standards of professionalism, training and probity within the private security industry, the Security Industry Authority (SIA) was created.

About the SIA

The SIA is the organisation responsible for regulating the private security industry. It is an independent body reporting to the Home Secretary, established in 2003 under the terms of the Private Security Industry Act 2001. It has two main duties. One is the compulsory licensing of individuals working in specific sectors of the private security industry; the other is to manage the Approved Contractor Scheme, which measures private security companies against a set of independently assessed criteria. The licensing requirements carry the force of law and will help prevent unsuitable or poorly trained people from working within the private security industry.

If a security provider knowingly deploys unlicensed security operatives to conduct licensable activities, then both the provider and the operative will be committing a criminal offence and may be subject to prosecution.

Licensing

Those working in the roles listed below in Great Britain may need an SIA licence.

- Manned guarding, including:
    - cash and valuables in transit – provided under contract;
    - close protection – provided under contract;
    - door supervision – provided under contract and in-house;
    - public space surveillance CCTV – provided under contract; and
    - security guarding – provided under contract.
- Vehicle immobilisation (immobilisation, restriction and removal of vehicles) – provided under contract and in-house (does not apply in Scotland).
- Key holding.

It is the activity undertaken that defines the need for a licence, not the job title. Manned guarding activities are defined as:

Workplace Law Network
www.workplacelaw.net

- guarding premises against unauthorised access or occupation, against outbreaks of disorder or against damage;
- guarding property against destruction or damage, against being stolen or against being otherwise dishonestly taken or obtained; or
- guarding one or more individuals against assault or against injuries that might be suffered in consequence of the unlawful conduct of others.

Those security operatives who are SIA licensed are easy to identify because, when on duty, they are required to wear their licence. There is an online register of licence holders on the SIA website where employees and the public can instantly check the validity of an SIA licence.

The Approved Contractor Scheme – providing extra quality assurance
To help drive continuous improvements in the quality of private security service delivery, the SIA manages a voluntary Approved Contractor Scheme (ACS). This for the first time provides a recognised hallmark of quality for suppliers of private security services and the assurance that the accredited provider has met a clearly defined and independently assessed set of quality standards throughout their business. Equally important, ACS accreditation enables buyers of private security services to distinguish between potential suppliers quickly, accurately and objectively. Approved contractors are demonstrably committed to customer service and the compulsory licensing of their staff. A list of Approved Contractors can be viewed via the SIA website.

Insurance
The Association of British Insurers (ABI) has issued guidance to commercial insurers and insurance companies about recognising the importance of SIA licensing. They are equally conscious of the commercial benefits of differentiating between 'the best and the rest' of security providers.

The ABI recommendations for insurers to consider when underwriting a risk are:

- On issuing or renewing policies and when claims are made, ensuring security providers or business owners are using licensed operatives.
- For property claims, consider whether policy conditions have been fully met if unlicensed security operatives have been employed.
- Liability insurers have noted the SIA licensing rules and will expect their customers to comply with these rules. Liability insurers may wish to ask their customers if they are employing SIA licensed staff.

The way forward
SIA licensing currently covers England, Wales and Scotland. Following a public consultation, the Northern Ireland Office recommended extending the remit of the SIA to Northern Ireland. This would create a single set of UK-wide industry standards.

The security industry and night-time economy are growing and important sectors. With qualified and professional security operatives, there is no longer a role for amateurs working in these positions of trust.

Sources of further information

Security Industry Authority: www.the-sia.org.uk

Association of British Insurers: www.abi.org.uk

Self employment

Andrea Bateman, BPE Solicitors

Key points

The purpose of this chapter is to help direct the minds of those who are considering 'jumping ship' and setting up their own business.

We look first at the legal differences between employed and self employed status. We then look at the issues to be addressed in starting up and running a business of your own successfully. Finally, we look at the implications for existing businesses in engaging the services of a self employed individual.

Employed versus self employed – what is the difference?

At this point I refer you to the chapter on *Employment Status (p.282)* which sets out the necessary considerations in addressing the question of 'Who is employed and who is self employed?' This chapter also sets out the legal consequences of such a distinction. In short, where:

- an individual is obliged to provide services personally; and
- there is mutuality of obligation between the two parties; and
- the individual is subject to 'sufficient' control at the hands of the person for whom he works,

the individual is likely to be an employee and thus benefit from unfair dismissal protection, redundancy payments, statutory notice, equal pay, maternity rights and sick pay, to name but a few. Assuming, however, that an individual is not or would rather not be an employee what are the considerations/implications for them?

Why might you want to become self employed?

There are many reasons why an individual may consider becoming self employed. For example, they may have been made redundant recently or indeed some time ago and are struggling to find work. Alternatively, an individual may be seeking more flexibility or control in terms of their work and, in particular, in terms of their working hours. This is often the case for individuals, both male and female, who wish to spend more time with their family.

What are the immediate and obvious concerns to being self employed?

Although there are many benefits to being self employed there are also a number of risks. For example, you will have to accept that:

- you will not necessarily earn a regular income;
- in practice, it is likely you will end up working long hours;
- you won't get paid when you are on holiday;
- you will have to make your own arrangements in terms of pension; and
- you will have to arrange adequate cover for sick leave.

From a personal perspective, you will also have to accept the lack of social contact with other employees, a transition that some people find very difficult.

Initial practical issues for those considering self employment

There are a number of issues to address in establishing your own business. For example:

What kind of business will you operate and how will you trade?

You will need to decide whether you are going to trade as a sole trader, a partnership or indeed, as a limited company. There are pros and cons to each option as well as financial considerations. Consequently, it is worth taking advice as to which format best suits your needs.

What about the finances?

You will need to register with HM Revenue and Customs on a self employed basis. From this, your income tax and national insurance position will become clearer. A reputable accountant will help you through the registration process and the daunting regime of self assessment and payments on account (if relevant). Your accountant will also help with VAT registration as and when your turnover reaches (currently) £64,000. If you need funding you will need to devise a strategy dealing with who you will ask, when, and produce relevant presentations for each potential investor. Depending on the nature of the business, you may have to address the issue of money laundering. You will have to consider suitable processes to address money laundering at the outset of any relationships and have suitable documentary evidence of compliance with the necessary regime. Once you are up and running you will need to establish a credible system for record keeping and decide how you will invoice clients e.g. weekly; monthly; at the end of a project. You will need to produce budgets, cash flows and so forth and ensure that you can pay your invoices and liabilities as and when they fall due for payment.

Where will you trade?

It may be that you intend to operate your business from your premises at home. Alternatively, you will need to find appropriate premises from which to operate. This may be an outright purchase or a rental property. Whichever option you choose you will have to establish whether you are required to pay business rates. You may also have to consider whether planning permission is required in terms of the use of the building or indeed whether any permits are necessary.

Marketing

To be successful, people will need to know about your business. You will, therefore, have to give serious consideration to how you will advertise your business. Options vary from flyers through the door to adverts in newspapers and appropriate trade journals or indeed on television. Much will depend on what you can afford and your target area. In any event, you may wish to utilise the expertise of external marketing / PR experts.

Insurance

This is an important area and you should obtain quotes before making the decision to set up on your own – for some, this cost will be prohibitive! You will need public liability insurance and probably occupier's liability insurance. Depending on the circumstances, you may also need employer's liability insurance. Whatever the situation, you are likely to need insurance for your premises both in terms of the building itself and the contents. If you have vehicles for use in connection with the business, they will have to be insured for business use.

Licences

Once again, your needs will depend on the nature of the business you are operating but you will need to check no licences are needed.

Health and safety

Your business premises will have to comply with all aspects of health and safety legislation. The Environmental Health department of your local authority will be able to provide all of the information you require and external Health and Safety consultants will conduct the necessary risk assessments for you and implement the necessary policies and procedures. Breach of health and safety law carries punitive penalties including, in some cases, imprisonment. It is a vast area of the law in which you should not seek to compromise.

Data protection

The Data Protection Act applies to all organisations no matter how small or large. Its purpose is to prevent the abuse of an individual's personal data. If you hold or use personal data, which includes information about any staff on your books, customers or client, you must comply with the eight principles contained within the Data Protection Act. As a rule of thumb, you should appoint an individual with responsibility for ensuring that your business adheres to the Data Protection Act. In addition, you may be required to register ('notify' if you adopt the language of the Act) with the Data Protection Commissioner, for which a small fee is payable.

Employing others

It may well be that you need to employ or engage other staff from the outset. Alternatively, this may become a necessity as and when your business expands. If so, you need to consider the capacity in which you wish to engage others e.g. as employees, as consultants, as casuals and, whatever their status, you need to look at the implications of it. For example, are they lawfully entitled to work in the UK and do you have the necessary paperwork to back up what you have been told in this respect? If they are consultants, who

is responsible for what? Have they got adequate insurance? How will you pay them? What if the relationship evolves and they are more akin to employees than consultants? If they are employees, once again you will have to consider whether they are allowed to work in the UK. You will also need the necessary paperwork to back this up. You will have to distribute contracts of employment and consider implementing appropriate policies and procedures. You will have to address health and safety issues in the workplace, even if the workplace happens to be the individual's home. You will have to be familiar with all aspects of employment law and consider your obligations in respect of holidays, sickness, maternity, paternity to name but a few. You will also have to consider the lawfulness of any decisions to dismiss!

Implications for other business of having self employed individuals on the premises

The concerns here are numerous. Set out below, however, are a couple of common misconceptions. A common 'nuisance value' Employment Tribunal claim relates to alleged 'self employed' consultants who, on termination of their contract for services, argue that they were actually an employee of the organisation to whom they provided their services. This is an extremely common claim in the IT sector but can happen in any sector of the working world. In light of this potential claim, steps have to be taken to ensure parties are clear from the outset as to what the nature of the relationship will be. Thereafter, the contract must reflect this intention and the practices adopted must do nothing to compromise this situation. Also, as a business you will be responsible for certain actions of consultants, contractors and indeed some visitors whilst they are on your premises. It should be made clear at the outset, therefore, what your policy is in relation to discrimination, for example. You will also have to consider health and safety.

See also: Employment status, p.282; Fixed-term workers, p.335; Part-time workers, p.559

Summary

We trust this chapter gives you a flavour of the considerations to be addressed in relation to self employed status. It can, by no means, address all of the issues but should help address your mind to the various concerns / implications that you will need to consider before launching on your own.

Sources of further information

HMRC: www.hmrc.gov.uk/selfemployed/

Workplace Law Network provides premium members with unrestricted access to a comprehensive range of online information – factsheets, case reports and daily news items – on employment, health and safety and premises management. Members also benefit from an online advice service and a free subscription to the *Workplace Law Magazine*. For more information email membership@ workplacelaw.net or call our membership services team on 0871 777 8881.

Shared premises / common parts

Kevin Boa, Pinsent Masons

Key points

- Tenants in occupation of shared premises are usually subject to a service charge imposed by the landlord for the provision of services. The services include repair and maintenance for which the landlord is responsible and insurance for the building or estate as a whole. The landlord will seek to recoup the cost of all services by the service charge.
- Tenants should carefully negotiate the provisions requiring them to pay for maintenance and repair so as to avoid incurring costs which may benefit the landlord's premises long after the expiry of their lease.

Service charge

The main issue for a tenant in shared premises is the payment of a service charge – what benefits it provides and obligations it imposes. The parties' interests will of course be contradictory. The landlord will want to try to recover all costs incurred in connection with the building and will want a free rein to decide what work is needed and who to charge it to. The tenant ideally will want to limit liability to basic services provided and for these to be reasonable amounts known in advance for budgeting purposes. A happy medium is found only by careful wording of the relevant provisions in the lease and a pragmatic working relationship between the landlord (or its managing agents) and the tenants.

Repair and maintenance

The lease will contain a clause requiring the landlord to maintain and repair the main structure and exterior of the building and the common parts.

The tenant will usually be responsible for internal repair and may be required to decorate the interior, usually every five years, leaving it in the same condition as when taking on the lease. Anything more onerous than this is an unnecessary burden on the tenant.

The tenant should ensure that the precise areas of the building contained in the common parts, for which the landlord has responsibility, are clearly identified in the lease to avoid later dispute and are sufficient for their use of the building. Such items as windows and doors could be either an integral part of the structure of the building or an internal fixture. The tenant should not wait for any dispute to arise before trying to decide who is responsible.

Any major repair works carried out will be reflected in an increased service charge. Tenants of new buildings should be vigilant that they are not asked to contribute towards the cost of the original construction of the building.

Repair or improvement?

A tenant does not have any input as to whether repairs are carried out on a cheaper or more expensive basis unless there is a specific reference in the lease for the landlord to obtain approved estimates. The landlord therefore could seek to add some expensive long-term structural repairs to the service charge which could be seen as an improvement rather than a necessary repair.

Tenants under a short-term lease should not be responsible for extensive long-term repairs and should ensure that the wording of the lease makes it clear that they are not required to contribute.

Insurance

It is usually the landlord's responsibility to provide adequate insurance cover for the building. The cost of this is recouped via the service charge. With shared premises this will invariably be by way of a block policy. The tenant should ensure that the lease contains a clause providing that:

- in the event of the building (or the means of access) being damaged or destroyed, the landlord is obliged to use the insurance monies to reinstate the building and make up the shortfall;
- the rent be suspended until the building is reinstated; and
- the tenant has an option to determine the lease if the building is not reinstated within a specified period.

Calculation of service charge

The lease will specify the proportion of the costs of the service charge. This may simply be by reference to a fair proportion, by reference to the relative floor size occupied by each tenant, or by some other method.

Tenants should ensure they are aware of exactly what services are included in the service charge (which should be scheduled in the lease), as, for example, a tenant on the ground floor does not want to pay a proportion of maintenance towards the lift (although in practice the landlord is unlikely to accept such a restriction).

The landlord can be required to certify, by way of a certificate issued by an accountant or surveyor, that the service charge is properly calculated in accordance with the lease.

See also: Dilapidations, p.193; Landlord and tenant: possession issues, p.444; Landlord and tenant: lease issues, p.448

Sources of further information

Workplace Law Network provides premium members with unrestricted access to a comprehensive range of online information – factsheets, case reports and daily news items – on employment, health and safety and premises management. Members also benefit from an online advice service and a free subscription to the *Workplace Law Magazine*. For more information email membership@workplacelaw.net or call our membership services team on 0871 777 8881.

Sickness leave

Nicole Hallegua, Berwin Leighton Paisner

Key points

- Contracts of employment and statements of terms must state whether or not the employer makes payments for periods of absence due to sickness and, if so, upon what terms.
- Certain qualifying employees are entitled to statutory sick pay (SSP), in respect of which, for a specified period, employers are responsible.
- When terminating the employment of those who are absent due to sickness (whether for conduct, capability or some other substantial reason), consideration must be given to (a) the fairness of the decision and the procedure followed; (b) the existence of permanent health insurance schemes; and (c) the question of disability discrimination.

Legislation

- Social Security Contributions and Benefits Act 1992 (as amended).
- Disability Discrimination Act 1995 (as amended).
- Employment Rights Act 1996.
- Employment Act 2002 (Dispute Resolution) Regulations 2004.
- DTI Guidance on the Employment Act 2002 (Dispute Resolution) Regulations 2004 and associated provisions in the Employment Act 2002 (May 2004).
- ACAS Code of Practice on Disciplinary and Grievance Procedures (June 2004).
- Disability Rights Commission Disability Discrimination Act 1995 Code of Practice Employment and Occupation (8 September 2004).

Sickness leave – entitlement to sick pay

Most employees have an entitlement (either contractual or statutory) to be paid sick pay from their employer while absent from work due to ill health.

Contractual sick pay

In practice, most employers operate company sick pay schemes that expressly outline each employee's contractual entitlement. Provided the employer pays to the employee the minimum level of remuneration he would be entitled to under the Social Security Contributions and Benefits Act 1992 (as amended) (SSCBA), the employer can opt out of the SSP scheme.

Statutory Sick Pay (SSP)

The legislative provisions dealing with payment of SSP are lengthy and technical. Broadly speaking, the SSCBA provides that all employees, subject to certain specified exceptions, are entitled to receive SSP from their employers. This entitlement is limited to 28 weeks in a three-year period. The weekly rate of Statutory Sick Pay for days of sickness from 6 April 2008 is £75.40.

To qualify for SSP, certain prerequisite conditions must be satisfied. Essentially these are as follows:

- The individual must be an 'employee', not a worker, during 'the period of incapacity for work' (PIW);
- The employee must have four or more consecutive days of sickness

(including weekends and holidays) during which he is too ill to be capable of doing his work;

■ The employee must notify his employer of his sickness leave (subject to certain statutory requirements and any agreement between them); and

■ The employee must provide evidence of his inability to do his normal job. This is usually done by self-certification (days one to seven inclusive) and a doctor's certificate (day eight onwards).

Those who do not, or no longer, qualify for SSP may be entitled to other social security benefits, e.g. incapacity benefit, statutory (and/or contractual) maternity pay, etc.

All employers have a statutory obligation to keep (and retain for at least three years) records for SSP purposes. As a minimum, for each employee, an employer must record PIWs and details of payments made (or not made) in respect of PIWs.

Sickness leave – dismissals

When dealing with sickness leave, a distinction should always be made between absences on grounds of longer periods of medically certificated illness (capability issue) and those bouts of persistent short absences caused by unconnected minor illnesses that may call for disciplinary action (conduct issue). In both dismissal scenarios, a potentially fair reason must exist and the employer must act reasonably in all the circumstances, and follow proper procedures which are compliant with the statutory minimum, in dismissing the employee as a consequence of the reason. Further, what may be considered fair and reasonable will vary according to the particular circumstances of each individual case.

Conduct

A dismissal on the grounds of conduct owing to persistent periods of absences from work should be fair provided the employer:

■ has reasonable grounds to believe the employee is guilty of misconduct;

■ before any disciplinary meeting, investigates the extent of and reasons for the employee's absences (thereby allowing the employee an opportunity to explain);

■ informs the employee of the level of attendance he is expected to attain, of the time within which he should achieve it, and that he may be dismissed if there is insufficient improvement;

■ thereafter monitors the situation, and offers support or assistance if appropriate, for a reasonable period prior to dismissal; and

■ follows a fair dismissal procedure which is compliant with the statutory minimum.

Capability

A dismissal on the grounds of incapability due to ill health should be fair where the employer:

■ investigates the employee's true medical position and prognosis for recovery (e.g. by obtaining a medical report with the employee's consent);

■ after considering the requirements of the business, the possibility of alternative employment and the likelihood of the employee returning to work in the foreseeable future, concludes there is no alternative but to dismiss;

■ consults with the employee about the possibility of his employment being terminated prior to dismissal; and

■ follows a fair dismissal procedure which is compliant with the statutory minimum.

Only when an employer obtains a clear prognosis of the employee's state of health will it be able to adequately assess the requirements of the business and what other alternative positions may be offered to the particular employee.

Sickness leave – dismissals and permanent health insurance (PHI) schemes

Where an employee has a right to receive permanent health benefits, the grounds on which an employer can dismiss are considerably restricted. In short, an employer will act unlawfully when it dismisses an employee who is in receipt of benefit under a PHI scheme. This is because there is an overriding implied term that an employer should not dismiss the employee while he is incapacitated and thereby deprive him of the very disability benefit that it is the primary purpose of PHI schemes to provide.

However, in such circumstances employers may be able to dismiss for good cause such as gross misconduct or for some other form of fundamental breach by the employee. Potentially, dismissal for capability or a genuine redundancy situation could also be a good cause for dismissal in these circumstances. What is crucial is that the 'good cause' must be something other than the ill health.

Sickness leave – dismissals and disability discrimination

Any worker who is dismissed in the light of his illness could potentially bring a claim under the Disability Discrimination Act 1995. To do this he would need to show that, by reason of the dismissal, the employer treated him less favourably because of his illness and that the illness constitutes a disability as defined by the legislation, i.e. "a physical or mental impairment which has a substantial and long-term adverse effect upon a person's ability to carry out normal day-to-day activities". If proven, the ultimate question then becomes whether the employer can be expected to wait any longer for the employee. To avoid a finding of discrimination and unfair dismissal, the employer will need to justify the reason for dismissing the employee and show that it made all "reasonable adjustments" as are practicable in the circumstances.

Sickness leave – notice rights

Where an employee, incapable of work because of sickness or injury, has his employment terminated with the statutory minimum period of notice and his contract of employment or statement of terms specifies normal working hours, he is entitled to receive a minimum hourly rate of pay during that notice period for any period during normal working hours in which he is too ill to be capable of working.

Where an employee who is incapable of work because of sickness or injury has his employment terminated with the statutory minimum period of notice and his contract of employment or statement of terms does not specify normal working hours, he is entitled to a week's pay for each week during that notice period when he is too ill to be capable of doing his work.

See also: Absence management, p.46; Discrimination, p.222; Dismissal, p.233; Leave, p.457

Sources of further information

ACAS: www.acas.org.uk

Slips, trips and falls

Jagdeep Tiwana, Berwin Leighton Paisner

Key points

Slips, trips and falls are the most common cause of injuries at work; 90% of them result in broken bones. The Health and Safety Executive (HSE) has initiated a campaign to reduce the number of slips, trips and falls in the workplace by 10% by 2010.

Legislation

- Health and Safety at Work etc. Act 1974.
- Workplace (Health, Safety and Welfare) Regulations 1992.
- Reporting of Injuries, Diseases and Dangerous Occurrences Regulations 1995 (RIDDOR).
- Management of Health and Safety at Work Regulations 1999.

Legal duties

The Health and Safety at Work etc. Act 1974 imposes a duty on all employers to take steps to ensure the health and safety of their employees and third parties (such as customers or workmen). This duty includes taking steps to control risks to such persons from slips, trips and falls. Employees are also under a duty to behave in a responsible manner to ensure their own safety and that of others around them. Additionally, they must make use of any safety equipment provided by their employer.

The Workplace (Health, Safety and Welfare) Regulations 1992 impose the specific requirement that floors must be suitable and in good condition. They must also be free from obstructions and people must be able to move around safely.

The Management of Health and Safety at Work Regulations 1999 impose a duty on employers to carry out risk assessments, including those relating to hazards involving slips, trips and falls. Once these have been highlighted, employers must put into place measures to prevent the risk of accidents arising from slips, trips and falls.

Risk assessment

The HSE recommends five steps in risk assessment of slips, trips and falls:

1. Look for slip and trip hazards (e.g. uneven floors, trailing cables, slippery surfaces – when wet or otherwise).
2. Identify who may be harmed and how (pay particular attention to older or disabled people).
3. Consider the risks and whether current safety measures adequately deal with these.
4. Record findings (if five or more employees).
5. Review the risk assessment regularly (particularly where there has been an accident involving a slip, trip or fall or where there have been significant changes in the workplace).

The HSE has issued specific mapping tools to assist managers and safety representatives to prevent accidents involving slips, trips and falls. These can be found on the HSE website, together with other useful information.

Good system

The HSE has highlighted the following as the requirements of a good system to prevent slips, trips and falls.

Planning

An employer should identify key areas of risk and work with employees to identify areas on the site giving rise to risk of slips, trips or falls. Employers should also take care when selecting floor coverings and equipment to prevent or reduce slip and trip hazards. This can be done by choosing anti-slip flooring and fitting splash guards.

Training

Staff should be trained in how to avoid accidents involving slips, trips and falls, including cleaning up spillages and not placing trip hazards in the workplace. Staff should also be trained on how to use safety signage to warn of slippery floors etc. and to wear suitable footwear.

Organisation

Work activities should be organised in a way that minimises the risks of slips, trips and falls and specific staff members should be given responsibility for ensuring that the workplace is kept safe. This can be done by ensuring the workplace is always well-lit, free from obstructions and tripping hazards (e.g. trailing cables) and that all spillages are cleared up quickly to prevent slipping.

Control

Records should be kept to ensure good cleaning and maintenance operations are being used. Checks should be carried out regularly to ensure safe working practices are being used.

Monitor and review

Employers should regularly review accident records and identify any areas where current safety arrangements are deficient. Steps should be taken to remedy any deficiencies highlighted. Employees should be encouraged to report any safety issues.

Common causes of accidents

The HSE has identified the main factors that it considers contribute to slips, trips and falls:

- *Flooring* – wet floors pose a well-known slipping hazard and ill-fitted or damaged floor coverings can lead to tripping. Floors should be regularly inspected and damaged flooring repaired. Spillages should be wiped up as soon as possible and safety signage used to warn of the hazards of wet floors.
- *Contamination* – contamination from oil, grease or even rainwater can make floors very slippery and it is therefore important that floors are cleaned thoroughly and rainwater is mopped up as soon as possible and safety signage used.
- *Obstacles* – the HSE estimates that 50% of all trip accidents are caused by bad housekeeping, so simple measures such as keeping areas clear of obstructions and work areas tidy can reduce the number of accidents.
- *Cleaning* – all workplaces will need to undergo cleaning but this can create slip and trip hazards, so cleaning is best done when the least number of people will be exposed to the risks of slipping or tripping (e.g. after the premises in question close to the public). When this is not possible, access to wet areas should be stopped and cleaning carried out in sections, using signs and/or cones. It is important to note that these will warn of a hazard, but will not prevent people from entering the area. Appropriate amounts of cleaning products should be used to remove grease and oil from floors.

- *Human factors* – instilling a positive attitude in staff and training them to deal with any hazards as soon as they arise will have a positive effect on workplace safety.
- *Environment* – environmental factors such as lighting, weather and condensation can have an impact on the risk of people suffering a slip, trip or fall. For example, excessive glare from sunlight on a shiny floor may prevent people from seeing a tripping hazard, or badly lit stairs will present a hazard. This can be reduced by using high visibility non-slip step edges.

- *Footwear* – the HSE recognises that footwear can play an important part in preventing slips, trips and falls while unsuitable footwear may contribute to an accident. Employers can reduce risks by providing non-slip footwear for staff or by implementing a footwear policy requiring employees to wear flat shoes which have a grip. This will not of course reduce the risk of slips or trips by customers or other third parties and additional steps may still be required. By undertaking a risk assessment and implementing good systems, the majority of accidents involving slips, trips and falls can be avoided.

See also: Accident invesigations, p.55; Catering: health and safety issues, p.124; Construction site health and safety, p.154; Workplace deaths, p.190; First aid, p.333; Health and safety at work, p.364; Working at height, p.395; Reporting of Injuries, Diseases and Dangerous Occurrences (RIDDOR), p.628; Risk assessments, p.639

Sources of further information

'Shattered lives' – HSE slips, trips and falls webpage: www.hse.gov.uk/slips/

Smoking

David Wright, Kennedys

Key points

Smoking has been banned in prescribed places in the Republic of Ireland since 2004, in Scotland since March 2006, in Northern Ireland and Wales since April 2007, and in England since July 2007. Employers and managers in charge of premises and vehicles to which the ban applies should:

- take reasonable steps to ensure staff, customers, members and visitors are aware that the premises and vehicles are legally required to be smoke-free;
- display 'no smoking' signs in smoke-free premises; and
- ensure that no one smokes in smoke-free premises or vehicles.

Relevant legislation

Prior to the Health Act 2006, which, along with a number of subordinate Regulations, introduced the smoking ban in England in July 2007, a combination of the Health and Safety at Work etc. Act 1974, the Management of Health and Safety at Work Regulations 1999 and the Workplace (Health, Safety and Welfare) Regulations 1992 required employers to take steps to assess and minimise the risks to their employees and visitors from environmental tobacco smoke in the workplace.

These 'health and safety' requirements, although still in existence, have been very largely overtaken by the recent 'smoke-free' legislation. At the present time, the nuts and bolts of the 'smoke-free' legislation in England is set out in the following Regulations:

- The Smoke-free (Premises and Enforcement) Regulations 2006 set out definitions of 'enclosed' and 'substantially enclosed' and the bodies responsible for enforcing smoke-free legislation.
- The Smoke-free (Exemptions and Vehicles) Regulations 2007 set out the exemptions to smoke-free legislation and vehicles required to be smoke-free.
- The Smoke-free (Penalties and Discounted Amounts) Regulations 2007 set out the levels of penalties for offences under smoke-free legislation.
- The Smoke-free (Vehicle Operators and Penalty Notices) Regulations 2007 set out the responsibility on vehicle operators to prevent smoking in smoke-free vehicles and the form for fixed penalty notices.
- The Smoke-free (Signs) Regulations 2007 set out the requirements for no-smoking signs required under smoke-free legislation.

Common law

Prior to the ban, in an employment law context, the courts and tribunals have tended to imply a right to protection for employees in the workplace, stating that there is a term implied into employment contracts that the employer will provide and monitor for his employees, so far as is reasonably practicable, a working environment that is reasonably suitable for the performance by them of their contractual duties. Applying this formula, it was held that a non-smoker was constructively dismissed (i.e. there was a fundamental breach of her employment contract) as a result of being required to work in a smoke-affected atmosphere, despite her protests. The smoking ban has reinforced this implied right.

Having said this, employers who choose to introduce anti-smoking measures that go beyond the requirements set out in the smoke-free legislation, for example by banning smoking anywhere on the premises, whether inside or out, must take care that by doing so they are not seen to be victimising smokers who may for many years have enjoyed an unfettered right to smoke in the workplace in order to avoid the possibility of antagonism and ill feeling.

The best way to avoid this problem is to have introduced a reasonable and carefully considered smoking policy, with the smoke-free legislation at its heart, and to have consulted employees on its introduction.

Outside the confines of employment law, employers also have a long-established duty of care under common law to take reasonable care for the health and safety of their workforce. The duty of care extends to the provision of a safe place and system of work.

UK statutory smoking bans

Scotland
On 30 June 2005, the Scottish Parliament passed the Smoking, Health and Social Care (Scotland) Act 2005, which introduced a complete ban on tobacco smoking in enclosed public places in Scotland from 26 March 2006. The Act makes it an offence for those in charge of 'no-smoking premises' to knowingly permit others to smoke there. Although there are defences of taking reasonable precautions to prevent smoking and having no lawful means to

prevent smoking, those convicted may be fined up to 2,500. It is also an offence to fail to display 'no-smoking' signs in such premises. The Act provides that culpable managers may also be prosecuted, as well as their employer companies.

Those convicted of smoking in 'no-smoking' premises may be fined up to 1,000.

The Prohibition of Smoking in Certain Premises (Scotland) Regulations 2006 add flesh to the Act's bones and contain provisions relating to the provision and display of no-smoking signage, giving effect to Schedule One of the Act which lists the types of premises that are prescribed to be no-smoking premises, defining key expressions such as premises and wholly enclosed, and setting out the levels of the relevant fixed penalties and other administrative matters.

In September 2007, 18 months into the ban, research suggested a 17% drop in the number of people admitted to hospital with heart attacks. In the previous decade, the annual reduction of heart attacks had been 3%. The Scottish Government said the findings highlighted the ban's "overwhelmingly positive effect".

England and Wales
In England and Wales, a consultation process to ban smoking in public places began in November 2004 with the publication of the UK Government's White Paper on Public Health. This included a plan to make enclosed public areas in England, including smoking rooms in offices and factories, smoke-free by 2008. The then Health Secretary, John Reid, announced that smoking restrictions were to be phased in with a ban on smoking in NHS and Government buildings in 2006, in enclosed public spaces in 2007 and in licensed premises by 2008. Only bars and public houses not preparing and serving

food and private clubs whose members voted to allow smoking were to be exempt from the ban.

In the event, after a series of well-publicised disagreements between MPs of all parties and between certain Cabinet ministers, the Commons voted to impose a ban on all enclosed or substantially enclosed public places and workplaces. The Health Act 2006, which devolved regulation-making powers on this issue to the Welsh Assembly, was followed by the publication in England and Wales of separate draft Regulations for consultation and bans took effect in April and July 2007 in Wales and England respectively. The requirements of both the English and Welsh smoke-free legislation are very similar.

What is the effect of the new legislation in England?

Overview
Employers and managers in charge of premises and vehicles to which the legislation applies should:

- take reasonable steps to ensure staff, customers, members and visitors are aware that the premises and vehicles are legally required to be smoke-free;
- display 'no-smoking' signs in smoke-free premises; and
- ensure that no one smokes in smoke-free premises or vehicles.

Which premises does the ban apply to?
Premises:

- that are open to the public;
- that are used as a place of work by more than one person; or
- where members of the public might attend to receive or provide goods or services, are to be smoke-free in areas that are enclosed or substantially enclosed.

Premises are 'enclosed' if they have a ceiling or roof and, except for doors, windows and passageways, are wholly enclosed either permanently or temporarily. Premises are 'substantially enclosed' if they have a ceiling or roof but there is an opening in the walls or an aggregate area of openings in the walls which is less than half the area of the walls.

The ban therefore includes offices, factories, shops, pubs, bars, restaurants, private members clubs and workplace smoking rooms. A 'roof' also includes any fixed or movable structure, such as canvas awnings. Tents, marquees or similar are also classified as enclosed premises if they fall within the definition.

Which vehicles does the ban apply to?
'Enclosed vehicles' are to be smoke-free at all times if they are used "by members of the public or a section of the public (whether or not for reward or hire)"; or "in the course of paid or voluntary work by more than one person, even if those people use the vehicle at different times, or only intermittently".

For example, a delivery van used by more than one driver, or which has a driver and passenger, must be smoke-free at all times. It should be noted that the Regulations do not extend to vehicles used for non-business purposes.

What signs should be displayed?
All smoke-free premises must display a no-smoking sign in a prominent position at each entrance that:

- is the equivalent of A5 in area;
- displays the international no-smoking symbol in colour, a minimum of 70 mm in diameter; and
- carries the words, 'No smoking. It is against the law to smoke in these premises,' in characters that can be easily read.

Workplace Law Network
www.workplacelaw.net

In addition, any person with management responsibilities for a smoke-free vehicle has legal duties to display a no-smoking sign in each enclosed compartment that can accommodate people.

What penalties can be imposed?
Smoking in a smoke-free premises or vehicle can attract a fixed penalty notice of £50 or a fine up to £200. Failure to display no-smoking signs in smoke-free premises and vehicles can attract a fixed penalty notice of £200 or a fine up to £1,000.

Failing to prevent smoking in a smoke-free premises or vehicle can lead to a fine up to £2,500.

The smoke-free legislation is enforced by a number of bodies, but primarily by district councils. There is no provision in the legislation for smoke-free offences to result in a review of a pub's licence.

Are there are exemptions from the smoke-free legislation?
There are some limited exemptions including the following:

- Private dwellings (with particular exceptions such as a communal stairwell);
- Designated bedrooms in hotels, guest houses, inns, hostels and members clubs (if they meet conditions set out in the Regulations); and
- designated bedrooms / rooms used only for smoking in care homes, hospices and prisons (if they meet conditions set out in the Regulations).

Latest research and compliance data
In England, the Department of Health has undertaken a series of surveys into the awareness and support of the new law by businesses. The latest results suggest a 98% level of compliance among all vehicles and businesses inspected between July 2007 and March 2008. The same research suggests that 87% of all premises and vehicles are displaying the correct no-smoking signage. Meanwhile, 87% of businesses reported that the implimentation of the new legislation had gone well or very well, with 40% saying that there had been a positive impact on the company against a mere 3% reporting a negative impact.

Less than three weeks after the introduction of the ban in July 2007, the first prosecution under the new legislation took place, resulting in a £500 fine for the licencee of a bar in Lancashire after he admitted 12 counts of failing to prevent smoking. There were a total of 19 court hearings for the same offence between July 2007 and March 2008 against a total of 49 fixed penalty notices issued and eight court hearings for signage offences.

The same period recorded 477 fixed penalty notices issued and eight court hearings for the offence of individuals smoking in a smoke-free premises or vehicle.

Earlier this year the High Court ruled that Nottinghamshire Healthcare Trust had not breached long-term psychiatric patients' human rights, by prohibiting them from smoking at a high security mental hospital.

International examples
In Dublin, there were a reported 2,000 job losses following the implementation of a ban on smoking in bars in March 2004, and the Irish Revenue Commissioner reported a 16% decrease in tobacco sales. Subsequent research suggests that airborne particulate matter, a feature of some pollution, decreased by up to 80% in pubs, and health and lung function of bar workers improved in the 12 months after the ban came into effect. The introduction of a ban on smoking in bars in New York allegedly saw a reduction in pollution levels

following the ban but a short term decrease of $28.5m in wage and salary payments.

In Norway, rather than implementing a complete ban, non-smoking areas and requirements for better ventilation are part of a 15-year staged process for the introduction of a ban. Norway banned smoking in bars, following the initiative in Ireland, and bar owners face the prospect of losing their licences if smokers are not persuaded to stop lighting up.

Other countries that have introduced bans or restrictions include Italy, Spain, Belgium, Sweden, the Netherlands, South Africa, Russia, Nepal and Tanzania. The State of California banned smoking in most indoor workplaces as long ago as 1995, with a temporary exemption for bars and casinos ending in 1998.

Introducing a smoking policy

All employers should by now have taken action to comply with the statutory smoking ban. In terms of the introduction of new or revised smoking policies to supplement or reinforce such action, an employer should consider both the form of the policy and the manner of its introduction. Whether a policy is reasonable or not will be a question of fact. However, as well as considering the implications of smoking bans, a prudent employer should take account of:

- the practicalities of the workplace;
- the nature of the business, including whether clients will be regularly visiting the building and whether employees are visiting clients at their homes;
- workplace opinion;
- assistance to smokers in adapting to the new policy;
- consultation with individuals and/or their representatives;

- ensuring that employees are fully aware of the possible sanctions for breach of the policy, including cross-references to the disciplinary procedure; and
- regular reviews of the policy for ongoing effectiveness.

Once a policy is in place it must be consistently enforced. It would, however, be sensible to support smokers during the early period of the policy and perhaps to avoid overly harsh sanctions during those early stages. Employers with activities in England, Wales, Scotland or Northern Ireland should by now have implemented appropriate procedures to ensure that their employees and others who access their premises refrain from smoking. Employers might find it helpful to approach the smoking ban in a similar way as many of them do to the wearing of Personal Protective Equipment. In other words, employers should:

- identify all those areas in which smoking will constitute an offence;
- alter the existing staff handbook or relevant procedures such that smoking in those areas will attract disciplinary sanctions;
- having publicised the alterations, make good on the promise to use them when there are reasonable grounds for doing so; and
- in the case of visitors, (i) make them aware of the company's policy, and (ii) eject them from the premises if the policy is breached. They should also take into account any increase in fire risk resulting from smokers gathering outside or even smoking surreptitiously. If practical, safe areas outside could be provided, distant from combustible materials and with suitably designed bins or buckets for smokers' waste.

See also: Discrimination,
p.222; Driving at work, p.244;
Occupational health, p.537;
Personal Protective Equipment,
p.568; Staff handbooks, p.666;
Vehicles at work, p.701

Sources of further information

Helpful guidance, including downloadable signage, can be accessed at the following websites:

England – www.smokefreeengland.co.uk

Wales – www.smokingbanwales.co.uk

Scotland – www.clearingtheairscotland.com

Northern Ireland – www.spacetobreath.org.uk

Since 1 July 2007 it has been illegal to smoke or to permit smoking in any workplace or public place in the UK. If you employ any staff or offer services to any members of the public Workplace Law Group's *Guide to Smoking Ban 2007* will prove essential reading to ensure compliance.

Written by Angela Philip, a barrister at Eversheds, this guide is designed to explain the many complex aspects of the smoking ban, and suggest ways in which employers, premises managers and service providers can keep in line with the legislation. Written in Workplace Law Group's jargon-free, plain-English style, this downloadable publication is an indispensable resource for all those affected by the ban. For more information visit www.workplacelaw.net/Bookshop/GuidesTo.

Staff handbooks

Jo Bradbury, Martineau Solicitors

Key points
- Ensure that staff handbooks are easy to read.
- Use a format that is easy to update.
- Reduce printing costs by publishing on your company intranet site.
- Ensure that all staff have access to the staff handbook.
- Ask new starters to sign to confirm they have read and understood the contents of the staff handbook.
- Build time into induction training to read the staff handbook.
- Clarify whether or not the contents are contractual.
- Review and amend policies regularly to reflect legislative changes and best practice.

Legislation
- Equal Pay Act 1970.
- Sex Discrimination Act 1975.
- Race Relations Act 1976.
- Employment Act 1989.
- Trade Union and Labour Relations (Consolidation) Act 1992.
- Disability Discrimination Act 1995.
- Employment Rights Act 1996.
- National Minimum Wage Act 1998.
- Working Time Regulations 1998.
- Employment Relations Act 1999.
- Part-time Workers (Prevention of Less Favourable Treatment) Regulations 2000.
- Fixed-term Employees (Prevention of Less Favourable Treatment) Regulations 2002.
- Employment Rights Act 2002.
- Information and Consultation of Employees Regulations 2004.
- Employment Equality (Age) Regulations 2006.

Purpose
Employers increasingly issue their staff with staff handbooks. Staff handbooks are an essential employee management tool which can be adapted to suit all organisations. They provide an essential element of good communication and can put in place a system of best practice for the employer and employee to follow throughout the course of an employment relationship.

Staff handbooks can vary considerably in terms of scope and length and, to this extent, can be tailored to suit the employment circumstances.

Once a staff handbook is assembled, employees can refer to one central source in order to clarify the employer's position with regards to any number of policies (including, for example, pay structures, holidays and absences, training, equal opportunities, disciplinary and grievance matters, redundancy, health and safety and so on).

Staff handbooks are also a very convenient way of inducting new members of staff to the structure and culture of an organisation.

Importantly, they can also be instrumental to employers in successfully defending Employment Tribunal claims.

Workplace Law Network
www.workplacelaw.net

Legal position

There is no legal requirement for an employer to publish a staff handbook. A Contract of Employment and/or a Section 1 Statement can adequately set out an employee's terms and conditions. However, certain terms and conditions are often too lengthy and cumbersome to include in the Contract / Section 1 Statement. Staff handbooks therefore provide an ideal solution to set out additional contractual information, together with other, non-contractual information which may be of key importance to both the employer and the employee.

Broadly speaking, a staff handbook will be made up of four sub-categories:

1. *Contractual issues* – these may include, for example, individual pay rates or enhanced redundancy provisions (over and above the statutory position) which are deemed to form part of an employee's terms and conditions of employment.
2. *Non-contractual issues* – these will encompass provisions which fall within the general statutory entitlement (such as statutory sick pay or maternity leave), together with more general company policies which are not considered to be part of the terms and conditions of employment (for example, use of the internet at work).
3. *Company-specific information* – including the hierarchy of the management structure, mission statements or a company history.
4. *Industry data* – this might include information about money laundering policies or quality standards within that field of work.

Crucially, employers must be careful when drafting Contracts of Employment / Section 1 Statements and staff handbooks to be absolutely clear about which parts of the staff handbook are contractual (by explicitly saying so in the Contract/Section 1 Statement) and which are not. For example, if a Contract makes reference to the disciplinary and grievance procedures being set out in the staff handbook, wording should also be inserted in the Contract to clarify that, for the avoidance of doubt, these policies do not form part of the employee's terms and conditions of employment. This means an employer will be free to raise and update policies and procedures.

This method also offers greater protection to the employer. For example, an employee should be prevented from successfully claiming breach of contract where the employer fails to complete a grievance investigation within the desired timeframe set out in its policy, provided that policy expressly states that the contents of the policy do not form part of the employee's Contract of Employment.

That said, recent developments in case law have shown that Tribunals are prepared to interpret disputed handbook provisions as creating contractual rights in favour of the employee, particularly where those provisions relate to remuneration (such as enhanced redundancy payments). It is therefore advisable for employers to separate contractual from non-contractual rights, or to expressly state the position (including a denial where provisions do not have contractual force) in order to eliminate any scope for ambiguity or dispute.

At various times, an employer may seek to rely on the policies set out in a staff handbook, for example during an Employment Tribunal claim. In order to do so successfully, it will be vital that the employer can demonstrate that the employee had access to, and full knowledge of, the contents of the staff handbook / relevant policy (including the latest version). One way to achieve this would be to ensure that all staff sign a document acknowledging that they have seen and/or have access to the staff handbook as amended from time to time.

Format

For staff handbooks to be effective, they must be easily accessible to all employees. The format in which the staff handbook is published will therefore depend on the type of organisation.

Some employers prefer to issue all staff with a hard copy of the staff handbook. This way, it is easy to monitor who has or has not received a copy of the handbook. Employees can be asked to sign a document to acknowledge receipt of the hard copy as evidence of this. It is advisable for hard copies to be produced in binders so that out-of-date sections can be removed and replaced as and when required. However, hard copy staff handbooks can be costly for the employer to produce, particularly where there are a large number of employees. Updating the sections can also be more onerous as new hard copy sections will need to be distributed, clearly identifying that they replace the previous section in order to avoid confusion.

Alternatively, employers are more often favouring intranet-based staff handbooks, which are particularly useful in large organisations provided that all employees have unlimited access to the information they contain, as and when required. Internet policies can be updated more easily and the information is available to employees instantaneously, without the need for costly or onerous distribution. However, employers must be careful to ensure that their employees are informed as and when changes are made to the staff handbook. Intranet-based staff handbooks are also preferred in paper-free

office environments, although it is helpful to provide a facility whereby relevant sections of the staff handbook can be printed off if an employee prefers to refer to a paper-based format. As above, it is also worth ensuring that members of staff sign a document to acknowledge that they are aware of the contents of the staff handbook and that they have access to this (as amended).

Employers should also be aware of their obligations under the Disability Discrimination Act 1995 and be ready to provide employees with the contents of the staff handbook in formats such as large type, Braille or audio, where it is reasonable to do so.

Updates

Given the fact that employment legislation is in a constant state of flux, staff handbooks and the policies within them can easily become out-of-date, reflecting bad practice or, at worst, unlawful provisions. It is therefore essential that each employer has in place a system which monitors and reviews the policies contained within their staff handbook. In this way, any necessary amendments can be made ahead of/at the time of changes to the law.

To the extent that staff handbooks incorporate terms and conditions for employees, any changes made to these terms and conditions should not be undertaken until consultation and agreement has been reached with the employees (or, where appropriate, employee representatives) as unilaterally imposed changes to terms and conditions are not enforceable.

Similarly, it is also considered best practice to consult with recognised trade unions / employee representatives whenever significant changes are made to any (non-contractual) policies set out by employers. This helps to maintain good employment relationships and can also support an employer in defending an Employment Tribunal claim if it can show that the employee was not only aware of the change but was consulted about, and agreed to, the change in a particular policy.

Key advantages

Staff handbooks can be crucial in ensuring that a consistent approach is taken across the board in dealing with any number of employees. This can avoid feelings of unequal treatment or discontent, and can also significantly limit the likelihood of Employment Tribunal claims being brought. For the employer, staff handbooks can bring harmonisation to a workforce that, previously, may have worked under different terms, conditions and policies.

Similarly, employees find staff handbooks user-friendly and know where to look in order to obtain specific information relating to their employment. In turn, this provides an additional advantage to the employer, who is not left to deal with queries which would otherwise crop up time and time again.

Drafting the Handbook

Some employers will produce their staff handbooks internally, within the human resources / personnel department. The same internal department would also then be responsible for updating the staff handbook as and when required. Alternatively, some employers seek legal advice in drafting and/or reviewing existing staff handbooks, in order to ensure that the policies are compliant with the latest legislative changes and views on best practice.

There is also widespread use of external guidance sources available to assist with the drafting of staff handbooks. Certain industries publish model documents

and contracts as precedents. Advice can also be sought from the DBERR website and the ACAS code of practice. Various policies can also be viewed and downloaded from the internet, although employers should be cautious of adopting such general-purpose policies without at least considering whether they meet the needs of the individual employer as well as the extent to which they are compliant with current legislation.

Content checklist:

- Absence / sick leave and pay;
- Collective agreements (if any);
- Deductions from wages (including recovery of overpayments);
- Disciplinary and grievance procedure;
- Equal opportunities / equality and diversity;
- Family-friendly policies including maternity, paternity and adoption leave, emergency time off for dependants and parental leave;
- Health and safety policy (this could be published as a separate document or handbook);
- Holiday leave and pay;
- Hours of work;
- Information and consultation arrangements (if any);
- Notice periods; and
- Pay and benefits (including overtime pay).

Optional:

- Bank holiday working;
- Bereavement / compassionate leave;
- Bullying and harassment;
- Communications;
- Company car;
- Company equipment (mobile phones, laptops, tools, etc.);
- Dress code;
- Drugs and alcohol;
- DSE eyesight policy (could be included in the health and safety handbook);

- Expenses procedure;
- Flexible working arrangements;
- Forms for in-house use;
- Gifts and hospitality;
- Housekeeping;
- Incapacity and capability;
- Induction;
- Internet and email policy;
- Introduction to the organisation;
- Jury service;
- Organisation chart / management structure;
- Organisation products and services;
- Performance management / appraisals;
- Redundancy;
- Reference policy;
- Retirement and pension benefits;
- Smoking;
- Stress;
- Termination of Employment;
- Time off for trade union representatives (if applicable);
- Training and promotion; and
- Whistleblowing.

Checklist of dos and don'ts

Do:

- ensure that you are familiar with current employment legislation and how this affects your policies and procedures;
- use bullet points, short sentences and paragraph subheadings;
- write confidently, concisely and directly;
- write formally;
- choose a format easy to update – loose-leaf or ring binders are helpful;
- try to make your handbook attractive to encourage staff to read it;
- think about including a frequently asked questions section (FAQS);
- consult senior managers and staff representatives when drafting new policies and procedures;
- get the contents checked from a legal perspective before publishing; and
- get it proofread to reduce errors or typing mistakes.

Don't:

- use scene-setting, padding or long lead-ins;
- use long paragraphs;
- use foreign phrases or Latin;
- use jargon, clichés or humour;
- be vague – this can lead to misinterpretation resulting in disputes with your employees; or
- ignore current employment legislation or best management practice.

See also: Employment contracts, p.273; Employment Tribunals, p.285

Sources of further information

ACAS guidelines on drawing up handbooks: www.acas.org.uk

Comprehensive, accurate and up to date policies and procedures are required by all employers to ensure that they comply with the latest employment law and health and safety legislation. Workplace Law Group has drafted a series of 21 complete and updated policies and procedures templates, covering all the major areas of risk to employers. All documents are issued electronically in MS Word format so that you can customise them for your organisation, and are accompanied by extensive guidance on the subject matter. For more information visit www.workplacelaw.net/Bookshop/PoliciesAndProcedures.

Stress

Nicola Cardenas-Blanco, Martineau Solicitors

Key points

- All employers owe a legal duty of care to their employees. Injury to mental health is treated in the same way as injury to physical health.
- Sixteen general propositions for bringing any civil claim for compensation for stress were provided by the Court of Appeal and approved as general guidance by the House of Lords. These are listed below (see Criteria for civil cases).
- A successful claim must show that, on the balance of probabilities, an employer had knowledge or deemed knowledge of the foreseeability of harm to a particular employee, so that the lack of his taking reasonable steps to, as far as is reasonably practicable, alleviate the risk of or prevent that harm occurring constituted a breach of duty of care to the employee, and that this caused the injury or loss.
- The HSE has urged employers to carry out risk assessments and implement measures to eliminate or control workplace stress or risk criminal prosecution. The HSE's Management Standards on stress (a web-based toolkit to help businesses comply with their duties) were published on 3 November 2004. Employers will need to take on board this HSE guidance in order to provide best practice in health and safety.

Legislation

- Health and Safety at Work etc. Act 1974.
- Management of Health and Safety at Work Regulations 1999.

Main cases

- *Stokes v. Guest Keen and Nettlefold (Bolts and Nuts) Limited* (1968) 1 WLR 1776, 1783.
- *Walker v. Northumberland County Council* (1995) 1 All ER. 737.
- *Sutherland v. Hatton* (2002) EWCA Civ 76, CA 05/02/02.
- *Barber v. Somerset County Council* (2004) UKHL13.
- *Hartman v. South Essex Mental Health & Community Care NHS Trust CA* (Civ Div) 19/1/2005.
- *Mark Hone v. Six Continents Retail Limited* (2005) EWCA Civ 922.
- *Edward Harding v. The Pub Estate Co. Limited* (2005) EWCA Civ 553.

Legal aspects of stress claims

All employers owe a legal duty of care to their employees. Injury to mental health is treated in the same way as injury to physical health.

Criteria for civil cases

A successful civil claim must show that, on the balance of probabilities, an employer had knowledge or deemed knowledge of the foreseeability of harm to a particular employee, so that the lack of his taking reasonable steps to, as far as is reasonably practicable, alleviate the risk of or prevent that harm occurring constituted a breach of duty of care to the employee, and that this caused the injury or loss.

A stress injury is not as immediately visible as, for instance, a broken leg, and the 16 propositions put forward by Lady Justice Hale in the Court of Appeal judgment of

Sutherland v. Hatton (and related cases) are still regarded as the best useful practical guidance as to whether or not a stress claim may be successful.

Nonetheless, every case does still depend on its own facts and in the later House of Lords case of *Barber v. Somerset County Council* Lord Walker preferred as a statement of law the statement of Swanwick J in *Stokes v. Guest Keen and Nettlefold (Bolts and Nuts) Limited* that "the overall test is still the conduct of the reasonable and prudent employer, taking positive thought for the safety of his workers in the light of what he knows or ought to know".

State of knowledge
Knowledge of the employee and the risks they are facing is key in both leading House of Lords cases on workplace stress. Lord Walker went furthest in the *Barber case* and stated that, where there was developing knowledge, a reasonable employer had a duty to keep reasonably abreast of it and not be too slow to apply it. Where the employer has greater than average knowledge of the risks, he may be obliged to take more than the average or standard precautions.

Knowledge is critical in the area of what is or is not 'reasonably foreseeable' in a civil claim. This was reinforced by the Court of Appeal case of *Mark Hone v. Six Continents Retail Limited*. In this case it was brought to the employer's attention that long hours were being worked and the employee was tired. It was held that it did not matter that the employer did not accept the level of the recorded hours as accurate as the fact the employee had been recording those hours was sufficient to indicate that he needed help and contributed to the "sufficiently plain indications of impending harm to health".

This may be contrasted with another Court of Appeal case of *Edward Harding v.*

The Pub Estate Company Ltd where, as manager, the claimant's hours were within his own control, no reduction in hours was requested, nor additional staff; complaints concentrated on working conditions. In this case, the Court of Appeal overturned judgment at first instance because they found no sufficient message was ever passed to the employers of a risk to the employee's health.

On deciding if a psychological injury was reasonably foreseeable after the event, it has been held that this is "to a large extent a matter of impression" (London Borough of Islington & University College London Hospital NHS Trust EWCA Civ 596 per Buxton LJ). Therefore, all factors that would go to make up such an impression should be monitored, such as working hours, increased workload, time off sick etc. as well as specific indications of stress from employees. This is therefore a matter to be considered on the individual facts of each case.

Part-time workers
However, time actually spent at work may well be a crucial factor in some cases. It was held in the Court of Appeal case of *Hartman v. South Essex Mental Health & Community Care NHS Trust* that it would only be in exceptional circumstances that someone working for two or three days a week with limited hours would make good a claim for injury caused by stress at work.

Confidential advice / health service
There are a number of precautionary measures outlined at the end of this chapter for employers to protect themselves against workplace stress claims and, in particular, the provision of a confidential advice service was thought likely to provide a good defence in the *Sutherland* case.

It was confirmed in *Hartman* that the mere fact that an employer offered an occupational health service should not lead to the conclusion that the employer had foreseen risk of psychiatric injury due to work-related stress to any individual or class of employee. An employer could not be expected to know confidential medical information disclosed by the claimant to occupational health. However, there may be circumstances where an occupational health department's duty of care to an employee requires it to seek his or her consent to disclose information that the employer needs to know, if proper steps are to be taken for the welfare of the employee.

Stress in other civil claims

Stress now raises its head more often in claims involving bullying and harassment, disability, discrimination and constructive dismissal. Failure to recognise and address stress issues in the context of these types of claim could result in significant liability for an employer. For instance, where an employee may establish that he falls within the definition of a disabled person under the Disability Discrimination Act 1995 and an employer fails to make reasonable adjustments to the workplace for this disability, compensation would also be payable for the psychiatric or physical injuries occurring from stress suffered as a result of this.

Sixteen propositions for stress claims

A summary of the 16 propositions stated in *Sutherland v. Hatton* is provided below.

General

1. The ordinary principles of employers' liability apply.
2. There are no occupations that should be regarded as intrinsically dangerous to mental health.

Reasonable foreseeability

3. The threshold question to be answered in any workplace stress

case was stated as: "whether this kind of harm to this particular employee was reasonably foreseeable". This has two components: (a) an injury (as distinct from occupational stress) that (b) is attributable to stress at work (as distinct from other factors).

4. Foreseeability depends upon what the employer knows (or ought reasonably to know) about the individual employees.
5. Factors likely to be relevant in answering the threshold question include:
   - the nature and extent of the work done; and
   - signs from the employee of impending harm to health.
6. The employer is generally entitled to take what he is told by his employee at face value, unless he has good reason to think to the contrary.
7. To trigger a duty to take steps, the indications of impending harm to health arising from stress at work must be plain enough for any reasonable employer to realise that he should do something about it.

Duty of employers

8. The employer is in breach of duty only if he has failed to take steps that are reasonable in the circumstances.
9. The size and scope of the employer's operation, its resources and the demands it faces are relevant in deciding what is reasonable; these include the interests of other employees and the need to treat them fairly (e.g. in any redistribution of duties).
10. An employer can only be expected to take steps that are reasonable in the circumstances.

Guidelines for employers

11. An employer who offers a confidential advice service, with referral to appropriate counselling or treatment

services, is unlikely to be found in breach of duty.

12. If the only reasonable and effective step would have been to dismiss or demote the employee, the employer will not have been in breach of duty in allowing a willing employee to continue in the job.

(However, in light of the lead judgment of Lord Walker in *Barber* that there is a requirement for 'drastic action' if an employee's health is in danger, it may be said that in the absence of alternative work, where an employee was at risk, ultimately the employer's duty of care would not preclude dismissing or demoting the employee at risk.)

13. In all cases, it is necessary to identify the steps that the employer both could and should have taken before finding him in breach of his duty of care.

14. The claimant must show that the breach of duty has caused or materially contributed to the harm suffered. It is not enough to show that occupational stress alone has caused the harm; it must be attributable to a breach of an employer's duty.

Apportionment

15. Where the harm suffered has more than one cause, the employer should pay only for that proportion of the harm suffered that is attributable to his wrongdoing, unless the harm is truly indivisible. It is for the defendant to raise the question of apportionment.

16. The assessment of damages will take account of pre-existing disorder or vulnerability and of the chance that the claimant would have succumbed to a stress-related disorder in any event.

It is not the case that one or other of the tests is more important; all 16 have to be looked at in respect of each individual case.

Criteria for criminal liability

There is no specific statute or other regulation controlling stress levels permitted in the workplace; therefore broad principles of health and safety at work will be applied as set out in the Health and Safety at Work etc. Act 1974 (HSWA) and the Management of Health and Safety at Work Regulations 1999 (MHSWR).

Where no action is taken by an employer on stress, he may be deemed to have fallen short of his duty to take all reasonably practicable measures to ensure the health, safety and welfare of employees and others sharing the workplace and to create safe and healthy working systems (HSWA).

Additionally, there is the requirement to undertake risk assessments of stress and put in place appropriate preventive and protective measures to keep the employees safe from harm (MHSWR).

Any breach of an employer's statutory or regulatory duties under health and safety legislation towards his employees giving rise to criminal liability may also be relied upon by a civil claimant as evidence of the employer's breach of duty in a negligence action and, indeed, in support of a claim for constructive dismissal.

Risk assessments

West Dorset Hospitals NHS Trust was the first organisation to have an improvement notice issued against it with the requirement that it assessed and reduced the stress levels of its doctors or other employees or face court action and a potentially unlimited fine. The HSE has urged employers to carry out risk assessments and implement measures to eliminate or control workplace stress or risk criminal prosecution.

It is therefore important that risk assessments for stress are undertaken, regularly reviewed and recommended actions implemented. Unlike civil litigation, any criminal prosecution carries with it the threat of an unlimited fine and/or imprisonment.

A general risk assessment of potential 'stressors' at work should be sufficient for most businesses but should additionally take into account any discrete categories of employees, such as night workers, the young and expectant mothers. But if an employer becomes aware of an employee at specific risk or who has raised any concerns, an individual risk assessment should be carried out for them, recommendations implemented and regularly reviewed.

Health and safety policy

It is further recommended that an employer's health and safety policy set out guidance on how stress should be dealt with and a clear complaints-handling procedure. In this way a company can show that it has followed its own procedures in dealing with any complaints and implementing any actions.

Conclusion

In order to protect themselves against enforcement action as well as employee claims, employers are advised to organise risk assessments of potential stressors, to make facilities such as counselling and grievance procedures available to employees, and to show a receptive and flexible response to complaints. In addition, compliance with the HSE Management Standards / Guidance will assist in showing that an employer has met the reasonable standard of duty of care required.

Combating stress: an employer's checklist

- No employer has an absolute duty to prevent all stress, which can be

as a result of interests outside work. However, once an employee has raised the issue of stress, an employer is under a duty to investigate properly and protect the employee as far as is reasonably practicable.

- Health monitoring – both through a confidential advice line and/or regular company medicals.
- Counselling – an employer who offers a confidential advice service, with referral to appropriate counselling or treatment services, is unlikely to be found in breach of duty. This is of course relative to the problem and the service provided but is a good indication that a proactive approach by an employer can protect him from stress claims and enforcement action.
- Pre-employment health check – this may allow vulnerable potential employees to be excluded from stressful roles. At a pre-employment health assessment the primary responsibility of the occupational physician is to the employer *(Katfunde v. Abbey National and Dr Daniel* (1998) IRLR 583).
- Regular medicals – these are a useful tool in alerting employers of any risks. However, medical confidentiality has to be observed and express consent given by employees for their clinical information to be shared with employers.
- Dismissal – in the absence of alternative work, the employee deemed at risk should be dismissed or demoted.
- Written health and safety policy – clear guidance in a company's health and safety policy on how stress should be dealt with shows that the company is complying with the health and safety regulations to provide a safe working environment for employees and enables staff to follow a set procedure. It would also stand as a defence where an employee fails to disclose that he is suffering

from stress because of ignorance of a company's procedures.

■ Equally, a bullying and harassment code should be in force and there should be a clear complaints-handling procedure.

■ Risk assessments should cover all workplace risks and should therefore include stress. HSE guidance on risk assessment can be found at www.hse.gov.uk/pubns/indg163.pdf.

■ Risk assessments should be regularly reviewed and recommended actions implemented.

■ Working time – employers can combat stress by monitoring and recording employees' working time with action

being taken if the benchmark set out in the Working Time Regulations 1998 is breached.

■ Implementation of HSE Management Standards / Guidance will assist in showing that an employer has met the reasonable standard of duty of care.

See also: Discrimination, p.222; Health and safety at work, p.364; Medical records, p.491; Mental health, p.496; Occupational health, p.537; Working time, p.767

Sources of further information

As part of the general duty to keep abreast of developing knowledge and practice, employers should be aware of the HSE's stress page at www.hse.gov.uk/stress/index.htm. This includes example stress policies and the HSE's Management Standards for workplace stress.

Additional HSE guidance includes an action pack *(Real Solutions, Real People* (ISBN: 0 7176 2767 5) priced at £25.). The pack includes a guide for employers and employees alike and an introduction to the Management Standards. Other HSE guidance in the form of free leaflets include the following: *Tackling stress: the management standards approach – a short guide; Making the stress Management Standards work: How to apply the Standards in your workplace;* and *Working together to reduce stress at work: A guide for employees.* These are available at the publications section of the HSE stress web page.

The Management Standards look at six key areas (or 'risk factors') that can be causes of work-related stress: 'demands', 'control', 'support', 'relationships', 'role' and 'change'.

The standard for each area contains simple statements about good management practice that can be applied by employers.

HSE guidelines such as these are voluntary and as such are not legally binding. They do, however, have evidential value. They assist the court in the interpretation of legislation and what the reasonable standard of duty of care owed may be. Therefore compliance with these Management Standards / Guidance will assist in showing the court that an employer has met the reasonable standard of duty of care required.

Strikes

Kerry Underwood, Underwoods

Key points

- Strike action is perceived as fundamental right, but there are exceptions.
- Industrial action does not, of itself, incur criminal liability either on the part of the organiser or the participator.
- If the employee was taking part in unofficial industrial action at the time of his or her dismissal, then subject to limited exceptions, he or she has no right to complain of unfair dismissal.
- A person is not entitled to be paid for the period while he or she was on strike.

Legislation

- Trade Union and Labour Relations (Consolidation) Act 1992.
- Trade Union Reform and Employment Rights Act 1993.

Right to strike

The right, or freedom, to strike in civil law is heavily restricted. It is in effect a right to leave after giving due notice. The right to organise is generally limited to a right to organise primary, but not secondary, industrial action; that is action against an employer directly involved in the dispute, about pay and other terms and conditions of employment or about other specified employment-related matters. Article 11 of the European Convention on Human Rights confers no express right to strike – see *Ministry of Justice v. Prison Officers Association* (2008) EWHC 239 (QB).

Where the industrial action is organised by or in the name of a trade union, then the union must hold a strike ballot and give the employer formal notice of intention to take industrial action.

Criminal law

Industrial action does not, of itself, incur criminal liability either on the part of the organiser or the participator. Criminal offences committed in connection with a strike, such as threatening behaviour, assault etc., are not subject to any special rules as compared with such acts committed otherwise than in connection with a strike.

Contractual liability

Industrial action does not normally incur liability in contract at collective level, but is often a breach of contract at the individual level; that is between employer and worker. The contract-breaker, the worker, leaves him or herself open to an action for breach of contract and this can have the effect of making the organiser, usually a trade union, liable in tort, generally for one or more of the following:

- Inducing a person to break a contract;
- Interfering with business by unlawful means;
- Indirectly interfering with a contract by unlawful means;
- Intimidation; and
- Conspiracy.

In relation to liability in tort there is a statutory defence available under section 219 of the Trade Union and Labour Relations (Consolidation) Act 1992 that the act was done in "contemplation or furtherance of a trade dispute". The issue of whether industrial action is a breach of the contract of employment depends on the terms of the contract, express or implied, upon the nature of the acts done or omitted to be done and the circumstances in which the industrial action took place. However in Case C-438/05 *Viking Line* (11 December 2007) and Case C-341/05 *Laval un Partneri* (18 December 2007) the European Court of Justice held that the free movement provisions of the EC Treaty, here Articles 43 (freedom of establishment) and Article 49 (freedom to provide services) impose obligations on trade unions which may make collective action unlawful.

Unfair dismissal

This is probably the most important area of the law relating to strikes. The Trade Union and Labour Relations (Consolidation) Act 1992 differentiates between unofficial industrial action (section 237) and official industrial action (section 238) and within official action gives special treatment to 'protected' industrial action (sections 238(2B) and 238A). If the employee was taking part in unofficial industrial action at the time of his or her dismissal, then subject to limited exceptions, he or she has no right to complain of unfair dismissal.

The exceptions are:

- jury service;
- family case;
- health and safety cases;
- working time case;
- specified employee representatives;
- whistleblowing;
- flexible working; and
- dependants' emergencies.

Dismissal takes place on the date the employment actually ends unless the

contract is terminated by notice, in which case the date of the dismissal is the date when notice is given (Section 237(5)).

Industrial action is unofficial unless:

- the employee is a member of a union and his union has authorised or endorsed the action; or
- he or she is not a member of a union but the industrial action has been authorised or endorsed by at least one of the unions involved; or
- none of the participants is a member of a trade union.

The question of whether a person was a member of a union is to be determined as at the time he or she began to take part in the industrial action, but the union membership is to be disregarded if it is unconnected with the employment in question (Section 237(6)). A union will have authorised or endorsed industrial action if it has done so:

- in accordance with the union's rules; or
- by the union's leadership as defined; or
- by some lesser union official or committee, provided that the union has not disowned the industrial action in accordance with section 21.

Pay

A person is not entitled to be paid for the period while he or she was on strike. The correct amount to be deducted is the pay for the period of the strike, not the loss to the employer – see *Cooper v. Isle of wight College* (2007) EWHC 2831 (QB).

Where a person has been involved in non-strike industrial action and given only partial performance of the contract of employment the employer is entitled to make an appropriate deduction from salary – see *Spackman v. London Metropolitan University* (13 July 2007), where a 30% deduction was upheld by the County Court.

See also: Dismissal, p.233; Trade unions, p.687

Sources of further information

Trade Union and Labour Relations (Consolidation) Act 1992: www.opsi.gov.uk/acts/acts1992/ukpga_19920052_en_1

Sustainability

Steve Cooper, Butler & Young Group

Key points

Responsibility for driving sustainability issues rests with various organisations
with some powers to create legislation having been devolved to the various local
administrations; however, the principles behind the drivers for change are broadly
the same. Rapid changes in the requirements that need to be complied with have
been and will continue to be made by those organisations.

Information sources for business

DBERR and DEFRA have joined together
to support UK business by providing a
government-funded programme of free,
confidential advice aimed at increasing
profitability and reducing environmental
impact. Envirowise provides free guidance
through a telephone advice line, onsite
visits, information resources, events and a
website.

Further information on environmental
regulations can be found in various
articles on this website while the UK
environmental regulators (the Environment
Agency in England and Wales, SEPA
in Scotland and the Environment and
Heritage Service in Northern Ireland) have
formed a partnership aimed at providing
free environmental guidance for small and
medium-sized businesses throughout the
UK. Their website – netregs – provides
information on environmental law by
business type and environmental topic.

The Kyoto agreement

In 1997 in excess of 150 governments,
including that of the UK, signed up to
mandatory targets for the reduction
of greenhouse gases at the Kyoto
Summit. The commitment under the
Kyoto Protocol to reduce greenhouse
gas emissions by 12.5% by 2008-12
(when compared to 1990 levels) has been

added to by a domestic target to reduce
carbon dioxide emissions by 20% by 2010
(again by comparison with 1990 levels). A
long-term goal was contained in the 2003
Energy White Paper to reduce carbon
emissions by 60% by the year 2050.

The Climate Change Programme

The UK Government believes that
climate change is the greatest long-term
challenge facing the world today. *The
Climate Change Programme*, published in
2006, sets out their policies and priorities
for action in the UK and internationally
together with a commitment to introduce
an annual report to Parliament.

This programme indicated that the various
sectors produce the following percentages
of greenhouse gas emissions (by end user):

- Business – 39%;
- Transport – 25%;
- Domestic – 24%;
- Agriculture, Forestry and Land
  Management – 7%; and
- Public Sector – 3%.

The subsequent Climate Change and
Sustainable Energy Act 2006 placed an
obligation on the Government to report to
Parliament on greenhouse gas emissions
in the UK and on action taken by them to
reduce these emissions. The first of these

reports was laid before parliament on 26 July 2007 and the second was published and laid before Parliament on Thursday 17 July 2008.

Annex B of this second report provides information on the next steps that are to be taken and includes programmes for:

- Complete the passage of the climate change bill through Parliament in Autumn 2008;
- First Phase II auction of the EU emissions trading scheme;
- Consultation on increasing the the level of the Renewable Transport Fuel Obligation;
- Successor to the UK voluntary agreements with car manufacturers;
- Expectation of agreement of a directive on aviation and emissions trading;
- Next phase of the smarter driving campaign; and
- Bio energy capital grants scheme, Round Five.

Energy Performance Certificates and the Code for Sustainable Homes
Energy Performance Certificates are needed for commercial buildings that are being sold, rented or constructed where the building is over 2,500 m². A requirement for them to be provided for commercial buildings of any size will come into force on 1 October 2008 at which time energy certificates will need to be displayed on public buildings over 1,000 m². Energy performance certificates are currently required for the sale or construction of all houses and it is proposed that this will also be the case for those that are privately or socially rented from 1 October 2008.

It is intended that the Code for Sustainable Homes will build on this new requirement:

- by providing a step change in sustainable home building practice;
- for those aspects of sustainability that are not currently contained within Building Regulations by setting new standards; and
- for homebuilders that go beyond current Building Regulation requirements by creating a method of recognising that work.

In 2004 more than one quarter of the UK's Carbon Dioxide emissions, one of the greenhouse gases, came from the energy used in heating and lighting homes. Projecting forward the current rate of home building by 2050 one third of the homes in use may have been constructed between now and then.

The Code for Sustainable Homes is seen as a method for reducing the energy demand of these new homes by recognising good environmental practice in nine categories:

1. CO_2 emissions;
2. Water use in the home;
3. Use of materials in construction;
4. Surface water run off from the building;
5. Production of waste and recycling during construction and by the household;
6. Pollution – by the insulants used in buildings and emissions from heating systems;
7. Health and wellbeing – daylight, sound insulation, private space and lifetime homes standards;
8. Management – advice to the occupants, considerate contractors, construction site impacts, security of the home; and
9. Ecology – value of the site, enhancements to the site, protection of features, changes in the ecological value and the ratio of floor area to buildings footprint.

The resulting star rating given to the home will depend upon the level of performance achieved in the nine categories. The lowest rating, a one star home, will achieve a 10% improvement in CO_2 emissions when compared to current Building Regulations. A six star home will be a zero carbon home which is defined as having zero net emissions of CO_2 from all energy uses within the home.

The Code utilises a mix of mandatory levels of performance with the ability to obtain additional points from other sections in order to achieve a star rating. For example a one star home must have CO_2 emissions that are 10% lower than current Building Regulation requirements, have a calculated water consumption of less than 120 litres per person per day and achieve minimum levels of performance for the materials used in construction, surface water run off, site waste management and household waste storage.

However, achieving these minimum levels of performance will not provide enough points to obtain the one star rating and additional points must be obtained from higher levels of performance in these areas or by meeting some of the requirements of other categories. A six star home will need to incorporate 90% of all that is in the Code.

See also: Building Regulations, p.81; Energy Performance, p.290; Environmental Management Systems, p.296

Sources of further information

Envirowise: www.envirowise.gov.uk/

Netregs: www.netregs.gov.uk/

There is a growing demand on employers to manage buildings more efficiently, thereby saving energy in the workplace. In 2006, new responsibilities were placed on building owners, surveyors, facilities managers and tenants to tackle energy efficiency in all new buildings and when refurbishing existing buildings, under the Energy Performance of Buildings Directive and Part L of the Building Regulations. Since then, there have been several key developments affecting workplace managers and adding weight to the Government's drive to cut carbon emissions and reduce the effects of global warming.

Workplace Law Group's *Energy Performance of Buildings 2008: Special Report* provides an in-depth insight into the implications of key developments in energy management and the requirements of legislation. For more information visit www.workplacelaw.net/Bookshop/SpecialReports.

Toilets

Andrew Johnston, PHS Washrooms

Key points
Most impressions of an organisation's buildings are formed in one of three key public spaces – loos, lifts and lobbies. These are the places you get a chance to win crucial ground in the battle for the hearts and minds (and wallets) of your customers, suppliers, employees and whoever else happens to find themselves on your premises. The loo, although only a semi-public space, can make a great difference to people's perceptions. There are obvious health and safety issues that need to be addressed and certain standards to be met regarding provision of facilities, but the smart organisation will always exceed these in terms of their specification, maintenance and cleaning regimes.

Legislation
■ Environmental Protection Act (Duty of Care) Regulations 1990 (amended 1991).
■ Water Industry Act 1991.
■ Workplace (Health, Safety and Welfare) Regulations 1992.
■ Disability Discrimination Act 1995.

Standard procedures
There are a number of relevant standards appropriate to washroom provision of which managers should be aware. The provision of facilities specified by the Workplace (Health, Safety and Welfare) Regulations 1992 (the 'Regulations') is covered below. The same Regulations also specify the provision of washroom equipment to include basic minimum standards. These include the following.

Water and soap dispensers
Regulation 21 of the Regulations states that "washing facilities ... must include soap or other suitable means of cleaning". In addition facilities must provide "a supply of clean hot and cold, or warm, water (which shall be running water so far as is practicable)".

Warm air dryers and paper dispensers
Regulation 21 of the Regulations states that "washing facilities ... must include towels or other suitable means of drying".

Sanitary disposal
The Approved Code of Practice for Regulation 21 advises that "in the case of water closets used by women, suitable means should be provided for the disposal of sanitary dressings".

Toilet roll holders
The Approved Code of Practice for Regulation 21 advises that in the case of water closets, "toilet paper in a holder or dispenser ... should be provided".

Disability Discrimination Act 1995
There are a number of other provisions that must be applied. The most high profile of these is compliance with the Disability Discrimination Act 1995, which is essential in giving access to washroom facilities. There are some very enlightened examples of this indeed, with at least one high profile and very large public building specified with disabled toilets in a ratio of 1:12.

In terms of waste disposal, under the Environmental Protection Act (Duty of Care) Regulations 1990 (amended 1991) there is a duty of care for any person responsible for controlled waste in their working environment to ensure that the waste they produce is handled and disposed of in a secure and correct manner. This is a legal responsibility and breaching of the duty of care is a criminal offence.

So, all waste should be stored and disposed of responsibly. Waste should only be handled by individuals or businesses that are authorised to deal with it. A record should be kept of all waste received or transferred through a system of Waste Transfer Notes (a document which must be completed and accompany any transfer of waste between different holders and held for two years).

In addition, under the Water Industry Act 1991, no items should be flushed that could cause a blockage within the sewer or drain. Complying with standards is one thing, but there are good reasons to see compliance merely as the minimum standard people expect. That is why many organisations, especially those with a vested interest in promoting hygiene such as restaurants and bars, go way beyond what is demanded of them by law or common practice.

People – including customers, employees, suppliers and other visitors – are very likely to judge an organisation on their impressions of the washrooms. This is the area that legislation sometimes fails to reach and which can only be achieved by looking at the design, specification, cleaning and maintenance of washrooms intelligently and in a structured way.

The environment
As well as standards dealing with hygiene and health and safety, there is a growing onus on organisations to treat water management as an important ethical concern. The efficient use of water plays a key role in environmental policy and one that will grow in relevance as the impact of climate change grows. Statistics from Envirowise have shown that offices alone waste around 310 million litres of water every working day and has estimated that a very few, simple and inexpensive measures could save industry as much as £304m a year. There are a number of such steps that building managers can take, both at the initial installation of washroom facilities and at retrofit, to ensure that water is used as efficiently as possible to both save money and help the environment. These can range from the straightforward to the more sophisticated.

At the most simple level, one of the most effective is a product such as an inexpensive water saving device which, when placed into a cistern, can save as much as a fifth of the water used by toilets. When you consider that around 86% of the 35 litres each office worker in the UK uses each day is simply flushed away, this can represent an enormous saving. Carelessly or maliciously left-on taps can also be a serious source of water wastage as well as causing floods, so it can be important to use push-action taps that deliver a set amount of water for hand washing.

A tap left on while brushing your teeth can use as much as ten litres of water, so imagine the impact of a tap left running indefinitely. It's obviously better to consider this during an installation, but some systems can be retrofitted to a wide range of tap types.

Automatic flushing urinals are extremely useful as a way of maintaining hygiene and are usually designed to be as efficient as possible in terms of the amount of water they use. Nevertheless they can also be extremely wasteful of water when the number of flushes is out of sync with the number of people using the facility. To help counter this, an intelligent water management system can regulate the flushing of the urinal to match the number of people using the washroom. The best systems work by using an infra-red sensor to count the numbers of people using a facility and adjust the flush rate accordingly. In sleep mode, the system maintains hygiene standards by flushing once every eight hours.

As well as addressing environmental concerns, the system also helps to save money; an average of around 70% when compared against an uncontrolled cistern and up to 30% against an unintelligent system. Defra is able to make recommendations about the best systems. Buyers should also look for products designed to have a minimal impact on the environment even when their main function is not environmental protection. These can include urinal sleeves which use enzyme-based bio-blocks rather than chemicals. The best designs will also minimise smells and so help to reduce water usage. It may also be worthwhile asking for any local by-laws regarding water management.

Allocation and the gender gap

The problem of allocating enough washrooms for people has always been with us. At the Great Exhibition of 1851, the engineer, George Jennings (who was also instrumental in introducing public conveniences to London and other cities and helped to develop the modern WC) was tasked with providing large scale 'elimination facilities' for the public for the first time. The toilets he introduced were reportedly used some 830,000 times over the 141 days of the exhibition, leading Jennings to acknowledge "the necessity of making similar provisions for the public whenever large numbers are congregated to alleviate the sufferings which must be endured by all, but more especially by females by account of the want of them."

This can be a sensitive issue. It's certainly a universal one. In 2005, New York introduced the Restroom Equity Bill. 2005 was an election year, and the issue, dubbed Potty Parity by local newspapers, became a significant feminist issue, driven by Mayor Bloomberg. The Bill is less about parity and more about recognising that women need more toilets than men so the legislation requires a two-to-one ratio for women's toilet facilities in new public venues including bars, restaurants and concert halls although venue owners can circumvent the rule by making all such facilities unisex.

In the UK, potty parity is enthroned to a certain extent by the Workplace (Health, Safety and Welfare) Regulations 1992, supported by a Code of Practice which gives precise details regarding the numbers of toilets and hand basins and

Table 1: Number of toilets and washbasins for mixed use (or women only)

Number of people at work	Number of toilets	Number of washbasins
1 – 5	1	1
6 – 25	2	2
26 – 50	3	3
51 – 75	4	4
76 – 100	5	5

Table 2: Toilets used by men only

Number of men at work	Number of toilets	Number of urinals
1 – 15	1	1
16 – 30	2	1
31 – 45	2	2
46 – 60	3	2
61 – 75	3	3
76 – 90	4	3
91 – 100	4	4

so on based on the numbers and sexes of employees. Again the Regulations try to ensure that women have access to more washrooms than men (see Table 1 and 2).

Conclusion

The Regulations are a useful guide. It is always important that you look at the wider picture when you are looking into the provision of these facilities. It is essential that you understand the culture of the organisation or bar or restaurant or venue or wherever before you specify anything. You can often make a good case for providing more and better facilities than you are advised to. Less is definitely not more where washrooms are concerned.

The UK Regulations also touch on the unisex issue which has been with us for some time but still seems to be unresolved. Whilst the UK regulations do not specifically mention unisex toilets, they do state "specific facilities for males and females may need to be provided, except where each toilet is in a separate room capable of being secured from the inside". The demand for unisex toilets is obviously still largely based on pressure of space but it is also dependent on new cultural attitudes that allow us to view them as acceptable. The consensus seems to be that they have their place but it is

incredibly important to be aware of the sensitivities surrounding their use.

Changing work practices can put all sorts of pressure on infrastructure like toilets and lifts, but you have to look at that on a case by case basis. As the office assumes more of a social and networking role for mobile employees, the more washroom facilities take on the qualities we expect from those we encounter socially. They are specified to a higher standard, there are more of them and they are cleaned more often.

Changing space standards, changing attitudes, changing social norms and the greater number of women in the workforce are continuing to have a profound effect on washrooms. People expect better facilities and they will often make a judgement about a firm or a venue based on what they encounter in the loo.

See also: Accessible environments, p.50; Building Regulations, p.81; Disability legislation, p.209; Discrimination, p.222; Human rights, p.413; Water fittings, p.734; Water quality, p.738

Trade unions

Pinsent Masons Employment Group

Key points

A trade union is an organisation consisting of workers whose main purpose is the regulation of relations between the workers and their employers.

Employers are prevented from offering inducements to their employees not to be a member of a trade union, not to take part in the activities of a trade union, not to make use of the services of a trade union and not to give up the right to have their terms and conditions of employment determined by a collective agreement. Further protection is provided to ensure that employees should not suffer detrimental actions for being a union member or using a union's services.

Legislation

- Trade Union and Labour Relations (Consolidation) Act 1992.
- Trade Union Reform and Employment Rights Act 1993.
- Employment Relations Act 1999.
- Employment Relations Act 2004.

Trade unions and collective agreements
In some industries, negotiated collective agreements exist relating to pay and terms of employment, and in some circumstances those agreements can also form part of the workers' contracts of employment.

A collective agreement may not always be enforceable between the union and the employer. However, the terms of a collective agreement may become incorporated into an individual employee's contract of employment, and so themselves become terms and conditions of employment.

Collective agreements can be incorporated if the employment contract expressly says so, or if the custom and practice in the industry is that the collective agreements are impliedly incorporated. However, some parts of collective agreements are not appropriate for incorporation.

Generally, once the terms of a collective agreement are incorporated into a contract of employment, they become terms of the contract and in some cases can remain in force even if the original collective agreement terminates.

Trade union recognition
The Employment Relations Act 1999 (ERA) created rules for trade unions to be recognised by employers on a statutory basis as long as certain conditions are fulfilled (see Statutory recognition below).

In general terms, however, 'recognition' of a trade union is important in a number of ways. If a union is recognised, employers will have certain duties, for example:

- to consult with the union and its representatives on collective redundancy situations;
- to disclose information for collective bargaining purposes; and
- to allow time off to employees engaged in trade union activities or duties.

In addition, employers are under a duty to provide information to and consult with recognised trade unions concerning TUPE transfers.

Statutory recognition

In certain circumstances, even outside the provisions of the ERA, trade union recognition can take place voluntarily. An employer can voluntarily recognise a trade union, either expressly by stating so or by clear conduct which shows an implied agreement to recognise that union.

Accordingly, an employer that actually enters into negotiation with a trade union about terms and conditions of employment, conditions of work, employee discipline, trade union membership, etc., may be deemed to recognise the union voluntarily.

However, the statutory procedure also allows the trade union to apply for recognition so that it can conduct collective bargaining regarding pay, hours and holidays. The procedures are complex and are set out in Schedule A1 to the Trade Union and Labour Relations (Consolidation) Act 1992 (TULRA), the legislation containing the recognition machinery introduced by Schedule 1 to ERA. To trigger the statutory procedure, the trade union must apply to the employer in respect of the workers who wish to constitute a bargaining unit (BU). A BU is determined by a number of factors which may result in a sector of the workforce being identified as a BU even though they may not have been the subject of separate negotiations in the past or even where the employer wishes to negotiate with the whole workforce.

The request to the employer must:

■ be in writing;
■ identify the relevant trade union and the BU; and

■ state that the request is made under paragraph eight of Schedule A1 to TULRA.

Further, the trade union must be independent and the employer must employ at least 21 workers.

The employer should, within ten working days of receiving the written request from the trade union, accept the request, reject it or offer to negotiate.

If the parties agree on the BU and that the trade union should be recognised in respect of the BU, that is the end of the statutory procedure.

However, if the employer rejects the trade union's request outright or fails to respond, the union can apply to the Central Arbitration Committee (CAC).

The employer or the trade union may request the Arbitration, Conciliation and Advisory Service (ACAS) to assist in conducting negotiations. If the employer proposes that ACAS assistance be requested, and the union fails to respond within ten working days of the proposal or rejects such a proposal, no application to the CAC can be made. This is provided that the proposal is made by the employer within ten working days of having informed the union of its willingness to negotiate.

The trade union may approach the CAC if no agreement is reached between the parties, and if the employer fails to respond to the request within the ten-working-day period. If the employer informs the union within ten working days that it does not accept the request but is willing to negotiate, then there is an additional 20 days for negotiation, starting the day after the first ten-day period ends.

If no agreement is reached at the end of the additional 20 day period, or if the parties agree a BU, but do not agree that the trade union is to be recognised, the trade union may apply to the CAC. On a practical note, if the employer reaches an agreement with the trade union that a ballot on recognition can take place, it may wish to include an undertaking by the trade union that the latter will not make another request for recognition for a period of time.

The CAC may accept the request if the initial request for recognition was valid and is on the face of it 'admissible'. The CAC will normally decide within ten working days of it receiving the request whether it may accept the claim. The CAC decides if the application is admissible by asking whether the trade union has 10% membership and whether the majority is likely to be in favour of recognition.

If the CAC accepts an application, but the BU has not been agreed, the employer must, within five working days, supply certain information about his workforce to the union and the CAC. If the BU has not been agreed by the parties, the CAC will try to help the parties to agree a BU within 20 working days of it giving notice of its acceptance. If the claim is not accepted by the CAC, this is an end to the statutory procedure.

If an agreement is reached between the parties, or if the CAC determines the BU, and this BU is different from the one originally proposed, then the validity test must be applied again.

If the CAC is satisfied that more than 50% of the workers constituting the BU are members of the trade union, it must usually issue a declaration that "the trade union is recognised as entitled to conduct collective bargaining on behalf of the workers constituting the BU", but may hold a ballot if any of the following three factors apply:

1. it is in the interests of good industrial relations; or
2. a significant number of the trade union members within the BU informs the CAC that they do not wish the trade union to conduct collective bargaining on their behalf; or
3. evidence leads the CAC to doubt whether a significant number of trade union members really want the trade union to conduct collective bargaining on their behalf.

If any of these conditions apply, or if the CAC is not satisfied that the majority of the workers in the BU are members of the union, then the CAC must arrange to hold a secret recognition ballot in which the workers constituting the BU are asked whether they want the trade union to conduct collective bargaining on their behalf.

Within ten working days of receiving the CAC notice, the trade union, or the trade union and the employer together, may notify the CAC that they do not want a ballot to be held. If a ballot is held in any event or if no objection is made, the ballot will be conducted by a Qualified Independent Person (QIP), who is appointed by the CAC. A QIP can, for example, be a practising solicitor.

The ballot must take place within 20 working days from the day the QIP is appointed, or such longer period as the CAC may decide. It may be conducted at a workplace, by post or by a combination of these two.

The CAC must inform the employer and the trade union of the result of the ballot as soon as it is reasonably practicable after it has itself been so informed by the QIP.

If a majority of the workers voting in the ballot, and at least 40% of the workers constituting the BU, vote in favour of recognition, the CAC must issue a declaration that the trade union is recognised as entitled to conduct collective bargaining on behalf of the BU.

The parties will then have a 30-working-day negotiation period in which they may negotiate with a view to agreeing a method by which they will conduct collective bargaining. If no agreement is reached, the employer or the trade union may apply to the CAC for assistance.

If an agreement still cannot be reached, the CAC must take a decision.

The Code of Practice: *Access and Unfair Practices during Recognition and Derecognition Ballots* gives guidance regarding the union's access to workers during the period of recognition ballots and the avoidance of unfair practices whilst campaigning during that period. Whilst the Code imposes no legal obligations, its provisions are admissible in evidence and will be taken into account by any court, Tribunal or the CAC where relevant.

> *See also*: Employee consultation, p.269; Health and safety consultation, p.372; Redundancy, p.618; Strikes, p.677; TUPE, p.697

Sources of further information

Central Arbitration Committee (CAC): www.cac.gov.uk/

ACAS: www.acas.org.uk

Training

Jill Bell, Anderson Strathern LLP

Key points
- Well trained staff can help businesses retain a competitive edge.
- Training staff in health and safety, basic employment law and equality and diversity issues will help reduce risk to the business.
- There is a statutory defence open to employers in discrimination legislation and, although it is a difficult test to meet, training in equality and diversity is one of the things that businesses can do to help them meet their obligations.

Legislation
- Health and Safety at Work etc. Act 1974.
- Sex Discrimination Act 1975 s41(3).
- Race Relations Act 1976 s32(3).
- Disability Discrimination Act 1995 s58(5).
- Race Relations (Amendment) Act 2000.
- Employment Equality (Religion or Belief) Regulations 2003 Reg. 22(3).
- Employment Equality (Sexual Orientation) Regulations 2003 Reg. 22(3).
- Disability Discrimination Act 2005.
- Employment Equality (Age) Regulations 2006 Reg. 25(3).
- Equality Act 2006.
- Corporate Manslaughter and Corporate Homicide Act 2007.

Why train your staff?
A business' most important resource is its employees. Giving employees the tools to enable them to excel is one way of making sure that they remain highly motivated and committed. Well-trained staff can be key to businesses achieving improved quality and increased productivity.

Well trained staff will give a business that competitive edge. Proper staff training will, of course, also help businesses manage risk. So, in terms of workplace law, where are the key areas where training will be of greatest benefit?

Health and safety
Every employer has a legal duty to ensure, so far as is reasonably practicable, the health, safety and welfare at work of all its employees. A breach of health and safety regulations can result in an employee being injured (with the possibility of a personal injury claim against the employer to follow). Even if no one is injured, a breach may also expose the business, and/or its responsible officers, to the risk of criminal prosecution.

This duty towards an employee specifically extends (HSWA s.2(2)(c)) to the provision of such information, instruction, training and supervision as is necessary to ensure the employee's heath and safety at work. A failure to provide such training etc. is an offence in its own right, and can of itself result in a criminal charge.

It is therefore essential that an employer trains its employees, where appropriate, in relation to matters such as lifting and manual handling and the proper operation of plant and machinery. And, of course, it follows that the provision of such training reduces risk for both employee and employer, all the more relevant since the coming into force of the Corporate Manslaughter and Corporate Homicide Act 2007.

An employer's duty to safeguard the health, safety and welfare of its employees extends to mental, as well as physical, health. Unreasonable stress at work can adversely impact upon the health of employees. Ensuring that staff are equipped with the skills to enable them to carry out their jobs can help to reduce stress. However, managers also need to be trained to identify signs of stress and to find ways of reducing it.

Basic employment law for managers
The increasing complexity of employment law can leave employers exposed if managers do not have a basic understanding of the main requirements of current employment legislation. The absence of such knowledge can lead to a decision to discipline or dismiss being made which may not stand up to scrutiny in an Employment Tribunal. There are therefore certain key areas where training for managers is required if a business is going to avoid exposure to possible claims.

In the first instance, managers need to be aware of the importance of the contract of employment and the basic statutory rights of an employee.

The procedures adopted by an employer are vital to the fairness of any decision made to discipline or dismiss an employee so every manager should be trained in the nature and application of the business' grievance and disciplinary procedures and should understand the basic requirements for conducting a fair and reasonable disciplinary process (*see 'Disciplinary and grievance procedures', p.216*).

Managers should also be aware of the potentially fair reasons for dismissal. They need to know what they should take into account when considering an appropriate sanction and what evidence they require to justify the decision that is taken.

It is also useful for managers to be aware of the potential costs to the business – in terms of money, time and damage to reputation – of not complying with current employment law requirements.

Equality and diversity
Increasingly, employers are becoming aware of the benefits of training their staff at all levels in equality and diversity issues. Included in this should be a basic grounding in discrimination law.

A key time of risk for employers can be during recruitment and selection where a lack of sound reasoning or inconsistent practices may leave a business exposed to accusations of bias. As the number of discrimination claims continues to rise, many organisations already make it compulsory for staff to attend recruitment and selection training. Part of this should be to ensure that all staff – not just managers – have a general awareness of the six prohibited grounds of unlawful discrimination.

In each piece of discrimination legislation (see above) there is a statutory defence open to an employer accused of discrimination. However, in order to establish such a defence, the employer has to be able to say that it took "such steps as were reasonably practicable" to prevent its employee doing whatever discriminatory act is being complained of. The bar for this test is set high. To have any prospect of being able to clear it, the employer will, at the very least, require to:

- have well drafted Policies and Procedures which are clearly communicated to its staff;
- ensure that staff are trained in the application of those Policies and Procedures; and
- train in equality and diversity issues more generally.

This training should include the provision of update sessions to ensure that knowledge and understanding is kept current.

All of this needs to be in place and operating consistently before an employer has any prospect of successfully making out a statutory defence.

Public Sector Duties

All public authorities have duties under the Race Relations (Amendment) Act 2000, the Disability Discrimination Act 2005 and the Equality Act 2006 to eliminate discrimination and promote equality of opportunity. In their supporting Equality Schemes, many organisations have made training of their staff a key element in meeting their obligations under these Acts. Having committed themselves to such a course of action, it is vitally important that those in the public sector meet their obligations. A failure to do so may lead to an Employment Tribunal being invited, in any discrimination claim, to consider that a lack of regard for equal opportunities has been shown. This could then lead to the establishment of an evidential basis for inferring discrimination.

Many public sector organisations are also using their procurement processes to meet their statutory duties to promote equality of opportunity. Those who have expressed an interest in providing services to such organisations may now be asked to demonstrate their own anti-discrimination practices and policies. It is therefore not unusual to be asked, for example, if all managers undergo compulsory training in equality and diversity. Apart from the obvious downside to the business of not providing such training, a negative answer can now also mean a lost opportunity. It is therefore becoming increasingly important for businesses looking for new opportunities to make sure they retain the competitive edge by putting such training in place.

See also: Bullying and harassment, p.95; Discrimination, p.222; Recruitment and selection, p.607; Workplace health, safety and welfare, p.772

Sources of further information

Workplace Law Training specialises in providing training and development in the areas of HR and employment law, health and safety, and premises management. We provide training in our own right, but are also approved by a number of leading professional institutes to teach accredited training programmes under their syllabus – notably the CIPD, IOSH, and NEBOSH. We run courses throughout the UK for a wide range of clients both in the public and private sectors. Our team of highly qualified trainers and consultants all have practical experience in the workplace as well as sound legal knowledge. We pride ourselves on our friendly, professional teaching style. For more information visit www.workplacelaw.net/ training/traininghome.

Trespassers and squatters

Joseph Murphy, Pinsent Masons

Key points

- A trespasser or squatter is a person who occupies land without the owner's consent. This extends to the airspace above land and to below ground level.
- The recommended remedy is for the landowner to obtain a court order to require the trespasser to leave. Self-help is not advisable as it is easy to commit an offence under the Criminal Law Act 1977. The police have rights to arrest trespassers in some cases but rarely use them.
- Trespassers have certain rights even though they are occupying land without the owner's permission.

Steps available to a landowner

Police

The police have powers to arrest and remove trespassers or squatters in certain circumstances:

- If there is evidence that a squatter has used force to break into a building – e.g. a witness has seen the squatter breaking a lock or window – then the police can arrest the squatter on suspicion of causing criminal damage. Once the squatters have been removed, the landowner can re-secure the premises.
- The police have powers to arrest a person for a breach of the peace and/or for the offence of aggravated trespass under sections 68 and 69 of the Criminal Justice and Public Order Act 1994. However, while the police may be prepared to use their powers in the case of disruptive trespassers who are seeking to prevent a lawful activity, they are less likely to do so in the more usual situation where land is occupied by passive squatters.

In practice the police tend not to get involved until a court order has been obtained from the civil courts.

Self-help

A landowner is entitled to use reasonable force to prevent a person from committing an act of trespass on his land. However, the use of reasonable force is not usually appropriate because of the following factors:

- It is a criminal offence under section 6(1) of the Criminal Law Act 1977 for a person to use or threaten violence to secure entry if there is someone present on the property who is opposed to entry. Violence includes violence to property as well as to persons and so an owner who smashes a window or a lock to gain access where there are trespassers in the building can commit a criminal offence even if he is the owner of the building.
- What constitutes reasonable force is a question of fact and degree and gives rise to considerable uncertainty.
- The use of any force can cause a situation to degenerate into violence.

Court order

There is a special procedure to obtain a possession order against trespassers or squatters. Generally a claim must be started in the County Court for the District in which the land is situated although in exceptional circumstances the claim can be brought in the High Court. Generally a hearing date will be given when the original application is issued by the court.

The trespassers must be served, in the case of residential property, not less than five working days before the hearing date and in the case of all other land not less than two working days before the hearing date.

Where the names of the trespassers are not known, the claim will brought against 'Persons Unknown' and service can be effected by attaching the claim form and any witness statements to the main door or some other part of the building where it is clearly visible, and by placing it through the letter box in a sealed transparent envelope addressed to the occupiers. Where the premises are not residential, service may be effected by placing stakes (to which the relevant documents are attached) on the land at prominent positions, again in sealed transparent envelopes addressed to the occupiers.

When a possession order has been obtained in the County Court, the landowner may have the matter transferred to the High Court for enforcement. This is by way of a High Court Enforcement Officer. This is more costly than enforcing through a bailiff, but generally ensures that enforcement will take place in a matter of days rather than weeks. There is also a procedure to obtain interim possession orders. The court issues the claim form and the application for the interim possession order, setting a date for the hearing not less than three days after the date of issue. All documents have to be served within 24 hours of the issue of the application.

If an interim possession order is granted, the defendant will be required to vacate

the premises within 24 hours, and it is a criminal offence if he does not. There are two potential difficulties with the interim possession proceedings. First, having made an interim possession order, the court sets a date for a hearing; hence there is a need for a second attendance at court. Second, it is not possible to get a court bailiff to enforce an interim possession order; hence, if the trespassers do not vacate the premises and the police cannot be persuaded to assist, it will be necessary to wait until after the second court hearing to obtain a warrant of possession such that the court bailiff will assist.

Squatters' rights

Surprising though it may seem, a person who is trespassing on another person's land does have certain limited rights. These rights have changed following the coming into force of the Land Registration Act 2002 on 13 October 2003:

- A person who has occupied another person's land without permission and has excluded the landowner from that land (e.g. by enclosing the land with a fence) for a period of 12 years prior to 13 October 2003 can become the legal landowner of the land he has unlawfully occupied.
- In order to become the legal owner, the possession must be obvious to the true owner of the land.
- If the landowner sells that land in the next three years up to 13 October 2006, the new owner will still be bound by the claim of the squatter. After that date, the squatter's claim will only survive a sale of the land if he is in actual occupation of the land in question.
- Following 13 October 2003, the squatter only needs to prove possession of the land for ten years.

However, the Land Registration Act 2002 has introduced a new three-part test that the squatter must pass to claim legal ownership of the land. It is expected that this will make it easier for the landowner to prevent the squatter from replacing him as the legal owner of the land even though the squatter has been in possession for the required ten years.

■ Adverse possession most frequently happens when an adjoining landowner extends his garden. However, it does occasionally occur with much bigger parcels of land and buildings. Consequently, once evidence of an encroachment or squatter comes to light, a landowner should take prompt action.

■ It is a criminal offence for a person to use or threaten violence to secure entry to a property occupied by a squatter if the squatter is opposed to that entry (Criminal Law Act 1977, section 6(1)). In practice this means that a landowner cannot force entry to a building unless he is satisfied that the squatter is not actually in the building at that time.

■ A landowner owes a limited duty of care to a trespasser and may be liable in damages for a trespasser injured as a result of a hazard on the land. This is particularly the case in respect of children.

The UK law in relation to adverse possession will not infringe human rights.

See also: Human rights, p.413; Landlord and tenant: possession issues, p.444

Sources of further information

Criminal Justice and Public Order Act 1994: www.opsi.gov.uk/acts/acts1994/Ukpga_19940033_en_1.htm

Land Registration Act 2002: www.opsi.gov.uk/acts/acts2002/20020009.htm

TUPE

Pinsent Masons Employment Group

Key points
One of the biggest employment law issues for workplace managers is the impact of the Transfer of Undertakings (Protection of Employment) Regulations 2006 (TUPE 2006) on the sale of a business or on a change of service provider. TUPE 2006 came into force in April 2006 and repealed and replaced the Transfer of Undertakings (Protection of Employment) Regulations 1981 (TUPE 1981). Where TUPE 2006 applies, it provides that contracts of employment and associated liabilities transfer by operation of law from the outgoing employer or service provider to the incoming employer or service provider.

Legislation
- Acquired Rights Directive 2001 (2001/23/ EC).
- Pensions Act 2004.
- Transfer of Undertakings (Protection of Employment) Regulations 2006.

Does TUPE apply?
TUPE 2006 applies to "a transfer of an undertaking, business or part of an undertaking or business situated immediately before the transfer in the United Kingdom to another person where there is a transfer of an economic entity which retains its identity (a 'business transfer')." Whether there has been a business transfer is not always straightforward. The key questions are:

- Is there any undertaking or entity?
- Does the undertaking retain its identity after the transfer?
- Has there been a change in employer?

The law in this area is notoriously uncertain, but there will ordinarily be a business transfer if there is a transfer of significant assets from the old employer to the new employer, or where a substantial proportion of the workforce transfers

in terms of skill and number. Case law suggests that the incoming employer cannot simply refuse to take on staff to avoid the application of TUPE.

In each case a general review of a number of key indicators is necessary to determine whether there has been a business transfer. These include:

- the type of undertaking being transferred;
- whether tangible assets (such as buildings, property, etc.) are transferred;
- whether intangible assets (such as goodwill) are transferred;
- whether the majority of employees are taken on by the new employer;
- whether customers are transferred;
- the degree of similarity between the activities carried on before and after the transfer; and
- the period for which activities cease (if at all).

TUPE also applies in a service provision change. A service provision change covers situations where a contract to provide a client (public or private sector) with a business service, e.g. office cleaning, workplace catering, etc., is:

- awarded to a contractor ('contracted out' or 'outsourced');
- re-let to a new contractor on subsequent re-tendering ('reassigned'); or
- ended with the bringing 'in house' of the service activities in question ('contracted in' or 'insourced').

There will not be a service provision change where:

- the contract is wholly or mainly for the supply of goods for the client's use;
- the activities are carried out in connection with a single event or task of short-term duration;
- there is no identifiable grouping of employees providing the service; or
- any organised grouping does not have, as its principal purpose, the provision of services to a particular client e.g. where employees provide services to a number of clients.

The original employer or service provider is known as the 'transferor' whereas the new employer or service provider to whom the business or contract is transferred is known as the 'transferee'.

Implications of TUPE 2006

A summary of the principal implications of TUPE 2006 is as follows:

- Employees who were assigned immediately before the transfer to the relevant business / service become employees of the transferee.
- The terms and conditions of their employment transfer to the transferee. All contractual terms transfer, including certain rights relating to occupational pension schemes.
- In broad terms, liabilities in relation to the transferring employees transfer to the transferee.
- Changes to terms and conditions of the transferring employees will be void if the sole or principal reason for

the change is the transfer itself or a reason connected with the transfer which is not an economic, technical or organisational reason (an 'ETO reason') entailing a change in the workforce.
- Any employee dismissals will be automatically unfair where the sole or principal reason for the dismissal is the transfer itself or a reason connected with the transfer which is not an ETO reason entailing a change in the workforce.
- Collective agreements and trade union recognition in respect of transferring employees usually transfer to the transferee.
- Obligations exist for both parties to inform and (in certain circumstances) to consult with employee representatives. Both transferor and transferee are jointly and severally liable for any failure by the transferor to inform and consult.
- Obligation on the transferor to provide the transferee with certain specified information about the transferring employees (e.g. their identity and age), known as employee liability information, at least 14 days before completion of the transfer.
- Right to make permitted variations to terms and conditions of employment on the transfer of an insolvent business provided the changes are designed to safeguard employment opportunities by ensuring the survival of the undertaking and the changes are agreed with appropriate representatives of the employees.

Which employees transfer?

Only those assigned to the business or service that is subject to the relevant transfer will transfer under TUPE 2006.

The key questions will be the amount of time they spend working for the business or providing the service, whether they are part of the organisational framework *~...*

COU...

(both together)

...sferor

...ne

...undertaking is

...oper investigation and
due diligence on the part of the transferee
can sort out whether such potentially
undesirable employees have been
'dumped' into the business.

Employees have the right to object to
transferring to a new employer. However,
if they exercise this right, their employment
terminates immediately. There will be
no dismissal and no resignation and
accordingly they will have no right to claim
compensation as a result. An exception
is that the employee would still have the
right to claim constructive dismissal if the
employer commits a repudiatory breach of
contract or because of actual or planned
detrimental changes to his terms and
conditions.

The worker must be an employee of the
transferor (not a self-employed contractor).

Changing terms and conditions
Changes to terms and conditions are void
(i.e. ineffective) if the sole or principal
reason is the transfer itself or a reason
connected with the transfer that is not
an ETO reason entailing changes in the
workforce.

Changes to terms and conditions are
potentially effective (i.e. effective, subject
to being agreed between the parties) if the
sole or principal reason is not the transfer
itself but is a reason connected with the

transfer that is an ETO reason entailing
changes in the workforce. One of the
predominant reasons for changing
terms and conditions is to harmonise
terms and conditions; in normal
circumstances this will not qualify as an
ETO reason.

There is no particular time period
following which a change will no longer be
connected to the transfer. It will simply be
a matter of fact as to whether the causal
link has been broken.

One way of circumventing this difficulty
is to terminate employment and to re-
engage on revised terms. If an employee
is dismissed for a reason connected to
the transfer, that dismissal is automatically
unfair. The employee would then have
the right to claim unfair dismissal. So this
route is only viable with the consent of the
employee.

Legal advice should be sought to manage
any change to terms and conditions the
reason for which could be considered to
relate to the transfer.

Information and consultation
Both the transferor and the transferee
must provide information and, if necessary,
consult with 'appropriate representatives'
(i.e. trade unions if they exist, or elected
employee representatives) of any
employees affected by the transfer.

The transferor and transferee must provide
the following information in writing to
the appropriate representatives of their
respective affected employees:

- confirmation that the transfer is to take
  place;
- when it will take place;
- the reasons for it;
- the 'legal, economic and social
  implications' of the transfer;
- any 'measures' that the transferor
  envisages taking towards the affected

employees (if there are no such measures, that should be made clear); and

- any 'measures' that the transferee envisages taking towards the affected employees (again, if there are no such measures, that should be made clear).

The transferee is under a duty to give information to the transferor as to the measures it intends to take in relation to the affected employees. If there are no 'measures' then there is no need to consult. Given the wide interpretation of 'measures' it is rare that there will be no need to consult. The information must be given sufficiently in advance of the transfer to enable proper consultation to take place if necessary. The consultation must be with a view to seeking agreement.

If either employer fails to inform and consult in compliance with TUPE, the representatives may present a complaint to an Employment Tribunal within three months of the completion of the transfer.

If the Tribunal finds that the complaint is well founded, it may order the employer who has failed to comply with the duty to pay appropriate compensation to affected employees. The amount of compensation will be that which the Tribunal considers just and equitable having regard to the seriousness of the failure of the employer in question to comply with their duties, and will not exceed an amount equal to 13 weeks' gross pay per employee. This is uncapped.

TUPE 2006 differs from TUPE 1981 in that it provides for the transferor and transferee to be jointly and severally liable for any award of compensation made by an Employment Tribunal for failure by the transferor to comply with the information and consultation requirements. The rationale on making the two parties jointly and severally liable is that, if such a liability were to pass wholly to the transferee, there would arguably be little or no incentive for the transferor to comply with the relevant information and consultation requirements.

See also: Contractors, p.160; Dismissal, p.233; Employee consultation, p.269; Employment Tribunals, p.285; Redundancy, p.618; Trade unions, p.687

Sources of further information

Workplace Law Group's ***TUPE Transfers 2007: Rights and Responsibilities Special Report*** is aimed at people who have to deal with TUPE issues on a regular basis, and sets out what the Transfer of Undertakings (Protection of Employment) Regulations (TUPE) 2006 legislation is intended to do, what it actually does and how the process may be managed. The report defines exactly what and who is transferred in a TUPE transfer (and what isn't), what the roles and responsibilities are of the transferor and transferee, and how the whole process should be managed. For more information visit www.workplacelaw.net/Bookshop/SpecialReports.

Vehicles at work

Kathryn Gilbertson, Greenwoods Solicitors LLP

Key points

- There are many specific industries where vehicles are designed and used for specific workplace tasks. These are beyond the scope of this chapter.
- Employers who need to provide vehicles as part of their safe systems of work must ensure that they put appropriate control measures in place.
- The safe system of work should include:
  - the workplace (vehicle routes, provision for pedestrians, signage);
  - vehicles (safety features, good maintenance);
  - employees (driver training, traffic hazard briefing, competence); and
  - vehicle activities (loading and unloading, refuelling or recharging, reversing, tipping, sheeting and unsheeting).

Legislation

- Health and Safety at Work etc. Act 1974.
- Workplace (Health, Safety and Welfare) Regulations 1992.
- Traffic Signs Regulations and General Directions 1994.
- Provision and Use of Work Equipment Regulations 1998.
- Road Traffic (General) Act 1999.
- Road Transport (Safety and Traffic Management) Act 1999.
- Management of Health and Safety at Work Regulations 1999.
- Heath Act 2006.
- Smoke Free (Exemptions and Vehicles) Regulations 2007.

Statutory requirements

An employer's principal legal duty is, so far as is reasonably practicable, to provide and maintain a safe system of work and to take all reasonably practicable precautions to ensure the health and safety of all the workers in the workplace.

The Management of Health and Safety at Work Regulations 1999 require that all employers assess the risks to the health and safety of their employees and of anyone who may be affected by their work activity. The risk assessment process should cover the following:

- Identification of all the hazards involving vehicles – moving vehicles, causing injury or damage by driving, loading and unloading or refuelling or recharging vehicles, maintenance;
- Consideration of the risks involved;
- Identifying the people involved;
- Evaluating the existing control measures;
- Recommending new control measures; and
- Recording the assessment.

It is important that all of the risks are addressed. Risks should be removed if possible or if not, risk control measures that will reduce the risks to acceptable levels be put into place. In relation to vehicles, the risk control measures will include safe systems of work.

The Management of Health and Safety at Work Regulations also require that employers shall:

- in entrusting tasks to employees, take into account their capabilities as regards health and safety; and
- ensure that employees are provided with adequate health and safety training on being recruited into the employer's undertaking and on being exposed to new or increased risks at the workplace.

The Workplace (Health, Safety and Welfare) Regulations place the following duties, in relation to vehicles, upon employers:

- The workplace shall be organised in such a way that vehicles can circulate in a safe manner.
- Traffic routes must be suitable for the vehicles using them.
- All routes must be suitably indicated.
- The workplace shall be maintained in an efficient state, in efficient working order and in good repair.
- Every floor in a workplace and the surface of every traffic route shall be kept free of obstruction.

This should be under constant review to ensure compliance.

The Provision and Use of Work Equipment Regulations 1998 place the following duties, in relation to vehicles, upon employers:

- To ensure that work equipment (which includes vehicles) is so constructed or adapted as to be suitable for the purpose for which it is used or provided.
- In selecting the work equipment, every employer shall have regard to the working conditions and to the risks to the health and safety of persons which exist in the premises or undertaking in which that work equipment is to be used, and any additional risk posed by the use of that work equipment.

- To ensure the work equipment is maintained in efficient working order and in good repair.

Common factors that will need consideration by employers in the majority of workplace situations are the following:

- Vehicle routes laid out to meet the needs of pedestrians and vehicles.
- Traffic routes appropriate to the types and quantities of vehicles.
- Safety features in place, e.g. signs and markings, barriers and humps.
- Reversing manoeuvres minimised.
- Safe parking for all drivers.
- Loading and unloading procedures arranged for safety.
- Vehicles fitted with all necessary safety equipment and features.
- Vehicles maintained in good working order.
- Driver selection and training procedures sufficient to ensure that employees asked to drive at work are suitably experienced and competent, and remain so.
- Adequate briefing on workplace driving hazards.
- Adequate supervision and inspection of workplace driving activities to ensure safe systems of work are being followed.

It is strongly advised for employers to put in place a written policy covering driving at work, which takes into account the factors mentioned above, not forgetting private cars used by employees for business use, for which employers are to have responsibility. This should ensure checks such as whether the car is insured for business, has a valid MOT etc. Recently a company successfully defended itself against a prosecution brought after an employee was killed whilst using a hand-held mobile phone. The company was able to show that their driving policy contained strict instructions prohibiting the use of mobile phones whilst driving.

The Health Act 2006 and the Smoke Free (Exemptions and Vehicle) Regulations 2007 provide that a vehicle that is used by the public in the course of paid or unpaid work by more than one person must be smoke-free. Consideration should be given to this when employees are using their own vehicles as well as company vehicles.

See also: Driving at work, p.244; Use of mobile phones at work, p.510; Parking, p.550; Smoking, p.660

Sources of further information

HSE – Workplace transport safety: www.hse.gov.uk/pubns/indg199.pdf

Workplace Law Group's *Driving at Work Policy and Management Guide, v.4.0* helps you cover yourself and your staff and ensure that your employees keep to the highest standards of safe driving at work. This comprehensive new edition of the policy and management guide updates several elements of the original including the implications of recent legislation such as the Health Act 2006, the Road Safety Act 2007 and the Corporate Manslaughter and Corporate Homicide Act 2007. If your business hasn't already got a driving at work policy in place, or your current policy is not up-to-date, this is an essential publication. The policy highlights the issue of liability should prosecution occur following a driving at work accident, and who might face prosecution as a result. For more details visit www. workplacelaw.net/Bookshop/PoliciesAndProcedures.

Workplace Law Group has also published the new and revised *Driving at Work 2008: Special Report,* updated from the bestselling first edition. As well as corporate manslaughter legislation the report considers changes to the Road Safety Act 2006, the smoking ban, mobile phones and the increasing number of environmental schemes affecting vehicles. Written by experts in the field, this new Special Report is packed with extensive, up-to-date, high-level research and provides a unique insight into practical measures required to comply with the law. For more information visit www.workplacelaw.net/Bookshop/SpecialReports.

Ventilation and temperature

Bob Towse, Heating and Ventilating Contractors' Association (HVCA)

Key points
- Requirements for the provision of ventilation to buildings are set out in the Workplace (Health, Safety and Welfare) Regulations 1992.
- These Regulations came into force on 1 January 1993 for new buildings and on 1 January 1996 for existing buildings.

The Regulations apply to a wide range of workplaces – not only factories, shops and offices but also, for example, schools, hospitals, hotels and places of entertainment. The Regulations replaced several pieces of older law, including parts of the Factories Act 1961 and the Offices, Shops and Railways Premises Act 1963.

General requirements

The Regulations require the workplace and the equipment, devices and systems to be maintained (including cleaned as appropriate) in an efficient state, in efficient working order and in good repair.

The Regulations do not go into detail, but the Health and Safety Commission (HSC) Approved Code of Practice (ACoP) – *Workplace Health, Safety and Welfare* – gives further guidance on how to comply.

Ventilation

Regulation 6 requires that "effective and suitable provision shall be made to ensure that every enclosed workplace is ventilated by a sufficient quantity of fresh or purified air".

It should be noted that this Regulation covers general workplace ventilation, not local exhaust ventilation for controlling specific hazardous materials or substances hazardous to health.

The ACoP states that workplaces should be sufficiently well-ventilated so that stale air, and air which is hot or humid because of the processes or equipment in the

workplace, is replaced at a reasonable rate. In many cases natural ventilation through windows or other openings may be sufficient, but mechanical ventilation or air conditioning may also be required to meet certain circumstances.

The ACoP also states that mechanical ventilation systems should always operate in a way which draws in some fresh air. One hundred per cent recirculation (no fresh air) is considered unhealthy.

All spaces that rely on mechanical means of ventilation should be supplied with outdoor air at a rate sufficient to dilute internally generated pollutants.

Ventilation should also remove and dilute warm, humid air and provide air movement which gives a sense of freshness without causing a draught. If the workplace contains process or heating equipment or other sources of dust, fumes or vapours, more fresh air will be needed to provide adequate ventilation.

The HSE guide, *General Ventilation in the Workplace,* confirms that a fresh air supply rate of eight litres per second per person should provide a clean and hygienic workplace in open-plan offices, shops and some factories. Higher fresh air supply rates of up to 32 litres per second per person are recommended for heavily contaminated buildings.

The Chartered Institution of Building Services Engineers (CIBSE) Guide A: *Environmental Design,* recommends the following outdoor air supply rates for sedentary occupants:

- Eight litres per second per person – non-smoking.
- Sixteen litres per second per person – 25% smoking.
- Twenty-four litres per second per person – 45% smoking.
- Thirty-six litres per second per person – 75% smoking.

Supply air quality
Air introduced from outside a building should be free from any impurities likely to be offensive or cause ill health. Outdoor air is generally considered acceptable provided that the air intake is not sited so that excessively contaminated air (such as might be found near flues, extract outlets or car parks) is drawn into the building.

The level of air pollution in some locations may mean that outdoor air is not suitable to introduce into a building unless it has first undergone adequate particle filtration.

Air that is recirculated should be adequately filtered before being redistributed within the building.

Maintenance
The ACoP requires that "any device or system used to provide fresh air to a building or space should be maintained in an efficient state so as to ensure that

the air produced or delivered is both suitable and sufficient for use within the workplace".

The term 'efficient state' relates to good working order and not productivity or economy. In particular, the plant should be kept clean and free from any substance or organism that may contaminate the air passing through it.

The ACoP refers to the need to "regularly and properly clean, test and maintain mechanical ventilation and air-conditioning systems to ensure that they are kept clean and free from anything which may contaminate the air".

Depending on use, compliance with this duty is likely to require a suitable system of maintenance, inspection, adjustment, lubrication and cleaning, as well as the keeping of accurate records.

CIBSE and the Heating and Ventilating Contractors' Association (HVCA) each publish a number of guides intended to assist in this purpose.

Temperature in indoor workplaces
Regulation 7 requires that "during working hours, the temperature in all workplaces inside buildings shall be reasonable".

The ACoP suggests that, in the typical workplace, the temperature should be at least 16°C unless much of the work involves severe physical effort, in which case the temperature should be at least 13°C.

These temperatures would be considered by most building occupants to be below comfort levels. However, the ACoP defines a reasonable temperature as one that should secure the thermal comfort of people at work, allowing for clothing, activity level, radiant heat, air movement and humidity.

For air-conditioned buildings in the UK, the CIBSE Guide A recommends a dry resultant temperature of between 21°C and 23°C during winter and between 22°C and 24°C in summer for continuous sedentary occupancy.

It is recognised that room temperatures in buildings without artificial cooling will exceed the summer values for some of the time but should not exceed 25°C for more than 5% of the annual occupied period (typically 125 hours).

See also: Building Regulations, p.81

Sources of further information

Chartered Institute of Building Services Engineers (CIBSE): www.cibse.org

Heating and Ventilating Contractors' Association: www.hvca.org.uk

Vibration

Simon Ient, Bureau Veritas

Key points

- The Control of Vibration Regulations 2005 came into force on 6 July 2005.
- The Regulations cover two aspects – Hand–Arm Vibration (HAV) and Whole-Body Vibration (WBV).
- There is a transitional period for exposure limits up to 2010 which applies to work equipment already in use before July 2007.
- Whole-Body Vibration exposure limits in the agriculture and forestry sectors are extended to 2014.
- Exposure limits may be exceeded during the transitional period providing you have complied with all the other requirements of the Regulations and taken all reasonably practicable actions to reduce exposure as much as you can.
- The emphasis of the regulations is on control and taking action, not on continual assessment.
- The Control of Vibration Regulations 2005 do not apply to work taking place in ships, boats or other vessels. Hand–Arm and whole-body vibration is separately dealt with under the Maritime and Coastguard Agency regulations, Statutory Instruments 2007 No. 3077.

Legislation

- Health and Safety at Work etc. Act 1974.
- Social Security (Industrial Injuries) (Prescribed Diseases) Regulations 1985.
- Supply of Machinery (Safety) Regulations 1992.
- Personal Protective Equipment at Work Regulations 1992.
- Reporting of Injuries, Diseases and Dangerous Occurrences Regulations 1995.
- Provision and Use of Work Equipment Regulations 1998.
- Management of Health and Safety at Work Regulations 1999.
- Control of Noise at Work Regulations 2005.
- The Control of Vibration Regulations 2005.

Whole-Body Vibration

Main points

- Exposure occurs when vibration is transmitted through the seat or feet.

Ill health symptoms

- Regular long-term exposure is associated with back pain and other muscle fatigue complaints.

Hand–Arm Vibration

Main points

Transmitted from work processes into workers' hands and arms. Common processes are:

- operating hand-held or hand-guided power tools; and
- holding materials being processed by machines.

Ill health symptoms

- Tingling and numbness in the fingers.
- Not being able to feel things properly.
- Loss of strength in the hands.
- Fingers going white (blanching) and becoming red and painful on recovery particularly in the cold and wet. Often

referred to as dead finger, dead hand or white finger.

Legal duties for both Whole-Body and Hand–Arm Vibration

Employers must:

- assess the vibration risk;
- establish if the daily exposure action value (EAV) will be exceeded;
- establish if the daily exposure limit value (ELV) will be exceeded;
- eliminate the risk or reduce exposure to a level as is reasonably practicable;
- provide health surveillance to employees who continue to be regularly exposed above the action value;
- provide information and training;
- consult trade union safety representatives or employee representatives on your proposals;
- keep records of the risk assessment and controls;
- keep health records for employees under health surveillance; and
- carry out regular reviews and take actions to reduce exposure.

Exposure action value

The exposure action value (EAV) is a daily (eight hours) amount of vibration exposure above which employers are required to take action to control exposure. Exposure is quantified in terms of the acceleration of the surface in contact with the hand. The acceleration of the surface is normally expressed in units of metres per second squared (m/s^2):

- For Whole-Body Vibration the EAV is a daily exposure of $0.5/s^2$ A(8).
- For Hand–Arm Vibration the EAV is a daily exposure of 2.5 m/s^2 A(8).

Exposure limit value (ELV)

The exposure limit value (ELV) is the maximum amount of vibration an employee may be exposed to on any single day. It represents a high risk above which employees should not be exposed:

- For Whole-Body Vibration the ELV is a daily exposure of 1.15 m/s^2 A(8).
- For Hand–Arm Vibration the ELV is a daily exposure of 5 m/s^2 A(8).

Estimating exposure

Care should be exercised in using manafacturers' vibration data. Check if the information represents the way you use the equipment. Specialist equipment and a competent person will be required if you want to obtain vibration measurements for your own tools. Many factors affect the readings and the experience of the competent person is important in achieving realistic readings. Table 1 demonstrates how vibration level and duration affect exposure.

The HSE has produced an exposure calculator at www.hse.gov.uk/vibration which can be used to assess each employee's daily exposure. Alternatively you can use the simple 'exposure points' system in Table 2.

Table 2

Multiply the points assigned to the tool vibration by the number of hours of daily 'trigger time' for the tool(s) and then compare the total with the exposure action value (EAV) and exposure limit value (ELV) points.

- 100 points per day = exposure action value (EAV).
- 400 points per day = exposure limit value (ELV).

Example

Someone using an angle grinder with a vibration level of 7 m/s^2 for five hours a day would reach the EAV (Exposure Action Value) level in one hour and the ELV (Exposure Limit Value) in four hours. In

Workplace Law Network
www.workplacelaw.net

Table 1 How vibration level and duration affect exposure. Source: HSE

Tool Type	Lowest	Typical	Highest
Road breakers	5 m/S^2	12 m/S^2	20 mS^2
Demolition hammers	8 m/S^2	15 m/S^2	25 m/S^2
Hammer drills/combi hammers	6 m/S^2	9 m/S^2	25 m/S^2
Needle scalers	5 m/S^2	–	18 m/S^2
Scabblers (hammer type)	–	–	40 m/S^2
Angle grinders	4 m/S^2	–	8 m/S^2
Clay spades/Jigger picks	–	16 m/S^2	–
Chipping hammers (metal)	–	18 m/S^2	–
Stone-working hammers	10 m/S^2	–	30 m/S^2
Chainsaws	–	6 m/S^2	–
Bruschutters	2 m/S^2	4 m/S^2	–
Saunders (random orbital)	–	7–10 m/S^2	–

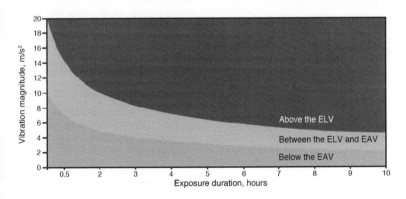

Table 2 Exposure points system

Tool vibration (m/s^2)	3	4	5	6	7	10	12	15
Points per hour (approx)	20	30	50	70	100	200	300	450

Vibration

. . . .

this example if the grinder is used for five hours a day the ELV has been exceeded by one hour.

Health surveillance

You must provide health surveillance for all employees who, despite your action to control the risk, are likely to be regularly exposed above the EAV.

Control measures

Alternative work methods

Try to find an alternative way of working that does not involve the use of vibrating tools or exposure to activities that create vibration.

Equipment selection

Ensure equipment is suitable and can do the work efficiently – if it is too small or not powerful enough it will extend the vibration exposure.

Have a policy in place for replacing old equipment and tools

Check the vibration data for equipment before purchase – choose equipment with the lowest vibration rating.

Workstation design

Devices such as jigs reduce the need to grip items.

Maintenance

Correct maintenance for equipment will lessen the likelihood of an increase in vibration, e.g. make sure cutting tools are kept sharp.

Work schedules

Limit the time to exposure, plan work, rotate employees.

Clothing

Provide the correct PPE.

Information and training

Inform employees of the risk assessment and the control measures and provide any training that may be considered necessary. Information to employees can include:

- instruction in the use of quipment viz. avoid gripping or forcing a tool or workpiece more than you have to;
- keep hands warm and dry;
- reduce smoking because smoking reduces the blood flow;
- massaging and exercising fingers during work breaks; and
- posture and manual handling training when taking into account whole body vibration exposure.

Health surveillance

You must provide health surveillance for all employees who, despite your action to control the risk, are likely to be regularly exposed above the EAV. This will provide you with useful feedback information on the effectiveness of your vibration control measures as well as monitoring those people at risk.

> *See also*: Health surveillance, p.392; Occupational health, p.537

Sources of further information

Vibration at work: www.hse.gov.uk/vibration

Violence at work

Kathryn Gilbertson, Greenwoods Solicitors LLP

Key points

For many people, perception of violence in the workplace is one associated with the physical violence we see occurring in the public sector – attacks on medical and nursing staff in accident and emergency units; attacks on paramedics attending a scene; attacks on police officers. That violence is the result of many factors of a situation coming together and is not uncommonly fuelled by anger and frustration, often including factors such as alcohol and drug consumption.

However, violence in the workplace extends beyond the stereotypical images that are described above. Violence can be physical or emotional, it can be a single outburst projected at a particular person; it can be a repeated series of attacks against a particular person or a particular group. The person or people carrying out the violence could indeed themselves have been a victim of violence in their own life.

Ultimately violence can and often does result in physical or emotional injury to its recipient and can have a significant effect on the lives of those around them.

Legislation

- Health and Safety at Work etc. Act 1974.
- Reporting of Injuries, Diseases and Dangerous Occurrences Regulations 1995.
- Management of Health and Safety at Work Regulations 1999.

Effects

The employer too can be affected by the consequences of workplace violence, financially and morally. Where workplace violence exists and is not managed, employers may well face low morale, high staff turnover, and difficulties in recruiting associated with an environment that is not conducive to healthy working and has a poor reputation in the public eye. Further financial impacts may occur from civil action and resulting compensation payments, prosecution and increased insurance premiums.

There has been a steady fall in recorded workplace violence since its peak in the mid-90s.

The Health and Safety Executive (HSE) defines work-related violence as "any incident in which a person is abused, threatened or assaulted in circumstances relating to their work".

There is a clear legal position in UK law with respect to prevention and management of workplace violence.

Section 2 of the Health and Safety at Work etc. Act 1974 requires employers, so far as is reasonably practicable, to ensure the health, safety and welfare of their employees. This duty includes providing a working environment that is safe and without risks to health.

The Management of Health and Safety at Work Regulations 1999 require employers to assess the risks to their employees and to take appropriate measures to prevent or reduce the risk.

Additionally, the Reporting of Injuries, Diseases and Dangerous Occurrences Regulations 1995 (RIDDOR) require employers to notify their enforcing authority in the event of an accident at work to any employee resulting in death, major injury, or incapacity to work three or more days. This includes accidents and injuries that occur as a result of any non-consensual physical violence done to a person at work.

The HSE continues to investigate and take action against incidents of workplace violence that come to their attention.

Most commonly, action is taken in the form of an improvement notice issued against the employer, although there have been at least two prosecutions against employers for incidents involving workplace violence.

Examples of enforcement action include an improvement notice against a local authority (council) requiring implementation of control measures for violence and aggression risks in home to school transport services. Another example is an improvement notice issued against an NHS Trust because they had not ensured:

- that staff at risk from violence and aggression were provided with adequate training in understanding and dealing with aggression in the workplace;
- that an adequate risk assessment was in place; and
- that a policy for managing violence to staff was in place.

It is essential that the employer complies with the current legal requirements in the UK and to demonstrate compliance the employer needs to ensure that they take the following actions when carrying out a risk assessment.

Identify the hazards
The employer should find out if there are problems with violence at work; consult with employees; ensure that suitable and sufficient risk assessments are carried out. This is not only a legal requirement but also critical to ensure that you get the right information in order to manage risks effectively.

Key elements:

- What is the perception of violence amongst employees?
- Is there evidence of verbal aggression in the workplace?
- Is there evidence of physical aggression in the workplace?
- Are there other factors influencing behaviours that can lead to violence and aggression, i.e. environmental factors; work patterns; training issues; organisational structure; and job design?
- Is your company or organisation dealing with customers and clients who may be emotionally fraught already, i.e. people facing redundancy; people who are ill; people who may already be facing prosecution and imprisonment? Existing frustration and anger can easily increase the incidence of violent incidents if not managed effectively.

Identify who is at risk and how they could be harmed
Many groups of people could be described as being 'at risk' of violence at work. Typical groups of at-risk individuals include those who are involved in providing services and are involved in direct communication with the public – for example, shop assistants; call centre operatives; nurses and doctors; couriers; teachers; security guards, etc.

It is important, however, to consider the less obvious 'at-risk' groups in your organisation – those representing authority such as line managers and HR managers; those who may be dealing with sensitive health issues such as occupational health professionals; and employees who travel off site or overseas where they may be at higher risk purely because of their nationality and/or ethnicity. An employer will need to carefully examine the work and work practices of their identified at-risk groups to determine how they could be harmed. For example, is it more likely to be verbal aggression rather than physical aggression; are there common incidents amongst those people such as physical assault with weapons?

Controls

Consider what controls you have in place and consider if those controls are effective. Ensure that you have in place:

- a system for reporting incidents, that encourages participation and provides appropriate confidentiality along with analysis of those figures to provide critical information on trends and the efficacy of controls;
- a policy that specifically addresses violence in the workplace; reporting incidents; debriefing from incidents; post-incident help and support; external legal assistance;
- other policies that may indirectly prevent violence in the workplace, i.e. policies and systems of work for loneworking; maintaining security in work areas; and to enhance organisational communication;
- good job design with employees provided with relevant information to

carry out their work safely, i.e. pre-travel briefings for work overseas or in high risk areas;
- training for employees to enable them to identify potentially violent behaviours and diffuse 'hot' situations; use personal protection measures and tactics when appropriate and be able to adjust behaviour accordingly;
- other appropriate physical controls relating to building layout and ambience which may include alternative methods of communicating, i.e. visual display boards, and alarm systems, etc.; and
- an environment that is clean and comfortable for employees, visitors and clients alike.

It is essential that control measures are relevant to the organisation and the risks it faces. The findings of the risk assessment should be recorded and the employer should have in place a system for monitoring, reviewing and auditing of control measures on a regular basis.

The most effective systems are those that have involved employee (and where appropriate public) consultation; have created a culture in which employees and visitors feel comfortable and safe; and demonstrate a balanced approach to the prevention and management of violence.

See also: Bullying and harassment, p.95; Reporting of Injuries, Diseases and Dangerous Occurrences (RIDDOR), p.628; Risk assessments, p.639

Sources of further information

HSE: www.hse.gov.uk/violence

HSE: Violence at work: A guide for employers INDG69 (rev)

Visitor safety

Andrew Richardson, Scott Wilson

Key points
- Employers have a duty to provide a safe environment for visitors to their premises.
- Children are less careful than adults and need more controls.
- The duty extends to uninvited visitors such as trespassers, and to tenants.
- Employers are liable for the actions of their employees who injure visitors.
- Employees must help their employer to ensure a safe and healthy workplace.

Legislation
- Occupiers' Liability Acts 1957 and 1984.
- Health and Safety at Work etc. Act 1974.
- Management of Health and Safety at Work Regulations 1999.

Occupiers' Liability Acts 1957 and 1984

From the employer's perspective, the Occupiers' Liability Act 1957 places a common law duty of care upon the occupier to all visitors to take such care as is reasonable to see that visitors will be reasonably safe in using the premises for the purposes for which they were invited or permitted to be there. The Act also points out that children will inevitably be less careful than adults.

The Occupiers' Liability Act 1984 amended the 1957 Act slightly to include a duty to unlawful visitors (e.g. trespassers) such that if:

- the occupier is aware of the danger, and
- the occupier knows the person could put himself at risk, and
- the risk is a risk that the occupier could reasonably be expected to do something about,

then the same common law duty of care is owed as is owed to lawful visitors.

Employers are also liable for the actions of their employees and, in relation to visitors, have a vicarious liability for those actions. If an employee injures a visitor during the course of his work, then the employer is liable.

Health and Safety at Work etc. Act 1974

Under section 3 of the Act an employer has a duty to "conduct his undertaking in such a way as to ensure, so far as is reasonably practicable, that persons not in his employment (e.g. visitors) who may be affected thereby are not thereby exposed to risks to their health and safety".

Section 4 requires that anyone in control of the premises or plant used by persons not in their employment should, so far as is reasonably practicable:

- ensure safe access and egress to the premises and plant; and
- ensure that plant or substances in the premises, or provided for their use, are safe and without risk to health.

These obligations are also transferred to any tenants of a building.

Section 7 places a general obligation upon all employees to take reasonable care of their own health and safety and that of others who may be affected by their own acts or omissions. They also have to cooperate with the employer so as to ensure that the employer can comply with all of the above statutory obligations.

Finally, under section 8, no person should intentionally or recklessly misuse or interfere with anything provided under the Act and other legislation in the interests of health and safety.

Management of Health and Safety at Work Regulations 1999

These Regulations identify a number of general duties that, if followed, will allow the employer to meet those obligations detailed in the Acts mentioned above. These are principally to carry out risk assessments and to set up emergency procedures.

All employers must assess the risks to health and safety of their employees and of anyone who may be affected by their work activity; this will include visitors. The risk assessment process should:

- identify all the hazards;
- consider the risks involved and identify the people involved (employees, visitors, the public);
- evaluate the existing control measures and recommend any new control measures;
- record the assessment; and
- review and revise the assessment as necessary.

It is important to address all of the risks, eliminate them if possible and, if not, put into place control measures that will reduce the risks to acceptable levels.

The Regulations also require employers to set up emergency procedures for serious and imminent dangers and to appoint competent persons to ensure compliance with those procedures. The procedures should cover all visitors to the premises.

See also: Health and safety at work, p.364; Trespassers and squatters, p.694

Sources of further information

L21 Management of Health and Safety at Work Regulations 1999 – Approved Code of Practice and Guidance (HSE Books, 2000) ISBN: 0 7176 2488 9 provides guidance to employers on managing risk to visitors and identifies any further documentation that is relevant.

Confidential waste

David Flint, MacRoberts Solicitors

Key points
- What is confidential waste?
- Implications of the Data Protection Act 1998.
- Penalties for non-compliance.
- Additional responsibilities for Public Authorities.
- Major changes: the disposal of IT equipment.

Legislation
- Data Protection Act 1998 (DPA 1998).
- Freedom of Information Act 2000 (FOIA 2000).
- Freedom of Information (Scotland) Act 2002 (FOISA 2002).
- Waste Electrical and Electronic Equipment (WEEE) Directive (2002/96/EC).
- Waste Electrical and Electronic Equipment Regulations 2004 (WEEE Regulations).

What is confidential waste?
Confidential waste includes any record that contains personal information about a particular living individual or information that is commercially sensitive. Examples include correspondence revealing contact details, personnel records, job applications and interview notes, salary records, Income Tax and National Insurance returns, contracts, tenders, purchasing and maintenance records and sensitive industrial relations negotiation material.

Implications of the Data Protection Act 1998
The DPA 1998 does not set out a standard way in which confidential waste should be disposed of. Businesses must ensure that the steps they are taking meet with the intention of the DPA 1998.

The DPA 1998 covers all computer records, information held in a relevant filing system, discs and CDs.

Companies have several responsibilities under the DPA 1998. They must ensure that data is not kept for longer than is necessary and also that when data is finished with it is destroyed in a safe and secure manner. Throwing files away into office bins in the hope that they will be adequately destroyed is not sufficient. Companies must take appropriate technical and organisational measures to prevent against unauthorised or unlawful processing of personal data and against accidental loss or destruction of, or damage to, personal data. The Act specifically states that in deciding the manner in which to destroy data, consideration must be given to the state of technological development at that time, the cost of the measures, the harm which might result from a breach in security and the nature of the data to be disposed of.

The issues that must be addressed with regards to confidential waste in a paper environment are different to those that must be addressed in an electronic environment. Special care must be taken when destroying electronic records as these can even be reconstructed from deleted information. Erasing or reformatting computer disks (or personal computers with hard drives) which once contained confidential personal information is also insufficient.

Although the DPA 1998 does not prescribe an exact method by which confidential records should be destroyed, employers should consider the following:

- Procedures regarding the storage and disposal of personal data including computer disks and print-outs should be reviewed.
- Waste paper containing personal data should be placed in a separate 'confidential' waste bin and shredded by a reputable contractor, who meets the new BS 8470 standard on securely destroying confidential waste and is registered and audited to ISO 9001:2000. It is also advisable to ensure that the contractor's employees are screened in accordance with BS 7858.
- If sub-contractors are used as data processors, a sub-contractor who gives guarantees about security measures and takes reasonable steps to ensure compliance with those measures should be chosen. Furthermore, a contract should be drawn up with the data controller and certificates of destruction of documents by the subcontractor should be issued as proof that the process has been completed.
- A standard risk assessment should be completed in order to identify threats to the system, the vulnerability of the system, and the procedures which can be put in place in order to manage and reduce the risks.

Penalties for non-compliance
Contravention of the DPA 1998 is a criminal offence. The maximum fine is £5,000. Individuals who suffer damage as a direct result of a contravention of the Act by a data controller are entitled to be compensated for that damage. Prosecutions under the DPA 1998 are becoming increasingly common. There is also a strong commercial incentive for businesses to protect personal data following the publicity of the recent TK Maxx scandal.

Additional responsibilities for Public Authorities
Section 61 of the FOISA 2002 and section 46 of the FOIA 2000 place additional responsibilities on public authorities regarding the management and disposal of their records. Section 61 and section 46 respectively state that it is desirable for public authorities to follow the Code of Practice on Records Management (the Code). The Code sets out various practices regarding the creation, keeping, management and disposition of their records. The implications of the FOISA 2002 and the FOIA 2000 are very far-reaching as the Code is applicable to all records in all formats, including paper, electronic, video and microfilm. It should be noted that the ambit of this definition is wider than that under the DPA 1998 and extends to all personal data.

The issues discussed in the Code affecting the disposal of confidential information can be summarised as follows:

- The disposition of records must be undertaken in accordance with clearly established policies which have been formally adopted by authorities and which are enforced by properly authorised staff. Authorities should establish a selection policy which sets out in broad terms the function from which records are likely to be selected for permanent preservation and the periods for which other records should be retained.

- Disposal schedules should be drawn up for each business area. These schedules should indicate the appropriate disposition action for all records within that area.
- A permanent documentation of any records destroyed showing exactly what records were destroyed, why they were destroyed, when they were destroyed and on whose authority they were destroyed, should be kept. The record should also provide some background information on the records being destroyed, such as legislative provisions, functional context and physical arrangement.
- Records should be destroyed in as secure a manner as is necessary for the level of confidentiality they bear.
- Authorities must have adequate arrangements to ensure that before a record is destroyed they ascertain whether or not the record is the subject of a request for information under the FOISA 2002 or the FOIA 2000. If a record is known to be the subject of a request under either the FOISA 2002 or the FOIA 2000, the destruction of the record should be delayed until either the information is disclosed or the review and appeal provisions have been exhausted.

Disposal of IT equipment

Companies, when disposing of their IT equipment, must act with extreme care in order to ensure that personal data is completely erased. Despite the fact that contravention of the DPA 1998 is a criminal offence, a study published by the University of Glamorgan's Computer Forensics Team revealed that around half of second-hand computers obtained from various sources contained sufficient information to identify organisations and individuals. This clearly illustrates that businesses are failing properly to delete highly sensitive information stored on their computers before they are sold on, and failing to meet the requirements of the DPA 1998.

There are various ways a business may dispose of its IT equipment responsibly. Shredding disks is considered to be the most effective way to destroy a disk and all the personal data that it contains. Where businesses wish to reuse a disk, unless they can adequately delete the files themselves, refurbishers or recyclers should be used.

The European Waste Electrical and Electronic Equipment (WEEE) Directive seeks to regulate the disposal of electronic equipment by requiring that member states of the European Union ensure that approximately 20% of their WEEE (around four kilograms per person in the UK) is collected and recycled. The Directive received effect in the UK on 1 July 2007. Manufacturers and importers of electrical and electronic equipment (EEE) are now responsible for financing the producer compliance regimes for the collection, treatment, recycling and recovery of WEEE. Such schemes will be monitored by the relevant environmental agency.

Retailers on the other hand must either offer customers a free exchange (or 'take-back') of WEEE for EEE, or help to finance public waste WEEE recycling services. The Regulations are reasonably specific about the sort of equipment that falls under their ambit and the sort of equipment that does not. Replacement peripherals and components, such as hard disk drives, are not considered WEEE under the Regulations except where they are inside equipment that is within their scope at the time of disposal.

Failure to comply with the WEEE
Regulations may result in a breach of the
DPA 1998 as well as considerable bad
publicity.

*The author acknowledges the assistance
of Valerie Surgenor and Fritha Wheeler-
Ozanne of MacRoberts TMC Group, in the
production of this chapter.*

See also: Data protection, p.186;
IT security, p.433; Personnel files
– recording information, p.571;
Waste management, p.7725;
WEEE – the Waste Electrical and
Electronic Equipment Regulations
and RoHS, p.744

Sources of further information

Information Commissioner: www.informationcommissioner.gov.uk

British Security Industry Association: www.bsia.co.uk

Hazardous waste

Mark Webster, Bureau Veritas

Key points

During 2005 Hazardous Waste Regulations (HWR) were made in England, Wales and Northern Ireland to revoke the respective Special Waste Regulations. The HWR provide a new system for the control of those wastes that are harmful to human health or the environment, or are difficult to handle. The Regulations provide a process for the control of such wastes from their production to their final disposal destination i.e. a cradle to grave documentation trail for the movement of hazardous waste. Amendments to the Special Waste Regulations 1996 were made in Scotland in 2003 to meet the requirements of the Hazardous Waste Directive.

The following chapter provides an overview of the requirements of the new Regulations and the key actions that producers should undertake to ensure compliance.

Legislation

- Special Waste (Scotland) Amendment Regulations 2003.
- Hazardous Waste (England and Wales) Regulations 2005.
- Hazardous Waste (Wales) Regulations 2005.
- Hazardous Waste Regulations (Northern Ireland) 2005 (as amended).

Summary of the key changes – England and Wales

- Special waste is now termed hazardous waste.
- All hazardous wastes must be characterised by codes from the associated List of Wastes Regulations 2005, using guidance issued by the Environment Agency (EA) / Scottish Environment Protection Agency (SEPA) for wastes with mirror entries in the List of Wastes to determine if such wastes are hazardous or not.
- An additional 200 types of waste are now classified as hazardous. Common office items such as fluorescent bulbs,

computer monitors, Ni-Cd, lead or mercury batteries and televisions are examples of newly classified hazardous wastes.

- Mixing of different categories of hazardous waste and the mixing of hazardous waste with non-hazardous waste is not permitted. It is important to note that each specific hazardous waste type cannot be mixed or co-disposed (i.e. batteries cannot be mixed with computer monitors).
- Producers of hazardous waste must undertake site premises notification with the EA and will receive a unique registration number (also known as a premises code) which is used in the issuing of consignment note numbers.
- Cessation of the requirement to pre-notify the EA prior to movement of hazardous waste in certain circumstances.
- Introduction of increased record keeping requirements – requirement on waste producers to maintain a register.

Scotland

- Scotland has met the requirements of the Hazardous Waste Directive by amendment of the Special Waste Regulations.

- Direct reference to the Directive is made in the definition of Hazardous Waste and the guidance issued by the EA/SEPA for wastes with mirror entries in the List of Wastes to determine if such wastes are hazardous or not.

- An additional 200 types of waste are now classified as hazardous. Common office items such as fluorescent bulbs, computer monitors, Ni-Cd, lead or mercury batteries and televisions are examples of newly classified hazardous wastes.

- Mixing of different categories of hazardous waste and the mixing of hazardous waste with non-hazardous waste is not permitted. It is important to note that each specific hazardous waste type cannot be mixed or co-disposed (i.e. batteries cannot be mixed with computer monitors).

- Introduction of increased record keeping requirements – requirement on waste producers to maintain a register.

Northern Ireland

- Special waste is now termed hazardous waste.

- All hazardous wastes must be characterised by codes from the associated List of Wastes Regulations 2005, using guidance issued by the EA/SEPA for wastes with mirror entries in the List of Wastes to determine if such wastes are hazardous or not.

- An additional 200 types of waste are now classified as hazardous. Common office items such as fluorescent bulbs, computer monitors, Ni-Cd, lead or mercury batteries and televisions are examples of newly classified hazardous wastes.

- Mixing of different categories of hazardous waste and the mixing of hazardous waste with non-hazardous waste is not permitted. It is important to note that each specific hazardous waste type cannot be mixed or co-disposed (i.e. batteries cannot be mixed with computer monitors).

- Introduction of increased record keeping requirements – requirement on waste producers to maintain a register.

The cross border movement of hazardous waste within the UK has been accounted for within the respective Regulations. Should you need to arrange such a cross border movement it is recommended that you seek advice from an appropriately qualified source. Refer to the document entitled *Consignment Notes: Cross Border Movements: A Guide to the Hazardous Waste Regulations* (HWR05) published by the EA.

Producer's responsibility (England and Wales)

Producers of hazardous wastes must ensure that their organisation (and individual locations) can fully demonstrate to regulators that they comply with all elements of the new Regulations. In order to ensure compliance, all producers must address the following actions:

- Register all premises which produce hazardous waste with the EA prior to any collection of hazardous waste. Please note that it is an offence to produce, remove or cause to be removed, or transport hazardous wastes from non-notified premises. Re-notification must be undertaken on an annual basis. Some premises may be exempt from registering their premises with the EA, for instance if they produce less than 200 kg of hazardous waste in a 12-month period (see below).

- Ensure that the consignee issues returns to the waste producer notifying the receipt of their waste. This requirement aims to close the loop by demonstrating that the disposal point receives the waste that was intended for its site, thus confirming that the waste followed its intended disposal route.

- Retain the quarterly returns provided to the waste producer by the waste management contractor for provision to the EA if requested. The information should include details of the wastes disposed of, the quantities and the location of treatment/disposal for each consignment of waste removed.

- Undertake and permit authorities to undertake inspections of waste management premises, procedures and documentation.

- Control consignment notes and effectively manage records.

- Whilst waste management contractors can be valuable partners in achieving compliance, the responsibilities for premises notification and provision and partial completion of the consignment notes rest with the waste producer.

Exemptions to premises notification (England and Wales)

There are exemptions to premises notification. The key exemptions are detailed under Regulation 23 of the HWR, which states that the following types of premises may be exempt:

- Office premises, to the extent that the hazardous waste arises from the use of the premises as an office;

- Shop premises, to the extent that the hazardous waste arises from the use of the premises as a shop;

- Premises used for agriculture within the meaning of the Agriculture Act 1947, to the extent that the hazardous waste arises from the use of the premises for agriculture;

- Premises of a description listed in:
  - paragraphs (a) to (e) of Section 75(5) of the Environmental Protection Act (1990); or
  - Schedule 1 to the Controlled Waste Regulations (1992);

- Premises at which waste electrical and electronic equipment is collected from others, to the extent that the premises are used for that purpose;

- Premises used by a dental, veterinary or medical practice, to the extent that the premises are used for that purpose; and

- Any ship.

Whilst these types of premises may be exempt they also have to ensure that they do not generate more than 200 kg in any given twelve month period and that the waste is collected by a registered carrier or an exempt carrier. Otherwise the premises must be notified to the EA. For more information on registering, refer to the appropriate section of the EA's website at www.environment-agency.gov.uk/subjects/waste, or contact the EA on 08708 502 858 (weekdays 9 a.m. to 5 p.m.) and refer to the documents entitled *Do I Need to Notify My Premises?, A Guide To The Hazardous Waste Regulations* (HWR02A) and *How to Notify Your Premises, A Guide To The Hazardous Waste Regulations* (HWR02B).

In addition to the above, if waste has been flytipped onto land (i.e. in contravention of Section 33 to the Environmental Protection

Act 1990), it may be removed from those premises without requiring notification of those premises, but would require a waste consignment note prior to removal and to be removed / transported by a registered waste carrier.

Finally, mobile service providers (e.g. mechanics) can be exempt from the HWR if they produce less than 200kg in one year and do not own any of the premises they work at. For more information refer to the documenet entitled Mobile Services: A Gude to the Hazardous Waste Regulations (HWR07) published by the EA.

Charges associated with the Regulations (England and Wales)
The notification of locations with the EA will result in one of the charges below:

■ £28 for each premises notified in writing;
■ £23 for each premises notified by telephone; and
■ £18 for each premises notified by electronic form.

Most waste management contractors will register premises for their waste producer customers, but it is the waste producer that is responsible for ensuring registration has occurred and for managing the use of

the unique premises code on sequential consignment notes. In addition to the registration fees that a company will have to pay there is also the potential for fines to be issued by the EA if the Regulations are not effectively implemented. Since April 2007 the EA has had powers under Regulation 70 of the HWR to issue Fixed Penalty Notices (FPNs) for certain environmental offences, such as:

■ failure to register premises;

■ failure to complete and store consignment notes; and

■ failure to apply for review of existing permit.

The FPN is currently £300, payable within 28 days of issue of the notice and if left unpaid the EA may resort to prosecution.

It should also be noted that hazardous waste disposal costs have increased due both to the decreased landfill disposal capacity following implementation of the Landfill Directive, increased waste treatment costs and also to the increased data return fees that waste management contractors are required to pay to the EA. There is therefore a real financial gain to be made in effectively reducing and managing the disposal of hazardous wastes.

See also: Recycling, p.614; Waste management, p.725; WEEE – the Waste Electrical and Electronic Equipment Regulations and RoHS, p.744

Sources of further information

The Hazardous Waste (England and Wales) Regulations 2005: www.opsi.gov.uk/SI/si2005/20050894.htm

Environment Agency – Dealing with hazardous waste: www.environment-agency.gov.uk/subjects/waste/1019330/1217981/?version=1

A considerable amount of information on waste management can be found on the EA's website: www.environment-agency.gov.uk

The Department for Environment, Food and Rural Affairs (Defra) also offers much information on environmental, including waste management, topics at www.defra.gov.uk/

The DTI's Envirowise programme can supply information and assistance via its helpline on 0800 585 794, or website at www.envirowise.gov.uk

WRAP works in partnership to encourage and enable businesses and consumers to be more efficient in their use of materials and recycling at www.wrap.org.uk/ or contact the helpline on 0808 100 2040.

NetRegs is a partnership between the UK environmental regulators – the Environment Agency in England and Wales, SEPA in Scotland and the Environment and Heritage Service in Northern Ireland – which provide free environmental guidance for small and medium-sized businesses throughout the UK. Help and advice is available by business type, environmental legislation and environmental topic and has useful links to other websites. www.netregs.gov.uk/netregs/ or telephone the EA National Customer Contact Centre on 08708 506 506.

National Industrial Symbiosis Programme (NISP) works directly with businesses of all sizes and sectors with the aim of improving cross industry resource efficiency via commercial trading of materials, energy and water and sharing assets, logistics and expertise. It engages traditionally separate industries and other organisations in a collective approach to competitive advantage involving physical exchange of materials, energy, water and/or by-products together with the shared use of assets, logistics and expertise. NISP is delivered at regional level across the UK. www.nisp.org.uk or telephone 0121 433 2650.

Waste management

Mark Webster, Bureau Veritas

Key points
The UK produces in excess of 330 million tonnes of waste annually – a quarter of which is from households and business. The remainder derives from construction and demolition, sewage sludge, farm waste and spoils from mines and dredging of rivers. Businesses handling, storing, transporting, treating and disposing of waste must be aware of a whole host of waste-related legislation to ensure compliance with the law and avoid prosecution.

Legislation

Listed below is some of the most pertinent legislation related to waste management activities, which implement many European Directives into UK law, together with pollution prevention and control (PPC) / environmental permitting, contaminated land and groundwater related legislation.

- Control of Pollution (Amendments) Act 1989.
- Environmental Protection Act 1990.
- Environmental Protection (Duty of Care) Regulations 1991.
- Controlled Waste Regulations 1992, plus subsequent amendments (1993).
- Landfill (England and Wales) Regulations 2002, and amendments (2004 and 2005).
- Environmental Protection (Duty of Care) (England) (Amendment) Regulations 2003.
- Packaging (Essential Requirements) Regulations 2003, and amendments (2004 and 2006).
- Special Waste (Scotland) Amendment Regulations 2003.
- Hazardous Waste (England and Wales) Regulations 2005.
- Hazardous Waste Regulations (Northern Ireland) 2005 (as amended).
- List of Wastes (England) Regulations 2005 (as amended).

- Environmental Permitting (England and Wales) Regulations 2007.
- Site Waste Management Plans Regulations 2008.

General guidance

Steps to consider in the overall process of waste generation through to disposal are outlined below.

Step One – Identify the types and sources of waste from your business
Firstly, create a list of each of the waste streams originating from your facility. This might include:

- general waste (day to day food items, food wrappers, etc);
- waste packaging materials;
- sanitary waste from toilets;
- medical waste from first aid or healthcare centres;
- building and other construction wastes; and
- waste oils from maintenance operations.

As a minimum, those responsible for waste management need to identify and separate out the different waste streams — inert, non hazardous and hazardous, in particular the latter which includes asbestos; lead-acid batteries;

electrical equipment containing hazardous components such as cathode ray tubes (e.g. televisions); oily sludges; solvents; fluorescent light tubes; chemical wastes and pesticides etc. — from other waste streams. The segregation of the differing waste streams needs to be at source.

The European Waste Catalogue (EWC) lists all wastes, grouped according to generic industry or process. Each identified waste type is allocated a six digit code. A waste is hazardous if it is classified as such in the EWC. Hazardous wastes are identified in the EWC with an asterisk (*).

Some wastes are classed as inert or hazardous outright whereas some wastes require prior assessment to determine which category they fall into. For instance inert wastes include glass, bricks, naturally occurring soil and stones (excluding topsoil and peat) whereas hazardous wastes include those that are explosive, flammable, corrosive or carcinogenic. The assessment is required to be undertaken by the 'owner' of the waste, or on their behalf by a third party and must be undertaken prior to recovery, reuse, recycling or disposal to account for relevant procedures to follow.

The Environment Agency (EA) has produced guidance to help waste categorisation in the document entitled *Guidance on Sampling and Testing of Wastes to Meet Landfill Waste Acceptance Procedures*. Useful information is also provided in the Landfill (England and Wales) Regulations 2002, and amendments (2004 and 2005) and in Technical Guidance document WM2 (updated in May 2008) which contains a consolidated version of the EWC and provides advice on the classification and assessment of hazardous waste. Also refer to the document entitled *What is Hazardous Waste?* (HWR01) published by the EA.

It is important to stress that at this stage, it is worth considering options available in the event of waste streams being classified as non-hazardous and hazardous as this will have inherent cost implications for waste management. It may be possible to treat the waste in some way so it is re-categorised to a non-hazardous or even inert waste.

If you are unsure about whether particular waste streams or wastes are inert, non-hazardous or hazardous and unsure of the most appropriate route for reuse, recycling or disposal it is advisable to first liaise with your local EA office or call the DTI-sponsored Envirowise programme (helpline 0800 585 794).

Step Two – Register with Environment Agency (if producing more than 200kg of hazardous waste per annum)
All businesses in England and Wales that produce hazardous waste have a legal duty to register their premises with the EA. The duty to notify premises rests with the producer of the waste. This would normally be regarded as the owner or occupier of the site. However, where waste is produced by a visiting mobile service, the duty may fall on the person operating that service. Hazardous waste producer registrations are valid for 12 months from the date of registration. In the event of premises continuing to produce hazardous waste after the initial 12-month period the registration must be renewed, up to one month in advance of the expiry date. Premises that fail to renew their registrations may be liable to enforcement action. Note that the EA will not inform premises to renew their registration. Each premises that is registered will be given a unique registration number or 'premises code'.

Some types of premises may be exempt from registering if they produce less than 200 kg of hazardous waste in any 12-month period. However, if exemption applies, e.g. office and shop premises, dental and doctors surgeries, some schools, charities and voluntary organisations, there is still a requirement to use a Hazardous Waste Consignment Note (HWCN) to accompany transfer of hazardous waste. In any event that it appears that the limit of 200 kg will be exceeded, the EA must be notified immediately and before the limit is exceeded. As an example, 200 kg equates to approximately ten small TVs; 14 lead acid batteries; 500 fluorescent tubes; five small domestic fridges.

Information required for registering as a hazardous waste producer includes the following.

Organisation:

- Name of organisation.
- Address and postcode of the applicant.
- Contact name of the applicant.
- Contact details for the applicant.

Sites to be registered:

- Name of organisation for which notification is required.
- Address and postcodes of all sites that require notification.
- Contact names and telephone number for contact person at each site to be registered.
- Previous registration number (if applicable).
- The Standard Industry Classification (SIC) code for the main activity that produces the waste (the 2003 UK SIC listing codes must be used and are obtainable from www.statistics.gov.uk/methods_quality/sic/downloads/UK_SIC_Vol2(2003).pdf)

- The number of employees working at the premises for which notification is required.
- Customer reference.
- Proposed notification start date.

Sites producing hazardous waste are required to provide separate registrations, although multiple sites can be registered on the same notification (up to a maximum of 2,000 premises). Therefore, a head office could register all its sites centrally, but each site would have a separate unique registration number and require a separate fee.

Applications for registration can be made using the internet, on disk, via email, by phone or on a paper form and each method attracts a charge of up to £28. Payment method depends on the method of registration. For more information on registering, refer to the appropriate section of the EA's website at www.environment-agency.gov.uk/subjects/waste, contact the EA on 08708 502 858 (weekdays 9 am to 5 pm) and refer to the documents entitled *Do I Need to Notify My Premises?, A Guide To The Hazardous Waste Regulations* (HWR02A) and *How to Notify Your Premises, A Guide to the Hazardous Waste Regulations* (HWR02B).

Step Three – Waste storage
Wastes should be appropriately and securely stored at all times to ensure compliance with the Duty of Care Regulations and must be prevented from causing pollution or harm. It is not appropriate to burn, bury or pour away wastes or indeed illegally dispose of them, for instance on another premises.

Fly-tipping is illegal and, under recent changes to Section 33 of the Environmental Protection Act (EPA) 1990 by the Clean Neighbourhoods and Environment Act 2005, can be punishable by fines up to £50,000 or 12 months' imprisonment (or both). If prosecuted in the Crown Court, the fine may be unlimited or five years' imprisonment. Since April 2007 the EA has had powers under Regulation 70 of the Hazardous Waste Regulations 2005 to issue Fixed Penalty Notices (FPNs) for certain environmental offences, including failure to provide evidence of being a registered waste carrier, failing to comply with laws on the Duty of Care and certain offences relating to managing hazardous waste as set out in the hazardous waste regulations. The FPN is currently £300, payable within 28 days of issue of the notice and if left unpaid the EA may resort to prosecution.

Step Four – Identify the most appropriate means of waste management

Regular reviews of waste management options ought to be undertaken – contractors' costs, escalating landfill tax and other measures make waste disposal expensive. For example, check whether wastes can be reused, recycled or reclaimed or indeed if the processes undertaken can be modified to reduce the amount, or even types, of wastes generated. Not only is this a more environmentally friendly and sustainable option, but it may have cost benefits too, in the short or long term.

Other examples include monitoring the use of raw materials, chemicals, water etc., with a view to reducing them, use of alternatives with low(er) environmental impact, use of oil interceptors and segregation of 'clean' and 'dirty' products to minimise the amounts of effluent or hazardous waste generated, or even introduction of compactors to reduce waste volume / bulk which therefore requires fewer waste collections. Each of these may have an impact on waste management and associated disposal costs.

Step Five – Select authorised waste carriers and disposal contractors

It is a legal requirement to transfer controlled waste by use of an authorised waste carrier such as a registered carrier or holder of an environmental permit (formerly a waste management licence), unless for instance you are carrying only your own waste to be disposed of or recovered, unless it is construction or demolition waste. Current exemptions include animal by-products, mines and quarries waste or agricultural waste, yet if these are mixed you will need to register as a waste carrier. However, this exemption is subject to change following a judgment in the European Court of Justice (CIWM, August 2007). Charities and voluntary organisations may collect or transport waste on a professional basis but must register with the EA as a waste transporter. Registration as an authorised carrier is still required even if waste is only occasionally transported.

Some commercial or trade wastes can be handled by your local authority's collection or disposal schemes, but check with them first. Ensure that waste contractors' authorisations are current and valid for your particular waste materials. Check actual copies of contractors' licences and, if unsure on any point, double-check with the EA. If you suspect any problems, suspend waste transfers and alert the EA.

Step Six – Maintain comprehensive records

All controlled waste (i.e. generated from households, commerce or industry) transfers / movements, intermediate storage, recovery, or disposal must be accompanied by a controlled waste transfer note (CWTN). This should include appropriate information such as a written description of the waste and name of the person to whom the waste is being transferred.

A transfer note should be completed for each individual transfer or, alternatively, a 'season ticket' can be completed which covers a pre-agreed (multiple) sequence of collections of small amounts of waste from more than one premises collected on the same vehicle and being delivered to the same consignee. Waste carriers or contractors will often provide this as part of their overall service. In addition all and each hazardous waste transfer must be accompanied by a hazardous waste consignment note (HWCN), even if from premises exempt from registration. The single movement HWCN is a three-part form and each part of the form should be completed. They are colour-coded and labelled as follows:

- Producer's / holder's / consignor's copy (White).
- Carrier's copy (Gold).
- Consignee's copy (Pink).

Each member of the chain has legal responsibility for ensuring that the procedures are followed and paperwork is all correct. Checking is not only in one direction. No one should accept waste from a source that seems to be in breach of the duty of care. Waste may only come either from the person who first produces or imports it or from someone who has received it.

All hazardous waste to be accepted at permitted waste management facilities must also meet minimum regulatory obligations relating to waste pre-acceptance, waste acceptance and waste storage. To find out how to meet the waste acceptance criteria of particular wastes, talk to your waste contractor or waste facility operator.

HWCNs must be kept on file for a minimum period of three years from the date on which the waste was transferred to another person or where it was disposed. It is the record holder's responsibility to ensure that all records are kept securely and are readily retrievable at all times. In the case of hazardous waste, a consignee (receiver of waste) must also keep detailed records showing the location(s) of where wastes are kept or deposited and provide returns to producers, holders or consignors.

For further details refer to the documents entitled *Consignment Notes: Multiple Collections, A Guide to the Hazardous Waste Regulations* (HWR03B), *Consignment Notes: Standard Procedure, A Guide to the Hazardous Waste Regulations* (HWR03A) *and Record Keeping. A Guide to Hazardous Waste Regulations* (HWR05) prepared by the EA.

Additional points for landlords or managing agents

A waste broker is an individual or company who arranges for the disposal or recovery of controlled waste on behalf of another party. Such arrangements will include those for the transfer of waste. Brokers do not handle the waste themselves or take it in their own physical possession, but control what happens to it.

Subject to various provisions, it is an offence for anyone to arrange on behalf of another person for the disposal or recovery of controlled waste if they are not registered as a broker. Anyone subject to the duty of care must ensure that, insofar as they use a broker when transferring waste, they use a registered broker or one exempt from the registration requirements.

Hence, where landlords (in the broadest meaning) or their managing agents, arrange for waste to be disposed of on behalf of their tenants, this may be a waste-brokering operation and the broker would have to register as a waste broker with the EA, prior to providing the service to the tenants. Speak to the EA in the first instance, if advice is required, or other specialists.

Additional considerations

As part of the bigger picture for waste management it is important to understand the legal definition of waste and implications of generating, handling, storing, transporting, treating and disposing of controlled waste. Cost considerations for each of these elements ought to be taken into account as waste disposal costs have increased over recent years due both to the decreased landfill disposal capacity following implementation of the Landfill Directive, increased waste treatment costs and also to the increased data return fees that waste management contractors have to pay the EA. There is therefore a real financial gain to be made in effectively reducing and managing the disposal of wastes and in particular hazardous waste types.

See also: Recycling, p.614; WEEE: The Waste Electrical and Electronic Equipment Regulations and RoHS, p.744

Sources of further information

A considerable amount of information on waste management can be found on the EA's website: www.environment-agency.gov.uk

The Department for Environment Food and Rural Affairs (Defra) website also offers much information on environmental, including waste management; topics at www.defra.gov.uk/

The Envirowise programme can supply information and assistance via its helpline on 0800 585 794, or website at www.envirowise.gov.uk

WRAP works in partnership to encourage and enable businesses and consumers to be more efficient in their use of materials and recycling at www.wrap.org.uk/ or contact the helpline on 0808 100 2040.

NetRegs is a partnership between the UK environmental regulators – the Environment Agency in England and Wales, SEPA in Scotland and the Environment and Heritage Service in Northern Ireland – and provides free environmental guidance for small and medium-sized businesses throughout the UK. Help and advice is available by business type, environmental legislation and environmental topic and has useful links to other websites: www.netregs.gov.uk/netregs/

National Industrial Symbiosis Programme (NISP) works directly with businesses of all sizes and sectors with the aim of improving cross industry resource efficiency via commercial trading of materials, energy and water and sharing assets, logistics and expertise. It engages traditionally separate industries and other organisations in a collective approach to competitive advantage involving physical exchange of materials, energy, water and/or by-products together with the shared use of assets, logistics and expertise. NISP is delivered at regional level across the UK: www.nisp.org.uk or telephone 0121 433 2650.

Comment...

Waste – out with the old, in with the new

Colin Malcolm has an MA in Environmental Management, is a Full Member of the Institute of Environmental Management and Assessment (IEMA) and sits on the IEMA Full Membership assessment panel. Colin has particular experience in working within industry on environmental legislation compliance and in particular IPPC; Environmental Management System implementation; training development and delivery; and waste, energy and resource efficiency auditing.

Industrial and commercial organisations producing and managing waste have become accustomed to a plentiful and regular flow of regulation governing how waste is stored, transferred and disposed. Waste legislation is currently one of the most complex and dense areas of environmental law and this trend shows little sign of slowing down. The Department for Environment, Food and Rural Affairs (DEFRA) has recently consulted on proposals to revise and tighten controls on the handling, transfer and transport of waste. The revised legislation, which is due to come into force in April 2009, represents the latest in a long-standing trend of regulation to control waste activities.

The Environmental Protection Act 1990 set the framework for much of the waste legislation applicable today, including one of the most widely recognised waste regulations, the Duty of Care. Since the Environmental Protection Act, a plethora of new Regulations have come into force to govern waste, the majority of which have been implemented to comply with European Directives.

Waste legislation has historically adopted many differing approaches towards the regulation of waste management, including generic compliance requirements, taxation, sector-specific measures and producer responsibility focus. Legislation in the early 1990s was driven by clear and generic compliance requirements such as waste transfer documentation and waste carrier licensing, while later years saw legislation incorporate the concept of producer responsibility through, for example, the Packaging Regulations. Green taxation, which has enjoyed significant recent publicity as a favoured regulatory approach, has been used to regulate the waste sector since 1996 through the landfill tax scheme. Individual business sectors have also been specifically targeted by waste law in a clear drive towards bespoke control measures. Recent examples include the End of Life Vehicles Regulations for the vehicle manufacturing sector; the WEEE and RoHS Regulations for the electronics sector and Site Waste Management Plan Regulations for the construction sector.

Notwithstanding the volume and scope of waste law, waste crime remains a significant problem with increases to flytipping and pollution the visible and prominent tip of a deeper problem of regulatory non-compliance. Increased costs associated with waste management and disposal undoubtedly provide a financial incentive for individuals and organisations to knowingly avert their responsibilities. However, many instances of poor compliance originate from a lack of understanding and awareness of compliance requirements.

The DEFRA consultation to update controls on the handling, transfer and transport of waste recognises that levels of compliance are clearly linked to the ease by which the Regulations can be understood by business. This is coupled with recognition that the existing regulatory framework is not set out in a manner that can be easily followed by businesses and that punitive measures have not typically acted as a strong deterrent.
The new Regulations are being structured and developed with a clear objective to improve transparency, the ease by which businesses and regulatory authorities can manage responsibility and by greater enforcement potential.

The second consultation stage, which closed on 8 September 2008, includes a draft of the proposed Regulations and these can be viewed from the DEFRA website at www.defra.gov.uk. DEFRA has also been conducting targeted campaigns around the country to raise the profile and awareness of the new Regulations. The revised Regulations will be redrafted once all consultation feedback has been reviewed; however changes are expected in the following areas:

- A revised, two-tier registration system for waste carriers;
- A new system of waste carrier display notification;
- Raised penalties for non-compliance and new Fixed Penalty Notices;
- Increased stop, search and seizure of vehicle powers; and
- A revised Code of Practice.

The new Regulations will revoke a significant amount of previous waste regulation including, in their entirety, the Controlled Waste (Registration of Carriers and Seizure of Vehicles) Regulations 1991 and The Environmental Protection (Duty of Care) Regulations 1991. Many other existing waste Regulations will be partly revoked, including, amongst others, the Waste Management Licensing Regulations 1994. The new Regulations can therefore be seen primarily as refreshing much of the early 1990s waste legislation with a revised framework and structure.

Streamlining regulation on the handling, transfer and transport of waste is without question an overdue exercise, as is the need to improve the ease by which compliance requirements can be understood and demonstrated. It is expected that the new Regulations will provide a framework by which businesses will find interpretation and compliance easier to follow. Furthermore, the addition of tougher penalties for non-compliance illustrates a commitment from central government to reverse increased trends in waste crime and also to provide greater regulatory teeth towards enforcement. Breaking down the complex and intertwined structure of waste law is undoubtedly a step forward as is the visible commitment to clamp down on those who flout compliance; however the level to which the new Regulations are able to demonstrate an improved system will only become apparent post-April 2009.

Water fittings

Steve Tuckwell, Water Regulations Advisory Scheme (WRAS)

Key points

- National Regulations or by-laws apply to all plumbing systems in premises that have a connection to the public water supply.
- The Regulations' purpose is to prevent waste, misuse, undue consumption, contamination and erroneous measurement of water supplied by a public water supplier.
- The installers and users of plumbing systems have a legal duty to comply with the Regulations or by-laws.
- All plumbing fittings and water-using appliances must be designed, constructed, installed and maintained to meet the requirements of the Regulations.
- In most circumstances, it is a criminal offence to begin the installation of water fittings or appliances, or to use them, without the consent of the water supplier.
- Consent is gained by notifying the water supplier in advance of installation work.

Legislation

- Water Supply (Water Fittings) Regulations 1999.
- Scottish Water By-laws 2004.
- Northern Ireland Water Regulations (legislation being updated).

The Water Supply (Water Fittings) Regulations came into force in England and Wales on 1 July 1999 to replace the suppliers' Water By-laws which had applied since 1989. The by-laws in Scotland were replaced on 4 April 2000, with technically identical requirements which have been updated as the Scottish Water By-laws 2004. Revised Regulations are in preparation in Northern Ireland which will update its Regulations so that there will be similarity throughout the UK. In this chapter, 'Regulations' refers to the legislation covering Scotland, England and Wales.

In all premises that have a public water supply connection, these Regulations control the design and installation of water systems, their maintenance and their disconnection, together with the use of the water that is supplied. They apply to pipework, including the underground supply pipe connecting premises to the water main, to all fittings such as pipes, valves, pumps and storage cisterns, and to all appliances, machines, sanitary ware and hosepipes that are connected to the plumbing system or receive water from it. The Regulations do not apply to premises that have no public water supply, e.g. those with only a privately owned borehole or well supply. However, the Regulations do provide a Code of Practice for plumbing systems used with private supplies, where prevention of contamination and waste of water are equally important.

Implications

What are the implications for workplace managers? It is important that the Regulations are complied with to protect all those using your premises against contamination of water for domestic purposes (bathing, cooking, drinking), to ensure reliable and robust plumbing systems, to obtain efficient use of water and to avoid criminal prosecution and possible claims for compensation from those affected by incidents.

The Regulations place duties on installers and users of plumbing systems as follows, but introduce a benefit too:

■   Give advanced notification and have the Water Supplier's consent for proposed plumbing work (new plumbing installations in all premises and changes in existing non-domestic premises).
■   All points of use must be adequately protected against contamination by backflow.
■   WCs and urinals must be installed and maintained to consume no more than permitted flush volumes.
■   Approved contractors are permitted to do certain types of work without the prior consent of the water supplier, so providing more flexibility in carrying out work. They also provide their clients with the reassurance of a certificate guaranteeing compliance of their work with the Regulations. These aspects are described more fully below.

Notification

The Regulations require prior notification to the water supplier of the intention to install any water fittings. The only exception is the extension of the water system of an existing house, which does not have to be notified unless there are certain specific items to be installed (see below). A table included in the Regulations lists certain types of fittings that need specific approval. Many of these relate to water conservation requirements such as the need to notify the installation of a bath having a capacity

of more than 230 litres; a pump drawing more than 12 litres per minute; a water treatment unit incorporating reverse osmosis, producing a waste water discharge or requiring the use of water for regeneration or cleaning; an automatic garden watering system; the laying of underground pipes outside the minimum depth of 750 mm or the maximum of 1,350 mm; and the construction of a swimming pool with a capacity greater than 10,000 litres being replenished automatically and from the water supplier's mains.

The remaining items requiring notification relate to contamination hazards such as the installation of a bidet with an ascending spray or flexible hose, and backflow protection devices designed to protect against the highest two categories of risk.

The written notification must include plans of the relevant parts of the premises, plans of the plumbing layout and fittings to be installed, and details of the person making the notification and that to whom a consent should be sent. Within ten working days of receipt of the notification, the water supplier must either grant consent, with conditions if necessary, or refuse consent, otherwise consent is deemed to have been given and installation can start. A leaflet summarising notification requirements is available on the WRAS website (www.wras.co.uk).

Suitability of fittings

There is no need to remove, replace, alter, disconnect or stop using any fittings that were lawfully installed under the by-laws before the Regulations came into force. However, in all new installations or modifications or extensions of existing systems, water fittings must comply – by being of an appropriate quality and standard and suitable for their intended purpose. To demonstrate that they are compliant, fittings must:

- carry an appropriate CE mark;
- conform with an appropriate European harmonised standard or European Technical Approval (ETA);
- be manufactured in accordance with an appropriate British Standard or an equivalent standard of a state that is a member of the European Economic Area; or
- comply with the performance specification approved by the 'regulator' (e.g. the Secretary of State).

Currently there are no relevant CE marks or harmonised standards available. Some water fittings with 'Kitemarks' are manufactured to relevant British Standards. The easiest way to demonstrate compliance of water fittings is to choose those that manufacturers have voluntarily submitted for checking by WRAS. These fittings and materials are assessed by the water suppliers' representatives themselves and are listed as WRAS Approved Products in the *Water Fittings and Materials Directory*.

The owner or occupier of the property is liable if installed fittings do not comply with the Regulations and if the installation has not been carried out 'in a workmanlike manner' – e.g. in accordance with an appropriate standard such as BS 6700 for the plumbing installations for domestic purposes in buildings.

Preventing contamination by backflow
If the usual direction of flow of water in pipes is reversed, there is a risk of contamination being drawn into the pipework from downstream appliances or processes and affecting drinking water supplies, either in the premises themselves or in adjacent premises. The Regulations define five levels of backflow risk ('fluid categories') according to the risk each represents to health and set out the acceptable devices for preventing backflow at each level of risk. When designing new

plumbing systems or making changes to existing ones, a risk assessment is required to determine the level of risk and suitable protective devices must then be installed. More information is given about this in the WRAS *Water Regulations Guide*.

Requirements for WCs and urinals
The maximum flush volume for new WCs is six litres and European-style drop valves, flap valves, flushing valves and flushing cisterns are permitted, provided they have undergone testing in accordance with a performance specification approved by the regulator. It is an offence to use valves and WCs that do not comply. Like-for-like replacements of already installed WCs exceeding six litres flush will still be permitted. WC cisterns no longer have to have an external warning pipe to indicate if the inlet valve is leaking. Instead an internal arrangement is permitted allowing water to run into the back of the WC pan via the flush pipe. Dual-flush WCs are reintroduced, but the smaller flush must not be greater than two-thirds of the larger flush.

Water saving
In June 2003 the regulator approved the retrofitting of devices into existing 7.5- or 9-litre 'by-laws' WC cisterns, which were installed before July 1999, to modify them to provide dual-flush or interruptible flush. This offers significant water savings for older premises. Cisterns used to be required for flushing urinals, but in non-domestic premises the Regulations permit automatic urinal control with water direct from the mains supply, via suitable backflow protection. This is a major water conservation initiative and workplace managers should now give consideration to taking advantage of it.

In addition to water conservation arising from the use of new types of WCs and urinals, the legislation makes reference to recycled or 'grey' water and the need to mark pipes carrying such water to reduce the risk of dangerous cross-connection with wholesome water.

Approved contractors

The Regulations define 'approved contractors' and give them certain benefits and responsibilities. They can be accredited by the water suppliers or other organisations authorised by the Secretary of State. Among the water suppliers in England and Wales, Anglian, Severn Trent, Thames and Yorkshire Water operate their own schemes; the remainder support the Water Industry Approved Plumbers Scheme (WIAPS) administered by WRAS. Members of WIAPS have demonstrated their experience in plumbing and knowledge of the Regulations. Names and addresses of WIAPS members are given on the WRAS website. Other schemes are operated by the Chartered Institute of Plumbing and Heating Engineering (formerly the Institute of Plumbing), the Association of Plumbing and Heating Contractors, and the Scottish and Northern Ireland Plumbing Employers' Federation.

Approved plumbers must give their customers a certificate of compliance for their work, which the customers can use as a defence in the event of any prosecution for non-compliance associated with the installation work. Approved plumbers can also undertake some types of work without the need for prior consent, which can provide flexibility for the timing of projects.

Practical conclusions

Workplace managers need to be fully aware of the legal requirements that the Regulations place upon the owners and occupiers of premises. Not only does this make sense to avoid possible prosecution and remedial costs if contraventions are found by the water suppliers that enforce the Regulations, but it will prevent contamination of drinking water in the premises and ensure efficient use of water.

Future changes

The Government plans to encourage the efficient use of water for domestic purposes in new and extensively refurbished premises by changes to the Building Regulations, introduced in 2009, which will require the plumbing system to be designed to meet an upper limit for water consumption per head. It then intends to revise the Water Supply (Water Fittings) Regulations to bring in limits for individual types of fittings (taps etc.), with the aim of using scarce water resources more effectively.

See also: Legionella, p.461; Toilets, p.683; Water quality, p.738

Sources of further information

The Water Regulations Advisory Scheme (WRAS) website provides downloads of advice leaflets and guidance notes, details of other publications, recent interpretations of the Regulations, and lists of WIAPS-approved contractors: www.wras.co.uk

Chartered Institute of Plumbing and Heating Engineering: www.iphe.org.uk/

Association of Plumbing and Heating Contractors: www.competentpersonsscheme.co.uk/

Scottish and Northern Ireland Plumbing Employers' Federation: www.snipef.org/

Water quality

Colin Malcolm, Bureau Veritas

Key points

Most commercial premises generate some form of liquid waste such as sewage, waste chemicals, cleaning effluents and contaminated surface run-off. There are three ways of disposing of these:

1. Into foul drains and sewers;
2. Into controlled waters, such as rivers or canals with or without treatment; or
3. Through licensed waste management contractors.

Legislation

- Environmental Protection Act 1990.
- Water Resources Act 1991.
- Water Industry Acts 1991 and 1999.
- Groundwater Regulations 1998.
- Anti-Pollution Works Regulations 1999.

Discharges to foul drains and sewers

Most sites have two drainage systems – surface water drains that remove storm run-off, and foul sewers that channel effluents towards sewage works. It is essential that you have a good understanding of the layout of the drains under your site so that discharges are made to the correct system.

If you discharge just domestic effluent to the foul drain, then you generally do not need a discharge consent. Discharge of anything else to these drains, such as process wastewaters, potentially contaminated surface run-off, condensate from compressors, cooling waters or detergents, is more likely to require a consent. Consents are usually issued by your local water company, such as Thames Water or United Utilities. Consents stipulate the volume and the strength of the effluent which you can discharge. If you are unsure whether you need a

consent, it is best to write to the water company to check.

Do not pour anything apart from domestic effluent into the foul drains. Foul drains flow to a sewage treatment works and, from there, into a watercourse. Oils or other chemicals poured into the drains cannot be treated by the sewage treatment works and so will contaminate the watercourse.

Discharges to storm drains

Storm drainage networks generally discharge directly to a local watercourse without treatment. Because there is no treatment, you must not discharge anything other than clean water to this system unless you have a discharge consent from the Environment Agency. Storm drains should only take rainwater from roofs, yards and roads. You should not wash spilled materials into the drains or wash vehicles in areas where the run-off will discharge into the storm system.

Oil water interceptors are often required in car park areas and capture spilled oils and fuel before they enter the storm drain. If interceptors are installed on your system, you should make sure that these are checked and emptied on a regular basis.

If you have any uncertainties about the need for a consent or if circumstances have changed since an original consent was approved or deemed unnecessary, stop the discharges and check with the Environment Agency as soon as possible.

In the event of any pollution incident involving contamination of controlled waters or land, notify the Environment Agency immediately (incident hotline 0800 80 70 60).

Waste disposal

Where there is no connection to mains sewers or where your effluent is too strong to be disposed directly to a sewer, then you will need to dispose of the liquid as waste.

Pollution prevention

Major prosecutions are often the consequence of a pollution incident that can be prevented or mitigated by careful design and planning. A comprehensive range of pollution prevention measures is essential to minimise the effects of incidents and limit potential liabilities:

- Make sure you know the types of environmental hazard that are present: what quantities there are, how they behave if released – physically, chemically and biologically – and what they could affect.
- Install portable or fixed pipe / pump systems to move liquids around site.
- Use suitable means of storage with adequate containment for all tanks, barrels and holding areas, including any pipes, valves and gauges. Closed loop systems are often an effective solution (e.g. for vehicle washing facilities). Containment structures need to be regularly inspected and maintained. Applying sealants to bund walls and floors protects against cracks, fissures and minor leaks. Ensure that all connections

are in good working order, and that any tanks or pipework that are being replaced are completely empty before dismantling.
- Where surface run-off may be contaminated with silts, heavy metals, chemicals or oils (e.g. car parks, access roads, yards, refuse compactors), potential pollutants should be controlled at source or before discharge by oil separators, gullies, raised kerbing, etc.
- Where significant construction work is undertaken, use a combination of alternative drainage techniques such as SUDS (sustainable urban drainage systems).
- Avoid underground storage and pipe systems wherever feasible. Where these are already installed, you may need to check for leaks. Pressure tests and sending cameras down the pipes can be very expensive but are cheaper than remediation.
- Protect facilities against accidental misuse, vandalism or other interference. Supervise deliveries; install alarm systems, lockable gates, doors and valves, etc.
- In the event of spillage, every effort should be made to contain the liquid – it must not be flushed away or allowed to spread except when there is a danger to life or health. Block off drain entry points or divert spills into holding tanks or 'sacrificial' areas.
- Provide 'spill kits' or sufficient absorbents as well as drain covers, seals and/or booms. Ensure that these materials are replenished regularly. Contaminated absorbent materials may require disposal by special waste contractors. Consider the health and safety implications of pollution incidents (risk assessment, provision of safety information, training and protective equipment).
- Train staff and contractors in correct disposal routines and emergency drills.

- Identify potential risks (e.g. risk of flooding if your site is on a floodplain) and maintain suitable contingency plans. As necessary, advise the relevant authorities, post key information (internal / external contacts, COSHH information, site plans, etc.) and provide equipment to deal with emergencies. Carry out regular drills.

Forthcoming legislation

The Groundwater Regulations 1998 are currently going through a consultation, with new Regulations expected to come into force in November 2008. The new Regulations will supplement existing regulations to protect groundwater in England and Wales. The new Regulations will:

- control groundwater pollution from historically contaminated land;

- use general binding rules or registration schemes for low risk activities;
- provide a more flexible, risk-based approach; and
- cover a wider range of substances.

Further information on the consultation can be found from DEFRA at www.defra.gov.uk

Conclusion

Make sure you have all necessary consents and that you comply with their requirements, including pollution prevention measures.

Reduce or eliminate liquid wastes wherever possible. A good environmental management system will help ensure compliance and avoid increasing liabilities.

See also: Environmental Management Systems, p.296; Legionella, p.461; Waste management, p.725; Water fittings, p.734

Sources of further information

The Environment Agency has a number of useful Pollution Prevention Guidelines (on containment structures, SUDS etc.) available at www.environment-agency.gov.uk.

Weather

David Wright, Kennedys

Key points
- Employers should consider weather conditions and their effect on the working environment when carrying out risk assessments.
- Air temperature is only one of many weather-related factors that should be considered.

Health and safety legislation

The Health and Safety at Work etc. Act 1974 (HSWA) requires employers to take all reasonably practicable steps to ensure the health, safety and welfare of employees at work.

A number of different health and safety regulations impose more specific duties that may require employers to take into account the effects of weather in order to comply with them.

The Workplace (Health, Safety and Welfare) Regulations 1992

Regulation 7 requires that the temperature of all indoor workplaces is 'reasonable' during work hours. The relevant ACoP goes on to explain that, subject to practicability, the temperature "should provide reasonable comfort without the need for special clothing" and that the minimum temperature should be 16°C or, if much of the work is physical, 13°C. The ACoP does not suggest a maximum temperature.

Regulation 11 provides that all outdoor workstations should, so far as is reasonably practicable, provide protection from adverse weather conditions.

The Personal Protective Equipment at Work Regulations 1992

Regulation 4 states that employees must be provided with 'suitable' PPE which is appropriate for conditions in the workplace. In terms of suitability, the ACoP suggests that consideration be given to environmental factors such as the weather if working outside.

The Management of Health and Safety at Work Regulations 1999

Various Regulations, e.g. 3, 16 and 19, and the ACoP, refer to the need to pay attention to the particular risks posed to young people and new and expectant mothers by environmental conditions such as extremes of temperature.

All potentially adverse weather, resulting in working conditions that are hot, cold, windy, icy, or wet, should be taken into account when employers undertake risk assessments, and appropriate measures should be implemented.

Hot weather

Exposure to sun can cause skin damage such as blistering and even skin cancer, which has become the commonest form of cancer in the UK. Exposure to heat can also cause symptoms of 'heat stress', from a mild inability to concentrate and increased irritability up to heat stroke. Although all workers should take steps to protect themselves, employers are also under a duty to consider implementing measures, outdoors or indoors, such as:

- shading employees from direct sunlight;
- the insulation of hot plant and pipes;

- the provision of fans or air-cooling plant;
- ensuring hats and other suitable clothing is worn;
- suitable rest breaks;
- scheduling work during a cooler time of day or year;
- additional supplies of drinking water; and/or
- educating workers.

There is no legal obligation for employers to provide suncream or sunglasses for outdoor workers but they should consider providing sun protection advice as part of health and safety training.

There was concern in 2005 when it was proposed that an EU Directive on optical radiation, originally intended to regulate the health and safety of workers regarding artificial radiation only, should be amended to cover natural radiation from the sun. The result would have been a specific requirement for employers to carry out risk assessments and devise measures to reduce the risks of sun exposure. In September 2005 however, after a vote by the European Parliament, the EU Commissioner for Employment, Social Affairs and Equal Opportunities, Vladimir Spidla, announced that the reference to sunlight would be removed from the Directive.

Cold weather

Just as for hot weather and hot conditions, employers should risk-assess their employees' workplaces and activities with the effects of cold weather in mind.

Possible risk mitigation measures include:

- the provision of mobile facilities such as heated cabins;
- warm drinks and sufficient breaks in which to have them and warm up;
- rescheduling work to warmer times of the year;

- systems of work to limit exposure, such as job rotation; and
- appropriate PPE for cold environments.

As far as the last of these measures is concerned, the House of Lords' decision in the case of *Fytche v. Wincanton Logistics plc* (2004) UKHL 31 provides some useful guidance. A lorry driver employed to collect milk from farms was provided by his employer with steel-capped safety boots to protect his toes from falling objects. In exceptionally wintry weather the driver's tanker became stuck on a remote snow-covered road. Although the employer's standing instruction in these circumstances was for drivers to use the cab telephone to call for help and wait to be rescued, this driver decided to dig himself out. One of his boots had a tiny hole in it and as a result freezing water penetrated and caused mild frostbite to the driver's little toe. He subsequently sued his employer on the basis that it had failed to maintain his boots in an efficient state, efficient working order and good repair as required by Regulation 7 of the PPE at Work Regulations 1992. Having failed at first instance and on appeal, the driver's case finally ended up in the House of Lords, who confirmed that the requirement to maintain was restricted to ensuring PPE was efficient for the purpose of protecting against the relevant risk. The boots had been adequate for the driver's ordinary conditions of work, the tiny hole did not constitute a breach of the employer's duty to maintain, so the driver's appeal was dismissed.

Travelling to and from work in adverse weather

Q: What happens if employees are unable to get into work because of adverse weather conditions?

A: Much will depend on whether or not the reason for non-attendance is reasonable, i.e. whether the employee has made a reasonable effort to get to work. An employee who fails to attend without a reasonable excuse is absent without leave and, subject to the terms of the employment contract, the employer may take disciplinary action which might include withholding pay. If the excuse for non-attendance is reasonable, and the employment contract allows it, the employer may still withhold pay or, if the employee enjoys more than the 20-day statutory holiday entitlement, require holiday to be taken. However, employers who allow time off with pay in these circumstances will often benefit from improved employee morale, attitude and loyalty, and a common sense approach should be adopted wherever possible. From a safety perspective, employers should be wary of exerting undue pressure on employees to drive to work in dangerous conditions.

And finally...

Although employers may often feel as though the law is stacked against them, requiring them to cross every single 't' and dot every single 'i' in the pursuit of absolute safety, the weather-related 1999 High Court case of *Groody v. West Sussex County Council* (1999) LTL 21/9/99 might give some comfort. An office worker employed in the County Hall offices in Chichester claimed she fell and was injured when she was dazzled by bright sunlight reflected off a photocopier and failed to see a step to a low platform. Despite the fact that she had successfully negotiated the step on a daily basis and again just prior to her accident and it had a fixed right-angled white edging, the worker alleged her employer was negligent in failing to (a) post a warning notice, (b) carpet the platform in a different colour to the rest of the floor, and (c) shade the windows to prevent sunlight from entering and reflecting off the photocopier. In deciding against the worker, the court held that the key question was whether it was reasonably foreseeable that there was a risk in clear weather, at certain times of the day and year, that the sun would shine directly into the office and, either directly or indirectly, by means of reflection, so distract the people inside from their activities as to expose them to harm. In the court's view, to state the worker's proposition revealed its absurdity.

See also: Outdoor workers, p.544; Personal Protective Equipment, p.568; Radiation, p.598; Ventilation and temperature, p.704

Sources of further information

HSE – thermal comfort: www.hse.gov.uk/temperature/thermal/index.htm

HSE – Sun protection: advice for employers of outdoor workers: www.hse.gov.uk/pubns/indg337.pdf

WEEE – the Waste Electrical and Electronic Equipment Regulations and RoHS

Phil Conran, BIFFA Waste Services

Key points

- The UK consumes around 1.7 million tonnes of electrical and electronic equipment (EEE) every year.
- The WEEE and RoHS Directives (2003/108/EC and 2002/95/EC) aim to minimise the impact of EEE on the environment.
- RoHS was implemented on time in the form predicted.
- Although implementation of the WEEE Directive was severely delayed, the Waste Electrical and Electronic Equipment Regulations 2006 (the WEEE Regulations) came into force in January 2007.
- An amendment was added in 2007.
- This chapter provides a summary of the requirements of WEEE and RoHS and highlights some key issues for Facilities Managers.

New WEEE Regulations

The WEEE Directive should have been in force in the UK by August 2005. The UK WEEE Regulations finally came into force on 2 January 2007 and were fully implemented on 1 July 2007.

Overview of the WEEE Regulations

The law on WEEE requires certain companies – known as 'producers' – to pay for the costs of the collection, treatment and recycling of WEEE for which they are responsible at the end of its useful life. This applies to any company that manufactures EEE, re-sells EEE produced by others under its own brand, or imports or exports EEE to an EU Member State. More limited obligations apply to distributors (including retailers) of EEE and, in certain circumstances, final business users.

WEEE: key features of the WEEE Regulations

- Regulations overseen by the Department of Business Enterprise and Regulatory Reform and regulated by the environmental Agencies (EA in England and Wales, SEPA in Scotland and the EHS in Northern Ireland.
- A national Distributor Takeback Scheme (DTS) has established a national network of Designated Collection Facilities (DCFs) to collect household WEEE.
- All 'producers' of EEE must register with a Government-approved Producer Compliance Scheme (PCS).
- Each PCS will:
    - register members with the the appropriate Agency;
    - provide all quarterly reports to the EA including the amount of EEE by category that its members placed on the market in the

preceding year and the quantities of WEEE collected, reused, treated, recycled and recovered;

– arrange on behalf of members the collection, transportation, treatment and reprocessing of the required amount of WEEE deposited at DCFs to meet their obligations; and

– arrange settlement at the end of each compliance period where under- or over-collection has occurred.

■ Each individual PCS must contractually agree with its members how the members share the costs of dealing with their aggregate WEEE obligations.

■ DCFs operate under a Code of Practice to govern collection of WEEE.

■ All WEEE must be taken to Approved Authorised Treatment Facilities (AATFs) for treatment, recycling and recovery.

■ Annual compliance periods are for calendar years other than the first year which was for six months from 1 July – 31 December.

■ The Environment Agency has national responsibility for receiving all quarterly data from PCSs and AATFs and for providing market share data to PCSs.

■ At the end of each year, the EA will calculate scheme market share obligations based on actual amounts of EEE placed on the market and the amounts of WEEE arising. Schemes will then be notified of their final obligations and will have to show how they have discharged them.

■ AATFs issue 'Evidence Notes' confirming treatment, recycling and recovery of quantities of WEEE. These are then used by PCSs to demonstrate compliance.

■ PCSs may trade Evidence Notes with other schemes.

■ Evidence must all be placed on a Government-controlled Settlement Centre used by the EA to track compliance and enabling trading of evidence between PCSs.

Scope of the WEEE Regulations

Products categories:

1. Large household appliances (e.g. white goods less cooling equipment).
2. Small household appliances (e.g. vacuums, irons, toasters etc.).
3. IT and telecoms equipment (e.g. computers, printers, calculators, phones, answer machines etc. but not displays).
4. Consumer equipment (e.g. radios, hi-fi equipment, electronic musical instruments etc. but not televisions).
5. Lighting equipment (but not household lighting).
6. Electrical and electronic tools (e.g. drills, saws, sewing machines etc., but excluding large stationary industrial tools).
7. Toys and leisure and sports equipment (e.g. train sets, video games, coin slot machines etc.).
8. Medical devices (e.g. dialysis machines, ventilators etc.) (Note that this category is not covered by the RoHS Directive at present – see below.).
9. Monitoring and Control instruments (e.g. smoke detectors, thermostats etc.) (Note that this category is also not covered by the RoHS Directive at present.).
10. Automatic dispensers (e.g. ATMs, vending machines etc.).
11. Display equipment (e.g. TVs and monitors).
12. Cooling equipment (e.g. refrigeration equipment).
13. Gas discharge lamps.

Are you affected?

For a preliminary guide, consider the questions below (definitive legal advice should be sought in every case).

1. Does your business:

- manufacture; or
- sell under its own-brand (even if manufactured by another); or
- distribute (which includes retailing and distance selling, e.g. via the internet); or
- import into the UK; or
- export into the EU, any electrical equipment not exceeding 1000 volts AC and 1500 volts DC?

If so go to Question 2.

2. Does that EEE fall into one of the above broad product categories? The products listed in these categories, taken from Annex IB to the WEEE Directive, are not exhaustive. For instance, commercial cookers would be counted under Category 1.

If so, go to Question 3.

3. Does your equipment fall into any of the exempt categories (described below)?

Exempt products:

- Part of another type of equipment that does not fall within the scope of the WEEE Directive (for example a car radio that would be included in the ELV Regulations);
- part of a fixed installation such as a heating system;
- Intended solely for national security / military use;
- Large-scale, stationary industrial tools;
- Household luminaires (this exception applies to WEEE only, not RoHS);
- Implanted or infected medical products; and

- Filament light bulbs (this exception also applies only to WEEE, not RoHS).

If not, go to Q4. If so, the new laws probably do not apply to your business. (Note there are other specific exceptions to the RoHS directive that may be relevant but are too detailed to be included in this chapter.)

4. Is the main power source of your product electricity?

If so, go to Q5. If not, the new laws probably do not apply to your business.

5. Is electricity needed for the product to perform its primary function? For example, could you use the product for the function for which it is designed without an electricity supply?

If so, the product in question may well be covered by these new laws.

If you suspect the new laws may be applicable to your business, you need to act now.

Practical implications

It will be a criminal offence not to comply with these various obligations.

There are no exemptions for small companies or persons handling only small quantities of WEEE.

Summary of key impacts

1. Producers

If you are a 'producer' the following are the key impacts upon you.

Compliance scheme membership

You will need to join a PCS and that PCS will need to register you with the EA if you wish to continue lawfully to place EEE on the UK market.

Household WEEE financing

Since 1 July 2007, producers (through their schemes) have had to pay for the cost of the collection, treatment, recovery and environmentally sound disposal of household WEEE deposited at designated collection facilities. Slightly more complex obligations apply in relation to B2B WEEE and these are addressed below.

Business WEEE financing

The rules regarding responsibility for business WEEE depend on whether the WEEE in question is historical business EEE (business EEE placed on the market before 13 August 2005 that has become WEEE) or new business EEE (business EEE placed on the market after 13 August 2005 that has since become WEEE).

If a producer has supplied or supplies new EEE to business users after 13 August 2005, it will be required to finance its treatment, recovery and disposal when that new EEE becomes waste in just the same way as for household WEEE, unless it contractually agrees otherwise with the business user in question. Subject to the provision below, it will not, however, have obligations in relation to historical (pre-13 August 2005) business EEE.

If a producer supplies new EEE to a business user after 13 August 2005 which replaces on a like-for-like basis historical EEE currently held by that business user, it will be required to finance the treatment, recovery and disposal of the original, replaced EEE – again unless it contractually agrees otherwise with the business user in question. This is so even though the same producer may not have supplied the original EEE at all.

'Like-for-like' purchases mean products that are intended to replace the relevant WEEE and are of an equivalent type or fulfil the same function on a common sense approach, even though not an identical replacement.

Buyers and sellers of business EEE should therefore be considering the position they intend to take on contractual allocation of liability for WEEE compliance and what language may therefore need to be introduced into standard terms of business for the sale / purchase of EEE.

If historical business EEE is simply disposed of without 'like-for-like' replacement, the business end-user bears the financing obligation (see below).

Product marking

Producers must also ensure that they comply with WEEE information and marking requirements. These require producers to mark all EEE they place on the market after 1 April 2007 with:

■ the designated symbol of a crossed-out wheelie bin with a date of manufacture or black bar underneath; and
■ the producer's identity.

RoHS compliance: restrictions on use of certain hazardous substances

Since 1 July 2006, subject to certain limited exemptions, producers must ensure and be able to demonstrate that their EEE products placed on the EU market, and the components in their EEE products (even if supplied by others), do not contain more than the prescribed amounts of lead, mercury, cadmium, hexavalent chromium, polybrominated biphenyls (PBBs) or polybrominated diphenyl ethers (PBDEs). Those prescribed amounts are shown below.

RoHS maximum concentration values:

■ up to 0.1% by weight in homogenous materials for lead, mercury, hexavalent chromium, PBB and PBDE; and

- up to 0.01% by weight in homogenous materials for cadmium.

RoHS exemptions
While the RoHS Directive essentially applies to all of the same products as WEEE, there are some very important additional exceptions. Some have already been specified. In addition you should note those below:

- For the time being, the RoHS requirements do not apply to products within categories 8 or 9 of Annex IB of the WEEE directive, namely Medical Devices (category 8) and Monitoring and Control Instruments (category 9).
- Specific applications of the prescribed substances are exempted, as specified in the Annex to the RoHS Directive itself as amended (for example lead in the glass of cathode ray tubes, electronic components and fluorescent tubes). Various further exemptions are being considered at present.
- The requirements of RoHS do not apply to spare parts for the repair of, or to the reuse of, EEE put on the market before 1 July 2006.

RoHS compliance and supply chain auditing
The UK has adopted a self-declaration approach to compliance. However, this is bolstered by risk-based market surveillance by the National Weights and Measures Laboratory. Technical documents and other information sufficient to demonstrate product compliance must be kept by producers for a minimum of four years and produced on request.

If your product contains materials supplied by third parties you should be carrying out adequate RoHS compliance auditing of your supply chain.

If you market your product in other EU Member States, you will need to find out what approach to implementation and compliance is being adopted in each state and ensure that your product is compliant there as well.

RoHS due diligence defence
A defence of due diligence is available in the UK to prosecution under the RoHS legislation, provided the business can show that it took "all reasonable steps and exercised all due diligence" to avoid committing the offence.

2. Distributors
If you are a retailer of, or otherwise provide, new EEE of any of the kinds described above to household users on a commercial basis, then these laws impose two key obligations which are described below.

Distributor obligations are policed by the Vehicle Certification Agency (VCA).

Free take-back of WEEE
- Since 1 April 2007, you have had to offer your customers free take-back of their WEEE when they make a 'like-for-like' purchase of new equipment. You may choose to comply with this obligation yourself (e.g. by in-store take-back or by collection-on-delivery, provided it is free of charge) or by participating in a Government-approved retailer compliance scheme offering WEEE take-back to consumers. In practice, the latter is likely to be the most convenient route for many retailers, particularly distance sellers.
- WEEE thus collected will then have to be properly disposed of by you (or the compliance scheme on your behalf) at a designated collection facility. This distributor take-back obligation does not apply to sales to business users.

Provision of information to customers

Also from 1 April 2007, retailers and other distributors must also take adequate steps to ensure that private householders are informed of:

- the WEEE take-back facilities available to them (either from the retailer / distributor itself or other facilities); and
- the meaning of the crossed-out wheelie bin symbol on products covered by the WEEE Directive;
- the role of users in private households in contributing to reuse, recycling and other forms of recovery of WEEE; and
- the potential effects on the environment and human health of WEEE.

It will be a criminal offence for any affected retailer / distributor not to comply with these duties.

Distributors have no obligations under the RoHS directive, which applies only to producers, and no obligations in relation to WEEE beyond the two identified above.

3. Business end-users

There are circumstances in which businesses can have obligations under the WEEE Directive even though they do not themselves produce or sell EEE.

Duties of business end-users of EEE

The end-user will assume full responsibility for financing the costs of the treatment, recovery and sound disposal of the WEEE only in the following cases:

- Where a business has purchased EEE before 13 August 2005 and does not buy 'like-for-like' replacement goods when it reaches the end of its useful life and is disposed of;
- Where a business has purchased EEE before 13 August 2005 and does replace it with 'like-for-like' goods, but agrees with its supplier to accept responsibility for the WEEE being replaced; and
- Where a business purchases EEE after 13 August 2005 and agrees with its supplier to accept responsibility for it when it becomes WEEE.

See also: Recycling, p.614; Waste management, p.725

Sources of further information

BERR: www.berr.gov.uk/sectors/sustainability/weee/page30269.html

Environment Agency: www.environment-agency.gov.uk/weee

SEPA: www.sepa.org.uk/producer/weee.htm

VCA: www.vca.gov.uk/enforcement/weee-enforcement.asp

List of PCSs: www.environment-agency.gov.uk/commondata/acro-bat/08_07_16_2028135.pdf

Transform Compliance scheme: www.transform-uk.net

Research has shown that many businesses are unaware of their duties under the Regulations, and with this in mind Workplace Law Group has produced the *Guide to WEEE 2007*, a downloadable publication that explains the varying responsibilities and roles under the new legislation. For more information visit www.workplacelaw.net/Bookshop/GuidesTo.

Wheelclamping

Dale Collins, Bond Pearce LLP

Key points

- Land owners and occupiers who allow their land to be used as a car park have the right to restrict that right to specified persons, e.g. those who have purchased and are using a valid ticket. Running with that right is the right to demand a payment for unlawful use and the ability to prevent the removal of unauthorised vehicles until such time as a payment is made.
- Where such a system is in place, however, the land owner or occupier must ensure that the person using the car park is aware of that fact to prevent actions for trespass and criminal damage being pursued.
- In accordance with the Private Security Industry Act 2001, since 3 May 2005 the wheelclamper must be licensed with the Security Industry Authority, failing which criminal offences are committed with, potentially, large fines being imposed.

Legislation

- Private Security Industry Act 2001.

Cases

- *Arthur v. Anker* (1996) 3 All ER 783.
- *Vine v. Waltham Forest London Borough Council* (2000) *The Times* 12 April 2000.
- Rowencroft Immobilisers.

The law

A private landowner has a right to take reasonable steps to protect his land, and any interest in that land, from harm. Anything placed on that land without his consent is a trespass. A trespass is an actionable tort (civil wrong) which gives rise to a claim in damages for compensation. It also gives rise to the right of 'self-help' – in other words, the ability to take action oneself to remove the trespassing article.

Clearly, vehicles parked unlawfully on private land are trespassing, and, although there may be no physical damage being caused by their being parked on the land, a claim can arise as damage does not need to be physical – it can arise from the landowner being unable to use that space. The car park owner or manager will want the car removed and the ability to claim immediate damages to represent the loss. He does not want to have to issue proceedings in court. The only way to do this is to ensure that the car is not removed without such payment being made.

The way to do this is through the use of wheelclamps.

However, the placing of a wheelclamp on another person's vehicle is itself a trespass, allowing the car owner to bring a claim for damages. In addition, should the installation of the clamp (or its removal) cause damage, the clamper could be liable for that damage and face a charge of criminal damage in the criminal courts.

Also, the wheelclamping itself does not remove the problem, i.e. the loss of car-parking space. In fact, it exacerbates the problem by potentially keeping the vehicle *in situ*.

Thus, in addition to the clamping, which is essentially a detention to secure payment of the fee, it is also necessary to have the ability to remove the obstructing vehicle. This removal can again cause damage.

So, from where do wheelclampers derive their authority preventing them being pursued or prosecuted?

It is all a question of consent.

Where it can be proved that the driver either saw or should have seen a sign prohibiting parking and warning that a wheelclamping regime was in place, the wheelclamping is lawful as the driver is said to accept, either explicitly or by implication, the consequences of his action.

This is best seen in the cases of *Arthur v. Anker* (1996) and *Vine v. Waltham Forest London Borough Council* (2000). In the former, the wheelclamper's actions were held to be lawful as the driver had seen the sign but decided to ignore it. In the latter, as the driver had not seen the sign prohibiting parking, she was found not to have consented to the wheelclamping and thus could recover damages.

In the *Vine* case, Lord Justice May stated:

"… a motorist who appreciates that there are warning signs obviously intended to affect the use of private property for parking vehicles, but who does not read the detailed warning, might, depending on the facts, be held to have consented to, or willingly assumed, the risk of a vehicle being clamped, if the unread warning sign in fact gives sufficient warning that trespassing vehicles would be clamped."

In other words, if the notices are such that it could not reasonably be argued that they were not seen, and if there were signs which made it abundantly clear what would

happen if unauthorised parking occurred, the court would infer consent.

Fee

What is a reasonable fee?

In the *Arthur* case, Master of the Rolls Bingham in his judgment stated:

"I would not accept that the clamper could exact any unreasonable or exorbitant charge for releasing the car, and the court would be very slow to find implied acceptance of such a charge."

In the *Vine* case the fee was £105, and in the *Arthur* case it was £40 to release the clamp and £90 plus storage to return the car. In both of those cases these fees were considered reasonable.

It is clear that the recovery of the costs associated with the wheelclamping scheme is acceptable, but if an attempt was made to make a large profit that would not be acceptable.

Removal

The problem with simply wheelclamping a vehicle which is illegally parked is that it does not free up the space – in other words, it does not solve the problem. The owners of a private car park are entitled, therefore, to reduce their losses by removing the vehicle, provided that removal is specified on the notice.

The additional difficulty with removal, however, is that there is an increased danger of damage being caused during the removal process. However, whether the trespassing owner will be entitled to claim for such damage will again be down to a question of consent. By parking unlawfully in the full knowledge that removal is a possibility, the driver is accepting that there may be some damage incurred, and provided that damage is not unreasonable or unexpected there should be no claim.

Practical guidance

Signage is vitally important in this area. Signs must be prominently displayed where they can be read and where they will be visible to anyone using that car park, and must include, as a minimum, the following information:

- The notice must specify that wheelclamping is in operation, the consequences of parking unlawfully and the cost of removal. (It may be worth considering that as well as written warnings there should be some type of pictogram making it clear that there is no parking except by permit.)
- The notice must contain the contact details for the removal of the wheelclamp (and that removal must be able to take place within a reasonable time).
- If the vehicle is to be removed that fact must be stated.

The British Parking Association (BPA) launched its Code of Practice for Parking Enforcement on Private Land and Unregulated Public Car Parks, Part 1: Vehicle Immobilisation or Removal, in April 2006.

The Code provides a model of best practice for individuals or organisations undertaking vehicle immobilisation or removal of vehicles on private land. Its main objective is to help raise standards in the parking sector and ensure that vehicle immobilisation and removal is undertaken in a responsible, effective and efficient manner.

The RAC Foundation for Motoring stated: "The RAC Foundation for Motoring wholeheartedly supports the BPA wheel clamping Code of Practice. It is concise, fair, workable and, above all, responsible and represents a genuine attempt to introduce a welcome element of reassurance into the sphere of off-street wheel clamping."

It continues:

"Whilst the Code is primarily directed at BPA members, themselves responsible organisations, it could and should be considered by the Security Industry Authority (SIA) as a model of good practice and be incorporated into the SIA Approved Contractors Scheme."

The document provides what is effectively good practice, including information on the types of vehicle that should not be clamped, expected release times to be achieved (usually no more than two hours and certainly never beyond four) and the types of sign to be used in car parks and to be placed on a vehicle following the clamping.

Other practical issues to be considered include the following:

- Photographing the car in relation to the sign (useful evidence).
- Checking the insurance position with regard to public liability.
- Training for those carrying out the wheelclamping and risk-assessing their tasks.

Recent developments

The Private Security Industry Act 2001 has been effective from 1 April 2003. The Act created the Security Industry Authority (SIA), whose job it is to regulate and oversee the private security industry, which includes those undertaking wheelclamping or vehicle immobilisation.

The 'Regulation' is by way of a licensing regime for those involved and the development of criteria for their professional training.

Not only do those working for wheelclamping firms have to be licensed; so, too, do in-house clampers.

There are two types of licence:

1. Front-line licence – for the clampers/immobilisers.
2. Non front-line licence – for the managers and supervisors of the clampers/immobilisers.

The front-line licence costs £245 and is valid for one year. A non front-line licence also costs £245, but is valid for three years. Before such a licence is issued, the individual will be checked out by the SIA (criminal record checks and so on) to ensure he is fit to hold a licence.

Undertaking clamping without a licence is a criminal offence for the individual, giving rise to a fine of £5,000 and/or six months' imprisonment.

In addition, the occupier of the land on which the wheelclamping takes place also commits an offence if an unlicensed clamper is working on his site. The only defence is that either he did not know that the person did not hold a licence or he took all reasonable steps to prevent such an unlicensed person from clamping on the land.

In the Magistrates' Court the penalty is the same as it is for the unlicensed clamper, but the matter may be heard in the Crown Court, where there is an unlimited fine and up to five years' imprisonment.

Where the occupier is a company, not only can the company be held liable, but, where it can be shown that a director, manager or similar officer consented to, connived in or was negligent as to the offence, then that individual can also be personally prosecuted.

The SIA has issued a guidance entitled *Get Licensed*, and this is available on its website (www.the-sia.org.uk). The SIA has the authority to withdraw (revoke) a licence

at any time if the licence holder fails to meet the licensing requirements. It will withdraw a licence if the licence holder:

- is not the person to whom the named licence should have been issued;
- does not have the training qualifications that were claimed on application;
- receives a conviction, caution or warning for a relevant offence; and/or
- loses, or did not have when they applied, the right to remain or work in the UK.

It may also consider taking away a licence if:

- the licence holder breaks the conditions on which the licence was issued;
- the SIA receives non-conviction information suggesting that there is a case for having the licence withdrawn; and/or
- the licence holder becomes subject to detention because of mental disorder.

There is also a power to suspend a licence, with such suspensions having immediate effect. The SIA states that it will consider suspension only where it is reasonably satisfied that a clear threat to public safety could exist if it did not suspend the licence. This usually means that a serious offence has allegedly taken place, where the licence holder has been charged but bailed. It will suspend a licence in other circumstances if it is in the public interest to do so. Since the regime became effective there have been ten revocations of vehicle immobiliser licences.

The SIA published, in April 2007, the SIA Enforcement Policy Code of Practice, which details its powers and how it will use those powers to ensure proactive and effective enforcement; this is also available on its website (www.the-sia.org.uk).

Conclusion

There is little doubt that the regulation of those who undertake wheelclamping (or more strictly vehicle immobilisation) on private land is needed. Examples of the boorish behaviour of some 'clampers' are many and varied, and it is such behaviour that the new regime was created to prevent.

- A man who broke down on a busy road pulled into the car park at a local pub. He went to find a phone box so that he could call out the RAC, leaving his 82-year-old disabled wife in the vehicle. Clampers appeared immediately and demanded that the woman move the car. Her disability prevented her from doing this, so they clamped the vehicle and demanded £80 for its removal.
- A clamper in London impounded a car without notifying the owner and then gave it to his daughter to drive.
- A hearse was clamped with a dead body in the back.
- Some clampers have demanded wedding rings, gold teeth or even sexual favours in lieu of payment.
- Clampers in Doncaster threatened to hold a mother's three-year-old daughter ransom.

Pending the introduction of the licensing regime, some local authorities took their own measures to curb bad practice. In May 2004, Portsmouth City Council and the local police sought and obtained an interim anti-social behaviour order against a wheelclamper who was responsible for the following incidents:

- Cars in a particular car park were all clamped on the blind side with no warning signs on the windscreens, resulting in their being damaged when the unwitting owners returned and drove them away, unaware that they had been clamped. One owner, who did £300 worth of damage to his vehicle, was laughed at and told to "get more glasses" when he challenged the clamper.
- A taxi driver taking money to his son to pay a clamping charge was also clamped and blocked in when he drove into the same car park.
- A man was clamped for the second time when he returned to the car park where he had previously been clamped. He returned because he had appealed the first fine, received no reply and went back to get the clamper's telephone number to follow up. His engine was running and he had pulled only slightly off the road.
- A woman who went to pick up her son took a short cut across a private car park in order to reach a side road. Her exit from the car park was blocked by the clamper demanding money even though her engine was running and her handbrake was not on.
- Clampers attempted to clamp two drivers who had executed three point turns in the road – even though only their rear wheels came in contact with the private car park.
- A woman with her children turned her car in the forecourt of a garage with no intention of stopping. A tow truck pulled in front of her and her car was clamped.

The order prohibits the clamper from:

- clamping without adhering to the British Parking Association codes of practice;
- clamping on land without the written authority of the legal occupier;
- clamping without signs clearly displayed warning of the use of wheelclamps;
- clamping or demanding money without producing the written authority of the legal occupier of the land and proof of identification;
- clamping or attempting to clamp a vehicle while the engine is running and occupied;

- blocking or attempting to block the pathway of a vehicle on the road or private land should the vehicle be occupied and the engine running;
- threatening, abusing or intimidating motorists where a wheelclamp has or is being applied; and
- inciting, encouraging, aiding or abetting any other person to undertake any of the above.

There are still rogue clampers out there, but they are being caught and punished. In May 2008, Rebecca Meakin was sentenced to serve four years' imprisonment after being found guilty to charges of blackmail, at Stafford Crown Court. She was the proprietor of Rowencroft Immobilisers, a clamping and towing service to private landowners in Staffordshire, West Midlands and Wiltshire.

In February 2006 a series of files were presented to the CPS for evidential review relating to incidents centred on two public houses in Staffordshire. At both locations Rowancroft Immobilisers were operating and incidents included allegations of assault, intimidation, theft and threatening behaviour.

The report review regularly showed an increase from the advertised £95 release fee to the £295 towing fee once the recovery truck had been called. This happened within minutes of the motorist parking because the recovery truck was already parked close by.

The company practice of only accepting cash or postal orders increased tension with motorists. When Rowancroft towed away vehicles they refused to state where they had been taken – significant evidence became available to show they were being abandoned on uncontrolled car parks or waste land.

The company had a P.O. box in Worcester as their business address and they used mobile telephone numbers for contact with victims. They were not registered for VAT, had no business bank account and were not a registered company. Records of income and expenditure were not maintained.

Rowancroft had a significant impact on police resources as members of the public were calling for assistance and officers were required to attend, sometimes leading to specific allegations, statements and arrests.

The basis of the blackmail enquiry was that it appeared that Rowencroft were making demands for money and reinforcing the demand with menaces:

- The motorists were prepared to pay £95 for the release of the clamp but £295 was demanded.
- In some cases the motorists were only on the car park for minutes or even seconds and were boxed in and not given the opportunity to drive away when the driver realised there were parking restrictions.
- Some victims parked, left the car park to call into a nearby shop and returned within a couple of minutes. It was considered that to clamp and demand £95 in these circumstances was not reasonable. When the motorist argued there should not be a charge, the fee would be increased to £295 on the basis that the tow truck was coming.
- There were never any allowances made for being elderly / disabled / a doctor on call / mothers with babies / other vulnerable people.
- The car was still on site, not hooked up or removed but a tow fee became payable at the discretion of the clamper.

The menaces were:

- the threat that the car would be taken away;
- the location that the car was to be taken to was never disclosed; and
- veiled threats of violence by the presence of 'heavies'.

See also: Parking, p.550; Vehicles at work, p.701

Sources of further information

British Parking Association: www.britishparking.co.uk

Security Industry Authority: www.the-sia.org.uk

Whistleblowers

Pinsent Masons Employment Group

Key points

- The Public Interest Disclosure Act 1998 protects workers from detriment as a consequence of disclosing wrongdoings on the part of their employer.
- To fall within the protection, the employee's disclosure must have been made in a certain way, about certain matters, to certain people.
- The definition of those protected under the Act goes beyond employees and includes contractors.

Legislation

- Employment Rights Act 1996.
- Public Interest Disclosure Act 1998.
- Public Interest Disclosure (Prescribed Persons) Order 1999.
- Public Interest Disclosure (Prescribed Persons) (Amendment) Order 2003 and 2005.

Protection

The Public Interest Disclosure Act 1998 has become known as the 'Whistleblowers' Act' because it protects workers who suffer detriment as a result of 'blowing the whistle' – disclosing wrongdoing – on their employers, provided that the informer goes through the correct channels.

To be protected, the worker must be able to show that:

- in his reasonable belief the disclosure relates to one of a list of specified wrongdoings; and
- the disclosure is made by one of six specified procedures to specified people.

List of wrongdoings

A protected disclosure is a disclosure made by a worker which in the reasonable belief of the worker tends to show that:

- a criminal offence has been, is being or is likely to be committed;
- a person has breached, is breaching or is likely to breach a legal obligation;
- a miscarriage of justice has occurred, is occurring or is likely to occur;
- the health and safety of an individual has been, is being or is likely to be endangered;
- the environment has been, is being or is likely to be endangered; or
- there is an attempt to cover up one of the above.

Procedures for disclosure

In order to be protected, the disclosure must be made only to the category of persons set out in the Act, not any person.

Any one of six methods of disclosing will be protected so long as the worker can show that he was justified in choosing that method.

1. Disclosure to employer / third party

The disclosure must be in 'good faith' (i.e. honestly, even if it is careless or negligent) and can be to the employer (e.g. telling the chairman that a director is fiddling expenses) or to a third party if one is involved (e.g. a supplier). A policy may also exist allowing workers to complain to a particular person (e.g. an external accountant).

2. Disclosure to legal advisor
A disclosure made "in the course of obtaining legal advice" will be protected even if it is not made in good faith.

3. Disclosure to ministers
A disclosure can be made "in good faith to a Minister of the Crown" if the employer is one appointed by an Act of Parliament (e.g. an NHS trust).

4. Disclosure to prescribed persons
The current list of 'prescribed persons' (see Employment Rights Act 1996, section 43F) is given in the Public Interest Disclosure (Prescribed Persons) (Amendment) Order 1999.

Specific persons are listed for particular purposes or industries including the HSE, Financial Services Authority, HM Revenue & Customs and Serious Fraud Office. The worker must reasonably believe that the information disclosed is substantially true and that it falls within the remit of the prescribed person.

5. Other external disclosure
Wider disclosures are possible to persons such as the media, police and MPs but to remain protected the worker must pass a number of tests.

In such a case, however, the worker must:

- make the disclosure in good faith and not for personal gain;
- reasonably believe that the information disclosed and allegations are substantially true; and
- show it is reasonable to make the disclosure, and that one of the following reasons is true:
  - the worker reasonably believes at the time of making the disclosure that he will be subjected to a detriment by the employer if disclosure is made to the employer or to a prescribed person; or
  - the worker reasonably believes that evidence will be concealed or destroyed if disclosure is made to the employer; or
  - the worker has previously made disclosure of the same information to the employer or to certain prescribed persons.

There is a list of considerations governing whether the disclosure is 'reasonable' or not. These are:

- the identity of the person to whom the disclosure is made;
- the seriousness of the wrongdoing;
- whether the wrongdoing will or is likely to continue or recur;
- whether the disclosure is made in breach of a duty of confidentiality which the employer owes to any other person;
- if the employee has previously disclosed substantially the same information to the employer, or to a prescribed person, whether they have taken action and what action they have taken or might have taken; and
- if a previous disclosure is made to the worker's employer, whether the worker complied with any whistleblowing procedure authorised by the employer.

6. Exceptionally serious failures
Where the wrongdoing is 'exceptionally serious', the other methods of disclosure can be overridden. However, the employee takes clear risks. He must:

- make the disclosure in good faith and not for personal gain;
- reasonably believe that information and allegations are substantially true;
- show that the wrongdoing is of an 'exceptionally serious nature': this

is a matter of fact (the worker could be mistaken, even if he believes it is serious – if wrong, he loses protection); and

- show it is reasonable for the worker to make the disclosure bearing in mind the identity of the person to whom the disclosure is made.

What can the worker claim?

Legal protection is given to workers who make a protected disclosure in certain specified circumstances (see above). They will have the right not to be subjected to any detriment by their employer on the ground that they have made a protected disclosure, and not to be dismissed and not to be selected for redundancy for this reason.

'Detriment' does not technically include dismissal. However, a dismissal will be regarded as automatically unfair if it is due to the worker making a disclosure, and no qualifying period of service is needed for a worker to bring such a claim of unfair dismissal. There is no limit on the amount of compensation that can be awarded.

Practical issues

Employers should consider introducing a whistleblowing policy, separate from disciplinary and grievance procedures, in order to encourage such matters to be resolved within the organisation and in a regulated manner. Further, any provision in a contract of employment purporting to prevent a worker from making a protected disclosure will be void.

See also: Dismissal, p.233

Sources of further information

ACAS: www.ascas.org.uk

Financial Services Authority: www.fsa.gov.uk

Public Concern at Work: www.pcaw.co.uk.

Work equipment

Fiona Montgomerie, Reynolds Porter Chamberlain LLP

Key points

The law relating to work equipment is found in specific statutory regulations which impose duties on all employers. These duties relate to the suitability, selection, maintenance and use of work equipment as well as training to be provided for those using work equipment.

In addition to statutory regulations, employers have common law duties in respect of work equipment.

Legislation

Provision and Use of Work Equipment Regulations 1998 (PUWER)

These Regulations form the core obligations concerning work equipment. PUWER is intended to cover all work equipment (except a ship's work equipment which is, generally, excluded from the Regulations) and to impose general duties. HSE guidance makes it clear that PUWER must be considered in conjunction with the Management of Health and Safety at Work Regulations 1999. These Regulations impose, in particular, a requirement for employers to assess risks to the health and safety of employees and others who are affected by work carried out on behalf of the employer.

To whom do the Regulations apply?

The Regulations apply to all employers. This includes the self-employed for the purposes of equipment which they use at work. The Regulations also apply to anyone who has control of work equipment, control of any person who uses or supervises the use of work equipment or control over the way such equipment is used.

What is work equipment?

This is defined as any machinery, appliance, apparatus, tool or installation for use at work (whether exclusively or not). This is a wide definition and extends to almost all equipment provided for use or used at work, including, for example, parts of machinery, desks, chairs, pens, trolleys and large machine presses. It may also include tools, etc., provided by the employee himself, provided they are used at work. This should not be overlooked and employers ought to consider including such equipment in maintenance checks, etc. However, a distinction does need to be drawn between equipment used at work over which the employer has control and that over which it has little or no control. This was considered by the Court of Appeal in *Smith v. Northamptonshire County Council* (2008) where it was held that a local authority was not liable for failing to maintain a ramp used by its employee at a person's house. For the authority to be caught by the Regulations it needed to have an element of control over the ramp. It did not and the ramp was not work equipment for the purposes of the Regulations.

General obligations

Regulation 4 – Suitability

Work equipment must be suitable (whether in its original state or when adapted) for the purpose for which it is used or provided. Suitability is interpreted in the light of risks to health and safety of those using the equipment, not merely from the point of view of acceptability for the job. Although a heavy burden for employers, it is not absolute. By way of example, work equipment which is ostensibly suitable but which is only rendered unsuitable because of the manner in which it is used by an employee is unlikely to be deemed unsuitable for the purposes of the Regulations. See *Mason v. Satelcom Ltd and East Potential Ltd* (2008). However, depending on the circumstances the employer might be in breach of Regulations 8 and/or 9 discussed further below.

Regulation 5 – Maintenance

This places an absolute obligation on employers to ensure that all work equipment is maintained in an efficient state, in efficient working order and in good repair. If machinery has a maintenance log, that log should be kept up-to-date. The significance of the absolute obligation should be understood. An employer is likely to be liable for defects in machinery or equipment, even though examination would not have revealed the defect. This underlines the importance of ensuring equipment is safe. A useful illustration is the case of *Stark v. Post Office* (2000). Mr Stark was a postman who had been provided with a bicycle to use when delivering mail. Part of the bicycle's front brake broke and lodged in the front wheel, which then locked. Mr Stark was thrown over the handlebars and injured. The court

accepted that even a 'perfectly rigorous' inspection would not have found the defect. Even so, the correct interpretation of the relevant regulation meant that the employer was still at fault. Equipment should, nevertheless, be inspected regularly and results of such inspections recorded.

Although the duty to maintain is absolute, it does not extend to removing transient or temporary conditions. Thus, failing to prevent rainwater accumulating on a step of a bus where the step was considered to be work equipment did not amount to a failure to maintain work equipment in *Green v. Yorkshire Traction Co Ltd* (2001).

Regulation 6 – Inspection

When the safety of work equipment depends on installation conditions, the employer must inspect after installation and before equipment is put into use for the first time, or after assembly at a new site or location. Similarly, if the equipment is exposed to conditions that may lead to a deterioration which could in turn lead to a dangerous situation, there must be regular inspections, as well as inspections each time such conditions occur. Results of inspections must be logged and kept until the next inspection is recorded.

Regulation 7 – Specific risks

Where use of work equipment is likely to involve a specific risk to health and safety, Regulation 7 provides that use of that equipment should be restricted to those given the task of using it and that any repairs, modifications, maintenance or servicing be restricted to those specially selected and trained to do this. It envisages removing such dangerous equipment from the general work population, reserving it for those individuals who are trained to use it.

Regulation 8 – Information and instructions

Employers must give adequate health and safety information to users of work equipment and, where appropriate, written instructions. It is the employer's responsibility to decide on which is the appropriate method of giving the information.

Regulation 9 – Training

This Regulation imposes a duty on employers to ensure that those using work equipment and also supervisors / managers, have received adequate training for the purposes of health and safety. Whether given orally or in writing the guidance should be easily understood by the person to whom it is being given. It should be noted that training is required for all persons who use work equipment, not just employees. Further, the requirement to train is ongoing and does not just apply on recruitment.

Specific requirements

Regulation 10 – Conformity with Community requirements

Work equipment must comply with EC requirements relating to health and safety information, instructions and kite marking.

Regulation 11 – Dangerous parts

There is an absolute obligation to ensure that effective measures are taken, in accordance with PUWER, to prevent access to dangerous parts of machinery. This Regulation is subject to the general requirement in Regulation 4, that work equipment must be suitable, but also deals in detail with requirements for guards and protection devices. The measures that employers must take are placed in a hierarchy comprising of four levels. The

'best' protection is a fixed enclosing guard; next, other guards or protection devices; followed by protection appliances, e.g. pushsticks; and, finally, the provision of training, guidance and supervision.

Regulation 12 – Protection against specified hazards

Employers must take measures to prevent or, where not reasonably practicable, adequately control exposure of those using work equipment to risks to health and safety from various hazards, including articles falling or being ejected from work equipment, work equipment catching fire and the unintended or premature explosion of work equipment. Regulation 12 does not apply in certain high-risk work areas where other specific regulations apply instead, e.g. Control of Asbestos at Work Regulations 1987; Noise at Work Regulations 1989; Control of Lead at Work Regulations 1998. Risk assessments should identify hazards and assess risks likely to arise from them.

Steps should then be taken to prevent the hazard arising. If this is not reasonably practicable, steps should be taken to adequately control exposure to these hazards.

Regulation 13 – High or very low temperature

There is an absolute obligation to ensure work equipment (which includes any article or substance produced, used or stored in the work equipment) has appropriate protection to prevent injury by burn, scald or sear if it is used at a very high or very low temperature. It is anticipated that the risk should be reduced by practical engineering means, i.e. insulation or shielding. If this cannot be done, consideration needs to be given to personal protective equipment. General requirements in respect of training and information apply.

Regulations 14–18 – Controls

These Regulations set out detailed obligations for the use of and provision of controls of work equipment. There are separate provisions for controls which start work equipment (Regulation 14), stop work equipment (Regulation 15) and emergency stop controls (Regulation 16). Regulation 17 imposes an absolute obligation on employers to ensure that all controls for work equipment are clearly visible and identifiable and Regulation 18 deals with an employer's obligations to ensure the safety of control systems.

Regulation 19 – Isolation from sources of energy

This sets out an employer's duty to isolate appropriate work equipment from power sources to prevent risks to employees' health and safety.

Regulation 20 – Stability

Work equipment or parts of such equipment must be stabilised as necessary, for the purposes of health and safety. Stabilisation can be effected by a number of means e.g. fastening or clamping.

Regulation 21 – Lighting

Suitable and sufficient lighting, taking into account the work being carried out, must be provided. This means the light provided must suit the job being carried out – this may mean special or additional lighting.

Regulation 22 – Maintenance operations

Appropriate measures must be taken to ensure that work equipment can, so far as is reasonably practicable, be maintained either when shut down or in such a way as to prevent risk to the health and safety of persons carrying out such maintenance.

Regulation 23 – Markings

All work equipment must be marked in a clearly visible way with any markings needed for health and safety reasons. This includes clear identification of controls, safe working loads and the contents of storage vessels. The purpose of this Regulation is to ensure workers know what they are dealing with.

Regulation 24 – Warnings

All work equipment must carry any warnings or warning devices appropriate for health and safety. Such warnings must be clear and easily understood.

Regulations 25–30

These deal with requirements relating to mobile work equipment, including forklift trucks and self-propelled work equipment and are discussed separately below.

Regulation 25

Requires employers to ensure no employee is carried on mobile work equipment unless it is suitable for carrying persons and has incorporated safety features.

Regulation 26

Imposes specific requirements relating to the need to stabilise work equipment ridden on by employees.

Regulation 27

Imposes a requirement relating to reducing the risk of forklift trucks rolling or overturning.

Regulation 28

Deals with safeguards which self-propelled work equipment should have to protect the safety of employees using it whilst it is in motion. Non-exhaustive examples include a requirement for the equipment to have a device for braking and stopping and facilities for preventing its being started by an unauthorised person. Other safeguards which may be required depend on the circumstances and environment in which the work equipment is being used and are set out in full in the Regulations.

Regulation 29

Deals with safeguards which apply to remote-controlled self-propelled work equipment. Where there is a risk to a person's safety when in motion, the equipment must stop automatically once it leaves control range and incorporate features guarding against crushing or impact.

Regulation 30

Imposes requirements relating to minimising risks from seizure of drive shafts.

Regulations 31–35

These apply to some power presses only and impose requirements in respect of guarding, examination, reporting and keeping of information. These requirements are set out in detail in the Regulations.

Consequences of breach of the Regulations

Any breach of the Regulations may give rise to both civil and criminal liability.

Guidance

The Regulations are accompanied by guidance. This contains some Approved Code of Practice material, as well as general information.

Other legislation

Although much of the law relating to work equipment is contained within PUWER, there are other statutory provisions which may apply to specific types of work equipment, which may need to be considered in conjunction with PUWER. These include:

- *The Personal Protective Equipment at Work Regulations 1992*. These govern equipment worn or held by employees and provided for safety.
- *The Lifting Operations and Lifting Equipment Regulations 1998*. These Regulations deal specifically with lifting equipment.
- *The Workplace (Health, Safety and Welfare) Regulations 1992*. Whilst not designed to deal with work equipment in some circumstances it may not be clear whether 'equipment' is, in fact work equipment – for the purposes of PUWER – or whether it forms part of the workplace itself. In the Court of Appeal case *PRP Architects v. Reid* (2007) a lift was work equipment but it was suggested that fire doors were more likely part of the workplace whilst in *Beck v. United Closures and Plastics Ltd* (2002) the Scottish Outer House decided that two heavy doors were work equipment. If in doubt, reference should be made to these Regulations which impose upon employers specific duties in relation to the safety of the workplace – particularly in respect of maintenance.
- *Employers' Liability (Defective Equipment) Act 1969*. This legislation imposes liability on an employer for injury to employees caused by any defect in equipment provided by the employer for use at work. If an employee suffers personal injury as a result of a defect in equipment and that defect is attributable to a third party, the injury will be deemed also to be attributable to negligence on the part of the employer (even if the defect could not have been discovered by proper examination). Although

primarily liable to the employee, the employer may be able to pass on some of the costs of liability to the supplier of the equipment.

Common law

An employer owes a duty to his employees to provide a safe system of work; a safe place of work; and safe fellow employees. That duty is non-delegable – employers cannot absolve themselves of the duty to take due care to provide a reasonably safe system of work; a safe place of work; safe fellow employees (*Wilsons & Clyde Coal Company Ltd v. English* (1938)). This duty includes the requirement to provide safe work equipment.

See also: Driving at work, p.244; Electricity and electrical equipment, p.252; Health and safety at work, p.364; Ladders, p.440

Sources of further information

INDG291 *Simple guide to the Provision and Use of Work Equipment Regulations 1998* (HSE Books, 1999) ISBN: 0 7176 2429 3.

L22 *Safe use of work equipment. Approved Code of Practice and guidance* (HSE Books, 1998, 3rd Edition 2008) ISBN: 978 0 717662 95 1.

L113 *Safe use of lifting equipment. Approved Code of Practice and guidance* (HSE Books, 1998) ISBN: 0 7176 1628 2.

Working time

Pinsent Masons Employment Group

Key points
- The Working Time Regulations 1998 (which implement the EC Working Time Directive into UK law) regulate hours worked, rest breaks and holidays.
- The BERR guidance notes should be read with the Regulations.
- Employees can opt out of the 48-hour week, and other rights can be softened or extended in 'special cases' or by agreement.
- The Regulations do not apply to some sectors, or to time which is not 'working time'.

Legislation

The Working Time Regulations 1998 came into force on 1 October 1998. They have been amended by the Working Time (Amendment) Regulations 2001 and the Working Time (Amendment) Regulations 2003 and the Working Time (Amendment) Regulations 2007.

BERR has issued guidance to assist companies to comply with the Regulations. The Regulations protect workers against working too many hours and not receiving proper rest, and allow them minimum paid holiday rights. Night workers have special rights (see *'Night working', p.527*).

Workers

The Regulations apply to 'workers' – i.e. not only to employees, but also to agency workers, freelance workers and those performing a contract for services. The Regulations do not apply to individuals who are genuinely self-employed. Young workers have special rights.

The Regulations do not apply to workers employed in some industry sectors including workers in the transport sector and sea fishing, other workers at sea, and certain activities of the armed forces, police or other civil protection services.

The Regulations were amended from 1 August 2003 to extend working-time measures in full to all workers in road transport (other than those covered by the Road Transport Directive), non-mobile workers in road, sea, inland waterways or lake transport, to workers in the railway and offshore sectors and to all workers in aviation who are not covered by the Aviation Directive.

Since 1 August 2004 the Regulations have also applied to junior doctors, with some exceptions and special rules.

48-hour week

An employer is expected to take all reasonable steps in keeping with the need to protect health and safety, to ensure that in principle each worker works no more than 48 hours on average in each working week. Young workers may not ordinarily work more than eight hours a day or 40 hours a week.

The average is calculated across a 17-week rolling reference period (which in certain circumstances can be extended).

Work for any employer is included, so care is needed if an employer knows or should know that an employee has more than one job. A worker cannot be forced to work more than these hours if the hours constitute 'working time'.

'Working time' is defined as any period during which a worker is "working, at his employer's disposal and carrying out his activity or duties"; any period during which the worker is receiving 'relevant training'; or any additional period which is agreed in a relevant agreement to be 'working time'. This leads to uncertainty, but working time will therefore not usually include, for example, a worker's time spent travelling to and from work or during rest breaks where no work is done. Recent case law has concluded that 'on-call' time constitutes working time if the employee is required to be in the workplace rather than at home.

The Regulations allow a worker to opt out of the 48-hour-week restriction by written agreement in a number of ways, including by way of an amendment to the individual's contract of employment, but it must be in writing and terminable by the worker on a minimum of seven days' (but not more than three months') notice. Even if a worker has agreed to opt out, he cannot be required to work excessively long hours if this creates a reasonably foreseeable risk to health and safety.

Where a worker has contracted out of the 48-hour week, the employer no longer needs to keep records showing the number of hours actually worked by the opted-out individual.

In these circumstances only a list of those who have opted out is necessary.

See EC proposals for change, below, for amendments to 'on-call' time and the opt-out provision following the political agreement at the meeting of EU employment ministers in June 2008.

Rest periods

The Regulations provide for rest periods to be given to workers.

Employers must provide that rest periods can be taken, but there is no need to ensure they are actually taken. The rest period is in addition to annual leave and can be paid or unpaid.

The provisions can be summarised as follows:

- There should be a minimum rest period of 11 uninterrupted hours between each working day.
- Young workers are entitled to 12 hours' uninterrupted rest in each 24-hour period.
- There should be a minimum weekly rest period of not less than 24 uninterrupted hours in each seven-day period.
- Days off can be averaged over a two-week period.
- Workers who work for six hours are entitled to a 20-minute break.
- There should be adequate rest breaks where monotonous work places the worker at risk.

Special cases

Workers can be asked to work without breaks in a number of 'special cases'.

Also, where special cases exist, the 17-week average period for the 48-hour week can be extended to 26 weeks. These include:

- where there is a 'foreseeable surge of activity';
- where "unusual and unforeseeable circumstances beyond the control of the worker's employer" exist;
- where continuity of service or production is needed (e.g. hospital care, prisons, media, refuse and

where a need exists to keep machines running);

■ where permanent presence is needed (e.g. security and surveillance); and

■ where there is great distance between the workplace and an employee's home, or between different places of work.

The basis of the special cases is that, if they exist, there is a reasonable need for work to be carried out quickly in a confined period. If because of one of the 'special cases' a worker is not able to take a rest break when he would ordinarily be entitled to do so, he should be allowed to take an equivalent rest break as soon as reasonably practicable thereafter.

Unmeasured working time

The provisions relating to the 48-hour week, night work and minimum rest periods will not apply where a worker's work is not measured or predetermined or can otherwise be determined by the worker himself.

Examples are managing executives or other persons who have a discretion over whether to work or not on a given day without needing to consult the employer.

The Working Time Regulations 1999 extended the scope of the unmeasured working-time exemption to include the concept of 'partially unmeasured working time', so that where a worker 'voluntarily' chooses to work outside the scope of the hours predetermined by his employer (more likely than not his contractual hours and any contractual overtime), only those hours which were predetermined by his employer will count for the purposes of calculating his working time. This has now been repealed following proceedings being issued by the European Commission against the UK that the exemption was not

permitted by the Working Time Directive and was therefore unlawful.

Annual leave

Since 1 October 2007 with the introduction of the Working Time (Amendment) Regulations 2007, statutory holiday entitlement has been increased for full-time workers to 4.8 weeks in each leave year and will increase again to 5.6 weeks on 1 April 2009. A part-time worker is entitled to 4.8 weeks' holiday reduced pro-rata according to the amount of days they work. Where a worker begins employment part-way through a leave year, he is entitled in that leave year to the proportion of the 4.8 weeks' annual leave which is equal to the proportion of the leave year for which he is employed.

There is no statutory right to take bank holidays but the October 2007 and April 2009 increases in annual leave will give full-time workers a further eight days' holiday to take account of bank holidays, although there is no right for the time off to be taken on bank holidays.

It is not possible to pay a worker instead of allowing annual leave to be made available save for the additional four days' holiday introduced post-1 October 2007, which can be replaced by payment in lieu during the transitional phase up to 1 April 2009.

Contractual holiday provisions should be checked to ensure enough holiday is given, but can also be used to fill in gaps in the Regulations, including, for example, in relation to the clawback of overpaid holiday pay when an employee leaves.

For the purposes of the statutory leave entitlement, workers are entitled to be paid a 'week's pay' for each week of annual leave. This is calculated in a particular manner. Effectively, where a worker is paid an annual, monthly or weekly amount to which he is contractually entitled, his holiday pay will be the weekly equivalent of that amount. However, where a worker receives a varying amount of pay each week which is not contractually provided for or agreed, a 'week's pay' must be calculated in accordance with the average amount of pay the worker received in the 12-week period prior to the date of payment. Specific pro rata rules apply to untaken holiday when an employee leaves.

The Regulations provide a right to stipulate when a worker can take his leave entitlement, including notice provisions for the employer and the employee.

Agreements
Various parts of the Regulations can be disapplied or softened by specific agreements.

A 'relevant agreement' is usually a contract between an employer and a worker.

A 'workforce agreement' means an agreement between an employer and its workers or their elected representatives.

Records
Employers must keep adequate records to show in particular whether the limits in the Regulations dealing with the 48-hour week and night work are being complied with.

The courts will expect employers to be able to show they are complying with the Regulations and policing working time.

Officers of the HSE are entitled to investigate an employer's working-time practices and can demand to see copies of its records.

Enforcement
The method of enforcing the Regulations depends upon whether the provision relied

upon is a limit or an entitlement. The HSE and local authorities are responsible for enforcing the limits set out in the Regulations.

Workers may present a complaint to an Employment Tribunal in connection with any failure by their employer to provide them with the relevant protections afforded by the Regulations. Where a worker is also an employee, and is dismissed as a result of exercising a right under the Regulations, his dismissal will be deemed to be automatically unfair.

It is automatically unfair to dismiss an employee for reasons connected with rights and entitlements under the Regulations. Employees may present a claim to an Employment Tribunal regardless of age or length of service.

EC proposals for change
Following the meeting between ministers at the EU Employment, Social Policy, Health and Consumer Affairs Council on 9 and 10 June 2008, the EU Council has published its proposed wording for a directive to amend the Working Time Directive. The agreed position is that the opt-out will remain but the following restrictions will apply:

- Workers will have to renew the opt-out in writing annually;
- Workers will be able to opt back in with immediate effect during the first six months of employment or up to three months after the end of any probationary period, whichever is longer. This means that the notice period for opting back in will be two months rather than the current three months;
- An opt-out will be void if signed at the same time as the employment contract;
- An opt-out will be void if signed within four weeks of starting work.

(This provision will not apply to workers who work for an employer for fewer than ten weeks in a 12-month period);

■ No worker can work for more than 60 hours a week averaged over three months unless permitted in a collective agreement or agreement. (This provision will not apply to workers who work for an employer for fewer than ten weeks in a 12-month period); and

■ Working time plus inactive on-call time cannot exceed 65 hours a week averaged over three months, unless permitted in a collective agreement. (This provision will not apply to workers who work for an employer for fewer than ten weeks in a 12-month period).

In addition:

■ The reference period for calculating the 48-hour week may be extended to six months, "for objective or technical reasons, or reasons concerning the organisation of work";

■ There will be a new category of time called 'inactive part of on-call time', which counts as neither working time not a rest period; and

■ Compensatory rest may be given after a 'reasonable period' rather than straight after the shift to which it relates.

The amended Directive is not yet in force and once in force the UK Government will need to legislate to implement it here.

> *See also*: Dismissal, p.233; Flexible working, p.338; Health and safety at work, p.364; Night working, p.527; Young persons, p.778

Sources of further information

BERR Working Time Regulations: www.berr.gov.uk/employment/employment-legislation/employment-guidance/page28978.html

Workplace health, safety and welfare

Kathryn Gilbertson, Greenwoods Solicitors LLP

Key points

The Regulations impose requirements in respect of the health, safety and welfare of the persons in a workplace. They do not apply to construction sites, temporary work sites and certain agricultural undertakings. They place requirements upon an employer and others in control of a workplace in relation to maintenance, ventilation, indoor temperature, lighting, cleanliness, room dimensions, the suitability of workstations, the condition of floors and pedestrian routes, together with providing toilet facilities, suitable washing facilities, supply of drinking water, the provision of suitable facilities for rest and to eat meals, as well as specifying the need to provide accommodation for the storage of outdoor clothing etc. All workplaces must be smoke-free.

Legislation

- Health and Safety at Work etc. Act 1974.
- Workplace (Health, Safety and Welfare) Regulations 1992.
- Health Act 2006.
- Smoke Free (Premises and Enforcement) Regulations 2006.

Workplace (Health, Safety and welfare) Regulations 1992

Regulation 5 – Maintenance of workplace and of equipment, devices and systems

These should be maintained in an efficient state, in efficient working order and in good repair. The Regulation creates an absolute duty that is not limited to what is reasonably practicable. Thus it is no defence to an employer to show that the cause of a lift failure could not be discovered. 'Efficient' is considered from the view of health, safety and welfare and not productivity or economy. Thus steps should be taken to ensure that repair and maintenance work is carried out properly.

Regulation 6 – Ventilation

Effective and suitable ventilation shall be provided to ensure that the workplace has sufficient quantity of fresh or purified air. Enclosed workplaces should be sufficiently well ventilated so that stale air and air which is hot or humid is replaced at a reasonable rate. Whilst it may not always be possible to remove smells coming in from outside, reasonable steps should be taken to minimise these. Air which is being introduced should be free from any impurity which is likely to give offence or cause ill health.

Regulation 7 – Temperature in indoor places

During working hours, the temperature in workplaces inside buildings shall be reasonable. Thus workers should be comfortable without the need for special clothing. Normally the temperature should be at least 16°c unless much of the work involves severe physical effort in which case the temperature should be at least 13°c. Where a reasonably comfortable temperature cannot be achieved throughout a work room, local heating or cooling should be provided. Thermometers should be available to enable persons to check the temperature of the workplace. These do not need to be provided in each work room. Site-specific risk assessments should be undertaken where heat stress or cold stress has been identified.

Regulation 8 – Lighting

Every workplace shall have suitable and sufficient lighting which should be, so far as is reasonably practicable, through natural lighting. Lighting levels should be sufficient to enable people to work without experiencing eye strain. Staircases in particular should be well lit, such that shadows are not cast over the main parts of the treads. Windows and sky lights should be cleaned regularly and kept free from unnecessary obstructions to admit maximum daylight.

Regulation 9 – Cleanliness and waste materials

Workplaces including furniture, furnishings and fittings shall be kept sufficiently clean. Waste materials should not be allowed to accumulate in the workplace except in suitable bins. Floors and indoor traffic routes should be cleaned at least once a week. Refuse should be removed at least daily.

Regulation 10 – Room dimensions and space

Every room shall have sufficient floor area, height and unoccupied space for the purposes of health, safety and welfare. Work rooms should allow enough free space for people to get to and from workstations and to move around within the room with ease. Eleven cubic metres per person is a minimum and this may be insufficient if the room is taken up with furniture etc. However, this figure does not apply to retain sales kiosks, attendance shelters etc.

Regulation 11 – Workstations and seating

A workstation must be suitable for the work being carried out in it and the person working within it. It shall provide protection from adverse weather, be arranged such that a person can leave swiftly if there is an emergency, and be provided with a suitable seat for them to carry out work whilst sitting. The workstation should allow the freedom of movement and the ability for the person to stand upright.

Seating should support the lower back and a footrest should be provided for any worker who cannot comfortably place their feet flat on the floor. Where visual display units (VDUs) are provided then employers should also refer to the Health and Safety (Display Screen Equipment) Regulations 1992.

Regulation 12 – Condition of floors and traffic routes

Floors should be of a sound construction without holes, slopes or an uneven or slippery surface so as to expose any person to a risk to their health or safety. Floors and traffic routes should be kept free from obstruction which may cause people to slip, trip or fall. Handrails should be provided on staircases except where they may cause obstruction.

Arrangements should be made to minimise the risk from snow and ice — which may involve gritting, snow clearing or the closure of some routes.

Regulation 13 – Falls or falling objects

Where there is a risk of a person falling a distance likely to cause personal injury or a person is likely to be struck by a falling object then secure fencing or coverings should be provided. Fencing should be provided where a person may fall two metres or more. Such fencing should consist of two guard rails at suitable heights. Fencing should be strong and stable to restrain any person or object falling onto or against it. Particular care should be undertaken where roof work is being carried out.

Materials should be stored and stacked in such a way that they are unlikely to fall or cause injury. This could be achieved through palletisation, or by setting limits for the height of stacks to maintain stability.

Regulations 14, 15 and 16 – Windows
Transparent or translucent surfaces (windows, sky lights, partitions, doors etc.) shall be made of safety material. Since there is a danger of breakage, glass doors and partitions should be marked to make them obvious. Safety glass which is laminated or toughened is recommended.

All windows and skylights must be able to be cleaned safely and consideration must also be given to any equipment that needs to be used when undertaking this cleaning.

Regulation 17 – Traffic routes
Workplaces should be organised in such a way that pedestrians and vehicles can move in a safe manner. Pedestrians and vehicles should be separated to enable people and traffic to pass near each other without any collision. This is particularly important where vehicles have to reverse into service yards, on to loading docks, or where pedestrian and vehicle routes cross. The use of signage, marked routes and segregation must be carefully managed.

Regulation 18 – Doors and gates
These should be properly constructed with devices to prevent them coming off their tracks or hinges during use. Thus any powered door should be able to be operated manually if the power fails. Doors and gates which swing in both directions should have a transparent panel positioned

to enable a person in a wheelchair to be seen from either side.

Regulation 19 – Escalators and moving walkways
These should work safely, and be fitted with emergency stop controls which are readily accessible and easily identifiable.

Regulation 20 and 21 – Sanitary conveniences and washing facilities
Sufficient facilities should be provided to enable everyone at work to use them without undue delay. They should be readily accessible, kept clean, adaequately ventilated and well lit. Washing facilities should have hot and cold running water, soap and a means of hand drying.

The minimum number of facilities required is:

- Up to five people – one toilet and one wash station.
- Six – 25 people – two toilets and two wash stations.
- One extra toilet and wash station for every subsequent 25 people.

For men a mixture of toilets and urinals can be provided.

Regulation 22 – Drinking water
Wholesome drinking water should be provided. It should be readily accessible and clearly marked that it is suitable for drinking purposes. It should not be installed in sanitary accommodation but be readily accessible in another location. Cups or glasses must be provided unless a water fountain is used.

Regulation 23 and 24 – Clothing
Employers should provide facilities for employees to change their clothing. This would include storage facilities for personal clothing not being worn at work, as well as special clothing to be worn at work that is not taken home. As a minimum this

could be a peg or hook for each worker in a changing room. The accommodation should allow clothing to dry and should be secure.

Regulation 25 – Facilities for rest and to eat meals

Rest areas should be large enough and have sufficient seats with back rests and tables for a number of workers likely to use them at any one time. The rest room shall include facilities to prepare or obtain a hot drink (such as a kettle, vending machine or canteen) as well as providing a means for heating their own food if hot food cannot be obtained in the workplace or reasonably near to it.

Health Act 2006
All workplaces must be smoke-free.

See also: Furniture, p.353; Working at height, p.395; Ladders, p.440; Lighting, p.469; Slips, trips and falls, p.657; Smoking, p.660; Ventilation and temperature, p.704; Water quality, p.738

Sources of further information

L24 *Workplace, Health, Safety and Welfare Approved Code of Practice and guidance* ISBN: 0 7176 0413 6.

INDG 244 *Workplace, Health, Safety and Welfare: a Short Guide for Managers* (HSE Books, 1997) ISBN: 0 7176 1328 3.

Work-related upper limb disorders (WRULDs)

Andrew Richardson, Scott Wilson

Key points

Musculo-skeletal problems of the arm, hand, shoulder and neck can be found across a broad range of work activities. These are properly referred to as work-related upper limb disorders (WRULDs). Often, especially where pain in the arm occurs among computer users, some forms of WRULD are referred to as repetitive strain injury (RSI). This can be confusing because RSI is not a medical diagnosis. For clarity and to avoid confusion, only WRULDs will be referred to in this chapter.

WRULDs is a generic term for a group of musculo-skeletal injuries that affect the muscles, tendons, joints and bones, usually in the hand, arm or shoulder, which are generally caused by frequent or repetitive movement of the arms, wrists and fingers.

ULDs can be caused by non-work activities. Employers need to ensure that the tasks they allocate to workers do not make the injury any worse.

WRULDs can be avoided by ergonomic improvements in the workplace, i.e. improving the interface between person and machine. The job must be matched to the person. Employers need to make adjustments to the task, workstation, work environment and/or work organisation.

Legislation

- Health and Safety at Work etc. Act 1974.
- Health and Safety (Display Screen Equipment) Regulations 1992 (as amended by the Health and Safety (Miscellaneous Amendments) Regulations 2002).
- Personal Protective Equipment at Work Regulations 1992.
- Manual Handling Operations Regulations 1992.
- Reporting of Injuries, Diseases and Dangerous Occurrences Regulations 1995.
- Provision and Use of Work Equipment Regulations 1998.
- Management of Health and Safety at Work Regulations 1999.

Dealing with WRULDs

WRULDs are musculo-skeletal disorders of the arm, hand, shoulder and neck. They can range from temporary fatigue or soreness of the limbs through to chronic soft tissue disorders such as tendonitis and carpal tunnel syndrome. Personnel can also suffer from occupational cramp. Symptoms of WRULDs include tenderness, aches, pains, stiffness, weakness, tingling, numbness, cramp and swelling.

WRULDs can be caused by forceful or repetitive activities or poor posture. They are widespread across a range of industries and jobs, but are particularly associated with the work of computer users and assembly workers.

Workplace Law Network
www.workplacelaw.net

The way that the workplace is arranged and managed can cause WRULDs or make existing medical conditions worse.

Employers have a legal duty under the Health and Safety at Work etc. Act 1974 and the Management of Health and Safety at Work Regulations 1999 to carry out risk assessments and put into place measures to prevent WRULDs and/or stop existing medical conditions becoming worse.

The HSE advocates the following management framework to all employers for dealing with WRULDs:

- *Understand the issues and commit to action*. Both the employer and employee should have an understanding of WRULDs and should be committed to carrying out actions to prevent them. Positive leadership, with a policy on WRULDs and the necessary systems in place, will help promote a positive safety culture.
- *Create the right organisational environment*. This should foster active employee participation and involvement, establish clear lines of communication and encourage employer–employee partnerships in carrying out the following steps:
  - *Assess the risk of WRULDs in your workplace*. Managers and workers should carry out assessments in a systematic way to identify the risks and prioritise them for action.
  - *Reduce the risks of WRULDs*. A process of risk reduction should be undertaken using an ergonomic approach. Where possible, risks should be

eliminated or reduced at source. Implementation should include the workforce, as it is more effective.
  - *Educate and inform your workforce*. The provision of education and information is vital. Training supports all aspects of this framework and should be ongoing, not a one-off task.
  - *Manage any incidence of WRULDs*. Employees should be encouraged to identify symptoms and to report them as soon as possible before they become persistent. Employers should respond quickly by reviewing the risks and introducing more effective controls. Employers must reassure employees that reporting symptoms will not prejudice their job or position. Early medical detection can stop further deterioration and aid return to work.
  - *Carry out regular checks on programme effectiveness*. This will ensure the framework remains effective and will improve its effectiveness.

Where workers use computer equipment, employers must comply with the requirements of the Display Screen Equipment Regulations – see *'Display screen equipment', p.238*.

See also: Display screen equipment, p.238; Health surveillance, p.392; Occupational health, p.537

Sources of further information

A free HSE leaflet – *Aching arms (or RSI) in small businesses* – which gives basic guidance information, can be downloaded at www.hse.gov.uk/pubns/indg171.pdf

Young persons

Pinsent Masons Employment Group

Key points
- A young person is a person who has ceased to be a child and who is under the age of 18 years. A child is a person not over compulsory school age, currently 16 years.
- Young workers have particular rights under the Working Time Regulations 1998, particularly relating to rest breaks and night work assessments.
- Particular hourly rates apply to young workers for national minimum wage purposes. General health and safety duties prevent young workers being used for work beyond their capabilities.

Legislation
- Children and Young Persons Act 1933 (as amended).
- Employment Rights Act 1996 (as amended).
- National Minimum Wage Act 1998.
- Working Time Regulations 1998.
- Management of Health and Safety at Work Regulations 1999 (replacing the Health and Safety (Young Persons) Regulations 1992).
- Working Time (Amendment) Regulations 2002.

General health and safety issues
Every employer should ensure that young persons employed by him are protected at work from any risks to their health or safety which are a consequence of:

- their lack of experience;
- their absence of awareness of existing or potential risk; or
- the fact that young persons have not yet fully matured.

Failure to do so may result in civil liability for a breach of statutory duty on the part of the employer.

Risk assessments
An employer should not employ a young person unless he has carried out a risk assessment to ensure that all relevant hazards and consequent risks have been identified.

In particular, an employer should consider:

- if the work is beyond the young person's physical or psychological capacity;
- if there is harmful exposure to radiation or agents which could be toxic or carcinogenic; or
- if there is a risk to health from extreme cold or heat, noise or vibration.

This risk assessment must take into account various issues such as the inexperience and immaturity of the young person, the nature of the workstation, the risks in the workplace including the equipment which the young person will use, and the extent of the health and safety training provided. An employer cannot rely on a risk assessment which had been previously carried out for a mature adult. Employers should consider

Workplace Law Network
www.workplacelaw.net

how these risks may be greater in respect of young persons than for other workers, and, if he is at significant risk from carrying out any task, a young person should be prohibited from undertaking it.

Daily rest
Young workers are entitled to a break of at least 12 consecutive hours in any 24-hour period.

Weekly rest
Young workers are entitled to a weekly rest period of at least 48 hours in each period of seven days (i.e. two days off each week). In addition, if owing to the nature of the work and because of technical or organisational reasons a young worker cannot take two days off per week, then the rest can be spread across 36 hours in a week.

Rest breaks while at work
If a young worker is required to work for more than four and a half hours at a stretch, he is entitled to a rest break of at least 30 minutes. A young worker's entitlement to rest breaks can be changed or excluded only in exceptional circumstances. If a young worker is working for more than one employer, the time he is working for each one should be added together to see if he is entitled to a rest break in a total four-and-a-half-hour period of work.

A young person's entitlement to breaks can be changed or not taken in exceptional circumstances only. The circumstances and 'special cases' are narrower than those for older workers and include the situation where no adult is available to do the work. Where this occurs, the worker should receive compensatory rest within three weeks.

Compensatory rest is a period of rest of the same length as the period of rest that a worker has missed.

Annual leave
Young workers have the same entitlements as adult workers in respect of annual leave. (Under the Working Time Regulations 1998, all adult employees are entitled to at least 4.8 weeks' paid annual leave, increasing to 5.6 in April 2009.)

Time off for study and training
Young persons who are not in full-time secondary or further education are entitled to take time off during working hours for the purposes of study or training leading to an external qualification (academic or vocational) which "enhances the young person's employment prospects". The length of time that can be taken is that which is reasonable in the circumstances, and the young person should be paid for the time taken off at his normal hourly rate.

Night work and health assessment
Young workers are given special protection as regards night work. Ordinarily they may not work at night between 11 p.m. and seven a.m. if the contract of employment provides for work after ten p.m. However, exceptions apply in particular circumstances in the case of certain kinds of employment.

Young workers require a health and capabilities assessment. Special consideration should be given to young workers' suitability for night work, taking account of their physique, maturity and experience.

In addition, all employers must offer young night workers a free health assessment before they begin working nights and thereafter on a regular basis. Young workers do not have to undergo a health assessment, but they must be offered one. All employers should maintain up-to-date records of health assessments.

National Minimum Wage

The National Minimum Wage Act 1998 came into force on 1 April 1999 and provides for the minimum level of pay to which almost all workers in the UK are entitled. Since 1 October 2004 most workers over 16 years of age have been covered by the Act. Following the introduction of the Employment Equality (Age) Regulations 2006 on 1 October 2006 minimum wage legislation could be challenged on the basis that it discriminates against people on the grounds of age.

Practical points to remember

Workplace managers should check:

- whether they employ young workers; and
- if they do, how many rest periods and breaks young workers are receiving.

If young workers are not receiving the correct rest periods, managers should consider:

- how these can be given; and
- whether the amount of hours worked can be reduced.

Managers should always ensure that:

- proper records of young workers are maintained, including details of health assessments;
- young workers are not involved in work which is particularly hazardous; and
- young workers are receiving the National Minimum Wage.

See also: Children at work, p.141; Discrimination, p.222; Minimum wage, p.504; Night working, p.527

Sources of further information

Workplace Law Network provides premium members with unrestricted access to a comprehensive range of online information – factsheets, case reports and daily news items – on employment, health and safety and premises management. Members also benefit from an online advice service and a free subscription to the *Workplace Law Magazine*. For more information email membership@workplacelaw.net or call our membership services team on 0871 777 8881.

Also available from Workplace Law

For further information on any of the products below call Workplace Law on **0871 777 8881** quoting promotion code **1843** or visit **www.workplacelaw.net/shop**. Prices of training and conferences may vary – call our training team for the latest dates and costs.

PUBLICATIONS

	Premium members	Standard members
Health and Safety Overkill Mug	£5.99	£5.99
Dodging Bullets - advice for employers on tricky legal situations	£8.99	£9.99
Facilities Management Legal Update 2008: Special Report	£80.10	£89.00
Guide to Business Continuity 2007	£35.99	£39.99
Guide to Dilapidations	£35.99	£39.99
Guide to Smoking Ban 2007	£31.49	£34.99
Guide to Flexible Working 2008	£31.49	£34.99
Guide to WEEE 2007	£31.49	£34.99
TUPE transfers 2007: Rights and Responsibilities Special Report	£80.10	£89.00
Fire Safety Documentation Pack 2007	£71.99	£79.99
BPF Consultancy Agreement version 2.0	£27.00	£30.00
Fire and Disability 2008: Special Report	£75.60	£84.00
Working with Contractors 2008: Special Report	£75.60	£84.00
Energy Performance of Buildings 2008: Special Report	£75.60	£84.00
Occupational Health 2008: Making the Business Case – Special Report	£71.10	£79.00
Facilities Management Contracts 2008	£71.99	£79.00
Sustainable Workplaces 2008: Special Report	£80.10	£89.00
Loneworking 2008: Special Report	£80.10	£89.00
Driving at Work 2008: Special Report	£75.83	£84.25
Corporate Manslaughter and Corporate Homicide Act: Special Report	£75.83	£84.25
Fire Safety 2009: Special Report	£42.13	£84.25
Making Buildings Accessible 2009: Special Report	£42.13	£84.25

POLICIES AND PROCEDURES

	Premium members	Standard members
Non-Contractual Disciplinary and Dismissal Policy and Management Guide, version 3.0	£44.99	£49.99
Non-contractual Grievance Policy and Management Guide, version 3.0	£31.49	£34.99
Risk Assessment Policy and Management Guide, version 3.0	£67.49	£74.99
Data Protection Policy and Management Guide, version 3.0	£31.49	£34.99
Health and Safety Policy and Management Guide, version 3.0	£53.99	£59.99
Smoking at Work Policy and Management Guide, version 3.0	£31.49	£34.99
Non-contractual Maternity Policy and Management Guide, version 3.0	£31.49	£34.99
Non-contractual Paternity Policy and Management Guide, version 3.0	£31.49	£34.99
Equal Opportunities Policy and Management Guide, version 3.0	£26.99	£29.99
Redundancy Policy and Management Guide, version 3.0	£31.49	£34.99
IT and Email Policy and Management Guide, version 2.0	£31.49	£34.99
Flexible Working Policy and Management Guide, version 3.0	£31.49	£34.99
Legionella Policy and Management Guide, version 3.0	£67.49	£74.99
Display Screen Equipment Policy and Management Guide, version 2.0	£49.49	£54.99
Waste Management Policy and Management Guide, version 3.0	£31.49	£34.99
Health and Safety Training Policy and Management Guide, version 3.0	£31.49	£34.99
Driving at Work Policy and Management Guide, version 4.0	£67.49	£74.99
Non-contractual Adoption Policy and Management Guide, version 2.0	£31.49	£34.99
Age Discrimination Policy and Management Guide version 1.0	£26.99	£29.99
Drug and Alcohol Policy and Management Guide version 1.0	£31.49	£34.99

Also available from Workplace Law

MODEL CONTRACTS

	Premium members	Standard members
Employment Contract and Management Guide, version 4.0	£31.49	£34.99

DISCOUNT PACKS

	Premium members	Standard members
Employment Law Policy and Procedures Series Discount Pack	£346.50	£385.00
Health and Safety Policy and Procedure Discount Pack	£337.50	£375.00
Employment Law Discount Pack	£299.00	£299.00
Premises Management Discount Pack	£279.00	£279.00
Health and Safety Law Discount Pack	£269.00	£269.00

PUBLIC TRAINING COURSES

	Premium members	Standard members
Workplace Law Training Brochure	£0.00	£0.00
IOSH Managing Safely Certificate	£719.10	£799.00
Certificate in Personnel Practice	£1,619.10	£1,799.00
NEBOSH: National General Certificate: Classroom	£1,619.10	£1,799.00
NEBOSH: National General Certificate: Blended	£1,079.10	£1,199.00
NEBOSH: National General Certificate: Elearning	£629.10	£699.00
NEBOSH: National General Certificate: Fast-track	£1,619.10	£1,799.00
Certificate in Employment Relations, Law and Practice	£2,024.10	£2,249.00

CONFERENCES

	Premium members	Standard members
10th Anniversary Facilities Management Legal Update	£719.10	£799.00
Fire Risk Management Workshop	£359.10	£399.00

IN-HOUSE TRAINING

First Aid appointed person	P.O.A.
First Aid at Work: Training	P.O.A.
First Aid refresher training	P.O.A.
Manual Handling - Train the Trainer: Training	P.O.A.
Manual Handling: Training	P.O.A.
Introduction to Health and Safety	P.O.A.
IOSH Managing Safely	P.O.A.
IOSH Directing Safely Certificate	P.O.A.
IOSH Working Safely	P.O.A.
Construction, Design and Management: Training	P.O.A.
NEBOSH National General Certificate	P.O.A.
NEBOSH Fire Safety and Risk Management Certificate, Module 2	P.O.A.
Fire Risk Assessment: Training	P.O.A.
Fire Warden: Training	P.O.A.
Evacuation Chair Use: Training	P.O.A.
Working at Height: Training	P.O.A.
Risk Assessment: Training	P.O.A.
Permits to Work: Training	P.O.A.
Building Regulations Update: Training	P.O.A.
Certificate in Personnel Practice (CPP)	P.O.A.
Certificate in Employment Relations Law and Practice (CERLAP)	P.O.A.
Managing Absence: Training	P.O.A.
Managing Appraisals: Training	P.O.A.
Managing Discipline and Grievances: Training	P.O.A.
Managing Poor Performance: Training	P.O.A.
Managing Recruitment and Selection: Training	P.O.A.
Managing Redundancy or Restructuring: Training	P.O.A.
Stress Management: Training	P.O.A.
COSHH Assessment: Training	P.O.A.
Display Screen Equipment - Assessors: Training	P.O.A.
Selection and Control of Contractors: Training	P.O.A.

Directory of information sources

Access Association
0113 2478102
www.access-association.org.uk

Acoustic Safety Programme
info@acousticsafety.org
www.acousticshock.org

Action on Smoking and Health (ASH)
020 7739 5902
www.ash.org.uk

Advisory, Conciliation and Arbitration Service (ACAS)
08457 474 747
www.acas.org.uk

Age Concern
0800 00 99 66
www.ageconcern.org.uk

Age Positive
0113 232 4444
www.agepositive.gov.uk

Alcohol Concern
020 7264 0510
www.alcoholconcern.org.uk

Asbestos Removal Contractors Association (ARCA)
01283 531126
www.arca.org.uk

Association for Project Safety (APS)
08456 121 290
www.aps.org.uk

Association for Specialist Fire Protection (ASFP)
01252 357 832
www.asfp.org.uk

Association of British Insurers (ABI)
020 7600 3333
www.abi.org.uk

Association of Building Engineers (ABE)
0845 126 1058
www.abe.org.uk

Association of Chief Police Officers (ACPO)
020 7084 8950
www.acpo.police.uk

Association of Consultant Approved Inspectors (ACAI)
020 7491 1914
www.acai.org.uk

Association of Consultant Architects (ACA)
020 8325 1402
www.acarchitects.co.uk

Association of Consulting and Engineers (ACE)
020 7222 6557
www.acenet.co.uk

Association of Industrial Road Safety Officers (AIRSO)
01903 506095
www.airso.org.uk

Association of Plumbing and Heating Contractors (APHC)
024 7647 0626
www.aphc.co.uk

Association of Security Consultants (ASC)
07071 224865
www.securityconsultants.org.uk

Association of Sustainability Practitioners
www.asp-online.org

Association of Technical Lighting and Access Specialists
0115 955 8818
www.atlas-1.org.uk

Automobile Association (AA)
0800 085 2721
www.theaa.com

Bathroom Manufacturers Association (BMA)
01782 747123
www.bathroom-association.org

Better Regulation Commission
www.brc.gov.uk

BioIndustry Association (BIA)
020 7565 7190
www.bioindustry.org

Blind in Business
020 7588 1885
www.blindinbusiness.co.uk

BRE Certification Ltd
01923 664100
www.bre.co.uk

British Approval for Fire Equipment (BAFE)
020 8541 1950
www.bafe.org.uk

British Association for Chemical Specialities
(BACS)
01423 700 249
www.bacsnet.org

British Association of Occupational Therapists
(BAOT) / College of Occupational Therapists
(COT)
020 7357 6480
www.cot.co.uk

British Association of Removers (BAR)
01923 699 480
www.bar.co.uk

British Automatic Fire Sprinkler Association
(BAFSA)
01353 659187
www.bafsa.org.uk

British Cement Association (BCA)
01276 608700
www.cementindustry.co.uk

British Chambers of Commerce (BCC)
020 7654 5800
www.britishchambers.org.uk

British Cleaning Council (BCC)
01562 851129
www.britishcleaningcouncil.org

British Fire Consortium (BFC)
01273 297274
www.tbfc.org.uk

Chartered Institute of Architectural Technologists
(CIAT)
020 7278 2206
www.ciat.org.uk

British Institute of Cleaning Science (BICSc)
01604 678710
www.bics.org.uk

British Institute of Facilities Management (BIFM)
0845 058 1356
www.bifm.org.uk

British Occupational Health Research Foundation
(BOHRF)
020 7317 5898
www.bohrf.org.uk

British Occupational Hygiene Society (BOHS)
01332 298101
www.bohs.org

British Parking Association (BPA)
01444 447300
www.britishparking.co.uk

British Pest Control Association (BPCA)
01332 294 288
www.bpca.org.uk

British Plastics Federation (BPF)
020 7457 5000
www.bpf.co.uk

British Property Federation (BPF)
020 7828 0111
www.bpf.org.uk

British Red Cross Society
0844 871 1111
www.redcross.org.uk

British Retail Consortium (BRC)
020 7854 8900
www.brc.org.uk

British Safety Council
020 8741 1231
www.britishsafetycouncil.co.uk

British Security Industry Association (BSIA)
0845 389 3889
www.bsia.co.uk

British Standards Institution (BSI)
020 8996 9001
www.bsi-global.com

British Woodworking Federation (BWF)
0870 458 6939
www.bwf.org.uk

Building Cost Information Service Ltd (BCIS)
020 7695 1500
www.bcis.co.uk

Building Research Establishment Ltd (BRE)
01923 664 000
www.bre.co.uk

Building Services Research and Information
Association (BSRIA)
01344 465 600
www.bsria.co.uk

Business Continuity Institute (BCI)
0118 947 8215
www.thebci.org

Business in the Community
020 7566 8650
www.bitc.org.uk

Cadw
01443 336 000
www.cadw.wales.gov.uk

Customer Contact Association (CCA)
0141 564 9010
www.cca.org.uk

Carbon Trust
0800 085 2005
www.carbontrust.co.uk

Central Arbitration Committee (CAC)
020 7904 2300
www.cac.gov.uk

Centre for Accessible Environments (CAE)
020 7840 0125
www.cae.org.uk

Centre for Corporate Accountability (CCA)
020 7490 4494
www.corporateaccountability.org

Centre for Effective Dispute Resolution (CEDR)
020 7536 6000
www.cedr.co.uk

Chartered Institute of Arbitrators
020 7421 7444
www.arbitrators.org

Chartered Institute of Building (CIOB)
01344 630700
www.ciob.org.uk

Chartered Institute of Environmental Health
(CIEH)
020 7928 6006
www.cieh.org.uk

Chartered Institute of Personnel and
Development (CIPD)
020 8162 6200
www.cipd.co.uk

Chartered Institute of Purchasing and Supply
(CIPS)
01780 756777
www.cips.org

Chartered Institution of Waste Management
(CIWM)
01604 620426
www.ciwm.co.uk

Chartered Institution of Building Services
Engineers (CIBSE)
020 8675 5211
www.cibse.org

Chartered Management Institute
020 7497 0580
www.managers.org.uk

Chartered Society of Physiotherapy (CSP)
020 7306 6666
www.csp.org.uk

Chemical Hazards Communication Society
(CHCS)
0844 636 2427
www.chcs.org.uk

Chemical Industries Association (CIA)
020 7834 3399
www.cia.org.uk

Chief Fire Officers' Association (CFOA)
01827 302 300
www.cfoa.org.uk

Chubb UK
0800 321 666(Chubb Fire)
01254 688 68 (Chubb Electronic Security)
www.chubb.co.uk

CIFAS (the UK's Fraud Prevention Service)
www.cifas.org.uk

CIRIA (formerly Construction Industry Research
and Information Association)
020 7549 3300
www.ciria.org.uk

Civil Contingencies Secretariat (Cabinet Office)
0207 276 1234
www.ukresilience.gov.uk

Clay Pipe Development Association (CPDA)
01494 791456
www.cpda.co.uk

Commercial Occupational Health Providers
Association (COHPA)
01933 232 373
www.cohpa.co.uk

Commission for Architecture and the Built
Environment (CABE)
020 7070 6700
www.cabe.org.uk

Commission for Racial Equality (CRE)
see Equality and Human Rights Commission

Concrete Society
01276 607140
www.concrete.org.uk

Confederation of British Industry (CBI)
020 7379 7400
www.cbi.org.uk

Confederation of Paper Industries (CPI)
01793 889600
www.paper.org.uk

Consortium of European Building Control (CEBC)
01473 748 182
www.cebc.eu

Constructing Excellence
0845 605 5556
www.constructingexcellence.org.uk

Construction Confederation
00870 898 9090
www.thecc.org.uk

Construction Health and Safety Group (CHSG)
01932 561 871 / 563 121
www.chsg.co.uk

Construction Industry Council (CIC)
020 7399 7400
www.cic.org.uk

CITB – Construction Skills
01485 577577
www.cskills.org

Contract Flooring Association (CFA)
0115 941 1126
www.cfa.org.uk

Contractors Health and Safety Assessment
Scheme (CHAS)
www.chas.gov.uk

Council of Registered Gas Installers (CORGI)
0800 915 0485
www.corgi-gas-safety.com

Cranfield Institute for Safety, Risk and Reliability
01234 750 111
www.cranfield.ac.uk/safety

Criminal Records Bureau (CRB)
0870 9090811
www.crb.gov.uk

Crown Prosecution Service (CPS)
020 7796 8000
www.cps.gov.uk

CSR Academy
020 7566 8650
www.csracademy.org.uk

Department for Business, Enterprise and
Regulatory Reform (DBERR)
020 7215 5000
www.berr.gov.uk

Department for Communities and Local
Government (DCLG)
020 7944 4400
www.communities.gov.uk

Department for Education and Skills (DfES)
0870 000 2288
www.dfes.gov.uk

Department for Environment, Food and Rural
Affairs (Defra)
0845 933 5577
www.defra.gov.uk

Department for Transport (DfT)
020 7944 8300
www.dft.gov.uk

Department for Work and Pensions (DWP)
www.dwp.gov.uk

Department of Health (DH)
020 7210 4850
www.dh.gov.uk

Department of Trade and Industry (DTI)
See Department for Business, Enterprise and
Regulatory Reform (DBERR)

Design Council
020 7420 5200
www.designcouncil.org.uk

Direct Gov
www.direct.gov.uk

Disability Matters
01794 341 824
www.disabilitymatters.com

Disability Rights Commission (DRC)
See Equality and Human Rights Commission

ELECSA Ltd
0845 634 9043
www.elecsa.org.uk

Electrical Contractors' Association (ECA)
020 7313 4800
www.eca.co.uk

Emergency Planning Society
0845 600 9587
www.the-eps.org

Employee Assistance Professionals Association
(EAPA)
01993 772 765
www.eapa.org.uk

Employers and Work-Life Balance
0207 976 3604
www.employersforwork-lifebalance.org.uk

Employers' Forum on Age (EFA)
0845 456 2495
www.efa.org.uk

Employers' Forum on Disability
020 7403 3020
www.employers-forum.co.uk

Employment Appeals Tribunal
020 7273 1041
www.employmentappeals.gov.uk

Employment Lawyers Association
01895 256972
www.elaweb.org.uk

Employment Tribunal
0845 795 9775
www.employmenttribunals.gov.uk

Energy Institute
020 7467 7100
www.energyinst.org.uk

Engineering and Construction Industry
Association (ECIA)
020 7799 2000
www.ecia.co.uk

Engineering Council UK (ECUK)
020 3206 0500
www.engc.org.uk

Engineering Employers Federation (EEF)
0800 458 1500
www.eef.org.uk

English Heritage
0870 333 1181
www.english-heritage.org.uk

ENTO (formerly Employment NTO)
0116 251 7979
www.ento.co.uk

Environment Agency
08708 506 506
www.environment-agency.gov.uk

Environment Council
020 7836 2626
www.the-environment-council.org.uk

Environment and Heritage Service (Northern Ireland) (EHSNI)
028 9054 6514
www.ehsni.gov.uk

Environmental Services Association (ESA)
www.esauk.org

Envirowise
0800 585 794
www.envirowise.gov.uk

Equality and Human Rights Commission
0845 604 6610
www.equalityhumanrights.com

Equal Opportunities Commission (EOC)
See Equality and Human Rights Commission

Ergonomics Society
01509 234904
www.ergonomics.org.uk

European Agency for Safety and Health at Work
+34 944 794 360
www.agency.osha.eu.int

Facilities Management Association (FMA)
07960 428 146
www.fmassociation.org.uk

Fall Arrest Safety Equipment Training (FASET)
01948 780 652
www.faset.org.uk

Federation of Environmental Trade Associations
0118 940 3416
www.feta.co.uk

Federation of Master Builders (FMB)
020 7242 7583
www.fmb.org.uk

Federation of Small Businesses (FSB)
01253 336000
www.fsb.org.uk

Federation of Window Cleaners (FWC)
0161 432 8754
www.nfmwgc.com

Financial Services Authority (FSA)
020 7066 1000
www.fsa.gov.uk

Fire Extinguishing Trades Association (FETA)
020 8549 5855
www.feta.org.uk

Fire Industry Association
020 8549 5855
www.fia.uk.com

Fire Industry Confederation (FIC)
020 8549 8839
www.the-fic.org.uk

FireNet International
www.fire.org.uk

Fire Protection Association (FPA)
01608 812500
www.thefpa.co.uk

Fire Service College
www.fireservicecollege.ac.uk

Food Standards Agency (FSA)
020 7276 8829
www.food.gov.uk

Fork Lift Truck Association (FLTA)
01256 381441
www.fork-truck.org.uk

Forum of Private Business (FPB)
0845 130 1722
www.fpb.co.uk

Friends of the Earth
020 7490 1555
www.foe.co.uk

Furniture Industry Research Association (FIRA)
01438 777700
www.fira.co.uk

Gangmasters Licensing Authority
0845 602 5020
www.gla.gov.uk

Glass and Glazing Federation (GGF)
0870 042 4255
www.ggf.org.uk

Greenpeace
020 7865 8100
www.greenpeace.org.uk

Groundwork UK
0121 236 8565
www.groundwork.org.uk

Hazards Forum
020 7665 2230
www.hazardsforum.co.uk

Health and Safety Executive (HSE)
0845 345 0055
www.hse.gov.uk

Health and Safety Executive for Northern Ireland
(HSENI)
028 9024 3249
www.hseni.gov.uk

Health and Safety Laboratory (HSL)
01298 218 000
www.hsl.gov.uk

Health Facilities Management Association
(Hefma)
www.hefma.org.uk

Health Protection Agency (HPA)
020 7759 2700
www.hpa.org.uk

Healthy Workplace Initiative (HWI)
www.newworkplaceinstitute.org

Heating and Ventilating Contractors' Association
(HVCA)
020 7313 4900
www.hvca.org.uk

Her Majesty's Treasury
020 7270 4558
www.hm-treasury.gov.uk

Historic Scotland
0131 668 8600
www.historic-scotland.gov.uk

HM Revenue & Customs
www.hmrc.gov.uk

Home Office
020 7035 4848
www.homeoffice.gov.uk

HSE Books
01787 881165
www.hsebooks.com

Incident Contact Centre Website
0845 300 9293
www.riddor.gov.uk

Independent Safety Consultants Association
(ISCA)
01621 874938
www.isca.org.uk

Industrial Rope Access Trade Association (IRATA)
01252 357 839
www.irata.org

Industry Committee for Emergency Lighting
(ICEL)
www.icel.co.uk

Information Commissioner's Office
08456 30 60 60
www.ico.gov.uk

Institute of Acoustics (IOA)
01727 848195
www.ioa.org.uk

Institute of Alcohol Studies (IAS)
01480 466 766
www.ias.org.uk

Institute of Customer Service (ICS)
01206 571716
www.instituteofcustomerservice.com

Institute of Directors (IoD)
020 7766 8866
www.iod.com

Institute of Environmental Management and
Assessment (IEMA)
01522 540069
www.iema.net

Institute of Food Research (IFR)
01603 255000
www.ifr.bbsrc.ac.uk

Institute of Hospitality
020 8661 4900
www.instituteofhospitality.org

Institute of Plumbing and Heating Engineering
(IPHE)
01708 472791
www.iphe.org.uk

Institute of Risk Management (IRM)
020 7709 9808
www.theirm.org

Institution of Civil Engineers (ICE)
020 7222 7722
www.ice.org.uk

Institution of Engineering and Technology
01483 313 311
www.theiet.org

Institution of Fire Engineers (IFE)
01608 812580
www.ife.org.uk

Institution of Gas Engineers and Managers
(IGEM)
01509 282728
www.igem.org.uk

Institution of Lighting Engineers (ILE)
01788 576492
www.ile.org.uk

Institution of Mechanical Engineers (IMechE)
020 7222 7899
www.imeche.org.uk

Institution of Occupational Safety and Health
(IOSH)
0116 257 3100
www.iosh.co.uk

Institution of Structural Engineers (IStructE)
020 7235 4535
www.istructe.org

International Facilities Management Association
[USA]
+1 713 623 4362
www.ifma.org

International Institute for Environment and
Development (IIED)
020 7388 2117
www.iied.org

International Institute of Risk and Safety
Management (IIRSM)
020 8741 9100
www.iirsm.org

International Lead Association
020 7935 6146
www.ila-lead.org

International Stress Management Association UK
(ISMA UK)
07000 780430
www.isma.org.uk

Investors in People
020 7467 1900
www.investorsinpeople.co.uk

Joint Industry Board for the Electrical Contracting
Industry (JIB)
020 8302 0031
www.jib.org.uk

Knowledge-Counsel
01344 779438
www.knowledge-counsel.com

Land Registry
020 7917 8888
www.landreg.gov.uk

Lift and Escalator Industry Association (LEIA)
020 7935 3013
www.leia.co.uk

Local Authority Building Control (LABC)
0844 561 6136
www.labc.co.uk

London Fire Brigade
020 8555 1200
www.london-fire.gov.uk

Low Pay Commission
020 7215 8459
www.lowpay.gov.uk

Mastic Asphalt Council (MAC)
01424 814400
www.masticasphaltcouncil.co.uk

Mind
0845 7660163
www.mind.org.uk

Mobile Operators Association (MOA)
020 7331 2015
www.mobilemastinfo.com

Motability
0845 456 4566
www.motability.co.uk

Motor Insurers' Information Centre (MIIC)
0845 165 2800
www.miic.org.uk

National Access and Scaffolding Confederation
(NASC)
020 7822 7400
www.nasc.org.uk

National Association for the Care and
Resettlement of Offenders (Nacro)
020 7840 7200
www.nacro.org.uk

National Association of Pension Funds (NAPF)
020 7808 1300
www.napf.co.uk

National Examination Board in Occupational
Safety and Health (NEBOSH)
0116 263 4700
www.nebosh.org.uk

National Federation of Builders (NFB)
0870 8989 091
www.builders.org.uk

National Federation of Demolition Contractors
(NFDC)
01784 456799
www.demolition-nfdc.com

National Group on Homeworking (NGH)
0800 174 095
www.homeworking.gn.apc.org

National Inspection Council for Electrical
Installation Contracting (NICEIC)
0870 013 0382
www.niceic.org.uk

National Institute for Health and Clinical
Excellence
0845 003 7780
www.nice.org.uk

National Pest Technicians Association (NPTA)
www.npta.org.uk

National Quality Assurance (NQA)
01582 539000
www.nqa.com

Health Protection Agency — Radiation Protection
Division
01235 831600
www.hpa.org.uk/radiation

National Register of Access Consultants (NRAC)
020 7735 7845
www.nrac.org.uk

National Security Inspectorate (NSI)
0845 006 3003
www.nsi.org.uk

National Trust
0845 800 1895
www.nationaltrust.org.uk

Natural England
0845 600 3078
www.naturalengland.org.uk

NHS Plus
www.nhsplus.nhs.uk

Noise Abatement Society (NAS)
01273 823 851
www.noiseabatementsociety.com

Northern Ireland Committee of the Irish Congress of Trade Unions (NIC.ICTU)
028 9024 7940
www.ictuni.org

Occupational Road Safety Alliance (ORSA)
www.orsa.org.uk

Office Furniture Advisory Service (OFAS)
01344 779438
www.ofas.org.uk

Office of Communications (Ofcom)
020 7981 3040
www.ofcom.org.uk

Office of Gas and Electricity Markets (Ofgem)
020 7901 7295
www.ofgem.gov.uk

Office of Government Commerce (OGC)
0845 000 4999
www.ogc.gov.uk

Office of Public Sector Information (OPSI)
www.opsi.gov.uk

Office of Water Services (Ofwat)
0121 625 1300
www.ofwat.gov.uk

Painting and Decorating Association (PDA)
024 7635 3776
www.paintingdecoratingassociation.co.uk

Patent Office
08459 500 505
www.patent.gov.uk

The Pensions Regulator
01273 811 800
www.thepensionsregulator.gov.uk

Planning Inspectorate
0117 372 6372 (England)/
029 2082 3866 (Wales)
www.planning-inspectorate.gov.uk

Public Concern at Work
020 7404 6609
www.pcaw.co.uk

Recruitment and Employment Confederation (REC)
020 7009 2100
www.rec.uk.com

Remploy
0800 138 7656
www.remploy.co.uk

Repetitive Strain Injuries Association (RSIA)
023 8029 4500
www.rsi.org.uk

RIBA Bookshops
020 7256 7222
www.ribabookshops.com

RICS Books
0870 333 1600
www.ricsbooks.com

Robust Details Ltd
0870 240 8210
www.robustdetails.com

Royal Association for Disability and Rehabilitation (RADAR)
020 7250 3222
www.radar.org.uk

Royal Automobile Club (RAC)
01922 727 313
www.rac.co.uk

Royal Environmental Health Institute of Scotland (REHIS)
0131 225 6999
www.rehisorg

Royal Incorporation of Architects in Scotland (RIAS)
0131 229 7545
www.rias.org.uk

Royal Institute of British Architects (RIBA)
020 7580 5533
www.riba.org

Royal Institution of Chartered Surveyors (RICS)
0870 333 1600
www.rics.org

Royal National Institute of the Blind (RNIB)
0845 766 9999
www.rnib.org.uk

Royal National Institute for Deaf People (RNID)
020 7296 8000
www.rnid.org.uk

Royal Society for the Prevention of Accidents
(RoSPA)
0121 248 2000
www.rospa.org.uk

Royal Society for the Promotion of Health
(RSPH)
020 7630 0121
www.rsph.org

Safety and Reliability Society (SaRS)
0161 228 7824
www.sars.org.uk

Safety Assessment Federation (SAFed)
020 7582 3208
www.safed.co.uk

St John Ambulance
020 7324 4000
www.sja.org.uk

Scottish and Northern Ireland Plumbing
Employers' Federation (SNIPEF)
0131 225 2255
www.snipef.org

Scottish Association of Building Standards
Managers (SABSM)
www.sabsm.co.uk

Scottish Building Standards Agency
01506 600 400
www.sbsa.gov.uk

Scottish Centre for Facilities Management
(Napier University) (SCFM)
0131 455 2642
www.sbe.napier.ac.uk/scfm

Scottish Environment Protection Agency (SEPA)
01786 457700
www.sepa.org.uk

Scottish Executive
08457 741 741
www.scotland.gov.uk/Home

Scottish Trades Union Congress (STUC)
0141 337 8100
www.stuc.org.uk

Security Industry Authority (SIA)
0844 892 1025
www.the-sia.org.uk

Security Institute
08453 707 717
www.security-institute.org

Sign Design Society
020 8776 8866
www.signdesignsociety.co.uk

Society of Light and Lighting (SLL)
020 8675 5211
www.cibse.org

Society of Occupational Medicine (SOM)
020 7486 2641
www.som.org.uk

Stress Management Society
08701 999 235
www.stress.org.uk

Suzy Lamplugh Trust
020 7091 0014
www.suzylamplugh.org

Systems Engineering and Management
Associates
001 626 793 7283
www.seama.net

Tailored Interactive Guidance on Employment Rights (TIGER)
See Direct Gov

Telework Association (TCA)
0800 616008
www.telework.org.uk

The Stationery Office
0870 600 5522
www.tso.co.uk

Think! Road Safety Website
www.thinkroadsafety.gov.uk

Trades Union Congress (TUC)
020 7636 4030
www.tuc.org.uk

Transco
www.nationalgrid.com/uk

United Kingdom Accreditation Service (UKAS)
020 8917 8400
www.ukas.com

Valuation Office Agency (VOA)
020 7506 1700
www.voa.gov.uk

Wales Trades Union Congress (TUC Cymru)
020 7636 4030
www.wtuc.org.uk

Water Regulations Advisory Scheme (WRAS)
01495 248454
www.wras.co.uk

Water Research Centre (WRc plc)
01793 865000
www.wrcplc.co.uk

Water UK
020 7344 1844
www.water.org.uk

The Welding Institute (TWI)
01223 899 000
www.twi.co.uk

Work Foundation
0207 976 3500
www.theworkfoundation.com

Working Balance
0161 217 2500
www.workingbalance.co.uk

Working Families
020 7253 7243
www.workingfamilies.org.uk

Working Well Together (WWT)
0845 27 27 500
www.wwt.uk.com

Workplace Law Group
0871 777 8881
www.workplacelaw.net

Join us

Join our 50,000+ membership base. It couldn't be easier

• •

Join the Network for free

Just go to **www.workplacelaw.net** and register to join as a free member.

Alternatively, call our membership services team and we'll complete your registration for you.

Join the Network as a premium member

You can use the membership quotamator at **www.workplacelaw.net/quotamator** to work out your own package, and change the rates on screen.

Then it's just a matter of applying online or calling our membership services team!

I'm already a member: I want to renew!

Renew online at **www.workplacelaw.net** or call our membership services team.

Save even more ... By renewing for two or three years, you can fix your current membership rate and save **£££**s.

Contact us

Chat to us online at **www.workplacelaw.net**

t 0871 777 8881
f 0871 777 8882
e membership@workplacelaw.net

Workplace Law Group
Second floor
Daedalus House
Station Road
Cambridge CB1 2RE

Workplace Law Network

Join the UK's fastest growing legal network
www.workplacelaw.net

Index

Workplace Law Network
www.workplacelaw.net

Index

....

Parking, 550–58
Civil Parking Enforcement, 551
disabled people and, 555–56
workplace parking levy, 551
Part-time workers, 559–61
definition of, 559
discrimination and, 559–60
Part-time Workers (Prevention of Less Favourable Treatment) Regulations 2000, 282, 559, 666
party walls, 77
Paternity and Adoption Leave Regulations 2002, 309, 310, 311
paternity leave, 138, 309, 310, 311, 532
Pensions, 562–65
life assurance and, 565
occupational, 564
personal, 564–65
stakeholder, 565
state, 562–63
Pensions Act 2004, 266, 562, 697
Permits to work, 566–67
Personal Emergency Evacuation Pans (PEEPs), 53, 205
Personal Protective Equipment, 568–70
Personal Protective Equipment at Work Regulations 1992, 568, 707, 741, 765, 776
Personal Protective Equipment Regulations 2002, 362, 568
Personnel files – recording information, 571–76
data protection, 573–74
relevant filing systems, 573–74
Pest control, 577–80
pests
definition of, 577
species of, 577
planning appeals, 583
planning control, breaches of, 582
portable appliance testing (PAT), 254
Power lines, 584–86
agreements relating to, 584
compensation and, 585
compulsory purchase and, 585
easements and, 584
installation of, 584
wayleaves and, 585
pregnancy, 484–87
Prevention of Damage by Pests Act 1949, 577–78
Private life, 587–91
Private Security Industry Act 2001, 646, 751, 753
Probationary periods, 592–94
prohibition notices (HSE), 327, 376, 378, 384
Property, buying and selling, 110–13
completion, 112
contracts, 111
title, 110–11
transfers, 112
warranties, 111
Property disputes, 595–97

evidence in, 595
professional advice in, 596
resolution of, 596
statutory time limits in, 596
Protection of Animals Act 1911, 577, 578
Public Electricity Supply Code, 586
Public Interest Disclosure Act 1998, 758
public liability insurance, 334, 418, 649

R v. Associated Octel (1996), 160
R v. Melvyn Spree, 248
R v. Raymond Knapman, 248
race discrimination, 225–26, 242, 343, 502
dress codes and, 242
Radiation, 598–601
Rates and revaluation, 602–06
Local Government Finance Act, 1988, 603, 606
non-domestic rates, 602–06
2005 Revaluation, 602–06
REACH: *see* Registration, Evaluation and Authorisation of Chemicals
'reasonably practicable', meaning of, 366–67
Recruitment and selection, 607–10
advertising, 608
interviews, 429–32, 609–10
job descriptions and, 607
shortlisting, 609
Recycling, 614–17
Redundancy, 618–21
consultation process, 619–20
payments, 618
References, 622–24
employees' claims, 623
Registration, Evaluation and Authorisation of Chemicals (REACH), 625–27
registration, 625–26
evaluation, 626
authorisation, 626
downstream users, 626
Regulation of Investigatory Powers Act 2000, 426, 522, 525, 556
Regulation of Investigatory Powers (Directed Surveillance and Covert Human Intelligence) Sources Order 2003, 525
Regulatory Reform (Fire Safety) Order 2005, 85, 124, 205, 258, 314, 322, 356–26, 330, 353, 469–70
Rehabilitation of Offenders Act 1974, 181, 182, 183, 277, 607, 609
Reporting of Injuries, Diseases and Dangerous Occurrences Regulations (RIDDOR) 1995, 628–32
representatives of employee safety, 373, 374
Responsible person, 51, 52, 148–149, 206, 314, 322, 325, 328, 330, 628
Restriction of the Use of certain Hazardous Substances in Electrical Equipment Directive, 744–50

Index